INTERNATIONAL HANDBOOK ON GENDER ROLES

INTERNATIONAL HANDBOOK ON GENDER ROLES

Edited by
LEONORE LOEB ADLER

Foreword by Nancy Felipe Russo

Greenwood Press
WESTPORT, CONNECTICUT • LONDON

Library of Congress Cataloging-in-Publication Data

International handbook on gender roles / edited by Leonore Loeb Adler ;
   foreword by Nancy Felipe Russo.
      p.   cm.
   Includes bibliographical references (p.   ) and index.
   ISBN 0–313–28336–2 (alk. paper)
   1. Sex roles—Cross-cultural studies.   I. Adler, Leonore Loeb.
HQ1075.I58   1993
305.3—dc20   92–45080

British Library Cataloguing in Publication Data is available.

Library of Congress Catalog Card Number: 92–45080
ISBN: 0–313–28336–2

First published in 1993

Greenwood Press, 88 Post Road West, Westport, CT 06881
An imprint of Greenwood Publishing Group, Inc.

Printed in the United States of America

The paper used in this book complies with the
Permanent Paper Standard issued by the National
Information Standards Organization (Z39.48–1984).

10 9 8 7 6 5 4 3 2 1

This volume is dedicated to my husband, Dr. Helmut E. Adler, who always showed me full understanding and agreement, while we explored and experienced the new and modern dimensions of the traditional gender roles.

Contents

Foreword

Nancy Felipe Russo

There is hardly a place in the world which has not been touched by the concerns of the women's movement in one respect or another.
—Lynne Iglitzin (1976a, p. xv)

In 1975, the United Nations proclaimed "International Women's Year," an impetus for expanding and connecting women's movements around the globe. This *International Handbook on Gender Roles* can be seen as an outcome of that internationalization of the women's movement. The rising expectations of women to be treated as full and complete human beings, with rights—even privileges, are of such profound significance that their impact and implications are yet to be fully comprehended. Women are creating a new world, restructuring old institutions and inventing new ones. The scholarship contained in these pages, which reflects the burgeoning scholarship on women and gender around the world, is a part of that important story.

As we face the next century, the need for such scholarship will become more critical. The decade of the 1980s brought alarming increases in illiteracy, unemployment, poverty, disease, and famine, all of which fall more heavily on women (Momsen, 1991). Just a few of the conditions that shape and are shaped by the position of women are the rise of religious fundamentalism and neoconservativism; the break-up of the Soviet Union and the realignment of national boundaries in Communist countries; the enormous debts of Third World countries and the realignment of the global economy that is changing the balance of power among nations; persistence of class and caste divisions that foster injustice, poverty, and racism; pervasive and escalating violence; population pressures and the pollution of the environment; pervasive illiteracy and declining systems of education; the breakdown of health delivery systems; the spread of AIDS and the changing nature of disease and illness together with their impact on society; the lengthening of the life span; the development and spread of reproductive technologies; the growing strength and pervasiveness of multinational corporations; and war (Momsen, 1991; O'Connell & Russo, 1991a).

That position continues to be hallmarked by social, economic, and political discrimination that undercuts our ability to respond to the challenges of the twenty-first century. As so eloquently stated in the preamble of the United Nations Declaration on the Elimination of Discrimination Against Women on November 7, 1967:

Discrimination against women is incompatible with human dignity and with the welfare of the family and of society, prevents their participation, on equal terms with men, in the political, social, economic and cultural life of their countries, and is an obstacle to the full development of the potentialities of women in the service of their countries and of humanity; . . . the full and complete development of a country, the welfare of the world, and the cause of peace require the maximum participation of women as well as men in all fields. (Boserup & Liljencrantz, 1975, p. 10)

Although women's status seems to be changing nearly everywhere, "in not a single country have women gone much beyond the reality gap—the contrast between doctrine and deed, pronouncement and enforcement, superficial rather than profound, change" (Iglitzin & Ross, 1986, p. xi). Socioeconomic advances and technological developments have changed women's lives across the globe and many countries have laws that prohibit discrimination against women in a variety of arenas. But legal protections for women are not uniform, and many countries, including the United States of America at this writing, have not even ratified the United Nations treaty to eliminate discrimination against women. Archaic laws and discriminatory practices continue to undermine women's access to and advancement in education, employment, and the political process, deprive them of assets, deny them liberty and dignity, and violate their physical and mental integrity and autonomy. Such practices have included female infanticide, suttee, genital mutilation, prostitution, child marriage, polygamy, arranged marriages, wife-selling, and prohibitions against birth control and abortion (in addition to this handbook, see also Andreas, 1971; Dwyer & Bruce, 1988; Iglitzin & Ross, 1976, 1986; Momsen, 1991; Morgan, 1984; Tinker, 1990).

Underlying these laws and practices are gender roles and stereotypes that reinforce traditional norms, values, and socialization patterns that rely on a view of women as different from and inferior to men. Women continue to be expected to find their central fulfillment as mothers and wives and are subordinated to men by social, economic, legal, and religious institutions—first to fathers and other male family members and then to husbands. They are dependent on fathers or husbands for housing and permission to participate in public life (e.g., to go to work, enter school, or travel) and are constrained in the economic sphere by their domestic and mothering responsibilities.

Women's work is characterized by subordination and service to men, and has been traditionally confined to care of family members, household work, provision of health care, shelter, and food, and support services in such roles as nurse, secretary, and teacher (Boserup & Liljencrantz, 1975). Women's jobs are lower status, low-paying jobs, and women are more likely to be unemployed. They are also denied credit, equal access to education, and opportunities for advancement. Further, wherever women find themselves they live with violence and the threat of violence and other forms of intimidation, including rape, battering, sexual harassment, sexual exploitation, and even sexual slavery (Barry, 1979).

Although women constitute one-half of the world's population, they perform two-thirds of its work, receive one-tenth of its income, and own less than one-hundredth of its property (United Nations, 1989, p. 3). There is a global trend towards "the feminization of poverty," which reflects a variety of factors, including lack of education and employment opportunities, growing numbers of female heads-of-households around the world, and failure of men to provide economic support for their wives and children. The latter is important for both married and divorced/separated women, as many countries do not require a husband to share his earnings with his wife—there is no concept of community property (Evason, 1991).

In 1976, Lynne Iglitzin provided a framework for assessing how much we know and how much more we need to know about the lives and circumstances of women in a particular country. As you read the pages that follow, consider how gender roles still reflect the domination of males and male-oriented values and beliefs across cultures and societies. (The five paragraphs that follow have been adapted from Iglitzin, 1976b, 1986.)

Is there a belief in "natural" differences between men and women that provides a rationale for a sexual division of labor? For example, the belief that women are the nurturant sex has been used to rationalize segregation of women into roles at work and in the home that involve nurturing and serving others, such as nurse, teacher, secretary, child-raiser, and household drudge. How are these beliefs transmitted from generation to generation in different cultures? Is the message uniform—that is, the same, whether in the home, at work, in school, in religious institutions, and in the media—or is it mixed? How strong are values and voices that provide alternatives to patriarchy, such as those represented by feminist groups or others who have made commitments to improving the social, economic, and political status of women?

In what ways is a woman's identity contingent on her relationships with men? Are women seen as the property of men? To what extent is a woman's access to resources dependent on men's discretion? To what extent are women without a significant male relationship—father, brother, uncle, husband, son, and so on—considered deviant? Do women have recourse when they are abused in or want to leave such relationships? Legalities aside, do suttee, dowries, dowry deaths, seclusion of married women, and other customs that enforce male control over women continue to be practiced?

Is a woman defined, first and foremost, as wife and mother, no matter what her other identities may be as worker or political or religious leader? Is the epitome of women's fulfillment being a wife and mother? Do women live vicariously through the accomplishments of the men in their lives such as husbands and sons? To what extent is women's behavior controlled so that she can serve men in these roles (e.g., through emphasis on the family and norms of chastity and marital fidelity applied to women but not to men)? Does a woman have autonomous control over her childbearing, that is, can she refuse sex with her husband and does she have access to safe and legal birth control and abortion? Is a woman motivated to bear many children in order to have sons as a defense against her economic insecurity should she lose her husband? Can she remain without children if she chooses without being ostracized?

Are women viewed as adults, with adult competencies, needs, motivations, and moral judgement, or are they considered childlike and in need of protection? Can they achieve a truly independent status? Must they have paternal protection via some sort of male relationship to survive—physically, socially, economically, or legally? Are women considered deviant and "open season" if they are alone, either by choice or circumstance? To what extent is homophobia used to socially control women and men and define women's respectability? Are women seen as potentially dangerous and corrupting (particularly sexually) if they are not controlled by men?

Are women confined to domestic spheres and kept from public life? Are business and politics the province of men? What are the sources of women's power, including the vote in democratic societies, but also including participation in actual decision-making councils? Are women's issues part of the national political agenda? Are there revolutionary movements that include women and women's issues in meaningful ways?

In reviewing conditions that undermine women's advancement, it is important to consider the effects of male violence against women. The international community has recently come to recognize the pervasiveness and severity of consequences of such violence and the role of traditional gender roles in supporting it:

In all countries and cultures, women have frequently been the victims of abuse by their intimates. They have been battered, sexually abused and psychologically injured by persons with whom they should enjoy the closest trust. This maltreatment has gone largely unpunished, unremarked, and has even been tacitly, if not explicitly condoned. (United Nations, 1989, p. 11)

Unfortunately, there has been a lag between recognition of the problem and research and programs that address it. As you read the chapters that follow, ask yourself how much we know and how much more we need to know, to understand and prevent violence and to help the women who endure it.

One cannot compare and contrast information on the lives and circumstances of women around the world without being impressed on the one hand with their similarity and on the other with their diversity. The sexual division of labor is pervasive but the actual activities assigned to various gender roles of men and understanding women's lives will not be achieved if we only focus on the activities of women in one sphere (public or private) at a time. Women's roles in the family, at work, and in the community are synergistic. Further, one sees the danger of generalizing from one culture to another when cross-cultural data broadens one's vision. This awareness is borne out in studies of women in development. Time after time, development programs that have sought to modernize developing countries have resulted in an improvement in the status of men and undermined the status of women. Ignorance about cross-cultural differences in the rights and responsibilities assigned to women and men has meant that in some cases where women's earnings provided food for the children, malnutrition has actually increased as a result of development programs that increased male income while lowering that of women (Dwyer & Bruce, 1988; Momsen, 1991).

To pursue the quest for knowledge to ameliorate the disadvantaged status of women will require a more sophisticated and in-depth examination of women's development, roles, and life circumstances around the world in all their diversity. New models and methods must be developed that will more accurately and appropriately reflect what is important in women's lives and help us to understand how gender shapes the lives and relations of women and men. Lessons from the history of psychology have revealed the androcentric nature of our knowledge, the inappropriateness of using psychological scales and other instruments developed in the context of male-oriented norms and values, the invisibility and devaluation of women's contributions and activities, and the use of psychological knowledge to reinforce stereotypes and justify discrimination against women (O'Connell & Russo, 1991b). For example, we have learned that a focus on paid employment does not provide a full picture of women's economic contributions to the family, and that a focus on women's weaknesses does not reveal women's strengths. In particular, effects of practices that exploit, degrade, and injure women (e.g., incest, pornography, rape, battering, sexual harassment) have been ignored or trivialized. For example, only recently have the physical and mental health effects of violence begun to be linked and investigated (see Goodman, Koss, & Russo, 1992 for a review).

We must learn more about both cross-cultural and subcultural variations in gender roles and circumstances that reflect the interaction of gender, race, age, ethnicity, class and caste, sexual orientation, able-bodiedness, and other factors that define identity and social status in various societies and cultures. It must be recognized that the difficulties in developing such complex approaches are compounded by continuing changes in gender roles and circumstances (O'Connell & Russo, 1991b). We must also explore women's strengths and strategies for transforming their disadvantages into challenges, and learn from and help one another.

As we approach the twenty-first century, scholars who study gender roles in different countries are increasingly communicating with and learning from each other. Leonore Loeb Adler is to be commended for her leadership and commitment in providing this forum for scholars to present their view of findings from such an impressive array of countries. One cannot read the chapters in this handbook without being struck by the emerging bodies of knowledge about gender roles and women's circumstances around the world. But while we can be excited by the amount of scholarship represented in these pages, there is clearly a long way to go before our quest for knowledge is completed. What is found in these pages represents an important step in the evolution of our knowledge about sex roles but it is one step in a long journey. It is hoped that this handbook will stimulate looking beyond cultural and national boundaries and encourage increased collaboration among scholars across cultures and countries in continuing the quest.

REFERENCES

Andreas, C. (1971). *Sex and Caste in America*. Englewood Cliffs, NJ: Prentice-Hall.

Barry, K. (1979). *Female Sexual Slavery*. Englewood Cliffs, NJ: Prentice-Hall.

Boserup, E., & Liljencrantz, C. (1975). *Integration of Women in Development: Why, When, and How*. New York: U.N. Development Programme.

Dwyer, D., & Bruce, J. (1988). *A Home Divided: Women and Income in the Third World*. Stanford, CA: Stanford University Press.

Evason, E. (1991). Women and poverty. In C. Davies & E. McLaughlin (Eds.), *Women, Employment, and Social Policy in Northern Ireland: A Problem Postponed?* (pp. 61–73). Belfast: Policy Research Institute.

Goodman, L. A., Koss, M. P., & Russo, N. F. (1992). Violence against women: Physical and mental health effects. Part I: Research findings. *Applied & Preventive Psychology: Current Scientific Perspectives*.

Iglitzin, L. B. (1976a). Foreword. In L. B. Iglitzin & R. Ross (Eds.), *Women in the World: A Comparative Study* (pp. xv–xvii). Santa Barbara, CA: Clio Books.

———. (1976b). The patriarchal heritage. In L. B. Iglitzin & R. Ross (Eds.), *Women in the World: A Comparative Study* (pp. 7–24). Santa Barbara, CA: Clio Books.

———. (1986). The patriarchal heritage revisited. In L. B. Iglitzin & R. Ross (Eds.), *Women in the World, 1975–1985: The Women's Decade* (2nd, rev. ed.) (pp. ix–xi). Santa Barbara, CA: Clio Books.

Iglitzin, L. B., & Ross, R. (Eds.). (1976). *Women in the World: A Comparative Study*. Santa Barbara, CA: Clio Books.

———. (1986). *Women in the World, 1975–1985: The Women's Decade* (2nd, rev. ed.). Santa Barbara, CA: Clio Books.

Momsen, J. H. (1991). *Women and Development in the Third World*. London: Routledge.

Morgan, R. (Ed.). (1984). *Sisterhood Is Global*. Garden City, NY: Anchor Press/Doubleday.

O'Connell, A. N., & Russo, N. F. (1991a). Women's heritage in psychology: Future directions. *Psychology of Women Quarterly, 4*; 677–78.

———. (Eds.). (1991b). Women's heritage in psychology: Origins, development, and future directions. Special centennial issue. *Psychology of Women Quarterly*, Whole No. 4.

Tinker, I. (Ed.). (1990). *Persistent Inequalities: Women and World Development*. New York: Oxford University Press.

United Nations, Centre for Social Development and Humanitarian Affairs. (1989). *Violence Against Women in the Family*. New York: United Nations [Sales No. E.89.IV.5.].

Introduction

Leonore Loeb Adler

The *International Handbook on Gender Roles* is a unique reference volume that not only serves scientists and professionals in a variety of disciplines but also is a valuable source of information to cross-cultural psychologists in academia, as well as in research at the library and in the field. It will inspire students to continue their studies and make further inquiries. In addition, the nonprofessional individual will find this volume good and interesting reading.

Each chapter is devoted to a particular country, and the chapters are arranged alphabetically for ease of use. The volume contains reports on representative countries from six continents. This *International Handbook* represents a great opportunity to compare men and women in a variety of ecologies. Each of the thirty-one chapters follows the same organization: an introduction; an overview; comparisons of life cycles between men's and women's gender roles: (1) infancy and early childhood, (2) school years, (3) young adulthood, (4) adulthood, and (5) old age; and a summary and conclusions. For each of these categories a short guideline elaborates on the contents to assure easy comparisons later on. While presenting the gender roles in a life-span developmental sequence, each chapter is written from an authentic *emic* (insider's) point of view. All the authors report about the countries and cultures where they lived and worked, which is the unique approach of this reference volume. On the other hand, the readers have an *etic* (outsider's) point of view when they compare the gender roles in the countries and cultures about which they read. The exposition of the life-styles follows a truly cross-cultural and cross-national approach. In addition to the same outline for all thirty-one chapters, the layout follows an orthogonal presentation, in which the reader can compare separate sections within each chapter, or else the reader can compare and analyze various topics or age groups among several chapters.

Comparisons serve to show similarities as well as differences. It is frequently more obvious and therefore easier to identify differences; in such cases the underlying causes for the variations can usually quite readily be explained. That may not be the case with similarities that exist in a variety of cultures and ecologies. Even within the same culture and country differences in gender roles may occur. In such situations the dissimilarities may be primarily due to tradition versus modernization and rural versus urban surroundings.

In many situations a rural environment seems more conducive to adherence to traditional customs, for example, female circumcision, which is more prevalent in rural settings than in urban communities. Among these rural settings are Egypt and South Africa (chapters 4 and 23; also see Ahmed, 1991; Okafor, 1991). This specific practice is mainly found in African societies, where old customs are followed obediently by maintaining the traditions. This then may be part of the reason for the greater resistance toward a trend of modernization. Such persistence remains, for example, in spite of the Egyptian government's efforts to discourage female circumcision.

On the other hand, similarities may often occur—with a variety of behaviors— in modern and modernizing countries. An illustration is an increase of single-parent families and a coincidence of unwed mothers—a topic that may or may not be discussed openly. Recently (spring 1992) such a situation was the focus of a sitcom (situation comedy) or a soap opera on U.S. television, when the character of Murphy Brown, a single woman, gave birth to an illegitimate baby. In response to this show, Dan Quayle, the then vice president of the United States of America, commented that this story line should not serve as a role model, since a father and a mother are needed to uphold the high family values and each child is entitled to be brought up by a father and a mother together. Radio and television commentators, as well as news reporters, were ready to point out that single mothers are more likely to face poverty, because many have reached only the lower levels of education, which often results in lesser opportunities to find high-paying jobs. (Some women, however, bachelor career women with well-paying positions and successful careers, do not want to miss out on motherhood.) It remains to be seen if the breakdown of the nuclear family will handicap the moral development of the next generation.

While basic similarities exist among most people worldwide with regard to the marital status of men and women, a great diversity of life-styles does occur. In most modern and Westernized countries monogamous marriages are the rule as well as the law. Currently in Africa (chapters 4, 17, 23, and 27) and in Haiti (chapter 8), as well as in some other parts of the world, polygamy is practiced. However, only very few places report the existence of polyandry. (See chapter 29 on Tibetan Societies.)

An interesting factor, which becomes more and more apparent in modernizing countries, is that matchmakers or go-betweens are not as prevalent as they used to be. It is reported, for example, that in Japan (see chapter 13) 70 percent of the marriages are ''love marriages.''

The traditional role for women is to take care of the household and the children, probably because a dichotomy exists between the genders on a biological basis. For instance, during the early part of the twentieth century, the domain of women's activities in Germany mainly included the "three Ks," which stood for *Kinder, Küche, Kirche* (somewhat freely translated into English as the "three Cs": child care, cooking, churchgoing).

However, very rarely are the negative aspects of motherhood—including "fatigue, curtailment of freedom, a damper on intellectual stimulation, and frustrated career opportunities" (Denmark, Schwartz & Smith, 1991; Lefley, 1991)—ever mentioned. Even in modern or modernizing countries the domestic duties are still regularly delegated to women, even in two-career families. Besides holding a part-time or full-time job, the woman is responsible for child care and household chores. Only in a few modern countries like the United States of America and Canada (chapters 31 and 32) can one find young fathers "helping out" with child-rearing practices and some domestic chores, though not all to the same degree of involvement that is expected of women.

In most countries and cultures families accord high status to men and therefore give primary importance to the birth of a son. Such family events are especially happily greeted and cherished in India and Sri Lanka (chapters 10 and 25). In contrast, the birth of a daughter is most often just tolerated, but not greeted with great joy. Even at the youngest age, as neonates, female babies are discriminated against in many cultures around the globe.

Women in the modern world aspire to equality with men, yet truly androgynous gender roles are still beyond women's reach, since the traditional sex stereotypes still prevail.

With regard to giving women "equal opportunities and equal pay for equal work," some inroads have been acknowledged, but only in isolated cases. In general there is agreement that equal education for boys and girls will lead to equal qualifications for jobs and careers (though that by itself does not guarantee equal pay). Higher education for daughters—who then could attain the higher-paying jobs—is used as a point of discussion when the dowry of the daughter is discussed with the future bridegroom's family in India (chapter 10). On the other hand, in Thailand (chapter 28), as well as in Egypt (chapter 4), the future bridegroom has to pay the dowry before getting married. However, a different situation exists in Moslem communities, since women hardly ever work outside the home; therefore, the prospective husbands prefer wives with less education than they have (Ahmed, 1991).

All the chapters in this *International Handbook on Gender Roles* discuss the educational conditions in the specific countries. The readers can compare rural and urban practices, as well as compulsory and voluntary commitments to education, especially with relation to the life-styles and the family background in which the children live. For example, the majority of children in primary and secondary school in Nigeria (chapter 17) come from polygamous homes; while in the United States of America (chapter 31) most of the children come from monogamous homes. The enrollment figures for higher education are far lower for young women than for young men; at this level the career orientations are divided by perceptions of "masculine" and "feminine" professions (see chapters 20, 24, 25, and 26 on Poland, Post-Soviets, Sri Lanka, as well as Taiwan, among others).

Some chapters present information on the establishment of laws in different countries to assure women's rights to equality. For example, in 1944 women received the right to vote in France (chapter 6); in Egypt (chapter 4) the constitution guaranteed women equal rights; and as recently as 1985 the Group of Women in Sports was founded in Australia (chapter 1) for equal media coverage with men. However, today's gender roles for the two sexes are still mainly oriented toward traditional lines (see chapters 5 on Finland and 21 on Portugal). Even more stereotyped are the gender roles in Mexico (chapter 15) and in Brazil (chapter 2), where the machismo role for men is very current.

Some research gives information on the attitudes of men and women. For example, in Brazil (chapter 2) men and women were asked about their opinion of what makes a good marriage; the men's responses were love, sex, and children, while the women's responses to the same queries were communication, trust, companionship, compatibility, and understanding. In Korea (chapter 14) men and women were asked about the job market. An impressive majority of the women felt that women could hold jobs outside the home, while significantly fewer men felt that way. Such investigations present the struggle for equality that women face in many areas around the world.

The continuing prevalence of traditional attitudes is probably part of the reason that women, compared with men, earn much less money for equal work. This is true for the United States of America (chapter 31), Canada (chapter 3), and New Zealand (chapter 15), where, even though legislation is in effect, women earn only about three-fourths of what men earn, and Maori women earn only 80 percent of what non-Maori women earn.

Another point can be made by comparing the workload between husbands and wives. For instance, in the Philippines (chapter 19) husbands are reported to work only two-thirds as much as their working wives, since they do no housework; instead, they can relax, drink, or socialize. In Turkey (chapter 30) women comprise about one-third of the active work force, since generally women's primary responsibility is her home and her children. However, it is reported that both men and women in Turkey endorse women's employment and think it is the road to the emancipation for women.

Other influences affect gender roles, as can be seen in Tanzania (chapter 27), where the African culture has been eroded due to the establishment of educational institutions and the influence of religiosity by missionaries. In other parts of the globe, such as Singapore (chapter 22), which is a Confucian society, filial piety is strongly valued. A still different approach is found in India (chapter 10), where reincarnation is an important religious belief. In Sri Lanka (chapter 25) the elderly, who live in a multireligious society, spend much time in church, temple, or kovil. Also in Poland (chapter 20) the reinstated Roman Catholic practices lead to a new dimension in the gender roles of the population. An interesting report is given in chapter 12 on Italy, where "in the major urban areas the old prejudices have been overcome"; however, "in the rural areas the traditional socialization customs still prevail, probably to some degree a reflection of the vestiges of the ancient virginity cult." While changes in women's status occur earlier in cities and urban environments, they happen later in rural communities. These changes, even though they may be slow in process—especially for the waiting women, as well as the working women—may bring along difficulties in adjustment and coping for both genders and different age levels. For example, in Peru (chapter 18) a "culture clash" exists between the traditional ways of life and the modern life-styles, though eventually acculturation is the result when the people from the Andean mountain regions migrate to, and settle in, the coastal urban areas. Similarly it is reported that children face an adjustment toward the ambiguous role models of their fathers and mothers. That is particularly so since parents in urban environments are caught in the trap of social change of gender roles; it seems necessary then to redefine the roles, when in fact the fathers may no longer be the only providers for the family. (See chapter 7 on Greece.)

Many adjustments have to be faced in old age. The elderly, especially the men in modern societies, have to adjust to their retirement; more women than men experience widowhood, and both sexes have to deal with increasing health problems. If the financial circumstances provide an adequate income, then old folks can spend time with their children, grandchildren, and great-grandchildren, which allows for some positive aspects of old age, regardless of gender roles. In the more traditional environments the aged parents are taken care of by their children; in more modern societies the elderly lead more independent lives, since many reside by themselves, though often close to their children or their friends. Frequently there is a role reversal between the frail, aging parent and the more vigorous younger generation. Often there are parallel situations of role reversals found among elderly couples, especially in modern settings, when older women can still find work outside the home after the husband has retired. Even those women who do not have a job can always find something to do and be active in their homes. On the other hand, in Brazil (chapter 2) one of the greatest problems for senior citizens may occur when the husband retires from his job but then begins to manage the household that was formerly the wife's domain. In the Philippines (chapter 19) the entire family plays a central role during the retirement years, and the Filipino women hold the purse strings of the family, even if the income cannot meet the basic necessities. Another interesting situation exists in the Israeli kibbutzim (see chapter 11). The members of these communities are assured of economic security; at the same time the social norms of the kibbutz encourage the older members to continue to work as long as they are able, and they are accommodated by being assigned less demanding jobs and fewer work hours. The kibbutz faces the problem of providing the elderly not only with physical care but also with meaningful social roles within the kibbutz community. Available statistics show an increased life expectancy within the kibbutz, compared with urban living, three years for women and six years for men.

By reading the chapters of this *International Handbook on Gender Roles*, one realizes that no country exists in isolation. Communication and the media are just about worldwide, and where they exist most often, the contact is instantaneous. Therefore modernization and technological specializations have an unprecedented global impact on the lives of people—both near and far—whether they live in similar or dissimilar environments or in different ecological and cultural settings around the world. The impact of modernization is undeniable and is continuously spreading, with only few exceptions, in the years since World War II. Therefore it is hoped that many areas around the globe follow suit and say, as Hong Kong (see chapter 9) does: "This country prides itself in its ability to maintain harmony within contrasts—as tradition is confronted by modern practices."

One of the aims of the *International Handbook on Gender Roles* is to gain greater insight into people's customs and manners, while providing the opportunity to achieve a better understanding of men's and women's gender roles. It is hoped that with more extensive knowledge and greater tolerance toward people living in different countries and cultures a congenial and harmonious coexistence can be achieved everywhere.

REFERENCES

All references cited in the Introduction are published in L. L. Adler (Ed.), *Women in Cross-Cultural Perspective* (New York: Praeger, 1991).

R. A. Women in Egypt and the Sudan. Chapter 9.
Denmark, F. L., Schwartz, L., & Smith, K. M. Women in the United States of America and Canada. Chapter 1.
Lefley, H. P. Foreword.
Okafor, N.A.O. Some traditional aspects of Nigerian women. Chapter 10.

INTERNATIONAL HANDBOOK ON GENDER ROLES

1

Australia

Marie O'Neill

INTRODUCTION

Australia is a very large country, about the same size as the United States of America. It is known as the largest island and the driest continent in the world. Its entire population numbers about 17.3 million, about 90 percent of whom live on the eastern and southern coastlands, where there is water and easy access. A sizable percentage of the Australian population is of mixed ancestry, as migration has been the most potent force responsible for the postwar increase in population.

Australia was colonized in 1788 by the British and is still a member of the Commonwealth. At the time of white occupation, about 300,000 Aborigines were living in the land, after a migration from Asia 40,000 years beforehand (Isaacs, 1980; Luling, 1982).

OVERVIEW

Comparisons of Equalities and Inequalities between Female and Male Individuals

In 1989 in Australia, Australian females earned 65 percent of total earnings of males (National Women's Conference, 1990). The same conference report pointed out that fewer women become managers or executives in the private sector than in many other Western, industrial countries. Clare Burton (1987) argues that including women at senior levels in the work force threatens men who have defined their own masculinity as deriving from inhabiting a space where women's concerns are definitively banned. The gap is seen to be widening, though the men reportedly remain unconvinced that many obstacles exist for women. The Organization for Economic Cooperation and Development (OECD) found that Australia in 1977 had the highest level of occupational segregation by sex of all the countries it studied.

Attitudes among women toward child care differ. Southern European women living in Australia emphasize the importance of children to a greater extent than do other women in Australia. For example, 70 percent of Southern European women agree that their most important role is mother, regardless of the nature of their career. Only 43 percent of Australian-born women agree with this statement.

Raddford (1990) reports that about 71 percent of the people at the lowest level of work in Australia are women, while only about 10 percent of women are at the top in the Senior Executive Service. Even so, the public sphere of work makes few concessions to the demands of the private sphere (Thiele & Grace, 1990). Professional women, on the whole, retain the bulk of the home responsibilities, and it is only recently that the need for child care has begun to be seen as an important economic issue (Raddford, 1990).

Maternity leave provisions have been made in Australia but are often ignored and are not equal between public and private sectors in respect to the paid and unpaid components. Mothers who stay at home to care for children are called dependent spouses rather than active career women (Edgar, 1990).

Edgar (1990) espouses the "re-education of boys and men to a broader view of their potential as parents." At present, "structures militate against even willing males caring more for their children." However, a historical decision in 1989 granted twelve months' paternity leave to men, thus enabling them to share responsibilities for children and helping women combine child rearing and work force participation (Glezer, 1990). In a maternity leave study carried out by the Australian Institute of Family Studies, it was found that in 10 percent of cases, child care was done solely by fathers, their wives working part-time.

Inequalities in employment are compounded by the fact that approximately 300,000 women are single parents. It is noteworthy that between 1981 and 1986 male parents heading single-parent families have almost doubled their reliance on Social Security benefits (Harrison, 1988). In 1986, of the 40,000 single fathers, 33 percent were not employed. Of the female single parents, 250,000 rely on Social Security, and "50,000 live in deplorable poverty" (Hall & ors, 1990). There is an overrepresentation in this group of aboriginal women and women of non-English-speaking backgrounds. The results are higher rates of morbidity, chronic illness, and disability, which are reported by women more than men in self-report surveys (National Policy on Women's Health, 1988).

A matter of growing concern is the extent to which male violence is tolerated against women in Australia. The law is seen to "support the traditional view that a man's home is his castle and that he represents the law in his own home" (Naffine, 1990). This is the case in heavily populated areas; also, in rural areas, isolation of country women, along with growth of rural poverty, lack of support services, and lack of confidentiality tends to increase the risk of family violence (Tom, 1990).

Non-English-speaking women have provided an important source of cheap labor in low-skill jobs. Their unemployment rates are also high, reportedly around 24 percent between 1970 and 1980. During their first ten years in Australia, when their family responsibilities are greatest and their social isolation is most acute, their job participation rates are highest (Martin, 1984). This leaves them open to stress and physical and mental disorders. These women are less likely to be able to participate in community activities geared to the English language and culture and less likely to be able to attend English language classes through which they might be educated to participate in casual or formal Australian social life. Many immigrant women never learn to communicate effectively in English.

In many areas of cultural life, gender differences are noticeable. For example, Australian women artists have long been undervalued for their achievements. In 1980, Janine Burke published the first history of *Australian Women Artists 1840– 1940*. She noted that the ''output of talented and sometimes prominent women artists . . . far outstrips the contribution of their contemporaries in either Europe or America . . . in a country traditionally hostile to women'' (Burke, 1980). The neglect of women's artistic accomplishments is reflected in such books as *100 Masterpieces of Australian Painting* (Splatt & Burton, 1977), in which not one woman artist is featured. Many women have become famous in music, but their achievements have been limited to performance. There is no record of any woman conductor in the *Macquarie Book of Events* (Fraser, 1983).

In 1985, it was found necessary to establish a Working Group on Women in Sports to address some of the issues concerning lack of media coverage for women's sports and to investigate some of the problems met by women's sports groups. These issues included gaining access to facilities, the promoting of participation, and obtaining funding from the government.

It was not until 1971 that equal pay conditions were established in Australia. This did not guarantee equal opportunity, however, as the statement for this was issued only in 1980, and the challenge to the principle of equal pay was constantly argued. During the 1980s Hester Eisenstein (1991), an American living in Australia, wrote of the ''conscious feminist strategy,'' which she saw growing as a strong force, aimed to place women in public service positions and in politics (''femocrats''). She remarked on the tardiness of the Australian academic community to encourage formal Women's Studies. ''Australian academic life is more austere and traditional. Interdisciplinary offerings have tended to be regarded with suspicion, and university curricula tend to remain divided along the boundaries of the traditional disciplines.'' Eisenstein attributed the lag to a resistance on the part of colleges, where the curricula were geared to vocational and professional areas.

Nevertheless, there is in Australia an increasing tendency for women to seek higher education. Female enrollments in higher education rose by 91 percent between 1975 and 1988. However, only small proportions of women are enrolled in science, engineering, and postgraduate courses (Rutter, 1990). Inequalities of opportunity exist between groups from country and urban locations, rural students being three times less likely to go on to a tertiary course than their urban counterparts (Tom, 1990).

Eisenstein (1991) was writing after certain important social changes had taken place in the 1970s, when sex inequality in school education was recognized as an issue. In 1975 a federal report was produced on ''Girls, School and Society,'' which concluded that different outcomes from schooling (e.g., success in mathematics) could not be attributed solely to innate differences between males and females, though major differences were being produced. Yates (1990) points out that this report was ''clearly influential in the way in which attention to gender and schooling has been developed in Australia.'' Other, more recent federal reports, such as ''Girls and Tomorrow'' (Commonwealth Schools Commission, 1984), referred to ''Girls, School and Society'' as the reference point. However, these early reports did not deal effectively with the daughters of non-English-speaking parents (including Aboriginal families), whose needs in the school situation were diverse. Tsolidis (1988) drew attention to the fact that this aspect was not addressed until ''The National Policy'' (See National Policy for the Education of Girls, 1987) was produced.

COMPARISONS BETWEEN MEN'S AND WOMEN'S GENDER ROLES DURING THE LIFE CYCLE

Infancy and Early Childhood

In traditional life, aboriginal children were born into a stable community and treated with love and pride by the men and women of the tribe. New babies were passed around the group to be admired, and the custom of being part of the group continued. Children were carried by their mothers everywhere they went until they could manage to walk by themselves. Aboriginal mothers let their babies feed at any time, and children continued to take breast milk long after they were walking. They were encouraged to hold their heads steady and to stand early. As toddlers they were left at the camp in the care of the old people. The child's basic needs were met in a nondemanding way, as the child learned by observation and by some direct teaching and games. When old enough to run around, boys were free to play, to remain with the women and girls, or to watch their fathers and uncles making tools and weapons. Girls were expected to help with food collecting, which was constant, to look after the younger children, and to learn skills such as net making and weaving. For all, work and play went hand in hand. Children and adults shared in games, songs, and dances (Fabian & Loh, 1980). Imagination in children was appreciated. If parents died, relatives would take care of the children. The laws and beliefs were introduced early in songs and legends and dances, as well as in games. Toys were made from natural materials. There was no competition, and therefore there was no failure. Many of these early attitudes toward child rearing have survived, especially those concerning belonging to the group and having relations upon whom the child can depend.

At times in the intervening period, aboriginal children of mixed blood would sometimes be killed or left to die, as they were considered to be a bad omen. Although much intermarriage with Europeans and Asians has taken place over the two centuries, aboriginal custom and lineage are now strongly supported within the culture (Edgar & ors, 1974). However, a grave decline in the health of Aborigines over this time has resulted in a significant increase in aboriginal infant mortality (Luling, 1982), at this stage only partly addressed.

The majority of new settlers in Australia have originated from England, Ireland, and Scotland. The British influence is still strong, though postwar migration from other parts of Europe has been encouraged. Lately, the Asian countries have been gaining more places. This cultural mix—that is, gaining settlers from different places—provides a complex picture in the study of gender issues, for "our culture is pluralistic, full of variety, color, conflicting interests and views of reality. Thus children from various groups, from diverse economic, ethnic and social situations, grow up differently in Australian society" (Edgar & Orrs, 1974). Also, the range of Australian experience for children has been vast, due to the nature of the country.

Preference for sex of child has not featured greatly in the traditional Australian population, except in some country areas or in established families where the tradition would have been for the son to become heir to the control of a business.

Australian culture of the 1990s tends to reflect a narrowing of the family circle in British descendants that is not matched in those families from other European nations. Hence, the new "migrant" child tends to have a wider but more close-knit family support system, with stricter rules and codes and more stress on gender-related rearing styles. This is evident from the earliest days.

A strong tradition of color-coding babies' clothing—pink for girls and blue for boys—is retained in Australian life. This is also associated with specifically colored and decorated rooms. The clothing trend is modified after babyhood. Children then often move into dresses (for girls) and pants (for boys), though climatic differences may interfere with this in informal living. After infancy, the commonality (teddy bears, rattles) of children's toys also changes, much along the lines viewed as American. Boys are often given cars, trucks, and other vehicles, as well as guns, assorted military toys, or TV cult-hero equipment. Girls receive dolls and related objects more commonly than other gifts.

A large percentage of young children in Australia attend preschool or child care centers, where toys, climbing equipment, and games are offered according to developmental needs, there being no planned allocation by sex discrimination. In well-equipped settings, all children have opportunities to play with a wide variety of objects. No sexual distinction can be made from the readings of descriptions of preschool needs for play or from observations of numerous preschools. Briggs and Potter (1990) emphasize that preschool "encourages a non-sexist curriculum, ensuring that girls feel comfortable handling hammers, saws and wheelbarrows and boys enjoy the dressing-up box and domestic corner." However, they report that parents sometimes express anxiety about the use of dolls by boys and often ban doll play at home, as they fear the boys will become effeminate. It is clear from observing children at preschool that young children tend to move into gender-related roles as mirrors of the male-female distinctions they witness and experience in their homes and as the early results of selective toy play have their effects, reinforced by their peers. Other life experiences also have their effect: girls and boys as young as four may participate in ballet (girls) or in football (boys). Davies (1989) suggests that "children recognize that they are not free as individuals to vary the way that gender is taken up."

School Years

Between 1 percent and 4 percent of children, up to adolescents, reported that they did no chores around the home (Amato, 1987). Primary school boys and girls mentioned making beds, tidying up bedrooms, and setting the table. Primary boys were more likely to take out the garbage, work in the yard, mow the lawn, and wash the car. Primary girls were more likely than boys to sweep or vacuum and take care of younger children. Traditional sex differences also emerged in the pattern of chores done by the secondary children. Ninety-five percent of children believed that they should help around the house.

Many Australian children spend as much time with their siblings as they do with their parents (Amato, 1987). Siblings are seen as major resources for children. The highest level of interaction occurs between primary school boys and their brothers. For most children there is a tendency to spend the most time with a sibling of the same sex. Playing games, working, talking, and watching television are the most common forms of interaction. Amato found that, despite day-to-day conflicts reported by children, most rate their relationships with siblings positively. Adolescents are even more likely than younger children to enjoy good relationships with siblings. Amato suggests that "as children mature, they sort out their conflicts with siblings and grow closer."

The legal (compulsory) age for entry to school in Australia is generally six years, though most children are attending by the age of five. "Being a Girl in an Australian School" (Commonwealth Schools Commission, 1987) reported that some primary schools "continue to use gender as a major organizing principle in almost all their activities, segregating boys and girls by the role, in lines outside the classroom, in disciplinary practices, and in a range of activities, notably sport." This would perforce increase the tendency for children to become set in their sex stereotyping.

In the early years of school, sex differences in groups and play materials can be quite marked (Briggs & Potter, 1990). These authors point out the educational and social dangers associated with this differentiation. For example, the disadvantages that accrue to girls who have no experience in early mathematical constructs. In many cases, the fault is seen as stemming from female teachers who "avoid mathematical and construction play areas and need to make conscious efforts to participate in traditionally male pursuits."

Girls frequently identified sports as an example of unfair treatment. The girls also saw the playing of sports, especially sports traditionally played by boys (e.g., soccer), as a source of problems with their families and the perception of their sex-related roles. Girls were more inclined to emphasize the social, rather than the physical, aspects of school sports and physical education. Some girls believed that males and females would relate to each other better generally if they played sports together, as they saw that males developed a strong sense of solidarity from the sports experience, while girls felt excluded from this. The report found that much depended on the attitudes of the principals and teachers involved in the schools. This point was more recently stressed by Margaret Clark (1990) in *The Great Divide: Gender in the Primary School*, in which she claimed that "change will not happen until school principals provide their support."

Some primary schools were putting great efforts into eliminating discriminatory practices. The same report mentions that girls were more likely to discuss their relationships with the opposite sex and to talk of their futures in the "wider context of adult life," while boys appeared to be less preoccupied with future relationships and with the work of parenting.

In 1988, 22.1 percent of female students attended all-female schools, compared with 19.5 percent of male students attending all-male schools. This included both government and nongovernment schools, where fees are charged. Thus, quite a large number of the youth of this country receive an education that biases their thinking, by virtue of their experiences in learning and play. Academic experiences also may vary according to the economic potential of the school, especially in the case of private schools. During the inquiry into a "National Policy for the Education of Girls in Australian Schools" (1987), it was noted that at several nongovernment secondary schools, teachers were aware that families tended to show greater support, financial and other, for the schools attended by sons than for their daughters' schools.

The inquiry revealed that at school "girls experience a great deal of what can only be described as intimidating sex-based harassment from males." This includes verbal innuendo, leering, bumping, and sexual graffiti. The issue of harassment and violence by male schoolchildren has been addressed recently by the federal government with their "Personal Development Program for Boys" (*The Gen*, January/February 1992). The program will include the teaching of "the construction of masculinity and femininity," conflict resolution, and communication skills to children from the sixth grade on. (*The Gen* is a federal publication of the Gender Equity Network, which involves teachers, students, and writers in discussions of gender reforms in schools.)

Gender preference for topic areas in school is best illustrated by the figures recorded for the final year of schooling, when decisions about future occupation are imminent. Overall, there has been an increase in the number of students completing the twelfth grade, but there has been no concomitant increase in the numbers taking university entrance subjects. This situation affects the future of girls in particular. Girls are under-represented in physical sciences, chemical sciences, higher mathematics, and computer sciences. Girls have higher representations than boys in history, languages, behavioral studies, biology, and the arts (Department of Employment, Education and Training, 1991). At the tertiary level, in 1989, more females than males completed higher education courses (46,961 versus 37,032). Female rates of entry for tertiary courses have been increasing more rapidly than those for males since 1975. Much of the difference, however, was made up in the "diploma" level, which accommodated education and nursing courses. Doctorates were gained by 723 males, compared with 308 females (Department of Employment, Education and Training, 1991).

Young Adulthood

Studies on subjective self-appraisal suggested that most Australian adolescents tend to have generally favorable self-concepts and feelings of self-adequacy (Heaven & Callan, 1990). Noller and Callan (1991) point out that by far the majority of young Australians "grow up in a family with their own parents who are married to each other." This assures the young, in general, of adequate opportunities to experience a degree of satisfactory socialization.

Noller and Callan (1991) show that females rate the problems in families as higher than do males. However, girls growing up with their parents view their family environments as more favorable. They rate their parents as more loving, affectionate, attentive, caring, sympathetic, accepting, strict, and overprotective and less abusive and inconsistent than did boys. This may suggest that adolescent boys do have more difficulty coming to terms with the particular social requirements of the average Australian family. Heaven and Callan (1990) relate this effect more especially to the early teen years. In the Noller and Callan (1991) study, on a scale of one (not at all) to six (highest), boys rated parents at a level of four or more points, as loving, affectionate, respectful, attentive, caring, understanding, sympathetic, and accepting. This reflects a high degree of cohesion within the family, though it is slightly less marked for boys than for girls.

Marjoribanks's (1987) proposition that parents' aspirations have a direct impact on female adolescents' educational aspirations and Heaven and Callan's (1990) finding that girls are more likely to be regarded by their teachers as interpersonally competent, obedient, and nonhostile may suggest that girls are more easily socialized as regards compliance with schooling. This would coincide with other studies quoted by Heaven and Callan that suggested that girls are more satisfied than boys with their academic performance and with their peer relationships. The literature suggests that for both boys and girls, parents were the most important influences in future-oriented decisions. Marjoribanks (1987) found this was particularly so with regard to the educational and occupational aspirations of male, working-class adolescents.

This last point may have a relationship to the standing of girls in employment, where they still experience disadvantage. "Girls have formed a minority of the teenage work force but a majority of unemployed teenagers during the past decade" (Porter, 1986). Porter argues that educational limitations placed on girls have given them a restricted range of occupations. "The girls' under-participation and under-achievement in mathematics, the physical sciences and technology significantly limit their post-school employment."

Porter contends that the education of girls does not build self-esteem and does not encourage creativity and inquiry in a way comparable to the education of boys. This leaves the girls with a restricted image of the future and liable to drift aimlessly into unsuitable employment. Women are shown to place greater importance on working relations, and men, on salary, job status, and prestige in the community (Neil & Snizek, 1987). Female dropouts are disadvantaged in terms of occupational choice and job access regardless of their school achievement, and this finding extends across social class, rural or urban residence, and migrant or Australian origin (Poole, 1981). Even in subgroups such as the severely intellectually disabled, gender bias in favor of males is an issue. Men have greater access to sheltered workshops, vocational training, and open work force environments than women (Grbich & Sykes, 1990).

Census statistics for 1992 show that more females aged 15–19 and over 20 were unemployed than were males of the same age and that this figure has increased consistently over the past year (Australian Bureau of Statistics, March 1992). At the same time, there were fewer women than men in the age group 15–24.

Overall, women comprise over a third of the paid work force, but "women do not see themselves (nor are they seen by others) as 'real workers' " (Rubinstein, 1982). This author argues that women retain an illusion that their working life is temporary until they marry and have children, despite the fact that most women work in paid jobs for most of their lives. This attitude interferes with initial job choice and tends to influence the retaining of unsatisfactory employment. Fems has discussed that the privatization of family life will increase as technological change forces more women out of work or into part-time work. This will serve to isolate women and keep the labor force weak. Jones (1983) considers that, while direct wage discrimination may have been virtually eliminated, occupational segregation by gender, discontinuous career patterns, and part-time employment continue to depress the earnings of women.

Adulthood

In Australia, 96 percent of parents are married (Noller & Callan, 1991). However, it is estimated that 16 percent of children will experience the divorce of their parents before the age of sixteen. There is a marked trend toward postponement of marriage to a later age, and it is estimated that 20–25 percent of today's young adult Australians will never marry (McDonald, 1991). Teenage marriage rates have significantly decreased. Seventy percent of teenage couples living together in 1986 were in de facto unions. Also, 30 percent of couples between ages 20 and 24 were living in de facto unions. Non-marriage relationships (especially among the young) have a much higher break-up rate than marriages, whether or not children are involved (Glezer, 1984). Associated with high break-up rate are domestic violence and substance abuse.

Differences are evident in some migrant groups. For example, the 1981 census showed that 26 percent of Lebanese women aged between 15 and 19 years were married, compared with 4 percent of Australian-born. Parental control is considered to be reflected in early marriage (McDonald, 1991).

In Australia the divorce rate declined after 1984, having peaked following the Family Law Act 1976. The tendency is for children to remain with their mother. This is so for all groups. Marriage is still the most popular form of union among the majority. Prior cohabitation is very common, though strong religious commitment restricts some couples as in many societies. Marriage after cohabitation appears to support commitment. However, the decline of the nuclear family is seen as progressing in Australia, while single-person households are increasing.

In intact families, the distribution of tasks to each gender has not changed appreciably over fifteen years (Findlay & Lawrence, 1991). Although men have increased their participation in household tasks, their contribution rarely comes close to that of their wives (Bryson, 1985). Women were seen to be responsible for cooking the meals, washing, shopping, keeping in touch with relatives, cleaning the house. Men repaired household equipment, put out garbage, did the gardening. Both decided how family income was spent, handled money on holidays, organized family holidays, listened to problems (Findlay & Lawrence, 1991). Glezer (1984) found that couples are less traditional than their parents, women now being more involved in the financial tasks.

Sex-stereotyping in Australia is noted in several other areas, notably in comparison of migrant cultures with Australian-born and especially related to women's perceptions. For example, Rosenthal and Grieve (1990) found Anglo-Australian women to be more romantic and more traditionally sex-typed, placing more importance on physical attractiveness and beauty. Szirom (1988) argues that current education programs are responsible for reinforcing limited views of female sexuality, as it is the male view of sexuality that is promulgated. The school is the agent of this style of socialization. In a study that investigated the relationship among sex role, age, and self-esteem for adults and youths, Moore and Rosenthal (1980) found that older females were more sex-stereotyped than younger females, but there were no generation differences in sex-stereotyping for the males. An interesting study in rural settlements among young people (Smith & Borthwick, 1991) found that sex-role stereotyping and homophobia were more prevalent in rural areas.

Old Age

Australia has an aging population, at least among the Australian-born. This is not true of the aboriginal population. Women may retire at the age of 60, while men are expected to work until they are 65. However, as the work force diminishes, early retirement has become more available, whether chosen or enforced. There is a tendency for elderly wives of retired men to continue to bear much of the responsibility for carrying out routine tasks, which prevents them from enjoying equivalent leisure in retirement (Dempsey, 1989). Although Australian women live longer than men, they suffer more physical and mental health disorders in their later years and are therefore more in need of care.

Among the aboriginal population, elderly women seem to have a more secure position than the men, with more stability of residence (Storer, 1985). This is in contrast to the general picture of the Anglo-Australian section, where distinct gender inequalities exist. Although elderly people generally have adequate and affordable housing compared with the population as a whole, in terms of housing tenure and costs, elderly women tend to fare less well than their male counterparts (Rossiter, 1986).

An increasing number of elderly people of Anglo-Australian stock are seeking retirement villages as security in health care. Such a move may, however, be binding and restraining financially. Many aged and disabled persons do not have access to this style of retirement, many of them living in poverty. They are more likely to be left alone when they are old and ill and are more likely to need publicly funded care, often in institutions (National Policy on Women's Health, 1988). Edgar (1992) has pointed out that the Australian government's recent preference for community care really means "family care," which usually means care by women. Consequently, at a time when elderly women may require assistance for themselves, they may be required to continue in the caring mode.

Healthy elderly persons often enjoy sporting activities. In retirement villages these are encouraged and may include aerobics, swimming, tennis, bowling. Many other hobbies are followed by these more fortunate citizens. Travel is encouraged, with some allowances for special rates. Access by wheelchair is mandatory in most situations.

SUMMARY AND CONCLUSIONS

Gender issues in the Australian scene have been viewed here as requiring much consideration and relentless attention. Despite several national inquiries and a strong development in Women's Studies, which produces major research, the position of women is far less well advanced than might have been predicted. Women remain a minority group, while constituting more than half the total population.

Some achievements are recognized: improved curriculum for girls, equality of wages, recognition of health needs, and increases in attendance at tertiary levels. Others are lagging, hidebound by tradition, political blocks, and, to some extent, discrimination against women whose values do not match the masculine ruling ideologies.

REFERENCES

Amato, Paul. (1987). *Children in Australian Families: The Growth of Competence*. New York: Prentice-Hall.

Australian Bureau of Statistics. (1992). *The Labor Force*. Canberra, Australia.

Bielski, Joan. (1980). Equal opportunities in life—Broadening the options for boys and girls. In Le Claire, L., & van Veendendall, C. J., *Children, the Community's Concern*. Canberra: Australian Pre-School Association.

Bottomley, Gill, & De Lepervanche, Marie (Eds.). (1984). *Ethnicity, Class and Gender in Australia*. Sydney: George Allen & Unwin.

Briggs, Freda, & Potter, Gillian. (1990). *Teaching Children in the First Three Years of School*. Melbourne: Longman Cheshire.

Bryson, L. (1985). Gender divisions and power relationships in the Australian family. In Close, P., & Collins, R. (Eds.), *Family and Economy in Modern Society*. Houndmills, Hampshire: Macmillan, 83–100.

Burke, Janine. (1980). *Australian Women Artists 1840–1940*. Collingwood, Victoria: Greenhouse Publications.

Burton, Clare. (1987). Merit and gender: Organizations and the "mobilization of masculine bias." *Australian Journal of Social Issues* (22).

Callan, Victor. (1986). *Australian Minority Groups*. Sydney: Harcourt Brace Jovanovich.

Clark, Margaret. (1990). *The Great Divide: Gender in the Primary School*. Carlton South: Curriculum Corporation.

Collman, J. (1979). Women, children and the significance of the domestic group to urban Aborigines in Central Australia. *Ethnology, 18* (4): 379–97.

Davies, B. (1989). *Frogs and Snails and Feminist Tails: Preschool Children and Gender*. Sydney: Allen & Unwin.

Dempsey, K. (1989). Gender exploitation and the domestic division of labor among the elderly: An Australian case study. *Australian Journal on Ageing, 8* (3): 3–10.

Department of Employment, Education and Training. (1991). Year 12 Subject Choice, 1984–1988. Australia.

Department of Employment, Education and Training. (1991). *School Leavers*. Canberra, Australia.

Edgar, Don. (1990). Mixed messages about children. *Family Matters* (27).

———. (1992). Look what's coming in family matters. *Family Notes* (1).

Edgar, Patricia, & ors. (1974). *Under Five in Australia*. Melbourne: Heinemann.

Eisenstein, Hester. (1991). *Gender Shock*. Sydney: Allen & Unwin.

Fabian, Sue, & Loh, Morag. (1980). *Children in Australia*. London: Oxford University Press.

Findlay, Bruce, & Lawrence, A. Jeannette. (1991). Who does what? Gender-related distribution of household tasks for couples, their families of origin and their ideals. *Australian Journal of Marriage & Family, 12* (1): 3–7.

Fraser, Bryce (Ed.). (1983). *The Macquarie Book of Events*. Sydney: Macquarie Library.

Glezer, H. (1984). Changes in marriage and sex-role attitudes among young married women: 1971–1982. *Australian Family Research Conference Proceedings, Volume 1; Family Format, Structure, Values.* Melbourne: Institute of Family Studies, 201–55.

Glezer, Helen. (1990). Fathers are parents too. *Family Matters* (27).

Grbich, C., & Sykes, S. (1990). Post school environments: Gender, curriculum and attitudes towards persons with severe intellectual disabilities. *Australian Disability Review* (2): 21–30.

Hall, Trish, & ors. (1990). Women and work: Challenges for the 1990s—A panel. In *National Women's Conference 1990 Proceedings.* Queanbeyan: Write People.

Harrison, Margaret. (1988). Major changes to Family Law Act. *Family Matters.* Australian Institute of Family Studies Newsletter, No. 20.

Heaven, Patrick, & Callan, Victor. (1990). *Adolescence: An Australian Perspective.* Sydney: Harcourt Brace Jovanovich.

Isaacs, Jennifer. (1980). *Australian Dreaming 40,000 Years of Aboriginal History.* Sydney: Lansdowne Press.

Jones, F. L. 1983. Sources of gender inequality in income: What the Australian census says. *Social Forces, 62* (September): 134–52.

Luling, Virginia. (1982). *Aborigines.* London: MacDonald.

McDonald, Peter. (1991). Migrant family structure. In Funder, Kathleen (Ed.), *Images of Australian Families.* Melbourne: Longman Cheshire.

Mackinnon, Alison. (1986). *The New Woman.* Netley: Wakefield Press.

Marjoribanks, K. (1987). Gender/social class, family environments and adolescents' aspirations. *Australian Journal of Education, 31* (1): 43–54.

Martin, Jeanne. (1984). *Non English-Speaking Women: Production and Social Reproduction.* In Bottomley, Gill, & De Lepervanche, Marie (Eds.), *Ethnicity, Class and Gender in Australia.* Sydney: George Allen & Unwin.

Moore, S. M., & Rosenthal, D. A. (1980). Sex-roles: Gender, generation, and self-esteem. *Australian Psychologist, 15* (November): 467–77.

Naffine, Ngaire. (1990). *Law and the Sexes: Exploration in Feminine Jurisprudence.* Sydney: Allen & Unwin.

National Agenda for Women Implementation Report. (1991). Canberra: Office of the Status of Women.

National Policy for the Education of Girls in Australian Schools. (1987). Canberra: Commonwealth Schools Commission.

National Policy on Women's Health: A Framework for Change. (1988). Canberra: Australian Government Publishing Service.

National Women's Conference 1990 Proceedings. (1990). Queanbeyan: Write People.

Neil, C. C., & Snizek, W. E. (1987). Work value, job characteristics, and gender. *Sociological Perspectives, 30*: 245–65.

Noller, Patricia, & Callan, Victor J. (1991). Images of the typical Australian family. In Funder, Kathleen (Ed.), *Images of Australian Families.* Melbourne: Longman Cheshire.

Poole, Millicent. (1981). *School Leavers in Australia.* Commonwealth Canberra: Schools Commission.

———. (1983). Influences on job choices of young women and girls—Problems of technological change. *Australian Educational Researcher, 10* (2): 24–46.

Porter, Paige. (1986). *Gender and Education.* Melbourne: Deakin University.

Raddford, Gail. (1990). EEO for women in the 1990s. In *National Women's Conference 1990 Proceedings*. Queanbeyan: Write People.

The Red Fems. (1982). The implications of technological change for women workers in the public sector. In Bevage, Margaret & Shute, Carmel (Eds.), *Worth Her Salt: Women at Work in Australia*. Sydney: Hale & Iremonger.

Rosenthal, Doreen, & Grieve, Norma. (1990). Attitudes to the gender culture: A comparison of Italian-Australian and Anglo-Australian female tertiary students. *Australian Psychologist, 25* (3): 282–92.

Rossiter, C. (1986). Housing tenure and costs of older Australians: Gender issues. *Australian Journal on Ageing, 5* (May): 4–12.

Rubinstein, Linda. (1982). Dominance eroticised: Sexual harassment of working women. In Bevage, Margaret & Shute, Carmel (Eds), *Worth Her Salt: Women at Work in Australia*. Sydney: Hale & Iremonger.

Rutter, Viki. (1990). Entrance, access, equity and employment—Factors affecting women in higher education. In *National Women's Conference 1990 Proceedings*. Queanbeyan: Write People.

Smith, V., & Borthwick, P. (1991). That's how it is: Gender and sexuality in rural Australia. *On the Level, 1* (1): 8–11.

Splatt, William, & Burton, Barbara. (1977). *100 Masterpieces of Australian Painting*. Adelaide: Rigby.

Storer, Des. (Ed.). (1985). *Ethnic Family Values in Australia*. Compiled by the Institute of Family Studies. Melbourne: Prentice-Hall.

Szirom, T. (1988). *Teaching Gender? Sex Education and Sexual stereotypes*. North Sydney: Allen & Unwin.

Thiele, B. & Grace, J. (1990). Negotiating the domestic division of labor. In National Women's Conference Proceedings, *National Foundation for Australian Women*, 129–52. Canberra, Australia.

Tom, Jean. (1990). Life has never been easy. In *National Women's Conference 1990 Proceedings*. Queanbeyan: Write People.

Tsolidis, G. (1988). Ethnic minority girls and self-esteem. In Kenway, J., & Williss S. (Eds.), *Hearts and Minds: Self-Esteem and the Schooling of Girls*. Canberra: Department of Employment, Education and Training.

Working Group on Women in Sport. (1985). *Women, Sport and the Media*. Canberra: Australian Government Publishing Service.

Yates, Lyn. (1990). *Theory/Practice Dilemmas: Gender, Knowledge and Education*. Geelong: Deakin University.

2

Brazil

Júlia Ferro Bucher and
Maria Alice D'Amorim

INTRODUCTION

Brazil is a country of 8.5 million square kilometers and approximately 150 million inhabitants. Today most of the population is mestizo, with mixed Portuguese, black African slave, and Indian ancestry. During the colonial period, Brazilian society was divided up into slaves (Blacks from Africa) and masters (white Portuguese).

The religious background is Catholic (coming from the Portuguese population) but also includes a strong spiritist tradition, including *candomblé* and other rituals (primarily originating in the black population), as well as beliefs in natural forces primarily inherited from the Indians. Protestant cults are increasing. However, today a great deal of religious syncretism may be found.

Brazilian culture is very diverse, varying according to regional population differences. For example, in the tropics (the Amazon region), Indian influence on food and on attitudes and behavior is strong. In the South, German, Italian, and Japanese immigration has influenced the cultural context. When we compare the two regions, we see that they are quite different. Many other variations are found in Brazilian culture as well.

Today the country is facing many social and economic problems, with great repercussions on the lives of men and women of all ages. Migration from the rural areas to the large urban centers, especially of men in search of better living conditions, often produces great family disintegration. In one study of migration to Brasilia, it was found that the husband migrates, while the wife and children stay at home. Some time after arriving in the city, he takes another woman, who becomes the mother of his children. With the passage of time, the wife and children who stayed home come looking for him, and he has to choose: he either stays with the most recent woman, with whom he has a new family, or with the wife and children who have just arrived. In this context, one of the two women will keep the children by herself, but not for long, and the cycle repeats itself (Ferro Bucher, 1991).

The Brazilian population is young. Approximately 37 percent of Brazilians are under 15 years of age. The rate of population growth is declining, as a consequence of the great reduction in fertility, which fell from 6.3 percent in 1966 to 3.3 percent in 1990.

Infant mortality is still very high. In 1989, the estimated mortality rate of children under 5 was 64/1,000, while life expectancy was 65 years.

Brazil is a country that is experiencing many changes, as may be clearly perceived through observation of the behavior of the people.

OVERVIEW

Relationships between men and women in Brazil are related to the prevailing values in the society. Today the country is passing through a period in which the prevailing values of patriarchal society are being rapidly transformed.

Bastide, in Ferro Bucher (1969), analyzing texts describing the behavior of men and women in the early fifties, wrote that they acted according to a principle that he called the double standard. Most men lived with their wives, a housewife and mother of the children legitimated by marriage, and with another woman, with whom they had a romantic and sexual relationship. The law was established as a function of this reality: descendance was considered only on the maternal side, in accordance with the Latin tradition *Partus ventrem sequitur*. Thus, the man was not responsible for those children who were not born under the protection of marriage.

In the colonial period, women and men were educated quite differently. Virginity was expected and even demanded of "family" women, who, through marriage, would become "family mothers." The other women, called *mulheres da vida*, were considered to be for sexual pleasure. Men were educated for extreme freedom, and virility was confounded with machismo (Freyre, 1964).

In the late sixties and through the mid-seventies, when the impact of machismo was still great, it came to be more intensely questioned due to the practice of men murdering their wives in the name of "defense of honor," when they suspected infidelity on their part. At first the men were absolved, because the alleged "defense of honor" was considered to be a sufficient motive to justify such an act.

In the early seventies, the women's situation began to be discussed. Countless changes in women's behavior began at that time, as the statistics show. In 1969, there were 100,000 women and 200,000 men studying at universities; by 1975 the numbers had increased to 500,000 women and 500,000 men. In just five years, the number of women had quintupled.

The same transformation occurred in the job market. In 1960, the economically active population represented 22.6 million persons, or 32 percent of the total population, and included 18.6 million men and 4 million women. In the period from 1970 to 1976, the female labor force doubled.

If the statistical indicators portray the differences and similarities in the experiences of men and women in Brazil, a study of the Brazilian legislation and constitution also points to important changes. Until 1962, the constitution placed married women at the same level as savages, spendthrifts, and pubescent minors. They needed their husband's authorization to do various things, including exercising a profession or engaging in commerce.

Women were emancipated in Brazilian legislation by Law 4121, Articles 233, 240, and 246 (1962), under which they attained the condition of companion of their spouse and collaborator in the family responsibilities and were authorized to exercise a remunerative profession different from that of the husband and to dispose freely of acquired property.

Among the motives for annulment of marriage, Article 219 specified that the husband could annul the marriage if the wife was deflowered, unbeknown to him. The taboo of lack of virginity was respected for many years and provoked absurd situations. Williams (1953:340) observed, "An attempt to adjust slowly changing ideas about sex to the iron rule of tradition may be seen in the not infrequent practice of restoring virginity by a surgical operation. Thus, at least what may be called the anatomic chance for marriage is thought to have been recovered."

Today, almost forty years after Williams's observation, things have changed a great deal. Lack of virginity is no longer a taboo, nor is virginity considered an indispensable prerequisite for marriage. The new constitution of 1988 states, in Article 5.I, that "men and women are equal in rights and obligations." It totally changes the relationship between the sexes when it makes explicit, in Article 226, paragraph 5, that "the rights and duties with reference to the conjugal relationship are exercised equally by man and woman."

COMPARISONS BETWEEN MEN'S AND WOMEN'S GENDER ROLES DURING THE LIFE CYCLE

Infancy and Early Childhood

In Brazil 3.5 million babies are born each year. Of these, many will grow up and develop within a family containing a father, mother, and other siblings, or in single-parent families. However, the number of children living in the streets, abandoned by their parents, is growing.

A study of parents' expectations regarding the sex of their children to be born did not show any significant difference between the expectations of the father and mother; both would like to have both sons and daughters (Ferro Bucher, 1991). Traditionally, boys and girls had culturally defined forms of play and differentiated playthings (dolls for girls and balls for boys). In modern Brazil, although video games are played by both sexes, they seduce the boys more, while the girls still prefer calmer pastimes.

Studies of accidents involving children also show that the growing number of female children involved in accidents is due to their assumption of responsibilities before they are old enough to handle them. This is especially true of young girls who are expected to take care of their siblings and of the house while the parents work all day (Ferro Bucher & Vale, 1987).

Relationships between the sexes in this phase of life have been little studied in Brazil.

School Years

The first aspect of gender role that affects children of school age is the difference in opportunity of access into the educational system. Rosemberg (1975), using census data, studied male and female enrollment rates, literacy level, and school achievement. She showed that the female population presents a lower level of literacy and school enrollment. However, this difference has been reduced over the years. The school dropout rate differs according to gender as well. Boys tend to leave school at no fixed point, while girls tend to finish one part and have trouble entering the following one, with a high dropout rate when finishing grammar school and at the moment of entering the university. Rosemberg's data indicate higher levels of achievement among female students compared to males, higher rates of graduation from the several levels, and a higher proportion of students attending each grade at the appropriate age.

Barroso and Mello (1975) studied access to higher education, professional choice, and performance on the university entrance exams, for male and female students. Their data showed that women have increased participation in higher education since 1956, the rate being 26 percent in 1956 and 40 percent in 1971. Their professional choices tend toward the humanities, with emphasis on psychology, sociology, education, and nursing. Today we find more women in some areas of medicine and in biology, law, and engineering. Despite better results in high school, their performance on the university entrance exam is often lower than that of their male peers. Differences in gender socialization create a fear of competing with men and a feeling that their professional life has to be adapted to the needs of raising a family.

Differences in gender socialization are reflected in studies of families' educational aspirations for boys and girls. Campos and Esposito (1975) studied mothers' expectations regarding their children's future occupations and educational attainments. Half of the mothers talked about their sons, the other half about their daughters. Middle-class mothers did not differ with respect to educational and occupational expectations for their sons or daughters. Lower-class mothers, however, had significantly higher expectations for their sons. They were supposed to go to college and become professionals, while the girls should finish high school and get routine jobs as secretaries or dental assistants. Using a list of masculine and feminine professions, the authors found that very few boys were expected to have feminine jobs, but among middle-class mothers a significant percentage of daughters could have masculine jobs. This may be an indication that gender roles are becoming less rigid.

As in many other countries, gender roles in Brazil are changing. Women have more access to education and suffer less discrimination at work. One should note that these advances do not interfere with the notion of the woman's main role as wife and mother. The opening up of new opportunities for work leads to double responsibility: professional duties and the care of children and the home, with very little help from men, especially since the social structure in Brazil still allows for even middle-class families to have some kind of hired domestic help.

Young Adults

This section presents studies about the perception of gender roles among several samples of female and male undergraduates. The general objective was to verify the beliefs and attitudes about personality traits and occupations related to feminine and masculine roles among Brazilian young adults.

Steinmann and Ramos (1974) studied the perception of the feminine role among groups of male and female undergraduates, professionals, and nonprofessionals of similar age. The scale used had 34 items; 17 described women as passive, home-oriented, giving precedence to the care of the family over professional activities; the other 17 items showed women as active, making important decisions in family matters, and willing to use their professional capacities. For the women in the sample two measures were used; they had to say how well the items corresponded to them (self-concept) and to the ideal woman. Men answered only the second measure. Results showed that female professionals and undergraduates perceived themselves and the ideal woman as active. Nonprofessional women chose passive items to describe themselves and the ideal woman, confirming some of the predictions made by the authors. Female subjects were also asked their opinion about men's perception of the ideal woman, and all three groups believed men would choose the passive role. Actually, professional men considered the active woman as ideal, undergraduates showed some ambivalence, and nonprofessionals preferred the family-oriented woman. The results show the women's dilemma well, wishing to be active and believing men to prefer them in a passive role.

In the Northeast of Brazil, the existence of gender-role stereotypes was studied by Radice (1987). Three groups of undergraduates received a list of 136 short descriptions, to choose those that best fit a man, a woman, and an adult, according to the group. For each concept, men, women, and adults, the 20 most chosen descriptions (75 percent) together formed a 60-item instrument for the following stage. Another group of 21 male and 29 female undergraduates had to classify the 60 descriptions according to their level of desirability for a person of undefined gender. Before the 60 descriptions were presented to the new group, they had undergone a content analysis that considered the male descriptions as related to instrumental and sexual dimensions; female descriptions were defined as belonging to emotional-expressive and submissive dimensions. Results were analyzed according to the subjects' sex: in both groups the highest level of desirability was obtained by the adult descriptions that were considered ideal for males and females, as an expression of the mature self. The least desirable descriptions were those containing gender stereotypes. Female subjects rejected a total of 11 descriptions, 8 feminine stereotypes such as submissive, obedient, and religious and 3 masculine ones: dominant, individualist, and competitive. Male subjects considered undesirable the same feminine descriptions, adding one more: "dislikes mathematics"; they also considered it undesirable to be dominant, moralistic, and a good politician. These results indicate that gender-role stereotypes still exist but are beginning to be rejected by young Brazilian adults.

In Brazil's capital, Brasilia, several studies about gender-role stereotypes were conducted by D'Amorim. The first one explored values and attitudes toward the future in a group of undergraduates (D'Amorim, 1987). Values were measured with a Rokeach scale adapted and validated for Brazilian use. A scale of attitudes toward the future (Nuttin, 1980) was the other instrument used. Results showed several significant gender differences for terminal values; women, more than men, value mature love, self-respect, inner harmony, self-realization, and a world at peace; men value, more than women, liberty, pleasure, social recognition, and a comfortable and exciting life. Instrumental values showed only two significant differences, with women valuing courage more than men and the latter giving more importance to self-control. As far as attitudes toward the future are concerned, only the dimension of difficulty yielded significant results, with women expecting more problems. The differences found in values and attitudes show women's need for self-respect and self-realization, values that men take for granted. Their pessimism toward the future could be explained by the difficulty felt in combining their domestic activities, leading to mature love and inner harmony, with the self-realization and self-respect to be obtained in the professional world.

Later studies (D'Amorim, 1988) tested the influence of behavioral information received on the gender typing of a stimulus person. Based on previous work by Deaux and Lewis (1984), three behavioral descriptions were used for male, female, and mixed roles. Three groups of undergraduates received one description each and were asked to evaluate the degree to which 12 personality traits and ten occupations would fit the described person. The male role description said: financial provider, leader of activities, head of the household, and responsible for its repairs; the female role said: source of emotional support, takes care of children, household manager and responsible for its decoration. The mixed role used two elements of each of the others: financial and emotional support, leader of activities, and takes care of the children. Personality traits and occupations had been classified as masculine or feminine, according to previous research (Deaux & Lewis, 1984). Results showed that subjects who read the feminine description considered the person as gentle, emotional, and understanding, with a high probability of being a nurse, teacher, or psychologist. The masculine description evoked the traits of self-confidence, competitiveness, independence, and persistence, with the person probably working as a dentist, broker, chemist, or salesman. The mixed description fitted a decided person, having more masculine than feminine traits and being able to work in both masculine and feminine professions. Results confirmed that a gender-linked message about someone's behavior at home determined the attribution not only of personality traits but also of professional occupations, on the basis of totally irrelevant information.

Adults

Gender-role stereotypes have been explored in several Brazilian studies. Goldberg, Baptista, Arruda, Barreto and Menezes (1975) studied the perception of the female role using the question "In your opinion, what are women like?" Answers were classified along a continuum from traditional to modern. Traditional answers included sweet, gentle, pleasant, helpful, polite, queen of the home, and others that exalted women's domestic role. Modern answers reinforced gender equality and showed some awareness of the changes in the female role. Although subjects of both sexes were relatively young, most presented the traditional point of view.

Salem (1980) found similar definitions of the female role in women of high, medium, and low socioeconomic level. In the author's opinion, this consistency is based on the social importance of women's domestic role; even when they pursue activities outside the home, women tend to attribute their main identity to domestic life.

In a later study with low-income women, Salem (1981) asked their perceptions of men and women. Men were described as free, irresponsible toward the family, and with greater earning power. Women were viewed as weak, needing protection, having greater responsibilities toward the children, and suffering more. The author concludes that men are considered as providers, with women having the procreative role, being responsible for their children's socialization and all domestic tasks.

Gender stereotypes in low-income women and men were studied in Brasilia by Raiser (1985), using a questionnaire of gender stereotypes with 30 items, 26 used to evaluate both men and women and four gender-related ones, two for each sex. The female role was described according to four dimensions: home, husband, children, and body. Responsibility for domestic tasks was the most frequent response, independent of sex or age, even when outside work is included, since it consists of domestic help. Submission to the husband and child care are an important part of the perceived female role. The body dimension, frequent among young men, involves the erotic aspects of young women's clothes. Male stereotypes relate to work, power, and freedom, including their responsibility as providers, their authority over the family, and the freedom to follow their inclinations, to the point of abandoning the family to establish a new one. Raiser (1985) concludes that women are defined as a function of men, their dimensions based on marital relations.

Metaperception results show that men expected to be seen by women with wider social receptivity and better physical appearance than they attributed to themselves. Women feel that men see them as more beautiful than their own evaluation, but also as less ethical, self-confident, and self-controlled than they perceived themselves. These metaperceptions are quite objective, corresponding to the way men and women perceive the opposite sex. According to the authors, the results differ from previous data; men perceived women more positively than themselves. Women's stereotypes, especially self-stereotypes, were not only defined as expressive but also included instrumental dimensions.

Nascimento (1988) studied the level of characterization of gender stereotypes, using content analysis. The subjects had to describe the attributes that best fit the categories of parent, executive, athlete, artist and student, and finally, men and women. Results showed that all male and female categories could be considered as basic ones, since they showed a significantly greater number of distinct attributes than common ones. Women, in general, gave more responses than men. Another result was that the general descriptions of men and women were not at a more abstract level of characterization than the other stimulus words offered, since they evoked the same number of responses as the others; the author concludes that besides using the general concepts of men and women, future gender-stereotyping research should also include other male and female subtypes that could contribute to a better understanding of the nature of stereotypes.

Sarti (1989) studied gender relation as perceived by women from a poor district on the outskirts of São Paulo. Her analysis of the data was based on the division of roles in the family. Viewed as "natural," such division rests on women's symbolic identification with home and men's with the street: the two universes are ruled by different moral codes, which may lead to defiance and mutual accusations. The analysis argues that gender relations bear on two principles: reciprocity, which establishes the complementary roles for men and women, and hierarchy, which establishes male authority over the family. Women's basic reference in the construction of their social identity lies in their domestic activities.

Male and female perceptions of domestic control were studied under matrifocal conditions, with data collected in a poor neighborhood of Recife. Expectations of strong male dominance are in contrast with a reality in which the basis for continuity and security of the domestic group is based on the women's side of the family. Using the concept of developmental cycles in the analysis of the domestic group, through the series of conjugal unions and separations, the author argues that gender defines how domestic cycles are lived (Scott, 1990).

Perceived causes for marital success and failure were studied with 80 married couples by Dela Coleta, Santamarina, and Castro (1986). There was agreement between men and women regarding the main causes of success, namely, understanding, compatibility, respect, love, education, trust, support, sex, money, honesty, luck, and good relations with in-laws; there was no agreement regarding perceived causes of failure except for lack of love, irresponsibility, jealousy, and problems with the in-laws. Some perceived causes of failure were blamed on women: lack of obedience, respect, and tolerance; neglect of home and husband; being bad-tempered, proud, stupid, shameless, and unfaithful. Men's responsibility was limited to drinking and gambling.

Dela Coleta (1989) studied married people by asking them the six main elements in a successful marriage. From among 58 elements, 17 reached the 10 percent criterion of agreement. Both sexes tended to value love as the main element in a successful marriage, followed by understanding, respect, fidelity, communication, and sex. Women mentioned respect between partners, friendship, and liberty almost twice as often as men; having children, patience, resignation, and effort were more frequently stated by men. To obtain not only frequencies but the relative values of each element for male and females, a second study was done with 62 couples aged 17 to 61, with an average of 12 years of marriage (Dela Coleta & D'Amorim, 1991). The subjects were asked to rank the 13 elements most frequently chosen, in the first study, as significant to a successful marriage. The general pattern of perceptions is similar across gender, with love as the most important value and money as the least; grouped in the middle are fidelity, honesty, respect, and communication.

Gender differences were found, with men considering love, sex, and children more important for a successful marriage than did women. Communication, trust, companionship, compatibility, and understanding were more valued by women.

Some studies refer to gender stereotypes in relation to work. Mello (1975) studied the distribution of teachers by sex and different levels of the school system. The data showed a predominance of women in the elementary schools (90 percent), about 50 percent in secondary schools, and a small participation at the university level (20 percent). Salary and prestige in the teaching profession were reduced by women's entrance. At all levels, even when they constitute the majority, the presence of women in administrative positions is small. Universities, while doing some gender-role research, have not yet acknowledged their role in the political side of this question.

Barroso (1975a) studied the participation of women in Brazilian scientific development, using data from the financing agencies and universities. The statistics show a very small percentage of women producing scientific knowledge in the main areas of research. Gender discrimination, parental expectations during the educational process, and the distribution of power and influence could explain such data. Even in the professions where women are in the majority, such as psychology and teaching, administrative positions are often held by men.

In another study (Barroso, 1975b), the author analyzes the psychological reasons for the low participation of women in scientific activities. Gender socialization, low self-concept, gender discrimination in school and work, the stress related to their double responsibilities (professional and domestic), and the lack of self-confidence felt by persons who disobey group norms are some of the explanations for the acceptance by women of subordinate positions without real power to change policies.

The Federal Council of Psychology (1988), in a national survey of psychologists in Brazil, found that 86 percent are women, but regional and federal councils are mostly presided over by men. At scientific meetings, the number of papers and lectures presented by men reaches 60 percent, showing them to be more productive or to enjoy more prestige than women (Rosas, Rosas & Xavier, 1988).

Old Age

In Brazilian culture, old age has the following characteristics, for both men and women. Demographic data show that average life expectancy in Brazil was sixty-five years in 1990. By the end of the nineties, the proportion of older people in the population will be 6 percent.

In 1978, life expectancy was 56.3 percent for men and 62.8 percent for women. According to data presented by Veras (1987), the increase in life expectancy in Brazil has been greater for women than for men. This is a consequence of different degrees of exposure to work risks and different attitudes toward disease and incapacities, regarding which women are more attentive to the appearance of symptoms and better utilization of the health services.

According to the report of the State University of Ceará on the Educational Project for Senior Citizens (Projeto de Ensino para a Terceira Idade), one of the greatest problems faced in conjugal relationships is due to the retirement of the husbands, who begin to manage the household—the erstwhile prerogative of the wife. In response to the countless marital problems, the project integrated the women into the course in preparation for retirement, including this dimension in the power relationship and life space of the couple.

Other studies have provided important data on this topic as well. A study of old age as a stage of human development shows that 6 percent of the Brazilian population, more than 7 million people, are over 60. The increase in the number of older people in recent years is related to socioeconomic level. Wealthy or even middle-class people may benefit from scientific and technological medical advances, but for the lower class, life expectancy is still around 53 years. Despite the increased prestige of old age in developed Western countries and in some Oriental ones, in Brazil old people are still viewed as infirm or at best nonproductive. Government retirement plans are inadequate; many people cannot retire without suffering great financial loss or risking starvation and destitution if their previous income was low.

SUMMARY AND CONCLUSIONS

In reviewing the literature on questions related to gender roles, incorporating studies that refer to these questions and pointing out certain statistical data, it becomes obvious that throughout history, attitudes and behavior have undergone changes, particularly in recent decades. Such changes have not been generalized throughout the country, however. There are points of resistance to change in the relationship between men and women, as well as organizations of men for machismo. In the state of Minas Gerais, such organizations have more and more taken on folkloric characteristics. Changes in legislation have also been extremely important in guaranteeing the rights of women. Contraception and women's increasing participation in education and the labor market have also given them greater autonomy, confidence, and respect. The crucial question concerns the need for integration of the male and female roles, not unchecked competition, which leads to a blind and meaningless escalation. This integration has become indispensable to the construction of solid structures at the personal, family, professional, and societal levels.

REFERENCES

Barroso, C. (1975a). Participação da mulher no desenvolvimento científico brasileiro (Women's participation in Brazilian scientific development). *Ciência e Cultura, 27* (6): 613–20.

———— (1975b). Porque são tão poucas as mulheres que exercem atividades científicas? (Why do so few women engage in scientific activities?). *Ciência e Cultura, 27* (7): 703–10.

Barroso, C., & Mello, G. (1975). O acesso da mulher ao ensino superior brasileiro (Women's access to higher education in Brazil). *Cadernos de Pesquisa, 15*: 47–76.

Bem, S. (1974). The management of psychological androgyny. *Journal of Consulting and Clinical Psychology, 42*: 155–62.

————. (1981). Gender schema theory: A cognitive account of sex-typing. *Psychology Review, 88*: 354–63.

Bonamigo, E., & Rasche, V. (1980). O processo de socialização da criança em famílias de classe popular (The socialization process in children of low-income families). *Psicologia: Teoria e pesquisa, 4* (3): 295–315.

Campos, M., & Esposito, Y. (1975). Relação entre o sexo da criança e aspirações educacionais da mãe (The relationship between child's sex and mother's educational aspirations). *Cadernos de Pesquisa, 15*: 37–46.

Constituição: República Federativa do Brasil—1988. Brasilia: Senado Federal, Centro Gráfico.

D'Amorim, M. A. (1987). Valores e atitudes em relação ao futuro em universitários brasileiros (Values and attitudes toward the future in Brazilian undergraduates). *Arquivos Brasileiros de Psicologia, 39* (4): 21–38.

————. (1988). Estereótipos de gênero em universitários (Gender stereotypes in Brazilian undergraduates). *Psicologia: Reflexão e Crítica, 3* (1-2): 3–11.

Deaux, K., & Lewis, L. (1984). Structure of gender stereotypes: Interrelationships among the components of gender label. *Journal of Personality and Social Psychology*, *36* (9): 927–40.

Dela Coleta, J. A., Santamarina, N. B., & Castro, S. A. (1986). Atribuição de causalidade a eventos naturais e acidentais em amostras de baixo nivel cultural (Causal attribution to natural and accidental events in low cultural samples). Technical Report, University of Uberlândia, Brazil.

Dela Coleta, M. F. (1989). Locus de controle e satisfação conjugal (Locus of control and marital satisfaction). Master's thesis, University of Brasilia, Brazil.

Dela Coleta, M. F. & D'Amorim, M. A. (1991). *Perceived causes of success and failure in marriage*. Paper presented at the Forty-ninth Annual Convention of the International Council of Psychologists, San Francisco.

Ferro Bucher, Júlia (1969). Contribution à une étude de la famille et la sexualité au Brésil. Master's thesis, University of Leuven, Belgium.

———. (1991). *Migration familiale, identité et changement socio-culturel. Actes do Troisème Colloque de l'ARIC*. Paris: Editions L'Harmattan.

———. (1991). Recasamento e recomposição familiar: Questões metodológicas, de linguagem e das teorias (Remarriage and family recomposition: Methodological, language, and theoretical questions). *Psicologia: Teoria e pesquisa, 6* (2): 155–69.

Ferro Bucher, J. and Vale, J. A. (1987). O acidente, o acidentado e o contexto sócio-familiar. *Arquivos Brasileiros de Psicologia, 39* (1): 95–108.

Freyre, Gilberto. (1964). *Casa grande e senzala* (The masters and the slaves). Porto Alegre: Globo.

Goldberg, M. A., Baptista, M. T., Arruda, N. C., Barreto, E. S., & Menezes, S. M. (1975). Concepções sobre o papel da mulher no trabalho, na política e na familia (Views about woman's role at work, in politics, and in the family). *Cadernos de Pesquisa, 15*: 86–123.

Mello, G. (1975). Estereótipos sexuais na escola (Gender stereotypes at school). *Cadernos de Pesquisa, 15*: 141–44.

Nascimento, M. C. (1988). Nível de categorização de estereótipos sexuais (Level of characterization of sexual stereotypes). *Psicologia: Teoria e pesquisa, 4* (2): 137–48.

Nuttin, J. (1980). *Motivation et Perspectives d'Avenir*. Louvain: Presses Universitaires de Louvain.

Radice, J. (1987). Papéis sexuais no nordeste do Brasil: Sua desejabilidade e possíveis consequências para a auto-realização da mulher (Gender roles in Brazil's northeast: Their desirability and possible consequences for women's self-realization). *Revista de Psicologia, 5* (1): 93–103.

Raiser, E. (1985). Estereótipos sexuais em favelados (Gender stereotypes in shantytowns). Master's thesis, University of Brasilia, Brazil.

Rosas, P., Rosas, A., & Xavier, I. (1988). Quantos e quem somos? (Who are we and how many?). In Conselho Federal de Psicologia (Ed.), *Quem é o psicólogo brasileiro?* (Who is the Brazilian psychologist?). São Paulo: Edicon.

Rosemberg, F. (1975). A escola e as diferenças sexuais (School and gender differences). *Cadernos de Pesquisa, 15*: 78–85.

Salem, T. (1980). *O velho e o novo. Um estudo de papéis e conflitos familiares* (The old and the new. A study of family roles and conflicts). Petrópolis: Vozes.

———. (1981). *Mulheres faveladas. Com a venda nos olhos* (Shantytown women. With closed eyes). Perspectivas Antropológicas da Mulher. Rio de Janeiro: Zahar.

Sarti, C. (1989). Reciprocidade e Hierarquia: Relação de gênero na periferia de Såo Paulo (Reciprocity and hierarchy: Gender relationships on the outskirts of São Paulo). *Cadernos de Pesquisa, 70*: 38–40.

Scott, S. (1990). O Homem na Matrifocalidade: Gênero, percepção e experiência do domínio doméstico (Men in matrifocality: Gender, perception, and experiences in the domestic domain). *Cadernos de Pesquisa, 73*: 38–47.

Steinmann, A., & Ramos, E. (1974). Percepções masculino-femininas do papel feminino no Brasil (Male-female perceptions of the feminine role in Brazil). *Arquivos Brasileiros de Psicologia Aplicada, 26* (4): 85–91.

Veras, R. P. (1987). Crescimento da população idosa no Brasil: Transformações e con-sequências na sociedade (Growth of the older population in Brazil: Transformations and consequences for society). *Revista Saúde Pública, São Paulo, 21* (3): 225–33.

Williams, J. (1953). The structure of the Brazilian family. *Social Forces, 31*:340–75.

3

Canada

D. Elaine Davis

INTRODUCTION

Canada is a vast region (9,976,139 square kilometers or 3,851,787 square miles) that lies in the northern part of the Western hemisphere. Its only land boundaries are with the United States of America on the south, where the border spans the North American continent, and in the northwest between the 60th and 70th parallels, shared with the state of Alaska. Otherwise, its borders are the Atlantic Ocean to the east, the Pacific Ocean to the west, and the Arctic Ocean to the north.

The country encompasses a great variety of geographical areas, ranging from seashores (which can be rocky or sandy, steep or sloping) to mountains, from forests to prairies, from rich farmland to tundra. Water bodies of every size and description are to be found all over the country. The climate is as varied as the surface features, yet much of the country is inhospitable to people; therefore most of the agricultural and trading activities take place near the southern border, where 72 percent of the population live (Statistics Canada, 1989).

Canada's people have come from many different backgrounds. The first people, aboriginal or native peoples, known as Indians and Inuit, have lived in this land for many thousands of years—long before it was known as Canada. In the early 1600s people from France began to settle here; in the early 1700s English-speaking people from the United States of America and from the British Isles also established settlements. Canada became a country in 1867 with four provinces and two official languages—French and English.

At present, there are ten provinces and two territories with a population of 25,354,064 (Statistics Canada, 1989). Many more nationalities are represented in that figure than those earliest settlers, and many have sizable communities.

Statistics Canada (1990) reports that there are over 100 different ethnic and cultural groups in Canada, of which about 25 percent have neither British nor French ancestry. This diversity gave rise in the 1970s to a policy of multiculturalism. Briefly, multiculturalism is a policy that encourages all ethnic groups to develop themselves as communities, therefore maintaining their cultural identity while being encouraged to share their culture and values with all of Canadian society.

OVERVIEW

The ethnic multiplicity in Canada, added to factors such as social strata and regional differences, means that there are wide variations in gender roles. Recent immigrants are more likely to conform to their country of origin than to Canada in terms of gender-role differences. Yet their children, for the most part, are educated in one of the two official languages. To work in Canada at any but the most menial jobs, one must be able to communicate in English and/or French. Further, the majority of radio and television programs and other media are in English or French and inevitably send messages about gender roles. Thus, over time, some assimilation of attitudes, life-style, and so forth must inevitably occur. At least theoretically, some influences extend outward from all ethnic groups to all others, including French and English; however, at present it would appear that the transcultural influence is much greater from the English and French majorities to the smaller groups. While this means that Canadian society is in constant flux, this chapter is an attempt to depict some gender-role attributes that seem to be somewhat generalizable to the present Canadian life span. It should be understood that these life patterns do not exactly fit all Canadians.

Before looking at the specifics of gender roles in life stages, it would be helpful to set the scene in terms of present-day laws and political realities. Equality between the sexes has come a long way since the early part of the century, when women were considered nonpersons and subject to male domination. In 1918 all Canadian women 21 years of age and older gained the right to vote for members of Parliament in federal elections. However, voting rights at provincial levels were and are governed by each individual province; thus full enfranchisement of women in each province occurred at different times. In 1940, the last province to grant voting rights to women was Quebec. (Newfoundland, which became the last province to become part of Canada in 1949, had enfranchised women in 1925.) In practice, Canadian women have been voting at about the same rate as men since the middle 1960s (Black, 1988).

In the 1960s and early 1970s, a number of federal and provincial groups were formed to promote public awareness of women's circumstances and to promote equality. As a consequence, the 1980s did bring a number of initiatives and changes at the governmental level with some positive results. For example, sexist language (the use of words that imply women do not do certain things, e.g., "salesman," and generic words like "man" to denote both genders) has been virtually eliminated in government documents; some women have been appointed to federal boards and commissions; a woman was appointed as Governor General; the first woman was appointed to the Supreme Court of Canada; and sizable allocations of money were provided to fund women's projects and groups. In addition, more women have been elected to various political positions. The elimination of sexist language in Canadian society and the representation of women in many organizations accompanied and often preceded the governmental changes; nevertheless the representation of women in positions of power in both the public and the private sectors remains far from equal.

In more personal spheres of life, in all of Canada, women and men are now more equal under the laws. For example, both women and men can own property; transact business and enter contracts on their own, that is, without the spouse's signature, unless communal property is involved; have equal access to (most) educational opportunities; and have equal access to work situations, promotions, and other work-related opportunities (with suitable qualifications). In actuality, however, discriminatory practice exists and is difficult to prove if complaints are taken to appropriate bodies. Also, each individual lives her or his life in a social-cultural milieu that often strongly affects how that life is lived, irrespective of the law. That milieu continues widely to transmit stereotypic, gender-specific messages, for example, that men are strong, tough, aggressive, independent, adventurous, competitive, do not show emotions, are ''breadwinners'' and that women are weak, expressive, gentle, aware of others' feelings, dependent, easily influenced, submissive, emotional. Furthermore, the characteristics attributed to males have been more valued.

A potent agent of transmission of gender messages is television. Although the number of women in some areas of broadcasting, such as newscasters, has increased markedly in recent years, one has only to turn on the television set to find, in short order, evidence of stereotypic portrayal of gender roles, both in advertising and in program content. The Canadian Radio-Television and Tele-communications Commission (CRTC) developed recommendations in the early 1980s to reduce stereotyping in the Canadian broadcast media that were disseminated to the appropriate broadcasting and advertising bodies. The CRTC then carried out a study that compared data from 1984 and 1988 to assess changes. Unfortunately, the results indicated few changes occurred in that four-year period in either English- or French-language broadcasting (CRTC, 1990).

The most distressing aspect of gender inequality in Canada is the large amount of violence directed against women by men. This is not to deny that violence against men also exists (sometimes even by women), but the preponderance of cases are directed against women. Intrafamilial violence against women (and children) has always existed, but it has finally ''gone public,'' and the immensity of the problem is alarming. In addition, assaults against women, including sexual assaults, have become so frequent that walking alone at night or parking in dimly lighted and unprotected areas has become terror-ridden for many women. While people not directly affected by violence against women may have been able to ignore its existence, one horrific event in 1989, now known as the Montreal Massacre, brought the issue to the foreground of attention all across Canada when fourteen female engineering students were shot by one young male. The suicide note discovered after he also shot himself was purported to be a diatribe against women. To end this overview in a somewhat more promising vein, many people—both men and women—have redoubled efforts to bring about social change that will make violence less acceptable as a way to deal with problems.

COMPARISONS BETWEEN MEN'S AND WOMEN'S GENDER ROLES DURING THE LIFE CYCLE

Infancy and Early Childhood

When it becomes apparent that a new child is to be born, usually the first question asked of prospective parents is "Do you want a boy or a girl?" Evidence reported for all of North America (Robinson & Salamon, 1987; Mackie, 1987) suggests a preference for sons as firstborn, but for sex-balanced completed families. A recent study (Krishnan, 1987) in Canada indicated similar results.

As soon as the child is born, its gender becomes a potent part of the socialization process, from choosing a gender-appropriate name to wrapping the baby in a pink (girl) or blue (boy) blanket. A birth announcement is sent and/or an announcement is put into the local newspaper giving the birth date, birth weight, name, and sex of the child. The widespread practice of dressing the child in pink or blue tends to continue while the child is an infant. This practice could even include the baby's disposable diaper, which, according to one current television advertisement, can be obtained in blue Oxford stripes for a boy or pink rosebuds for a girl! Even when a baby's clothing does not conform to the "color code," it is unlikely that a boy will be dressed in pink. For a formal occasion, a girl infant or young child will often be seen wearing a frilly dress, whereas a boy will be seen in some variation of trousers. But in more informal situations unisex clothing has become common; that is, both sexes wear rompers or pants. Interestingly, females tend to have more choice and more variety in clothing styles throughout their lives.

Studies cited by Robinson and Salamon (1987) suggest that comments about babies in their first twenty-four hours by parents tend to differ according to their sex (even when no differences exist by observable criteria); for example, girls are said to be cute, delicate, weak, and beautiful while boys are described as strong, alert, and well coordinated. Also, the authors cited differing interpretations of nine-month-old babies' similar reactions to a stimulus in an experimental situation—anger for boys, fear for girls.

There is some suggestion that parental behavior begins to differ according to the child's gender soon after birth, with girls getting more attention in the form of talking and looking and boys receiving more physical contact. Girls tend to be treated as more fragile than boys, with the result that boys are allowed more freedom to explore their environment; after about six months of age, boys receive more feedback, both negative and positive, than girls. As development proceeds, more concern is evidenced when boys engage in gender-inappropriate behavior. Proscriptions for boys continue outside the home environment by such socialization agents as schools and peer groups. This emphasis on gender-inappropriate proscriptions tells boys what not to do or be (boys don't cry; don't be a sissy), but leaves what to do up in the air. It has been suggested that this gives rise to anxiety about appropriate future behavior. On the other hand, while less attention has been paid to little girls' socialization, some research indicates gender-role learning may be anxiety arousing for girls also, because girls are encouraged to engage in activities that are deemed gender-appropriate but are not as valued as those of males (Robinson & Salamon, 1987).

Toys provided for children are likely to reinforce gender socialization. In the first two years, boys and girls receive many of the same toys (e.g., stuffed animals and educational toys), but that practice quickly changes. Boys tend to receive more toys and more categories of toys that encourage creativity, visual and spatial manipulation, and actions oriented toward the outside world (e.g., vehicles, construction and military toys, sports equipment) while girls' toys tend to be oriented toward the world inside the home (e.g., dolls, miniature domestic equipment) (Robinson & Salamon, 1987; Mackie, 1987). The depiction of toys as gender-specific can be seen in the commercials on children's shows on Saturday morning television and in current (1991) issues of popular catalogs, such as Sears and Consumers Distributing.

Further influence on gender socialization is provided by access to media—children's books and television. Books teach as they entertain, and, in general, the messages serve to reinforce differential gender roles: females tend to be underrepresented; male characters play more active roles and are active in a greater variety of situations than females; and stereotypic, "gender-appropriate" behavior is common (Robinson & Salamon, 1987; Mackie, 1987). Some books have appeared in recent years that attempt to portray more balance between genders; however, to date there has been no systematic survey of the availability or sales of such books. Two newspaper journalists recently reported being very frustrated when they looked for nonstereotypic books for their children. Barnett (1987) was especially dismayed at the depiction of gender in picture books for very young children, and Valpy (1989) was incensed by the treatment of fathers in books as taking no part in the care of children in modern-day families.

Television is more than just one of the media. Its influence is pervasive in contemporary life. Most children watch so much television that it has been referred to as the "electronic baby-sitter," and it has greatly reduced the amount of time spent by earlier generations in reading and playing games. In addition to the supplantation of other activities, concern has been expressed that young children (under 8–10) cannot sort out real from unreal in the many messages received via television. Content analysis of cartoons, commercials, and most other programs directed toward children indicates gender stereotyping patterns similar to those in books. Indications are that the more time children spend watching television, the greater their acceptance of traditional gender stereotypes (Robinson & Salamon, 1987; Mackie, 1987).

Mackie (1987) summarizes some differences that begin to occur in play activities by preschool children in their third year. Children begin to show preferences for same-sexed playmates, and they begin to show differences in the type of play. Boys tend to engage in more rough-and-tumble, aggressive play in a struggle for dominance. When they play together, children tend to adopt roles from the same gender; that is, girls are mothers, sisters, daughters, and boys are fathers, brothers, sons. When changeovers occur in role-playing, they are generally in the form of girls playing male roles; however, recent observations show that some boys are, at times, playing parts previously in the female domain, such as tending babies.

School Years

From about the time children enter school until puberty, they are said to be in the game stage (Mackie, 1987). However, in general, girls continue to play, while boys "game." Activities continue to be sex-segregated, and boys' activities tend to be evaluated more positively than those of girls. Girls tend to engage in less structured, small group activities that emphasize interpersonal skills and cooperation such as tag, jumping rope, hopscotch, and playing with dolls. Boys, on the other hand, tend to play more competitive games with definite structure and rules, such as hockey. The emphasis on sex-segregated and team-oriented sports activities is carried over into the school curricula throughout the school years. While female participation in sports seems to be increasing, sports activities have generally been deemed more important for boys in learning skills, such as emotional control and taking orders, that will enable them to be successful in the world of work.

As evidenced by play patterns, children learn much by observation and by overt messages. But as they grow older, children are given some opportunities to learn tasks by doing them. Traditionally, children's tasks were largely divided into gender-specific duties, with indoor chores being done by girls and outdoor ones by boys. Yet such attitudes appear to be changing, partly due to the pragmatics of increased numbers of women in the work force. One study (Luxton, 1987), which researched attitudes of working women in a small northern community, found that in a minority of households, tasks for children were strictly divided according to gender; that is, girls were taught and assigned "household" duties such as setting the table, washing dishes, and making beds, while boys were assigned no such responsibilities. But in more than half of the households, boys were also expected to learn and take on some of the same duties.

Canadian schools are accessible to all children; indeed, children are required to attend school until at least age sixteen. Gender socialization is continued by school agents, such as teachers, guidance counselors, and textbooks. However, changes are occurring in schools also. Gaskell and McLaren (1987) report that dramatic changes have taken place in books that are published for use in the primary grades: both genders are equally represented, and females are represented in nontraditional roles. Even so, the authors go on to say that the use of the new texts remains far from universal. They further suggest that other curriculum indexes, such as the number of female authors on reading lists and the number of women in history texts, convey the message that women are not as important as men.

Children begin to think about what they will do when they grow up at an early age. One recent project (Labor Canada, 1986) surveyed 700 elementary schoolchildren between the ages of six and fourteen and found evidence of sex-role stereotyping in future career aspirations and evidence that some change is occurring. Many girls indicated they would like to work in a career that is traditionally masculine or equally represented by males and females, while nearly all the boys chose traditionally masculine careers. Both boys and girls said they expected men and women to engage in many of the same occupations. Girls, however, were more likely to be caught up in the idea of being a mother and staying at home with small children; they appeared to have little awareness of the many years they are unlikely to have dependent children at home.

The lack of congruity between the reality of the present work world, where the majority of women work outside the home much of their lives, even when they have small children, and perceived reality, where women are mostly at home until children are older, may contribute, in part, to the continued differences between what have been considered as ''girl subjects'' and ''boy subjects.'' Typically, girls tend to study such areas as English, history, music, art, business, and home economics. Boys, more usually, study math, chemistry, physics, computer science, and industrial arts. The choice of such subjects in high school leads to different study areas in university and different occupations.

One area, mathematics, has been extensively examined in terms of differential achievement between males and females, since it is considered to be a key subject area for future science careers. Mura, Kimball, and Cloutier (1987) reviewed some studies regarding gender differences in math achievement that indicated that few differences exist before age fourteen. In high school and beyond, they found that males perform better on standardized achievement tests, but not higher on classroom-based tests. Generally, the authors found that when background and experience are similar, achievement is not discrepant between males and females. They suggest, then, that females' lower participation in science occupations is not entirely due to being ''filtered out'' by inadequate math background. A small study conducted by the authors in a Quebec high school provided some evidence that young women tend to attribute success in math not to their ability, but to their efforts, while boys attributed their success to ability. It was suggested that ''ability'' might be viewed as a construct that spans time, whereas effort may not be as great in the future, depending on other demands on one's time. This could relate to the other major gender difference—

expectations of future work plans. More young women expected they would not work outside the home or would work only part-time while their children are young, and they expected their spouses to work full-time. Males primarily expected the opposite pattern; that is, they would work full-time, and their wives would not.

Young Adulthood

The late teens and early twenties are a time of future orientation when young men and young women face decisions about work, further education, and relationships—essentially, questions of identity. These questions are made even more difficult in an age of economic and political uncertainty, high divorce rates, and the increased pace of change.

In regard to work, a survey of fifteen- to twenty-four-year-old Canadian youth (Posterski & Bibby, 1987) indicated that both young men and women espouse equality of job opportunities and equal pay for work of equal value, yet 59 percent of males and 42 percent of females also believe that young children are likely to suffer if a mother works outside the home. This attitude is more clearly exemplified by Gaskell (1988), who interviewed youths in a working-class neighborhood in Vancouver. The predominant ideology by both males and females was that women may work, but the work will be less valued than that of men (i.e., women will receive lower pay) and may be interrupted by childbearing and child rearing. Even so, many of the young women expected that staying at home with children would be boring and isolating and thus viewed the possibility of joining the work force at some time in their future as positive. Young men, on the other hand, expected to spend a lifetime in the work force. While their job plans were viewed as mostly independent of marriage plans, anxiety was evidenced about possible failure to fulfill their perceived role as "breadwinners." Of course, many young adults are already working. The previously mentioned survey (Posterski & Bibby, 1987) found that approximately 30 percent were working full-time (more males than females), 30 percent were working part-time (more females than males), 30 percent were students not working, and 1 percent were neither working nor in school. However, fewer than half were very satisfied with their work.

For young adults who go on to postsecondary education, the picture, at first glance, appears to be more equal. Labor Canada statistics (1990) indicated that women constituted 51 percent of enrollment in full-time university bachelor and first professional programs, over 54 percent in community college full-time programs in 1988–1989, and even higher percentages in part-time programs. While these numbers are encouraging, women continue to be overrepresented in traditionally female areas of study such as education, fine/applied arts, and the health professions and underrepresented in engineering/applied sciences and mathematical/physical sciences. Women have made gains in the social sciences and agricultural/biological sciences, where they constituted more than 56 percent of enrollment. Women have also made gains in enrollment in master's and doctoral programs—the greatest are again in the traditionally female areas.

Young adulthood, a time before many have their own family responsibilities, tends also to be exemplified by pleasure-seeking activities. The Posterski and Bibby (1987) survey found that young adults list friendship (93 percent) and music (88 percent) at the top of the list of sources of enjoyment. Other enjoyments listed by more than 50 percent of those surveyed were relationships with parents (70 percent still live with parents), relationships with girlfriends/boyfriends, stereo, dating, television, sports (males), and reading (girls). All of these activities have the potential to continue differential gender socialization.

Friendship patterns for young adults are often associated with groups where social constructions tend to be different for males and females and tend to induce conformity to traditional gender-role patterns, such as females' deferring to males, cheering them on, acting in supportive roles rather than taking the lead, and taking care of "housekeeping" functions. A participant-observer study by Batcher (1987) in a mall in a Toronto middle-class, suburban setting provided evidence for the preceding statements. The group, consisting of both males and females, had somewhere between thirty and sixty members, some of whom were in evidence most of the open hours of the mall. While young women in the study expressed the viewpoint that "girls today can do anything" (p. 150), in actuality they were very much constrained by the opinions of the group members, especially those of males. Some young women told the researcher that they downplay interests and activities that are deemed "different," for example, playing classical music on the piano, reading, or excelling at studies.

The second highest source of enjoyment for young adults, music, according to evidence cited in Mackie (1987), consists primarily of rock music (80 percent of all records sold in Canada). This music is generally created by young males and is tailored for male audiences, and its lyrics tend to depict women in either erotic roles or, less frequently, in nurturing roles. Neither of these images is conducive to a view of gender equality. According to the author, some of the latest music, New Wave, actually depicts rape and murder, a truly horrifying trend.

The development of sexual maturity brings new differences for young women and men. A young woman begins to experience herself as a sex object when males whistle at her, stare at her, and make comments about her physical appearance. A young man begins to understand his sexuality as an expression of power. Both platonic and nonplatonic relationships begin to form between the sexes and are important for both sexes in trying to figure out their places in the scheme of things. Social relationships between the sexes vary from attending the same parties, cabarets, and dances to more formal "dating" arrangements. Dates still tend to be initiated by males and paid for by them, at least at the beginning of a relationship, although females may initiate flirtation. Later in dating relationships, females may take some responsibility for planning dates and may sometimes pay their own way on dates. The activities in which young adults engage while in a dating relationship can encompass a wide variety. Yet there seems to be a trend to spectator types of amusements (e.g., watching movies or videos, watching sports events, and listening to music), involvement in drinking alcohol, and getting into sex.

In regard to sexuality, the Posterski and Bibby (1987) survey reports that more than 80 percent of Canadian youth say premarital sexual activity is OK when people love each other. Mackie (1987) suggests that females are more likely than males to view love as a prerequisite for sex. Males still tend to pressure young women to ''show their love'' or ''help them release pressure'' by giving in to sex. Yet the responsibility for birth control is primarily expected to be the woman's. Unfortunately, birth control information and availability are too often limited, and over 40,000 Canadian teenage women become pregnant each year (Nolte, 1987). A similar situation exists in regard to acquired immunodeficiency syndrome (AIDS). Young adults report knowledge of AIDS and say they believe it has had an impact on sexual practices in Canada, yet when asked if any change has occurred in their own behavior, four out of five said, ''No'' (Posterski & Bibby, 1987).

Adulthood

The majority of Canadian young adults face three major tasks—selecting a mate and developing a relationship with that person, having children and parenting them, and developing competence in a work setting. In the mainstream culture, mate selection is generally accomplished by ''falling in love.'' (Minority cultures, as noted in the introduction, may follow customs that derive from their cultural backgrounds.) Falling in love is usually accompanied by physical manifestations such as quickened pulse, fluttery stomach, inability to concentrate, and so forth—symptoms that in other situations would be labeled as anxiety, anger, or excitement! Although this sort of romantic love sounds completely random, most Canadians choose mates from similar socioeconomic and ethnic backgrounds. Males tend to be somewhat older, taller, better paid, and better educated than their mates. Relationship styles tend to differ according to gender, with women's preferring emotional closeness and verbal expression and men's preferring to give more instrumental help and sex (Mackie, 1987).

Following from the romantic love notion, marriages are entered into by mutual agreement, with the male generally the one to mention the possibility—or to ask. When a couple have agreed to marry, a ring is often given to the woman to make the intent to marry public. Practically, the ring serves to announce to other males that this woman is spoken for; no such symbol is evident for the male. The engagement period may last for months or years and may depend on such things as finishing educational programs, economic stability, and so forth. If a couple has this type of formal engagement period, they will likely be married in a formal setting, often a religious one, with family and friends in attendance and with a reception or party afterward. Traditionally, the bride's parents would pay for most, if not all, of this extravaganza; however, economic realities in the present-day world may mean that the couple pays much of the expense themselves. Of course, many people do not possess the economic means to get married in such style and thus may be married in a civil ceremony with only a few persons in attendance.

Traditionally, in Canada, a woman assumed the man's last name and therefore "assumed a new identity." Today some women keep their own last name, and in other marriages both partners assume a hyphenated last name consisting of both their names; however, the majority continue to follow the traditional pattern. Nonetheless, newly married partners both find themselves in a different reality than before, and while their roles are guided by past familial and societal experiences, new living patterns need to be negotiated, involving nearly all aspects of their lives. Partners enter marriage with expectations that the relationship will fulfill needs (in varying degrees for men and women) for companionship, affection, understanding, social support, sex, reproduction, and security (Greenglass, 1987; MacDaniel, 1988). After the couple are married, they usually set up a household of their own, separate from relatives. While some couples may live near parents, many do not and therefore receive little assistance or emotional support from family.

When both partners are working at the time of marriage, both tend to continue to work until the birth of the first child, at which time some women leave the work force permanently or for some years. Others may enter the part-time labor force. Labor Canada (1990) reported that in 1989, of all individuals over fifteen, almost 58 percent of women and nearly 77 percent of men were in the work force. Women constituted more than 44 percent of the total labor force. More women than men were working part-time (women, 24.5 percent; men, 7.7 percent), yet more than 75 percent of working women were working full-time. Sixty percent of married women were working, and while many Canadians express the opinion that mothers with small children should not work outside the home, in 1989 over 62 percent of women with pre-school children were, in fact, working. Younger women and women with higher levels of education were more likely to be in the work force. However, nearly 60 percent of women were working in lower paid and lesser valued clerical, sales, and service occupations. On the average, women workers earned approximately 65 percent of male earnings. Even in professional areas, women earned less than men.

The preceding percentages represent a large increase in the number of working women in recent decades. While many factors play a part in this increase, evidence cited in an article by Greenglass (1987) suggests that the majority of women are employed due to economic need. Even so, she cites further evidence that suggests that employed women have higher self-esteem, more self-confidence, and a greater sense of personal competence than housewives. This sense of psychological well-being, along with the benefits of the paycheck, seems to be a plus. However, there is a negative side—working married women are still largely responsible for housework and child care, in essence giving them two jobs. This means that time must be taken from other activities in order to get everything done. This results in role strain; when a woman is raising a family and pursuing a career (as opposed to ''just working''), even greater role strain is experienced. In some instances, men are taking more responsibility for household chores, but a recently released report from Statistics Canada cited in a local newspaper (''Study Shows,'' August 1991) showed that women continue to do the bulk of housework and child rearing and that male contribution in such areas has actually decreased slightly in the past decade.

The current average age at which a Canadian woman marries for the first time is 22.5 years (Gee, 1988). A recently released Statistics Canada report (''Women Delay,'' September, 1991) indicated that 41 percent of first births in 1988 occurred to women under twenty-five. This represented a dramatic shift since 1971, when 70 percent of first births occurred in that age range. A marked increase occurred in the over-thirty age category—18 percent, up from 7 percent. MacDaniel (1988) reported that the Canadian birthrate in the early 1980s was 1.7, an all-time low. So, Canadian women are having fewer children, and are waiting longer to have them, and some are opting not to have children at all. Gee (1988) suggests that the people who are delaying are likely from the well-educated, successful middle class. Some of the many factors that contribute to the low birthrate are the increase in the number of women in the work force, inadequate day care, limited extended families, and the increased cost of raising children. MacDaniel (1988) also cites evidence that having children may not be considered as crucial to life satisfaction for women as was true in former years.

It is very difficult to make definitive statements about family activities, since these can be nearly as varied as different families. In general, in Canadian families that are not in crisis, family activities prior to children's teen years are often centered about keeping children interested and happy. The previously cited Statistics Canada survey (''Study Shows,'' August 1991) presented data that more than half of all parents spend an average of two hours a day with their children. In addition to doing things with children, parents with higher economic resources may provide them with learning opportunities, such as lessons in music, dance, swimming, tennis, or skating. Some of the time spent with children probably involves watching television, since the same survey showed Canadian adults watching television more than two hours per day (more time for men than for women).

The number of other adult activities may be restricted when children are young, particularly for women. These can be quite varied and, to some extent, may be different for men and women. For example, many women engage in sewing, knitting, and other household craft activities that would be extremely rare activities for men; many men (and only a few women) may engage in woodworking or mechanical activities; generally, more men than women go hunting or fishing;

and in sports, men, more than women, are involved in team activities, such as hockey and basketball. There is a trend toward more individual pursuits for both men and women, such as walking, jogging, swimming, weight lifting, and other aerobic activities.

While most Canadians intend to marry for life, data from Statistics Canada (1986) suggest that about one-third of marriages can be expected to end in divorce. This is no doubt due to a variety of factors, but for whatever specific reasons, divorce or separation is likely to occur when the relationship is considered untenable by at least one of the partners. Many persons who divorce remarry—a greater number of men than women. A new term—blended family—has been coined to describe the situation in which partners have children from a previous marriage. Divorce is a difficult and painful process, and there are frequently battles over division of property and custody of children. In recent years, property laws have been passed that presumably make property division more equal than it was in the past, yet Crean (1988) presents evidence that equal division is still not a reality, particularly when the wife has not worked outside the home for part or all of the marriage. This appears to be because housework and raising children are not deemed as valuable as "breadwinning." Women who have not developed job skills often live at a poverty level after divorce, and when children are involved and living with the mother, support payments for the children are frequently not enforced. Custody arrangements have typically favored the mother, who has usually been the primary caregiver prior to separation. In recent years there has been a trend toward joint custody and father custody. Crean also indicates that if a custody case goes to court, the man is more likely to win, even in some cases when evidence of child abuse by the father was presented. She suggests that rather than being a move toward equality, this is another form of discrimination toward women and is due in large part to the generally greater financial resources and greater power of men.

As people pass into middle age, reassessments of their lives are common. Neither men nor women particularly welcome middle age, since Canadian society, like most Western societies, is youth-oriented. In middle age, people begin to notice changes in their physical appearance; they begin to think in terms of how many years may be left to them and to think about hopes and dreams still unfulfilled. Many men begin to put more focus on families just at the time when many women, who are becoming more free from taking care of children, begin to focus outside the family to work or perhaps to gain additional education. When marriages withstand these new strains, this period may be a time for an increase in shared activities and a decrease in economic concerns (Mackie, 1987). For women who live alone in middle age, the picture is not so optimistic—a recently released study by Statistics Canada reported in a local newspaper ("Plight," December 1991) indicated that 29 percent of women aged fifty-five to sixty-four lived alone in 1986 and more than 50 percent of these were living below the Canadian poverty line.

Old Age

The proportion of older people in Canada (arbitrarily set at sixty-five and over) has dramatically increased in recent years, due partly to increased longevity rates and partly to lower birthrates. Many writers make a distinction between the young old (65–74) and the old old (75 and over); this distinction will be used occasionally in the paragraphs to follow. Women are overrepresented in the sixty-five and over ages, with the imbalance greatest among the old old (Dulude, 1988).

Typically, in Canada, the later stages of life have been viewed negatively; that is, older people have not been especially valued. There is evidence that these negative attitudes are changing somewhat as older people become more visible in various roles and are more positively portrayed on television (Novak, 1985; Roadburg, 1985). Furthermore, as Mackie (1987) suggested, holding a negative attitude toward older people is more uncomfortable than having a negative attitude toward other groups, since chances are great that the individual holding the negative view will eventually join the group of "old folks."

The convergence of social roles begun in middle-aged males and females expands in the later years. Older people tend to be regarded as sexless and are often referred to by such monikers as senior citizens, old folks, or the elderly, rather than men and women. Marriages that have survived into the later years tend to be happier than at other stages of life—couples do more things together and are less restricted by gender roles (Dulude, 1988). Attitudes of older people regarding the level of satisfaction in their lives are generally positive; that is, the majority indicate a high degree of satisfaction (Roadburg, 1985; Connidis, 1989). People who express satisfaction tend to be in good health, to live with a spouse or family, to see their children often (when they have children), and to have an adequate income.

There are negatives for many people, however. Traditionally, the losses in later years were believed to be somewhat gender-equal—men losing a major source of their identity at retirement and women often losing their husbands. However, recent research (Dulude, 1988; Mackie, 1987) suggests that for most men, retirement is not as negative an event as was previously thought and, in fact, is often regarded positively. This may be partly due to preretirement socialization while they are still in the work force. Furthermore, more and more women also go through retirement. Both men and women whose spouse has died report that as the most devastating event that has happened in their lives. However, women most often experience this loss. Women's life expectancies are longer than those of men, and the tendency for men to marry women younger than themselves means that widowhood is much more likely for women. Also, when men's spouses die, they are much more likely to remarry, often to a younger woman. Figures reported by Dulude (1988) show that in 1983, among Canadians between sixty-five and sixty-nine, more than 80 percent of men were

married, compared with 60 percent of women; for those eighty and older, half of the males and only 15 percent of women still had a spouse.

Another factor associated with satisfaction in the later years is adequate income. Here again, many more women than men live at or below the Canadian poverty level. This is most frequently true of the many women who live alone or with nonrelatives. While Canadian social programs provide some income for anyone who does not have one, it is too low to provide necessities, let alone any extras. Pension plans, both government and private, have been designed to benefit full-time participants in the labor force (primarily males) and the people they support (Dulude, 1988; Roadburg, 1985). However, as the various statistics already mentioned in this chapter show, many people, especially women, do not fit into either of these categories. Pension reform with the intent to provide better provisions for all Canadians has been discussed for some years but has not become reality.

Older people live in a variety of situations. The majority vastly prefer independence and, if they own homes, prefer to live in them as long as possible (Novak, 1985; Roadburg, 1985). In addition, independent living may involve other arrangements within the general community (apartments, condominiums, trailer homes, low-rent housing, and so on). Other independent arrangements might be in an age-segregated situation, such as a retirement community or a low-rent "senior citizen" apartment complex. Healthy young old people are more likely to be able to live in independent situations.

While the majority of older Canadians are healthy (Novak, 1985), health does deteriorate with age—and with the deterioration, independence may be lost. While there is some movement toward more home-based services to provide assistance for older people to remain in independent living situations, many become dependent and must live in some sort of collective situation, such as rooming houses, nursing homes, and the like. Some move in with children or other relatives—this usually being the least preferred option. Again, women make up the largest part of this dependent group of the old olds. The quality of care provided in institutional and family settings varies greatly. In family situations, daughters or wives of the old, "the women in the middle," are often burdened with care of the dependent parent or spouse with little or no outside help. This group is likely to increase as the population ages. New government services to aid such caregivers have been proposed but as yet have received little support (Dulude, 1988).

At the top of the list of factors associated with satisfaction in the later years is good health. While the majority of older Canadians do enjoy health, many also experience health problems, more as they age. Some of the diseases that are likely to be experienced by older Canadians are diseases of the circulatory system, cancer, kidney disease, diabetes, Alzheimer's, and Parkinson's. Canada has one of the most complete government-sponsored health care systems in the world, and most older Canadians are pleased that when they do get sick, they will receive decent health care (Novak, 1985). The system is not problem-free,

and most agree that more community-based services (e.g., home nursing visits) and more preventive programs need to be put in place. There have been trends in both these directions. One example of a government-supported, preventive program that has caught on with many older people is "Participation"—activities geared toward keeping people of all ages more physically fit and, thereby, healthier.

Some people continue to be involved in work activities in the later years. Many organizations have a mandatory retirement age of sixty-five (currently being challenged in the courts), but in some situations it is possible to disengage from work more gradually by working part-time, teaching one course, acting as a consultant, and so forth. In other cases, people may go into completely new work activities—paid or volunteer—that may be less pressured and more under individual control than previously.

Leisure activities, on the average, become somewhat more sedentary as people grow older, yet the amount and type of activities continue to vary nearly as widely as before. Many older people continue to engage in similar types of activities as when they were younger. The living situation, marital status, and economic situation also influence the types of activities. For example, some retired couples travel extensively. Generally, when older people are married, they tend to be involved in more active pursuits, while those alone tend toward indoor activities that facilitate interaction with others (Roadburg, 1985). Many population centers in Canada have developed senior centers (many with government funding), which offer a variety of recreational and social activities. Many social and cultural events are available at a discount for "seniors." Across the country new educational opportunities are available to older people; the best-known of these is Elderhostel, which offers courses and dormitory accommodations during nonacademic periods in participating universities in several countries, thus allowing a relatively inexpensive travel/learning experience (Novak, 1985).

SUMMARY AND CONCLUSIONS

The information presented in this chapter indicates that while vast changes have occurred in recent decades, gender equality is still far from a reality in present-day Canada. Much of the evidence could be seen to imply a sort of social determinism. Indeed, if one knows such things as a person's gender, social class, and ethnic background, there may be some basis for predictability of behavior, attitudes, and so forth. Yet, gender socialization is extremely complex, and people exhibit great variability of behavior even within similar parameters. People continue to learn, to think, and to make choices throughout the life span. If more egalitarian choices are made both at the personal level and in public policies, more Canadians may be able to enjoy a higher quality of life.

Throughout the chapter mention has been made of areas where changes could be made to bring about greater gender equality. Some of these include pension reform, equal pay for work of equal value, equality of educational and work opportunities, more sensitive portrayal of gender roles and more equal gender representation in the media, and more equal representation in political and management areas. Perhaps most important of all for future gender equality would be to raise and educate children in a way that does not promote gender as a basis for categorizing behavior and attitudes.

REFERENCES

Barnett, V. (1987, April 19). Books still toying with role models. *Calgary Herald*, p. B1.

Batcher, E. (1987). Building the barriers: Adolescent girls delimit the future. In Nemiroff, G. H. (Ed.), *Women and Men: Interdisciplinary Readings on Gender* (pp. 150–65). Canada: Fitzhenry & Whiteside.

Black, N. (1988). The Canadian women's movement: The second wave. In Burt S., Code L., & Dorney, L. (Eds.), *Changing Patterns: Women in Canada* (pp. 80–102). Toronto: McClelland & Stewart.

Connidis, I. (1989). The subjective experience of aging: Correlates of divergent views. *Canadian Journal on Aging, 8*(1):7–18.

Crean, S. (1988). *In the Name of the Fathers: The Story Behind Child Custody*. Toronto: Amanita Enterprises.

CRTC. (1990). *The Portrayal of Gender in Canadian Broadcasting: Summary Report 1984–1988*. Ottawa: Minister of Supply and Services Canada.

Dulude, L. (1988). Getting old: Men in couples and women alone. In McLaren, A. T. (Ed.), *Gender and Society: Creating a Canadian Women's Sociology* (pp. 205–20). Toronto: Copp Clark Pittman.

Gaskell, J. (1988). The reproduction of family life: Perspectives of male and female adolescents. In McLaren, A. T. (Ed.), *Gender and Society: Creating a Canadian Women's Sociology* (pp. 146–68). Toronto: Copp Clark Pittman.

Gaskell, J., & McLaren, A. (1987). Introduction. In Gaskell, J., & McLaren, A. (Eds.), *Women and Education: A Canadian Perspective* (pp. 5–20). Calgary: Detselig Enterprises.

Gee, E. (1988). The life course of Canadian women: A historical and demographic analysis. In McLaren, A. T. (Ed.), *Gender and Society: Creating a Canadian Women's Sociology* (pp. 187–204). Toronto: Copp Clark Pittman.

Greenglass, E. (1987). A social-psychological view of marriage for women. In Nemiroff, G. H. (Ed.), *Women and Men: Interdisciplinary Readings on Gender* (pp. 290–302). Canada: Fitzhenry & Whiteside.

Krishnan, V. (1987). Preference for sex of children: A multivariate analysis. *Journal of Biosocial Science, 19*(3):367–76.

Labor Canada. (1986). *When I Grow Up: Career Expectations and Aspirations of Canadian Schoolchildren*. Ottawa: Minister of Supply and Services Canada.

———. (1990). *Women in the Labor Force: 1990–91 Edition*. Ottawa: Minister of Supply and Services Canada.

Luxton, M. (1987). Two hands for the clock: Changing patterns in the gendered division of labor in the home. In Salamon, E. D., & Robinson, B. W. (Eds.), *Gender Roles: Doing What Comes Naturally* (pp. 213–26). Toronto: Methuen.

MacDaniel, S. (1988). The changing Canadian family: Women's roles and the impact of feminism. In Burt, S., Code, L., & Dorney, L. (Eds.), *Changing Patterns: Women in Canada* (pp. 103–28). Toronto: McClelland & Stewart.

Mackie, M. (1987). *Constructing Women and Men: Gender Socialization.* Toronto: Holt, Rinehart, & Winston.

Mura, R., Kimball, M., & Cloutier, R. (1987). Girls and science programs: Two steps forward, one step back. In Gaskell, J. & McLaren, A. (Eds.), *Women and Education: A Canadian Perspective* (pp. 133–49). Calgary: Detselig Enterprises.

Nolte, J. (1987). Sexuality, fertility and choice: On becoming a woman in the eighties. In Nemiroff, G. H. (Ed.), *Women and Men: Interdisciplinary Readings on Gender* (pp. 202–23). Canada: Fitzhenry & Whiteside.

Novak, M. (1985). *Successful Aging: The Myths, Realities and Future of Aging in Canada.* Markham, Ontario: Penguin Books.

Plight of older women said to be worsening. (1991, December 3). *Evening Telegram*, p. 1.

Posterski, D., & Bibby, R. (1987). *Canada's Youth "Ready for Today": A Comprehensive Survey of 15–24 Year Olds.* Ottawa: Canadian Youth Foundation.

Roadburg, A. (1985). *Aging: Retirement, Leisure and Work in Canada.* Agincourt, ON: Methuen.

Robinson, B. W., & Salamon, E. D. (1987). Gender role socialization: A review of the literature. In Salamon, E. D. & Robinson, B. W. (Eds.), *Gender Roles: Doing What Comes Naturally* (pp. 123–42). Toronto: Methuen.

Statistics Canada. (1986). *Marriages and Divorces.* Ottawa: Minister of Supply and Services Canada.

———. (1989). *Focus on Canada: Canada's Population from Ocean to Ocean.* Ottawa: Minister of Supply and Services Canada.

———. (1990). *Focus on Canada: Ethnic Diversity in Canada.* Ottawa: Minister of Supply and Services Canada.

Study shows women do bulk of household work. (1991, August 22). *Evening Telegram*, p. 15.

Valpy, M. (1989, October 11). Fathers fare poorly in children's books. *Toronto Globe and Mail*, p. A8.

Women delay motherhood. (1991, September 4). *Evening Telegram*, p. 19.

4

Egypt

Nicholas V. Ciaccio and Omnia Sayed El Shakry

INTRODUCTION

Egypt lies in the northeast corner of Africa and is part of the Sinai Peninsula, which is usually thought of as part of Asia. Egypt is an Arab country in the Middle East with a long and illustrious history dating back to pharaonic times, many millennia ago. In the south it borders the Sudan, and in the west it shares a border with Libya. To the north Egypt extends to the Mediterranean Sea and a 600-mile coastline, and in the east it borders for 1,200 miles on the Red Sea. Because of the Suez Canal, which cuts through northeast Egypt, it provides a trade route between Europe and Asia. Egypt's entire land area covers 386,000 square miles, of which most is desert, but 3.6 percent is inhabited, mostly along the fertile Nile River valley. Of the estimated population of 48 million people, 49.6 percent are women (Ahmed, 1991). Egypt has a high rate (2.8 percent) of population growth annually. However, the population, of mostly large families, has a high mortality rate due to many prenatal, infant, and maternal deaths.

The basic realities that affect Egypt today are poverty, illiteracy, high birth increase, and chronic unemployment. Any discussion of gender roles must be seen within these parameters. Fully one-half of the population live at or below the poverty line. One-half of Egyptian women are in their childbearing years, with 1 million "new arrivals" coming every nine months. Life expectancy for males is 59 and for females, 60. Yet Egypt has produced the greatest number of female university professors, lawyers, doctors, and poets among the nations of the Arab world (Ciaccio, in preparation).

OVERVIEW

While the authors recognize these accomplishments, they address the concerns of the majority of Egyptian women and men as they live their daily lives. The university professor is the exception; the woman living in two rooms with five children, managing on less than $800 per year is the rule (Ciaccio, in preparation). The authors intend to discuss these factors as they impinge on the lives of Egyptian men and women. The discussion might be seen as grim by some, but in fact, much social progress has taken place in the last ten years. Social service policies, literacy programs, and welfare and development projects have changed the picture dramatically.

However, any discussion of gender roles in Egypt must be placed firmly within the Islamic context, as Islam constitutes the fundamental organizational background of Egyptian society. Egypt's citizens are predominantly Sunni Muslims; only 8 percent are Christians (Farag, in preparation). Islam is, therefore, the most significant rationale behind the delineation of men's and women's roles. The ideology derived from Islam directly impacts the roles and statuses attributed to women (Nelson, 1984).

Briefly, the conceptual base of Islam consists of the following: the Quran (the holy book revealed to the prophet Muhammed), the Sunna (sayings and traditions of the prophet), and Shari'a law. Islam emphasizes the complementary nature of the sexes and dictates their roles accordingly (Saleh, 1972; Nelson, 1984). Women are placed under male guardianship to ensure the safeguarding of morality. Marriage is considered a contract between a man and a woman, and a woman must give her consent for a marriage to occur. Divorce, on the other hand, is a prerogative of men (Quran, Sura 2:227). Females are entitled to inheritance rights and the ownership of property, but they inherit one-half the portion that men inherit (Quran, Sura 2:11). Of course, these rules are being challenged daily by women, Jehan el Sadat being one of the leaders of a new sociolegal order; while religious leaders also argue over these dictates, real change has been slow.

The woman's chief role is still seen to be mother and wife. The Quran specifies the nature of the relationship between husband and wife: "Men are the protectors and maintainers of women, because God has given the one, more [strength] than the other, and they support them from their means" (Quran, Sura 4:34).

Obedience and respect for their husbands are considered a duty for Muslim women. It is therefore within this general framework that men's and women's roles are shaped. Gender ideologies, however, are far too complex to be attributed solely to religion, and in Egypt social and cultural conditions, influenced by Islamic belief and tradition, contribute to the demarcation of gender roles.

COMPARISONS BETWEEN MEN'S AND WOMEN'S GENDER ROLES DURING THE LIFE CYCLE

Infancy and Early Childhood

In Egypt, and elsewhere in the Middle East, there exists a definitive preference for sons. Sons can carry the family name and provide future economic support for the family (Tomeh, 1983; Hatem, 1986b). A daughter, on the other hand, often does not contribute economically to her nuclear family. Above all, females require supervision to guard against any type of moral indiscretion; and since they can jeopardize the entire family, they are often seen as a source of anxiety (El Saadawy, 1980; Tomeh, 1983; Hatem, 1986a, b).

To have a boy, in traditional interpretation, fosters the belief that fathers who have sons are immortal. Women, especially those who live in rural areas, often feel that their value depends on their ability to bear children, especially sons (Minai, 1981). Fertility appeared to be lower for educated women, working women with a high income, and women in large cities. It also appeared that in rural areas agricultural work by women—and also men—seemed to be conducive to having more children (Ahmed, 1991). However, it is a heavy physical burden for women continually to give birth and nurse babies. A study conducted in Egypt a few years ago showed that 97 percent of rural mothers were breast-feeding their babies (Al-Ahram, 1985).

If a girl survives infancy in her poverty-stricken environment, as soon as she can walk, she will be given tasks and work to do. It is regrettable when one considers that she has to help at home, and therefore she cannot attend the cost-free primary school (Galal el-Din, 1984).

The pressures women feel from their husbands and from society in general to bear sons inevitably lead them to value the birth of a son. The parents' feelings toward their daughter, their wish for her to have been a son, will be communicated unintentionally or otherwise (Hatem, 1986b). Hence, many females grow up in an environment where they experience hostility and learn from an early age that it would have been better to have been born a male (El Saadawy, 1980). Throughout their childhood, males and females are socialized to behave in gender-appropriate manners. Female children are expected to help their mothers with household responsibilities, while male children are discouraged from doing so (Hatem, 1986b). Female children are also placed under more restrictions, and they must constantly be aware of their behavior and manners (El Saadawy, 1980). Ultimately, female children are raised in a more circumscribed domestic context, where they are prepared for their future roles as wives and mothers.

School Years

The cognitive development during the school years was the focus of research by Ramadan A. Ahmed (1981, 1989). He tested and compared Egyptian and Sudanese children by assessing the development of number, space, quantity, and reasoning concepts. Ahmed tested schoolchildren at the ages of 6, 8, 10, and 12 years; these age groups corresponded to Piaget's "concrete operations" stage and the beginning of the "formal operations" stage. The fathers' socio-economic status and their educational level were also recorded. The results were most interesting. On the whole the results showed that cognitive abilities and intellectual performances steadily improved with age. These findings were in line with Piaget's postulates that children systematically developed their cognitive abilities, which increased with age. The Sudanese children achieved higher conservation scores than their Egyptian counterparts on the concept of quantity, which was probably more relevant both ecologically and culturally. On the other hand, the Egyptian schoolchildren received higher conservation scores than their Sudanese counterparts in the tasks on space and reasoning concepts. When the same students were tested on two intelligence tests (Raven Progressive Matrices Test and the Wechsler Intelligence Scale for Children), the Egyptian students received higher scores, especially on the Raven Progressive Matrices. Ahmed (1989) also found that the socioeconomic status and the educational level of the fathers, as well as the children's sex differences, had only weak and statistically *non*significant effects upon cognitive development.

The maintenance of female chastity as a form of preservation for the family, especially male honor, has acquired high cultural value in Egypt and other Middle Eastern societies (Smock & Youssef, 1977; El Saadawy, 1980). This has led to stringent controls on the behavior and conduct of women. In Egypt, these have ranged from complete sexual segregation to female circumcision. Whereas Islam requires modesty and chastity for both sexes (Quran, Sura 24:30), the women seem to bear the onus of the constraining cultural concept of "honor." Some authors (Sabbah, 1984; Mernissi, 1985; Ghassoub, 1987) have argued that underlying Islam and the Muslim tradition is an anxiety about female sexuality. Women's sexuality is perceived as being (hyper)active and in need of supervision because of its potential for creating *fitna* (Mernissi, 1985). *Fitna* in Arabic means chaos and, alternately, a beautiful woman, the implication being that women, through their seductiveness and beauty, have the potential capacity to create disorder and destruction in the community (El Saadawy, 1980; Mernissi, 1985). Among the controls imposed upon women's sexuality in Egypt today is the insistence upon premarital virginity and circumcision.

Premarital virginity is considered a sine qua non for women in Egypt. This, coupled with the view that marriage is the most appropriate option for women, leads to an inordinate emphasis on the demonstration of virginity at the time of marriage. El Saadawy states that "Arab society still considers that the fine membrane which covers the aperture of the external genital organ is the most cherished and most important part of a girl's body" (El Saadawy, 1980). Thus the concept of honor of a female and her entire family is contingent upon an intact hymen; "the concept of honor and virginity locates the prestige of a man between the legs of a woman" (Mernissi, 1985). This code of "morality" absolutely applies to women of all social classes. Sexual experience in the life of men is a source of pride, but in the life of women, it is a source of shame (El Saadawy, 1980).

The extent to which female chastity is valued is demonstrated also by the practice of female circumcision. Female circumcision still exists in Egyptian society despite governmental decrees (Assaad, 1980). According to conservative figures, 75 percent of Egyptian women are circumcised (Assaad, 1980). This figure may be as high as 98 percent among the lower rural classes (El Saadawy,

1980). Parental education appears to be an influential factor in determining whether a female child will be circumcised or not (Assaad, 1980; El Saadawy, 1980; Farag, in preparation).

Circumcision can be divided into four categories. In first-degree circumcision, only the tip of the clitoris and a portion of the labia minora are removed. In second-degree circumcision, the labia minora and part of the clitoris are removed; and in third-degree circumcision, the entire labia minora and clitoris are removed. In fourth-degree or "pharaonic" circumcision, the labia minora, labia majora, and the clitoris are removed. In Egypt the most commonly performed circumcisions are first and second degree. Women between the ages of seven and eleven are usually circumcised by midwives or, much less frequently, by trained doctors and nurses (El Saadawy, 1980; Ciaccio, in preparation).

The effects of female circumcision are numerous. In terms of immediate effects, it is not uncommon for the girl to suffer from shock, hemorrhaging, infection, inflammation, urinary disturbance, and severe pain, often due to the unhygienic nature of the procedure (Assaad, 1980; Denny & Quadagno, 1988).

Despite the deleterious effects of circumcision, it continues to exist. It is perhaps the supreme example of the perpetuation of custom and tradition in Egypt, in spite of governmental and religious sanctions. The primary manifest intent of circumcision is the preservation of female premarital virginity and chastity during marriage. Circumcision is believed to protect women from "losing their honor" by quelling their incipient sexual desires. Many parents also fear that an uncircumcised daughter will be unable to marry (Assaad, 1980; Hany, 1990). Other reasons for circumcision sometimes cited are cleanliness, the belief that the clitoris virilizes a woman, and the erroneous belief that Islam requires it (Hany, 1990).

What message is Egyptian society giving females by physically amputating an integral part of their sexuality? Women are not expected to derive pleasure from sex; in fact, they are often physically prohibited from doing so. They are socialized to believe that their sexuality is something to be ashamed of and hidden. Indeed, this view is reinforced constantly throughout the childhood of females and is epitomized by circumcision.

Young Adulthood

In Egypt it is believed that a woman can best realize her role in society through marriage. Women derive a great deal of their status from their fulfillment of their wife-mother role (Smock & Youssef, 1977). Since women are highly restricted prior to their marriage, they themselves often view marriage as an alternative of greater freedom (Smock & Youssef, 1977; Tomeh, 1983; Ciaccio, in preparation). Thus, both women and their families place great emphasis on the importance of marriage. Furthermore, few viable options outside marriage and motherhood exist in Egypt, since unmarried women of any age are expected to live with their kin groups (Smock & Youssef, 1977).

Marriage in Egypt often does not depend on individual choice; rather it is viewed as an agreement between two family groups. Although some families may not actually select mates for their children, they are almost always involved in approving their children's decisions and facilitating marital negotiations (Tomeh, 1983; Rugh, 1984). The true rationale behind such marriages is that they strengthen already existing kinship ties (Rugh, 1984). In the case of nonendogamous marriages, family members often assist in finding prospective spouses (Tomeh, 1983). Choices of partners appear to be motivated by matching characteristics such as socioeconomic status, education, attractiveness, and "moral" factors between the couple, rather than notions of romantic love (Rugh, 1984). Once a male has decided on a prospective bride, his parents contact the parents of the woman, and negotiations begin (Tomeh, 1983). These "negotiations" include the setting of the *mahr* or dowry, a sum of money or a gift given to the bride (Barakat, 1985).

Ideally, the future couple are to get to know one another during their engagement period. Male-female relations outside marriage and the period of engagement are generally frowned upon (Tomeh, 1983).

Once married, the Egyptian woman is expected to concentrate on her familial duties, which include obedience and respect for the husband, caring for the household, and producing and raising children. But it is important to note that women are accorded a great deal of respect within the family, insofar as they perform their duties as wives and mothers well (Smock & Youssef, 1977).

The issue of family planning has received great attention in Egypt, due to governmental campaigns aimed at the reduction of the birthrate. Women in Egypt, as elsewhere in the Arab world, have a high birthrate, 37.5 percent in 1988 (Central Agency for Public Mobilization and Statistics [CAPMAS], 1990). A variety of factors have influenced fertility in Egypt. These include early marriage, especially in rural areas, with childbearing beginning soon after, short intervals between births, and the emphasis placed on having sons. Additionally Islam espouses a view compatible with pro-reproductive norms. Nevertheless, there exists a controversy about birth control in Islam, and religious authorities are often of conflicting opinions (Smock & Youssef, 1977; El Saadawy, 1980).

More importantly, however, women in Egypt have a keen interest in procreation, because by bearing children, a woman guarantees herself a degree of security vis-à-vis her husband (Smock & Youssef, 1977). A woman who cannot bear children may be divorced by her husband, or he may take on a second wife (Tomeh, 1983). Furthermore, a woman's prestige is enhanced, in the eyes of both her husband and the community, when she bears children, especially sons (Smock & Youssef, 1977). An important factor that serves to reduce fertility is education (Farag, in preparation). Education usually entails a delay in marriage and subsequently in childbearing, as well as a rechanneling of women's goals to include suprafamilial activities such as employment (Farag, in preparation). The control of fertility patterns by women implies a control of sexuality and is an important step toward female liberation in the Arab world.

The legal rights of women with respect to marriage and divorce are firmly codified in the personal status laws of Egypt. These laws are based on the principles of Shari'a (Islamic law). According to these laws, marriage is validated through a contract between two consenting adults (Hussein et al., 1988). The *mahr* (dowry) and *mu'akhar* should be stated in the contract. The *mahr* could be any sum, and it is used by the bride and becomes her property. The *mu'akhar*, on the other hand, is a sum that is set aside and is paid to the wife in case of divorce (Mohsen, 1974). The *mahr* and *mu'akhar* are felt to protect the economic interests of the bride.

Perhaps the most controversial issue concerning the personal status law is the unilateral right of the husband in divorce. A husband may divorce his wife simply by stating, "I divorce you" three times, and there need not be any specific grounds for divorce. A wife, however, may ask for a divorce under certain circumstances, some of which are:

• a husband's absence for a year or more
• a husband's imprisonment for three years or more
• mental or physical illness (Hussein et al., 1988)

Women's participation in education and employment is a critical indicator of their status in society. Women in Egypt have made very definite progress in this respect, yet many inequities remain. For example, illiteracy in Egypt is a major national problem. An estimated 52 percent of the population, aged 15 years and over, are illiterate, with a breakdown of 37.1 percent male and 66.2 percent female (*UNESCO Statistical Yearbook*, 1990). Education in Egypt is compulsory between the ages of 6–15, yet more males begin school and more females drop out before completing their primary education (State of Egyptian Children, CAPMAS & UNICEF, 1988). Although the percentage of females enrolled in all levels of the educational cycle has increased consistently since 1952, their enrollment still lags behind that of men.

According to the CAPMAS *Statistical Yearbook* (1990), the proportional distribution for students in primary education for the year 1988–1989 was 55.8 percent male and 44.2 percent female. For that same year the distribution of students in secondary education was 61.5 percent male and 38.5 percent female, while in higher education it was 66.2 percent male and 33.8 percent female. These figures represent a remarkably sizable increase from 20 years ago.

Women were first granted the right to a university education in Egypt in 1928, and the number of female university students has been increasing steadily since then (El Guindi, 1983). In 1929 there were 29 female university students (Hussein et al., 1988), and in 1987 there were 253,814, accounting for 33 percent of all university students (*UNESCO Statistical Yearbook*, 1990). Additionally, the ratio of male to female students has been decreasing. According to figures for 1987, the most popular fields of study for university women were, in descending order:

1. humanities, religion, and theology
2. commerce and business administration
3. education
4. medical science and health-related fields
5. law (*UNESCO Statistical Yearbook*, 1990)

Table 4.1
Population in 1986, 10 Years and Over by Educational Status and Sex

Status	Urban		Rural	
	Male	Female	Male	Female
Illiterate	26.5%	44.7%	47.1%	75.8%
Read & Write	25.4%	20.8%	26.4%	13.5%
Primary	8.5%	7.7%	6.0%	3.4%
Over Medium	30.6%	23.7%	17.8%	6.7%
University	8.8%	2.9%	2.2%	0.2%
Not Stated	0.3%	0.3%	0.3%	0.4%

Source: CAPMAS, *Statistical Yearbook* (1990).

The relatively low rate of female education cannot be understood outside women's socioeconomic and cultural context. Since women's primary roles in society are still viewed by many in terms of marriage and motherhood, the importance of formal education is naturally deemed low by the masses. Among the upper socioeconomic classes, however, the situation is completely reversed, with education often being seen as a favorable factor in marriage prospects. Economic factors definitely play a role in limiting women's education. If families are unable to support the education of both their sons and daughters, they will prefer their.sons (Smock & Youssef, 1977). Parents feel it is more important for the son to be educated, since he will be able to work and assist the family later, and he will be the one to support his own family in the future. Thus, from a purely pragmatic viewpoint, the education of sons is a better long-term investment for parents. In the rural setting, the discrepancy between males and females in education is more significantly marked (see Table 4.1).

On an underlying level, the education of women inevitably leads to a challenging of the gender hierarchy. The more women become educated, the more they will become aware of the inegalitarian nature of gender relations (Farag, in preparation).

Smock and Youssef (1977) point to the existence of a "false consciousness" among Egyptian women. They contend that not many Egyptian women view themselves and their condition outside or within the family as oppressed. Ciaccio (in preparation) offers an entirely different view. He argues that many Egyptian women, regardless of social class, are increasingly sensitized to the current gender inequities and point to the demands for full and equal participation in their society. Female education engenders an increased awareness of, and demand for, sociopolitical rights and a possible restructuring of values regarding marriage and the family (Farag, in preparation).

Adulthood

Egyptian women have not managed to make as much progress in the domain of employment as in education. Women in Egypt have a substantial number of legal rights with respect to employment. The legal rights pertaining to women and work are outlined in the Egyptian constitution, international conventions, and Egyptian laws (Hussein et al., 1988).

The 1971 constitution (Article 14) guarantees men and women equal rights to hold public positions. Additionally, Article 11 protects maternal and childhood rights and ensures the reconciliation between women's familial duties and public or societal work. The Egyptian government has also approved the International Convention on the elimination of all forms of discrimination against women and has codified it by Presidential Decree #434, 1981. Article 11 of the above convention calls for the elimination of all discrimination against women in order to allow women the right to equal employment opportunities with men, the right to equal pay, the right to choose an occupation, the right to career advancement and security, and the right to social security and health benefits. It calls for the elimination of discrimination against women due to marital or maternal status, through such measures as the prohibition against firing women because of marriage or pregnancy, providing paid maternal leave, and social services such as child-care centers.

The following specific Egyptian laws protect the woman's right to work:

• Laws 47 and 48 (1978). These laws pertain to the public sector and ensure women the right to two years' unpaid maternity leave for a maximum of three times and the right to paid maternity leave for three months.

• Law 137 (1981). This law pertains to the private sector and grants women 50 days' paid maternity leave and one year's unpaid maternity leave. It also prohibits the employment of women in jobs "detrimental to their health or morals or in strenuous jobs." Finally, it requires employers with over 100 female employees to provide nursery facilities. (Hussein et al., 1988)

The legal provisions for female employment in Egypt are relatively comprehensive and equitable in nature. The reality of female employment in Egypt, however, is dismal. Labor statistics for Egypt and much of the Arab world tend to be unreliable and inconsistent (Sullivan, 1981; Hijab, 1988). Nevertheless, International Labor Organization (ILO) statistics for the year 1989–1990 indicate that 13.5 percent of the female population is economically active (ILO *Yearbook of Labor Statistics*, 1989–1990: See Table 4.2). Statistics for the year 1984, compiled by the Central Agency for Administration and Management, indicate that females account for 17 percent of government employees and 15 percent of

Table 4.2
Economically Active Population by Sex and Age Group, 1989–1990

Age	Activity Rate of Total Population	Males %	Females %
0 - 14	8.2%	9.8	6.4
15 - 19	27.8%	40.8	13
20 - 24	47.6%	71.5	24.4
24 - 29	49.9%	79.3	21.5
30 - 39	49.9%	81.7	19.3
40 - 59	57.6%	98.5	15.7
60 - 64	45.4%	84.4	7.7
65 +	47.5%	72.5	23.7
Total	31.6%	49.3	13.5

Source: ILO, *Labor Statistics Yearbook* (1989–1990).

the work force in the public and private sectors combined (Hussein et al., 1988). Furthermore, the number of female employees increased in a number of fields, including insurance (41.7 percent), tourism and aviation (40.1 percent), culture and information (39.2 percent), and elementary school teaching (97 percent). The fields in which the number of female employees has decreased are agriculture (16 percent), defense and justice (13.9 percent), and health services (9.4 percent) (Central Agency for Administration and Management, 1984, as cited in Hussein et al., 1988).

Social class differences are as salient in the domain of employment as they are in education. Upper-middle-class women and their families appear to have more positive attitudes toward female employment than their lower-class counterparts (Mohsen, 1974). Women in upper classes have the financial means to employ household and child-care help, thus limiting their domestic duties (Mohsen, 1985). In addition to this, their level of educational attainment is such that the employment they are able to obtain is relatively well paying, usually in the private sector (Mohsen, 1985). The lower middle classes, on the other hand, encounter more obstacles with respect to work, although they are most in need of supplemental income. These women cannot usually afford to hire help to aid with their domestic duties or send their children to day-care centers; thus their decision to work entails a difficult balancing between their occupational and familial and household duties. Beyond that, they may meet resistance from their husbands and the community, even if the extra income is badly needed (Rugh, 1984).

Although women's participation in the labor force has increased over the years, the majority of women in Egypt do not seek employment outside the home. The primary focus for females remains marriage and childbearing; hence most economic activities are considered peripheral to women's main role. Women who are employed are expected to carry complete responsibility for care of the household with little or no help from their husbands (Hussein et al., 1988). This creates a tremendous strain on women who are expected to work and attend to their familial responsibilities with the same proficiency as before employment (Rugh, 1984). Furthermore, social supports for working women are meager. Services that facilitate the employment of mothers, such as child-care centers, are not readily available or affordable (Hussein et al., 1988). Employers often ignore their legal obligation to set up nurseries when over 100 women are employed (Hussein et al., 1988). In addition to the lack of tangible social support, women must also contend with the decisively negative cultural attitudes toward female employment (El Saadawy, 1980). Furthermore, socioreligious movements in Egypt during recent years have called for women's return to the home and her "natural" role as wife and mother (see al Bahi, as cited in Hoffman-Ladd, 1987). Social disapproval stems from the overtly public role of women who work. Women who work outside the home are felt to jeopardize their femininity and their married and maternal life and risk the "harmful" consequences of freedom experienced by the "Western woman" (see al Bahi, as cited in Hoffman-Ladd, 1987). Female employment entails increased interaction with males in the workplace and in the use of public transportation. As such, the single woman is felt to be placed in a precarious position, since her morality is no longer safeguarded by her male family members (Hoffman-Ladd, 1987; Hijab, 1988). The negative attitude toward female employment is not peculiar to Egypt but rather occurs in Arab societies in general. Therefore, a woman who decides to seek employment incurs not only a greater workload but often social censure as well. Within the context in which some women are benefiting less from the outside employment compared with the hardships they endure, their reluctance to seek paid employment is more comprehensible.

Old Age

The Egyptian government has given special attention to the problems of the elderly, both men and women. While there were 3.6 percent of the total population who were 65 years and up in 1976, statistics showed that in 1985 the number of elderly people had increased to 2.5 million individuals or 6.5 percent (Central Agency for Public Mobilization and Statistics, 1978; Al-Ahram, 1985).

To help the elderly citizens in Egypt, the government, as well as private social associations, focused on providing assistance in terms of medical and social care. A number of clubs and homes were established that provided the elderly with health care, social services, and psychological support. There are about 2,000 elderly persons who live in 35 homes in Cairo and Alexandria that were established by the Ministry for Social Affairs in Egypt; and in addition 10,000 members are accommodated and served in 18 clubs for older persons. Furthermore, more than a million elderly people, both men and women, enjoyed the benefits of monthly pensions that were established in 1970 by presidential decree (State Information Service, 1983).

SUMMARY AND CONCLUSIONS

Many women in Egyptian society continue to challenge the male vision of reality (Ciaccio, in preparation). While many continue to seek the advocacy of males, they now want to choose for themselves, rather than merely being told what is best for them. Women's continued participation in education and employment, deriving prestige and status from activities outside the home, is forcing a reinterpretation of gender hierarchies and a new degree of independence incompatible with current sex-role ideals.

REFERENCES

Ahmed, L. (1982). Western ethnocentrism and perceptions of the harem. *Feminist Studies*.

Ahmed, R. A. (1981). Zur Ontogenese der Begriffskompetenz bei ägyptischen Kindern in Abhängigkeit von sozialen und kulturellen Entwicklungsbedingungen. Ph.D. diss., Karl-Marx Universität Leipzig, Sektion Psychologie, Leipzig.

————. (1989). The development of number, space, quantity, and reasoning concepts in Sudanese school children. In Adler, L. L. (Ed.), *Cross-Cultural Research in Human Development: Life-Span Perspectives* (Chapter 2). New York: Praeger.

————. (1991). Women in Egypt and the Sudan. In Adler, L. L. (Ed.), *Women in Cross-Cultural Perspective* (Chapter 9). New York: Praeger.

Al-Ahram (1985, January 2). Egyptian daily newspaper in Arabic.

Al-Ahram (1985, January 11). Egyptian daily newspaper (in Arabic).

Assaad, M. (1980). Female circumcision in Egypt: Social implications, current research, and prospects for change. *Studies in Family Planning*.

Barakat, H. (1985). The Arab family and the challenge of social transformation. In Fernea, E. (Ed.), *Women and the Family in the Middle East*. Austin: University of Texas Press.

Central Agency for Public Mobilization and Statistics (CAPMAS). (1978). *Detailed Results of the 1976 General Census in Egypt* (in Arabic). Cairo.

————. (1990). *Statistical Yearbook*. Arab Republic of Egypt: CAPMAS.

Ciaccio, N. V. (in preparation). *The Children of Egypt Speak*.

Denny, N., & Quadagno, D. (1988). *Human Sexuality*. St. Louis: Times Mirror/Mosby College.

El Guindi, F. (1983). Veiled activism. Egyptian women in the contemporary Islamic movement. *Femmes de la Méditerranée*.

El Saadawy, N. (1980). *The Hidden Face of Eve: Women in the Arab World*. London: Zed Books.

Farag, O. (in preparation). *Strategies for Sustainable Development in Egypt*.

Galal el-Din, M. E. (1984). The discrimination between men and women and its reflections on woman's positions and her role in the society. (In Arabic.) *Journal of the Social Sciences, 12* (3): 7–35.

Ghassoub, M. (1987). Feminism or the eternal masculine in the Arab world. *New Left Review*.

Hany, D. (1990). *Female Circumcision in Egypt*. Unpublished.

Hatem, M. (1986a). The enduring alliance of nationalism and patriarchy in Muslim personal status laws: The case of modern Egypt. *Feminist Issue*.

————. (1986b). Underdevelopment, mothering and gender within the Egyptian family. *Arab Studies Quarterly*.

Hijab, N. (1988). *Woman Power: The Arab Debate on Women at Work*. Cambridge: Cambridge University Press.

Hoffman-Ladd, V. (1987). Polemics on the modesty and segregation of women in contemporary Egypt. *International Journal of Middle Eastern Studies*.

Hussein, A., et al. (1988). *The Legal Rights of Egyptian Women: Between Theory and Implementation*. Arab Republic of Egypt: Cairo Document #5004.

International Labor Organization (ILO) (1989–1990). *Yearbook of Labor Statistics*.

Mernissi, F. (1985). *Beyond the Veil: Male-Female Dynamics in Muslim Society*. London: El Saqui.

Minai, N. (1981). *Women in Islam: Tradition and Transition in the Middle East* (p.91). London: John Murray.

Mohsen, S. (1974). The Egyptian woman: Between modernity and tradition. In Matthiasson, C. (Ed.), *Many Sisters: Women in Cross-Cultural Perspective*. London: Free Press.

————. (1985). *New Images, Old Reflections: Working Middle-Class Women in Egypt*. Austin: University of Texas Press.

Nelson, C. (1984). Islamic tradition and women's education in Egypt. In S. Acker et al. (Eds.), *The World Yearbook of Education*. London: Nichols.

Quran, trans. Y. Ali. Arab Republic of Egypt: Dar el Kitab al Masri.

Rugh, A. (1984). *Family in Contemporary Egypt*. Syracuse, NY: Syracuse University Press.

Sabbah, F. (1984). *Women in the Muslim Unconscious*.

Saleh, S. (1972). *Women in Islam: Their Status in Religious and Traditional Culture*.

Smock, A., & Youssef, N. (1977). Egypt: From seclusion to limited participation. In Giele, J., & Smock, A. (Eds.), *Women: Role and Status in Eight Countries*. New York: John Wiley.

State Information Service, Ministry of Information, the Arab Republic of Egypt. (1983). *Highlights on the Five-Year Plan for Economic and Social Development in the Arab Republic of Egypt*. (In Arabic.) Cairo: Ministry of Information.

Tomeh, A. (1983). The traditional and modern Arab family. *Journal of South Asian and Middle Eastern Studies*.

UNESCO. (1990). *UNESCO Statistical Yearbook*. Paris: UNESCO.

UNICEF & CAPMAS. (1988). *The State of Egyptian Children*. Arab Republic of Egypt: Dar al Kitab al Masri.

5

Finland

Liisa Husu and Pirkko Niemelä

INTRODUCTION

Finland is a northern European country, sharing several cultural and institutional features with the other Nordic countries: Denmark, Norway, Sweden, and Iceland. The country has common borders with Russia in the east, Norway in the north, and Sweden in the north and northwest. With an area of 338,000 square kilometers (130,502 square miles), Finland is one of the largest countries in Europe.

However, the population of Finland is only 5 million; in this respect Finland is one of the smallest European countries. Population density is low: 16 per square kilometer. The population is concentrated in the south and west, with 65 percent living in towns. The metropolitan area around the capital, Helsinki, has nearly 1 million inhabitants. Half of the population are in the labor force. The population is homogeneous: 93 percent speak Finnish, and 6 percent speak Swedish, the two official languages. The population is also homogeneous in their religious affiliation: 88 percent belong to the Lutheran Church of Finland. Population growth continues to be slow. The birthrate is on the same level as in most European countries, about 1.7. The proportion of people over 65 has grown more rapidly in Finland in the 1970s and 1980s than elsewhere in Europe; in 1990 it was 13.5 percent (Valkonen, 1990).

For years, Finland was part of the Swedish kingdom. In 1809 the country became an autonomous Grand Duchy of Imperial Russia. Finland gained independence in 1917. During World War II, Finland was initially at war with the Soviet Union in the Winter War of 1939–1940 and 1941–1944. Later Finland fought Germany in Lapland in 1944–1945. The country was, however, never occupied by foreign troops. In the wars Finland lost around 100,000 men from its population of 4.5 million. Subsequently, the area of Karelia had to be ceded to the Soviet Union, and its 400,000 inhabitants resettled in Finland. A devastated Lapland was rebuilt, and heavy war reparations were paid to the Soviet Union. After World War II, Finland experienced a very rapid economic and social development. The shift from an agrarian society to a postindustrial society was one of the most rapid in Europe. In a global perspective, Finland is one of the wealthiest countries of the world.

Finland is a multiparty parliamentary democracy. The 200-member Parliament is elected every four years, and the president of the Republic is elected every six years in free elections. The cabinets are usually coalitions. There is a strong tradition of local government: 460 municipalities are responsible for organizing and financing basic services, many of which are partly state-subsidized.

Finland has a mixed economy. The economy is based largely on private ownership. The extensive public sector offers free basic education and primary health care, social security, various cultural services, and subsidized public transport. Health care and social welfare are organized and run by the municipalities and funded by the municipalities and the state. This is possible because municipalities can levy their own taxes.

Basic social security for all residents is guaranteed by compulsory social insurance. Compulsory social insurance insures all persons for old age, disability, sickness, and unemployment. The entitlement is based on residence. In the last decades social insurance has developed so that it both guarantees a minimum income and takes into account the level of earnings. Minimum security does not depend on tax payment of insurance premiums.

OVERVIEW

Finnish women are often considered more integrated throughout society than their sisters in many other countries. Ancient findings suggest that this phenomenon might have long roots. The Roman historian Tacitus (c.98 B.C.) describes in Germania the "wild and horribly poor" Fenni: "The same hunt provides food for men and women alike; for the women go everywhere with the men and claim a share in the prey" (Manninen, 1990).

At the site of the earliest cultural settlements in Finland, Astuvansalmi in the Finnish Lake District, interesting rock engravings have been found that support Tacitus's claims. One of these "depicts a typically mythical hunting scene of elks, hunters, horned shamans and, oddly enough, two women. These women have caused archeologists a real headache because one of them carries a bow" (Manninen, 1990). A female figure sporting a bow is a virtually unknown character in rock engravings.

Viking period (A.D. 800–1000) grave findings also suggest that during that time there were women who played important public roles in their communities. One grave finding revealed a woman with two magnificent swords beside her, and another showed a woman with a curled-up man buried under her feet (Manninen, 1990). After these times the possibilities of women were influenced by the church, which gained a foothold in Finland in the thirteenth century. The idea of women's inherent weakness or of women as "imperfect men" created to serve men guaranteed that women had fewer opportunities and rights in society (Manninen, 1990).

From very early times women have had a strong impact on the cultural life of Finland, both as creators and as consumers. For at least six centuries women have participated in all the main literary genres and forms: narrative lyrical poetry (ballads and legends), song lyrics, early forms of drama (rites), and narrative prose (fairly tales and stories) (Apo, 1989). Women's oral poetry included highly valued forms, such as the laments that were transitional rites, entertainment, and children's poetry.

The national epos *Kalevala* describes several strong female figures: Louhi, a mighty matron, who was a leader of her tribe, witch and warrior, and the mother of Lemminkäinen, who fetched her son from death.

Finnish is a Fenno-Ugrarian language. The language does not use gender as a grammatical category. Finnish has no equivalents to "he" or "she" but uses instead only one pronoun, *hän*, referring to both males and females.

In recent international comparisons (Population Crisis Committee, 1988; Human Development Report, 1990), Finland has been given high ratings in gender equality. The majority of women are wage earners, and women under forty are already slightly better educated than men and are playing an increasingly active and prominent role in politics compared with most other countries.

In spite of all this, many persistent gender inequalities can be discerned. The Equality Act prohibiting discrimination came into force in 1987. The law is, however, complaint-based and has had little effect on the deep structural roots of gender inequality. The wage gap between men and women is still a reality and broadened in the 1980s. Education and working life are gender-segregated. Education is not as useful a resource for women in the labor market as it is for men. In comparison to their male counterparts, women with the same educational experience do not achieve equal positions in the labor market (Anttalainen, 1986; Pöntinen, 1991; Olennainen, 1990, 1991). The double burden of working women is a reality for most women in Finland: they work full-time outside the home but still bear the main responsibility for household chores, performing 65 percent of them (Niemi & Pääkkönen, 1989).

Health differences between Finnish men and women are considerable: in 1989, life expectancy at birth was 70.9 for men and 78.9 for women. Female health is good by international standards, and women's life expectancy has grown continuously. Compared with other Western, industrialized countries, the life expectancy at birth of Finnish men was one of the lowest and is the lowest in the Nordic countries (Vogel, 1991). The difference in life expectancy between men and women in Western, industrialized countries is greatest in Finland. However, the life expectancy at birth of Finnish men has increased by two years from the 1979 calculation level (Vogel, 1991). In 1986 female life expectancy at birth was higher in Finland than in such countries as Denmark, France, Great Britain, or the United States of America.

While overall health in Finland is good and mortality figures for Finnish women are on the same level as in the other Scandinavian countries, mortality of males over 25 years is higher than in most other industrialized countries. This is mainly due to cardiovascular diseases. The number of deaths from coronaries among middle-aged men is near the world peak. There is also a notable excess of male mortality due to accidents, suicides, and lung cancer (*Health*, 1990).

COMPARISONS BETWEEN MEN'S AND WOMEN'S GENDER ROLES DURING THE LIFE CYCLE

Infancy and Early Childhood

Infant mortality in Finland is among the lowest in the world. This is mainly due to the effective system of maternity and child health care centers. Since the 1940s it has been compulsory for local authorities to provide these centers. The centers are accessible to all parents and infants regardless of means or locality. They provide free service, regular inoculations, and support for families. Except in sparsely populated areas, maternity and child health care centers are near to every family. Ninety-nine percent of children are born in hospitals.

Most children have mothers and fathers who work full-time outside the home. Only 12 percent of women work part-time. In 1989 85 percent of mothers with children under 18 years and 78 percent of mothers with children under 7 years belonged to the work force. The majority (76 percent) of mothers with 3 or more children under 18 years also belong to the work force (*Women & Men in Finland*, 1991).

Day-care arrangements are therefore of crucial importance. Day care has been a major issue in national and local policy of the 1980s and early 1990s. Facilities have increased rapidly, almost meeting the demand. Also, other reforms intended to facilitate the combining of work and family responsibilities have developed in the 1980s and early 1990s.

The Finnish day-care system started about 100 years ago. It has been built up systematically, since 1973 by means of legislation. The government has laid down minimum standards for the quality of day care and subsidizes the costs. Local authorities are responsible for the organization of day care, both family child minding and kindergartens, as they are for all other social and health services. Not all day care is a municipal monopoly, but in fact almost all kindergartens are municipal. Many children under three are cared for in private families. Municipal child minders contract to the municipality, which pays their salary and controls the quality of the care. Child minders may work in their own home or in the children's. In all municipal day-care forms, parents pay an income-related fee to the municipality. Children of parents with a modest income level are offered municipal day care free of charge.

Most municipalities also run evening and night care for children of shift workers and afternoon care for schoolchildren. Day-care centers are staffed by qualified children's nurses, social educators, and preschool teachers.

At the beginning of 1990, a new system was initiated guaranteeing parents with children under three the choice of either a municipal day-care place or a home care allowance to pay for nonmunicipal day care. This allowance is a compensation for not using the municipal system. In practice, the majority of families have until now used this allowance to enable the mother to care for the child at home. Parents with children under school age have a right to shorten their daily or weekly working hours. Those with children under three are partly compensated for loss of income due to shortened hours.

The right to choose either a municipal day-care place or home care allowance will gradually broaden so that by 1995 all parents with children under school age will have this right.

At day-care centers and school, boys and girls have different games, interests, and relationships with other children and with teachers and other staff. Girls enjoy day care and school activities more than boys and adapt to day care and school much better. Boys have more learning difficulties and receive more remedial instruction. Boys have more socioemotional problems. Their problems, more than girls', disturb others. Boys, more often than girls, are removed to the special classes, where 88 percent of the children were boys in the late 1980s.

There are now new attempts to develop day care and school activities so that boys will adapt better. The Turku project (Keskinen, personal communication, 1991) started from the observation that the day-care staff was more negative toward boys than girls. The goal was to pay more attention to the different developmental needs of the boys and girls, in the daily interaction between the staff and the children. Therefore staff caring for 3 to 6 year old children were given supplementary training and supervision. As a result the boys were observed to be more capable of making contact with both adults and other children.

The greatest effects were that the staff came to accept the difference between boys and girls and to accept boys' greater need for activity and interest in technical equipment. The staff now organize more activities for the boys than previously, for example, in sports, and provide boys with more toys they want to play with. Earlier house rules, for example, prohibiting war toys, have been abolished. When the rule that skipping ropes could be used only for skipping was abolished, the boys could use them for lassos and lianas, like Tarzan. Also one day a week, wrestling was allowed. Though boys now wrestle more often than before, they also play more with teddies and dolls and are more interested in domestic work. The boys appreciate play with equipment like computers and TV remote controls; they report at home that now they can do "real men's work" at day care while girls report at home that the boys tease them less.

The main goal of the Turku project was to clarify and support boys' and girls' respective identity developments so that day care could offer models for both masculine and feminine development. The names of day-care groups, which have traditionally been names of flowers, for example, "bluebells," now can be, for example, "beavers." This trend did not separate boys from girls nor restrict their possibilities or models.

The staff was now also interested in ways of activating girls and increasing alternatives for both boys and girls. The staff is now concerned that the girls are very sensitive to the expectations of adults, fulfill the expectations of the staff, and perhaps act less from their own needs.

Several books about boys' development have recently been published in Finnish. For example, Jouko Huttunen (1990) has studied the significance of the father's gender role for his sons. He found that a masculine father, exhibiting paternal control, contributes to his son's androgynous development. The relatively high number of studies on boys' psychological development, as well as the new trends in the day-care and school systems, suggests a growth in concern for Finnish men's illness and early death.

School Years

The formal education system in Finland is public. Over 90 percent of formal education costs are covered by the state or local authorities. The normal educational system is composed of the comprehensive school, vocational and professional educational institutions, and the universities. Comprehensive school is compulsory for all 7 to 16 year olds. The syllabus is essentially the same for all pupils. After completing the comprehensive school, all pupils are eligible for further education: general education provided in the senior secondary schools (3 years leading to matriculation examination) or vocational education provided in the vocational and professional institutions. Gender equality is mentioned as a goal in all school laws. The realization of this goal in everyday practice is another matter.

Studying is more common among women in all age groups except 16–17. In 1990, 37 percent of women and 26 percent of men aged 20–24 years were studying. In the fall of 1990, 58 percent of those entering senior secondary school were girls. In the late 1980s about 45 percent of the age group matriculated, 36 percent of the men and 54 percent of the women (*Education*, 1991).

Education is clearly gender-segregated. In 1989 no field of vocational and professional education had equal proportions of women and men. Male-dominated areas include mathematics, computer science, trade, craft, industry, engineering, agriculture, forestry, fishery, transport, and communications. Women are in a majority in teacher training, fine and applied arts, humanities, commercial and business administration, medicine and health, home economics and domestic science, and service trades (*Education*, 1991).

In vocational and professional educational institutions, admission is most difficult for those applying to the institutes of health care and social services, which are traditionally popular among girls. On the other hand, male-dominated schools specializing in timber, mechanical engineering, and metal work are easiest to enter. Often nearly all applicants are admitted. On average, 60 percent of the applicants are admitted to vocational and professional schools. Of those applying, this represents over 70 percent of the boys and a little over 50 percent of the girls (*Education*, 1991).

In the 1960s, girls were taught more domestic science and boys had more practice in physics and chemistry. Now schools are coeducational, and the curriculum is formally the same for boys and girls; only physical education and sports are segregated. Attempts have been made to have girls taught sports by a male teacher and boys aerobics by a female teacher. The former practice of segregated teaching of crafts has been formally abolished; formerly, girls focused more on knitting and needlework while the boys concentrated on woodwork. Handicraft is taught as a common subject in the first two school years. In the third grade, the pupils have to choose either textile work or technical work. Although the system is gender-neutral, still over 90 percent of girls choose textile work, and over 90 percent of boys choose technical work. This results in a situation where boys are introduced to applying natural science and technology more than girls and diminishes the possibilities to attract girls to study natural sciences. According to the school laws, both textile and technical crafts should be taught as a common subject for boys and girls until the end of seventh grade. This is not the case today, and thus the current practice is against the school laws, as has been pointed out by the Equality Ombudsman (Räsänen, 1992).

The value of equality between the sexes is not taught as a separate subject. The goal is that it should penetrate every school subject and be integrated in all teaching. Whether or not schools officially attempt to educate children about equality, there is accumulating information on the existence of the hidden agendas that affect children's conceptions of equality. For example, girls are expected to obey rules while boys are expected to be more "individual" and thus have more freedom. In comparison to girls, boys receive more criticism and discipline from teachers, but they also receive more attention and interest. Girls are expected to be careful, painstaking, and thorough while boys' carelessness and negligence are accepted as a sign of creativity and contempt for unnecessary pettiness.

The existence of this hidden agenda toward schoolchildren is also revealed in the hierarchy of the staff. Sixty-five percent of the teachers were women in the late 1980s, but most principals were men. Only 14 percent of lower grade school, 22 percent of higher grade school, and 17 percent of upper secondary school principals are women. Until 1988, there was a quota of 40 percent male students for teacher training. Now the quota has been abolished as it is against the Equality Act, and male trainees number only 10 percent.

Gendered structures in the Finnish school system have been studied by Elina Lahelma (1990). Throughout the comprehensive school, girls' achievements are better than boys'. During the 1980s, girls achieved better grades in every subject in the final years of comprehensive school. However, there was little difference between girls' and boys' grades in physics, mathematics, technical subjects, and textile handicraft. Also, in upper secondary school, girls' school achievement was better, with the exception of chemistry and mathematics. The same pattern was observed in the matriculation examination, in which 50 percent of the girls and 44 percent of the boys received the highest or second highest grade in 1988. An extensive course in mathematics was taken by 55 percent of the matriculating boys but only 22 percent of the girls. Extensive mathematics courses are an important gatekeeper for further studies in many fields. Boys also tend to receive better grades in mathematics tests than girls.

In international educational achievement tests, boys tend to perform better in science than girls. In Finland boys have received better grades in all natural sciences, the differences growing with age. In the seventies the difference between boys and girls in Finland was larger than the international averages in all subjects (Comber & Keeves, 1973). These differences have diminished since the 1970s. Still the difference between Finnish boys and girls in physics is very large; the difference is larger only in Poland (*Science Achievement*, 1988).

Lahelma concludes that girls receive better grades in school but that differences between girls and boys are not so great in standardized tests. Excepting their worst grades, boys have perhaps achieved the schools' goals for cognitive development better than girls. Boys' better achievements in standardized "objective" tests have been used to suggest that Finnish schools favor girls. However, one can ask, Which is better, to have better grades or to be better qualified for life after school?

Diversity in school achievement is greater among boys: there are more very successful and more very unsuccessful boys (Tarmo, 1986). This demonstrates that boys may get more attention than girls in school. They are selected more thoroughly but are classified into losers and winners. Girls tend to appear as mediocre to the teachers (Lahelma, 1990).

Young Adulthood

For a long time Finnish women have been eligible for vocational training, up to the highest levels. The first Finnish female upper secondary school student graduated in 1870 while the first female university student graduated in 1892. In 1922 and after that, over half of the upper secondary school students were women, and after 1950 over half of the matriculating students were women.

The universities opened officially to women in 1901. It was possible, however, for women to enter university studies before that with dispensation. As early as 1892–1893 female students made up 3 percent of all students. In 1895 the first woman received her doctoral degree in medicine, and in 1897 the first woman gained her Ph.D. Finland had the first female physician in the Nordic countries. Finnish female architects graduated in the 1890s were among the first female architects in the world.

After 1987 women formed over half of those graduating from Finnish universities. The proportion of women obtaining a doctoral degree has grown rapidly, and in 1989 reached 30 percent. Women obtain the doctorate two years later on the average than do their male counterparts (Räty, 1991).

University education is somewhat less segregated than vocational and professional education. About one-third of all applicants are admitted. In 1990, 51 percent of all university students and 56 percent of new university students were women. Mathematics, computer science, and engineering are the only male-dominated subjects. Female-dominated subjects included teacher training, humanities, medicine and health, home economics, and domestic science. In all other studies neither sex exceeds 60 percent of all students (*Education*, 1991).

Several studies have attempted to explain the difference between boys' and girls' vocational choices. Prior to entering upper secondary school, girls are more active in researching their career and discussing their choices than are boys. However, they have lower professional goals when they get older. They often choose a career that fits in with motherhood, while boys, reaching out for their own career, consider that it is their duty to guarantee the livelihood of the family.

To improve boys' and girls' knowledge of nontraditional careers, there have been experimentations where the boys worked in a typical women's profession and the girls in a typical men's profession. At first the students were against this experimentation, but after starting, they were in favor of it.

Both boys and girls include work and family among their most important plans in their lives (Niemi, 1988). Whether or not students are oriented toward traditional gender-role careers, girls appreciate getting vocational training and work experience before motherhood. They usually plan not to stay home with their children but to have two-earner families.

Female adolescents consider these plans in their sexual behavior also. There are, in international terms, few teenage pregnancies: 11.8 childbirths per 1,000 15 to 19 year old females in 1989. Adolescents use contraceptives well. Abortion is not used as a method of contraception, although it is fairly inexpensive. Among 15 to 19 year old female adolescents there are only 14.6 abortions per 1,000 individuals (1989). Furthermore many of these abortions are due to the failure of condoms or the minipills. The successful use of the contraceptives among adolescents is due, at least partly, to the educational work of school health nurses.

Several Finnish studies have reported that when girls grow older, their self-esteem decreases. Rauste-von Wright (1987) in a longitudinal study asked respondents aged 11, 13, 15, and 18 to evaluate their own self-image, their ideal self-image, and their normative self-image (the way they believed others expected them to be), on scales of intelligence, energy, and so on. Both boys and girls wanted to be successful, able, and popular, in a calm and relaxed manner, without any "human weaknesses." Between 11 and 15 years of age, the girls' ideal self-images changed in the direction of what could be traditionally regarded as "masculine." The value for emotionality decreased, while the value for leadership and initiative increased. It would appear that the girls were becoming more ambivalent toward features "typical" of their own sex.

As to the normative self-image, there was little difference between the sexes. The only clear age-related trend was that the girls felt greater pressure toward being matter-of-fact at ages 15 and 18 than at age 13.

The assessments of self-image differ between the sexes, and differences increase with age. In comparison with boys, girls rated themselves as more emotional, more impulsive, and less energetic. Self-esteem was operationalized in terms of the difference between self-image and ideal self-image. It was lower for girls than for boys. The sex difference in self-esteem, not significant at age 11, was significant at ages 13, 15, and 18.

In the same study, Rauste-von Wright (1989) measured adolescents' satisfaction with their bodies. At all age levels, males were more satisfied with their physical features than were females. Females tended to be dissatisfied with their weight while males tended to be satisfied with their shoulders at all age levels.

Adulthood

During the 1980s nearly half of Finland's labor force were women. In international terms, labor force participation of Finnish women has traditionally been very high. One explanation is that Finland remained an agrarian society until the 1950s. The rapid industrialization and expansion of the service sector produced a rising demand for labor. During the 1960s and 1970s this demand was almost totally satisfied by female workers (Anttalainen, 1986; Jallinoja, 1980), not by immigrants, as in many other countries.

However, women's waged labor was already common during the first phase of industrialization. In the capital of Helsinki, 39 percent of women of working age were in waged labor as early as 1870. By 1900 this figure was 55 percent (Jallinoja, 1980). It remained around this level until the 1960s. During this first phase, the proportion of nonmarried women was quite high among women of working age. This facilitated the use of a female work force. The tradition of women's working outside the home made it easier to accept women's waged work during the phase of rapid industrialization. Marriages became more common after World War II, and both unmarried and married women could be used as female waged labor (Jallinoja, 1980). By 1950 nearly half the female labor force were married women, and by 1980 the figure was 65 percent (Anttalainen, 1986).

School lunches and canteen facilities provided by employers are important factors making possible both parents' full-time work. Schools and kindergartens serve a warm lunch for children during the school day. The free school lunches started in the 1940s. In the 1970s canteen facilities provided by employers increased rapidly. Nowadays the majority of the population may have a warm lunch for subsidized costs during their working or school day (Haavio-Mannila, 1984).

The labor market is strongly gender-segregated in Finland as it is in other Nordic countries. This segregation has not diminished since World War II. Since the 1950s, 4–8 percent of the labor force have been working in a gender-balanced occupation in which the female to male ratio is 41 to 60 percent. Eight out of ten women and eight out of ten men are working in fields where over half of the employees are of their own sex. That education is clearly gender-segregated enforces gender segregation in the labor market (Anttalainen, 1986; Allen et al., 1990).

Higher education does not produce equal positions for women and men. In prestigious occupations, as among engineers, doctors, or lawyers, internal labor markets are gender-segregated. Female lawyers are seldom hired for prestigious and highly paid positions in the private sector. In the public sector they most often work in the middle or lower steps of the hierarchy (Silius, 1992).

Gender segregation of wages is partially explained by women's and men's working in different positions. Recent studies have, however, proved that this is only a part of the explanation. A more important reason is that the same work or work of equal value is not paid equally for men and women. In percentage, the wage gap diminished up to the beginning of the 1980s. Then it stagnated at a level of 75–80 percent. In hard currency, the gap has even grown since 1982–1983.

A characteristic of the wage structure in Finland is that women's wage levels generally end where men's start. A wage level at which most women are under it and most men over it can be identified. Two-thirds of women end up at the wage level that is passed by two-thirds of men (Anttalainen, 1986; Olennainen, 1989, 1990). Only in the late 1980s was the wage gap broadly acknowledged as a problem in collective bargaining and also in the public discussion.

The average size of a family was 3.12 persons in 1987, compared with 3.72 persons in 1960, and families tended to have 1.75 children on the average, compared with 2.27 in 1960. As of 1989, 41 percent of women and 43 percent of men were married. The predominant family type, constituting 54 percent of families, is a married couple with children. Twenty-eight percent of families are married couples without children, 14 percent of families are composed of mother and children, 2 percent are composed of father and children, and 2 percent are unmarried couples with children (*Women & Men in Finland*, 1991). Divorces are increasing. In 1990 there were 24,000 marriages and 13,000 divorces. According to Niemelä et al. women manage their life better after divorce than men, and many women choose not to marry again, while the men remarry more readily.

Cohabitation has became a common and accepted way of life. In 1989 16 percent of all couples lived together without marriage. An unmarried couple living together is recognized now as a couple by many authorities, and changes in legislation are currently under way in order to make cohabitation and marriage more equal forms of family legally. Cohabitation serves as a kind of preliminary phase preceding marriage. The earlier negative attitude toward women's choosing to have a child alone has been reduced. Abortion is readily available, and therefore nobody is forced to have a child against her will.

Families with children receive several income transfers that compensate families an estimated 20 percent of the extra costs due to the children. These income transfers include tax deductions, child allowances, child home care allowances, maternity benefits, child maintenance allowances, and parent's allowances. The child allowances are paid monthly for all children under 17 regardless of the family's economic state. All mothers, during each pregnancy, receive a maternity benefit pack, unique in the world. It contains basic clothing for the newborn and several requisites for baby care.

Apparently men are becoming more interested in parenthood. In most hospitals it is possible for fathers to attend the delivery. Over 80 percent of fathers attend the delivery of their first child and also participate in childbirth preparation classes before the delivery. Fathers not attending delivery are frequently asked to explain their behavior by friends and relatives. A father with pram or strollers is not an unusual scene in the streets.

A marrying couple may choose as their common family name the name of either the wife or the husband, according to the Family Name Act from 1986. Also they may each retain their own family name. The majority of the marrying women still follow the traditional practice and take the family name of their husband.

Combining work with parenthood is a practice facilitated by the Finnish welfare state's extensive support system. Parental leave is a legal entitlement subsidized by the state. Currently one is allowed 275 days (excluding Sundays and public holidays), 30–50 of which can be taken before the birth. The first 100 days can be taken only by the mother, but the remaining days can be divided between the mother and father. Maternity leave is lengthened by 60 days if one has two or more babies. Parental benefit is also paid to adoptive parents for 234 days.

Paternity leave was institutionalized in 1978. The father is entitled to paternity leave with allowance to stay at home with the mother during the first two weeks after childbirth. Furthermore he is entitled to take one week's paternity leave at any chosen time during the mother's parental leave. Since 1985 parental leave can be taken by either parent but not simultaneously. They can also take turns. Parental leave is predominantly used by mothers. Thirty-five percent of fathers took parental or paternity leave in 1989, but only 2 percent took both. Most fathers (34 percent) took the short leave in connection with the birth, but only 3 percent took the longer parental leave.

Since 1985, either the father or the mother has had the right to take leave to care for his or her child until the child is three years old. The Employment Contracts Act assures job security for any parent who uses this home care leave. In 1989 about 46 percent of mothers who had been wage earners before childbirth (35 percent of all mothers) and 0.6 percent of fathers took the leave. This home care leave was least popular among two very different groups of women: the most highly educated ones, apparently for career development reasons, and women without any vocational training, perhaps for economical reasons. Only 15 percent of families on child-care leave used the maximum time of three years.

In 1906 Finnish women simultaneously gained suffrage and eligibility to enter

Parliament. Finland was the first nation in the world to allow the latter, electing the first woman Member of Parliament (MP) in the world a year later. In the first parliamentary elections, 10 percent of those elected were women. Since that time women have increased their influence and visibility in both local and national politics. After the 1960s women's and men's voting activity has been at the same level, and in the latest elections women voted somewhat more actively than men. Women have always made up at least 8 percent of the total MPs, a level that many Western, industrialized countries, for example, France, Great Britain, and the United States of America have reached only in recent years. As of 1992, this percentage was 38.5 percent, larger than in any other country. However, it is becoming increasingly evident that the democratically elected, political decision-making bodies in which women have been able to put a foot in the door are losing decision-making power.

On the other hand, women in Finland have been active pioneers of the welfare state as participants in public policy and legislative activities (Sinkkonen & Haavio-Mannila, 1981). The welfare state has not been given to women; they have actively participated in creating it.

Women are less visible in the local political arena. In the municipal councils for 1988–1992 only 27 percent of delegates were women. There are great territorial differences: in the area around the capital, nearly half the delegates in many councils are women, while in the countryside there are many municipalities with very few female decision makers.

For political parties the current trend is to have at least one woman in a visible post among the leadership. There are no quotas for women in any party nor serious discussions to establish them.

In the 1992 cabinet, 7 of the 17 ministers were women. The gender-based division of labor is apparent on this level too: women most often hold posts in the traditional female domains of social affairs and education. Between 1926 and 1991 a woman was appointed to the cabinet 63 times, 46 times as minister of education or social affairs (Kuusipalo, 1991). In recent years there have also been female finance, justice, or foreign trade ministers, but these are exceptions. The minister of defense in two subsequent cabinets in the early 1990s was a woman, and, according to polls in the fall of 1991, she is one of the country's most popular politicians. In common with another female politician also polled as popular, she is notable for refusing to use political jargon common among most Finnish politicians. These two female politicians are also popular candidates for the next president of the Republic to be elected in 1994. The president of the Republic has considerable power in the Finnish political system and has always been male.

Top female politicians have also broadened the politician's image: the female minister of social affairs and health became pregnant and gave birth to a daughter during her period of office. She took a short maternity leave whereas her husband took parental leave to care for the child.

Today in creative cultural life, women manage more and more intermediary, public relations tasks whereas men occupy the leading positions. Women work as organizers in local and national cultural administration, as municipal cultural officers, or as secretaries of provincial art committees (Eskola, 1990). Only in recent years have a few women achieved top positions in cultural life.

Women make up a relatively large minority (37 percent) of those working in artistic occupations (Liikkanen, 1988). Internationally this is rather high (Eskola, 1990; Karttunen, 1988; Heikkinen, 1989). Women in 1986 represented 40 percent of those working in visual arts; 42 percent of writers and critics; 32 percent of film directors; 47 percent of theater, opera, and ballet performers; 30 percent of musicians; 25 percent of photographers; 32 percent of architects; and 66 percent of industrial designers (Liikkanen, 1988).

Art as a hobby is common among Finnish people. In comparison to men, women are more active in local cultural activities and more frequently the "consumers" of culture, comprising the majority of audiences for theaters and classical music concerts. Women more often visit art exhibitions and libraries, read, sing, draw, and write. They act slightly more than do men, who are more active as amateur musicians. Light music concerts and cinema attract women and men equally (Eskola, 1990).

Old Age

The population is aging: the proportion of people over 65 is estimated to reach 25 percent of the population in 2030. Especially the oldest age group is growing due to the improved standard of living. There is a growing ratio of old people living alone.

Because nearly all women work outside the home and because of large internal migration and dense housing, it is not very common that grown-up children can take care of their old parents. Public old-age care has been institution-centered, but there is a tendency to shift from institution care toward more open care. The guiding principle of old-age welfare is to enable old people to go on living at home as long as possible.

Services that municipalities offer for the elderly include short-stay rehabilitation, service-housing, home help, home nursing, meals on wheels, supplemented housing services such as bathing and laundry, and transport services.

The general retirement age is 65 in the private sector and 63 in the public sector. Early retirement has become common in Finland: in 1990 only 29 percent of women and 24 percent of men retired at the allotted age. The real retirement age is thus lower, and it is lower now than ten years ago. In 1989 the average pension age, including disability and unemployment pensions, was around 59 years.

All pensioners who are disabled or over 65 get a basic, flat-rate pension. Any person either not receiving earnings-related pension or receiving a very small one is guaranteed a minimum pension. Earnings-related pension is proportional to pay and length of service. Because women's earnings are smaller and their working lives are shorter, their earnings-related pensions are smaller than men's. The full old-age pension amounts to 60 percent of one's salary after 30–40 years of service. Pensions are taxable income.

Those under 55 can get a disability pension. Women and men are equally likely to retire between 55 and 64. Those who do so have many options: disability pension, individual early pension, or war veteran's pension. These pensions assume that the person is either disabled or long-term unemployed. In some fields, however, it is possible to retire even earlier.

Women, more often than men, receive unemployment pension, while men receive disability pension, which is granted by application. Women's applications have been rejected 1.5 times more often than men's during the last 20 years. According to data gathered in the Equality Ombudsman's Office, this difference exhibits a pattern and is systematic. The causes are being investigated by this office in the application and acceptance procedures. The laws regulating the retirement system are gender-neutral.

SUMMARY AND CONCLUSIONS

According to many traditional indicators of gender equality such as education, labor force participation, and political power, Finland is far ahead of most countries. In a country where younger women are already slightly better educated than men, where women constitute the majority of the wage earners, and where the male excess mortality is nationally very high, one often hears the claim that Finnish women are too strong.

The overall picture of Finnish women might seem rosy. However, if one looks at the situation of women in more detail, one sees the picture changing. Equal possibilities do not produce equal results in Finland or any other country. Women are well educated, but education is strongly gender-segregated. Even if girls receive better grades in school, the school does not prepare them for working life as well as it prepares boys. Even if women make up half of the wage earners, the labor market is strongly gender-segregated, and there is no change in sight. Finnish women's working days are long because after a full working day, household chores are still mainly women's responsibility. The wage gap is a reality and has increased over the last 10 years. Stress has increased, especially in women's jobs (Lehto, 1991). Even if women are active and visible in politics, many important decisions are not made by the democratically chosen political arenas where women have a foot in the door.

On the other hand, good education and a long tradition of working women make it impossible to ignore the demands of women or to treat them as a reserve labor force. "What would happen if all Finnish women went on strike?" has sometimes been hypothesized; schools, hospitals, kindergartens, and other community services and banks, parts of industry, insurance companies, shops, and restaurants would close down. Society would be totally paralyzed and come to a standstill.

In Finland sexism has been a problem with no name until recent years. The fact that, in spite of women's high education and intensive labor force participation, women are still the second sex has usually been explained by referring vaguely to "attitudes" that have to be changed. Women's issues, such as a persistent wage gap, have only in recent years started to receive more attention as legitimate matters. On the other hand, issues like violence against women and sexual harassment, which also exist in Finland, were rejected until the late 1980s.

In recent years there have been more and more signs suggesting that gender contradictions are hardening. In 1991 many female professionals were elected to top positions in key art institutions. National art museums, the National Theatre, the Helsinki City Theatre, and the Finnish Film Foundation all received female directors. All of them were highly educated, experienced, and competent in their area. In particular, the art museum nominations were strongly criticized by male critics, who wrote about a "female mafia" of female directors suspected of favoring female artists—even before they had started work.

The Nordic welfare state has often been characterized as a "girl's best friend." The economic crisis Finland experienced in the early 1990s might teach Finnish women that nothing—not even the safety net that the welfare state has offered—can be taken for granted. This could have a radicalizing effect and result in an even broader mobilization of women in politics and in the women's movement.

REFERENCES

Allén, Tuovi, Laaksonen, Seppo, Keinänen, Päivi, & Ilmakunnas, Seija (1990). Palkkaa työstä ja sukupuolesta. Tutkimus palkkaeroista Suomessa 1985. Tilastokeskus: Tutkimuksia 169, Helsinki.

Anttalainen, Marja-Liisa. (1986). Sukupuolen mukaan kahtiajakautuneet työmarkkinat Pohjoismaissa. Tasa-arvoasiain neuvottelukunta: Naistutkimusmonisteita, 1.

Apo, Satu. (1989). Suullinen runous—vuosisatainen traditio. In Nevala, Maria Liisa (Ed.), Sain roolin johon en mahdu. Keuruu: Otava.

Comber, L., & Keeves, J. (1973). Science Education in Nineteen Countries. An Empirical Study. Stockholm: Almqwist & Wicksell.

Education in Finland. (1991). Helsinki: Central Statistical Office.

Eskola, Katarina. (1990). Women as creative cultural workers and users. In Manninen and Setälä, The Lady with the Bow. The Story of Finnish Women. Helsinki: Otava.

Haavio-Mannila, Elina, Jallinoja, Riitta, & Strandell, Harriet. (1984). Perhe, työ ja tunteet. Porvoo-Helsinki-Juva: WSOY.

Health Care in Finland. (1990). Ministry of Social Affairs and Health.

Heikkinen, Merja. (1989). Tilannekuva kirjailijoista. Taiteen keskustoimikunnan julkaisuja 5. Helsinki: Valtion painatuskeskus.

Human Development Report. (1991). United Nations Development Program. New York: Oxford University Press.

Huttunen, Jouko. (1990). Isän merkitys pojan sosiaaliselle sukupuolelle. Jyväskylä: University of Jyväskylä.

Jallinoja, Riitta. (1980). Miehet ja naiset. In Valkonen et al. (Eds.), Suomalaiset. Yhteiskunnan rakenne teollistumisen aikana. Porvoo: WSOY.

Karttunen, Sari. (1988). Taide pitkä - leipä kapea. Taiteen keskustoimikunnan julkaisuja 2. Helsinki: Valtion painatuskeskus.

Kuusipalo, Jaana. (1991, July 21–25). Women's power in the Finnish welfare state: Obstacles and opportunities. Paper presented at the Fifteenth World Congress of the International Political Science Association, Buenos Aires.

Lahelma, Elina. (1990). Tyttöjen ja poikien koulu. Peruskoulu ja lukio sukupuolinäkökulmasta. Unpublished licentiate thesis, University of Helsinki, Department of Pedagogics.

Lehto, Anna-Maija. (1991). Työelämän laatu ja tasa-arvo. Naisten ja miesten työolojen muutoksia 1977-1990. Komiteamietintö 1991:39, Tilastokeskuksen tutkimuksia 189. Helsinki: Tilastokeskus.

Liikkanen, Mirja. (1988). Kulttuurin ja joukkoviestinnän ammateissa toimivat 1970,1980 ja 1985. Kulttuuri ja viestintä 1988:1. Helsinki: Tilastokeskus.

Manninen, Merja. (1990). Finnish women's opportunities before the 19th century. In Manninen, Merja, & Setälä, Päivi, The Lady with a Bow. The Story of Finnish Women. Helsinki: Otava.

Manninen, Merja & Setälä, Päivi. (1990). The Lady with a Bow. The Story of Finnish Women. Helsinki: Otava.

Niemi, Iiris, & Pääkkönen, Hannu. (1989). Ajankäytön muutokset 1980-luvulla. Tilastokeskuksen tutkimuksia 153, Helsinki.

Niemi, Päivi. (1988). Adolescents and the Family. Images and Experiences of Family Life in Finland. Annales Universitatis Turkuensis, Series B, 181. Turku: University of Turku.

Olennainen työssä. Sosiaali- ja terveysministeriö, Tasa-arvojulkaisuja, Sarja B: Tiedotteita 2. 1989.

Olennainen työssä. Yhteenveto lausunnoista. Sosiaali- ja terveysministeriö, Tasa-arvojulkaisuja, sarja C: Työraportteja 1. 1990.

Pöntinen, Seppo. (1990). Koulutuksen kehityslinjoja. In Riihinen, Olavi (Ed.), Suomi 2017. Jyväskylä: Gummerus.

Population Crisis Committee. (1988, June). Country rankings on the status of women. Population Briefing Paper 20, Washington, DC.

Räsänen, Leila. (1992). Tytöt ja fysiikka. Thesis in sociology, University of Helsinki.

Räty, Teuvo. (1991). Naisten näkyvyys tieteessä paranemassa? Naistutkimustiedote, 11: 3.

Rauste-von Wright, Marja-Liisa. (1987). On the life process among Finnish adolescents. Summary report of a longitudinal study. Commentationes Scientiarum Socialium, 35.

——— (1989). Body image satisfaction in adolescent girls and boys: A longitudinal study. Journal of Youth and Adolescence, 18: 71–83.

Science Achievement in Seventeen Countries. A Preliminary Report. (1988). International Association for the Evaluation of Educational Achievement (IEA). Exeter: Pergamon Press.

Silius, Harriet. (1992). Den kringgärdade kvinnligheten. Att vara kvinnlig jurist i Finland. Turku: Åbo Academy Press.

Sinkkonen, Sirkka, & Haavio-Mannila, Elina. (1981). The impact of the women's movement and legislative activity of women MPs on social development. In Rendel Margarita (Ed.), *Women, Power and Political Systems*. London: Groom Hel.

Social Insurance in Finland. (1990). Ministry of Social Affairs and Health.

Social Security and Health Care in Finland. (1991). Ministry of Social Affairs and Health. Helsinki: Government Printing Center.

Social Welfare in Finland. (1990). Ministry of Social Affairs and Health.

Säntti, Riitta. (1990). Hoitovapaan käyttö ja lasten hoitomuodon valinta. Sosiaali- ja terveysministeriö, kehittämisosaston julkaisuja 1.

Tarmo, Marjatta. (1986). Tytöt ja pojat koulututkimuksen valossa. Jyväskylän yliopisto: Kasvatustieteellisen tutkimuslaitoksen julkaisuja 370.

Valkonen, Tapani. (1990). Väestönkehitys. In Riihinen, Olavi (Ed.), *Suomi 2017*. Jyväskylä: Gummerus.

Vogel, Joachim. (1991). *Social Report for the Nordic Countries. Living Conditions and Inequality in the Late 1980's*. Copenhagen: Nordisk Statistisk Skriftserie, *55*.

Women and Men in Finland. (1991). Helsinki: Central Statistical Office.

6

France

Roseline D. Davido and Mary Ann O'Donoghue

In Memoriam: Lisette Pâquerette Fanchon

INTRODUCTION

Modern France has combined elements of the industrial orientation of northern Europe with the humanistic exuberance of the Mediterranean south. The centralizing tendency of French nationalism has welded into a certain homogeneity a broad grouping of originally diverse peoples, such as the peasants of Brittany on the northern border, the urban-oriented merchants of Alsace on the eastern border with Germany, and the mountain-dwelling Basques at the nation's southern border with Spain.

France has historically been a rural land of pastoral beauty, less inclined than other European countries to abandon the land for the drive toward industrialism. The post–World War II modernization of France, however, quickly turned an agricultural nation into an urban nation. In the last few decades over 6 million people have emigrated from the farms and have moved into new jobs in the rapidly expanding urban centers. That relocation, spurred in part by the rebuilding of the nation's infrastructure, lowered farming's share of the work force from 38 percent to 8 percent (Ardagh, 1991).

In the five decades since the end of World War II, the population of Paris has climbed from 4.5 million to over 9.0 million, while 57 other urban areas in France have expanded to populations in excess of 100,000. The population of France steadily declined throughout the 1930s, with an overall drop of almost 14 percent in that decade. The decline dramatically ended in the post–World War II economic boom. From a total population of 41 million at the start of World War II in 1939, the nation expanded to a population in excess of 60 million at the beginning of the 1990s. This surge, which represented a national growth of almost 50 percent over half a century, was stimulated by a government policy of providing generous subsidies to families (Ardagh, 1991).

France has been a major force in the building of the European Economic Community and, in contrast with the more conservative policies of England, has provided continuous support for the elimination of all trade barriers within Europe. The September 1992 national referendum, in which French voters approved a single European currency by the year 2000, has been hailed as a decisive step in the movement toward a unified Europe.

Men and women of France, who, contrary to common perceptions, remain somewhat traditional in their attitudes and behaviors, have demonstrated in this free election their openness to change.

OVERVIEW

Regional diversity, population variables, and the movement toward European unity have contributed to new dimensions of gender roles in France. The history of France has provided numerous examples of unique portrayal in regard to gender roles, for example, Joan of Arc, Napoleon, Marie-Antoinette. The vast majority of men and women, however, have followed the more traditional paths of role identification. Women in France have historically tended to the needs of family and home, while men have followed the traditional roles linked to their work as peasant farmers, merchants, artisans, and craftsmen.

Various nuances in these roles have been associated with class distinctions. Centuries ago the aristocracy tended to marry for economic and political reasons, with a pattern of liaisons accepted as a pragmatic accommodation to arranged marriages. Many of the women involved in liaisons with members of the upper class were not members of that class but used liaisons as a vehicle to gain wealth and independence. This process was epitomized in the liaisons of Louis XIV and the noblemen who were members of his court (Durant & Durant, 1963). The male and female members of lower social classes did not have comparable opportunities to deviate from the accepted gender roles of father-laborer or mother-homemaker-laborer.

The French Revolution of 1789 promised liberty and equality for all social classes. It did not, however, have an immediate impact on French society in terms of gender roles. The pattern of class distinctions, which separated French society on the basis of income, education, and occupation, endured with only minor modifications up to the end of World War II in 1945. Six years of occupation by a foreign power (Germany), followed by a liberation completed with the assistance of other nations, were instrumental in the establishment of a new national approach to gender roles. Women in France gained the right to vote in 1945 and, as part of a process of revision of French law, were granted key business rights formerly confined to males, such as the right of wives to start new businesses and the opportunity to maintain a bank account distinct from that held by a husband.

Gender roles in France reflect the evolution of male and female roles that has occurred throughout Western society in the decades since World War II. In France, as in most European nations, men continue to play dominant roles in the major arena of home and work. Women have made modest gains in achieving expanded roles in political, economic, and social life. This chapter examines the factors responsible for the changes in French gender roles in terms of the process of gender identification. Specifically, how are male and female gender roles in France undergoing change in the developmental stages of infants, children, adolescents, and adults?

COMPARISONS BETWEEN MEN'S AND WOMEN'S GENDER ROLES DURING THE LIFE CYCLE

Infancy and Early Childhood

Gender identification begins at birth with the expectations and interactions expressed by parental behavior patterns. The assigning of specific colors as a means of identifying male and female infants, such as blue for boys and pink for girls, occurs in France as it does throughout Europe and North America. Hospital personnel are major contributors to the early assignment of gender roles in France, where over 99 percent of all births now occur in hospitals (Fremy & Fremy, 1992). French parents have a preference for one male and one female child as the ideal family unit, as reflected in the common French expression "a royal share," a situation that occurs when a family has one male and one female child. Women in France constitute a majority of the population, since women have a longevity rate that exceeds males by almost four years.

French companies with more than 100 employees are required to provide one year of parental leave to either the mother or father of an infant as part of a national policy of assuring direct parental involvement in early child care. A national system of subsidies to families is used to provide benefits to parents from the fifth month of pregnancy up to three months after birth, with total funding of the expenses of delivery and hospitalization. Seventy percent of all mothers do not return to employment until their children reach two years of age. Day-care centers, nursery schools, and a system of registered helpers who visit homes have expanded through government-funded programs. This pattern of assistance may be responsible for the decreasing rate of grandparents who reside in the homes of families with young children.

Gender roles in France continue to be reinforced through toys and gifts to children. These gifts and toys are gender-specific, although children receive some encouragement to play with toys that are stereotypically associated with the opposite sex (Editions du CNDP, 1989). Le Camus (1987) reported that the majority of mothers and fathers in France are bound to traditional gender roles in caring for young children. Eight-year-old children, participants in a gender-role investigation, displayed the male and female attitudes traditionally associated with gender roles in France (Editions du CNDP, 1989). Children of that age are attending school.

School Years

Ninety-seven percent of French children have begun formal education by the age of five; school attendance is mandatory from ages six to sixteen. The public school system, which is free to all children, is staffed by teachers regarded as civil servants. All schools have a formal set of provisions regarding students who require special classes. The decisions regarding the special placement of students are made by commissions composed of teachers, Parent-Teacher Association (PTA) members, physicians, school psychologists, and school administrators.

All public schools are coeducational, with an established policy of encouraging cooperation among male and female students from earliest years. The majority (97 percent) of private schools in France are maintained by Catholic organizations, supported by the voluntary contributions of Catholics, who constitute slightly over 90 percent of the total French population (Fremy & Fremy, 1992). The balance of private schools either are nondenominational or have affiliations with Jewish or Protestant groups. Most private schools operate at the elementary level.

High schools in France are conducted on the basis of a five-day week, with an annual total of school hours that range from 180 to 200. During this time spent in educational institutions, traditional gender stereotypes are fostered. French schools, while emphasizing academic excellence, encourage traditional gender-role identification. The unconscious attitudes of teachers and the individual academic advising of students, as well as the textbook content, are basic vehicles that strengthen gender stereotyping. Textbooks routinely present husbands as active manipulators of their environment, while wives are frequently presented as passive acceptors of the situations in which they perform their tasks (Frappat, 1975). The stereotypes are not reality.

Research reports indicate that females outperform males in most aspects of high school studies, possibly because there is a smaller number of female students in attendance after the age of sixteen. Girls have been found to score higher on the General Studies Baccalaureat and have received more honorable mentions than boys (Duru-Bellat, 1992). Female students prefer literature and history as majors, while most male students choose science or mathematics. This preference pattern places female students at a distinct disadvantage in a nation where acceptance into higher education is primarily based on performance in science and mathematics (Baudelot & Establet, 1992). There has been no major effort on the part of educators to change the current disproportionate representation of males in the sciences.

The established pattern of educational stereotyping has an impact on the social life of French students. The "good young woman" is hardworking, docile, and conforming; the "good young man" is creative, special, and independent. In vocational schools, attended almost exclusively by young people from the working class, the pattern of stereotyping is congruent with a dominant belief held by members of the French working class: hard work leads to success in life. Success, when it is achieved by young female students, is attributed to their work habits rather than to their level of education. This is congruent with the traditional perception of female students as members of a group with limited choices. Male students are regarded as high-potential individuals with the qualities most likely to produce success.

A pattern of coeducation in French schools, originally adopted in an effort to end gender discrimination, has not attained its anticipated outcome. An extensive investigation of self-attribution patterns among French students found that the educational system tended to reinforce a divergent type of identification among males and females (Baudelot & Establet, 1992). Females chose adjectives such as passive, calm, and accepting from a list of items to be used in describing their outlook on life. Males chose terms such as active, excited, and self-centered when asked to describe their approach to life.

The role of educational institutions in developing these perceptions can be documented. The textbooks, used at various levels of French education, routinely present women as housewives with no major responsibility outside the home. Males are presented as involved individuals, skilled in business affairs, and prepared to act decisively when necessary. The textbook patterns of stereotypical behavior are reinforced by the career choices encouraged by school personnel. A recent research project (Lage, 1991) investigated the change in perceptions of ten- to eleven-year-old students and fourteen- to fifteen-year-old students when introduced to the possibility of careers in technology. The younger students considered boys and girls to be equally competent in technical fields, and they evaluated a female computer enthusiast as a very attractive person. The older students, however, did not consider boys and girls to be equally competent in technical fields, and they regarded a female computer enthusiast as an unusual and unattractive individual.

It is important to note that both male and female students considered a girl's interest in computers as an indication of loneliness. Lage (1991) concluded that a widely prevalent model of feminine identity, based on stereotypes of feminine passivity and lack of key skills, may explain the absence of interest in computer technology observed among female students in French high schools. National research reports have indicated that school expectations, as advanced by school personnel and the larger society outside the school, continue to reinforce the established gender-role tradition, which subordinates the potential roles of females to those of males (Guichard, 1988).

Young Adulthood

Adolescents and young adults in France appear to be abandoning the rebelliousness of the generation of the 1960s and the 1970s. A rising rate of unemployment among younger workers has made it necessary for many young adults to continue to live with their parents. The earlier generation's emphasis on freedom and independence from established authority, whether family or government, has been reduced by a rising level of economic difficulties in French society. Young males and females are now indicating that their family can be a source of major support in difficult times (Cressard, 1992).

Equal pay for equal work has not yet been achieved in the French workplace. Female employees, who now constitute 43 percent of the total work force, receive only 68 percent of the compensation provided to male workers in comparable positions. Salary inequities between males and females are proportionately greater at higher career levels. Males tend to dominate in those occupations linked to production or finance, while females choose occupations that are service-related, such as teaching, health, and social service. Although the number of women professionals has been rising, these workers tend to be concentrated within a relatively small number of occupations characterized by salary levels lower than those prevalent in the majority of professions in France (Insee, 1991). Women's salary level, relative to males', conforms to a basic characteristic of compensation in France, that salary inequities between men and women are proportionately greater at higher levels of career success (Ehrlich & Vinsonneau, 1988).

Dating and mating trends among young adults in France now represent a distinct break with the earlier pattern of traditional sex roles. Cohabitation prior to marriage has become a socially accepted practice. Female members of the working class retain the traditional French preference that mothers of small children should not be employed, but women with more education are opting for motherhood and employment in increasing numbers (Fagnani, 1992).

Adulthood

France's legalization of abortion, combined with the widespread availability of birth control techniques, has led to a number of major changes in the behavior patterns of French women. Gender roles have been somewhat altered for female adults who now have options in their sexual behavior and childbearing patterns. Marriages in France are occurring at a progressively later age in the case of both men and women; women now tend to marry at 25, while the average age at marriage for men is 27. France's divorce rate tripled between 1970 and 1985, with approximately 30 percent of all marriages in the 1990s projected to end in divorce (Insee, 1991). Child support and alimony are requested in slightly over half of all divorces, with decisions made by the courts on an individual basis. Decisions with regard to the custody of children may be reached on the basis of agreement between parents, or custody may be determined by a magistrate. Fifteen percent of children of divorced parents live in families considered ''reconstructed,'' which means a combination of stepparent, parent, children, and stepchildren.

Changes in society are linked to changes in the political picture. In the French National Assembly there are 33 female and 544 male deputies. Edith Cresson became the first woman prime minister in 1991. She was succeeded by a man after one year. Nevertheless, her achievement reflects the influence of the women's movement, which emerged as a political and social force in the early 1970s. The women's movement has not experienced an outstanding growth pattern, but it has been credited with a role in the advances made by women in the workplace and in political life (*Journal Officiel*, 1989).

Old Age

Many elderly men and women live alone in a nation where widowed parents are not expected to live with their children. An estimated 9 percent of the elderly population now live in senior citizen homes where their expenses are paid by relatives or by plans that provide income by mortgaging the property or possessions of the elderly person.

A pattern of retirement at age sixty-five is followed by most men and women in France. Old-age pensions, which had formerly been among the lowest provided by European nations, have been slowly rising. Pension payments assigned to women tend to be about 60 percent of the payments provided to men, a situation that is linked to the lower lifetime salary pattern experienced by women. However, all retirees can benefit from travel discounts provided by government-owned transportation systems.

Gender roles are sometimes reversed in old age. French women, who have a longer life span than men and who tend to be healthier in their advanced years than men, must frequently assume the decision-making role formerly exercised by their husbands. Greater female longevity produces a pattern in which many women spend the final segment of their lives without the possibility of subordination to a husband: the number of females alive at age 95 in France exceeds the number of males alive by five times.

SUMMARY AND CONCLUSIONS

Gender roles in France can be regarded as evolving from a more traditional pattern of role assignments. Infants continue to be provided with clothes and toys that are gender-specific. Children of nursery school age, however, are subject to gender expectations that reflect an evolution toward a somewhat different pattern of gender identification. The sexual behavior and gender interaction patterns followed by adolescents would seem to signal a clear break with the earlier pattern of stereotypical expectation. Adult males and females are experiencing a degree of liberation in the choice of careers. Progress has been made in opening once male-dominated professions to women, but a substantial difference continues to exist in salaries provided to men and women for comparable work. Women with higher levels of educational attainment now have increasing opportunities in areas such as politics, where gender roles are undergoing a slow but significant change. The traditional dominance of males in legal matters involving families is also undergoing change, with females playing a greater role in family patterns altered by a rising divorce rate. Older men and women sometimes reverse roles when the better health of females places them in a position of responsibility for their less healthy male counterparts. The total pattern of changes in gender roles in France reflects an adaptation to a broad range of social and economic changes in the national environment. The unification of Europe, with its acceleration of changes in family and work patterns of behavior, can be expected to lead to additional changes in gender roles within France.

REFERENCES

Ardagh, J. (1991). France, *Encyclopedia Americana* (International edition), *11*: 690–701.

Baudelot, C., & Establet, R. (1992). *Allez les filles*, Éditions du seuil.

Cressard, A. (1992). Les metamorphoses adolescentes. *Le Monde de l'Éducation, 193*: 46–47.

Durant, W., & Durant, A. (1963). *The Age of Louis XIV*. New York: Simon & Schuster.

Duru-Bellat, M. (1992). *L'École des filles*. Editions l'Harmattan.

Editions du CNDP. (1989). *L'éducation des filles*. French as a foreign language series (videotape).

Ehrlich, M., & Vinsonneau, G. (1988). Representations differentielles des sexes: Attributions et prises de roles dans les équipes de travail. *Bulletin de Psychologie, 41*: 785–801.

Fagnani, J. (1992). Vers un retour des femmes au foyer. *Femmes, 20*: 70–73.

Frappat, B. (1975). Les manuels scolaires à la source des préjuges. *Le Monde, 23*.

Fremy, D., & Fremy, M. (1992). *Quid 92*, Editions Robert Laffont.

Guichard, J. (1988). The French school system and sexual differentiation of social roles. *International Journal for the Advancement of Counselling, 11*(4): 323–32.

Insee. (1991). Contours et caracteres, *Les Femmes*.

Journal Officiel de la République Française (1989). Avis et rapports du Conseil Économique et social.

Lage, E. (1991). Boys, girls, and microcomputing. *European Journal of Psychology of Education, 6* (1): 29–44.

le Camus, J. (1987). Les pratiques de nursing chez les parents d'enfants de créche. *Enfance, 40* (3): 245–61.

Leclerq, J., & Rault, C. (1989). Les systèmes éducatifs en Europe. *Editions la Documentation Française, 6*.

7

Greece

Diomedes C. Markoulis and Maria Dikaiou

INTRODUCTION

Greece consists of a jagged peninsula with a long coastline and many islands. The mainland is a country of high mountains running in a northwest-southeast direction. The cities of Athens (capital) and Thessaloniki, densely populated due to the internal migration movement, are the main centers of economic, cultural, and intellectual activity. Greece is a homogeneous country, both in terms of its people's ethnic origin and in terms of religion (about 97 percent of the population are Greek Orthodox, the state religion). The life-style is a mixture of Eastern and European habits.

Life expectancy is among the highest in Europe. The marriage rate is 5.9 percent per 1,000 inhabitants, whereas the number of children per woman (in reproductive age) has fallen. In 1986 it was 1.6 percent per woman (National Statistics Service of Greece [NSSG], 1989).

Education, from the elementary to the tertiary level, is free and compulsory up to the age of fifteen. Greek society is educationally oriented, with one out of three teenagers enrolled in some kind of educational program. During the last ten years a number of new universities have been established, while serious efforts were undertaken toward the reformation of the educational system.

Greece contributed enormously to European civilization. Art, science, literature, philosophy, and political thought reached their summit during the fifth century B.C. Preserving their ancient tradition, Greek people continue to be able merchants and traders and receive travelers with hospitable welcome, especially in the more out-of-the-way villages.

OVERVIEW

Sociologist Dumon (1991) has argued that marriage and parenthood constitute the two major aspects of the family institution. Both aspects can be better understood if we consider certain family policies that formed its background in Greek society. Before we discuss matters related to marriage and parenthood, however, it is essential to describe briefly the position of women in recent years with respect to education and work.

Data from the National Statistics Service show that in 1981 both genders had equal access to primary and secondary education. At the tertiary level, female students made up 41 percent of the student population, whereas in 1984–1985 the proportion reached 46 percent. As far as the various fields of study are concerned, female students represented large proportions (75–85 percent) in humanities and only 7–9 percent in science (Deliyanni-Kouimtzi, in press).

An issue that began to be hotly debated in the early eighties concerned gender discrimination, particularly, sexism in education. In 1976 a wide range of educational changes was introduced, but their effect on gender discrimination was minimal. New organizational measures were again introduced (Law 1268/82, Article 4), but despite considerable progress toward the abolishment of discrimination on the grounds of gender (specifically in the content of primary and secondary textbooks), a number of educational sociologists consider the issue still unsettled (Deliyanni-Kouimtzi, in press).

In the labor market, women made up 32 percent of the work force. As shown in Table 7.1, 67 percent of working women were married and 47 percent were 25–44 years of age. About 40 percent of the female work force was concentrated in the service sector, while in the primary sector and in specific sectors of industry the female proportion was about 37 percent and 17.4 percent, respectively.

COMPARISONS BETWEEN MEN'S AND WOMEN'S GENDER ROLES DURING THE LIFE CYCLE

Infancy and Early Childhood

Greek studies dealing with attitudes toward genders and with child-rearing practices are scarce. Dikaiou, Sakka, and Haritos-Fatouros (1987) compared two groups of Greek migrant mothers, one from the home and one from the receiving country, with a nonmigrant group on an attitude questionnaire concerning child-rearing practices such as training the child with regard to participation in home duties, keeping clean and tidy, self-reliance, and social behavior toward visitors and ways of dealing with the child's obedience/disobedience, favor-seeking behavior, and food and sleeping problems.

A factor analysis of the data showed that, overall, migrant mothers were similar in their practices toward boys as compared with girls, except for one case: the returnees were more overprotective toward boys than girls. Thus, the

Table 7.1

Coefficient of Participation in the Work Force According to Sex and Age Groups, 1974, 1984 (Urban and Suburban Areas)

	1974		1984	
Age	Men	Women	Men	Women
14	9.3	5.3	6.8	3.7
15-19	30.0	17.9	24.7	20.1
20-24	58.2	34.6	71.1	48.4
25-29	92.5	30.5	95.0	50.8
30-44	96.7	24.5	97.7	43.7
45-64	80.9	15.0	78.3	24.1
65+	13.5	1.6	10.3	1.8

Source: X. Petrinioti, "Women's Work. Some Statistical Data," *O Agonas tis Gynaikas, 45* (1990): 36.

authors argue that sex differentiation is overridden by the influence of social and economic pressures related to the migrant status in both the home and host countries.

Sex-specific differences were found only among the nonmigrant (control) mothers who had been constantly influenced by the cultural environment, which is probably promoting stereotyping. Mothers were more controlling and restrictive for girls and more permissive for boys. However, as will be seen later on, stereotyped role treatment of boys and girls varies according to the rural versus urban environment under which families are living.

School Years

There are no direct studies on gender preferences for school subjects. Some information can be detected from studies in allied fields, such as mothers' attitudes toward the education of their children, mostly based on interviews (Doumanis, 1983; Moussourou, 1985). In this line, 952 mothers of preschool children in Athens were asked about the kind of education they would like for their son or daughter (Moussourou, 1985).

The majority of these women reported that they would let the child make the choice. However, mothers were less ambitious for their daughters than for their sons; only a small proportion of women wished their daughters to become scientists whereas the opposite was true for sons.

The same study pointed out that there is a strong relationship between educational and occupational background of the mother, on one hand, and expectations held about the child's education, on the other. The more educated the mother, the less stereotypic the expectations. This applied particularly to female children. Less-educated mothers have been found to be more rigid with regard to the number of options a daughter has. These mothers prefer a traditional role for their children, that is, to graduate from school and get married.

Males and females exert similar types of behavior in interacting with same-sex peers, matched for grade, under cooperative versus competitive conditions. These findings have been reported in a series of studies (Georgas, 1985a, b; 1986; 1987) in which Greek children in sixth, seventh, and eighth grade were observed while discussing, in groups of three persons, the solution of a Mastermind problem. As the author of these studies argues, competitive behaviors, like "verbal aggression," "disapprovals," "pushing other's hand away," "obstructing other's participation," and "passive rejection of task, withdrawal from the field," were observed in both sexes.

Similarly, "discussion of tactics," "suggestions," "encouraging others' efforts," "self-assertion and leading," and "enthusiasm" were observed for both sexes in the cooperative conditions. Also, the interactions of the children during cooperative conditions in all studies were characterized by the forming of a boundary between themselves and the experimenter: whispering, hands in front of face to hide whispering from the experimenter, heads together and arms around each other's shoulders, as if the experimenter was an outsider.

This boundary, held in common by males and females, is reminiscent of Triandis and Vassiliou's (1972) description of the in-group. They found that within the in-group, members observed marked cooperative behaviors and positive feelings, but members not in the in-group were perceived with suspicion and hostility. Although the authors defined the in-group in Greece as members of the family, friends of the family, or those concerned with self, the children in the above studies were classmates and the interactions of males and females in the cooperative condition were similar to their description of in-group behavior of Greek adults. Similar results were also found in later studies (Dikaiou, 1989) in which peer interactions of eighth-grade children were observed under semi-experimental, cooperative conditions. "Supportive or positive responses to requests for help and information" were found in both sex groups. In addition, "insults and acts of physical aggression such as snatching material, occupying others' space, pushing or grimacing" were expressed by both boys and girls.

Young Adulthood

Studies of the Greek milieu (Friedl, 1962; Campbell, 1964; Triandis & Vassiliou, 1968; Vassiliou & Vassiliou, 1973; Dragona, 1983) show that socialization practices inherent in the traditional/rural versus modernized/technological environments are different. In the traditional environment (Kiountouzis & Vassiliou, 1981), people are organized on the basis of cooperation and interdependence; boys and girls move from childhood to adulthood roles and status through participation in family work. In wheat growing, for instance, the plowing is done by male adults and children, and the hoeing and weeding are generally done by females. This is also the case in the cotton fields. Irrigation of cotton and other crops is men's work. In tobacco cultivation, men do the plowing, but women tend the small plants, which must be handled expertly. The division of labor appears to follow a simple sexual symbolism: men do the tasks that require organization and strength, and women work where nurturing and care are needed. For this reason, too, men have no part in domestic work, which would be regarded as degrading. Thus, roles in this society are limited and clearly defined. There is no doubt in the minds of the community about what is proper and what is improper action, and, as a result, behavior within these roles is strongly supported. In this way, a strict conformity centrally relating to the family is achieved (du Boulay, 1974). The roles of men and women are complementary and clearly defined. Thus conflicts and role confusion are prevented. Consequently, in the case of children no difficulties are encountered in developing the proper identification (Spinelli, Vassiliou, & Vassiliou, 1970).

At this point, it would seem inadequate to limit the term *traditional milieu* to rural environment, in terms of its geographical determinants; rather, the specific boundary structuring of the system defines the extent to which a given milieu would be characterized as traditional or not (Kiountouzis & Vassiliou, 1981). Boundary structuring refers to the values, goals, and information-processing and decision-making mechanisms that are characteristic of every system (Vassiliou & Vassiliou, 1980). In the traditional community, where the in-group (immediate family, relatives, friends of friends, neighbors) is the most important social unit, the values and goals are shared by all in-group members. Information is processed and decisions are made always in the context of the in-group. The individual (male or female) has been socialized in such a way that he or she is ready to accept the values, goals, and mode of behavior already adopted by older males and females (Dragona, 1983). Thus socialization processes underlying the male and female roles present a stability and continuity over different generations.

However, rapid and increased urbanization in Greece for the last twenty years, tourist development, vast spread of mass media, and consumerism propagated as a way of living have all led to changes in the sociocultural environment. Thousands of people have moved to big cities. In their new environment parents and children are thrown into small apartments of a crowded building, in a densely populated, impersonal neighborhood in which people have neither the time nor the means to become psychologically and culturally "urbanized" (Emmanuel et al., 1976).

The process of socialization, right from the child's very early years, is a process of incorporation into a lonely world. The children "imprisoned" within the four walls of their home as well as within the mother-child relationship, are entirely cut off from any kind of "community." They are loved, protected, and endlessly provided with goods and comfort. However, the child, whether of school age or as a young adult, has no responsibility toward his or her in-group's needs. Despite the fact that the child, son or daughter, receives the whole family's attention, being deprived of all group participation (both in the social and in the family context), which could foster psychosocial differentiation, means that she or he is left as an isolated unit (Vassiliou & Vassiliou, 1982). More specifically, the daughter of the nuclear family, contrary to her rural counterpart, is offered an inadequate female model for identification (Moussourou, 1985; Dragona, 1983). She sees that her mother has shifted away from the traditional role of obedience and attendance to her husband's needs toward a vague and unclear perception of her role. Consequently the mother feels unhappy as a housewife and seems to be exploited, victimized, and useless. The mother as a career woman feels equally unhappy with herself (Stamatopoulou-Igglesi, 1989). Accomplishment of her new goals is far from complete; the mother seems to be torn between the competing demands of her husband, her children, her career, and society at large (Christea-Doumanis, 1978; Vassiliou & Vassiliou, 1982). Furthermore, in the urban context the daughter is deprived of her traditional in-group space and finds it very difficult to develop the peer girl-to-girl relationships that in the rural culture were the corridor to group participation.

Sons are also faced with ambiguous father models. In the urban environment, the man, still "father-provider," simply produces money through wages, something anyone could do in the newly formed reality. In the traditional environment, where the administration of the family property was collective, the interests of all members were taken into consideration, the man represented and negotiated the interests of his wife and children (Campbell & Sherrard, 1968; Hirschon, 1989). In reality, the father was cut off from the psychosocial and socio-economic transactions in which he was involved in the traditional community. Now his position is lowered and somehow downgraded; the new reality demands of him that he find a new role that will meet the demands of the new complexity. In sum, theorists and researchers point out that children at all ages are faced with ambiguous parental models since parents are caught in the trap of social change and are trying to redefine their roles. As a result, children are pushed toward academic achievement, leaving no room for real group participation that could foster role differentiation (Vassiliou & Vassiliou, 1982). Finally, some information about socialization and dating/courtship issues can also be detected from studies concerning the problems of young people today. In a cross-cultural study (Gibson et al., 1991) in which Greek adolescents, 13 to 15 years of age, were compared with adolescents from other countries, similarities, as well as differences, between the two sexes were found.

With regard to the former, males and females responded in similar ways to the question of what problems bothered them most. Regardless of country and socioeconomic grouping, both sexes reported problems relating to school, identity, and family. Males and females were also similar with respect to problems such as sexuality (becoming sexually active) and dating/courtship; this referred to fears about never being in a relationship, pressures resulting from an existing relationship, or even social and familial restrictions that limit the subject's ability to choose a partner freely.

These results seem to suggest that males and females are very much alike today in many of their perceptions of their worlds. Besides these similarities, however, some differences were found. Male adolescents expressed school problems more frequently but family and interpersonal concerns less frequently than did females. The latter mainly reported problems of self-confidence in relation to identity.

These findings are compatible with studies that show that females need help in developing an identity, that they are more uncomfortable in the outside world than they are among their own families, and that they feel more comfortable in nurturing than in achieving. On the other hand, males who are reinforced for success in the outside world need assistance whenever that success becomes difficult to attain (McIntosh, 1991).

Adulthood

Until 1983, legislation governing family relationships in Greece dated from 1946 and expressed the social values of a former age (Symeonidou, 1988). With the amendment of family law, the "patriarchal" family, which had for years been protected by law and which was perpetuated through economic, social, and educational practices, was legally abolished. Underlying the family law amendment was the belief that both men and women have equal rights within the family context. The new legislation reflected the acknowledgment of women's changing role in society. For instance, no distinctions or discriminations are now made on the grounds of gender with regard to marriage, separation, and divorce. However, changes in legislation do not necessarily result in attitude changes relating to the above and other issues associated with gender roles. In 1986, three years after the introduction of the civil marriage institution, only 9 percent of marriages were carried out in this manner (National Statistics Service of Greece [NSSG], 1989).

The marriage rate has changed very little during the last years. It was 6.47 percent per 1000 inhabitants in 1980, 6.92 percent in 1982, and 5.9 percent in 1986 (National Statistics Service of Greece [NSSG], 1986, 1989). As we noted earlier, however, the mean number of children per woman (in reproductive age) has fallen below replacement level since 1981, and in 1986 it was 1.6 children per woman.

Under the law previously in force, the husband was the head of the family and was responsible for decision making on matters relating to the family. The wife's duties were confined to the care of the household. In order to ensure that she made a financial contribution to the family, her parents were obliged, in accordance with their financial possibilities, to provide property or some other asset as dowry. From a legal point of view things have now changed. The institution of dowry is abolished, and the couple can jointly decide on matters relating to marriage. Patriarchal authority has given place to care by both parents for underage children. This means that upbringing and education of children are the joint duty and right of both parents. If the parents are divorced, the exercise of parental care is determined by the court and may be assigned to one or both parents, if it is so agreed. The parent to whom parental care has not been assigned has the right of personal communication with the child. Despite all these changes, however, and the major alterations that came about in legislation involving the family, women continue to shoulder the main responsibility for the upbringing of children, and, in most cases of separation or divorce, women undertake the custody of children (Symeonidou, 1989).

Besides family responsibilities, women are also working outside the home. For instance, the increase of women's participation in the labor force between 1981 and 1986 for the age group 45 to 64 years, from 23 percent to 35 percent (National Statistics Service of Greece [NSSG], 1984, 1986) underlines women's double working role: inside and outside the home. The occupational role is, however, still considered secondary and supplementary (Katakis, 1984). Stereotypic role divisions in both the private and the public sectors of life continue to exist for women regardless of their employment status. Research (Haritos-Fatouros, Sakka & Dikaiou, 1988) shows that the mother's predominant responsibility is to look after the child's upbringing: satisfy the child's basic needs, teach and supervise behaviors toward others, and help out with homework. Fathers are more concerned with financial matters. In this line, Moussourou (1985) reports that only 5 percent of those males who agreed to share responsibilities actually became involved in the child's upbringing. A gap between males' attitudes and task-sharing behavior within the family is also found in ongoing research. Males, being used to a traditional model, find it hard to adapt to the new reality, whereas women face conflicts between the occupational role and the traditional role of wife and mother. This conflict seems to exist across age groups, at least for the working women (Harila, 1990).

Early studies in Greek culture show that besides the gender differences, both men and women share some common attributes in their relationships with others (Triandis & Vassiliou, 1972). Within the in-group (immediate family, relatives, friends, friends of friends, and neighbors) relations are ruled by interdependence and the enactment of the Greek concept of *philotimo* (love of honor). *Philotimous* behavior implies that the person behaves properly according to in-group norms, is honest and respectful, and loves and helps others (Friedl, 1962; Vassiliou, 1966; Triandis & Vassiliou, 1987; du Boulay, 1974). Vassiliou and Vassiliou (1973) found that Greeks associated the concept of *philotimo* with such concepts as honesty, respect, love, conscientiousness, morality, and duty, while it is also seen to lead to respect and obedience, honesty and sincerity, success, progress, and humaneness. Through his or her *philotimo* each member contributes to the family's honorable status (Lee, 1955).

In the traditional milieu, marriage was planned through the efforts of the in-group, which had as its main objective its own socioeconomic betterment, while at the same time individual needs were met. Marriages were nearly always arranged, and the married couples and their children continued to live in the context of either the husband's or the wife's in-group in constant interrelation and interdependence with their community. Research has shown that in the Greek milieu all roles seem to be either superordinate or subordinate (Triandis, Vas-siliou, & Nassiakou, 1968). There has been a tendency for high-status in-group persons to show high superordination while the low-status in-group members do not hesitate to show the proper subordination. The male role seems to be the dominant and the superordinate, while the woman is expected always to take a subordinate position. This has also been verified by more recent studies (Mous-sourou, 1985; Stamatopoulou-Igglesi, 1989).

For the woman, her individual interests are synonymous with the interests of the group, and by attending to the needs of others, she is supposed to satisfy her own needs. For example, by bearing a child, she gives the family strength and hope for the future and secures to herself status and prestige (Vassiliou, 1966; Vassiliou & Vassiliou, 1982). Later studies, however, show that bearing a child is not necessarily associated with the betterment of a woman's position in the family; many women face problems of psychosocial adjustment after childbirth, given the fact that the social support provided by the traditional environment no longer exists (Dragona, 1987; Sueref, 1991).

Among the various family roles that have been studied in Greece (Harila, 1990; Triandis et al., 1968) the husband-wife role is seen as least intimate. Additionally, Vassiliou (1966) has found that a successful and happy marriage is seen by Athenians as dependent on mutual understanding and mutual conces-sion rather than love. The central family role seems to be, still today, that of parent-child, mainly the mother-son role, which is viewed as more reciprocal than other family roles (Dragona, 1987). The woman's role, which has not changed considerably by her becoming a wife, changes dramatically by her becoming a mother. From the moment she assumes that role she is highly idealized, respected, and obeyed (Vassiliou, 1966).

Old Age

Life expectancy at birth in Greece is among the highest worldwide. In 1986, the percentage of the population aged 65 years and above was 12.3 percent, and it is expected to increase to 14 percent by the year 2001 (Emke-Papadopoulos, 1982; Tzougas & Tziafetas, 1989). Although in industrialized countries 5–8 percent of the aged live in institutions, in Greece this percentage is very low (about 0.5 percent), and the great majority of senior citizens continue to live in the community. Most have some kind of family support from their sons and/or daughters with whom they cohabit or who live in the same vicinity (Symeonidou, 1989).

However, the lack of systematic, relevant studies does not allow us to analyze psychosocially the dynamics of family relations with respect to the elderly. Information about both the status of the elderly in the community and the type of support they are receiving comes mostly from demographers, economists, and/or sociologists. In this respect recent research (Pitsiou, 1986; Amira, Georgiadis & Teperoglou, 1986) indicates that in provincial and semiurban areas there is an informal support system between members of a family, other relatives, and neighbors, who offer substantial help in daily chores such as cooking and washing, as well as providing social contact to senior citizens. This situation has significant benefits but may also lead to difficulties for the family. On one hand, it enables the elderly to play an active and useful role in the community. In many cases, for example, they may even have a significant role in looking after grandchildren while parents are at work. However, if they are chronically ill, disabled, or bedridden, the main burden is on the individuals who care for them. The institution of family help in which individuals who are unable to care for themselves receive state care has not yet developed in Greece, with the exception of a few isolated initiatives in a few neighborhoods (Symeonidou, 1989). Therefore the responsibility usually falls on the family, most often on women. The underlying assumption reflected in this situation seems to be that it is the family's responsibility to bear expenses and provide care and support for aged relatives. This becomes even more evident if we take into account the low pensions and lack of real support from the state in the form of specialized services, home help, or provision of equipment and the often appalling conditions to be found in old people's homes. It also coincides with the values of Greek society, where there is a very strong commitment to mutual help, especially within families, and where families prefer to take care of their members themselves rather than allow the state to take over responsibility since they believe it is their obligation to do this. In addition, there is a general mistrust of the quality of care the state welfare services are able to provide.

However, some efforts have been made recently to change the situation with the development of the KAPI, which are open day-care centers for the aged. These centers employ a team consisting of a social worker, doctor, nursing staff, a psychotherapist, an occupational therapist, and a home assistant, who, in certain circumstances, visits the aged in their homes. Emphasis is given on helping those in most need. These centers attempt to deal with the social and psychological problems the elderly face as well as basic problems of health; they have also set up programs that aim to encourage senior citizens to spend their spare time constructively and to participate in the social and cultural life of the community. Even though at present the centers can meet the needs of only 6 percent of senior citizens, they have been enthusiastically supported (Amira, Georgiadis, & Teperoglou, 1986). Most recently, measures like financial support and housing loans have been taken to encourage the family to cohabit with its elder members. This helps to strengthen the family unit, leads to mutual help between generations, and certainly prevents the aged from withdrawing from social life.

SUMMARY AND CONCLUSIONS

Two clearly observable features seem to emerge from the examination of sex and gender differences. First, where empirical data are used to illuminate the life cycle of men and women, what is demonstrated is a lack of systematic studies, especially during the last ten years. Second, the existing studies do not always deal exclusively with gender roles but only with differences in the attitudes of parents (mostly mothers) or in the behavior of children. Because of this, the first two sections regarding infancy and childhood are based merely on attitudinal data and/or observational data concerning differences found between males and females in interaction.

A more realistic picture of gender roles is given by the two sections on young adulthood and adulthood. It is beyond doubt that in the last decade a number of changes have been introduced in the country's legal system. These changes constitute an advance toward greater gender equality. However, the gap between the rhetoric of legislation and the reality of everyday life is evident, especially in the rural areas and the older generation. This must not be taken to mean that changes in mentality and attitudes are negligible. The proportion of women in high schools or universities today is greater than it was 20 years ago. Young men and women share common views about gender roles and equality and expect to share most of housing and financial responsibilities with their future partner (Harila, 1990). Whether or not these expectations will be met, we do not know. In the public sector adults up to 45 would seem to be less clear about their gender roles than young adolescents. Although the latter sound more hopeful about the realization of gender-role equality, the former seem to be caught in the trap of social change. Traditional role divisions are in conflict with new demands of men's and women's responsibilities inside and outside the home, and people thus often find themselves in a state of confusion and doubt. Social parameters like education or family policies have not led to dissolution of these conflicts. Women, more than men, still remain a relatively disadvantaged group. This disadvantage, however, takes different forms in the rural versus the urban environment of the Greek cultural context.

REFERENCES

Amira, A., Georgiadis, E., & Teperoglou, A. (1986). *The Institution of Open Care for Elderly in Greece, Ministry of Health and Social Security*. Athens: National Center of Social Research.

Campbell, J. (1964). *Honor, Family and Patronage*. Oxford: Clarendon Press.

Campbell, J. & Sherrard, P. (1968). *Modern Greece*. London: Ernest Bern.

Christea-Doumanis, M. (1978). The cultural function of the mother-child interaction. Ph.D. diss., University of Lancaster.

Deliyanni-Kouimtzi, K. (in press). Greek primary school reading texts as an example of educational policy for gender equality. *Gender and Education.*

Dikaiou, M. (1989). Peer interaction in migrant children. Observational data and parents' evaluations. *International Migration, 27*: 49–67.

Dikaiou, M., Sakka, D., & Haritos-Fatouros, M. (1987). Maternal attitudes of Greek migrant women. *International Migration, 25* (1): 73–86.

Doumanis, M. (1983). Mothering in Greece: From collectivism to individualism. *Behavioral Development*: A Series of Monographs. New York: Academic Press.

Dragona, Th. G. (1983). The self-concept of preadolescents in the Hellenic context. Ph.D. diss., University of Aston.

———. (1987). *Birth.* (In Greek.) Athens: Dodoni.

du Boulay, J. (1974). *Portrait of a Greek Mountain Village.* Oxford: Clarendon Press.

Dumon, W. (1991). *Family Policy in EEC Countries.* Lueven: Katholike Univeteit of Lueven.

Emke-Papadopoulos, I. (1982). Le Vieillissement demographique en Grèce: Causes et cousequences. *Population, Travail.* Paris: Chomage, Economica, pp. 183–220.

———. (1990). Vieillissement demographique et la vie des personnes agées en Grèce. Athens: Institut National D'Études Démographique 5.

Emmanuel, A. et al. (1976). The family of today and tomorrow. *Helliniki Iatriki, 45* (5):203–29.

Friedl, E. (1962). *Vassilica, a Village in Modern Greece.* New York: Holt, Rinehart, & Winston.

Georgas, J. (1985a). Cooperative, competitive and individual problem solving in sixth grade children. *European Journal of Social Psychology, 15*: 67–77.

———. (1985b). Group interactions and problem solving under cooperative, competitive and individual conditions. *General Psychology Monographs, 3*: 349–61.

———. (1986). Cooperative, competitive and individualistic goal structures with seventh grade Greek children: Problem-solving effectiveness and group interactions. *Journal of Social Psychology, 126*: 227–36.

———. (1987). Effect of intelligence on group interactions and problem solving: Cooperative, competitive and individual goal structures with Greek children. *International Journal of Small Group Research, 3*: 16–37.

Gibson, J. (1991). Youth and culture: A seventeen nation study of perceived problems and coping strategies. *International Journal for the Advancement of Counselling, 14*: 203–16.

Harila, D. (1990). Stereotyped perception, couple's roles and satisfaction in marriage. (In Greek.) Master's thesis, Aristotelian University of Thessaloniki.

Haritos-Fatouros, M., Sakka, D. & Dikaiou, M. (1988). A study of migrant mothers: Return home and role change. *International Journal for the Advancement of Counselling, 11*: 167–81.

Hirschon, R. (1989). *Heirs of the Greek Catastrophe. The Social Life of Asia Minor Refugees in Piraeus.* Oxford: Clarendon Press.

Katakis, Ch. (1984). *The Three Identities of Greek Family.* (In Greek.) Athens: Kedros.

Kelperis, Ch., et. al. (1985). Youth: Use of time and interpersonal relations. *Review of Social Research, 57*: 83–144.

Kiountouzis, Ch., & Vassiliou, V. (1981). Variations in boundary-structuring in rural couples. Paper presented at the Second Mediterranean Congress of Social Psychiatry, Undine, Italy.

McIntosh, P. (1991). Feeling like a fraud: Panic and wisdom in women and girls. Plenary address presented to the International Round Table for the Advancement of Counseling, Oporto, Portugal.

Moussourou, L. (1985). *Family and Child in Athens*. (In Greek.) Athens: Hestia.

Pitsiou, E. (1986). *Life-Styles of Older Athenians*. Athens: National Center of Social Research.

Spinelli, C., Vassiliou, V., & Vassiliou, G. (1970). Milieu development and male and female roles. In Seward, G. & Williamson, R. (Eds.), *Sex Roles in Changing Society*. New York: Random House.

Stamatopoulou-Igglesi, C. H. (1989). Patterns of female identity in Greek society. (In Greek.) Ph.D. diss., University of Ioannina.

Sueref, A. (1991). Pregnancy, couple's relations and depression. (In Greek.) Master's thesis, Aristotelian University, Thessaloniki.

Symeonidou, H. (1988). Employment and fertility of women in the greater Athens area. Ph.D. diss., University of London.

———. (1991). Family policies in Greece. In Dumon, W. (Ed.), *Family Policies in EEC Countries*. Leuven: Katholic University of Leuven.

Triandis, H. C., & Vassiliou, V. (1972). A comparative analysis of subjective cultures. In Triandis, H. C. (Ed.), *The Analysis of Subjective Culture*. New York: Wiley.

———. (1987). Frequency of contact and stereotyping. *Journal of Personality and Social Psychology*, 7: 316–28.

Triandis, H. C., et. al. (1968). Three cross-cultural studies of subjective culture. *Journal of Personality and Social Psychology*, 8: 1–42.

Tzougas, J., & Tziafetas, G. (1989). The impact of international migration on fertility: An econometric population model. *International Migration*, 27 (4): 581–94.

Vassiliou, G. (1966). Aspects of parent-adolescent transaction in the Greek family. In Caplan and Lebovici (Eds.), *Adolescence: Psychosocial Perspectives*. New York: Basic Books.

Vassiliou, G. & Vassiliou, V. (1973). The implicative meaning of the Greek concept of philotimo. *Journal of Cross-Cultural Psychology*, 4 (3): 326–41.

———. (1980). Boundary structuring during psychotherapy: To counteract psychophrenic disorganization. Paper presented at the International Symposium of D.A.P. on Psychotherapy of Schizophrenics, Munich.

———. (1982). Promoting psychosocial functioning and preventing malfunctioning. *Pediatrician*, 11 (1–2): 90–98.

8

Haiti

Chavannes Douyon, Jeanne Philippe, and Cynthia Frazier

INTRODUCTION

The country of Haiti is located on the western third of the island known as Hispaniola, which is the second largest island in the Caribbean. The Dominican Republic occupies the eastern portion of the island, with Cuba located to the northwest and Jamaica to the southwest. Haiti, meaning "land of mountains," was the original name given to the region by the Taino Arawak Indian inhabitants. The name of the island was changed to Santo Domingo during the Spanish colonization (1492–1697). When the western third of the island of Hispaniola was ceded to France under the Treaty of Ryswick in 1697, the name was changed to Saint-Domingue. It was not until Jacques Dessalines declared independence in 1804 that the original name of Haiti was reinstated.

Haiti occupies approximately 27,750 square kilometers (10,715 miles), with a population of approximately 6 million inhabitants. Nearly 2 million Haitians, comprising 25 percent of the population, reside in the urban centers of Port-au-Prince, Cap-Haitien, and Les Cayes. The highest concentration of inhabitants (75 percent) is found in the rural interior regions of the country. The population density is 170 per square kilometer (approximately 2.6 miles).

Haiti is regarded as the world's first independent black republic. Seventy-five percent of the population is black, of African descent. The remaining 25 percent is characterized by a range of racial traits resulting from miscegenation, primarily between white Europeans and black Africans. The official language is French, which is spoken by only 10 percent of the population, whereas Creole is spoken by all Haitians. Similarly, the official religion is Roman Catholic, but the popular religion is voodoo. Voodoo is based on the universality of the spirit, or life force, reminiscent of African animist beliefs. Voodoo lacks the formalized structure of other religions but, nonetheless, operates as an important verbal (non-written) system of social and cultural communication.

Haiti is considered the poorest country in the Western hemisphere. The infant mortality rate is 130 per 1,000. Average life expectancy is 48 years. The national wealth is primarily controlled by the minority urban elite. The minimum wage is currently 15 gourds per day (U.S. $1.50). Estimates indicate that 78 percent of the rural population live at or below the poverty level despite the fact that most own their own property. Since many cannot support their families on such small plots, they have cleared land to cultivate. Unfortunately, this has led to uncontrolled deforestation, which has worsened drought conditions and lowered agricultural productivity, resulting in food shortages. Primary, secondary, vocational, technical, and university education is provided by the government. Despite the fact that education is required by law, the illiteracy rate is estimated at 80 percent of the population.

OVERVIEW

To understand current gender roles in Haiti, it is important to understand the historical development of racial and social class differences, which has greatly influenced the roles of male and female. It is useful here to provide a brief review of racial and class inequalities that have preceded gender-role inequality.

Originally inhabited by the Tainos, the island of Hispaniola was colonized first by the Spanish. Christopher Columbus landed on the northern coast of Haiti in December 1492. The Tainos were enslaved to mine gold and serve as domestic help. By 1502, the Tainos population had dwindled due to harsh treatment. The Spanish then began importing slaves from Africa to replenish the labor supply. As the gold reserves were exhausted, the Spanish sought new sources in Mexico and Peru, leaving the colony of Santo Domingo unprotected from raids by the French and the British. By 1697, France acquired possession of the western portion of Hispaniola (Saint-Domingue) and maintained the system of slavery to amass wealth by trading predominantly sugar and coffee.

This colonial system of slavery foreshadows present conflicts between rich and poor and between upper and lower classes. The French, or *grand blancs*, enjoyed the wealth at the expense of the black slaves. Another class emerged known as mulattoes, or *gens de couleur*, who were children of white fathers and black slave mothers. According to the *French Code Noir* of 1685, mulattoes were entitled to own property, including slaves, although they were not permitted to enter certain professions, to live in France, or to intermarry with whites. Mulattoes had to wear different clothing than whites and were subjected to segregation in public places. Blacks slaves, who outnumbered both whites and mulattoes, had no rights under French law and were subjected to severe, inhumane treatment. The colony of Saint-Domingue was called "a mill for crushing negroes as much as for crushing sugar cane."

In August 1791, black slaves staged an organized revolt, led first by Boukman and later by Toussaint l'Ouverture, that resulted in the abolition of slavery in February 1793. As the white privileged class was destroyed, yet another class emerged known as the. *nouveaux libres*, or freed slaves (the class to which Touissant belonged). Touissant established Saint-Domingue's autonomy by establishing an authoritarian state under France's suzerainty. Independence from France was declared on 1 January 1804, by Jean-Jacques Dessalines, who then named himself Emperor Jacques I. France did not recognize Haiti's independence until 1825, in exchange for an enormous indemnity. This debt, in part, became influential in Haiti's dependence upon external resources and the devastation of the economy in the years to come.

Internal strife continued as Haiti split into a northern province, ruled by the black King Henri Christophe, and a southern state governed by the mulatto President Alexandre Pétion. Many landowners moved from the plantations to the city to establish businesses and to enter professions. Urban Haitians, aspiring to a French style of behavior, began speaking French, rather than Creole, and practicing Catholicism, rather than voodoo. Thus a major social class difference between urban and rural Haitians emerged around language and religion. Furthermore, the incorporation of a European social order based on skin color intensified the internal conflict between light-skinned and dark-skinned Haitians. Haiti was not reunified until 1820 under Pétion's successor, Jean-Pierre Boyer.

The first black republic experienced a succession of political leaders and increased financial indebtedness to the United States of America and other European countries. After rioting resulted in the death of President Sam in July 1915, the United States of America occupied the country for nearly twenty years. During the occupation, elected officials of the government were primarily mulatto, due in large part to American racism and preference for light skin over black.

The strife between the mulattoes and blacks continued until 1957, when François Duvalier was elected president. Duvalier, known as "Papa Doc," won the election largely due to his *noiriste* appeal to the black middle class in the urban centers and the black landowners and peasants in the rural districts. Duvalier gave blacks a more significant role in government with increased authority and status. Many were employed in Duvalier's personal national guard known as Toutons Macoutes, later renamed Voluntaires de la Sécurité Nationale (VSN). VSN were responsible for the arrests of those who expressed opposition to Duvalier policy. In 1964, Papa Doc declared himself "president for life" and remained so until his death in April 1971. He was succeeded by his son Jean-Claude, "Baby Doc," who was only nineteen at the time of succession. In 1980, Jean-Claude married Michèle Bennett, whose father was a prominent member of the mulatto urban elite. Subsequently, the base of power shifted from the black middle class to the mulatto upper class. Baby Doc remained in power until 1986, when political and social conditions forced his ouster. Since that time, Haiti continues to experience frequent political change due to internal strife and natural catastrophe.

This historical review illustrates the inequalities among Haitians based on race and socioeconomic class. While the male is generally considered superior to the female, one's skin color and socioeconomic status also must be considered. In rural areas of Haiti, where 75 percent of the population is concentrated, men are considered superior on the basis of physical prowess, emotional control, and leadership aptitude. Men make decisions independently about family affairs and are not held accountable. Rural women accept a submissive and dependent role to maintain equilibrium within the family system and the community.

Both men and women work the land. Women typically are responsible for planting seedlings, harvesting the crop, and transporting it to market to sell. In addition, they are responsible for the cooking, household maintenance, and child care. Men are responsible for the heavier tasks of farming and the more intellectual tasks of regulating the finances of the family or community. Under the practice known as *placage*, a male farmer who has several plots to cultivate may have a principal wife and a concubine at each site who works the land and oversees his personal interests. At each site, the woman uses song and dance to foster a sense of family. The peasant farmer is responsible for the welfare of each female partner and the children she has borne. In essence, rural women and their children have become the property of men.

Ironically, no gender inequality exists in the voodoo religion. Both men and women are likely to be summoned by the spirits to become voodoo priests. A *houngan* (male) or *mambo* (female) voodoo priest serves as a community doctor in the rural areas. Both have knowledge of plants that are used for medicine and possess the power to heal.

As land has become scarce and rural poverty has increased, many Haitians have migrated to the urban centers to work. As a result, cities like Port-au-Prince have become overcrowded without adequate housing, sanitation, schools, and health facilities. Women living in these urban slums work for extremely low wages at menial jobs (e.g., in assembling factories or as maids for wealthy families). Some entrepreneurial women, known as a Madame Sara, obtain financial independence by importing items in bulk to sell to local street vendors for a small profit. Due to high unemployment, women may be the only wage earners in the family. In spite of this economic advantage, women still believe that men possess the authority and leadership in the family.

Among the middle class, composed of teachers, professors, public administrators, attorneys, physicians, accountants, technicians, and business owners, the distinction between gender roles is less pronounced. At this level, women generally obtain the same education as men. With equal education, women can attain economic independence and professional stature in the community. However, they must continue to manage the children and household affairs since many middle-class men are physically and psychologically absent from family life. In spite of economic independence, women usually do not act independently. Decisions concerning finances and expenditures must receive authorization from the man, who remains the head of the family, as is practiced among the lower class.

Women and men are considered equal among the upper class. All decisions, whether related to the management of business, home, or social affairs, are mutually determined. Women are as likely as men to secure high-level positions in government and business, although, in conflict situations, a decision is ultimately determined by the man with the support of the woman. Vestiges of the traditional role of male authority are still evident among the upper class.

This basic inequality between male and female appears in each phase of life from infancy to old age.

COMPARISONS BETWEEN MEN'S AND WOMEN'S GENDER ROLES DURING THE LIFE CYCLE

Infancy and Childhood

Among the rural majority, a son is preferred over a daughter, particularly the firstborn. A man often praises a woman when a son is born. He may bestow upon her a gift, such as a small parcel of land, or he may legally marry her. The birth of a daughter engenders great disappointment. She is often considered an unnecessary burden to the father since a female can become pregnant. During this life phase, a boy receives more attention than a girl from the mother. The mother binds the waist of the son with cloth to ensure future sexual prowess. Similarly, his penis is often stimulated, caressed, and given an endearing nickname such as "little pigeon" or "little goat." The genitalia of the female are considered inferior. In infancy until early childhood, a boy is kept unclothed with exposed genitalia. Conversely, an infant girl is dressed in a hooded jumper, which is later replaced with a long blue dress and a scarf to cover the head.

A son is allowed to nurse longer than a daughter to strengthen physically the boy's developing body and to foster an affectionate temperament. Weaning may be abruptly ended at the mother's discretion. The time period required to toilet train a boy is shorter than for a girl. This difference may be due to the emphasis placed on male independence. A mother may foster dependence in the female by assisting with toileting in spite of the child's self-sufficiency.

In the rural regions of the country, females are socialized to be more dependent physically, emotionally, financially, and socially. Males are permitted to display a wider range of behavior than females. For example, boys are allowed to be physically active (e.g., climb, jump, run) and to display aggression (e.g., fight). Typical male toys during early childhood include handmade objects such as kites, slingshots, and fishing poles. Likewise, females receive hand-sewn dolls. Since children begin working with their parents at a young age, there is little time for play. By the age of five, gender identification is expedited by same-sex segregation. That is, a boy joins his father in daily activities (e.g., chores, farming) or meeting with other men in the village. A girl assists the mother with household chores, child care, planting, or harvesting.

The customs of the urban middle class are similar to those of rural Haitians, with some exceptions. For example, the preference for a son may be disguised as the mother's wish for her first son to look like the father. At this social class level, child-rearing practices are more strict regarding toilet training, control of anger and aggression, sexual curiosity, and dress. These restrictions are more oppressive for females, who are required to be neat, reserved, disciplined, submissive, and kind. Girls are rarely allowed to socialize outside the home, whereas boys enjoy more freedom within and outside the home. Parental identification is often diffused within middle-class families since children experience close emotional attachments to significant family members residing within the same household (e.g., uncle, aunt, grandfather, grandmother, cousin).

The customs of upper-class Haitians reflect a blending of Haitian and Western beliefs and behaviors. For example, an infant generally spends most of the day in close physical and emotional contact with a lower-class nanny, who imparts traditional values about gender. A combination of breast and bottle feeding is employed until weaning is concluded between the third and fifth months. Spoon and finger feeding are gradually added, making the weaning a more natural process. The fundamental beliefs of Haitian culture infiltrate the upper ranks as a result of socioeconomic class interaction and interdependence.

In general, aggression, competition, and rivalry are not encouraged or tolerated among children in Haitian society. Children are raised to be respectful and submissive to adults. Physical punishment is commonly practiced, particularly within lower-class families, to discipline disobedient children.

School Years

In Haiti, education is free and compulsory. The government provides six years (ages 6–12) of primary and seven years (ages 12–19) of secondary schooling. The Haitian Department of Education issues a diploma upon completion of secondary school. Religious organizations provide private schooling, primarily in urban areas. Alternative schooling is offered by the French and American governments. Each provides a certified diploma, which is valid when applying for admission into the respective country's college/university system.

Since attendance is not enforced, children in rural areas often do not begin school until the age of eight. They may attend only three days a week since they must assist their parents with work on the land or within the home. While rural boys generally are encouraged to continue attending primary school longer, rural girls usually stop attending class by the age of 10. Only 14 percent of rural children ever complete a primary education.

Among the middle class, primary schooling begins at age six. They usually attend public schools. Some middle-class parents enroll their children in private parochial schools, if financially able. Great emphasis is placed on education and academic success as the only means to reaching higher social status. As a result, the education of the boy is given greater priority due to the cultural importance of the male in the determination of political, economic, and social affairs. However, middle-class females do complete secondary schooling and/or college. Most often, middle-class students continue their education in Haitian universities. If finances permit, students may attend college in Europe, Canada, or the United States of America. Females tend to prefer different topic areas than males, such as literature, history, nursing, teaching, psychology, and secretarial/administration courses. Boys initially study social studies or literature during primary and secondary school but often shift to scientific and technological disciplines, such as biology, medicine, engineering, statistics, management, law, and economics at the university level.

Children of the upper class are able to attend the most elite schools. With the advantage of wealth, they often begin attending school at between three to five years of age, in private nursery schools or kindergartens. Generally they complete their secondary education in the elite, private French or American school systems. Both males and females are likely to attend the most prestigious universities in Europe, Canada, or the United States of America. Females tend to study the same disciplines as men. Upon completion, upper-class students attain high-level positions within government, private industry, or family-owned businesses.

Young Adulthood

Typical behavior displayed during young adulthood varies according to social class. Among peasants of rural communities, sexual maturity is reached earlier by males (age 12) than by females. Rural boys are now allowed to play cards and attend cockfights with the men of the community. Tobacco smoking and drinking rum and *clairin* (alcohol made from sugarcane) are acceptable behaviors. At this age, males are considered independent and are afforded personal freedom to socialize. Rural females, however, mature between ages 15 and 25. They are not permitted to socialize outside the home. On occasion, they may go to social events during the day, but never after the sun sets. Consequently, a young man may have the opportunity to meet a young woman only at a dance during the village feast or en route to market, church, or the river. While most young adults are curious about sex, the female outwardly resists. Often the male uses ''force'' to overcome her ''protestations.'' Public display of affection is never permitted.

Socialization among young adults of the middle class is not encouraged by parents, who are concerned that the attainment of an education and a professional career will be jeopardized by the development of a sexual interest. Despite this concern, males are permitted to socialize freely, while females, at this age, are encouraged to preserve their virginity. Typical social activities include sports, movies, dances, and parties.

Socialization among upper-class young adults is less restrictive and inhibited. Both males and females are able to socialize openly. However, they socialize only with those of the same social standing. Membership to private country clubs offers the opportunity to play tennis, golf, sail, and swim. Upper-class young adults can afford to travel more extensively and to frequent fine restaurants and nightclubs.

Adulthood

Adulthood is generally marked by the decision to live with someone in *placage* or to marry legally. Marriage in Haiti reflects the resilience of tradition in the rural communities versus the assimilation of European customs in the urban middle and upper classes.

When a peasant finds a woman who will accept his love, he must send a letter of proposal to her family. This letter is usually written on colored paper by the most educated in the community. The proposal must be delivered to the woman's family by the eldest member of the man's family. If her family accepts the proposal, he then builds a house on a parcel of land in his family *lakou*, or physical/social space. After the house is completed, the man and woman may be married before the priest. Usually, however, the couple lives in *placage* since legal marriage may pose an additional expense. She continues to be called *mamzelle* (Miss) until she has lived faithfully with her husband for several years. Then, she may be referred to as *madame* (Mrs.).

Once married, the wife resides in the *lakou* of the husband's extended family. All members of the *lakou* are linked by ties of kinship or marriage. They all serve the same gods in the voodoo religion and participate in family worship ceremonies. In this relationship the wife is submissive to the husband, who is the object of respect and admiration. For example, the wife gives the choice portion of food to the husband; the bed linens are often arranged for him alone.

Rural men enjoy their leisure time by gathering to play cards, smoke, drink, and exchange stories. Women have little leisure time. They gather to wash, cook, bathe, or sell produce at the market. When they do congregate, they often chew or smoke tobacco and share riddles to amuse themselves. The couple generally continue living in *placage* unless the man decides to leave. The children remain with their mother.

In the urban communities, marriage customs reflect European traditions. After a couple has been engaged, a religious ceremony in the church is performed. The bride wears white to symbolize purity and is accompanied by bridesmaids. Wedding guests enjoy a festive reception, complete with food, champagne, and dancing. After the honeymoon, the couple begin their married life and have children of their own. Divorce and custody of children are ruled by the law. Generally, children remain with the mother except in rare cases where the court has ruled in favor of the father.

Old Age

Once again, cultural attitudes and behaviors regarding old age are determined by socioeconomic class and community. In lower-class rural communities, the aged man is elevated to a position of the highest social importance. He now conducts the family worship voodoo ceremonies. All the women in his *lakou* care for him and bring him food each day. Everyone refers to him as *Papa*, and he calls each *mon enfant* (my child). He spends his time by telling tales and reciting proverbs. Young children are often presented for the old man to hold since it is believed that he has the power to repel evil spirits. When he dies, the women wear mourning clothes and praise his virtues. The rural man enjoys higher social status than a woman, even during old age. The aged woman is fed and cared for by her daughter.

In urban areas, aging is characterized by a shift from independence to dependence as a result of loss of partner or income. In Haitian society the major social support for the elderly comes from the family (Frazier & Douyon, 1989). The aged father or mother of the middle class takes up residence with his or her adult children if they are willing and financially able to support him or her. The father, however, no longer plays a significant role in family affairs and may feel useless and demoralized.

The aged man or woman in the upper class is likely to remain at home by hiring the support services needed to live independently of his or her family. When medical attention or hospitalization is necessary, he or she may seek assistance abroad.

SUMMARY AND CONCLUSIONS

Haitian society today is rapidly changing due to the impact of Westernization and the ongoing struggle for equality and freedom. In 1987, the new Haitian constitution declared total equality of sexes and recognized the civil rights of all Haitians. As a result of political and social change, gender distinctions appear to be less pronounced. However, the ability to earn continues to be the more significant factor in determining personal value in Haitian society. Similarly, job opportunities dictate what educational direction both men and women now pursue, which often eliminates gender preferences.

To date, 15 women have been appointed as ministers in the different governments that have succeeded that of President François Duvalier. In addition, other women have been chosen to serve as mayor of Port-au-Prince and as judges on supreme and civil courts of justice. Furthermore, the president of the third provisional government was Ertha Trouillot, the person responsible for organizing a democratic and free election in Haiti between 1990 and 1991.

Comparable changes toward equality of the sexes have occurred within the family, educational, and cultural institutions of Haiti. However, these changes have not come without conflict within individuals and between generations. As a result, the world's first black republic continues to struggle and change today.

NOTE

All statistical data cited in this chapter are estimates extracted from documents published by the World Bank, the United Nations, and the U.S. government.

REFERENCES

Alexis, Gerson. (1970). *Le concept de chance en Haiti*. (These de licence.) Port-au-Prince, Haiti: Faculté d'Éthologie.

Bijoux, Legrand. (1982). *Contrôle de la chance dans le milieu Haitien*. Traditions et Innovations Cours International d'Été: La femme Haitienne en milieu rural. Collection CHISS, 175–82.

Constitution de la République d'Haiti. (1987). Haiti, West Indies: Presses Nationales.

Douyon, Chavannes. (1982). *Image de soi de la femme Haitienne en milieu rural*. Traditions et Innovations Cours International d'Été: La femme rurale en Haiti et dans les Caribes, 183–204.

Frazier, Cynthia L., & Douyon, Chavannes. (1989). Social support in the elderly: A cross-cultural comparison. In L.L. Adler (Ed.), *Cross-Cultural Research in Human Development: Life-Span Perspectives*. New York: Praeger.

Liburn, James. (1982). *Las castas y las classe*. Pueblo Haitiano, 243.

Prince, Rod. (1985). *Haiti Family Business*. London: Latin American Bureau.

Rubin, V., & Schaeldel, R. (1982). *The Haitian Potential: Research and Resources*. New York: Teachers College Press, Columbia University.

9

Hong Kong

Agnes Yinling Yu

INTRODUCTION

Hong Kong is a Cantonese name meaning Fragrant Harbor. It traces its political origins to China. Geographically it is located at the mouth of the Pearl River (Jujiang) in the province of Guangdong, in southern China. About a century and a half ago, Hong Kong was a sleepy little fishing village, inhabited by fisherfolk, pirates, traders, and a few farmers on the mainland. After China was defeated in the Opium War of 1841, the island of Hong Kong was ceded to Britain in the Treaty of Nanking in 1842. In 1860 the Kowloon peninsula was added to the cession, and in 1898 the New Territories was leased to Britain for 99 years. All this land came to be known as the British Crown Colony of Hong Kong.

The Colony, which consists of 235 small islands, covers 370 square miles. Most of the land is made up of barren hills, of which only 10 percent are inhabitable. The majority of the population is concentrated on both sides of the Hong Kong harbor, on the Kowloon peninsula and the northern shores of the Hong Kong island. Hong Kong has a population of close to 5.5 million (Lau & Kuan, 1988), of whom 98 percent are of Chinese descent. The other 2 percent consist of Caucasians from Europe and North America, a well-established Portuguese community tracing its origins to the trading days, and small communities of East Indians. Because of the intermingling of cultures, Hong Kong has developed a cosmopolitan outlook.

Chinese immigrants came to Hong Kong during several periods, pre–World War II, postwar, and thereafter. They came predominantly from the rural regions of southern China from Quangdong, Fujian, and Swatow. After the liberation of China, the more urbane Chinese from Shanghai and other urban centers came to settle in Hong Kong. These Chinese immigrants came from different ethnolinguistic groups, with their respective Chinese dialects and customs.

Contemporary Hong Kong society consists of 57 percent Hong Kong–born residents. The remainder of the population is made up of a small number of expatriates and a sizable number of first-generation Chinese from neighboring China. Thus Hong Kong can be considered a community of immigrants. Whether native or foreign born, the majority of Hong Kong residents consider their society instrumentally as a place to make a living and to prosper (Ikels, 1983), where they can live in a semblance of democracy in the form of personal freedom and free enterprise. It is a haven of capitalism and consumerism, where competition is the way of life.

In the 1950s Hong Kong functioned economically as an entrepôt. As the wheels of industrialization turned in the 1960s, Hong Kong's economy was characterized by cottage industries, the manufacture of plastic goods and toys (plastic flowers!), and textiles. The major industrial change occurred in the 1970s, when industries took off and propelled Hong Kong to a market and consumer-driven society (Lau & Kuan, 1988).

The 1990s are said to be Hong Kong's twilight years as a colonial enclave; it will be returned to China in 1997. In its brief history, it has metamorphosed from a colonial outpost and entrepôt in the South China Sea to an internationally renowned and commercially vibrant metropolis. Although the people of Hong Kong can trace their recent origins from traditional China, it is a distinct Chinese society in many ways, although the processes of Westernization and moderni-zation have dramatically changed the traditional characteristics of the people. Within the last decade a frenetic change of pace was noted (Lau & Kuan, 1988), unsurpassed by any period in its history. This process of change touches upon the lives of the old and young, male and female. The ramifications of this frenzied process make Hong Kong, and in particular the people of Hong Kong, a fas-cinating subject of study for social scientists from East and West.

OVERVIEW

Hong Kong is a unique society that prides itself in its ability to maintain harmony within contrasts. It is a place where East meets West, where tradition confronts modern practices, where the old face the young, and the rich encounter the poor. Within the family the contrasts can be easily observed. Tremendous changes have occurred in the Hong Kong Chinese family within a generation, changes that would have normally taken generations to develop in a more con-ventional society.

In view of its Chinese roots, the Hong Kong Chinese were traditionally gov-erned by Confucian dicta, for example, that certain positions in the society are inviolable: the common people had to defer to the emperor or those in power, the wife to the husband, and the children to the elders. The rules of conduct in a Confucian society did not presuppose equality. In fact, equality or inequality was never questioned. Harmony or the preservation of order was the key to a peaceful society. If the order of society were violated, then disorder and chaos would prevail. Because of the Chinese emphasis on harmony, behaviors were stipulated to maintain conformity. Children were socialized to recognize their place in the social order. Remnants of these practices are still seen today in contemporary Hong Kong society, particularly in the way parents socialize their young and the way the sexes interact with each other.

The push for Westernization and modernization in Hong Kong society has eroded traditional values, and old practices are giving way to new behaviors in order to keep in tune with current realities. Since Hong Kong's livelihood depends mainly on its capacity to provide highly fashionable and technologized consumer goods to the West, cross-cultural communication in business dealings demands that the Hong Kong Chinese modify and adapt their rules of conduct between themselves and foreigners. Unlike their Chinese compatriots in China, who were inward-looking for many years, the Hong Kong Chinese have had almost 150 years to find socially acceptable ways to deal with foreigners. In addition, Hong Kong society has been exposed to Western ways of administration, which colors the way the people will think and behave. As the Hong Kong Chinese began to take on new behaviors for economic survival, this inevitably changed their behaviors among themselves.

Researchers (Cheung, Lam & Chau, 1990; Ho, 1977; Mitchell, 1972a; Salaff, 1981; Yu & Bain, 1985) into Hong Kong life-style have generally identified a traditional versus modern orientation, a social class-education-work status differentiation in the social behaviors of the Hong Kong Chinese. These works form the bases in this chapter for the interpretation of the development of gender roles.

COMPARISONS BETWEEN MEN'S AND WOMEN'S GENDER ROLES DURING THE LIFE CYCLE

Infancy and Early Childhood

Hong Kong parents usually are not that far removed from their traditional Chinese roots, since the majority of them were reared by parents who were Chinese immigrants. As first-generation Hong Kong parents usually came directly from neighboring China, they brought with them their respective traditions and customs, usually of rural origins. Now, however, these ideas are often juxtaposed with the more modern and Westernized ideas of child rearing, from books written by Dr. Benjamin Spock and others. As a society that pursues trends and fads, the Hong Kong Chinese try to adapt their ways to ones that are most expedient, including the rejection of traditional ways.

In a traditional agrarian society, the number of offspring in a family is an important factor in economic survival. The more children a family can produce, the more assured the family will be of assistance in farm work. Children also act as insurance for security in old age, particularly in a society where pensions are unheard of.

While this type of thinking is still prevalent among the more traditional Hong Kong parents, among the professional and better educated, the size of a family is no longer an issue. These people are in pursuit of quality of life and better living standards.

In modern China there is still a definite preference for male offspring. In a patriarchal society, males could inherit the family names and pass those on to their children. Perpetuity of the family is a long-held Chinese tradition that has not been eroded by time. Female offspring are seen as temporary members, to be passed on to another family at marriage. Hong Kong parents are no exception to this Chinese tradition: Mitchell (1972b) found that Chinese mothers are more likely to reject their daughters than their sons, and they also spend less time with their daughters than their sons, although, among the more educated Hong Kong parents, the sentiment for the male child is not as strong as it is among the working-class, tradition-oriented parents (Salaff, 1981).

Ho (1977) described two stages in child-rearing practices among Chinese parents. In the earlier stage, from birth to around 6 years, parents have a "nurturing" function: the provision of nourishment, love, daily care, shelter, and basic necessities. At this age level, the child is seen as incapable of "understanding" anything. Thus parents need to take an attitude of kindness, indulgence, and lenience toward the young child.

Cheung, Lam, & Chau (1990) discovered differences in child-rearing behaviors between the traditional, less-educated and the professional, better-educated Hong Kong Chinese parents. The former group tended to be more concerned with control and instilling obedient and compliant behaviors in their children. The latter group tended to be more tolerant and allowed their children to become more assertive and independent. Their findings also revealed that boys have the tendency to be trained to be more assertive than girls; girls are less verbally and physically aggressive than boys; and children from the modern, professional families are generally less physically aggressive. Mitchell (1972c) further found that Hong Kong parents tend to use conditional love as a discipline measure to control behavior of boys.

It was also found (Ho, 1977) that fathers played more with their male offspring, and Mitchell (1972a) discovered that the more educated the parents were, the more likely they were to play with their children. In another study (Yu & Bain, 1985) class differences were found in the availability of toys for the children. The professional class tend to provide more Western, education-oriented toys than their working-class counterparts. Generally, boys have access to more assertive types of toys (cars, building blocks, transformer toys, weapons) whereas girls play with passive types of toys (dolls, stuffed animals, playhouses, cooking sets). Boys tend to engage in more physical activities (sports) than girls. However, both boys and girls spend much time in television watching.

In dress codes, Hong Kong parents tend to follow the universal color pattern, pink or red for girls, blue or gray for boys, supplemented by a variation of colors. A Western influence can definitely be discerned in children's fashion, which is a result of Hong Kong's being the manufacturing center for upscale international fashion.

In recent decades, a trend for higher education and more exposure to Western ideas among young parents in Hong Kong is evident. A change in child-rearing practices is observed, partly because of knowledge gleaned from the media sources and partly because of government efforts in educating young parents and the rising standard of education, with the result that the gap in sex differences in child rearing is increasingly being narrowed.

School Years

From about age 6 on, Ho (1977) noted that Chinese parents tend to take a "teaching" or "training" function rather than the earlier "nurturing" function. There is a concern to instill in their young socially acceptable behaviors, for the goal of formation of a moral character. Among Hong Kong Chinese families, birth order defines how siblings relate to each other. Deference to the older sibling prevails, following Confucian traditions, and between twins, the firstborn twin has the right to claim authority over the later-born sibling. Between the sexes, the male siblings are generally allowed more freedom from household duties when sisters are present. Among working parents, it is common to see the oldest daughter assuming child care and household duties while the parents are at work. But the assumption of these duties does not necessarily give the daughter authority over a male sibling (Salaff, 1981).

During the school-age years, boys have the opportunity for more education, more often than girls. Generally, Hong Kong parents are very concerned about their children's academic achievement, and they would take over all household duties so that their children would have adequate time to spend on schoolwork. According to Mitchell (1972a) the higher the socio-economic status and educational level of the parents, the more likely they are to set higher educational goals for their children. More parents, however, aspire for their sons to pursue a university education than their daughters, and the better-educated mothers, especially, tend to have higher educational goals for their sons. In Hong Kong, the level of education and educational achievement are seen as tickets to social mobility and job opportunity. In this regard, male offspring are seen as future heads of households with concomitant financial responsibilities. In working-class families, it is not unusual to see female offspring forsake their education so that their brothers can have a chance for more or higher education (Salaff, 1981). However, if the female child possesses superior capabilities and can secure government funding for a place in secondary school, she will be encouraged by her family to stay in school. In financially capable families, the distinction between the sexes in terms of educational opportunities is not as pronounced.

In Hong Kong the pursuit of a particular discipline of study often determines an individual's subsequent career opportunities (Mitchell, 1972c). However, the selection of the field of study often depends on the intellectual or academic capability of the student. Even with the rising level of education among females, the male offspring are encouraged to pursue fields of study related to medicine, science and technology, and business. The nonacademically oriented males are usually channeled into industrial or work-related apprenticeships. Their female counterparts are encouraged to pursue white-collar work, such as secretarial training, although the more capable females tend to pursue teacher training, nursing, social work, or business education. However, for high-achieving females, science and technology studies are no longer the preserve of males. Cheung and Tam (1984) found that male self-esteem is positively related to socioeconomic status, academic achievement status or prestige of the school, and selection of academic stream (Anglo-Chinese versus Chinese, science versus arts, academic versus vocational), while in contrast, female self-esteem is related only to socioeconomic status.

Generally, during the school years in a highly competitive society such as Hong Kong, Chinese parents will do anything within their ability to secure educational opportunities for their young. Intellectual and academic development are seen as the stepping-stones to upward mobility and financial security. All efforts of the family and the child are channeled toward academic achievement. Although some gender differences in practice are still discerned, in the main, the capability of the child, whether male or female, becomes the determinant of educational opportunities, in the family, in the educational system, and in the broader society.

Young Adulthood

The end of school years signals the end of a phase of development and the period of dependency. Young Hong Kong adults now enter a phase of independence and responsibilities for themselves, a time to repay the parents' efforts in nurturing and supporting them. It is also the time the young adult begins to develop an interpersonal network that will fulfill a social function. The individual will start preparing for the eventuality of marriage and family.

In the urbanized, industrialized, and modernized setting of Hong Kong, the young adult now embarks on a career. In the competitive world of market economics, career opportunities are often determined by international market trends. Fortunately, in the Colony, the current trends provide ample opportunities in the manufacturing, service, sales, high-tech, semiprofessional, and professional areas. Depending on one's level of education and career training, there is always a niche where an individual may fit in the scheme of career opportunities. At the lower socioeconomic level, gender differences are more pronounced (Salaff, 1981), and there is a higher proportion of females in the manufacturing sector (garment manufacture, electronic assembly).

In the service sector, where workers will be exposed at times to Western clients (hotels and restaurants), a certain level of English proficiency is generally required. The level and stream of education a worker has had now become important factors in securing employment; there is no noticeable gender differentiation in this area. However, chefs in exclusive hotel restaurants are still mainly males, while females tend to be hostesses. In the sales sector, contingent upon the type of consumer goods, males appear to dominate. In the semiprofessional area, such as teaching, social work, and office work, more females are evident. However, male clerks in offices and banks are quite common. In the professional areas where a high level of expertise and educaton is required, especially at the upper executive levels, a higher percentage of males is found. This is not surprising, as parental aspirations support education of sons, rather than daughters, at the postsecondary levels.

Outside work, the young adult can now begin to enjoy some freedom in the form of leisure pursuits, unlike the school years, where social activities are often constrained by studies. Socioeconomic differences are evident (Ng, 1984) in social and leisure activities among young people in Hong Kong. Males tend to engage in more physical activities (sports, ball games, outings) than do females. Males also tend to have a wider variety of leisure activities, all to establish a social network from which to develop an opportunity to advance their careers. Females, on the other hand, tend to engage in more socializing activities (shopping, visits to teahouses, picnics), either in the company of work colleagues of the same sex or in a mixed-sex setting. Females also spend more of their leisure time in developing interest activities or household skills (such as cooking classes, knitting). Salaff (1981) pointed to the phenomenon of working-class girls, who are now freed from the pressures of household duties in exchange for their economic support of the family. Their share of the housework is now assumed either by their mothers or by younger siblings. Salaff further noted that even with their economic contribution to the family, which is sometimes substantial, these females are still not accorded the status within the family that a male sibling would enjoy. However, these females may now have the time to pursue selfimprovement classes, as in English language classes or academic upgrading for those who had to leave school earlier to join the work force. Attendance at evening or extramural classes for self-improvement among both male and female workers is a common phenomenon in Hong Kong. This provides additional skills for competing in a demanding job market, thereby affording chances for upward mobility.

The young adult years are also the time to learn to socialize and meet prospective mates. Reflecting the early missionary influence, many schools in Hong Kong are still segregated by sex. With heavy academic demands, students often do not have the time or the occasion to socialize with members of the opposite sex. When the school years are over and with the young adults embarking on careers, the opportunity is there for them to socialize and date. Among the Hong Kong Chinese, group dating is quite acceptable. This provides the opportunity for them to meet prospective boyfriends or girlfriends through an acceptable social channel, their colleagues, friends, relatives, or youth organizations. Dating as a couple is taken seriously, for this is associated with marriage. Dating is not usually contemplated until the young adult is nearly finished with schooling. Among the working class, where daughters have to provide support for their families, parents usually discourage serious dating, for fear that an early marriage may terminate their daughters' financial support for the family (Salaff, 1981). Daughters usually have to wait until such times as their younger siblings are almost finished with their schooling. Thus it is not uncommon to see young Hong Kong females become engaged for two or more years and often wait until they are in their mid-20s before contemplating marriage. The males often wait until they are in their late 20s, with their careers established, before they marry. Generally, the impact of education is felt in the institution of marriage among the Hong Kong Chinese, for it is now common to have longer courtships among the more educated couples; in addition, free choice is the rule rather than the exception.

Adulthood

Adulthood is the time for serious consideration of selecting a mate in marriage. Living in a modern, urbanized society, where exposure to Western norms of behavior is commonplace, Chinese adults now insist on freedom of choice in the selection of their mates. Unlike their parents' generation, where the traditional practice of arranged marriages prevailed, this is no longer acceptable to Hong Kong adults. However, these adults will generally allow their parents to offer their approval of the union. Legalized unions are the acceptable norm; cohabitation of a couple without the benefit of marriage is still frowned upon. In the case of the eldest offspring, particularly a male, a wedding banquet to cement the union is practically compulsory. In working-class families, sometimes it may take the whole family several years to save sufficient funds to pay for the ceremony. Travel weddings, where the couple marry in a private ceremony and then embark on a honeymoon, are becoming more popular because of the amount of money the couple may save. Mitchell (1972b) and Salaff (1981) found that females tend to marry up in the socio-economic scale. In mate selection, young women now tend to look for compatibility, capability, and work and earning potential in prospective mates (Salaff, 1981). Females are implicitly taught that once they marry, their loyalty to the family will switch from their birth family to their husbands'. Married working females should rank their employment second in importance to their family, their children, and their husbands, in that order.

Chinese tradition used to stipulate that young marrieds lived patrilocally, with the parents of the groom, but the experience suffered by the previous generation, usually the woman's mother, may be enough for the mother to support her daughter's reluctance or refusal to live with the in-laws. In light of rising educational levels for females and their increasing employment, young couples, particularly among the better educated, are now insisting on a neolocal living arrangement, that is, living independently (Mitchell, 1972a). It has now become more acceptable for the husband to live with his wife's family, particularly if her family has the financial means and the availability of space to house the married couple. Mitchell further found that Hong Kong parents want their sons to bring their wives into the household, but they do not want their daughters to live with their respective parents-in-law.

Once a couple is married, it is customary for them to start a family soon. Chinese people tend to be suspicious of birth control before the start of the family, for fear that the chemical properties may ruin fertility. When birth control is practiced, usually after the birth of the desired number of children, it is usually incumbent upon the woman to take the responsibility. Once a baby is on the way, the wife customarily devotes herself full-time to the infant, as Chinese families are still child-oriented. Among the affluent families, the mother can receive additional help from nursemaids or nannies. Among working-class families, the mother usually stays home with her young until they are old enough to be cared for by other adults, sometimes by the older siblings.

The fact that better-educated working females are becoming more common-place is beginning to change dramatically the structure of authority in the Chinese household. In traditional times, deference and authority belonged to the male. In the modern Chinese household, particularly where there is a working mother, authority and decision making are being negotiated by the couple (Mitchell, 1972a; Wong, 1981), and among professional families, shared authority becomes the norm. Among working-class families where both men and women work, the sharing of household duties, such as grocery shopping, cooking, cleaning, child care, and household maintenance, is becoming more acceptable; however, part-time working mothers still engage in double duty, working outside the home as well as being the main homemaker. Professional working couples, of course, have access to hired help. Even though the traditional male superiority in a Chinese household is eroding, few females are given the authority to make all decisions concerning household affairs (Wong, 1981). One dramatic change in the Hong Kong Chinese household is that the conception of the father as the authority figure no longer holds true.

An impact of education on marriage is in the communication pattern of the married couple. It appears that the higher level of education the couple has, the more open the communication (Mitchell, 1972b). Couples who communicate more tend to engage in more joint activities outside the home. Some of these activities may be couple-oriented (such as going to movies), while others may be family-oriented (watching television, going to teahouses, family outings, visits with friends and relatives). As long as there are dependent or unmarried children in the home, the parents' efforts and activities generally are child-oriented. There is a Chinese saying that the parents work is never finished until their children are settled and can start their own families.

Traditional practice prohibits divorce among Chinese couples. However, in a modern society and with Western influence, divorce is occurring more often among Hong Kong Chinese couples. Among couples in long-term marriages, there are now more wives who complain of unhappiness in the marriage (Mitchell, 1972b). However, these tend to be marriages where there is little communication between the couple, where the marriage is generally characterized by a short courtship and a stricter delineation of responsibilities between male and female, with males holding the authority role, and where couples tend to have limited education. In cases of divorce involving children, they are considered to be the property of the father, who has custody. But there are more wives who are contesting child custody. Nevertheless the old conception that the wife must bear the cross of an unhappy marriage still prevails in modern society. Probably this is due to the wife's more dependent financial status. Remarriage for the male is more acceptable, particularly if the first wife could not bear him any children or if he is widowed. Concubinage, the taking of a secondary wife, has not been legal in Hong Kong since 1971. Remarriage for the divorcée or a widow is generally still frowned upon (Mitchell, 1972a). As traditional practices fade, to be replaced by more modern ones, the institutions of marriage and family will have to adapt to new mores.

Old Age

Hong Kong Chinese generally believe in filial piety as a family virtue and an expected behavior required of all children. Theoretically, according to Confucian values, Chinese seniors should be able to enjoy their golden years with respect, honor, and security, surrounded by their children and grandchildren. In an overcrowded and urban society that prides itself on its industrial progress and free enterprise, traditional values are often clouded by modern values, and this may influence the way the younger generation views the concept of the family, particularly the traditional extended family. In Hong Kong, young couples aspire to have nuclear families, following the Western tradition so often portrayed in the media, free from the interference of in-laws. The older generation, most of whom are still steeped in their rural Chinese traditions, often have to contend with ideas and experiences alien to their customary expectations. In some instances, elders who came as refugees do not have children residing in Hong Kong, and they may be faced with loneliness in old age, away from their children and kinship support. In other instances, elders have children married to Hong Kong-born-and-bred individuals, who may not subscribe to traditional values. Thus the golden years may bring unexpected and heartrending adjustments, for both the Chinese elderly and their adult children, between the old and the young, the traditional and the modern.

Ikels (1983) identified several factors impacting on the adjustment of the elderly in Hong Kong. These relate to education, economic resources, and the availability of descendants or kin. She also pointed to gender differences at this stage in life. Chinese men, who, as males, had the benefit of more education, were more literate than their female counterparts. Consequently, they held better-paid jobs, which could put them in a more enviable financial situation than the

females. These factors could significantly affect how men adjusted to their retirement years. For example, it is not uncommon in Hong Kong to see elderly
Chinese men who frequent teahouses, where they meet and chat with friends,
who read the newspaper, or who go for walks with their pet birds. These are
socially acceptable activities often accorded elderly men. The majority of elderly
women of the present generation, on the other hand, had little or no formal
schooling and are generally illiterate (Ikels, 1983). Subsequently, whatever jobs
they held tended to be low-skilled, with low job security; in their old age, they
need to rely on others, usually their children, for sustenance. Traditional expectations also confine them to their families, where they spend their days helping
in family chores. Their usual pastimes do not go beyond the joys of the radio
or television or just sitting and resting after the day's work is done. Because
they are unable to read proficiently, the pleasure of reading is denied them. For
those unfortunate females who have no descendants or kin, their future is pre-
dictably gloomy. They have to spend their aging years searching for part-time
or casual employment or relying on government or charities for support.

With retirement come a decline in income and a devaluation in social status.
For the privileged, educated, and professional individuals, the change of status
is softened by the recognition that they still have something to contribute to
society, their knowledge and experience, and they usually do not have financial
worries but are self-sufficient. If they are not living with their adult children,
then they can rely on hired help to take care of their daily living. In fact, they
can truly enjoy the proverbial golden years. These individuals are the rare exception among the Chinese elderly in Hong Kong; the majority of the elderly
have to recognize that their wage-earning years are now over as a result of aging
and deteriorating physical or mental faculties. In this particular free enterprise
society, they are not eligible for pensions or income securities since such benefits
are for the privileged few who are employees of the government or large corporations. The change from a self-reliant to a dependent status is drastic. They
often have to rely on traditional expectations to pull them through this adjustment
period. Here, the practice of the patrilocal residence pattern provides a safety
net in their old age. Since throughout their adult life, they have expended their
efforts to support their children, especially their sons, now is the time for their
efforts to be repaid. Their sons are now obligated to provide for their aging
parents' needs, in the form of shelter, food, and necessities. The loss of income
from the elderly parents and the added expense of supporting them can put
constraints on the workng-class family. These constraints could be financial,
physical, or emotional, creating stress on the entire family.

Health or illness could be a problematic issue for the Chinese elderly. The
educated, Westernized younger generation accepts Western medical practices as
a convenient and superior way to treat illness; the more traditional older generation is still reliant on traditional Chinese medical practices for ailments. In
Hong Kong there is government support for Western medicine, making it easily
available for the masses (Ikels, 1983), but Chinese medicine does not qualify

for government support. Those who frequent Chinese practitioners have to pay from their limited resources. For the traditionally minded elderly, the treatment of illness is cultural and psychological, rooted to beliefs and practices handed down from generations and crucial to their well-being; in the absence of a culturally sensitive health care system in Hong Kong, illness in old age can cause undue burden for families.

In a rapidly advancing technological society that still maintains traditional roots, old age can be challenging years for the Chinese elderly; society does not make adjustments for them or give them the deference and security they have worked for all their lives. They have to make major adjustments in order to accommodate their adult children, changing societal and cultural values, and the perpetual problems of aging. In this sense, the Hong Kong Chinese elderly may not be alone; they are joining the universal problems of aging in a Western society.

SUMMARY AND CONCLUSIONS

The study of gender roles in Hong Kong society has generated some interesting findings. Unlike other countries, where gender-role development can take its natural course through generations, in Hong Kong it is telescoped within a short time, sometimes in one generation. Besides the time factor, there are other significant factors in gender development: socioeconomic status, level of education, professional status, continuity of traditional practices, exposure to Western influences, and residence status. Each in its own way intervenes in every stage of life of the Chinese male and female in Hong Kong. In a rapidly changing urban society, these help to bridge the gap between the sexes and promote more equality and sharing in gender roles, at least among the younger generation.

In the early years of childhood, dramatic changes in child-rearing practices among the young Hong Kong parents can be observed, even though a modicum of tradition still remains. As the parents become better educated, they are adapting to more Western customs, which are consistent with the structural and economic changes in their society; as a result many of the ways in which they bring up their children are not unlike those of North America or Western Europe. Whether they will reach the level of the androgynous child is questionable, as Chinese young parents will continue to search for their identity in an increasingly Westernized society.

Inevitably, Chinese youngsters in the school years cannot escape the march of progress. The social prestige placed on a Western education, which ultimately determines their place in the social and economic order, affects the way they interact with each other and how they will progress in society. Parents insist on educational achievement for their children, as educational achievement is a strong force toward social mobility. The fact that education is usually reserved for the intellectually and academically capable, male or female, has helped to break down old gender barriers, albeit mostly for the elite. For the bulk of the student population, remnants of educational streaming based on gender still prevail. However, industrial progress and market economy will likely shape the future of education and interpersonal behaviors between the genders in Hong Kong.

As young Chinese adults step into the work world, they inevitably come into contact with peers and colleagues. In the work setting, traditions are gradually taken over by industrial and economic demands for high technology and professional expertise. Gender delineation is not markedly noticeable here, for it is the highly skilled individual who wins out in the competition. In the social setting, where young adults are planning for their future, socialization and dating practices still follow traditions. This is where young men and women learn to play out their socially assigned roles in a formal society. Socioeconomic status and level of education are still major determinants of the social order, regulated by gender, among young adults in Hong Kong society.

Rising levels of education and increasing numbers of working women are unfolding phenomena among maturing Chinese adults in Hong Kong. This population must now come to terms with different demands within the family and in the broader society. The phenomena usher in changes in the social structure of the family. With working wives and working daughters making substantial contributions to the family coffers, their cries for structural changes in traditional authority must be heard. Male superiority is replaced by nearly equal power and share of responsibilities between the marriage partners. Stereotypical expectations and behaviors are questioned by both men and women, in particular in regard to patrilocal residence patterns; the nuclear family is rapidly becoming the norm of future Hong Kong families.

The present generation of Chinese elders can be considered pioneers in the emerging social order in Hong Kong. Unlike the past, where old age demanded deference and accommodation from the younger generation, the elderly now have to make significant adjustments. Tensions exist between new and old, traditional and modern practices. However, insufficient time is given to this group to iron out the problems, and among these senior citizens traditional gender roles and values are still flourishing. Unfortunately, the elderly are the victims of a changing society. But the ultimate victim is still the female, stripped of social, economic, and individual power in families and in the society.

Looking at the adaptation trends in Hong Kong's brief history, one can see a Western tide sweeping over the Colony at a rapid rate seldom seen anywhere in the world. As twilight casts its shadows over this British colony with a Chinese face, one cannot help but wonder what new economic and political changes or uncertainties it will bring to the society, in particular to the Chinese family. Will the Hong Kong Chinese men and women follow the existing Western order, or will they adapt to the realities of becoming part of the People's Republic of China? Will gender development among the Hong Kong Chinese be arrested or accelerated in the next fifty years? This will be another chapter in Hong Kong's history.

REFERENCES

Cheung, F. M., Lam, M. C., & Chau, B.T.W. (1990). Caregivers' techniques and preschool children's behavior in Hong Kong. In Chan, B.P.K., & Smilansky, M. (Eds.), *Early Childhood in the 21st Century: A Worldwide Perspective* (pp. 403–12). Hong Kong: Yew Chung Education.

Cheung, T. S., & Tam, S. Y. (1984). *An Analysis of the Self-Esteem of Adolescents in Hong Kong.* Hong Kong: Center for Hong Kong Studies.

Ho, D.Y.F. (1976–77). Traditional patterns of socialization in China. *Psyche*: 7–39.

———. (1986). Chinese patterns of socialization: A critical review. In Bond, M. H. (Ed.), *The Psychology of Chinese People* (pp. 1–37). Hong Kong: Oxford University Press.

Ikels, C. (1983). *Aging and Adaptation: Chinese in Hong Kong and the United States.* Hamden, CT: Archon Books.

Jacobs, J. B. (1975). Continuity and change in the contemporary Chinese family. *Asian Survey*, *15* (8): 882–91.

Lau, S. K., & Kuan, H. C. (1988). *The Ethos of the Hong Kong Chinese.* Hong Kong: The Chinese University Press.

Mitchell, R. E. (1972a). *Family Life in Urban Hong Kong, I and II.* Taipei: The Orient Cultural Service.

———. (1972b). Husband-wife relations and family-planning practices in urban Hong Kong. *Journal of Marriage and the Family*, *34*: 134–46.

——— (1972c). *Pupil, Parent and School: A Hong Kong Study.* Taipei: The Orient Cultural Service.

Ng, P.P.T. (1981). Social factors contributing to fertility decline. In King, A. Y. C., & Lee, R.P.L. (Eds.), *Social Life and Development in Hong Kong.* Hong Kong: The Chinese University Press.

———. (1984). *Social-Demographic Patterns of Leisure Behavior of Adolescents in Hong Kong.* Hong Kong: Centre for Hong Kong Studies.

Richard, Abbott M. (1983). *Masculine and Feminine—Sex Roles over the Life Cycle.* Reading, MA: Addison-Wesley.

Romer, N. (1981). *The Sex-Role Cycle: Socialization from Infancy to Old Age.* Old Westbury, NY: Feminist Press.

Salaff, J. W. (1981). *Working Daughters of Hong Kong.* Cambridge: Cambridge University Press.

Wong, A. K. (1972). *The Kaifong Associations and the Society of Hong Kong.* Taipei: The Orient Cultural Service.

Wong, F. M. (1975). Industrialization and family structures in Hong Kong. *Journal of Marriage and the Family*, *37*: 985–1000.

———. (1981). Effects of the employment of mothers on marital role and power differentiation in Hong Kong. In King, A.Y.C., & Lee, R.P.L. (Eds.), *Social Life and Development in Hong Kong.* Hong Kong: The Chinese University Press.

Yu, A. Y., & Bain, B. C. (1985). *Language, Social Class and Cognitive Style: A Comparative Study of Unilingual and Bilingual Education in Hong Kong and Alberta.* Hong Kong: Hong Kong Teachers' Association.

10

India

Nalini Deka

INTRODUCTION

India is in Southeast Asia. It is separated from Central Asia by the natural barriers of the great Himalayan range, from West Asia by the Arabian Sea, and from the nations of the Far East by the Bay of Bengal. Its neighbors are Pakistan in the northwest, China and Nepal in the northeast, and Bangladesh and Burma in the east. Peninsular India is bounded by the seas and the Indian Ocean. Sri Lanka, its southernmost neighbor, is separated from the mainland by a few miles of ocean.

The total land mass measures some 2,012.5 miles from south to north and some 1,862.5 miles from west to east. Much of India's landmass lies between the equator and the tropic of Cancer, and therefore it has largely a tropical climate; nevertheless, a wide variety of climatic contrasts may be observed. The dry desert of Rajasthan contrasts with the wet humidity of Assam, and the below zero–degree temperatures of Himachal and Ladakh contrast with the equatorial heat of Kerala and Tamilandu.

India is the second most populated nation of the world. The total population of India in 1981 was 685,184,692, increased to 843,930,861 on 1 March 1991. The decennial growth of population has been 23.5 percent. The overall density of population in 1981 was 216 persons per square kilometer, but it rose sharply to 267 persons per square kilometer in 1991 (Bose, 1991). There has therefore been an increase of 51 persons per square kilometer in the country during the decade.

The sex ratio (number of females per 1,000 males), as recorded by the 1981 census, is 929, as against 934 in the 1991 census. The sex ratio has therefore declined in the country during the decade.

OVERVIEW

The 1991 census carried out by the government of India reveals a very disquieting trend with respect to sex ratios in the northern and southern states of India. The number of missing women in the Hindi-speaking northern belt, comprising the states of Uttar Pradesh, Bihar, Madhya Pradesh, Rajasthan, Punjab and Haryana, Himachal, Jammu and Kashmir, is much higher than in the southern states of Karnataka, Maharashtra, Tamil Nadu, and Kerala. The shortfall of women in India was worked out by Dreze and Sen (1989) by comparing the sex ratio of India with that of sub-Saharan Africa (an area ravaged by droughts and famines). This economically backward region has a sex ratio of 1,022 whereas India, with a better gross national product (GNP), compares poorly. According to Dreze and Sen (1989), there are 41 million missing women in India, and more than two-thirds are accounted for by the Hindi-speaking states. The relatively richer states of Punjab and Haryana have much lower ratios than Andhra Pradesh and Orissa, which are relatively poorer. Thus poverty, though an important variable, is not the only determining factor for the missing women in India.

Nagaraja (1991), in his article on gender trends, observes that a low sex ratio is basically a reflection of the role played or position held by women or of their deprivation relative to men. He examines the reasons for the large number of missing women. Assuming that there is a likelihood of an undercount of females in the census and that the sex ratio at birth favors the male (generally about 105 male babies are born to every 100 females), nonetheless one cannot account for the massive shortfall by these two factors alone. The single most important factor then is greater female mortality in relation to the mortality of males over the past several decades. The greater female mortality at birth and during the period of childhood reflects the degree of discrimination against the female child in India. The girl child is deprived of adequate nutrition and medical care during the crucial years of early childhood. The infant mortality rate between birth and four years for females (36.8 per 1,000 population) is significantly higher than that of males (33.6), and again it is higher during the childbearing age (15–34 years) because of complications during pregnancy and childbirth. This clearly reflects the sociocultural prejudices against girls in India.

In terms of demographic data, the status of women in the southern states of India is marginally better than that of their counterparts in the north. The north-south division essentially means that (1) while discrimination against females does exist, it is lower than in the north and (2) the consequences of discrimination, particularly in terms of greater female mortality, appear to be less damaging in the south (Nagaraja, 1991).

Why does the south have a lower gender discrimination than the north? Several social, cultural, and economic factors contribute to this. The literacy level for females from the southern states (49.76) is much higher than that for females from the north (25.07). The participation rate in nondomestic work is higher for women from the southern states. According to the 1981 census, 26.96 percent of the women from the southern states were working while the corresponding number for the north is only 15.56 percent. The pattern of sex-role identity in the north places the women in a much more disadvantaged position.

COMPARISONS BETWEEN MEN'S AND WOMEN'S GENDER ROLES DURING THE LIFE CYCLE

Any comparison of the gender roles of men and women in India must take into account the historic traditions, customs, and rituals that have shaped the social life of its inhabitants.

Hindus make up 83.82 percent of the total population, 10 percent are Muslims, and only 3 percent are Christians. The Sikhs, Buddhists, and other communities make up the remaining 3 percent (Census of India, 1981: 2–3). Thus the Hindus are overwhelmingly the dominant community in India. Therefore the traditions and customs of the Hindus are examined in the description of the life cycles of men and women in India.

In the Hindu tradition the image of the human life cycle, or *dharma*, has been given in the *Dharma Shastras*[1] (600 B.C.). *Dharma* represents the law, moral duty, or right action. It is the means by which a person achieves everlasting peace.

According to Kakkar (1978), the understanding of one's *Swadharma*, or role, occurs through the narration of stories and parables by mothers, grandmothers, and others in the circle of the extended family. *Dharma* is not only the principle of individual action and social relations but also the ground plan for an ideal life cycle. It defines the tasks at the different stages of life and the way each stage would be lived. Like modern theories of personality, the Hindu model of *Ashramadharma*[2] envisages development in a succession of stages. The stepwise progression from one stage to the next requires the performance of certain tasks and the realization of certain virtues. The Hindu model of *Ashramadharma* has been schematically compared with Erikson's psychosocial stages in Table 10.1. The similarities between the two models are indeed interesting and illuminating as both theories proceed along the same basic premise, except that one is in the form of religious prescription for attaining *moksha*[3] while the other has clinical implications for mental health.

Thus each stage or *ashram* clearly demarcates the role assigned to the male at different stages of his life cycle, but it provides little direction to the female in the performance of her tasks. Her *dharma* lies in fulfilling the different roles assigned to her. Of her own destiny and fate she has no control. Thus the identity of the Hindu women is not an independent notion but a series of role relationships as daughter, daughter-in-law, wife, and mother. She achieves the highest status as the mother of a son.

Many of the inequalities between men and women seen in today's modern India can be attributed to the influence of the Aryan religious practices—ritual

Table 10.1

Comparison of the Schemata in the Development of the Life Stages

ERIKSON'S SCHEME		HINDU SCHEME	
Stage	Specific Task (Crisis): and 'Virtue' (Favorable Outcome)	Stage	Specific Task and 'Virtue'
1. Infancy	Basic & Trust vs. Mistrust: Hope	Individual's prehistory- not explicitly considered	Preparation of the capacity to comprehend <u>dharma</u>
2. Early Childhood	Autonomy vs. Shame, Doubt: Selfcontrol		
3. Play Age	Initiative vs. Guilt: Purposefulness		
4. School Age	Industry vs. Inferiority: Competence	1. Apprenticeship (<u>brahmacharya</u>)	Knowledge of <u>dharma</u>: Competence and Fidelity
5. Adolescence	Identity vs. Role Confusion: Fidelity/Devotion		
6. Youth	Intimacy vs. Isolation: Love	2. Householder (<u>garhasthya</u>)	Practice of <u>dharma</u>: Love and Care
7. Adulthood	Generativity vs. Stagnation: Production/Care	3. Withdrawal (<u>vanaprastha</u>)	Teaching of <u>dharma</u>: Extended Care
8. Old Age	Integrity vs. Despair: Wisdom	4. Renunciation (<u>samnyasa</u>)	Realization of <u>dharma</u>: Wisdom

Sources: Sudhir Kakkar, *Identity and Adulthood* (Delhi: Oxford University Press, 1979); and E.H. Erikson, *Identity, Youth, and Crisis* (New York: Norton, 1968).

roles—prescribed in the ancient religious texts: the Vedas and the Shastras. The Aryans were primarily a patriarchal pastoral society. Their gods were males, as mentioned in the *Rig Veda*—Brahma,[4] Vishnu,[5] and Shiva.[6] The later Vedic texts, however, included important female deities. According to Chattopadhyay in the pre-Aryan societies of Mohanjodaro and Harappa, matriarchal and materialistic, *prakriti*,[7] the female principle, was fundamental. The female goddess was therefore the principal deity. The Aryans, on the other hand, were philosophical, idealist patriarchs and emphasized the predominance of the male principle *purusha*.[8] When the Aryans overran these cultures, they absorbed and assimilated the deities of these tribes. This constituted the smaller traditions of the Hindu belief system. The gods of the Aryans in the smaller tradition were provided with consorts; for example, Lakshmi the goddess of wealth was the wife of Vishnu, and Durga Parvati was the wife of Shiva. The social supremacy that the female enjoyed in the pre-Vedic period was undermined and displaced by the male-dominated Vedic traditions. The degeneration of the female role can be directly traced to Manu, who, in about the third century B.C. is supposed to have codified the ritual roles and practices of males and females in the *Manusmriti*.[9] The role assigned to the woman was inferior, and at all times, from birth to death, she was governed, disciplined, and shaped to serve her lords and masters. Thus the *Manusmriti* was essentially "fiercely misogynist." Henceforth until the advent of Islam, there was a gradual depletion of the female status and position in the Hindu life-style.

The "Bhakti movement" in India provided some relief to the oppressed female, as the path of devotion set up no barriers of caste and sex. Further, the movement was a people's revolt against domination of the upper caste and Brahmin priests and the lifeless rituals of Vedic Hinduism that they preached. A number of Bhakti poets were women, who chafed at the strictures of the household and family and the numbing triviality of household chores. The women's writings of this period (about A.D. 1000) reflect the struggle of women against their prescribed roles as daughters, wives, and daughters-in-law. The only route for escape was to don the mantle of a woman devoted to God (e.g., Akkama Devi,[10a] Mirabai[10b]).

At the turn of the twentieth century the role and status of women in India reached its *nadir*. The long period of subjugation to alien cultures (first Islamic and then the British) created a strong xenophobia among the Hindu elite and middle class. The accompanying feelings of insecurity led them to adopt practices such as child-marriage and *sati*[11] to protect their cultural identity. Since the female was the repository of family honor, she was to be protected. The only way to do this was to adopt the *purdah* and enclose her within four walls, to marry her off before puberty, and coerce her to commit self-immolation in the event of her husband's death. The upper-caste and middle-class Hindu women were completely confined to their homes. The realm of work and activity did not extend beyond the four walls of their homes. The birth of a girl was viewed as a curse, and female infanticide was practiced in several communities in India. The infamous practice of *sati* was also common among the Rajputs of Rajasthan and Punjab. Social reformers like Raja Ram Mohan Roy and Ishwar Chandra Vidya Sagar fought hard against the Hindu fundamentalists to remove these unsavory practices from Hinduism, to bring society back to the path of *dharma*. Industrialization in the West also had an impact on the educated, upper middle-class, urban Hindu families. Victorian views were assimilated through books and writings, and the image of being a well-bred gentlewomen, with no useful (economic) skills, was cultivated. The home chores were assigned to the mem-sahib's servants,[12] and leisure time was spent in a round of clubs and mindless gossip. At the same time the woman of rural India remained immersed in the multiplicity of her various roles and continued to suffer behind the *purdah*, or the veil of modesty, which she was forced to wear.

Infancy and Early Childhood

Lives of women without children
Like oxen hired out
Like a plantation leaf discussed after a meal.
—Translated from a Kannada folk song by Taijiswini Niranjan

This southern Indian folk song very poignantly underlines the importance of becoming a mother in India. An Indian woman comes into her own only after she has given birth to a child. A host of rituals accompanies the birth of a baby. Some of these rituals are common to the birth of a child of either sex, while several are observed only at the birth of a son.

All Indians, whether from the south or the north, strongly desire a son. Vedic verses pray that sons will be followed by still more male offspring—never by females (Kakkar, 1978). All prayers and entreaties mentioned in the *Atharvaveda*[13] are for a son, never for a daughter, since the birth of a daughter is viewed as a necessary burden to be borne—at best for a while—until she is old enough to be married. At the birth of a son, the entire household rejoices, sweets are sent for, and conch shells are blown. All those who attended the mother during the birth are handsomely rewarded. The daughter-in-law's position and status are enhanced the moment she becomes the mother of a baby boy. All her needs are immediately attended to, and the mother-in-law prepares special sweets mixed with herbs and clarified butter, which are believed to increase the supply of milk for the infant.

Kakkar (1978) observes, "Women's folk songs reveal the painful awareness of inferiority . . . of this discrepancy at birth, between the celebration of sons and the mere tolerance of daughters." This is not to say that the birth of a baby girl is never welcomed. The first female child for a couple is always welcomed, even though no elaborate celebrations are held. She is described as *Lakshmi*, the harbinger of wealth and prosperity, and blessings are showered on her so that "her birth may be followed by that of a male child."

In parts of northern India significant rituals are attached to the thirteenth and fourteenth days after birth. These are auspicious days when the mother emerges from her confinement and is allowed to meet with friends and relatives. Folk songs extolling her good fortune for having delivered a son are sung, and there is much exchanging of gifts. The young mother's parents send expensive gifts to her parents-in-law, and all members of the husband's family, especially other sisters and brothers and their wives, are given a set of clothes (saris and suits), according to the economic level of the in-law household.

The birth of a male child has *dharmic* significance, since several important religious rites and sacraments, especially at the time of death, must be performed by sons only. According to the Vedic tradition the soul of the parents will not achieve *moksha* if the ceremonies are not performed by the son. Thus those unfortunate people who have no male heirs generally adopt a child from among their kin to ensure their peace in the other world.

This obvious gender discrimination against girls has certain economic reasons attached to it. The daughter is viewed as an economic burden, since she takes away a considerable part of the family's wealth as her dowry. In villages, poor farmers often get into a debt trap in order to provide for a daughter's wedding and dowry. Besides, her contribution is toward only domestic chores since no self-respecting father would send his daughter out to work and earn money. This is still the scenario in the villages and small towns of India. In the large cities and urban industrialized townships, women have made rapid progress. In nuclear families with only one or two children, this gender discrimination is gradually disappearing. A girl is being trained to become economically independent.

Despite the social and cultural directives against the girl child, daughters are not denied affection. Generally, mothers are protective and indulgent toward daughters, and they are treated with solicitous concern. Often the brothers are told not to disturb their sisters, as they are *paraya dhan*, belonging to someone else, and, like guests, must soon leave forever. The mother-daughter relationship is deeply empathic, for the mother knows that, like herself, her daughter too must go away and take her place among strangers.

The young girl in India acquires her feminine role not only from her mother, who is the primary role model, but also from others, including aunts, cousins, grandmothers, and sisters, who make up the extended family. Thus a girl imperceptibly absorbs all the skills for becoming a good daughter-in-law in the process of interacting with the other women in her extended family (Kumar, 1989, 1991).

The mother-infant son relationship is indeed unique to the Indian experience and has been the focus of much anthropological and psychoanalytic attention. The infant son is completely indulged from the time of his birth. He is fed on demand, sometimes well beyond the infancy period. Thus there develops a deep and intimate attachment between the mother and the son, which lasts until the son starts school. The infant son is constantly in contact with his mother. All his wishes are instantly gratified, and at the slightest sign of distress he is picked up and given the breast—not necessarily that of the mother. The son often sleeps with the parents until he is five or six years old. There is very little toilet training, and the child takes his own time to learn to control his bowels.

Thus the period of infancy and early childhood in traditional Indian homes is essentially a period of love and nurturing, rather than love and control. In the modernized nuclear families of the cities, the gender discrimination is not readily apparent. Usually the urban nuclear household consists of two children and the parents. Toilet training and weaning are deliberate tasks, but handled in a less traumatic fashion compared with the custom of some Western parents. Very seldom is a child admonished for soiling his clothes. Usually some kind of household help is available, which makes the task of parenting easier.

In terms of dress there is little gender differentiation during early childhood. Generally the very comfortable, loose garment resembling a frock is worn, even by boys, till children are able to walk. Once the toddler is mobile, the choice of clothes becomes gender-specific. The boy may wear only an undergarment, but the girl child is modestly covered. According to Veena Das (1979), the treatment of the body in childhood emphasizes separate value orientations for boys and girls. At an early age girls are made aware of their femininity. A visit to the bazaar usually means the purchase of bangles, dolls, and artificial jewelry for the girls and some kind of mechanical toy for the boys. However, in general, in rural India, little boys play outside their homes with sticks, old tires, slings, and so on. They are seldom seen to play with toys. While a boy is encouraged to go out and play, from early childhood the play activity of little girls is confined to their home.

School Years

The end of childhood for the upper-caste male children in the traditional Hindu homes is marked by a ceremony called the *Upnayana*, or the sacred thread ceremony. This also marks the boy's entry into the male world when his intense relationship with his mother is severed. This sudden break from the nurturant mother often appears traumatic to the boy; he is then admonished to bear it like a man. The father usually appears to be a cold and distant figure, who has to be respected and obeyed. The father-son relationship is usually a formal one without the close attachment that was so characteristic of the mother-son relationship.

The son is sent to the school selected by the father; he is expected to study hard and obey his *guru*, or teacher, and lead the life of a *brahmacharya*.[14] The masculine identity of the child is nurtured and gradually strengthened under the firm hand of male members of the family other than the father. The father does not appear to the child to be a friend or ally, but a difficult taskmaster, and the boy's resentment and anger are often directed against the father.

In the urban nuclear setup, however, the boy's relationship with the mother is never so drastically severed. The father begins to take on the role of a teacher and disciplinarian as soon as the boy enters the primary level of education. The girl, on the other hand, does not experience this sudden and traumatic break so early. She continues to remain in an affectionate relationship with her mother and gradually adopts her nurturant role as she enters puberty.

Since the young girl in India is always the repository of the family honor during the different stages of her life cycle, her entry into school is also perceived in the same light. It is widely acknowledged nowadays in all castes and communities that girls, too, must be taught to read and write; nonetheless school is considered essential for the boy and not for the girl. Sending the girl to school means one less hand to help with the domestic chores. The concerted campaign by the government to change these attitudes in rural India has yielded some results. The fifth All India Educational Survey carried out by the national Council of Educational Research and Training in New Delhi revealed that the percentage of enrollment of girls in the primary to secondary school was consistently lower than that of boys. By Class V (the fifth grade), the enrollment figures drop sharply for girls and so does the drop-out rate. The drop-out rate for the girls of Class I (the first grade) is nearly 70.04 percent, whereas that of boys is 60.7 percent. This indicates that there is socioeconomic discrimination against the young girls. If the family cannot afford to send all the children to school, it is usually the eldest girl in the family who is deprived of education.

In Class VIII (the eighth grade) the enrollment figures are an appalling 17.7 percent for girls, as compared with 51.82 percent for boys. This dramatic decrease can be attributed to puberty, when the girl is twelve or thirteen and therefore not allowed to mix and play with boys. The family honor requires that she be confined to the home and remain in the company of other female members of the household until she is suitably married.

It is hoped that all the efforts being made by international and national agencies will improve the enrollment figures for girls in the 1990s. In order to lower the drop-out rate, it is essential that the attitudes of parents change. In modern India more and more young men are moving to the cities for employment and in the process are perceiving the need for wives who are at least literate. Thus with greater urbanization the hold of traditional attitudes is gradually weakening.

At all times during the period of his education the boy is reminded of the fact that he has to be the breadwinner and look after his parents in their old age. It is essential, therefore, for the boy to crystallize his future role and work toward it. He has the choice to select his role and future identity to the extent the economic status of the family allows; but for the girls there is only one identity, to be a homemaker. Any other role is viewed as secondary to the primary one. During the 1960s and 1970s the educational policy for girls emphasized the need for subjects in secondary schools that would be suitable for them in their role as a housewife and mother. Thus education, too, was made an instrument for confining the female to her traditional primary role.

The new subject in secondary schools, colleges, and universities that should prepare women generally for a job is home science (home economics). Through this subject women are to be given the necessary basic training that prepares them for the three roles that Indian society prescribes for them: (1) the housewife-mother role (which still has priority), (2) the economic role (which acquires ever greater importance with growing economic pressures), and (3) the role of service to society (which belongs to the ideal of the Indian woman since the independence movement) (Report of the Education Commission, 1964–1966: 314).

The preferred subjects for girls in secondary schools are generally the humanities, home science, and the arts, while for boys there are science and business courses. Among most southern Indian families, along with the formal education, the girl is taught to be proficient in music, either vocal or instrumental, at an early age. Dance is taught to enhance the girl's grace and carriage. These subjects are also taught at the university level. The young girl is encouraged to aspire to become a teacher, rather than a doctor, administrator, or engineer as these would seriously jeopardize her primary role as mother-housekeeper. The major aim of education is to improve marriage prospects.

No household chores are assigned to the boys in the family who are encouraged to go on for higher education. Only those chores that require a visit to the market for purchase of goods and groceries, which normally is not performed by the girls in the family, are given them. The girl is expected to serve her brother his meals, wash up, and look after his sundry needs, while the son is free to loaf around with his pals and cronies.

The girl's peer group is limited to her immediate neighborhood. She can meet her friends and go to their homes only with permission. Usually leisure time is spent in learning sewing or embroidery, exchanging a recipe, or other such skills that will enhance her prospects as a match. Thus in the traditional household the girl's upbringing is strictly monitored, and all traits toward self-assertion and independence are quickly suppressed and nipped in the bud. The boy, however, is brought up with relatively less discipline, since he is not expected to learn any household chores; he grows up into a young man totally dependent on the female for a number of tasks related to his toilette, food, and general appearance.

Young Adulthood

Youth is a distinct and important period in the life cycle of the individual. It ends the period of childhood and adolescence and starts the period of productive adulthood. Psychologically this period has been viewed as a period of crises. Erikson refers to it as the period of identity (role) confusion, since young men at this stage have not yet crystallized their future role and goals. Most young men experience this state of confusion and express it in a variety of forms. Many find life meaningless, competition "abhorrent," and the need to achieve "stifling" or "petty bourgeoise." This phenomenon is seen among some Western youths and among the educated urban middle class in India.

Modern Indian society, having broken with its traditional past, is going through a period of transition. Old beliefs, attitudes, and social structures have, at best, weakened or are changing, though, as yet, no new values have taken their place. Thus Indian society as a whole is in a state of Eriksonian confusion. At present the structured society of the past has become fragmented, as it cannot provide solutions to the present problems. On one hand, there exists a strong desire for self-sufficiency, independence, and individuality, but on the other hand, a pathetic clinging to ancient rituals persists to give some semblance of continuity with the past. With such a scenario the problems of the young become further accentuated and express themselves in militancy, terrorism, and a revolt against the establishment. Consequently, defining their role in society becomes a daunting task indeed for males and females.

The way Indian society has to some extent resolved this problem is to extend the period of study from Class XII (twelfth grade) to college. A Bachelor of Arts or Science (B.A. or B.S.) is viewed as imperative for a young man, as well as for a young woman, among the urban middle class. In India higher education is almost free; therefore all levels of society can aspire to give their youths some kind of college or university education. This period of three years that young men and women spend in a liberal arts college is a means of postponing their making a decision with regard to their future role as active participants in society. This keeps the youths from getting into trouble. It also provides an opportunity to select and discard different ideologies, roles, and value systems. Colleges and universities therefore function as "tension-release systems" in the current society. Only a small number of fortunate young men and women are able to gain admission into the prestigious technical institutions, which prepare them for a specific career. For the vast majority an arts education merely provides a certificate stating "education unemployed."

Rural India lacks an adolescent culture. The burden of adult responsibilities falls quickly on young people, and they have to learn the appropriate skills (housework or agricultural chores for young women and some form of artisan or mechanical work for young men) in order to contribute to the family maintenance. A large number of young men seek employment in the borderline sectors in cities and busy metropolises, which leads to the creation of urban slums that, in turn, have their own distinct culture and problems.

An important feature of both urban and rural youth is the prolonged dependency on the father and the family for all decisions with regard to their future career and role in society. A vocational choice is seldom based on aptitudes and interest, but instead it is based on the expectations the father has for his son. The economic burden for training a young man in the skills of a vocation is borne entirely by the family, sometimes at the cost of educating their daughters. Most often a girl is married by the time she is 15 to 16 years old. According to the 1981 census the mean age of marriage of rural girls was 16.51 whereas for urban girls it was marginally better at 17.63 years (Saxena, 1989).

Education is an important variable determining the mean age of marriage. It has been observed that as the educational level increases, the mean age when young women get married also increases; and this is true for both rural and urban women (Saxena, 1989). Among the modern, middle-class, urban families, more and more people are realizing the need to give their daughters higher education, though the future social roles of females will define educational needs and goals. Not only is the instrumental value of education different for young men and women, but there are no clear specifications for women's higher education. The possibility of a young woman getting educated is determined by factors such as whether the girl is likely to be married, whether there are girls' colleges or institutes available in the vicinity, whether there is sufficient household help, and so on. Neera Desai in her report on Research in Women's Education (1983–1988) observes, "In a society where marriage is obligatory for a woman, a situation is created in which she will pursue her studies as long as marriage is not settled."

Subjects like psychology, sociology, social anthropology, and education are viewed as women's disciplines. The colleges offering these subjects in Delhi are all women's institutions. Only one coeducational college offers psychology, and there, too, more females sign up for these courses than do males.

Westernized parents are not too pleased to send their daughters to coeducational institutions, as this fact may mar the chances of making a good match. The predominance of women in the faculties of arts at various universities has important implications for access to jobs and important positions in later years.

Several private and government-aided polytechnic institutions are now providing opportunities to young people for developing skills in areas of office management, computer system analysis, software programming, interior decoration, fashion designing, journalism, hotel management, food and nutrition, and so on. Most of these institutions are co-educational; therefore, the gender bias gradually, at least in vocational courses, is fast disappearing. One disadvantage is that these institutes are only in the big cities and are expensive. Unfortunately they do not cater to the needs of the vast number of rural and semiurban young people.

Interaction between the sexes during the period of matriculation is usually frowned upon. Men are not allowed to enter the women's institutions except during cultural festivals. Young women generally seek the company of their own gender, though a few who have the opportunity to have a boyfriend do so on the sly. Similarly, boys and young men tend to stay with their own male peer group.

A young man is not supposed to express openly his desire for female company. The elders in the family keep a sharp eye on their sons and daughters to see that they do not deviate from the norms of the society. The practice of dating at this stage of life is therefore negligible. Whatever dating or meeting between the sexes that takes place is usually on the sly or occurs under the sharp eyes and supervision of parents or teachers. Of late some enterprising young men and women have tried to select their life partners during their period of college education, but not many are successful, since young men and women at this stage are still economically dependent on their parents. The parents' cooperation or consent determines whether the couple will ultimately marry.

The mass media and films, particularly Hindi cinema, also have an impact on the attitudes and values of young men and women and reinforce the gender stereotypes existing in society. Most films from the studios of Bombay depict females as sex objects: feminine, delicate, and desirable; while the macho image is emphasized for males. It is no wonder, therefore, that teasing, harassing, molesting, and rape are on the increase in the busy metropolises of India. The female role is being constantly devalued by the mass media, and a most unsatisfactory image is being created. This has an extremely negative impact on the young minds watching such films, advertisements, and serials. Of late the government has given strict orders that programs depicting women as inferior to men not be shown on the national network. But only time can change the entrenched attitudes and values of Indian society.

Adulthood

The period of adulthood corresponds to the *Grihasthaya*, or householder stage, of the *Ashramadharma*. Consequently, marriage and responsibilities of a family are the primary tasks for both genders. Marriage is obligatory for the females but can be optional for the male.

Intimacy, which, according to Erikson, precedes the movement from young adulthood to adulthood, is (according to Hindu tradition) a consequence of shared responsibilities, procreation, and sensuality. There is therefore no intermediate phase of courtship leading to intimacy. The bride for the boy or the groom for the girl is selected by the family, keeping in mind caste, status, and familial requirements.

The rules that govern marriage among most communities of northern India specify that (1) the bride must come from a different village than the groom, (2) she must be of a different clan, or *gotra*, (3) there must be no consanguineous link between the couple, and (4) the couple must be of the same caste (Sharma, 1980).

The matchmaker is usually the village Puorhit or Brahmin. In the punjabi households the elder aunts and sisters-in-law often suggest brides for the young man of their own patriarchal homes. The prospective brides and grooms are generally discreetly looked over during family functions, such as weddings and festivals. The concurrence of the couple is obtained after these brief meetings. It is the matchmaker's responsibility to ascertain the merits and demerits of the boy or girl in question and also to communicate the amount of dowry appropriate to the status and position of the boy's family. The giving of dowry, or *stridhan*, is obligatory for the girl's father, according to the traditional pattern of marriage, or *kanya daan*. The giving away of the daughter is viewed as a religious duty ordained in religious texts and essential for the achievement of merit in the other world.

One important consequence of marriage for the girl is that she moves out of the familiar environment of her own natal family into the completely strange and unfamiliar home of her husband and in-laws. This is the most traumatic event for the girl, especially since the future is a completely unknown quantity among unknown people. Young women in India therefore have a very ambivalent attitude toward marriage. On one hand, they yearn for an intimate relationship and their own home, but on the other hand, the thought of breaking all ties with their familiar natal home appears very threatening. On account of this formidable feature of marriage and womanhood, daughters are given differential treatment and are indulged by their father and mother in their own natal homes.

The departure of the bride from her natal home (*peke*) to her in-law's home (*saure*) has been the subject of several folk songs and couplets. The intense sorrow and grief expressed by all the older female members reenact their own experience and trauma on the departure from their own natal homes. The ritual songs sung at the time of the bride's *doli*, or departure, emphasize the break with all familiar ties, with mother, father, brothers, sisters, peer group, and friends; joining the other family, she has to seek the love and approval of her in-laws from then on. The ideal of Indian womanhood is personified by Sita, the heroine of the epic *Ramayana*, and the ideal of Indian manhood is described in the character of Rama, the hero of the epic. The legend of Rama and Sita is recounted a number of times and generally forms the theme of folk plays and devotional songs.

Sudhir Kakkar (1978) closely examines the influence of this myth in the crystallization of a Hindu woman's identity and character. Kakkar observes that the ideal of Indian womanhood incorporated by Sita is chastity, purity, gentle tenderness, and a singular faithfulness that cannot be destroyed or even disturbed by her husband's rejection. Rama, on the other hand, has all the traits of a godlike hero, yet he is also fragile, mistrustful, jealous, and a conformist, both to his parents' wishes and to social opinion. Thus he is an ideal son and brother but not an ideal husband or father. These expectations an Indian woman incorporates gradually into her inner world. The social relations between a husband and wife are also governed by these idealized images of Rama and Sita and are incorporated into the self.

The bride of the Hindu family is first a daughter-in-law and then a wife. The primary duties are toward her husband's parents and his brothers and sisters, rather than toward her husband. She is expected to be obedient and compliant with the wishes of the elder women in the family. The mother-in-law generally views her daughter-in-law as a usurper of her son's affections and tries all means to minimize the opportunities available to the young couple for the development of intimacy. A son enamored by the guiles of his young wife is likely to forget his duties as a son and brother.

The bride's position in the family undergoes a dramatic change once she becomes pregnant. Motherhood confers upon her a status and crystallizes her identity as a woman in a way no other event in her life cycle does. It is her ultimate good fortune if she gives birth to a son; her position in the family is firmly established.

The impact of Western values of individuality and sexual equality has to some extent weakened the sexual stereotypes operating in HIndu society. However, they are still present in a disguised form, even among the highly educated and Westernized Indian elite.

For the educated Indian woman the additional role of a wage earner has become superimposed on her other roles of mother, wife, and daughter-in-law. This then is a factor contributing to role strain and role conflict experienced by the urban working woman in India.

Discrimination between the sexes is a dominant feature of the employment scene in India. The work participation rates for males and females are a sad reflection of this sociocultural reality. According to Saxena (1989), the largest number of females is to be found under the category of farm workers. Of course, the rate of females in the household industry is also higher than that of males, both in rural and in urban areas. Thus the occupational profile reflects the presence of a gender bias in the choice of occupation.

The traditional occupation for urban, middle-class, educated women is teaching. Most studies carried out on working women are on women teachers; the second largest group is employed in office work, followed by the health sciences. As these jobs are considered less prestigious, there is relatively less competition from males. Nevertheless the total work participation of females in all sectors is still much below that of males; 51.23 percent of males are employed, compared with only 14.44 percent females (Census of India, 1981; Paper 3 of 1982). Mies (1980) observes that the primary reason for women seeking employment outside the home is economic pressures of modern living. A large number of upper-class, educated women, however, choose professions that satisfy their needs for self-actualization, while some others do so because of a desire to use their leisure time more profitably.

In the Ramanamma study nearly 40 percent of the sample reported that they sought employment in order to collect money for their dowry. Today many middle-class families are finding it extremely difficult to manage the large dowries being demanded by prospective grooms and their families; therefore, in order to make a respectable match, women must perforce work to mitigate the burden on their fathers. A few upper-middle-class women work in order to maintain their highly Westernized life-style, which has become a feature of young professional couples who are living in nuclear units in the larger cities. Apart from this purely economic aspect, the desire to become independent and move out of the traditional constraints of the Sita identity is another significant element that has entered into the psyche of Indian women.

The activity outside the home has not changed the basic ideology regarding sex roles and sex-based divisions of labor. Despite the fact that women are bringing in substantial salaries and doing equal work, household chores remain the domain for women. Women, too, consider the fulfillment of both their family obligations and their professional obligations as legitimate and are of the opinion that they are compatible.

Role strain and role conflict are phenomena common to the working woman of any status or community today and sometimes can be a cause of marital discord and separation. Women who earn more than their husbands and have a superior work status often find it extremely difficult to accept a subordinate position in the family hierarchy, leading to marital conflict and maladjustment (Kapur, 1973).

Leisure time in India is generally spent on family activities. Males can still venture out to clubs, recreation centers, and so on, but women prefer to spend their leisure time with their children. Saxena (1989), in her microanalysis of the decision-making domains of Indian women, reports that nearly 66.7 percent of the graduate working women in her study opted for household work as the first choice for using leisure time and 36.6 percent of postgraduate women opted for spending time with the family. Thus in real terms there is hardly any leisure time available to working women in India. Leisure time for the middle-class male means relaxing at home or visiting relatives and friends. The life-style of Indian males tends to be more sedentary than that of their Western counterparts. Membership in health clubs and sports clubs remains restricted to the upper classes. Watching television and the VCR then becomes the only leisure activities that the middle class can afford. The upper class, of course, is the "leisure class" in all cultures, but their life-styles do not reflect the reality of the Indian life-style today.

Old Age

In the 1990s a significant proportion of the Indian population is 60 years and older. According to population pundits, there will be nearly 76 million Indians over the age of 60 at the turn of the century. The life expectancy of men and women has vastly increased from what it was a few decades ago. Life expectancy today is over 62 years for men and 65 years for women, whereas ten years ago it was just 55.4 years for males while females were marginally better (55.7 years). Improved health standards and medical breakthroughs have ushered in an era of longevity which can prove to be either a boon or a disaster, depending upon the way society recognizes and handles the problem of the aged.

Traditionally in India (this is still true of rural India, which constitutes 70 percent of the population) the onset of old age was not viewed with anxiety. People in the fourth *ashrama* or the stage of *vanaprastha* (see Table 10.1) were given their due respect and revered. Silver hair and a wrinkled face were signs of wisdom and experience. The aging patriarch or matriarch always remained a figure of authority. Usually the village Panchayat or council consisted of five elder, prominent members whose word was law for the rest of the village community. The elderly men constituted the decision-making body. All matters regarding the well-being of the village community, including matters relating to property disputes, family honor, festivals, and marriages, were discussed in these gatherings. The village folk generally abided by the decisions arrived at in the Panchayat. The elderly male members therefore continued to provide advice and direction to the younger members of their community. Elderly women, however, did not figure in the decision-making council. It is only recently that some village Panchayats have allowed the representation of women. In communities where women contribute equally to the village economy, the government has ensured that they take part in the decision-making councils.

The deference accorded to senior women is directly proportionate to their years. Thus a woman who is a much-respected elder citizen of her village does not mind adding a few years to her age to establish her advisory status. Even today the onset of old age is not viewed with as much anxiety as it is in the West. The appearance of gray hair and wrinkles is inevitable, and therefore the women in India accept their age gracefully. The average Indian woman does not try to hide her age or compete with younger colleagues for male attention. Physical appearance is not at a premium in this society. Modesty, grace, and qualities of head and heart are more important assets than physical beauty, which is short-lived and fleeting. Therefore, the onset of old age need not translate into loss of self-esteem or into self-devaluation. Nalini Singh, a well-known television personality on the Indian television network, interviewed several young, middle-aged, and elder women with regard to their need to ''look good.'' The program telecast on 5 June 1992 covered a cross-section of women who were regular visitors to the different beauty parlors in Bombay. The responses to the question ''Why do you come to the beauty parlor?'' were varied and reflected the new awareness to look attractive and feel fit. Generally, the feeling was that it was necessary to look well groomed and neat at all ages. One respondent pointed out that a visit to the beauty parlor gave her confidence in meeting and interacting with people, while another observed that she liked to look dignified and well appointed. Indian women do not, as a rule, hanker after a youthful figure or a flawless skin after they have become mothers. Motherhood bestows on women a status and identity that transcend all other maidenly images of lissome beauty. The matronly figure of middle-age affords the woman a sense of security, so that she can move around freely without comment or innuendo.

Menopause for the woman in rural India is still a welcome phase in the life cycle, for it relieves her from the drudgery of childbirth year after year. It is quite common to find women producing children even after the eldest is married off. Thus menopause affords women the much sought after freedom from recurring pregnancies.

At menopause a woman is expected to relinquish sexual relations with her husband. Husbands may even be admonished for seeking sexual satisfaction or for unseemly behavior. Passing into the stage of Vanaprastha, elderly women gradually relinquish their control over the household chores as soon as the daughter-in-law crosses the threshold. In traditional homes the mother-in-law still remains the ''authority'' whenever customary rituals have to be performed or relationships maintained. Sundry chores and tasks are performed by the daughter-in-law, but all decisions of expenses and running of the home remain with the old matriarch.

In the urban setup, men in their fifties must face the fact of impending retirement, reduced physical fitness, and, in an increasing number of cases, a reduced sex drive. Men, like women, do not aim at physical fitness. The routine of home-office-home is occasionally interrupted by festivals, social obligations, parental demands, and illness. This leaves no time for exercise and other healthy activities.

Club memberships are confined to the upper classes, where older men and women prefer to spend their time playing bridge or poker in the evenings and golf in the mornings.

The aging, Indian, middle-class male is typically a potbellied, balding, harassed-looking figure who must cope with the increasing requirements of his family members with a diminishing income. The major anxiety of the head of the family at this stage of life is to ensure his daughters' marriages and his sons' careers. It is a matter of shame for a father to have an unmarried daughter. To this end all efforts are made to find a suitable match and collect a sufficient dowry.

A daughter's marriage and a son's career often lead the family to incur debt, wipe out all savings, and in several cases may also require the sale of ancestral land and property. The parents, therefore, as they enter old age, become dependent on their sons for their maintenance.

At retirement most middle-class men go through a period of depression as they face the future with diminished energies and without any particular interest or hobby to look forward to. More than the female, the male finds himself at loose ends. The earlier role of being the head of the family and the provider suddenly ends, leaving a vacuum in their lives. Lacking a specific social role, males begin to experience a sense of devaluation and reduced self-esteem, till they come to terms with the new stage of life and begin a new pattern of existence dependent on their children for security and care.

The social roles of women in old age begin to diminish gradually. Some seek mental peace by immersing themselves in the reading of scriptures and pilgrimages to sacred places, temples, and so on. Those who are dependent on their sons take on the responsibility of looking after their grandchildren. As more and more young women take up professional careers, old parents pitch in by helping to look after their children's children. Thus they remain enmeshed in the cobweb of relationships well into their dotage. There are only a fortunate few who can live their independent lives surrounded by servants and experience the freedom to develop their interests, hobbies, and so on and contribute meaningfully to the social welfare of their community.

The status of grandfather or grandmother is endowed with several privileges in Indian society. Despite the change in family structure and the increase in nuclear families, grandparents are still respected and revered. Looking after one's old parents is considered *punya*, that is, it earns merit in the afterlife. A son who does not look after his old mother or father is not respected in society. There are nowadays an increasing number of cases where the old have been abandoned by their kith or kin or left in an old people's home, but these cases are few.

The rapid urbanization and reduction in living space are affecting the lives of old and young alike. This march toward rapid modernization is making old people more and more alienated from the present generation. Tensions of having to live with the young, uncaring generation are forcing many old couples to move away and live separately from their children. The death of a spouse further increases the sense of loneliness, and many old people experience depression and suicidal thoughts. Lack of social security makes the old entirely dependent on their sons for support. This inevitably leads to conflict with daughters-in-law; therefore, interpersonal tensions tend to persist in the life-styles of the elderly. The old widower feels more redundant than the old widow, as women tend to be more involved with their grandchildren and continue to perform the small chores of repairing and darning, pickling and preserving, that continue to provide meaning to their existence. The old man, on the other hand, begins to find himself increasingly becoming a burden, and therefore there are far more cases of depression and involutional melancholia among old men than among old women.

Increasingly, a number of organizations—Helpage, Agecare, Karmika—have responded to the need for developing programs for the aged, in order that their lives can be more meaningful and that the extended gray period of life is spent in self-satisfying roles and productive work. The old cannot be discarded like used paper; a society that is callous in its attitude toward the frail and elderly will some day destroy itself.

The period of *sanyaas*, the last of the five stages, requires the old to detach themselves from all worldly desires, relinquish all relationships, and prepare themselves for their final journey—not an easy task. Only one who has lived a full life and has known all pleasure and sorrows can truly be a *Samnyasa* and await the final event.

SUMMARY AND CONCLUSIONS

The developmental features of gender-role identity reflect the deep impact of tradition, custom, and religion on the psyche of Indian men and women. The ancient law books—the *Dharmashastras*—assign a subservient role to the woman in Hindu society. From birth the discriminatory child-rearing practices contribute to the development of a negative self-image in girls. The male child gets a greater share of parental affection, and little effort is made to curb his natural impulses till the time he begins school.

In childhood the girl is constantly made aware of the fact that she is a burden. Her behavior is closely monitored by her parents and relatives, so that she imbibes the traits required for serving the male in the multiplicity of roles prescribed by the *Shastras*. The girl's education is also geared to her final role of homemaker and mother. The school drop-out rate is much higher for girls than for boys, as the burden of household chores falls heavily on girls. Boys are given very few household chores; the effort is to train them to adopt the role of the breadwinner and head of the family.

The father's primary duty is to select an appropriate groom for his daughter, as soon as she is of marriageable age. Selection of a mate is based on commonality of caste, class, and religion rather than on love and intimacy. The adequacy of the girl's training in her natal home is judged by the ease with which she adjusts into the role of a dutiful daughter-in-law and devoted wife among strangers in the strange environment of a village or city. The boy's primary duty is toward his parents and other members of the extended family. The wife merits attention only occasionally.

Motherhood establishes the status and identity of the daughter-in-law in her husband's home. The birth of a male child and the rituals attached to it further serve to reinforce inferiority about her own sex.

Work outside the home is a phenomenon related to economic pressures generated by modern standards of living. Most women seek employment in home-related industries, teaching, or health services. Gender discrimination in choice of careers is present because these careers enable the woman to balance her role of a homemaker, mother, and money earner. The more demanding jobs of administrator, business executive, and consultant (which are considered male preserves) threaten the primary role and are therefore generally not considered ideal for women.

Old age sees a man and a woman immersed in the duties of grandparents managing their son's children. Respect and reverence formerly accorded the elderly are now fast diminishing, as more and more young men move away from the joint family structures to the nuclear units of the city. Elderly citizens find themselves redundant and useless. They do not fit into the modern life-styles of their children and find themselves an embarrassment. Many old couples prefer to live their lonely lives in the village among familiar surroundings and their own peer group, somehow eking out an existence while waiting for occasional visits from their sons and daughters.

The imperceptibly enculturated, stereotyped gender roles of a dutiful daughter, a devoted wife, and a loving mother, which Indian women have displayed in the different periods of their life cycle through the centuries, are now gradually giving way. A more assertive, discriminating, independent, and liberated image is fast replacing the traditionally submissive and sacrificing one. Women have become aware that they cannot continue to be treated as second-rate or subhuman citizens in a world tailored to support the dominance of men over women.

The numerous surveys carried out by the government on the status of women in India have revealed the deeply entrenched attitudes of discrimination in rearing girls and boys in rural and urban areas alike. In recent times special efforts have been made by both governmental and nongovernmental agencies to eradicate the sex-stereotyped images of men and women in society. This is not an easy task. Even today, despite the promulgation of several laws, the mass media show women in stereotyped roles. The figure of an attractive model is essential for selling men's shirts and pants, while household gadgets always depict the woman in the role of a harassed housewife. Indian cinema is the worst perpetrator of discrimination against the female. Nearly all films exhibit violence against women. The woman is always shown as a sexually attractive, dim-witted, prancing female with little ambition except for marrying the first guy who falls in love with her. This degrading image is responsible for the increasing violence in real life toward women.

Today, a concerted campaign has been launched by women's organizations, such as the Progressive Organization of Women and the Organization for the Independence of Women to focus the attention of all right-thinking people toward sex discrimination tests, sex-linked abortions, dowry deaths, and so on. These organizations have worked for changes in attitude through street plays, documentaries, and films, so that the traditional stereotypes are not perpetuated.

The National Council of Educational Research and Training is now remodeling textbooks in order to remove sexist bias in education. However, much remains to be achieved, as a large number of rural men and women steeped in ignorance cling closely to their traditional roles and continue to perpetuate the same discrimination and bias in the rearing of their daughters and sons.

NOTES

1. *Dharma Shastras* are treatises on Dharma, the earliest being Gautama's *Dharma Shastra* (c. 600 B.C.). See Kane's history of *Dharma Shastra*.

2. *Ashramadharma* are the four stages of life in the Hindu tradition. *Ashrama* refers to stage.

3. *Moksha* is freedom from the cycle of birth, death, and rebirth.

4. Brahma is the "creator," first god of the Hindu trinity.

5. Vishnu is the "preserver," second god of the Hindu trinity.

6. Shiva is the "destroyer," third god of the Hindu trinity.

7. *Prakriti* is the female principle of Sankhya.

8. *Purusha* is the male principle of Sankhya.

9. *Manusmriti* are treatises on *Dharma* written by Manu circa 300 B.C.

10a. Akkama Devi was a woman poet of the twelvth century.

10b. Mirabai was a woman poet of the fifteenth century. (See Tharu & Lalita, 1991.)

11. *Sati* is self-immolation of the wife on the funeral pyre of the husband, practiced in India till the beginning of the twentieth century.

12. The lower castes were employed as servants in the homes of the upper castes. The cooks, however, always belonged to the upper caste. The lower castes performed the chores of washing, cleaning, sweeping, and maintaining the house.

13. *Atharvaveda* is the fourth and the latest Veda, largely consisting of priestly spells and incantations.

14. *Brahmacharya* is the stage of apprenticeship and learning and practicing celibacy. See Table 10.1.

REFERENCES

Bose, A. (1991). *Population of India, 1991 Census: Results and Methodology*. Delhi: B. R. Publishing House.

Cormack, M. (1961). *The Hindu Women*. Bombay: Asia Publishing House.

Das, V. (1976a). Indian women. Work, power and status. In Nanda, B. R. (Ed.), *Indian Women: From Purdah to Modernity*. New Delhi: Vikas Publishing House.

———. (1976b). Masks and faces. An essay on Punjab kinship. *Indian Sociology*, *10*(1):1–30.

———. (1979). Reflections on social constructions of adulthood. In Kakkar, S. (Ed.), *Identity and Adulthood*. Delhi: Oxford University Press.

Dreze, J., & Sen, A. (1989). *Hunger and Public Action*. Oxford: Clarendon Press.

Kakkar, S. (1978). *The Inner World: A Psychoanalytic Study of Childhood and Society in India*. Delhi: Oxford University Press.

———. (Ed.). (1979). *Identity and Adulthood*. Delhi: Oxford University Press.

Kapur, P. (1973). *Love, Marriage and Sex*. Delhi: Vikas Publishing House.

Kumar, U. (1989). Mother-in-law, son, and daughter-in-law: A developmental analysis of the relationships in the Hindu social context. In Adler, L.L. (Ed.), *Cross-Cultural Research in Human Development: Life-Span Perspectives*. New York: Praeger.

———. (1991). Life stages in the development of the Hindu woman in India. In Adler, L.L. (Ed.), *Women in Cross-Cultural Perspective*. New York: Praeger.

Mies, M. (1980). *Indian Women and Patriarchy*. New Delhi: Concept.

Nagaraja, K. (1991, May 25–June 7). The missing women, Frontline, *National Press*, Madras.

Tharu, S., & Lalita, K. (Eds.). (1991). *Women's Writings in India; 600 B.C. to the Present*. Delhi: Oxford University Press.

Saxena, M. (1989). Indian women in Asia: Beyond the domestic domain (pp. 17–150). RUSHAP Series on Monographs and Occasional Papers, UNESCO Principal Regional Office for Asia and the Pacific, Bangkok.

Sharma, U. (1980). *Women, Work & Property in North-West India*. London: Tavistock.

11

Israel

*Dafna N. Izraeli and
Marilyn P. Safir*

INTRODUCTION

This chapter sketches the major gender themes of Israeli society as they are woven into the socialization process over the life course. Viewing the cultural fabric through a gender lens, it begins by focusing on the significance of Israel as a relatively new state, as a Jewish state, as a state under siege, and finally as a family-oriented society. Whereas each condition contributes a different dimension to gender relations, the underlying gender theme is that men and women are partners in the collective, but with unequal standing in the partnership: men are the senior partners, women the junior partners.

The population of Israel (5 million in 1991)[1] is composed of a number of socially significant national/religious groupings: Jews (82 percent), Moslems (14 percent), Christians (2.3 percent), and Druze (1.7 percent). Almost all non-Jews are Arabs. The focus of this chapter is limited to the Jewish majority.

The great majority of Israel's Jewish population are immigrants or their Israeli-born offspring. Between 1948 and 1960, more than 1,250,000 Jewish immigrants arrived, and immigration accounted for 65 percent of the net population. Most came as refugees from the Moslem countries of North Africa and the Middle East and from the ghettos and concentration camps of post–World War II Europe. Immigrants from the former, more traditional, economically less-developed countries are known locally as Orientals or Easterners, and immigrants from the latter and the more modern, industrialized countries of Europe and North and South America are known as Ashkenazim or Westerners. The Easterners, the numerical majority, as a group, have lower education, occupational status, and income and less access to the valued resources of Israeli society. The women are doubly disadvantaged as both Easterners and women (Bernstein, 1983). The

condition of Easterners, especially of the younger generation, is currently ex-
acerbated by the competition for resources created by the recent waves of immigration.

In 1990 and 1991 over 350,000 immigrants arrived in Israel, the great majority
fleeing the Soviet Union. A very large proportion is privileged with higher
education, especially in technological fields. It is difficult to predict how this
new wave of immigration will affect Israeli society. The immediate impact is
high rates of unemployment for both Israeli-born, especially new entrants into
the labor force, and immigrants, with unemployment significantly higher for
women in both groups. The future impact of this immigration on gender relations
is ambiguous. Socialized within the communist system where full employment
for women was the norm but where women also managed the home under
conditions of scarcity, with little assistance from their husbands, women tend
to view a demanding career more as an additional burden than as an opportunity
for self-fulfillment. Given the option, many prefer part-time employment.

OVERVIEW

Both men and women are partners in the collective of Am Yisrael (the nation
of Israel), but they serve the collective in different ways, and their contributions
are valued differently (Izraeli, 1992). The biblical metaphor of woman as "help-
mate" to man, created from his rib to play an important but secondary role, is
prototypical of the structure and tenor of gender relations.

Israel is a relatively new state and, like all new states, bears the imprint of
its early beginnings. Its institutional infrastructure was established by young
Zionist pioneers ideologically driven by the vision of a Jewish homeland reconstructed on principles of social justice and equality. They came during the early
decades of this century, mainly from Eastern Europe, most without parents and
in peer groups of single men and women, although women were a small minority.
These women expected to be equal partners with the men in the emerging
agricultural collectives. Disappointed by their exclusion from the valued activities
of nation building, the women pioneers founded the first-wave feminist movement within the Zionist socialist movement in Palestine (Izraeli, 1981).

Israel is officially a Jewish state. The Jewish orthodox tradition supplies an
additional theme in the composition of gender relations. Israel was established
(1948) as a homeland for the Jewish people and a refuge from the persecutions
of other nations. Religious and traditional Jewish holidays are national holidays.
Matters of marriage and divorce are the sole jurisdiction of religious courts
(Moslems and Christians have their own courts). These courts are presided over
by rabbinical (male) authorities who make their decisions according to religious
codes of law in which women are subordinate to men.

Gender is a major organizing principle of the Jewish religion. The Hebrew
language as a metaphor for the culture has no neutral terms—all nouns are either
masculine or feminine, and verbs are conjugated accordingly. The phallocentric

narrative of the rabbinical tradition is reflected in the following *midrash* (rabbinic tale), meant to compliment women—that God granted women intelligence equal to man so that man would respect and heed her. Whereas the tradition treats woman as subordinate to man, it also emphasizes man's dependence on woman and his obligations toward her and sets limits on the husband's patriarchal rights with regard to his wife.

Among European Jews, prior to World War II, women frequently managed the family store and engaged in commerce. However, Torah learning, the study of the most holy books and the most valued activity of Jewish life, was closed to women. The ideology that emphasized gender role differences and the importance of family life and the value placed on women's distinctive contributions within the family sustained their sense of partnership within the community.

Israel is a society under siege. The Jewish community in Palestine has been in conflict with its Arab neighbors since the early decades of the century and with the State of Israel since its inception (1948). National defense, a sine qua non of national survival, was elevated to a "religious" ideal. Those associated with it provided the heroes of the new mythology. All the heroes are men. In later decades they became the major reservoir for recruitment to the political and economic elites. Very few women fill positions in the military that provide access to those channels of mobility. As in the pioneering society and traditional Jewish life, women have always participated in defense as helpmates to man, as junior partners, essential but secondary and needing special protection. Organizationally the Women's Corps (Chen) is the responsible authority for training women soldiers and for judicial matters involving women soldiers. All work assignments, however, are general military manpower decisions.

Both men and women do compulsory military service; women's service, however, is shorter than that of men, they do not engage in combat, and they are rarely called for reserve duty. Whereas the man serves the collective during his active lifetime through reserve army service, the woman's contribution is linked to her role as mother and her responsibility for her family, to which she is expected to give priority.

COMPARISONS BETWEEN MEN'S AND WOMEN'S GENDER ROLES DURING THE LIFE CYCLE

Israel is a family-oriented society. Family stability is the rule, although the divorce rate has been on the increase in the last decade and especially in the last two years as a consequence of high divorce rates among recent Soviet immigrants. For women, the choice of whether to have children or to pursue a career is not part of the repertoire of options. Marrying and having children are cultural imperatives for both men and women. Only 5.7 percent of women are never married by age 40 (3.7 percent for men)—up from 3 percent a decade ago. Only one out of six Jewish marriages and 1 out of 10 Moslem marriages end in divorce. Most Christians are Catholic, and divorce in this community is rare.

Few births occur out of wedlock—1.2 percent, with a quarter of these births by women over 35. Over 90 percent of all households with children under 18 are two-parent households. Median age of first marriage for Jews is 22.5 for women and 25.9 for men; for Moslems, 19.9 for women and 24.2 for men; for Christians, 22.5 for women and 27.4 for men; and for Druze, 19.1 for women and 23.8 for men. Among those with a college education, however, the median age of first marriage is significantly higher.

Infancy and Early Childhood

Children are considered essential for a happy marriage, and a childless couple is not considered a family (Bar-Yosef, Bloom & Levy, 1978). The great importance attributed to having children is reflected in the fact that in vitro experimentation and services are highly developed in Israel, where the number of centers for every 1 million people is four times greater than in the United States. All treatments for infertility are covered by health insurance.

The fertility rate in 1990—the average number of children a woman may bear in her lifetime—was 3.02. During the last 30 years the fertility rate has dropped dramatically: among first-generation Easterners from 5.4 to 3.1, among Moslems from 8.2 to 4.7, among Christians from 4.6 to 2.6, and among Druze from 7.2 to 4.1. Among Israeli-born and first-generation Westerners, it has remained stable (2.8 and 2.3, respectively). Decrease in fertility is associated with women's increasing levels of education and age of marriage. Among Jews, however, the best single predictor of fertility rate is religiosity. Among the ultraorthodox groups, six plus is the norm.

Almost all babies are born in the maternity ward of a general hospital and are delivered by nurse-midwives. The hospital stay for mother and child is four days or less. Infants are cared for by over 900 well-baby clinics run by the Ministry of Health throughout the country. First contact with the clinic is made during pregnancy when women come for checkups and can attend prenatal classes with their husbands. A husband's participation is a relatively new phenomenon and varies with the couple's education and social class—the higher it is, the more likely both will participate and the husband will be present during the delivery.

Jews traditionally have a preference for male children and especially for the first child's being male. A male child was traditionally referred to as a *kaddishel*— a term of endearment for one who mourns (only the male is obligated to pray) after the death of a parent. Mothers are more likely than fathers to prefer daughters, who are less likely than sons to be wounded or killed in combat. All male infants are circumcised on the eighth day after birth (health permitting). On that occasion a large party is held, often catered in a hired hall to which a large number of guests are invited. The event symbolizes the entry of the male infant into the covenant between God and the people of Israel. Although the circumcision is a religious ritual, it is also observed by those who are nonreligious. There is no equivalent ceremony for girls, although in recent years a growing number of younger couples have begun to celebrate the birth of a daughter. Arab society also shows a strong preference for sons. Whereas among Jews the daughter is viewed as always staying close to her family, among Arabs she is viewed as a temporary resident who will eventually become a part of her husband's family.

During infancy, gender differentiation is minimal. Even among the ultraorthodox, where sex segregation in play and education is very stringent, differences are minimal until age three, when boys receive their first haircuts. Clothing in stereotyped pink or blue is often given to a newborn as a present. However, unisex dressing is generally the norm for play (jeans in winter and shorts in summer) for both sexes through preschool. Social life revolves around the children. Small children often accompany their parents to family and social events, for which they are more likely to be dressed in stereotypical fashion. Child care continues to be the primary responsibility of the mother.

Visitors are impressed with the freedom of the Israeli child, who spends a great deal of time playing out in the open. Because of the mild weather between March and November, most youngsters play outdoors, and active play is common for both sexes. Cooperative play appears much earlier than in the United States of America because of early interaction in neighborhoods and early attendance in preschool programs. Israelis consider children's early participation in nursery settings valuable for their development, especially of social skills and independence. Jewish children begin prekindergarten classes at age two. In addition, there are day-care centers for working mothers operated by women's organizations and subsidized by the Ministry of Labor and Social Welfare. Payment is on a graded scale according to family size and income. These centers, open from 7:30 A.M. to 4:00 P.M., accept children from 6 months and are viewed as a positive solution for working women. There are not enough places in such centers, however, to meet the demand. If a willing grandmother is not available, then a child care worker (*metapelet*) is hired for home care. Between 3 and 4 years the child usually moves into prekindergarten, sponsored by the Ministry of Education. In 1988, 67 percent of two-year-olds, 92 percent of three-year-olds, and 99 percent of four-year-olds were in some preschool setting. Similar provisions for day care and prekindergarten settings have not been widely available among the Arab population. To remedy this situation, centers to train early childhood workers have been set up in Acre and Nazareth by Arab women's groups.

School Years

All children begin kindergarten during the year of their fifth birthday. School attendance is compulsory for both sexes from kindergarten through age 15 and free through the end of high school at age 18. From the prekindergarten stage right through primary school, the school day ends around noon or shortly after, following which children come home for the main meal. This arrangement seriously curtails mothers' ability to take on full-time employment. Public schools require students to wear a school uniform; girls may wear skirts or pants. In the government-subsidized schools of the more orthodox sector, education is sex-segregated, and clearly differentiated clothing is the rule.

The kibbutz family is generally more egalitarian, with more role sharing than its city counterpart. Child rearing in the kibbutz is very different from the traditional urban pattern. Until the late fifties, children in all kibbutzim lived in separate age-graded, mixed-sex children's houses. Over the last three decades there has been a move, spearheaded by women, toward children's sleeping in their parents' home. Only a few kibbutzim belonging to the more ideologically committed movements still maintain separate sleeping quarters. Nonetheless, children are communally reared. The child enters the infants' house at six weeks. She or he becomes part of a peer group that lives together until age 12–14, when the children leave the kibbutz for a regional kibbutz boardingschool. The child's mother visits the infants' house during work hours to nurse the child, and the child spends late afternoon and early evening with his or her parents before being returned to the infants' house.

In addition to strong peer ties, kibbutz children experience multiple mothering, as the person (*metapelet*) responsible for the child's care within the infants' house and her helpers are women. The role of the biological parents is basically expressive (loving), as training and discipline are taken over by the *metapelet* and later the class teacher-educator, who spends more time with the child on a daily basis than do the parents. Keller (1983), who summarized the positive effects of multiple mothering, stated that the reduction of the role of the biological mother has resulted not in maternal deprivation but in increased mothering from several figures. The biological family is thus a less complex system for the kibbutz child than for children generally, since the mother and father roles are relatively undifferentiated in their emphasis on affection, permissiveness, and nurturance toward the child. Nonetheless, research (Safir, 1983) indicates that these boys and girls are more sex-stereotyped and more conforming than their city cohorts, probably a result of the significantly greater sex typing in the division of labor in the kibbutz compared with the city.

The peer group is a very important socializing influence in Israeli society. Birthdays are celebrated in primary school with the whole class. By third or fourth grade, the class meets for a weekly night party at the home of one of the children. The youth movement (including scouts), while more significant in the past, is another activity where both boys and girls join with their classmates in fourth grade and continue to meet twice a week through the end of high school. Many same- and cross-sex adult friendships are begun during this preadolescent period.

Primary school is followed by junior high school. In an attempt to enhance ethnic integration and close the educational gap between Easterners and Westerners, comprehensive regional junior and senior high schools were established in the 1970s, to which children were bused from a variety of neighborhoods.

The extent of success of this project is still an issue of debate among educators. Easterners continue to perform significantly lower on ability and achievement tests, attributable to lower socioeconomic status (SES).

While girls' records of achievements are equal or superior to those of boys, their performance on ability tests is significantly poorer than that of boys. Lieblich (1985) reported that boys begin to surpass girls on verbal intelligence tests by age nine, and by age eleven their verbal IQs are significantly higher than those of girls. Safir (1986) found that gifted girls lost points by not taking "risks" on ability tests when compared with their 7–9 year old male peers. Lieblich and Safir suggested that teachers, by reflecting the cultural preference for boys, may provide girls with a psychological environment that negatively affects their self-esteem. BenTsvi-Mayer, Herz-Lazerovitz, and Safir (1989), in fact, demonstrated that primary school teachers view boys as more outstanding than girls despite their avowed statements that boys and girls are equally talented.

As the boy infant is singled out at birth by ritual circumcision, at thirteen he participates in a Bar Mitzvah ceremony, signifying his passage from childhood to manhood and his assumption of religious duties. The ceremony takes place during prayer services in the synagogue. In addition a large party, usually catered in a hired hall, is held. It is not unusual for 200–500 guests to be invited to the party. The Bar Mitzvah is celebrated by both religious and secular families. There is no equivalent rite of passage for girls, although some celebration of a girl's coming of age (at 12 years) is becoming widespread. At the end of the ninth grade, children are channeled into either an academic or a vocational high school on the basis of their grades and ability tests. Weaker students transfer to vocational high schools. Pupil population at these schools consists of 55 percent boys and 45 percent girls. Graduates of the majority of these schools are ineligible to sit for matriculation examinations. All students in academic high schools follow the same program of studies in grade 10. During the last two years of high school, they choose between different specializations. Girls are overrepresented in the humanities, proportionately represented in biology, and underrepresented in the mathematics, physics, and computer specializations: 31 percent of the girls, compared with 47 percent of the boys, take advanced mathematics, and only 7 percent of the girls, compared with 25 percent of the boys, take advanced physics. These gender differences in high school have long-term negative repercussions for women's integration in high-tech occupations.

Young Adulthood

Dating patterns vary but begin earlier among the secular and less traditional elements of the population. Children in grammar school speak of having a girlfriend or boyfriend, but pairing usually occurs within the peer social group. The couple does not go on a date by itself until mid to late adolescence. Platonic friendships are common. Casual dating is not the norm, and once two people form a couple, they continue to date for a minimum of several months. It is not uncommon for couples formed at age 14 ultimately to marry. The large majority, however, are formed during army service or later at the university. The pair often participates as a couple in family functions, but the families do not meet formally until the couple decides to marry.

Adulthood

There is no official period of engagement. Couples usually announce their decision to marry two to three months before the wedding date. In recent years premarital cohabitation has become more common and more normatively acceptable. This trend is also reflected in the relatively later marital age among nonorthodox, educated girls. The religiously orthodox attend religious schools, which have separate classes for boys and girls, and a large proportion of boys go to all-male boarding high schools and come home every second or third weekend. The clubs of the orthodox youth movements are similarly segregated by sex. Dating is viewed as preparation for marriage, and relationships not likely to lead to marriage are discouraged and short-lived. Orthodox girls and boys marry younger than the national average. Legislation has made 18 the age of consent for girls (with parents' permission, at age seventeen) to prevent marriage among minors prevalent among the ultraorthodox and very traditional groups in both the Jewish and Arab communities. Among the ultraorthodox, matchmaking is still the norm. Hassan (1991) claims that Arab women in these ultratraditional communities have no freedom in mate choice.

Kibbutz members virtually never marry a member of their own peer group with whom they have grown up. Marriage partners are usually chosen from younger or older groups, peers who joined as adolescents, members of other kibbutzim, or nonmembers. Since kibbutz life is organized around family, there is no role for the single person. Singles feel isolated and are more likely than marrieds to leave, as are kibbutz members who marry nonmembers. Therefore, the kibbutz movements sponsor special programs, parties, and trips for kibbutz singles, whose primary purpose is to provide opportunities for them to meet and marry one another, increasing the probability of their remaining in a kibbutz.

Israel was the first, and is still one of the few, states that have universal compulsory military training for both men and women. Marriage, pregnancy, and motherhood, however, are grounds for compulsory nonconscription for women while religious conviction is grounds for voluntary nonconscription. Some 65 percent of each cohort of women and 97 percent of men are drafted. Ultraorthodox men may get military deferment while they continue to pursue their religious studies and in effect are often not conscripted. Approximately 25 percent of each cohort of women are released on religious grounds. The proportion released because of marriage or pregnancy has declined over the years and is currently negligible.

Women serve two years, men three. Officer training obligates the recruit to sign up for an extra year, during which he or she is paid as part of the professional military. Functionally, most army roles are segregated by sex, and from point of intake throughout army service, men and women follow separate career paths. Nevertheless, army service has been found to have a significant, positive impact on women's self-esteem and occupational aspirations (Bloom & Bar-Yosef, 1985).

The two decades following Independence (when fighting units were consolidated but not greatly expanded) brought about a continuous restriction of women to more traditionally female (clerical) jobs and an increase in the sex segregation of occupations. The shortage in human (male) resources following the Six-Day War (1967) precipitated a more extensive use of women in non-traditionally female jobs to increase the number of men for combat units. The anticipated shortage of high-quality males and the intensification in the use of sophisticated technologies led the army to reevaluate its policies regarding the most efficient use of women (Izraeli, 1979).

In 1976, 210 out of 709 jobs (29.6 percent) were open to women, the majority of them clerical jobs. Since 1984 the range of jobs filled by women has expanded greatly (60 percent by the end of 1985), and there is continued experimentation to break down the barriers to women's integration. New technologies create new occupations for which the more educated women soldiers are well suited. However, the fact that women do not serve in combat units, their shorter period of service (two years compared with three for men), their disinclination to sign up for an additional period of army service, their release upon marriage, and their negligible availability for reserve duty remain major disincentives to intensifying the investments in women's training and to expanding the number of jobs available to them. Female career officers reach a glass ceiling at the lower ranks as a result of their lack of combat experience.

Between 1961 and 1990, the proportion of the population with higher education increased from 9 percent to 25 percent (26 percent of the males and 24 percent of the females). The proportion of women among the student body more than doubled, from less than 25 percent to 50 percent. During the last decade the major developments have been the growth in the proportion of women among graduate students and their movement into previously male-dominated specializations. In 1988–1989, among recipients of university degrees, women were 51 percent of recipients of the first degree, 45 percent of the second degree, and 39 percent of the third degree. That same year, women constituted 51 percent of the students for the first degree, 49 percent for the second degree, and 42 percent for the third degree. Although they are still overrepresented in traditionally female academic niches, they are entering new fields in growing numbers. In the academic year 1988–1989, among first-degree students, women represented 74 percent of those enrolled in the humanities, 49 percent in the social sciences, 43 percent in mathematics and the sciences, 43 percent in law, 37 percent in medicine, and 31 percent in business and administration, but only 15 percent in engineering and architecture—most in architecture.

There are over 670,000 women and 980,000 men in the civilian labor force.

Between 1954 and 1990 the proportion of women in the civilian labor force grew from 21 percent to 41.1 percent, but that of men declined from 79 percent to 62.3 percent. Among Jewish women the figure reached over 46 percent but among minority women it was only 15.2 percent (up from 7.2 percent in 1970). Women joined the labor force in response to the demand created for educated workers by the growth in public and community services (primarily education and health) as well as financial and business services from the end of the 1960s to the mid-1970s. At the same time, growing military and defense-related needs absorbed men from the civilian sector, shrinking the pool of those available for the civilian economy, a trend intensified by the growth in the number of students in the universities. In most cases the demand for labor came from occupations such as teaching, social work, and clerical work, where women already had a foothold. In others it came from occupations previously closed to women, such as bank tellers, where, unable to attract men in sufficient numbers, employers were compelled to hire women. In addition, new occupations that initially had no clear sex label, such as in the fields of computers and human resource management, were receptive to women. The demand for labor during the 1970s increased opportunities for older women who had previously encountered difficulty competing for jobs (Izraeli, 1988).

An analysis of gender trends in the age distribution of the labor force during the last 20 years reveals the following. For men there is a general small decline for all age groups. For women there is a drop in participation rates among women aged 24 and under, due largely to the prolongation of school education and partly to an increase in the percentage of women inducted into the army. Peak participation by age in 1970 was 18–24, in 1975 it was 25–34, and since 1984 it is 35–44. This upward drift reflects an increase in the proportion of older women with higher education. The proportion of married women in the labor force grew from 25.3 percent in 1967 to 47.3 percent (51.7 percent among Jewish women) in 1990. In addition, the presence of small children has become less of a deterrent to women's employment. In 1990, almost 54 percent of all Jewish women with youngest child aged up to one year and almost 60 percent of all Jewish women with youngest child aged 2–4 were in the labor force; among the women with 13 and more years of schooling, the figures were 68 percent and 79 percent, respectively. The current age distribution for Moslem, Christian, and Druze women resembles that of Jewish women in 1970, with participation peaking at 18–24 and then declining. The majority of Arab women in the labor force work until marriage or the birth of the first child and then leave the labor market. The pattern, however, is changing among the growing number of educated semi-professionals where continued labor force involvement after marriage is becoming the norm.

Differences in labor force participation among Jewish women from different ethnic groups may be attributed primarily to differences in educational attainment. The more educated a woman is, the more likely she is to have a job. This applies to Arab women as well, although the effect of education is not as powerful as it is for Jewish women. The lower employment rates found for first- and second-generation women from Asian and African countries become negligible when we compare women with the same levels of education. Furthermore among those with 16+ years of education, the employment rates for women are the same as those for men. The female labor force is, on the average, more educated than the male labor force. The median years of schooling in 1987 were 12.5 for women and 11.8 for men.

Additional changes facilitated the entry of women with small children. Early in the 1970s, the number of day-care centers was tripled as part of government policy to encourage female labor force participation. There are today some 1,000 child-care centers—subsidized and supervised by the Ministry of Labor and Social Welfare—for over 90,000 children aged up to 3 years. Furthermore, many of the new job openings permitted part-time employment or were concentrated in the public sector where work schedules could be better synchronized with school schedules. Half-time workers are entitled to a proportionate share of all benefits enjoyed by full-time workers, including tenure. In addition, rising expectations for a materially more comfortable style of life created greater reliance of the family on a second income.

During the last decade shrinking employment opportunities resulting from the slowdown in economic growth since the end of the 1970s and the Soviet immigration since the end of the 1980s slowed the upward drift in female employment rates. Although unemployment rates for women have been consistently higher than for men, the gender gap in unemployment doubled in 1990 compared with previous years.

Israel adopted most of the maternity laws proposed by the International Labor Organization in the 1950s and 1960s. They were based on the assumption that women are the natural caretakers of children and need to be protected in their roles as mothers from exploitation by employers. Employers may not fire a woman on grounds of pregnancy, provided she has worked for the employer at least five months before becoming pregnant. Women are obligated to take 12 weeks' maternity leave with 70 percent pay, covered by Social Security. In 1988, labor laws were changed to enable either parent to take the additional 9 months as parental leave without pay. Many labor contracts permit a nursing mother, during the first year after the birth, to take off an hour a day at the employer's expense and permit mothers of young children to work one hour less a day at the employer's expense. Either parent may take sick leave to care for family members.

While the family is valued by both sexes, it impacts differently on men and women's occupational roles. Husbands invest the same amount of time in housework and child care whether wives are employed or full-time homemakers (Peres & Katz, 1983). A study of 137 dual-career couples (Izraeli, forthcoming) in which both husband and wife were physicians found that women spent two-thirds of the total hours spent by the couple in family work. However, wives' earnings affected husbands' participation. Among physician couples where wives contributed 50 percent or more of the family income, husbands reported spending more time in child care and errands (but not in domestic work) than husbands whose wives contributed less than 50 percent of the family income.

The fact that men serve in the army reserves through age 50–55 for up to 45 days a year also intensifies the sex division of labor in the household and how they feel about it. Comparing a sample of Israeli career women at mid-life with a similar group of women from the United States, Lieblich (1991) observed that Israeli women were less resentful of their husbands' lack of participation in both child care and housework and experienced less role conflict. She explains this difference by the lesser importance Israeli women attribute to their careers and the greater centrality of the mother/wife/helpmate roles to their identity.

The induction of a son or daughter into the army (at 18 years) rarely leaves the parents with an empty nest. More often, the result is an intensification of parenting, especially of mothering. The household revolves around the army leaves of the young soldier. He or she may return home one to three weekends a month, bringing the dirty laundry that needs washing and careful ironing. Favorite foods and cakes are prepared. When the soldier is not home for a long period, mother often sends him or her packages with homemade goodies. The middle-aged woman, even if she is employed, often helps her married children by baby-sitting for her grandchildren and providing other personal services.

A study of women and men working in technological professions (Etzion, 1988) found that moving into middle age affects men and women differently. Women tend to become more self-confident and to experience less role conflict and less burnout than similar younger women while the opposite is true for men, who show signs of greater burnout, boredom, and dissatisfaction than younger men.

Old Age

Women generally welcome retirement more than men do and are better prepared for it. In a series of studies of couples over the life span, focusing on the elderly couple, Friedman (1987) found a shift in the power balance, with women feeling more powerful and less vulnerable in the relationship and men less so than in earlier periods. She argues that women make greater investments in establishing social ties and consequently enter old age with more supportive social networks of friends and kin than do men.

The centrality of family life includes concern for aging parents. Elderly parents tend to live in the same city and rarely more than a drive of an hour or two from one of their offspring. Among larger families living within the same city, care for elderly parents may be shared among the offspring, with most of the responsibility falling on the woman, whether daughter or daughter-in-law, although among Eastern Jews males traditionally play an active role in caring for parents and meeting their physical needs. With the growth in the number of elderly but the decline in number of children they have to care for them and women's entry into the labor market, care for the elderly is emerging as a serious social problem.

The number of elderly citizens (65 + years) has increased almost fivefold since 1955, and their proportion in the population grew from 3.9 percent to 9.5 percent. Women constitute 54 percent of all those 65 years and older. The elderly are also growing older, with 41 percent of the elderly over 75 years. Approximately 92 percent of the elderly live in private homes, that is, in noninstitutional settings; of these, approximately 44 percent live as couples, 38 percent live with other family members, and 19 percent live alone (75 percent women). Regardless of where they live, however, it is very likely that at some point they will require and expect to receive intensive attention from offspring, most likely from a daughter. A sizable proportion of women consequently experience the middle-age squeeze—supporting children who are launching their careers, caring for grandchildren, and being responsible for aging parents.

The availability of institutional alternatives lags far behind demand, and most of those built in the last decade are geared to the wealthy and healthy among the aging population. Almost all the 500 + kibbutzim in Israel were established and initially populated by young people, often before marriage. Today the more established kibbutzim are more than 50 years old and have a sizable elderly population. Furthermore, life expectancy for women in the kibbutz is 3 years more than for their urban counterparts, and for men it is 6 years more. While the economic structure of the kibbutz relieves its members of financial insecurity, social norms encourage older members to continue working as long as they are able to. As members age, they may move into a less demanding job and work fewer hours. In a society where social status is greatly influenced by the individual's contribution to the collective, the kibbutz faces the problem of providing not only physical care for the aging but also meaningful social roles for them to play within the kibbutz community.

SUMMARY AND CONCLUSIONS

This review of the dominant gender themes in people's lives over the life course highlights the contradictory pulls of a tradition that is valued but that is also problematic with regard to women's status. This chapter focuses on the opportunities inherent in modernity, which also entail new tensions and conflicts. Jewish tradition emphasizes the centrality of family life and motherhood to women's identity. Jewish tradition also carved out a role for women that was separate and not equal to that of men. The centrality of the military in Israeli society, not likely to change until Israel's survival as a state appears less precarious, deepens the gender inequality. Public policy in the form of collective labor agreements and legislation provides working mothers with protection and, together with women's organizations, provides subsidized child care. This enables women to combine family and work but confines most married women to part-time jobs or those in the female niche. The short school day and the inadequacy of services for working parents constrained women from making the heavy investments in the labor force that are necessary to advance their careers and that are made by their male counterparts. The current focus on peace negotiations, the high rate of unemployment, and need to absorb the Soviet immigration make it more difficult to get public attention, including that of women, for gender inequalities in society. Nonetheless, women's increased education, participation in the labor force, and pressure applied by feminist organizations have greatly increased public sensitivity to these issues. These and macrolevel contextual factors permeate the socialization process at the microlevel and shape gender development over the life-course.

NOTE

1. Unless otherwise specified, all statistical data are taken from the *Statistical Abstract of Israel*, *42*, 1991, and from the Labor Force Survey for the relevant year.

REFERENCES

Bar-Yosef, Rivka, Bloom, Anne R., & Levy, Tzveia. (1978). *Role Ideology of Young Israeli Women* (Research report). Jerusalem: Hebrew University, Work and Welfare Research Institute.

BenTsvi-Mayer, Shoshana, Herz-Lazerovitz, Rachel, & Safir, Marilyn P. (1989). Teacher's selections of boys or girls as prominent pupils. *Sex Roles*, *21*: 231–47.

Bernstein, Deborah. (1983). Economic growth and female labor: The case of Israel. *Sociological Review*, *31*: 263–92.

Bloom, Anne R., & Bar-Yosef, Rivka. (1985). Israeli women and military experience: A socialization experience. In Safir, Marilyn, Mednick, Martha T., Izraeli, Dafna, & Bernard, Jessie (Eds.), *Women's Worlds: From the New Scholarship*. New York: Praeger.

Etzion, Dalia. (1988). Experience of burnout and work and non-work success in male and female engineers: A matched pairs comparison. *Human Resource Management*, *27*: 163–79.

Friedman, Ariella. (1987). Getting powerful with age: Changes in women over the life cycle. *Israel Social Science Research: A Multidisciplinary Journal* (special issue on women in Israel, Dafna N. Izraeli, guest editor), *5*: 76–86.

Hassan, Manar. (1991). Growing up female and Palestinian in Israel. In Swirsky, Barbara, & Safir, Marilyn P. (Eds.), *Calling the Equality Bluff: Women in Israel*. New York: Teacher's College Press.

Izraeli, Dafna N. (1979). The sex structure of occupations: The Israeli experience. *Journal of Work and Occupations*, *15*: 404–29.

———. (1981). The Zionist women's movement in Palestine, 1911–1927. *Signs: Journal of Women in Culture and Society*, *7*: 87–114.

———. (1988). Women's movement into management. In Nancy Adler and Dafna N. Izraeli (Eds.), *Women in Management Worldwide*. New York: M.E. Sharpe.

———. (1992). Culture, policy and women in dual earner families in Israel. In Suzan Lewis, Dafna N. Izraeli and Helen Hootsmans (Eds.), *Dual Earner Families— International Perspectives*. London: Sage.

————. (forthcoming). Money-matters: Spousal income and family/work relations. *The Sociological Quarterly*.

Keller, Suzanne. (1983). The family in the kibbutz: What lessons for us?. In Michal Palgi, Joseph Blassi, Menachem Rosner & Marilyn P. Safir (Eds.), *Sexual Equality: The Israeli Kibbutz Tests the Theories*. Philadelphia: Norwood Press.

Lieblich, Amia. (1985). Sex differences in intelligence test performance of Jewish and Arab school children in Israel. In Marilyn P. Safir, Martha T. Mednick, Dafna Izraeli & Jessie Bernard (Eds.), *Women's Worlds: From the New Scholarship*. New York: Praeger.

————. (1991). A comparison of successful Israeli and American career women at mid-life. In Swirsky, Barbara, & Safir, Marilyn P. (Eds.), *Calling the Equality Bluff: Women in Israel*. New York: Teacher's College Press.

Peres, Yohanan, & Katz, Ruth. (1983). Stability and centrality: The nuclear family in modern Israel. *Social Forces, 59*: 687–704.

Raday, Frances. (1991). The concept of gender equality in a Jewish state. In Swirsky, Barbara, & Safir, Marilyn P. (Eds.), *Calling the Equality Bluff: Women in Israel*. New York: Teacher's College Press.

Safir, Marilyn P. (1983). Sex role education/socialization in the kibbutzim. In Palgi, Michal, Blassi, Joseph, Rosner, Menachem, & Safir, Marilyn P. (Eds.), *Sexual Equality: The Israeli Kibbutz Tests the Theories*. Philadelphia: Norwood Press.

————. (1986). Nature or nurture effects on sex differences in intellectual function. *Sex Roles, 14*: 581–90.

————. (1991). How has the kibbutz experiment failed to create sex equality? In Swirsky, Barbara, & Safir, Marilyn P. (Eds.), *Calling the Equality Bluff: Women in Israel*. New York: Teacher's College Press.

12

Italy

Rosemary Merenda and Marina Mattioni

INTRODUCTION

Italy is a predominantly mountainous peninsula (surface area: 301,262 square kilometers or 116,317 square miles) jutting out into the Mediterranean Sea. While the Alps separate it from the rest of Europe, the Apennine chain runs down the length of the boot. Nevertheless, it is a densely populated country with 57,103,833 inhabitants (as of 20 October 1991), approximately 190 per square kilometer (.6 square mile). Although for centuries the geographic area of Italy had a fundamentally agricultural economy, the Italians live for the most part in cities and towns. Only rarely do families live independently, at least 10 kilometers (6 miles) from some urban center. With few natural resources, Italy now thrives economically on the production of goods and services. Meanwhile, its agricultural activity (including olive oil, wine, cheese, fruits, and vegetables for exportation) does not even cover all the country's needs. It has been a full member of the European Economic Community since its creation in 1957.

Even though united in terms of culture and language since ancient times, Italy was unified as a single nation only in 1861. But more than 130 years of unification have yet to cancel out the profound differences between an industrialized north with a strong agricultural base (Val d'Aosta, Piedmont, Lombardy, the three Veneto provinces, Liguria, Emilia, and Tuscany) and a backward south made up primarily of large estates employing day and/or migrant workers. In contrast, the central provinces, with Rome the capital as the focus, have become an enormous bureaucratic center. These divisions still exist today, in part, in the popular culture: the north has developed a more secular mentality, whereas the south still feels a strong influence of the Catholic church.

Demographically, Italy is heading toward a zero population growth. For the first time in recent years the birthrate has been only slightly higher than the death rate. For example, in the 1987–1989 period, there were 9.9 births per thousand inhabitants and 9.3 deaths. While this is true overall, the same does not hold for the southern part of the country—the so-called Mezzogiorno—which maintains relatively high birthrates and low death rates, and so a natural population increase higher than the rest of Italy. Meantime, with a longer life span than men's (73 years), women (79.7 years) have gradually taken over the majority of the population, now 51.42 percent.

A further indication of the aging of the Italians shows up in the scholastic population. During the 1990–1991 school year, university students represented 14 percent of the total, and elementary school children, 31 percent. The same figures twenty years before were, respectively, 7 percent and 52 percent.

As for population distribution by age, in 1986 0-to-19-year-olds constituted 26.5 percent of the total, 20-to-59-year-olds, 54.5 percent, and those over 60, 19 percent.

OVERVIEW

Despite the fact that Italy became a modern nation in 1861, it was a monarchy until 1946, that is, until the end of World War II, at which time it became a constitutional democratic republic. One of the first decrees of the provisional government, even before the actual creation of the republic, was to give Italian women the vote for the first time in history. They then made use of the decree, dated 1 February 1946, for the first time on 2 June 1946, choosing a republic over the monarchy and electing the members of the Constituent Assembly: 21 women were elected out of 556 deputies.

The Constitution represented a compromise between an American model of democracy and the ideals of solidarity and equality deriving from popular political parties (in particular reference to the partisans who fought in the Resistance). This is evident right from the first article, which states clearly that Italy is a democratic republic founded on the work principle. Most significantly, the Constitution established for the first time the moral and legal equality between men and women (Article 3),[1] further specified in terms of work (Article 37).[2]

To attain this recognition on the part of the law, Italian women had to go through 2,000 years of blatant discrimination. As such, only an outline of the role women played over the centuries can lead to an understanding of the new life they were initiating in 1946. And also to the realization that, while the situation was changing drastically for women from a legal standpoint, a comparative evolution on a practical level would be very slow in coming.

In the cradle of civilization in the entire Mediterranean area, women were held in high esteem as childbearers. In almost all the ancient cultures (Minoan, Phoenician, and so on) there were traces of fertility cults identified with powerful goddesses, such as Astarte. The picture changed dramatically with the birth of the classical culture in the Mediterranean area and with the Hebrew culture in the Near East, for both followed a strict patriarchal model. Women were always and everywhere discriminated against and kept on the outskirts of society. Excluded from the exercise of power in religious, political, and social life, they were considered physically weaker and intellectually inferior.

While, in Athens (the fifth to fourth centuries B.C.), women were not free to leave the home and enjoyed no political rights (about a century later, in fact, Aristotle developed his theory about the natural diversity and consequent inferiority of women), in Rome, the situation was significantly different. Although lacking in political rights, women—no longer segregated in the home—gradually acquired more freedom of movement and greater autonomy, on the condition they were *cives*, privileged citizens of Rome. In Roman society women were, in effect, always figures of great respect, queens of the household. They were entrusted with the primary task of educating their children, preparing them to become Roman citizens.

Toward the end of the Republican age, during the imperial period, some women belonging to illustrious families succeeded in having a determinant influence on public affairs. These women initiated a process of progressive emancipation through the increasingly more frequent practices of divorce and abortion, but this extreme freedom concerned only a very few women. With the corruption of common morality, women of the lower classes were left exposed to the arrogance and abuse of wealthy Romans.

In the first century A.D. early Christianity brought a message of freedom for all women. Christ was the first man to defend adulteresses and to exhort women to cultivate the heart and soul. Among the early Christians, women spread the message of Christ and even faced martyrdom, no matter what their civil/social status was.

When, however, Christianity became the state religion of Rome under Constantine in A.D. 313, the dignity Jesus had introduced for women began falling under the negative influence of the original patriarchal society. In the early centuries A.D. the fathers of the Western church identified women with Eve, original sin, and the devil. They established for women a strict hierarchy of roles, with the virgin in first place, the widow in second, and the mother only in third. St. Ambrose defined the Virgin Mary as mother of salvation, in contrast to Eve, mother of the race (Epist. 63, 33, PL 16). St. Jerome went even further, saying that death came from Eve, life from Mary, because "now that a virgin has conceived and given us a Child, the chain of malediction is broken." This mystical idealization of women arose from the cultural necessity of Christians to spread a feminine image in contrast to the stereotype of the virtuous Roman matron/mother "who tends the hearth and spins the yarn."

The cult of virginity had, at the same time, positive effects on the life of women. By giving themselves to religion as virgins or widows, women had an honorable means for freeing themselves from subjugation to men and relative family duties. The incredible number of women who abandoned home and family to follow St. Jerome, who spent all their material wealth to visit holy places and to assist the poor, reveals how the Roman women converted to Christianity once again achieved a significant degree of autonomy in the fourth to fifth centuries A.D. The growing number of monasteries, as well as the scholastic reform of Charlemagne, allowed women a more systematic access to culture from the ninth century on. All during the High Middle Ages convents for women became centers of culture and teaching, even for young girls (nobles especially). Some abbesses acquired an authority equal to that of bishops.

Lower-class women, meanwhile, maintained a profound knowledge of more earthly matters, natural remedies, and so on. Medicine and science in the Middle Ages were not completely closed to women. The prestigious Salerno Medical School had a few women experts in medicine, authors of medical papers on physiology. The most famous of these was Trotula (eleventh century), who wrote the first gynecological tract attributed to a woman: she knew that abstinence from sexual activity was not good for the health (in an era in which a permanent state of virginity was considered healthy). She was so prominently known that one century later Chaucer mentioned her in his *Canterbury Tales*.

Then, from the end of the twelfth century on, city-states began emerging throughout Italy, giving rise to a new urban middle class of artisans, traders, and so on and to a relative cultural development. Italian took over from Latin as the main spoken and written language. New models of male-female relations arose accordingly. First was an idealized form of love, that of the knight for his lady. Successively, with the ''dolce stil novo'' and Dante Alighieri, the woman became an angel on earth guiding the poet toward God. While, at this point, a modern idea of love was being nurtured in literature, daily reality was quite different. Around the fourteenth century, the merchant Giovanni Morelli wrote a book of memoirs for his son encouraging him to choose a wife according to the same criteria by which he would buy a cow: healthy, submissive, hard-working, prolific (in order to have lots of male children).

In the same period, however, lived one of the brightest figures in Italian history: St. Catherine, patron saint of Italy. A true mystic, St. Catherine wrote a series of fervent letters to the Pope in Avignon to have him return to Rome. And she succeeded in this most unusual and arduous endeavor.

During the Renaissance only a very few women intellectuals and artists made a mark on the period (poetesses Gaspara Stampa and Veronica Gambara, art patrons Isabella d'Este and Vittoria Colonna, painters Sofonisba Anguissola and Artemisia Gentilleschi). In order to exercise an artistic activity, women had either to be wealthy and powerful or to accept certain compromises. Meanwhile, many women treating illnesses with popular cures were tried as witches. This was true up until the seventeenth century.

In the eighteenth and nineteenth centuries, the most important development for women concerned the degree of literacy in the area of the country north of Florence. The ability to read and write increased exponentially in urban communities, particularly among women.

When the time finally came for unification, in 1861, many women of both lower and upper classes played a role. The newly formed Italian kingdom-nation, however, did very little for them. Women could not vote and earned less money than men for the same work. The only women who gained widespread respect were queens, noblewomen involved in charity work, and distinct figures such as Grazia Deledda, Nobel prizewinner for literature. The only truly accepted feminine models were the self-sacrificing wife and mother, the devoted nun, or the dedicated spinster schoolteacher.

The Catholic church, as ever one of the major influences in Italian society, was instrumental in imposing these stereotypical role models. These same role models were further glorified through rhetoric all during the fascist regime (1922–1943). For example, Benito Mussolini awarded medals to mothers of big families (ten to twelve children).

In light of a similar history, the dramatic change in the status of Italian women that came with the establishment of the democratic republic in 1946 takes on all the more importance. In the more than forty years since the issuing of the constitution, much has been achieved in Italy in terms of male-female equality. Especially in the last two decades, thanks to pressure from women's associations and the women's movement in general, all previous situations of inequality in Italian laws have been eliminated. Particularly noteworthy in this respect was the Family Rights Reform Law of 19 May 1975, according to which all differences between husband and wife were abolished and replaced with a standard of complete equality.

It is also true that in daily life, in the application of the laws, a lot of direct and indirect indiscrimination due to a persistence in the Italian culture to consider women inferior to men occurs. There remains a strong tendency not to recognize on a practical level women's right/responsibility to make their own individual decisions in determining their life with others and as a part of society as a whole. While today women choose a variety of life experiences—a job, a family/personal relations, study, leisure—they nevertheless come up against a material and symbolic organization of society still based on a division of sexual roles. Working women currently represent 33 percent of the overall labor force in Italy, but they have almost total responsibility for running the household. Women are, moreover, expected "naturally" to take care of others (children, the sick, the elderly) and to take on positions in the working world without decisional power, status, or great economic compensation.

Indicative of the rigid patriarchal mentality that continues to pervade many aspects of Italian society are the words of a father from a small town near Rome in defense of his son, accused of the rape of two young girls in 1984. Before the entire court, he stated: "I have three daughters; two are married. The youngest is always at home; she goes out only to do the shopping, and even then in the company of her sisters. The way I see it, my daughter has to live like this until she gets married. Women have to live like this."

COMPARISONS BETWEEN MEN'S AND WOMEN'S GENDER ROLES DURING THE LIFE CYCLE

Infancy and Early Childhood

Elena Gianini Belotti, a prominent Italian early childhood expert and Montessori teacher, published in 1973 an analytical study on the differences in Italy between male and female child-rearing practices. This text has become a major reference for both feminists and educators in Italy and throughout Europe. Even though the situation is improving somewhat, today Belotti's book, *Little Girls*, is still pertinent to the great majority of the Italian population.

As in all historically peasant cultures, families give primary importance to the birth of a male child. The female child, meanwhile, is wanted—if she is wanted at all—on the basis of a sort of scale of convenience: girls are more affectionate, more grateful; they are sweet and playful, fun to dress; they are more company in the home, as well as a help with the housework.

This preference becomes all the more striking after birth, during breast-feeding. Belotti explains how Italian women breast-feed male infants far more willingly than female ones. Right from the first months of life, the mothers encourage a certain greediness in suckling on the part of males as a sign of natural (and positive) aggressiveness but inhibit the same on the part of females as an unnatural sign of indelicacy. In other words, mothers already start training the girls for a life of "spirituality" and self-sacrifice. The same difference of attitude shows up in physically caring for the infant. For example, in changing diapers, the mothers fondle lovingly the male infant's genitals, while for the female's they reserve only an aseptic cleansing. This difference comes through in the Italian language, which has tens of nicknames for the male child's genitals but only two for the female's.

Mother-daughter relationships are, therefore, generally much more problematic than mother-son relationships, right from the early months. This becomes evident in typical conflicts. Mothers confess to being more anxious, nervous, and insecure when bringing up a son; and yet they find it an easier undertaking. They do not blame any of the troubles encountered in raising a girl on themselves, but rather on the "difficult nature" of girls. All in all, mothers themselves recognize that they are stricter with girls.

The impact this can have on the psychological makeup of women is underlined by Italian philosopher Luisa Muraro in her essay entitled *L'ordine simbolico della madre* (*The Symbolic Order of the Mother*). In it she clearly states that the patriarchal society treats the love between mother and son as its most precious heritage: it is the hearth of fervent desires, the kitchen of sublime endeavors, the workshop of the law. She even goes as far as to say: "If there is something for which I envy men it is this culture of mother-love in which they grew up." According to Muraro, in Italian society there is no similar rapport between mother and daughter. Female nihilism can be referred directly back to the cultural absence of a true mother-daughter experience.

The same pattern shows up all through the years of child rearing. As children begin expressing their own individual personalities, mothers outrightly seek to modify these personalities in line with specific sexual stereotypes. That is, they encourage the naturally aggressive male child and discourage a similar female child in their behavior, and vice versa for naturally low-key and apparently passive children.

This entire process reveals itself openly through the various accessories of life. Today, not only mothers but nursery/kindergarten teachers, whether consciously or unconsciously, still encourage sexual stereotyping through the selection of clothes, toys, and games for the children: the traditional blue, guns, building blocks for boys; pink, dolls, and playing house for girls. At the same time, in recent years, thanks to the efforts of feminism and even to the evolution of consumer trends, the situation has changed somewhat, especially in the urban areas of the north. As in all the rest of the industrialized world, in Italy, too, children of all ages dress willingly in jogging suits, jeans, and sneakers and use colorful knapsacks as their carryalls. But in another respect Italy is unique. Given the tremendous importance of fashion today in Italian life at all levels (the textile/apparel industry is in fact the country's first and foremost in terms of manufacturing), children tend to be keenly interested in, and aware of, quality, trendy clothing expressing differences in male and female roles: little boys like to dress up in jackets and ties, little girls in pretty dresses, often in takeoffs of designer models.

In other ways, however, in recent years there have been important signs of change on a sociopolitical level. Whereas, before, only women could become nursery and kindergarten teachers in Italy, now men are also invited to undertake the profession. Fathers, too, have been encouraged to participate more actively in the nurturing and raising of their children. Specifically, in 1977 the legislature passed a law providing fathers with the option to take paid paternity leave in order to care for a newborn while the wife goes to work. Just recently (1991) this option was extended to include the care of a newly adopted child as well.

School Years

As a natural extension of gender discrimination in child-rearing practices, in Italian families brothers and sisters have always played vastly different roles. While girls had to help with the housework, boys were granted infinitely more freedom; while boys were encouraged to express their independence, girls were instructed actually to serve their brothers as sweet nonentities and enjoy doing so. Today, however, gender differences between brothers and sisters are no longer as underlined as in the past: at least in urban areas of the north, both participate in family chores.

Meanwhile, on an elementary school level (where 90 percent of the teachers are female), discrimination still shows up to a significant degree. In textbooks for primary schools, the woman who works outside the home, who enjoys prestige and has responsibilities remains an unfamiliar figure. In face of similar prejudices, parents' associations are increasingly raising their voice in protest.

As the children continue their schooling, distinctions become less marked, also because a more even distribution of male/female teachers evolves. While in junior high, two-thirds are still women, by high school there is a fifty-fifty split between the two.

In Italy school attendance is obligatory and free for eight years (ages 6 to 14): specifically, five years of elementary and three of junior high. In practice, high school attendance is optional. Whereas up until the early 1960s a majority of the state schools divided the classes by gender, now at all levels of education, even in parochial schools, all classes are fully integrated. Yet once students reach high school, a natural division takes place in terms of scholastic direction. This fact is important in Italy because there are distinct schools for the various classical, scientific, artistic, technical, and clerical programs. Students must choose their orientation early on and stick to it until graduation. While changing schools is possible, it is not recommended. Both sexes attend the first three kinds of high school on an equal basis; males make up the great majority of the population in technical schools, and females are the majority in clerical ones.

On a university level the first departments in which a significant number of women enrolled—in the years between the two world wars—were the humanities and, to a lesser extent, law, medicine, and architecture. Now, instead, women also enroll willingly in departments once the stronghold of males, such as physics, engineering, mathematics, chemistry, veterinary medicine, and agricultural science. Since Italian universities are primarily state-run and open to all those who want to attend (the only prerequisite is a high school diploma), enrollment costs are extremely low. Yet in Italy university graduates still make up a small fraction of the population. In 1981, for example, only 2.8 percent of all Italians had a university degree: 2.1 percent of all women, 3.6 percent of all men. (According to a 1991 census report, while 25 percent currently enroll in a university, only 8 percent complete their studies.) Especially in provincial and rural communities, a degree represents not only a means for achieving professional status but also— and in some cases, even above all—an element of prestige for the entire family. This is, of course, far truer for males than for females.

Young Adulthood

In Italian tradition socialization customs between the two sexes were extremely rigid, to some degree a reflection of the vestiges of the ancient virginity cult. While today in major urban areas most of these old prejudices have been overcome, in provincial and rural ones they still occur. Of particular interest in this regard is the case in 1989 of the young Sicilian girl, Lara Cardella, from the small town of Licata, who wrote a first novel, an immediate best-seller, *Volevo i pantaloni* (*I Wanted Trousers*), in which she described in emotional detail the repression teenage girls still suffer within the family. According to the picture portrayed by Cardella, in many cases parents are still obsessed with the good name of the family: in other words, no wearing miniskirts, no licking an ice-cream cone in public, no meeting with boys after school. This book had such a big impact on Italian society—highly ambivalent about being depicted in such terms—that it set off a national controversy through the media. At one point the mayor of Licata even went on television to claim this image of Sicilian society was unjustified. Meanwhile, lots of young girls from towns in many parts of the country wrote letters to various newspapers and magazines saying that they indeed encountered similar forms of repression.

On a different level, socialization practices have undergone major changes in the last two decades. Whereas traditionally, young adults followed strict dating customs, often finding a partner at an early age and becoming officially engaged, today teenagers and young people in general enjoy a more open and flexible system of social relations, especially in the big cities. Girls can have more than one boyfriend without getting stigmatized as frivolous. Meanwhile, marriage is no longer the principal aim of relations of the sexes at this period in life. In contrast, formerly, young people had to be officially engaged simply to go out on a date. As part of the same evolution, young single women are no longer seen as spinsters but rather as modern, independent-minded individuals. Specifically in this regard, virginity is no longer a value to be defended for most Italians (for 52.7 percent of the population, according to a 1991 poll); in fact, most young people have their first complete sexual encounter between ages 16 and 20.

At this point, however, an important note must be made. Although many things have changed in terms of socialization practices among young adults in Italy, one remains the same. Due to a variety of factors—including the high cost of living but also a willingness to enjoy, well into the twenties, all the comforts of home—Italian young adults still tend to live with their parents until they get married, even if they have a fulfilling and well-paying job.

In terms of employment, however, the situation in Italy among males and females is extremely mobile. On 10 April 1991, the Italian legislature passed a special equal opportunity law aimed at eliminating all forms of sexual inequality relative to scholastic and professional training and access to jobs; favoring a diversification in women's selection of jobs and managerial training; promoting inclusion of women in jobs where their presence is minimal and/or low-level; and encouraging a better balance of professional and domestic duties between the two sexes. No less than a National Equal Opportunity Committee was established within the Italian Ministry of Labor to oversee the application of the equal opportunity law and to promote positive actions to further its effectiveness.

Even before this new law favoring their professional rise went into effect, Italian women were getting more new jobs than men. In 1989, for example,

114,000 of the 176,000 new jobs created went to women. In effect, women are currently running 429,000 businesses throughout the country. At the same time, women account for only 3.3 percent of all executives in Italy, whereas female factory and office workers make up 52 percent of the overall women's labor force. Yet the situation is destined to improve because, according to the new law, companies employing women will receive special benefits and those not employing women will receive fines and even punishment (exclusion from bidding for government projects).

There is a further aspect of this new socioeconomic reality. Today's youths represent for the first time a generation bombarded by consumer ideology putting accent on the present as the only time and space dimension. While before, in line with the traditional peasant mentality emphasizing saving money as the only means for emerging from a condition of subordination, putting funds aside for the future was of primary importance (e.g., girls saved up to have a lavish trousseau for the day they would marry), now both sexes spend their earnings freely on consumer goods and entertainment.

Adulthood

Until a few years ago in Italy the whole process of getting married was an extremely elaborate affair. Even the poorest families would spend all their savings and even go heavily into debt to assure their children *un bel matrimonio*: a church full of flowers, a magnificent wedding gown, a lavish banquet for hundreds of guests, expensive wedding favors for one and all, and a sumptuous trousseau of hand-embroidered linens. In exchange, the guests were expected to give the newlyweds very expensive presents. Now, instead, an increasing number of young couples, especially in major urban areas, opt for a more simple and sometimes only a civil (instead of religious) ceremony. There is another interesting aspect in regard to marriage in Italy. Traditionally and still today, becoming husband and wife also means most specifically getting *sistemati*, an exquisitely Italian expression signifying "settled for life." This means, particularly for women, that their place in society has been permanently and safely established.

From an institutional viewpoint, up until the Family Rights Reform Law in 1975, in marriage women were in an inferior position in respect to their husband. With the law all distinctions of rights/responsibilities between marital partners were eliminated: both husband and wife now must meet the needs of the family in relation to their respective material possibilities and professional/domestic capacities. Adultery, moreover, is no longer a crime (until 1968 it was, but only for wives!). On a material level, unless otherwise specified (with a *separazione dei beni*, a legal separation of worldly goods), couples now enjoy a situation in which everything acquired after the marriage is considered the property of both husband and wife to the same degree. This holds for everything except personal items, no matter who paid for the goods, property, financial holdings.

As for household duties, the classic figure of the Italian male as king of his own private realm is fading somewhat among the new generations. Young husbands share certain tasks with their wife, mostly those related to cooking, shopping, and child rearing. Women, however, still handle the great bulk of the cleaning. This is true whether the wife has a job outside the home or not.

Divorce has been legal in Italy only since 1970. The law in question was passed after an arduous battle against the Catholic-oriented political parties, which even made an unsuccessful attempt to abolish it by means of a popular referendum five years after it went into effect. This was the first time ever in the history of the republic that the Catholic groups suffered such a bitter defeat. But in another respect the Catholic church won. While divorce is now allowed in Italy, it can be granted only after three years (up until 1987 five years) of legal separation.

In separating, the economically better-off partner must continue supporting the other in the manner he or she is accustomed to, until the other contracts a second marriage. The family home is assigned to the one who gets custody of the children, no matter who actually owns it. Refusal to pay alimony/child support is a crime punishable with a fine and/or one year in prison. A wife or husband receiving alimony—if not remarried—can demand 40 percent of her or his ex-spouse's severance pay relative to the years they were married. She or he can also (again if not remarried) collect the spouse's pension in case of death.

In seeking to protect family rights, both during marriage and afterward, Italian law has particular regard for working mothers. Maternity is considered not only a personal/family value but a social one as well. Working mothers thus enjoy special benefits during pregnancy and after giving birth; some of these benefits are extended also to fathers. No woman can be fired from the start of the pregnancy until the child is twelve months old or until three months after delivery if the baby is born dead. During the pregnancy and up to seven months after delivery, women who remain on the job are absolved from heavy and/or dangerous duties. In any case, they are obliged to stay home from work from two months before the due date to three months after delivery. They have the option of staying home six months during the child's first year of life and as long as necessary if the child becomes ill during the first three years of life. All this is with almost full salary.

The state also provides family-planning centers guaranteeing pregnant women all the necessary social and medical services. Abortion has, in fact, been legal in Italy since 1978. During the first ninety days of pregnancy, a woman can get an abortion on the basis of a simple request; afterward, she can get one only if her life is in danger or if the fetus is severely malformed. If the woman is underage, she needs the consent of a parent or guardian; otherwise, she needs a judicial decree. The state pays for all assistance.

While the family is still fundamentally the focus of Italian life and children tend to be spoiled by their parents, recreational time spent together as a unit is not all that common, other than Sunday outings and the typical month's vacation at the beach in August. Most Italian families spend their evenings at home watching television. Another classic Italian ritual is enjoying the weekend soccer matches either at the stadium or on TV, an activity fathers and sons enthusiastically share.

Old Age

Whereas in peasant culture the elderly had considerable status as the holders of wisdom and important practical knowledge (in particular regard to farming and the preserving of agricultural products for future use), in modern industrial Italy the most that old people can hope for is a dignified autonomy. Frequently this is a futile hope, because to a great extent today's elderly receive pensions that have not kept up with the rate of inflation. This is why many are forced to live with children. In any case, in Italy children are obliged by law to provide materially for their parents when they lack the sufficient means on their own.

In another respect, however, the elderly in Italy are unusually well-off. Thanks to the Italian national health care plan, they enjoy complete medical coverage. Even most medicines are, for all practical purposes, free. Meanwhile, nursing homes remain an unpopular (and rare) solution.

One of the favorite pastimes of the elderly in Italy is spending time with, and taking care of, their grandchildren, often in the official role of baby-sitter. This is particularly true in the case of working daughters and/or daughters-in-law, because today Italians still dislike referring to someone outside the family for the task. Other activities of elderly men include spending time with friends, sitting at the local bar, chatting, and/or playing cards. Meanwhile, the women mostly stay at home, going out only for the daily grocery shopping ritual or for attending morning mass.

In recent years, however, both state and religious groups have become more active in organizing leisure pastimes for senior citizens. These include gym classes, ballroom dances, outings, short trips abroad, even special educational programs. The elderly in Italy also enjoy discount rates for the movies, theater productions, and public transportation.

SUMMARY AND CONCLUSIONS

Today women in Italy have come a long way. Formerly prominent figures such as the old lady always dressed in black, perennially in mourning, and the young girl kept excessively within the safety of the home are gradually dying out. But the ideology and inherent prejudices of twenty centuries of a patriarchal mind-set and strict Catholicism are still deeply rooted in male and female psyches. Despite wide-ranging legislation in favor of equality—intrinsically beneficial to both men and women—attempts are frequently made, especially on the part of reactionary Catholics, to cancel out or at least diminish the effects of the laws. The Pope, ever a dominant presence in Italy, feels it his right and responsibility to emphasize the traditional teachings of the church (only in 1968 did Pope Paul

VI officially establish for the first time in papal history that sexual intercourse between husband and wife was admissible, good even, for purposes other than procreation).

Indications of this underlying negative mentality inevitably surface from time to time. For example, while public brothels were officially shut down in Italy in 1958 by the Merlin law, prominent male intellectuals, nostalgic about this period of state-approved female subjugation, occasionally propose their reopening.

A new law that would make rape a crime no longer against the family but against the individual has been under consideration, without passage, in the Italian Parliament now for fourteen years.

Only in the early 1980s was the article regarding *il delitto d'onore* (the husband's prerogative to murder his unfaithful wife for purposes of maintaining his personal honor) eliminated from the Constitution. But in the summer of 1991 the question came up again when a man who had in fact killed his spouse for infidelity got a major reduction in his sentence in the court of appeals because the judges deemed the provocation factor an important extenuating circumstance.

As for the problem of sexual harassment, Italians of both genders remained incredulous during the Judge Clarence Thomas/Anita Hill case in the fall of 1991 because in Italy similar harassment is not only quite common but considered a normal aspect of male-female relations. For one thing, it is not a crime under Italian law. For another, Italian men tend to feel, even after repeated rejection, that all their advances are welcome (a 1991 trade union–sponsored poll reported that 70 percent of the male population believes women appreciate this type of flirting).

All these signs of chauvinistic behavior do not go unnoticed by the female population, especially in the case of women with roles in the various political parties. While in the 1970s the feminist movement showed up predominantly in the streets, now the battle for women's rights is fought primarily on an institutional level and with long-range insight. Of particular interest in this respect is the proposal for a new law that would modify the rhythms of modern life. It is an original, courageous proposal without precedent in Europe, encouraging both men and women to reevaluate well-established life-styles. Based on the principle that time is not money, it calls for a thirty-five-hour workweek; paid leaves for men and women for personal motives, as well as unpaid leaves for reasons of study or other reasons; and a division of household and family-oriented chores equally between the two sexes. Women are the protagonists of this ambitious project. After all, today's major social/cultural transformations have their roots in the evolution of female psychology, for women are changing from passive creatures who accept a certain destiny and role to dynamic, unpredictable beings who take charge of their individual lives.

In conclusion, how do Italian men and women see themselves today? Perhaps the most precise image of women emerged from a study conducted in 1990 by the Makno Research Institute. It revealed that women are extraordinarily modern and autonomous figures who work for three basic motives: economic independence, interest in the professional activity per se, and contact with others. Meanwhile, marital aspirations appear on a sharp decline. Whereas twenty years ago 68 percent of young women dreamed of encountering the ideal mate, now only a modest 7 percent put finding a husband at the top of their wish list. This does not mean they are uninterested in falling in love and getting married. Rather, it reflects that they realize establishing an equal partnership on a meaningful basis is difficult, and so they realistically focus on a more concrete objective: professional fulfillment.

In regard to men, a 1991 survey of 800 males age 18 to 65 revealed an Italian male self-image quite different from the one portrayed in official statistics, an image characterized by low self-confidence and no arrogance, a wobbly self-concept in this transition period from the traditional lord-and-master figure to the who-knows-what? of today. According to 70.6 percent, male power has diminished in respect to female power in Italy in the last ten years. As philosopher Umberto Galimberti succinctly points out, "Anthropologically, twenty years is too short a time to assimilate in full the process of women's liberation." Social relations analyst Anna Del Bo Boffino goes on to explain, "The pill gave women the right to choose, broadening the gap between reality and the male fantasy world—a big blow for men to accept." Meanwhile, psychoanalyst-sex therapist Willy Pasini maintains not only that men are still very fearful of female initiative and boldness but that herein lies the reason for the current interest in paternity (specifically, the idea: If I cannot be a man, at least I can be a father). Thus men are discovering values formerly the exclusive territory of women.

NOTES

1. "All citizens are equal before the law regardless of sex, race, language, religion, political beliefs, and personal/social conditions. It is the task of the Republic to remove obstacles of a social/economic nature which . . . hinder the full development of the individual person" (Article 3 of the Italian Constitution).

2. "The woman who works has the same rights and commands the same pay as the man who works. Working conditions must allow the fulfillment of her essential function in the family" (Article 37 of the Italian Constitution).

REFERENCES

Bassi, Tina Lagostena. (1991). *L'avvocato delle donne, Dodici storie di ordinaria violenza (The Women's Lawyer, Twelve Stories of Ordinary Violence)*. Milan: Arnoldo Mondadori.
Bellocchio, Lella Ravasi. (1987). *Di madre in figlia (From Mother to Daughter)*. Milan: Raffaello Cortina.
Belotti, Elena Gianini. (1973). *Little Girls*. Milan: Giangiacomo Feltrinelli. (English translation published in 1975, London: Writers and Readers Publishing Cooperative.)

Bertini, F., Cardini, F., Leonardi, C., & Fumagalli Beonio Brocchieri, M. T. (1989). *Medioevo al femminile* (*A Feminine View of the Middle Ages*). Milan: Gius. Laterza & Sons.

Cardella, Lara. (1989). *Volevo i pantaloni* (*I Wanted Trousers*). Milan: Arnoldo Mondadori.

Del Bufalo, M., Di Cristofaro Longo, G., Dini, A., Moscato, M., Parasassi, G., & Remiddi, L. (1991). *Pagine Rosa, Guida ai diritti delle donne* (*Pink Pages, Guide to Women's Rights*). Rome: Presidenza del Consiglio dei Ministri.

Istituto Poligrafico e zecca dello stato. (1991). *Azioni positive per la parità uomo donna nel lavoro* (*Positive Actions for Male/Female Equality in the Workplace*). Rome.

La repubblica. (9 August 1991): Storia d'Italia in cifre (The history of Italy in figures); (3 September 1991): Un marito supertradito uccide sempre per ira (A superbetrayed husband always kills out of anger); (12 October 1991): La gioventù del tutto e subito (Today's young people: Wanting it all and now); (13–14 October 1991): La verginità? Meglio conservarla (Virginity? It's better to keep it); (16 October 1991): Le proposte alle colleghe? Per i maschi italiani è normale (Making advances to female colleagues? For Italian men it's normal). Rome.

L'espresso. (18 August 1991): Una legge lunga quattordici anni (A law fourteen years long); (20 October 1991): Quando comanda lei (When she's the boss). Milan.

Mattioni, Marina. (1990). *Dossier Donne '90* (*Special Report on Women in the '90s*). Milan: Edimoda.

Morelli, Giovanni di Paolo. *Ricordi* (*Recollections*).

Muraro, Luisa. (1976). *La signora del gioco, Episodi della caccia alle streghe* (*The Lady of the Game, Episodes of the Witch Hunt*). Milan: Feltrinelli.

———. (1991). *L'ordine simbolico della madre* (*The Symbolic Order of the Mother*). Rome: Riuniti.

Panorama. (28 July 1991). Ma che uomo sei (What kind of man are you). Milan.

Ranke-Heinemann, Uta. (1988). *Eunuchi per il regno dei cieli* (*Eunuchs for the Kingdom of God*). Hamburg: Hoffman und Campe. (Italian translation published in 1990, Milan: Rizzoli Books.)

Turco, Livia. (1990). *Le donne cambiano i tempi* (*Women Change the Times*). Rome.

13

Japan

*Seisoh Sukemune,
Toshiyuki Shiraishi,
Yoshiko Shirakawa, and
Junko Tanaka Matsumi*

INTRODUCTION

Japan is an island nation situated off the eastern coast of Asia. Extending some 2,000 miles from northeast to southwest, the Japanese Archipelago consists of four main islands of Honshu, Shikoku, Kyushu, and Hokkaido, as well as more than 4,000 smaller islands. Japan has a population of 124 million. Because the whole country is so mountainous, more than 60 percent of the people are concentrated in less than 3 percent of the total land area, which makes Japan one of the most densely populated nations in the world. Japanese men and women have maintained ethnic homogeneity for more than 20 centuries and have built an extremely disciplined culture with numerous sex-differentiated codes for social behaviors.

Historically, Japan has undergone a rapid and drastic sociocultural change during the last 150 years from a hierarchically oriented feudalistic society to unprecedented modernization and industrialization. Japan's international economic advancements were particularly noteworthy after World War II. After the defeat in World War II, from 1945 to 1952 Japan was forced to undergo occupation by the United States of America under General Douglas MacArthur, who initiated a sweeping change in the basic education and legal system with a goal of developing democracy in Japan. The new Japanese constitution, which went into effect in 1947, underscores the nature of a series of sociocultural changes. The new constitution provided that the emperor is no longer a "living god" and is now "the symbol of the State." For the first time the legal equality of the sexes was guaranteed in the constitution:

There shall be no discrimination in political, economic or social relations, because of . . . sex. . . . Marriage shall be based only on the mutual consent of both sexes . . . with regard to choice of spouse, property rights, inheritance, choice of domicile, divorce and other matters pertaining to family. . . . Laws shall be enacted from the standpoint of individual dignity and the essential equality in the sexes.

Both men and women have the right to vote at the age of 20. Women were first given the right to vote and to stand for office in 1945. In 1985 an Equal Employment Act was enacted, giving a fresh impetus to the employment of women, who amounted to 36 percent of the work force in 1987 (Beasley, 1990). Thus, it appears that there is now a firm legal ground to practice equal rights of Japanese men and women.

Yet, despite the postwar legal provisions, the Japanese cultural sentiment continues to reflect *Danson-johi*, which may be translated as the predominance of men over women in many areas of the lives of Japanese men and women. As will be shown in this chapter, the rapid postwar social and technological changes occurred against the historical background of male-dominated, hierarchical familial and social structure, with numerous codes of sex-differentiated role behaviors in both public and private situations. The present chapter examines the extent to which the fundamental conceptions of the traditionally sex-differentiated roles of Japanese men and women have accommodated to technological changes in Japan.

OVERVIEW

Despite technological and legal changes, Japan continues to function as a very stable society without any drastic shifts in family roles. Japanese parents are dedicated to the education of their children through very hard work. The overall familial stability is based on traditional cultural practices derived from Confucian philosophy, which emphasizes the network of particularistic obligations and responsibilities that the individual assumed as a member of his or her family or immediate community (Nakane, 1970). Even today, Japanese men are intensely committed to the occupational role and women to the domestic role. These sex-role specializations (Lebra, 1984) have long been reinforced by the Confucian philosophy that men and women are not openly to interact in public or to switch social roles once they reach the age of seven.

Japanese people have traditionally valued family lineage by transmitting the family name through the eldest male child. Under the prewar family system, the eldest son, *chonan*, would inherit the family property and assume the duty of paying respect to the ancestors. In families without a male heir, a daughter may marry a man who would assume his wife's name to ensure the continuation of the family.

Today with the new legal provision, the eldest son is no longer entitled to an automatic inheritance of the family property; however, he is still considered responsible for supporting and caring for his aging parents. Marrying an eldest son, therefore, implies serving and taking care of the in-laws. Women's domestic role in such a household is highly prescribed. It can become a full-time job to be perfected. Such an intense involvement with the domestic role has delayed Japanese women from turning their attention to a larger social role outside the home (Lebra, 1984). To evaluate fully this situation, it is necessary to turn the attention to the development of sex roles in the context of Japan's history of long feudal experience supported by Confucian philosophy.

COMPARISONS BETWEEN MEN'S AND WOMEN'S GENDER ROLES DURING THE LIFE CYCLE

Infancy and Early Childhood

Japanese studies of child-rearing patterns and cross-cultural research on mother-child interaction have documented that Japanese parents' attitudes and behavior toward their child differ according to the sex of the child. According to Kashiwagi (1986), who has conducted a series of empirical studies on the development of sex roles in Japanese children and adolescents, sex-differentiated discipline occurs in nearly 80 percent of Japanese homes. Girls are expected to conform to the traditional female role more than boys. She also found that while boys showed more positive opinion of parental discipline, girls held a more negative view of parental discipline. Boys are, in fact, treated more permissively than girls in Japanese families (Hara & Wagatsuma, 1974).

Cross-cultural developmental studies also reveal some of the unique parenting styles of Japanese mothers. Japanese mothers are intensely involved with their infants through nonverbal communication. They stay physically close to the infant (Caudill & Weinstein, 1969). According to Caudill (1974), Japanese mothers encourage dependency in the child through physical proximity. The relationship between the child and mother is assumed to be emotionally close (Caudill, 1973; Markus & Kitayama, 1991). Takahashi (1986) found that in Ainsworth's situation Japanese infants rated high on the proximity/contact dimension.

This Japanese emphasis on interdependence rather than independence since infancy encourages parental discipline that is based on social conformity. The child's behavior is judged according to how the child is able to adjust and accommodate to specific others (Azuma, 1984). In their longitudinal investigation of family influences on school readiness and achievement in Japan, Hess and his colleagues (1986) found that in situations requiring discipline with their preschool children, Japanese mothers frequently emphasized the potentially deleterious consequences of the act (e.g., how shameful the act appears to others) rather than the mother's authority. Japanese mothers also appealed more frequently to feelings. On the whole, Japanese mothers expected the child to be compliant, polite, and emotionally mature.

In contrast to the active parenting role played by Japanese mothers, Japanese fathers assume a dominant authority role, but, in reality, they generally do not actively participate in child rearing. As a result, alliance is often formed between the mother and the child in the Japanese family. Japanese fathers are more intensely involved with their occupational role outside, leaving them little time to attend to their children.

Within the child-oriented Japanese family structure, there are a number of special days assigned to celebrate festival events, which serve to reinforce sex-role socializations. On these special days both fathers and mothers are typically seen to celebrate together and appreciate the Japanese value of *kodakara*, which means children as treasures.

Shichi-go-san (the seven-five-three festival) is the festival for boys and girls of three, boys of five, and girls of seven. These three ages are considered very important for children. They are dressed in their best traditional outfits and are taken to a Shinto shrine on 15 November by their parents, who give thanks for their good health and pray for future blessings. *Kodomo-no-hi* (Children's Day) is nationally celebrated on 5 May as predominantly the Boys' Festival *(tango-no-sekku)*. The Girls' Festival is celebrated 3 March with traditional Japanese dolls, or *hinamatsuri*.

Between ages 1 and 3 Japanese boys like to swing and play several ball games, while girls like to play pretend activities and draw pictures. At ages 4–6 ball games are liked by boys, while girls prefer pretend play. With age boys become more actively involved in physical play, such as *sumo*, a traditional Japanese wrestling, which has a history of 300 years, while girls become accustomed to various static and elaborate play activities, such as *origami*, paper folding, which stimulates creativity and fosters dexterity (Hirayama et al., 1988). There are also exclusively sex-linked extracurricular activity clubs, such as the drama, music, cooking, handicrafts, *sado* (flower arrangement), and volleyball clubs for girls (Nakamura, 1986).

More recently computer games called Famicom (family computer) and Nintendo games are extremely popular for both boys and girls. According to a survey (Yuji, 1992), about one-third of children, aged four to five years old, own game software.

School-aged boys like to play TV video games (19 percent) and make plastic models (5 percent), while school-aged girls prefer TV games (16 percent), jump rope skipping (12 percent), or elastic band skipping (5 percent) (Nippon Sogo Aiiku Kenkyusho, 1991). The average time that children play TV video games is about three hours a week, and approximately 60 percent of elementary school children have experienced playing TV video games (Mori, 1992).

How much time do Japanese boys and girls actually have to enjoy playing? In recent years the increased academic pressure both in and out of school has led Japanese children to sacrifice their play time to various learning engagements even after school and during school ''vacation'' time.

The Japanese education system was reformed after World War II. In 1947 a new compulsory educational system was established in accordance with the new Constitution and under strong American influence. Compulsory education was extended to six years of elementary school and three years of junior high school. Higher education included three years of high school and four years of college or two years of junior college. With education made compulsory through 12 years of schooling, girls receive as much education as boys through junior high school, although they fall off at higher levels.

Education in Japan has been evaluated highly by international scholars (e.g., Vogel, 1979), and at nearly 100 percent, Japanese people rank among the highest in literacy. Japanese children outperform American children in mathematics as early as first grade (Stevenson et al., 1986). Compulsory education in Japan is based on a detailed national curriculum, a long academic calendar year, structured classroom settings, and discipline, among other features.

To evaluate fully the impact of contemporary education on Japanese children, it is necessary to note the widespread existence of *juku* or *yobiko*, a private cram school, which children attend after regular school hours, in order to prepare for competitive entrance examinations to prestigious schools. *Juku* schooling may start as early as preschool for some children, and by the time college-bound students enter high school, close to 50 percent of them attend *juku* to cram knowledge to survive the "examination war" (Inagaki, 1986).

Much more academic pressure and competition are exerted on boys throughout the school system. For male students, successful entry to a good university is an indispensable step to build future occupational status. By contrast, female students are under much less academic pressure. They generally lack career aspirations. This is due in part to a historical lack of equal employment opportunities and their domestic role specializations. Girls are expected to take a special class such as homemaking in order to develop domestic skills. This type of sex-differentiated curriculum has been supported by societal expectations that boys are to develop a career and girls are to preserve family lineage through marriage and child care duties.

In Japanese families women tend to control almost all household duties. Mothers thus assign household chores to children. Both boys and girls are expected to help their mothers with various household chores. Some of the sex differences can be found in the assignment of these chores and seem to reflect sex-differentiated socialization practices. According to a survey (Nippon Kodomo o Mamoru Kai, 1983), the three most common chores for girls are helping meal preparation (35 percent), making *Futon* beds (31 percent), and taking care of pets (22 percent), while for boys, they include making *Futon* beds (27 percent), taking care of pets (16 percent), and shopping (15 percent). More girls than boys are instructed to help mothers sweep *tatami* floors (18 percent versus 6 percent) and do laundry (13 percent versus 1 percent). Girls as early as kindergarten are differentiated from boys in their domestic roles.

Young Adulthood

One of the most distinguishing features of the life of young adults in Japan is their struggle to survive the academic competition. The aforementioned academic pressure in and out of school has resulted in a large percentage of Japanese adolescents attending higher education. As many as 34 percent of high school graduates go on to colleges or universities. Japan ranks second to the United States in number of students enrolled in universities (Ministry of Education, 1975). There is a biased distribution of majors among male and female students, with a heavy concentration of females in literature, music, or home economics. Males are overrepresented in natural science, medicine, and law.

Most two-year junior colleges are open only to women. Many of these schools are looked upon as finishing schools for future brides. Other junior colleges train men and women in practical and specific vocations, including nursery school teacher, primary school teacher, and clinical technicians.

Many high school graduates who have failed in the competitive university entrance examination attend *yobiko*, cram preparatory schools, to prepare for their second try the following year. These students are called *ronin*, which literally means "lordless samurai" because they have no place to belong to.

The impact of pressure-laden schooling and the family structure with relative absence of father due to his role commitment outside is significant for the sex-role development of young men and women in Japan. Young women particularly stand out as experiencing a clash between the traditional role and the role they themselves expect to fulfill in contemporary Japan. For example, Japanese women, even in high school, perceive discrepancy between their own role expectation and that of their mothers (Yamaguchi, 1989). They perceive that their mothers expect them to be more "feminine" (e.g., "child-rearing," "self-sacrificing," "warm," "sensitive"). Fathers also expect their daughters to be more traditionally feminine. This discrepancy between self-expectation and felt parental and societal expectation reaches its peak at the university level. The results suggest that young Japanese women experience a role strain (Kashiwagi, 1986; Lebra, 1984). Further, while almost 80 percent of Japanese female junior college students accept their female sex role and look to their mothers as a model, those who reject this role report relationship difficulties with their mothers (Toda & Katada, 1987).

Accepting or rejecting one's sex role for Japanese college students seems to relate to their self-concept. Yamamoto, Matsui, and Yamanari (1982) found that Japanese female students were significantly more negative in their self-evaluation than male students. Despite legally guaranteed equality, young Japanese women continue to see themselves inferior to men. Such results suggest that at least some Japanese women are experiencing difficulty in fulfilling sex-role expectations (Kashiwagi, 1986).

Adulthood

Adulthood in Japan is nationally celebrated on 15 January as *Seijin-no-hi*, day for coming of age, when people reach the age of 20. The local government plays host to them at a ceremony. Women wear a *kimono* made especially for this occasion, while most men wear a Western suit. At age 20 Japanese men and women gain the right to vote and the freedom to marry without parental consent. They can also drink *sake*, rice wine, and smoke legally.

For young Japanese women the period in their life between the completion of their schooling and their marriage offers them a sense of freedom and independence. Most women during this time enter the labor market. Those with lesser education commonly work in light industries, such as in textile and electric appliance factories, or service-oriented jobs, such as waitresses or salesgirls. Those with more education are likely to work as secretaries or "O.L.," "office ladies," as Japanese call them. Both groups of female workers are considered temporary, and for the most part they are denied positions of lifetime employment, which is almost always given to male workers.

The educated career woman does exist in Japan but in fewer numbers than in most industrialized, Western countries. For Japanese women, teaching at a school is one profession where they can fully exercise their capabilities. In fact, more than half of all elementary school teachers are women. Compared to the past there are today more female judges, administrative and executive officers, school principals, Diet members (i.e. members of Parliament), police officers, and even Self-Defense Force members, even though their numbers are still extremely small. Women are also found among driving school teachers, public prosecutors, prison policewomen, firefighters, and patrol police officers.

It is expected that women's advance into the Japanese labor market will gradually increase in various traditionally male-dominated skilled sectors. In unskilled areas this increase is much more accelerated, particularly among married women as they enter the labor market in their mid-thirties, on a part-time basis, after their children go to school. Women earn only slightly more than half of males' salaries, and gender wage differentials are increasing (Beasley, 1990). Thus, even though nearly 40 percent of the Japanese work force consists of women, most of them work in insecure jobs without benefits accorded to men.

Traditionally, marriage in Japan was considered a relationship between two households rather than two individuals. Further, Confucian teachings prohibited a man and a woman to interact intimately in public, and romantic love was looked down upon. Marriage served to preserve the family name; therefore, a deliberate and careful investigation of the wealth and social status of the potential couple was conducted by the matchmaker. Arranged marriage has a structural significance in terms of perpetuating the family name. In her field investigation of constraint and fulfillment of Japanese women, Lebra (1984) found that the Japanese women she interviewed revealed that they did not have autonomy in responding to marriage proposals.

According to a survey conducted by the Japanese Ministry of Health in 1992, 87 percent of all marriages are love marriages based on mutual consent, and 13 percent are arranged marriages. These statistics show a 15 percent decline in arranged marriages in the past 10 years. Arranged marriages are, however, still practiced among 30 percent of Japanese men and women who are more than 30 years of age. The mean age at first marriage for Japanese men is 28.2, and for women it is 25.7.

In prewar Japan, when education was still segregated by sex, *joggako*, the girl's high school, was oriented toward teaching young women to be brides and mothers. Students learned domestic skills, such as cooking and sewing, as well as good manners. Today, such training has shifted to the women's junior colleges. Japanese women from more affluent homes take private lessons in traditional arts of *kado*, flower arrangement, and *sado*, tea ceremony, both of which emphasize discipline and control. Contemporary Japanese women continue to take these art lessons as part of bridal preparation.

There are no counterpart lessons or premarital preparations for Japanese men. Their desirability, at least externally, is determined on the basis of their education, occupation, and, more traditionally, their social status in terms of family background.

Most weddings are held according to Shinto rites. At the shrine, after the bride and groom have exchanged vows, they drink in turn from each of a set of "three" sake cups. A Shinto priest, the matchmaker couple, parents, and other relatives also take part in the wedding ceremony. There is usually a formal introduction of the family members and relatives. Other couples are married in Buddhist or Christian ceremonies. The newlyweds usually depart on their honeymoon trip after the banquet.

Married women in their role as housewives assume responsibility for household affairs. As the Japanese economy has developed and a large labor shortage emerged, almost all households have to take full responsibility for household chores without hired help. Today Japanese homes are equipped with various sophisticated electrical appliances. Such technological advances have freed time for homemakers; however, child rearing continues to be a primary female responsibility. In addition, women assume almost all the household responsibilities, including home finances and children's education. Men function as wage earners, and they do not spend much time at home with their wives and children due to long hours of work and commuting.

The intense involvement by men with the occupational role within Japanese hierarchical social structure has literally created father-absent homes, as Japan's industrial and business activities expand both nationally and internationally. There is a special category of job situation called *tanshinfunin*, which means that a husband lives separately from his wife and children for business reasons. Due to the extreme importance placed on children's education, Japanese parents choose not to move together; instead, the husband alone transfers to a new business assignment, including one in a foreign country. Consequently, in such father-absent homes, children's education and socialization fall on the mother's shoulders.

It is evident from the examples of *tanshinfunin* cases that Japanese family structure is centered around parent-child relationships rather than a conjugal relationship between wife and husband. This conception of marriage partly explains the low divorce rate in Japan. Japanese couples may have to wait until the husband's retirement age to enjoy common leisure activities. In short, adulthood for Japanese men and women is characterized by long hours of hard work and dedication to children's education. One may conclude that Japan's postwar economic advancement has been supported by the traditional Japanese sex-role specializations, as women fulfill the domestic role and men fulfill the occupational role.

Old Age

Today Japan enjoys the world's longest average life expectancy of 74 years for men and 81 for women. It is expected that by the early twenty-first century the population of elderly citizens will reach close to 20 percent. A national medical insurance system for the elderly provides that all senior citizens are entitled to medical services.

About 60 percent of Japanese elderly people live with their children. Increasingly, young Japanese couples prefer to live separately from their parents. However, the number of shared households by a married couple and the parents has actually increased since 1975 (Morgan & Hirosima, 1983). While most Japanese families are nuclear families in urban areas, there are still many extended families in rural areas.

There are two types of extended families. In one, the grandparents live under the same roof as the younger family members, and in the other, each household lives in its own home on the same ground. In either case, there is a close interaction between grandparents and grandchildren.

In a study investigating whether women's changing roles have resulted in generational differences in attitudes toward gender-appropriate roles and responsibility for the care of the aged in Japan, Campbell and Brody (1985) found that Japanese women favored egalitarian roles. Japanese women of all three generations agreed that the care of the elderly is a family responsibility. Older Japanese women in particular did not think they should hire outside help to take care of a parent. Japanese women are expected to take care of their in-laws. With increased life expectancy the younger Japanese wife may live with her mother-in-law until she herself is a grandmother.

It is not rare for aged people to engage in professions on a full-time or part-time basis long after retirement age. Retirement age was established at 55 before the war. Today lifetime male employees usually retire between 55 and 60. Pensions begin at age 60. Since pensions alone are not adequate to support the cost of living, many Japanese men seek full-time or part-time employment opportunities after retirement age. In general, Japanese employers tend to keep their workers until retirement age, and even after that, they are frequently referred to another employer within the same occupational hierarchy. Employment opportunities for the elderly are increasing due to labor shortage. In addition, reflecting the increased longevity, many elderly return to structured learning by utilizing the University of the Air or media educational programs.

After fulfilling their roles as parents and grandparents, Japanese men and women continue to be involved with extended family affairs, but with a much reduced sense of responsibility. They engage in various leisure activities, including visiting temples and shrines, participating in group-based recreational programs at community centers, and playing certain sports, such as gateball. Gateball is a popular outdoor sport among elderly men and women throughout Japan. Discount tickets are offered for senior citizens on public transportation.

SUMMARY AND CONCLUSIONS

Japan has undergone a rapid and drastic social change since the Second World War and has become a nation of super economic power, with its men and women achieving the longest life expectancy in the world. The postwar educational reformation within the hierarchical social structure has created unprecedented academic pressure, culminating in the "examination war," particularly for Japanese male adolescents. With a long prewar history of Confucian-influenced moral values, Japanese men and women have followed strict behavior codes and role specializations, with apparent male superiority in almost all spheres of social life.

Externally, it appears that the social behaviors of Japanese children and adults have changed to reflect egalitarian roles; however, much remains unchanged. For instance, Japanese wives no longer trail behind their husbands in public, but most Japanese wives still call their husbands *Shujin*, which means head of the family. Japanese husbands in return still call their wives *Kanai*, which means inside the house. Japanese women's role continues to focus, for the most part, on domestic activities, and women, in fact, control the entire household budget and education of their children. Men spend long hours at work and mingle socially mostly with their colleagues in the same organization.

Generational differences in sex-role behaviors are observed; for example, many young women and men walk arm-in-arm in public places. Despite these changes, Japanese women are experiencing role strains in their quest for self-fulfillment. This is consistently reflected in various studies that indicate young Japanese women's perceived discrepancy between their own role expectation and that of society and their parents. This discrepancy increases as they make progress in higher education. Nevertheless, arranged marriages are still practiced through the mediation of a matchmaker, and women fulfill the structural role of marriage by preserving family names.

Japanese individuals are socialized to value interdependence with others through a particular interpersonal network. Developmentally, Japanese mothers indulge their children and maintain close emotional and physical proximity with their infants. Doi's (1981) concept of *amae* (dependency) has thus been linked to the development of the Japanese self, which emphasizes interdependence among individuals (De Vos, 1985; Johnson, in press). The sense of self is defined according to one's social network and roles within it. Interaction in Japanese society is determined according to a particular set of rules and rituals. Thus, it is often said that Japanese adults have two views of things. One is that "a rule is just a rule," which refers to *tatemae*, and the other is that a rule can sometimes be changed depending on circumstances, which refers to *honne* (Sukemune, 1983). This means that what one says and does will be different depending on specific situations and how one positions oneself relative to others. This relativistic or particularistic attitude may have been acquired during Japan's feudalistic era. Many Japanese adults tend to behave along these lines. They may say "yes" when their intention is negative. Gender roles among Japanese adults may also be understood according to this duality of public practice and personal intent.

NOTE

We are indebted to Dr. David Schwalb, Koryo International College, Nagoya, Japan, for his assistance with the English version of this article. The authors would also like to thank Mr. Hiroki Yuji, Hiroshima University, for his assistance in library research.

REFERENCES

Azuma, H. (1984). Secondary control as a heterogeneous category. *American Psychologist, 39*: 970–71.
————. (1986). Why study child development in Japan? In Stevenson, H., Azuma, H., & Hakuta, K. (Eds.), *Child Development and Education in Japan* (pp. 3–12). New York: W. H. Freeman.
Beasley, W. G. (1990). *The Rise of Modern Japan*. New York: St. Martin's Press.
Befu, H. (1986). The social and cultural background of child development in Japan and the United States. In Stevenson, H., Azuma, H., & Hakuta, K. (Eds.), *Child Development and Education in Japan* (pp. 13–27). New York: W. H. Freeman.
Campbell, R., & Brody, E. M. (1985). Women's changing roles and help to the elderly: Attitudes of women in the United States and Japan. *Gerontologist, 25*: 584–92.
Caudill, W. (1973). Tiny dramas: Vocal communication between mother and infant in Japanese and American families. In Lebra, W. P. (Ed.), *Mental Health Research in Asia and the Pacific* (Vol. 2, pp. 25–48). Honolulu: East-West Center.
Caudill, W., & Weinstein, H. (1969). Maternal care and infant behavior in Japan and America. *Psychiatry, 32*: 12–43.
De Vos, G. A. (1985). Dimensions of the self in Japanese culture. In Marsella, A., De Vos, G. A., & Hsu, F. (Eds.), *Culture and Self*. London: Tavistock.
Doi, T. (1981). *The Anatomy of Dependence*, rev. ed. Tokyo: Kodansha International.
Hara, H., & Wagatsuma, H. (1974). *Shitsuke* (Child discipline). Tokyo: Kobundo.
Hess, R., Holloway, S., NcDevitt, Azuma, H., Kashiwagi, K., Nagano, S., Miyake, K., Dickson, W. P., Price, G., & Hatano, G. (1986). Family influences on school readiness and achievement in Japan and the United States: An overview of a

longitudinal study. In Stevenson, H., Azuma, H., & Hakuta, K. (Eds.), *Child Development and Education in Japan* (pp. 147–66). New York: W. H. Freeman.

Hirayama, M., Ando, M., Takano, Y., Takamura, K., Nomura, T., Fukaya, M., Moriue, S., & Yunoki, F. (Eds.). (1988). *Encyclopedia of Modern Children* (in Japanese). Tokyo: Chuohoki.

Honna, N., & Hoffer, B. (Eds.). (1986). *An English Dictionary of Japanese Culture*. Tokyo: Yuhikaku.

Inagaki, T. (1986). School education: Its history and contemporary status. In Stevenson, H., Azuma, H., & Hakuta, K. (Eds.), *Child Development and Education in Japan* (pp. 75–92). New York: W. H. Freeman.

Johnson, F. A. (in press). *Dependency, Interdependency and Amae: Psychoanalytic and Anthropological Observations*. New York: New York University Press.

Kashiwagi, K. (1986). Personality development of adolescents. In Stevens, H., Azuma, H., & Hakuta, K. (Eds.), *Child Development and Education in Japan* (pp. 167–85). New York: W. H. Freeman.

Lebra, T. S. (1984). *Japanese Women: Constraint and Fulfillment*. Honolulu: University of Hawaii Press.

Markus, H. R., & Kitayama, S. (1991). Culture and the self: Implications for cognition, emotion, and motivation. *Psychological Review*, 98: 224–55.

Ministry of Education. (1975). *A Basic Survey of Education in Japan*. Tokyo.

Morgan, S. P., & Hirosima, K. (1983). The persistence of extended family residence in Japan. *American Sociological Review*, 48: 269–81.

Mori, S. (1992). *Education Based on Philosophy of Play*. Nagoya: Reimei.

Nakamura, T. (1986). Boys' and girls' participation in extra-curricular activities in elementary school. *Child Psychology*, December, 76–85.

Nakane, C. (1970). *Japanese Society*. Berkeley: University of California Press.

Nippon Kodomo o Mamoru Kai. (1983). *White Paper on the Japanese Child*. Tokyo: Kusado Bunka.

Nippon Sogo Aiiku Kenkyusho (Ed.). (1991). *A Yearbook of Japanese Children: 1991–1992*. Nagoya: Chuoshuppan.

Nittetsu Human Development. (1988). *Nippon: The Land and Its People*. Tokyo: Gakuseisha.

Stevenson, H., Lee, S., Stigler, J., Kitamura, S., Kimura, S., & Kato, T. (1986). Achievement in mathematics. In Stevenson, H., Azuma, H., & Hakuta, K. (Eds.), *Child Development and Education in Japan* (pp. 201–16). New York: W. H. Freeman.

Sukemune, S. (1983). Japan, Japanese children and adults, and Japanese psychology today. *International Psychologist*, 24 (2): 16–18.

Takahashi, K. (1986). Examining the strange-situation procedure with Japanese mothers and 12-month-old infants. *Developmental Psychology*, 22: 265–70.

Toda, K., & Katada, Y. (1987). Experimental analysis of the conscious structure of the sex-role-acceptance in the female adolescents: Among the girl students in their final period of moratorium in Hokkaido. *Japanese Journal of Psychology*, 58: 309–17.

Vogel, E. F. (1979). *Japan as Number One: Lessons for America*. Cambridge, MA: Harvard University Press.

Yamaguchi, M. (1989). Two aspects of Masculinity-Femininity II. *Japanese Journal of Psychology, 59*: 350–56.

Yamamoto, M., Matsui, Y., & Yamanari, Y. (1982). The structure of perceived aspects of self. *Japanese Journal of Educational Psychology, 30*: 64–68.

Yuji, H. (1992). A survey of TV games among preschool children. Unpublished manuscript.

14

Korea

Tae Lyon Kim

INTRODUCTION

The Korean peninsula, located in northeastern Asia, is bordered on the north by China and gazes at Japan to the east. The country was divided into south and north by the Demilitarized Zone at roughly the 38th parallel. The land area of South Korea is 38,276 square miles, and its population is 42 million. Korea experiences four distinct seasons, with an average temperature of 60 degrees Fahrenheit.

Koreans and other Asian people share similar characteristics, such as physical appearance. However, Koreans remain independent and distinctive in their culture, language, clothing, and cuisine. The Korean language is regarded as a member of the Altaic family, which includes such tongues as Manchurian and Mongolian. Although Korean has no linguistic relationship with Chinese, centuries of close contact with China have resulted in the absorption of a large number of Chinese characters into Korean.

OVERVIEW

From ancient times to modern society, gender roles have been characterized by a uniform emphasis on biological differences. This focus continues to provide an easy justification for a dichotomous conception of gender roles. In particular, traditional Oriental philosophy has had at its root a system of cosmic forces that recognize man as positive, valuable, strong, and active and as provider of life resources and woman as negative, valueless, weak, and passive and as recipient of life resources. Traditional Korean society has adopted this delineation of gender roles, thereby placing women in positions subordinate and inferior to those of their male counterparts.

This philosophical baseline has greatly contributed to constructing and maintaining a fixed conception of gender roles and has shaped individual self-identification. Korean society, influenced by Confucianism for over 1,000 years, applies several restrictions on women's behavior: physical and psychological segregation of women from men, mandatory subservience of women, confinement of women to their homes, and rejection of women from social activities. Under the principles of Confucian ideology, women observe the virtues of three submissions: to their fathers, their husbands, and their sons.

These traditional concepts of gender roles as perceived by Korean people appeared to be influenced by the so-called modernization period of the Japanese occupation of Korea. However, Japan, the colonizing country, also viewed gender roles in a stratified manner. Korea's own struggles with new and changing definitions of gender roles impaired its ability effectively to advance Korea's modernization.

Further, in 1948, Korea became independent under the name of the Republic of Korea and adopted a constitution that declared such liberal democratic ideals as separation of powers, equality before the law, and guarantees of fundamental human rights. In 1950, the Korean War began and left in its wake a society deprived of the opportunities to practice the declarations of equality and human rights of the 1948 constitution. Rather, of prime concern to the war-torn Korean citizenry were issues of survival through rebuilding and redeveloping their country. Korea's current economic success remains a legacy of the intense focus placed on efficiency and production.

Amid this environment of "reconstruction," the issue of gender roles, in the context of social equality, has remained safely shielded behind economic or political debates, that is, the resolutions of labor troubles or the potential threats of communism. Various autocratic governments further perpetuated the maintenance of dichotomous conceptions of gender roles by ignoring and subverting issues of human rights and equality.

Continuous efforts to improve women's legal and social positions persist despite historical obstacles. Clearly, people in contemporary Korea are experiencing changes in attitude and perceptions of gender roles.

COMPARISONS BETWEEN MEN'S AND WOMEN'S GENDER ROLES DURING THE LIFE CYCLE

Infancy and Early Childhood

Traditionally, the principles of Confucian ideology served as the primary influence on the behavior and customs of the Korean family. The male-oriented teachings of Confucianism stress the patriarchal role of men, the importance of family lineage, and the significance of paying homage to ancestors. As such, men predominate over women, and sons are preferred over daughters. That is, the patriarchal family system places a premium on male roles in customs, such as worshiping ancestors, parents' dependence on their sons, male leadership in family rituals, male superiority in economic matters, male adeptness in social situations, and finally, the dominant belief that men "adopt" their wives into their families after marriage. In sum, traditional Korean families prefer sons, believing that only sons can continue the family lineage and that sons have the duty of caring for their parents.

Today, the significance of sons has diminished, largely due to increasing numbers of people who are educated or are experienced in cultural exchanges and aware of different values. Still, Koreans generally prefer sons over daughters. When a mother gives birth to a son, she feels relief, pride, and joy because she believes she has fulfilled one of her fundamental duties to her parents-in-law. When a daughter is born, the mother usually feels disappointed and consoles herself with the thought that her daughter can be helpful to her. Nevertheless, many mothers hope for sons the next time or continue to give birth until they bear sons.

Such a preference for sons results in the high baby boy-baby girl ratio of 117 to 100, considerably higher than the world average of 103 to 100 (Korean Women's Development Institute [KWDI], 1989). Many Korean parents today try to limit the number of children they have to one or two, and they wish for at least one son. To that end, many women consult with specialists to ascertain the sex of the fetus. This practice has led to an increasing number of abortions and ultimately to sexual imbalance in the structure of the population. In response to this problem, the Korean Ministry of Health and Social Affairs recently enacted a law prohibiting doctors from conducting gender tests before the actual delivery of the child.

Throughout Korean history, the preference for sons has been widely accepted. Still predominant in contemporary Korean society, this preference has had the adverse effect of producing a sexually imbalanced generation, as evidenced in the male-female ratio of young children. This phenomenon raises serious concern about the destruction of sexual balance naturally maintained in human ecology.

The development of child behavior and personality evolves within the basic family unit. Parents have the greatest influence on their children's thinking and behavior. Korean parents who demonstrate a strong preference for sons have attitudes and expectations of their sons that are distinct from those of their daughters. Depending on the sex of the child, different colors and shapes in clothes, blankets, toys, and interior design are selected. The colors selected for daughters, for example, are mainly in the order of pinks or reds, while those selected for boys are generally of blue or brown tones. Korean parents appear to stress the emotional development of daughters and to emphasize strength and the intellectual development of sons.

Toys are similarly picked according to sex. Cars, toy guns, and sporting goods are chosen for boys, while musical instruments, dolls, and play dishes and utensils are given to girls. Boys play with building blocks or with toy cars, which develop their sense of space and analytical skills; with toy guns, which enhance aggressive and independent characters; or with mechanical toys, which contribute to their intellectual development. In contrast, girls play with musical instruments, dance, play with dolls, or play house in order to develop emotional capabilities and social skills (Lee, 1989). Accordingly, 95 percent of young girls have dolls, while the same percentage of young boys are prohibited from playing with dolls (Lee, 1989). Such differences in selecting toys, based on a child's sex, reflect parents' differing attitudes regarding gender.

Finally, differences due to gender are noted in the use of words. *Strong* and *courageous* are considered masculine and thus are used to describe boys. Girls, on the other hand, are expected to be kind and submissive in order to be feminine. Girls are brought up to be passive and dependent, while restrictions are rarely imposed on boys, who are raised to be active and independent. Therefore, Korean girls experience different patterns of socialization than their "brothers" since parents have preconceived ideas about gender roles and deep-rooted preferences for sons.

School Years

Birth order affects the quantity and quality of interaction between Korean parents and their children. Korean parents expect more of their firstborn children. Firstborns are expected to excel in academic achievement and extracurricular activities. As influenced by Confucian teachings, this fact is especially true for firstborn sons, who therefore tend to become more gender-stereotyped than other children. Firstborn sons are likely to be more masculine than their brothers (Choi, 1983).

Typically, responsibilities in Korean households are divided by gender. Men are expected to be the financial supporter, while women tend to the housekeeping. Surveys among Korean teenagers suggest differences in attitudes toward gender roles (Lee, 1983). Lee listed fifteen household chores. Among them, garbage disposal, farm work, and carrying heavy loads—which are regarded as men's work—were mainly carried out by male students, while few of them said they did the cooking, laundering clothes, washing dishes, grocery shopping, or baby-sitting—chores frequently performed by female students. Both male and female students consider household chores women's work, not men's.

The Korean constitution stipulates that all people, regardless of sex, age, or social status, shall have equal opportunity for education. Accordingly, elementary school attendance is compulsory for both boys and girls. More than 95 percent of Korean students—both boys and girls—attend elementary school (Ministry of Education, 1990).

As the level of education increases, however, differences based on gender become evident. In 1960, for example, the ratio of boys to girls in Korean high schools was 72 to 28. Significant increases are noted for both sexes; that is, by

1990, boys constituted 83.3 percent of the high school population, a twelvefold increase, and girls made up 69.3 percent, twenty-six times larger than in 1960. However, a striking gap between the sexes continues.

Male students outnumber female students by a rate of 71 to 29 by the time they reach college. Female college students constitute less than one-third of the entire college population. Further, the percentage of women who ultimately receive university degrees is considerably smaller than that of their male counterparts. The percentage of men achieving a Bachelor of Arts degree is 37.58 percent, while women trail behind at 21.11 percent. Similarly, for a Master of Arts degree, 6.74 percent of the graduates are men, and 1.53 percent are women, and for a doctorate, 0.581 percent are men and 0.068 percent are women (Ministry of Education, 1990). Clearly, the disparity of attendance between men and women increases with the level of education.

In general, the school environment dictates the different roles expected of both sexes. The structure of the school itself invites adherence to basic gender distinctions. In Korean elementary schools, for instance, most teachers are women, while the school principals, with few exceptions, are men. Moreover, the small number of male teachers take dominant roles in major projects at school. Daily performances and activities are also divided depending on sex.

Korean schools contribute to preexisting definitions of gender roles in two specific areas: (1) different curricula are maintained for male students and for female students and (2) teachers manifest different expectations for their students based on sex.

The curriculum for female students attempts to foster certain ''feminine'' traits, for example, warm-heartedness, kindness, generosity, and caring. In contrast, the male students' curriculum targets characteristics such as sincerity, diligence, creativity, strength, and progressiveness. For example, female students in middle school must take mandatory courses in home economics and vocational training, including such subjects as woman as consumer and as childbearer. Male students must take compulsory courses in technological training, which prepare them for future production and management positions in society.

A study on the perception of gender differences of junior high and high school students suggests varying preferences for certain subjects depending on sex (Sae-Hwa Chung, 1989). According to the study, male students generally prefer mathematics, science, physical education, and manual training, while female students prefer language, English, music, and home economics. This study points to the fact that although the total number of students rose in the past decade, education at school continues to stress traditional gender roles.

Similar conclusions can be made about different preferences for certain majors between male and female university students (KWDI, 1989). Typically, the majors chosen by male students are in the order of engineering (which heads the list), social science, language, literature, and education. In comparison, female students make up 56.0 percent of all art majors, 56.7 percent of those majoring in education, a mere 3.4 percent of engineering students, and 4.9

percent of majors in marine biology and fisheries (KWDI, 1989). These figures suggest that deep-rooted, sex-stereotyped divisions remain firmly embedded in the female student's perceptions.

Young Adulthood

Industrialization in Korea resulted in mass migration of young people from rural areas to cities. In the process of adjusting to modern society, which rewards efficiency and individual performances, young Koreans have come to espouse the spirit of equality and individualism that has ultimately led to a change of views about marriage. Whereas traditional Korean society has emphasized the continuation of family lineage and prosperity to the family, contemporary society stresses the significance of marriage to a spouse to fulfill individual happiness.

Usually in the past, the first meeting with the future spouse was at the wedding ceremony, but this is no longer practiced in modern marriages. Naturally, dating has become an important part of life for young Korean adults. Also noteworthy is the different significance of dating as a result of relatively rapid social changes. In the past, simply going out once or twice was acceptable, leading ultimately to frequent meetings where young Koreans were encouraged to marry. Discrimination as a function of sex and male-oriented conceptions of sex, however, remains solidly ingrained in Korean society. When asked their opinions about premarital sex between men and women, Korean women generally accepted their fiancés premarital sexual experiences, while most men expressed a strong dislike for their future wives' sexual experiences before marriage (KWDI, 1989). In sum, dating or merely having meetings with the opposite sex is widely accepted by Korean society, but women's premarital sexual experiences are harshly criticized by men and even by other women.

Women are further discriminated against because of their gender in the job market. Attitudes toward women who work vary according to the sex of the respondent. A Korean Women's Development Institute study posited the question, "What do you think of women having jobs?" While 83.5 percent responded positively to the question, more than 15 percent reacted negatively (KWDI, 1989). Also, 91.6 percent of the women answered that females could have jobs, while a significantly lower percentage of men felt that women should not work. This KWDI study showed Korean men's relatively conservative nature concerning working women.

When KWDI asked, "Why do you want to work?" 48.2 percent of the women respondents said, "To earn money" as their primary reason, while 25.9 percent answered, "To have my own work," and 24.7 percent responded, "To develop as a human being," among other reasons. Most of the women who worked because of financial necessity said that they would quit working as soon as they reached a level of economic stability. Other women with careers, working for reasons other than necessity, said that they would continue to work anyway (35.1 percent), while 13.1 percent of these women said they would work "until they got married." These figures suggest that many Korean women still do not understand the concept of having "lifelong jobs" or permanent careers.

In professional and administrative positions, men outnumber women by a rate of 72.6 to 27.4. In recent years, the percentage of women in the total work force increased to 4.2 percent, but this figure remains modest compared with the total number of working men. Further, most of the women in the current work force participate primarily in industries such as agriculture, forestry, and fishery, rather than in professional or white-collar positions.

Scholastically, working women continue to stagger behind their male counterparts. Most working women are elementary school graduates and have not pursued advanced academic degrees. Studies show that the academic degree achieved by women inversely relates to the number of women in the work force. Simply put, women are receiving higher levels of education in increasing numbers, but this does not necessarily translate into a growing population of working women. The male population in the work force, in contrast, is characterized by an even distribution of educational levels. The low employment rate among highly educated women indicates that women do not generally make significant contributions to economic activities in proportion to their academic background. This fact suggests that women do not have equal access to professional and white-collar positions.

Adulthood

Generally, adult self-identification depends on getting married, starting a family, and gaining status in one's profession. These processes are related to social interactions between the genders, with different sex-stereotypical roles. That is, women identify themselves in their roles as mother and wife, while men relate to their function as breadwinners for their families.

In Korea, marriage is considered a developmental stage that everyone should experience. For men, the "proper age" for marriage is between the ages of 26 and 27, that is, after graduation from university and after compulsory military service. On the other hand, women generally marry at the age of 23 or 24, after their college graduation. Women who do not attend college usually marry at even younger ages.

According to a KWDI study, the factors for selecting spouses can be classified into four categories: (1) *parental arrangement*: parents choose their children's spouses, (2) *parental introduction*: parents or third parties (matchmakers) recommend a spouse and then allow the children to make the final decision, (3) *parental consent*: children choose their own prospective spouses that parents either approve or disapprove, and (4) *child autonomy*: children choose their spouses regardless of the parents' opinions.

The manifestation of these four factors depends significantly on the socioeconomic circumstances. For example, in families of middle to high income, parental introduction of the prospective spouses occurs most frequently. In contrast, parental consent of children's marriage plans is widely used among working-class families. In all, child autonomy in mate selection is rarely practiced in Korea.

In general, the use and popularity of each of the practices listed above change with generations. Among housewives who are over 46 years old, more than half (54.9 percent) were married through parental arrangements. Of the marriages among young adults now, 37.8 percent are allowed through parental consent, while the percentage of arranged marriages has decreased to 30.9 percent. Evidently, the factors important to spouse selection in Korea have shifted away from arranged marriages to love marriages.

While older generations stress social and economic status (family and academic background), people of the younger generation express more interest in marriage as a harmony of both emotion and personality and of similar preferences and hobbies. Unlike in the past, middle-class young adults are now selecting their spouses by focusing on the person himself or herself, rather than on his or her family background.

Customarily, the Korean bride is to present gifts to her bridegroom's family and relatives. Another form of *honsu* requires the bride to purchase appliances and furniture for her new family home. *Honsu* emerges as an important social problem due to the increasing number of women who are forced by their in-laws to get divorced because they could not provide enough *honsu*.

Koreans generally believe that housework is too trivial to be performed by men. Most men who do housework are disdained and ridiculed. Rather, housework, considered unimportant and worthless, remains the responsibility of women. Regardless of whether she has a job outside the home, a woman is expected to take care of the housework in her home. Husbands rarely share the burden.

According to a survey of 235 working women and 265 non-working women in Seoul, not even one woman reported that her husband helped with cooking, washing clothes, or ironing (KWDI, 1986). Working wives can generally get outside help, such as a maid, to complete the housework. In low-income families, however, working wives must do the menial work both in the workplace and at home. In short, sex stereotyping pervades Korean households with regard to individual duties and responsibilities. Women are strictly responsible for housework.

Adherence to these rigid roles may contribute to marital problems. According to a survey of 300 homemakers married for less than five years, however, marital problems stemmed from trouble with in-laws, economic difficulties, personality differences, and communication problems. Most frequently, lack of communication between husband and wife caused the conflict. The Seoul Central Office for Family Advice showed that, based on their study, the causes leading to divorce were extramarital affairs (27.9 percent), problems related to children (14.8 percent), personality differences (11.9 percent), conflicts between mothers-in-law and daughters-in-law, and physical abuse by the husband (8.4 percent).

By Korean law, fathers reserve all rights and obligations over their children in the case of divorce. Fathers, not mothers, are awarded custody of their children. Many Korean mothers, who fear losing their children and who do not have their own financial resources, do not consider divorce, but instead remain unhappily married. However, recent action has been taken to reduce the extent of paternal rights. Such changes promise increasing divorce rates and more active participation of women in economic activities.

The current wave of change in Korean society brings with it new conceptions of gender roles. Amid these changes, deep-rooted traditional values persist that cause great confusion for women as mothers, wives, or professionals. Those who devote themselves to caring for their families feel frustration at their lack of self-development, while many career women feel trapped between traditional gender roles and changing conceptions of women. In reality, the percentage of middle-aged women who have outside jobs remains small.

Old Age

As with other countries with increasing standards of living and progressive development of medicine, Korea is experiencing lower mortality rates and a longer life span, which results in a growing population of elderly people. Korea's population of senior citizens (over 60 years old) has increased from 3.4 percent in 1960 to 3.9 percent in 1980 to 4.5 percent in 1990. By the year 2000, the increase is expected to reach 6.0 percent (Rhee, 1990).

The philosophy of Confucius has traditionally been the primary influence on Korean behavior and customs. Under the teachings of Confucius, filial obligation has been regarded as the basic code of conduct and the most important moral principle. Hierarchical order valued under Confucian thought has transcended the parent-child relationship in the society in general, requiring the young to respect, honor, and obey the elderly.

In the traditional Korean family, the oldest member typically had the authority to decide on family matters. In contemporary society, however, this power has shifted from the elderly to the nuclear family in general. The advent of modern technology and science has further undermined the elderly's power of experience and wisdom. Elderly men, in particular, have lost their position of authority and the center of power in the family. Elderly women, however, continue to exert their influence in the family, especially in the realm of housekeeping, albeit to a lesser degree.

A social policy for the welfare of senior citizens has not yet been fully developed in Korean society. This shortfall can be attributed to an unprecedented growth in the population (due to improving standards of living and medical technology) and to the teachings of Confucius, which place responsibility of the elderly within the confines of the family over society. According to a sample survey conducted by the Korean Gallup Poll (Korea Survey, 1983), 96 percent of Korean senior citizens live with their families.

According to Cho (1990), elderly men outwork their female counterparts by a rate of 30 percent to 9.6 percent, respectively. They participate actively in agriculture and fisheries (44 percent) and in the management of small businesses (26.9 percent). A mere 1.9 percent work as technicians, white-collar professionals, or administrators—all areas necessary for industrial growth.

Differences can also be noted in the employment rate between the elderly residing in cities and the elderly in rural communities. In Korean cities, senior citizens constitute a small 5.4 percent of the work force, while 42.3 percent of the work in rural areas is done by the senior citizens of the community. This disparity suggests a shortage of jobs for the elderly in big cities.

Cho's report concludes with the elderly's general concerns with health problems, which relate directly to their satisfaction with their lives. More than half (55 percent) of the elderly women interviewed believed they were not healthy. Elderly men similarly had little faith in their health (46 percent). In general, the older this population becomes, the more apt they are to believe they are not healthy.

Differences between men and women can be found in the degree of dependency. Traditionally, women have depended on men in nearly every respect. As such, a spouse's death has been much more stressful and painful for women than for men. After their husbands' deaths, older women experience financial difficulties, social isolation, and loneliness. Women who have been satisfied with being just "someone's wife" lose their identity after their husbands die. The male-oriented tradition has compelled Korean women to identify with their fathers, husbands, or sons, which is especially true of the older generation. As a result, widowed women often turn to their sons for identification. Their sons frequently lack the ability to satisfy their mothers and feel unduly burdened by this responsibility. Inevitably, conflict arises between mothers and sons.

Gender differences concerning marital status are similarly striking. In Korea, single women outnumber single men. According to a report of the Economic Planning Board (1983), 79.9 percent of elderly men are married, while the corresponding number of 24.3 percent for women is considerably lower. The wide gap is due to the fact that (1) women have longer life expectancies than men, (2) women marry at younger ages than men, and (3) men remarry at a higher rate than women.

According to a study on the intent to remarry, 31.7 percent of the respondents reported that they wished to remarry, while 68 percent said they did not want to remarry. The gender differences were as follows: 61.8 percent of the male respondents answered that they wanted to remarry, while only 22.7 percent of the women responded similarly. Of this population, 38.5 percent of the men and 15.5 percent of the women desired remarriage "to stop the loneliness." Men, at a rate of 15 percent, said they wanted to remarry to be cared for by their new wives. However, 32.1 percent of the women responded they would not take on the obligation of caring for another by being remarried. These figures suggest that elderly women continue to live with the psychological and social responsibilities of the traditional concepts of marriage.

In Korea, only a small number of the elderly have financial independence. Most are supported by family members. According to a study by Yoon (1983), 78.2 percent of Korea's senior citizens depend on their children financially. The remaining 21.8 percent work or live off their property incomes. Those who are ill are cared for by family members—daughter-in-law, wife, husband, and daughter. Most senior citizens do not work (80 percent); instead, they tend to their homes and care for their grandchildren. Old women, in particular, help with the housework.

According to a Gallup survey on the elderly's leisure activities, 32.5 percent of elderly men attend social gatherings, usually held at parks, or attend schools for the elderly; 16.3 percent visit their children or friends; and 2.5 percent go to church. In contrast, elderly women remain at home (39.4 percent), take care of their grandchildren (24.9 percent), and help with the housework (14.5 percent). In sum, 78.8 percent of elderly women do ''women's work'' at home.

SUMMARY AND CONCLUSIONS

Traditional gender roles as characterized by Confucian principles continue to lose significance as more women receive higher education and begin careers. Koreans are confused by the transition from traditional role divisions between the sexes and the new role divisions in modern society.

Further, revolutionary changes concerning gender roles can be predicted with Korea's rapid industrialization and modernization. Housewives will be able to spend less time doing household chores as a result of the recent wide availability of electrical appliances and of the current trend for smaller families. As more families have fewer children, the hours devoted to child rearing will be shortened. Thus, smaller Korean families can expect higher standards of living and longer life spans.

In many respects, Korean society has begun to accept women in its social and economic milieus. However, it still puts restrictions on women's activities by emphasizing the traditional role divisions. These deep-rooted differences in gender roles are most apparent in the home. While women's power is weakened by being confined to the home, men gain power in the society as a result of this confinement.

As such. Korean women are confused about their own understanding of gender roles. They anguish between what they learned through education and what, in reality, is imposed by society. Men, for their part, share in the confusion. They remain torn between the traditional, conservative position and the new concepts of gender divisions. Underlying these contrasts, the fundamental theme remains: gender division, coupled with psychological traits, such as self-esteem, has greatly influenced individuals to reassess their own social roles.

Rational gender roles bring forth rational and efficient social progress. With this in mind, the confusion Koreans experience today can be interpreted as an inevitable transition in the process of moving toward gender equality. Although such changes take place slowly, they will happen gradually. Efforts to realize these great changes pave the road to ultimate success.

NOTE

The capable assistance of Ms. Patricia Shin is gratefully acknowledged.

REFERENCES

Cho, B. E. (1990). Intergenerational family solidarity and life satisfaction among Korean aged parents. *Journal of Korea Gerontological Society, 10*: 105–24.

Choi, Bo-Ga. (1983). The influence of the family environmental factors towards gender role attitudes. Ph.D. diss., Busan University, Busan, Korea.

Chung, Sae-Hwa. (1989). The study on the gender role attitudes between male and female high school students. Master's thesis, Ewha University, Seoul, Korea.

Economic Planning Board. (1983). *Annual Report on Economically Active Population Survey*. Seoul.

Kim, J. U. (1972). Parent-child relationship in the Korean family, *Non Chong. Journal of the Korean Cultural Research Institute*.

Korean Institute for Family Planning. (1978). *Statistics on Population and Family Planning in Korea*, Vol. 1. Seoul: Korea Institute for Family Planning.

Korea Survey (Gallup Poll). (1983). *Family Life and Educational Value System*. Korean Public Opinion Series No. 2. Seoul: Korean Survey (Gallup) Polls.

———. (1987). *Lifestyles and Belief Systems of Housewives*. Korean Public Opinion Series No. 7. Seoul: Korea Survey (Gallup) Polls.

Korea Women's Development Institute (KWDI). (1985). *White Paper*. Seoul: KWDI.

———. (1986). *Survey on Employment Status of Women: Married Women Only*. Seoul: KWDI.

———. (1988). *Strategies for the Improvement of Women's Problems*. Seoul: KWDI.

———. (1989). *Women and Development II*. Seoul: KWDI.

Lee, Soon-Hyon. (1983). Study on the gender role attitudes of high school students. Master's thesis, Dongkuk University, Seoul, Korea.

Lee, Yong-Sung. (1989). The influence of the family environmental factors towards gender role attitudes. Master's thesis, Chunman University, Kwangju, Korea.

Ministry of Education. (1990). *Annual Statistical Report of the Ministry of Education*, No. 1990, Seoul.

Rhee, K. O. (1990). The theoretical framework and indicators of social care for the aged. *Journal of Korean Gerontological Society, 10*: 147–62.

Yoon, H. Y. (1983). Developmental stages and psychological maladjustment: Psychology in late adulthood. *Journal of Korea Gerontological Society, 3*: 5–15.

15

Mexico

Rogelio Diaz-Guerrero and Maria Lucy Rodriguez de Diaz

INTRODUCTION

The official name of the country is United States of Mexico. It is a federal representative republic that is divided into 31 states and one Federal District (DF). In the Federal District, Mexico City, founded in 1325 as Tenochtitlan by the Aztecs, has been dismally growing very much beyond the DF limits to the north, the east, and the west, until it is likely that, as we are writing these lines, it has close to 20 million inhabitants. The Federal District harbors the government of the republic. The president is elected by direct popular vote to govern for a period of six years but can never be reelected. He exercises the executive power. The legislative power is represented by the Congress; 300 deputies are elected by a majority of votes in each one of the 300 electoral districts. One interesting aspect of Mexican democracy is that, besides these 300 elected deputies by majority, there are 200 deputies divided proportionally among those political parties that do not obtain 60 or more representatives, by simple majority, and that will obtain at least 1.5 percent of the votes—an innovative idea to give representation to the minorities.

The total population of Mexico, which as we write has probably reached 90 million people, is fundamentally youthful. Fifty-one percent are between zero and 19 years of age, and 31 percent between 20 and 39 years. Only 4 percent are more than 65 years of age. Illiteracy is less than 10 percent, ethnically around 75 percent of the population is Mestizo with varying amounts of Indian and Spanish blood. Around 15 percent are still pure Indians, and 10 percent are Caucasian. Spanish is the language spoken. Approximately 7 percent of the Indian group are bilingual in their indigenous language and Spanish, and no more than 1 to 2 percent speak only their own language. There are, however,

52 different languages still spoken in Mexico. It must be acknowledged that when the Spaniards arrived in Mexico in 1519, there were 8 million Indian people living in the very large number of valleys surrounded by mountains. This accounts not only for the variety of languages spoken but also for the incredibly rich and varied folklore and indigenous art that can still be admired in Mexico.

OVERVIEW

It is still difficult to try to apply Western standards, particularly U.S. standards, to the problem of equality and inequality of the gender roles in Mexico. The concepts of equality and inequality in the United States of America have traditionally become linked exclusively to the dimension of power. In Mexico, fundamentally, it appears, because of its history, equality and inequality are judged by at least two categories: power and love. Diaz-Guerrero (1975) wrote, speaking of Mexico:

Its whole sociocultural historical background is based upon the union of a conqueror— the powerful, the male, the Spaniard—and the conquered—the female, the subjugated, the Indian. . . . Sometime, somehow, consciously or unconsciously, this relationship crystalized into a decision that seems to hold the key to most dealings both within the Mexican family and within the Mexican socioculture. The decision was that all power was to be in the hands of the male and all love was to be in the hands of the female. (Pp. 15–16)

The dynamics, advantages, and disadvantages of this dichotomous way of understanding equality and inequality were explored later (Diaz-Guerrero, 1988).

This dichotomy, however, proved very handy to understand why a cross-cultural study (Peck & Diaz-Guerrero, 1967) found that, generally, Mexican male students in Mexico had a higher level of respect for women than did their American counterparts. Respect, in effect, in Mexico as compared with the United States of America, is often given more in terms of affiliation than in terms of power, which explains another striking result in the same study: Mexican male students scored high respect for beggars while American students scored very low respect.

Traditionally, power is bestowed on women through affiliative channels. This explains that in a number of studies, around 90 percent of the people said yes to the question, "Is the mother for you the dearest person in existence?" and may explain why the Virgin and not Jesus is the highest religious symbol. That women feel secure in this way of allotting power may explain why, in an early study (Diaz-Guerrero, 1952), to the question, "Do you believe that women's place is in the home?" 91 percent of men above 18 years of age in a sample in Mexico City answered yes but also 90 percent of the women agreed. Agreement by women with this proposition has decreased intensely in the last decades, as we shall see later on. This is likely related to the modern and strong Western trend to utilize only one dimension for the determination of status, that is, power.

COMPARISONS BETWEEN MEN'S AND WOMEN'S
GENDER ROLES DURING THE LIFE CYCLE

The tradition in Mexico has been that sons are highly preferred to daughters. However, in a national study (Leñero-Otero, 1968) strongly biased toward urban and more affluent couples, most of the parents have no preference for either boy or girl. For those who did have a preference, only males, in a proportion of 2 to 1, preferred sons rather than daughters. But that there is a definite bias preferring the male over the female gender is illustrated by an unpublished study carried out by R. Diaz-Guerrero in 1959 in 17 high schools in Mexico City. Among 120 questions, one said, "Is it better to be a woman than a man?" Only 1 percent of the boys agreed, and, what is more interesting, only 15 percent of the girls agreed with the statement. These results are somewhat backed by the fact that in a cohort study (Diaz-Guerrero, 1974) that was carried out in the same 17 high schools in 1959 and 1970, to the opposite question, "It is much better to be a man than a woman," a fourth of the girls in the sample answered affirmatively.

Accumulated evidence about the roles of the sexes in Mexico tends to corroborate—with the possible exception of Mexicans with high school or more education completed (about 16 percent of the population)—the Mexican pattern regarding gender roles as described 37 years ago by Diaz-Guerrero (1955). Matters of love and sex, at times intermingled with power, seem to run through the entire patterning. However, later in this chapter we deal with what seems to be known regarding the Indians of Mexico and stress the intense modernization, particularly in the last few years, that has taken effect in Mexico, as reflected in the data that have, most of the time, been obtained from people with high school and university education.

Infancy and Early Childhood

The dynamics of the Mexican family are rooted in two fundamental propositions: (1) the absolute supremacy of the father and (2) the necessary and absolute self-sacrifice of the mother. The mother's role has always implied abnegation, which involves the denial of any and all possible selfish aims.

In the beginning the Mexican baby gets anything and everything. Infants are deeply loved, fondled, and admired—for the first two years of their existence. Relatives, usually many of them, participate in this activity. At the same time, slowly in the first two years and then much more actively, children are taught that they must obey, without question, the wishes of their parents. In addition to obedience, children learn humility, courtesy, and genuine respect for authority. Thus, a well-brought-up child may not yet be able to pronounce his own name, but when asked what it is he will invariably follow his answer with *para servirle* or *a sus ordenes* ("to serve you" or "at your orders"). When words alone are not sufficient to instill in the child this sense of obedience and respect, physical punishment is used.

Although the preference to have a son is prevalent in many societies, in Mexico this preference is more intense. In fact, the birth of a girl—unless she appears after two, but preferably three, boys—is somewhat of an emotional tragedy. Historically, the virility of a man whose wife gave birth to a girl was considered questionable. In addition to this stigma, the birth of a girl is undesirable for several reasons: (1) it means a bad economic break; (2) it imposes on the family the physical and emotional strain of guarding the girl's honor (to lose one's virginity prior to marriage would threaten the fundamental premise of femininity and self-sacrifice in the female); (3) even marriage, the ideal solution, necessitates the intrusion of a strange male into the family; and (4) if she fails to marry, she will become a *cotorra*, literally, an "old female parrot," who constantly burdens the family with neurotic complaints. A girl is seen as an asset to the family only in the sense that she will serve her older brothers, thus allowing the wife more time to care for the husband.

The role expectations for the male child include, above all, that he must grow up to assume the dignified role of a male. There must be no deviation from the traditionally masculine recreational activities of young boys. Any demonstration of feminine interests is met with instant disapproval by older brothers, uncles, cousins, and even by the boy's mother. Older children discriminate against younger ones on the basis that they are not sufficiently male (*macho*) to participate in their games, which become progressively more "masculine." The younger children, therefore, look forward with longing to the attainment of greater virility.

School Years

The child-rearing practices in Mexico for boys and girls are clearly different. Boys are encouraged to be rational and to act; girls are encouraged to be emotional, sentimentally expressive, and passive. A number of studies covering subjects in primary and secondary schools have clearly shown a tendency for girls to score lower than boys in cognitive intellectual tasks (the WISC, the Raven) and to show, significantly more than boys, the Mexican pattern (in comparison with the American) of response to the Holtzman Inkblot Test (HIT) (Holtzman, Diaz-Guerrero & Swartz, 1975). This implies more rejection of the plates, more localization, less movement, less integration, less hostility, and so on (Diaz-Guerrero & Lara Tapia, 1972).

In the Holtzman, Diaz-Guerrero, and Swartz study cited above, of as many as 18 replications of different psychological tests, applied to Mexican and American children of both sexes from age 7 to age 18, it was considered that nothing could explain the results better than a different style of coping with problems. Diaz-Guerrero (1967), at the end of a search for a general explanation of the most obvious differences in the behavior of Mexicans and Americans, postulated the existence of different styles of coping with the problems of everyday life.

He considered that Americans were active copers; that is, when confronted with a problem, they would try to solve it by changing the environment—interpersonal, social, or physical. On the contrary, it was postulated that when Mexicans were confronted by a problem, they would try to solve it by modifying themselves. This fundamental interpretation of the findings was later corroborated by generally low but persistently significant correlations across several studies between a measure of active versus self-modifying coping style and several of the HIT scores that characterized the Mexican pattern of response to the test. In the general population of Mexico, it is believed that this response pattern remains the same at all ages.

The female child must grow up to her destiny: superlative femininity, the home, maternity. Little girls amuse themselves with dolls and playing house. They must stay away from the rough games of the boys, for, as the educated people explain, it would not be ladylike to participate in them. This idea is based apparently on variants of the widespread belief that if a girl should run or jump, she would become a man. Very early the little girl starts helping her mother with home chores—an area of taboo for the male child. In order to acquire greater femininity, the little girl must start learning delicate feminine activities like embroidery or lace making. Later in life she may learn painting, music, poetry, literature, or philosophy. But even as a little girl, she must always dress like a female, keep neat, and be graceful and coquettish. It is interesting to note that one of the postulates under which Mexican public education has labored for years is that one of the main goals of education is to make men more typically male and women more typically female.

During the entire childhood signs of virility in the male are courage to the point of temerity, aggressiveness, and not running away from a fight or breaking a deal (*no rajarse*). But both the boy and the girl must be obedient within the family. Paradoxically, a father will feel proud of the child who did not run from a fight in the street but at home may punish him severely for having disobeyed his orders regarding street fights. This appears to mean that the child must be masculine, but not as much so as his father.

Adolescence and Young Adulthood

During adolescence the sign of virility in the male is to talk about or act in the sexual sphere. He who possesses information and/or experience regarding sexual matters is inevitably the leader of the group. Prepubescent boys are coldly discriminated from the *albures* (words with a sexual double sense) sessions of adolescents on the basis that they are not sufficiently masculine to participate. Girls, instead of being avoided, are now the alluring goal of the males. During adolescence comes a peculiar phenomenon. The pursuit of the female unfolds in two aspects. In one the adolescent searches for the ideal woman—the one he would like to convert into his wife. She must have all the attributes of the perfect feminine role. She must be chaste, delicate, homey (*hogareña*), sweet, maternal, dreamy, and religious and must not smoke or cross her legs. Her face must be beautiful, especially her eyes—but not necessarily her body. Sexuality takes a very secondary role. In the other aspect the adolescent searches for the sexualized female with the clear purpose in mind of sexual intercourse. Here the roundness of her lines and their quantity are determinant factors. The male Mexican's female ideal implies breasts and hips, particularly hips, far broader and far more quivering than are considered proper in the United States. It is even more interesting to note that in every case as soon as the individual has found the woman he may idealize, ipso facto, all other women become objects for the sexualized search and tempting objects of seduction.

As adolescence advances into youth and adulthood, the extreme differentiation among feminine objects loses some of its momentum. Although the entire expression of sexuality is still open only to lovers or prostitutes, it is also true that the youth or the adult with matrimonial intentions will, before making his decision, attend a little more to the quality and quantity of the secondary sexual characteristics of the female. It is well to repeat, however, that even in this case chastity and the other factors of femininity continue to weigh heavily.

From adolescence on, through the entire life of the male, virility is measured by sexual potential and only secondarily in terms of physical strength, courage, or audacity. These other characteristics of behavior, as well as still other, subtler ones, are even believed to be dependent upon sexual capacity. The accent falls upon the sexual organs and their functions. The size of the penis has its importance. The size of the testicles has more, but more important than the physical size is the "functional" size. It is assumed the sexual organs are functioning well when (1) the individual acts efficiently in sexual activity or speaks or brags convincingly of his multiple seductive successes, (2) he speaks or actually shows that he is not afraid of death, (3) he is very successful in the fields of intellectuality, science, and so on.

In each of these cases the common people, who put things crudely, will say, "That guy has plenty of nuts (*muchos huevos*)!" or will say that he has them very well placed. This sociocultural proposition of profound depth and breadth seems to embrace in its scope the majority of the Latin American people. A Cuban physician once told how one of the Cuban presidents had gone alone into a large military post where the commanding general was preparing a coup d'état. Man to man, the president made the general confess and made him a prisoner of his former followers. The Cuban physician summed up the story by saying: "Oh! What a man; his testicles are bigger than a cathedral." Not only is the monumental size attributed to the testicles amazing in this remark, but also amazing is the inclusion in one sentence of the two opposing sociocultural premises: the testicles, virility, and the cathedral, the female set of values.

After the termination of grade school, the female is returned to the home. It is not feminine to have an advanced education. During adolescence women learn more and more the varied aspects of their roles. Now substituting for, now helping the mother in her care and attention to the males, she irons, washes, cooks, sews buttons, purchases socks and undershorts for her brothers, and is supposed to fulfill the most menial needs of her brothers. The brothers, in turn, are the faithful custodians of the chastity of the female. On the basis that nothing can happen to the sister if there are no male strangers around, even innocent courtships, where well-intentioned gentlemen talk through the railings of a window with girls, are viewed with suspicion. As a consequence, these gentlemen are the objects of hostility and are seen from the corner of the eye, and the family artilleries are ready to shoot in case such a boyfriend dares to hold the hand of the sister. Precautions are taken to such an extreme that often the friends of the father or brothers are never admitted into the homes—except, of course, if there is a fiesta, at which time there is a breaking down of most restrictions. At any rate, in this fashion the girl is prepared to give and give—and receive little or nothing. But during adolescence and youth a Mexican woman experiences her happiest period. In effect, she is sooner or later converted into the ideal woman for a given male. Then she is placed on a pedestal and is highly over-evaluated. The girl in this period receives poems, songs, gallantries, serenades, and all the tenderness of which the Mexican male is capable. Such tokens are numerous, for the male has learned very well in his infancy, through his relations with his mother, a very intensive and extensive repertoire for the expression of affection; and, as a part of the maternal ideals, romanticism and idealism dig deep into the mental structure of the Mexican. At any rate, our Cinderella, who has heretofore given all and received nothing in exchange, enters into an ecstatic state as a result of this veneration, this incredible submission—as a slave to a queen—of the imposing, proud, dictatorial, and conceited male. Many years later the Mexican female again experiences an ecstasy of the same quality when her children consider her the dearest being in existence. But this is not surprising, as both expressions of sentimentality are only branchings of the same fundamental phenomenon: the set of maternal values.

Adulthood

Soon after the honeymoon, the husband passes from slave to master, and the woman enters the hardest test of her life. The idealism of the male rapidly changes toward the wife as a mother. To make matters worse, the wife cannot be considered a sexual object in a broad sense. Mexican husbands repeatedly indicate that sex must be practiced in one way with the wife and in another with the lover. The most common statement refers to the fear that the wife might become too interested in sex if he introduced her to the subtleties of this pleasure. At other times this fear is expressed in a clearer fashion by saying that the wife might become a prostitute.

The husband must work and provide. He knows nothing, nor does he want to know anything, about what happens in the home. He demands only that all obey him and that his authority be unquestioned. Often, after working hours, he joins his friends and leads a life no different from that he led when unmarried.

Toward his children he shows affection but, before anything else, authority. Although he does not follow them himself, he demands adherence to the "maternal" religious concepts. Often, however, he imposes the authority of his moods and his whims. He is satisfied if his children obey him, "right or wrong." There is therefore again the premise of unquestioned authority. The wife submits and, deprived of the previous idealization, must serve him to his satisfaction "the way mother did." Since this is not possible, the husband often becomes cruel and brutal toward his wife.

Finally, even the undisputed authority of the male in the home and in all other functions in relation to the female may be explained by the fact that he has testicles and she does not. Incidents like the following are very common among university students. If one of Mexico's relatively few career women obtains high grades, one or many of the male students will exert himself to express with a serious face and in a loud whisper that he knows from reliable sources that this student has already missed several menstruations. Americans would leap to the conclusion that the girl is pregnant, but in Mexico the implication is that she is becoming a male.

Old Age

Scholars dealing with the problem of man, tribe, and state among the Aztecs concur that old age, for both male and female, had many a privilege. In fact, in Tenochtitlan (the earliest Mexico City) all decisions regarding law and order and power rested in the elders of the clan, the twenty tribal units that made up that city-state. Respect for the aged has remained strong in today's Indians of Mexico and has unequivocally filtered to present-day, mainly mestizo population.

Almost every old person in Mexico is either an *abuelo* or *abuela* (grandparent). Children in Mexico are strongly socialized to love and respect their *abuelos*, who, in turn, are expected to play, chat with, and spoil their grandchildren. Traditionally, elders are seldom placed in homes for the aged or hospitals. Unbelievable sacrifices are made to care for them until death in the homes of their children. Giant urbanization is beginning to erode these traditions. A sign of these times is the government's implemented INSEN, the National Institute for the Senescence, which endeavors to help senior citizens (sixty and older) constructively to nourish their lives. Old age in Mexico is also endowed with wisdom; an old and often quoted proverb has it that "mas sabe el diablo por viejo que por diablo": the devil knows more because he is old, rather than because he is the devil.

It is interesting that whatever little is known from studies verifies most beliefs regarding the status of old age in Mexico, including a widespread belief that *abuelas* are more important than *abuelos*.

In the early sixties Peck and Diaz-Guerrero (1967) were able to define the meaning of respect for more than 1,000 university students in Mexico and the

United States of America. Later Diaz-Guerrero (1975) determined to whom and to what degree this respect was bestowed. In general, Mexicans, to a statistically significant degree, accorded more respect to the extremes in age—the very young and the elderly—and to the female sex. More specifically, while both old people and grandparents received high respect in both societies, it was significantly higher in Mexico.

Curious data (Diaz-Guerrero, 1982) obtained with the Spanish Language Semantic Differential (Diaz-Guerrero & Salas, 1975) show that Mexico City high schoolers evaluate ''myself'' much below their evaluation of grandfather and grandmother and the latter slightly higher than grandfather. Regarding strength, they see themselves insignificantly above the grandmother, who is followed by the grandfather. Only in dynamism do these adolescents score themselves high above the grandmother, who, again, but this time significantly, is above the grandfather. This raises the question as to whether the Mexican grandmother is perceived as a special case in the world. Comparing the scores for her concept to the mean scores obtained by Osgood (Osgood, May & Miron, 1975: 433) in comparable high schoolers from 23 language cultures, the case can be made that she is seen as better, equal in power, and more quiet. Without question these Mexican grandmothers are highly valued.

It may be difficult to find a source specifically dedicated to the study of gender roles among the different groups of Indians in Mexico. In their study of the Indians in the social classes of Mexico, Pozas and H. de Pozas (1972) distinguished between those groups that cultivate their own fields and those that emigrate and work for others *a destajo* (this is a common work contract, where people are paid by the amount of work that they have produced). For the groups tilling their own land, these authors stress that they follow closely the traditions and values transmitted through generations. They follow closely the ways that were supported by their pre-Hispanic ancestors. In pre-Hispanic days gender roles were strictly maintained:

The child, if a boy, was shown toy weapons and tools which the parents placed in his hands guiding them in the motions of use. If the child were a girl, the parents made her pretend to weave and spin with toy instruments. A name was given to the child at this time. A boy was often named from the date of his birth . . . two flowers, seven deer, or from an animal like Netzahualcoyotl (hungry coyote), or from an ancestor like Moctezuma, the younger . . . girls' names frequently were compounded with the word for flower, Xochitl. (Vaillant, 1960: 115–16)

Pozas and H. de Pozas (1972) point out that authority is exercised by the father, but that the woman maintains equality with the man in marriage, since both complement each other in their different working roles, forming an indispensable unit to satisfy the needs of the family. It is interesting that recently Rodriguez (1990), studying 143 parents and sixth grade schoolchildren in a Nahuatl-speaking town and a mestizo town in the mountains of the State of Puebla, found that to the statement ''The father should always be the boss in the home,'' 69 percent of the Indians were in agreement, compared with 83 percent in the mestizo town. While the majority in both towns agree that authority should be in the hands of the father, significantly more individuals agree with that statement in the Mestizo than in the Indian town.

When Indians migrate (Pozas & H. de Pozas, 1972), they bring along their family, wife, and children and carry the indispensable tools to prepare the food (*ollas, metates, comales,* and so on). When working *a destajo,* both the wife and the children participate in the work in the fields. They also help to construct an abode to protect the family from the elements. Women, besides, prepare the daily food, wash, and make the clothing for the family. They are also fundamental in maintaining what in Mexico is called the ''harmony of the family.'' Furthermore, Indian women often manage the budget of the family and invest it with great care. In contrast, the authors point out that in the rural, non-Indian areas, women do not work in the fields. In the rural areas there was an increasing tendency to eliminate women and children from all work in the fields. Because of Western influence the authors feel, the pattern of women in the home and men in the fields is finally standardized. (An often cited exception are the Zapotec descendants in Oaxaca. These women are as close to heads of the household as can be found in Mexico.)

Mexican anthropologists have generally accentuated the great diversity of folklore and customs across the Republic of Mexico. Recently, Bonfil Batalla (1987), making use of considerable interesting information on diversity across Mexico, concludes that there is almost an irreconcilable conflict between the pre-Hispanic and the Spanish beliefs. This generalized statement contrasts with the findings of careful research. Almeida et al. (1987), reporting on a study carried out in 1978, found no difference in scores on a questionnaire dealing with traditional beliefs, particularly about gender roles, between sixth grade children in Mexico City and their counterparts in a Mestizo town and an Indian town in the mountains of Puebla. The questionnaire, a one-factor scale, contains statements such as the following: ''Men are more intelligent than women,'' ''A child should always obey his parents,'' ''Men are naturally superior to women,'' ''The father must always be the boss in the home,'' ''The place for women is in the home,'' ''Women should be docile,'' ''Men should wear the pants in the family,'' ''It is much better to be a man than to be a woman,'' and ''Young women should not go out alone at night with a man.'' These authors found no difference in the scores on this scale among fathers, mothers, and children in the Indian town. In the Mestizo town, mothers were significantly more traditional than fathers and than their children, and in Mexico City, both parents, more so the father, were less traditional than their children!

This study led Rodriguez (1990) to replicate the research in two towns. It became a cohort study, ten years later, of sixth grade children and their parents, in the same schools, in the same towns, and with historical time as the independent variable.

In her analysis of variance of these two towns by two historical times, 1978 and 1988, only time was significant. In the sixteen-item, one-factor scale cited above, the mean score was over 13 in the two towns in 1978 and averaged 12.6 in 1988. While significant, this difference indicated that traditionalism had diminished in 10 years' time only a little more than half a score point. In her secondary statistical analysis, item by item, Rodriguez found that the trend toward change is toward diminishing the authority of the parents and the superiority of the male over the female. These findings corroborate a study carried out earlier by Diaz-Guerrero (1974) in a cohort study in 17 high schools in Mexico City carried out in 1959 and again in 1970. The results at that time pointed out again relatively small but significant differences in items dealing with the authority of the parents, with the superiority of the male over the female, and with the submission of women. As in Rodriguez's study the tendency was toward less traditionalism.

Elu de Leñero (1969) published a book under the title *Hacia Donde Va la Mujer Mexicana* (Where are the Mexican women going?). Taking advantage of a quasi-national survey of the Mexican family, intended to give information about family planning practices, she included a number of questions intended to test what could be considered masculine and feminine in Mexico. Interestingly, she asked more than 5,000 married men and women of this sample between 20 and 50 years of age about the number of years they completed in school. She found that 10 percent of the women were illiterate and 8 percent of the men, but that more women than men have completed their studies up to 12 years of schooling, which is partially explained by the fact that above 12 years of schooling, men have completed studies in the proportion of 20.8 percent to 6.3 percent. She concludes that, much more often than would be expected, women in Mexico in her sample are completing high school education. She believes this may be due to the fact that there are a greater number of opportunities for them at this level of training. From several questions, the author concludes that most domestic activities are fundamentally in the hands of women. However, with regard to the use of money, males usually handle the finances, four to six times as often as females.

From another set of questions, the author concludes that the areas where women have greater authority are in elaborating the monthly budget, selecting the school for the children, and determining the punishment that is imposed on the children when they have seriously misbehaved. The areas where the man is the final authority are the selection of his job, the decision of whether the wife should work or not, and the decision about having or not having more children. It is unfortunate that this study did not include questions about aspirations and activities or jobs of women outside the home.

From the sources consulted it is likely that no more than 15 percent of the women of Mexico are gainfully employed. This appears to be the case, for instance, in the study carried out by Muñoz Izquierdo (1987). In his quasi-national survey of individuals between 13 and 72 years of age, he found that only 46 percent of the total sample were gainfully occupied. Of these, 69.7

percent were men. Unfortunately, only in two of his 35 tables analyzing attitudes toward work does he utilize sex as the independent variable. In achievement motivation he finds no difference between those women and men, and in his table about level of occupation and sex, it is interestingly shown that in high positions, women are more represented than men, 47 to 33 percent. There is no difference in percentages for the level of white-collar workers, but blue-collar workers are more often to be found among men. No difference is to be found among peasants or people who work on their own. Since Mexico has a number of women deputies (fifty for the LIV Legislature, 1988–1991) representing people in the Congress and several women governors, it may be fair to conclude that women who decide to enter the working force in Mexico have greater opportunities to reach a higher position. Actually, however, in a quasi-national sample in a study by Leñero-Otero (1968), when women were asked if at the moment of answering the questionnaire, they were gainfully employed, 89 percent of them said no.

SUMMARY AND CONCLUSIONS

Almeida and Sanchez de Almeida (1983) report on a unique cross-cultural study dealing with psychological and other factors affecting change in women's roles and status. The study, sponsored by the International Union of Psychological Science and supported by the International Social Science Council (United Nations Educational, Scientific, and Cultural Organization [UNESCO]), was carried out in four countries, two developed and two developing: the United States of America, France, Tunisia, and Mexico. As these authors, speaking for the principal investigators in the four countries, point out, "The project was focused on . . . dimensions of perceived masculinity-femininity, sexual stereotypes, sexual self-concepts, coping styles, educational aspirations and expectations, and occupational values" (p. 14). The theoretical sample, not completed in all 4 countries, was to study 600 subjects, half of them males and half females, one-third of the sample to be obtained from the last year of junior high school, 15 years of age; the second group from the last year of senior high, age 18; and the third group from the second year of college, age 20. Half of the sample came from technical schools, and half of the sample came from the usual academic institutions. Subjects came from a broadly defined middle class.

The first striking result of this study is that age (in this case, amount of education) did not affect most of the dependent variables either in Mexico or in this four-nation total sample. Gender patterning, beyond junior high, seems to be generally frozen. The second striking result of this cross-cultural study, given the possible diversity of social class and other characteristics in the four samples, is the homogeneity obtained in the results, which must be ascribed to the similar amount of education. Thus, there were no gender differences in regard to educational aspirations and expectations. All students answered the question "What is the highest level of school you would want to attend?" and the responses, showing aspiration and expectation, range from a score of 1, none or some grade school, to 9, Ph.D. or professional degree.

As expected, on the measure of sex-role stereotypes and masculinity-femininity (Spence, Helmreich & Stapp, 1974), males scored higher on masculinity and females higher in femininity. However, it should be noted that both men and women scored sufficiently high in characteristics stereotypically considered proper to the opposite sex to support the conclusion that sex-role stereotyping is decreasing among students from the 4 countries. A third surprising result was that females, across the four samples, have a more active coping style than males. With the only exception of the American sample, women score higher on self-assertiveness and appear as more internally controlled, bold, and independent than men. This rosy picture is, however, tarnished by the fact that in occupational values, the male and the female pattern of preference mirrors that reported by Diaz-Guerrero (1972). In that study of 6,400 10- and 14-year-old children, from the fourth and eighth school grade, respectively, boys and girls from seven countries, it was found that the occupational values held by girls were altruism, esthetics, self-satisfaction, intellectual stimulation, security, associates, and variety. In contrast the values held by boys were management, success, creativity, prestige, economic returns, and following one's father. The girls preferred intrinsic values, the boys extrinsic ones. With this exception, however, the authors summarize the results in the following way: ''Our data reveal that changes are occurring in the basic assumptions that underlie sex roles and sex identity and that the trend is moving towards greater equality in the status given to each sex. At least this is the case for males and females that have been incorporated into the educational systems of these four countries'' (pp. 31–32).

Almeida, Rodriguez, Mercado, Rivero and Sanchez de Almeida (1983) discuss at greater depth the results of this study for male and female students in Mexico. The measuring instruments utilized in the Mexican study (all in Spanish) were a demographic questionnaire, including the importance of marriage versus work, the desired number of children, and educational aspirations and expectations; the personal attributes questionnaire (Spence & Helmreich, 1978); the work and family orientation; the views of life test (Diaz-Guerrero, 1973; Diaz-Guerrero & Iscoe, 1984); the occupational values inventory; and the semantic differential scales (Osgood, Suci & Tannenbaum, 1957; Diaz-Guerrero & Salas, 1975).

The authors first refer to the intriguing finding that the female students in the Mexican sample give less importance to marriage, compared with work, than the male students. This goes flagrantly against the usual sex-role stereotype in Mexico, as does the fact that they desire, on the average, fewer number of children (2.08) than do males (2.29). It should be stated here that the sample in Mexico did have 600 subjects, 300 from technical schools and 300 from the usual academic careers, and that 3 ages, 14, 17, and 20, were equally represented. As in the large sample, age differences were generally insignificant and were not considered. Another unexpected finding were the similar results with regard to both sexes in educational aspirations and expectations. The mean educational aspiration was an average of 7.43 out of 9, and the expectation was an average of 6.88 out of 9.

The authors point out that their results confirm Spence and Helmreich's (1978) statement that masculinity and femininity in personality characteristics are not opposites of a continuum and that each has to be conceptualized and measured independently. They found significant differences for both the masculinity score for self and the femininity score for self, in terms of sex and academic orientation. The range of the data demonstrated that both dimensions were valued by both sexes. Thus, the group means for masculinity range from 18.8 (female technical students) to 21.0 (college male students), out of a maximum score of 32. The group means for femininity range from 20.2 (male technical students) to 22.2 (college female students), out of a maximum score of 32. Regarding sex stereotypes, the female students in the study showed more progressive views than the male students as far as the images of the ideal man and the ideal woman were concerned. The female students would like men to have more feminine traits and women more masculine traits; that is, they appear to be more interested in androgyny, which has been found to be related to more effective functioning (Spence & Helmreich, 1978).

On top of all of the above it was found that in achievement motivation, as measured by the WOFO, there were no sex differences for either mastery, work, or competitiveness. Finally, the scores on the self-assertive coping style favored the females, and there was no difference between the sexes on internal control, boldness, or independence.

The authors conclude: "The results discussed so far indicate that significant change is taking place in Mexico in the basic assumptions held by male students, and particularly by female students, in relation to sex roles and sex identity. This has been shown in terms of the importance given to marriage as compared with work, number of children desired, masculinity, femininity, sex-stereotypes, achievement motivation and coping style" (p. 79).

The authors are, however, very cautious about this statement, because of the findings with the semantic differential and with the occupational values in the same study. In effect, male subjects rated themselves on "I as a male" and "I as a student," and female subjects rated themselves on "I as a woman" and "I as a student." Although there were no differences—which is important—in regard to evaluation and activity of the concepts, males rated themselves significantly more potent than females both as persons and as students. The authors state: "The prevalence of a certain rigidity in sex roles is further confirmed by two results. Males gave significant higher ratings than females for evaluation, activity and potency when confronted with the stimulus: 'my ability at traditional masculine tasks'; males consistently gave significant lower ratings than females for the three dimensions when confronted with stimulus: 'my ability at traditional feminine tasks' " (p. 79).

Additionally, the analysis of variance performed with the 15 occupational

Table 15.1
Analysis of Variance (N = 200) of Affiliative Obedience

	Private High		State High	
	Men	Women	Men	Women
$\overline{X}$	8.58	8.02	8.34	9.10
σ	1.71	1.84	1.93	1.77

Note: Translated from Perez-Lagunas (1990).

values show that the traditional value systems for occupation prevail among Mexican students. Women scored higher than men on intrinsic values such as altruism, intellectual stimulation, esthetics, and variety, while men gave higher ratings than women for extrinsic values such as prestige, tendency to follow father's occupation, independence, management, and creativity.

The results of this large study lead the authors to conclude:

On the whole, the obtained contrasting results reveal that even though there is a decrease in the psychological barriers to the equality between the sexes, there is still a long way before the basic assumptions held in relation to sex roles and status can be considered instrumental in promoting the norm of non-discrimination towards women. Furthermore, our results could generalize with some reservations only to the student population of Mexico City. Several other background factors such as stratification and subcultural value systems should be taken into account to get a more global picture of the psychological factors affecting women's role and status in Mexico. (Pp. 79–80)

It is certainly not simple to try to find out the reasons for the contrasting results obtained in the Almeida et al. study. We prefer to understand such a contrast in terms of the generalized and often not clearly verbalized cultural beliefs that we discussed in the first sections of this chapter. It will be of interest to consider in this context the recent research by Perez-Lagunas (1990). She utilized Diaz-Guerrero's (1986) more recent scale of historic-sociocultural beliefs. Observe in Table 15.1 the results for the analysis of variance for the factor of affiliative obedience. Hers was a sample of 200 subjects, half males and half females, half from a private senior high and half from a state senior high. The range of scores was from 0 to 12, and the theoretical mean was 6. There was a significant interaction of sex by school, indicating that the men in the private school and the women in the state school were most affiliative obedient, while the women in the private and the men in the state school were least affiliative obedient. These results confirm the results of other studies that in several of the factors of the historic-sociocultural premises, men in private schools (higher social class) are becoming more traditional, and women in the same schools are becoming less traditional. While the opposite, the normal Mexican pattern remains in the state schools with subjects of lower social classes. What is happening

Table 15.2
Analysis of Variance (N = 200) of Virginity

	Private High		State High	
	Men	Women	Men	Women
$\overline{X}$	8.46	7.40	8.06	8.84
σ	2.09	2.13	2.17	2.41

Note: Translated from Perez-Lagunas (1990).

Table 15.3
Analysis of Variance (N = 200) of Machismo

	Private High		State High	
	Men	Women	Men	Women
$\overline{X}$	7.90	4.90	7.94	4.76
σ	2.21	1.35	1.71	1.15

Note: Translated from Perez-Lagunas (1990).

in the private schools is just the opposite of the "normal" polarization pattern of Mexico: women are more obedient and prone to abnegation than men. It is important, however, to indicate that in all cases the means are over the theoretical mean of the questionnaire, and in one case almost two standard deviations above it. Affiliative obedience continues to be an important cultural characteristic of the Mexican population across sex and social class. As indicated above and as seen in Table 15.2, the very same significant interactions have developed in regard to the factor of virginity.

Only in the factor of machismo, a scale badly skewed in favor of the males, is there a large difference between the scores of the males and the females, as can be seen in Table 15.3. Almost all of the women in the sample are rebelling to the statements "Men are more intelligent than women" and "Submissive women are the best," but not so much to the statement "It is much better to be a man than a woman." This explains that although the means of the women are below the theoretical mean, the standard deviation indicates that some women, those who are educated, will go above the theoretical mean, even for machismo. As was pointed out at the beginning, high school students and above form only 16 percent of the population.

Clearly, much change is occurring in Mexico regarding sex-role stereotypes and the status of women. The fundamental remedy for this to take place is amount of education. However, it is extremely clear that liberal education is not enough and that probably it will be indispensable to develop courses that will make Mexicans very conscious of the historic-sociocultural premises that they adhere to and that much open discussion needs to be carried out regarding this matter. Diaz-Guerrero (1974) summed up this problem as follows:

There is a little doubt that women in Mexico have been assigned a tough role. Much data . . . show that the area where Mexican women have been affected most is in their cognitive and intellectual development. We are convinced that this is the area in which there is need to make changes in order to permit Mexican women to completely develop their intellectual potential. On the other hand, it is a common observation that Mexican women have a large number of opportunities for the development of their emotional and sentimental life and their specific role of femininity. There are also data that indicate that Mexican women in general are happy with their role. On the other hand, it is very clear, however, that they are less and less satisfied with the opportunities that are offered for their intellectual, cognitive and professional development. If Mexican society does not want these unsatisfied needs of the Mexican woman to lead her to provoke a polarization of the sexes, as is observed at present in the United States of America, and if the large number of sentimental, affective, romantic, and loving values that have always united men and women in Mexico is not to be lost, then Mexican society must increase by loving means the number of opportunities for the Mexican women. (Pp. 15–16)

The intriguing results of Acuña-Morales's extensive research (1991) on the relation of gender roles to self-concept in Mexican college students appear to support this thinking. Contrary to previous findings in the U.S.A. and elsewhere, femininity correlates higher with a good self-concept than does masculinity. True androgyny continues to be the best predictor of a good self-concept, but it is precisely because of this that much thought must be given to these findings. Also, the self-concept utilized in Acuña-Morales's research was developed in Mexico (La Rosa & Diaz-Loving, 1991), and, as an American self-concept scale may be partial to instrumentality, a Mexican scale can be partial to expressiveness. Culture seems, therefore, inevitably intertwined with both the gender roles and the self-concept.

REFERENCES

Acuña-Morales, L. A. (1991). Estructura factorial del inventario de roles sexuales de Bem en Mexico: Roles sexuales y su relacion con el autoconcepto. Ph.D. diss., Universidad Nacional Autonoma de Mexico, Mexico, D.F.

Almeida, E., & Sanchez de Almeida, M. E. (1983). Psychological factors affecting change in women's roles and status: A cross-cultural study. *International Journal of Psychology*, *18* (1–2): 3–35.

Almeida, E., Rodriguez, G., Mercado, D., Rivero, M., & Sanchez de Almeida, M. E. (1983). Psychological characteristics of male and female students and the status of women in Mexico. *International Journal of Psychology*, *18* (1–2): 67–81.

Almeida, E., Ramirez, J., Limon, A., De la Fuente, E., & Sanchez de Almeida, M. E. (1987). Aplicacion de la prueba de premisas socioculturales en tres medios escolares culturalmente differenciados. *Revista de Psicologia Social y Personalidad*, *3* (1): 35–49.

Bonfil Batalla, G. (1987). *Mexico Profundo, Una Civilizacion Negada*. Mexico City: CIESAS/SEP.

Diaz-Guerrero, R. (1952). Teoria y resultados preliminares de un ensayo de determinacion del grado de salud mental, personal y social, del mexicano de la ciudad. *Psiquis*, 2, (1–2): 31–56.

―――. (1955). Neurosis and the Mexican family structure. *American Journal of Psychiatry*, *112*, (6): 411–17.

―――. (1967). Sociocultural premises, attitudes and cross-cultural research. *International Journal of Psychology*, 2 (2): 79–87.

―――. (1972a). Una escala factorial de premisas historico-socio-culturales de la familia mexicana. *Revista Interamericana de Psicologia*, 6 (3–4): 235–44.

―――. (1972b). Occupational values of Mexican schoolchildren. *Totus Homo*, 4 (1): 18–26.

―――. (1973). Interpreting coping styles across nations from sex and social class differences. *International Journal of Psychology*, 8 (3): 193–203.

―――. (1974). La mujer y las premisas historico-socioculturales de la familia mexicana. *Revista Latinoamericana de Psicologia*, 6 (1): 7–16.

―――. (1975). *Psychology of the Mexican, Culture and Personality*. Austin: University of Texas Press.

―――. (1982). El Yo del Mexicano y la piramide. In Diaz-Guerrero, R., *Psicologia del Mexicano*. Mexico, D.F.: Trillas.

―――. (1986). Historio-sociocultura y personalidad: Definicion y caracteristicas de los factores de la familia mexicana. *Revista de Psicologia Social y Personalidad*, 2 (1): 15–42.

―――. (1988, October 27, 28). El amor y el poder en la sociocultura mexicana. *Excelsior*.

Diaz-Guerrero, R. & Iscoe, I. (1984). El impacto de la cultura iberoamericana tradicional y del estres economico sobre la salud mental y fisica: Instrumentacion y potencial para la investigacion transcultural, I. *Revista Latinoamericana de Psicologia*, *16* (12): 167–211.

Diaz-Guerrero, R., & Lara Tapia, L. (1972). Diferencias sexuales en el desarrollo de la personalidad del escolar mexicano. *Revista Latinoamericana de Psicologia*, *4* (3): 345–51.

Diaz-Guerrero, R., & Salas, M. (1975). *El Diferencial Semantico del Idioma Español*. Mexico City: Trillas.

Elu de Leñero, M. C. (1969). *Hacia donde va la mujer mexicana?* Mexico City: Instituto Mexicano de Estudios Sociales, A.C.

Helmreich, R. L., & Spence, J. T. (1978). The Work and Family Orientation Scale (WOFO): An objective instrument to assess components of achievement motivation and attitudes towards family and carrier. *JSAS Catalog of Selected Documents in Psychology*, 8 (35): MS 1677.

Holtzman, W. H., Diaz-Guerrero, R., & Swartz, J. D. (1975). *Personality Development in Two Cultures*. Austin: University of Texas Press.

La Rosa, J., & Diaz-Loving, R. (1991). Evaluacion del autoconcepto: Una escala multidimensional. *Revista Latinoamericana de Psicologia*, *23* (1): 15–33.

Leñero-Otero, L. (1968). *Investigacion de la familia en Mexico*. Mexico City: Instituto Mexicano de Estudios Sociales, A.C.

Muñoz-Izquierdo, C. (1987). Actitudes ante el trabajo. In Medina, A. H. & Rodriguez,

L. N. (Eds.), *Como Somos los Mexicanos*. Mexico City: Centro de Estudios Educativos, A.C.

Osgood, C. E., May, W. H., & Miron, M. S. (1975). *Cross-Cultural Universals of Affective Meaning*. Urbana: University of Illinois Press.

Osgood, C. E., Suci, G. J., & Tannenbaum, P. H. (1957). *The Measurement of Meaning*. Urbana: University of Illinois Press.

Peck, R. F., & Diaz-Guerrero, R. (1967). Respeto y posicion social en dos culturas. *Proceedings of the 7th Interamerican Congress of Psychology* (pp. 79–88). Mexico City: Sociedad Mexicana de Psicologia, A.C.

Perez-Lagunas, E. R. (1990). Las premisas socioculturales y la salud mental en estudiantes preparatorianos. Master's thesis, Universidad Nacional Autonoma de Mexico, Mexico, D.F.

Pozas, R., & H. de Pozas, I. (1972). *Los Indios en las Clases Sociales de Mexico*. Mexico City: Siglo XXI Editores.

Rodriguez, M. L. (1990). Efectos del tiempo historico en el tradicionalismo de la familia mexicana medidos a traves de las premisas historico-socio-culturales en dos comunidades Nahuatl. Master's thesis, Universidad Iberoamericana, Mexico, D.F.

Spence, J. T., & Helmreich, R. L. (1978). *Masculinity and Femininity*. Austin: University of Texas Press.

Spence, J. T., Helmreich, R. L. & Stapp, J. (1974). The Personal Attributes Questionnaire: A measure of sex-role stereotypes and masculinity-femininity. *JSAS Catalog of Selected Documents in Psychology*, 4: 43.

Vaillant, G. C. (1960). *The Aztecs of Mexico*. Baltimore, MD: Penguin Books.

16

New Zealand

Lise Bird

INTRODUCTION

New Zealand is the name given by Dutch explorers to the group of islands they encountered in the southern Pacific Ocean in the late 1700s. However, the three main islands were already settled by the Maori people. The name Aotearoa, "land of the long white cloud," is a common Maori name used to refer to the country. The founding document for New Zealand was the Treaty of Waitangi, signed in 1840 between representatives of the Maori tribes and Queen Victoria, though there continues to be controversy over whether the treaty has been honored. In 1986 the population of New Zealand/Aotearoa was 3.3 million, of which approximately 9 percent were Maori (versus 49 percent in 1858). The population also includes about 3 percent Polynesians from other Pacific Islands in the region, smaller populations with ancestry from India, Fiji, or China, with most of the remaining population being of northern European (mainly British) ancestry. New Zealand is interesting in that a commonly used term for citizens of European origin is *pakeha*, a Maori term that refers to pale strangers or those "other" than Maori. The Maori population is somewhat younger overall than the *pakeha* population. In the 1986 census[1] the main religions of the country were Church of England (24 percent of adults), Presbyterian (18 percent), Catholic (15 percent), or no religion (16 percent), with a further 8 percent objecting to the question.

Urban drift has affected New Zealand as much as other countries, with most people (84 percent) living in towns with more than 1,000 people. In recent years recession has been hard on the economy, with unemployment estimated at around 10 percent in 1991. New Zealand still has a high percentage of home ownership (77 percent in 1986). With a formal examination system in place for 15-year-olds in 1988, 20 percent of students left school without any formal qualifications (approximately one-third of these were Maori), though recently the number leaving school early has been decreasing.

OVERVIEW

In 1893, after years of feminist groundwork, New Zealand was the first country to give women the vote. Political activity for many women around the turn of the century was closely associated with the Christian temperance movement (Bunkle, 1980). The middle of the century saw the rise of a comprehensive "welfare state" and lessening of visible feminist activity. A special committee of Parliament (in the unicameral system) was established to look specifically at the position of women in New Zealand society in 1975. The committee's findings focused on inequalities in the educational attainments and job prospects for women. As a result of raised awareness about gender inequalities, in the 1970s women were appointed as advisers on policies concerning employment and education of women. This was an example of the raised level of concern about gender inequality that arose as part of the "second wave" of the feminist movement. However, there had been feminist activity throughout the century, for example, in the trade union movement and in the Maori Women's Welfare League.

A governmental Ministry of Women's Affairs, with a permanent head of department, was established in 1984 to look after women's issues relating to equality in matters of government policy. A wing of this ministry, Te Ohu Whakatupu, focuses on issues important to Maori women, such as programs to help Maori women establish businesses. Today many women are in important positions in government, including heads of government ministries (i.e., departments of the civil service). Though a minority of parliamentary representatives are women, in 1991 two of these women were cabinet ministers in charge of government policies on finance and social welfare.

Women did not have legislation fully guaranteeing equal pay in both the private and public sectors until 1977. In the late 1980s women in New Zealand earned only three-quarters as much as men in average wages. Further, Maori women earned about 80 percent of the pay that non-Maori women earned (Horsfield & Evans, 1988). Comprehensive legislation to address pay equity, in which occupations were to be opened to assessment to determine any gender bias in rates of pay across jobs, was enacted in 1990 but repealed shortly afterward when a Labor government was succeeded by a more conservative National party government.

There has been a considerable amount of active work, both voluntary and state-funded, in a number of areas of women's concerns. Rape Crisis is a well-established network that provides counseling and support for women who have been sexually assaulted. There is a national network of Women's Refuges for women seeking safe accommodation away from violent partners. The Help Foundation provides assistance for people coping with the aftermath of childhood sexual abuse. Most secondary schools and tertiary educational institutions have procedures set in place to deal with complaints regarding sexual harassment, though there is also current concern from a number of trade unions about legislative changes that may weaken the enforcement of sexual harassment grievances in the workplace.

Health is a major area of concern for women in New Zealand. A major controversy of the 1980s was an exposé of a medical research study that allowed women with suspected cervical cancer to go untreated as part of a control group, without the consent of the participants (see Bunkle, 1988). This issue led to the establishment of a cervical cancer screening program, which is currently being implemented around the country.

COMPARISONS BETWEEN MEN'S AND WOMEN'S GENDER ROLES DURING THE LIFE CYCLE

Infancy and Early Childhood

Most prenatal care and obstetric care during the first two weeks after an infant's birth is provided to parents free by the state. There is legal provision for all women to take up to 14 weeks' unpaid maternity leave and for fathers to take two weeks of paternity leave, with possible extensions of this leave for up to 12 months for one parent during the child's first year of life (or first year of adoption, if that child is under 5 years of age). An employer is not allowed to terminate the parent's employment during that time.

New Zealand's infant mortality rate was 10 per 1,000 live births in 1989. Unexplained deaths of infants under one year continue to be a health issue of concern. Other prominent health concerns for young children in the country have been the high rates of childhood asthma, ear infection, and injuries from accidents.

There is little direct evidence of preferences for sons among New Zealanders. When first-year university students studying education were asked what sort of family they would like to have in the future, two-thirds stated a preference for a boy first and a girl second and for a three-child family (see Smith, 1988).

In New Zealand/Aotearoa, as in many other countries, children are labeled from birth by gender. English pronouns require that the child's gender be known, and baby clothes and accoutrements still tend quite regularly to be coded pink or blue, though many parents in the last 15 years or so have attempted to be less stereotyped in their attitudes to their daughters and sons. Jane and James Ritchie (1970) did a follow-up study of Sears, Maccoby, and Levin's (1957) classic child-rearing study, interviewing Maori and *pakeha* mothers of 4-year-olds. Though they discussed few gender differences in children, there appeared to be very stereotyped roles for mothers versus fathers. Fathers were described as having a "taboo on tenderness" while the "bleakness of motherhood" was considered an area of concern (pp. 155–56). In a later analysis of the data the Ritchies (1978) found that mothers reported putting greater restrictions on girls, for example, in being less tolerant of aggression and more concerned with neatness and obedience. They also appeared to be more tolerant of dependency and passivity and to have closer emotional ties to daughters. The Ritchies also suggested that New Zealand fathers appeared to be more concerned than American fathers about appropriate gender roles for their sons.

Early childhood centers have been sites for some important studies of gender stereotyping and gendered activities in young children, perhaps because of the high involvement of New Zealand in the early childhood setting. Play centers and kindergartens have for some time offered widening opportunities for girls to take up more active play and, perhaps to a lesser extent, for boys to be involved in more nurturing activities. Studies of the early 1970s (e.g., Bell, in Department of Education, 1976) found that certain preschool activities, such as sand or block play, were more likely to be boys' domains, while other activities, such as painting or family play, were those where girls were more likely to be found. Interesting studies of the 1980s (e.g., Meade & Staden, 1985; Smith, 1985) looked at interventions in early childhood settings to see how adults working in early childhood centers might be able to alter the fixed gender patterns. The studies found that while short-term changes could be implemented, making longer-term changes to gendered activities was more problematic. Theorizing about gender in childhood has probably moved from a liberal focus on changes in adult behavior at a microlevel earlier in the 1980s, toward recent greater concern with interlinked systems that make gender inequalities a ubiquitous part of the social fabric that is difficult to change.

Early childhood education has been a very dynamic area for women in New Zealand. Kindergartens emerged late in the nineteenth century, and a range of other early childhood centers emerged in this century. Notable among these is the play center movement, which gathered momentum in the 1940s, and in the 1980s another movement evolved within the Maori community: Te Kohanga Reo, or indigenous language nests, to nurture children in the Maori language in traditional settings. Language nests in Pacific Island languages have also sprung up. Over 90 percent of 4-year-olds in New Zealand attend some kind of early childhood care or education center on a regular basis (see Meade, 1988).

School Years

Schooling in New Zealand is compulsory from age 6 to age 16, though most children start elementary school at age 5. An overview of child-rearing practices in the country historically and of research on parent-child interaction and parental beliefs can be found in Podmore and Bird (1990). In many ways the lives of children, at least *pakeha* children, are similar to those of children in other English-speaking countries.

A detailed historical account of play patterns in New Zealand from 1840 to

1950 was mapped out by Brian Sutton-Smith. This showed clearly that most play activities for *pakeha* girls and boys were differentiated by gender, with girls traditionally having more sedate and "ladylike" forms of play. In commenting on changes in children's play from 1950 to 1980, Sutton-Smith pointed out the greater physical activity on the part of girls in recent times, with girls appearing to be the ones still playing traditional games, creating a historical reversal by gender. Boys' playtime, on the other hand, has become more and more focused on the organized sports popular with adults, such as rugby, cricket, and soccer.

In the secondary school system, there are notable gender-typed patterns in choice of school subjects. Girls are much more likely than boys to choose shorthand/typing, clothing and textiles, biology, home economics, and languages and far less likely to choose technical graphics, workshop subjects, agriculture, and physics. However, English, general science, geography, economics, and mathematics are taken by similar numbers of girls and boys. Educational disadvantage falls heavily on Maori students, as 33 percent of girls leaving school with no formal academic qualifications are Maori and only 4 percent of women at universities are Maori (O'Neill, 1990).

Friendship for adolescents is a major focus of energy, both for same-gender and cross-gender relationships. "Going out" with a member of the opposite sex is a common activity, though there is a great variety of cultural practices involved. In her study of teenagers in New Zealand, Alison Gray (1988) found that the old "double standard" was alive and well: responsibility for any consequences of sexual activity was more likely to taken by girls than boys. Sex education in schools was a controversial topic in New Zealand well into the 1980s, and recent studies (see Gray, 1988, for a summary) decry the lack of information New Zealand teenagers have about contraception and sexually transmitted diseases. In 1983, about 6,750 teenage girls became pregnant, of whom 29 percent had abortions and 55 percent had ex-nuptial births, with 23 percent giving the babies up for adoption. For lesbian and gay teenagers, coming to grips with their sexuality in a supportive atmosphere is particularly difficult (Gray, 1988), though homosexual law reform of 1986 removed legal sanctions regarding sexual activity between consenting males aged 16 or over.

In tertiary education, gender-typed choices are still common for subject areas. For enrollments in trades courses in 1988, women were more numerous only for hairdressing (91 percent), while 1 percent or less of women trained to be butchers, carpenters, fitters, and turners or mechanics. For students training to work in the education sector, 99 percent of kindergarten, 81 percent of elementary, and 54 percent of high school trainees were women. For the small percentage of students taking university subjects in 1985, about 50 percent of students were female. Proportions of women taking law (46 percent) and medical subjects (42 percent) were similar to those of men, though women were more likely to be enrolled in arts (70 percent of enrollments), rather than science (36 percent), economics or business studies (37 percent), or engineering subjects (11 percent) (Horsfield, 1988).

Young Adulthood

Women's participation in the labor force has increased in recent decades. In 1986 approximately 48 percent of women worked in paid employment; 39 percent of women worked 20 or more hours a week (Horsfield, 1988). The range of jobs taken by women has expanded somewhat in recent years, though it is still more likely that women, rather than men, will be involved in clerical work (34 percent versus 8 percent, respectively), service work (13 percent versus 6 percent), or professional and technical work, including nursing (18 percent versus 13 percent). Men are more likely to be involved in transport and industrial work (44 percent versus 14 percent), agricultural and forestry work (13 percent versus 7 percent), and administrative and managerial work (7 percent versus 2 percent).

The government department of statistics is monitoring unpaid work undertaken in society. One study showed that while men's hours of work per week, including paid work and household work, were essentially the same whether or not their wives worked, women at home reported that they worked fewer hours than men, while working wives worked on average two hours more per week, giving them a sixty-eight-hour week (Fletcher, 1978).

Adulthood

New Zealand's population had a "baby boom" phenomenon about 1960, which has affected various population trends. The age at first marriage in 1970 dropped to its lowest point with couples in their early twenties, but in 1988 it was back to its level of late in the last century, being on average age 25 years for women and age 27 years for men. An interesting feature of census data gathering in New Zealand in recent times is that there is no attempt to differentiate legal and de facto marriages, as had been done in earlier decades. The 1986 census estimated that 62 percent of adult women and men live in husband-and-wife relationships.

Divorce rates have risen this century, with estimates of the dissolution rate being about 10 percent (Swain, 1986, cited in Smith, 1988). Since 1981 there has been only one ground for divorce, that the marriage has irreconcilably broken down. Custody of children after divorce or legal separation tended in 1988 to be given more to mothers (74 percent) or as divided custody to both parents and/or a third party (15 percent), rather than fathers alone (11 percent). About half the custody orders in 1988 concerned legal marriages that had broken down. Fathers who had been in legal marriages were more likely to receive custody than fathers who had not been legally married to the mother.

Of households in New Zealand in 1986, 69 percent contained only one family, consisting of at least one parent and his or her child(ren). About 19 percent of dwellings had only one person living in them, while 6 percent had other types of family compositions and 6 percent had groups of people not related to each other.

An interesting study by Jan Cameron (1990) looked at the reasons that *pakeha* adults in New Zealand decide to become parents. Though parenthood seemed to be an important issue for generational continuation and as a rite of passage for adulthood, there was a great variety of responses to the issue of child rearing, showing the complexity of the personal issues involved.

Approximately one-third of marriages in New Zealand consist of "reconstituted" families where at least one partner was married before (Smith, 1988). There is a growing minority of single parents, usually mothers, raising children on their own (Smith's estimate, 1988, is one in every seven families). Stresses within single-parent families were documented in an Auckland study (Clay & Robinson, 1978), which pointed to great stress on families, at least for the short term, and variable effects on children, depending on a number of other factors (e.g., violence, economic security). An economic safety net for single families has been in place since 1973, with the creation of a single welfare category, the "domestic purposes benefit," available to single partners who wish to remain at home to raise children; at present there is a basic level of financial support available until the youngest child is seven years old.

Average family size in New Zealand was about 2.1 children in 1988, a figure that has dropped steadily from 1960 through the 1980s. The average age for a woman having her first child has, like the ages at first marriage, slowly dropped during the century to its low point in the 1950s. A new mother in 1988 was likely to be about age 27.

Though cricket is a popular summer spectator sport, rugby is the national game, and support for the national team, the All Blacks (named for their uniform), has led on occasion to national protest, especially in controversies over sporting contacts with South Africa during the 1980s. Phillips (1987) has described the importance of rugby for the development of masculine identity in the *pakeha* male, though the appeal of rugby would appear to be widespread among men of all cultures in New Zealand.

Old Age

Life expectancy in New Zealand is about 77 years for women and 72 years for men, though *pakehas* tend to outlive Maori by 4–5 years. Population projections suggest that New Zealand will grow older into the next century, as the baby boomers of the 1960s get older. In Maori communities elders are given the highest status in community life. Though decisions are made through complex processes of negotiation and consensus, views of elders are held with great respect. In contrast, as in most Western societies, older people in the *pakeha* community have less social status as "retired" persons eligible for government benefits.

In 1986 21 percent of men and 7 percent of women over age 60 were still in the paid work force. However, there is a notable drop in income for people who have reached retirement age, though a majority of elderly have freehold ownership of their homes. Eligibility for government assistance is expected to rise from 60 years to 65 years, and the issue of government funding for the elderly was the subject of much controversy in 1991. There has been some controversy about the level of welfare benefits available to the elderly of the current generation that will not be available for future generations, due to the economic recession (e.g., Thomson, 1991).

The 1986 census showed that most New Zealanders over age 65 (94 percent) lived in the community rather than in institutions, suggesting a reasonable level of health and mobility for most older people. The leisure activities of older people tend to be extensions of activities of interest in their earlier years, with gardening, lawn bowls, craftwork, television, and family activities being popular (Koopman-Boyden, 1986). The most common health ailment for all people over 60 years is circulatory/heart diseases.

Of older people living in the community, approximately 56 percent were married, 32 percent lived alone, 10 percent lived with other family members, and the rest lived with other people; most older people in New Zealand also appear to have relatives living nearby (Koopman-Boyden, 1987). Older people who are Maori or from other Pacific Island backgrounds are much more likely than *pakeha* elders to live in extended family settings. For older people who need considerable help at home, Koopman-Boyden has found that female family members are more likely than males to be the caregivers, who in about half the cases were daughters of the elderly person. Sons or sons-in-law appeared to be more likely to help with domestic chores, such as mowing lawns.

SUMMARY AND CONCLUSIONS

Huge changes in the lives of women have taken place this century in New Zealand/Aotearoa. From a narrower range of educational and life choices in the rural life of a century ago, women today choose a greater range of educational and career options. Despite the gains made by a small number of women who hold important positions in government and industry, there still tends to be segregation of the work force by gender, with women being more likely to be found in service and caring areas, on lower rates of pay. For many women, the working day has become longer, with the stress of jobs added to demands of housework and child care.

Some exciting gains of the 1980s, such as pay equity legislation, have been overturned, and there has been controversy over the role of policy advisers on women's issues in various wings of government. During the 1990s economic recession, provisions for health care, education for older returning students, and welfare for caregivers have been substantially cut. These changes have probably had their greatest impact on women. The influences of women's perspectives on state provision and monitoring of health, education, social welfare, and employment issues will be the sites of contention in the 1990s. Though there is reason for optimism, there is also concern about the never-ending need for those who care about women's issues to keep refighting the battles of earlier struggles.

NOTE

1. Information from the 1986 census came from a variety of sources, notably the *New Zealand Official Year-Book 1990* (Wellington: Government Printer).

REFERENCES

Bunkle, P. (1980). The origins of the women's movement in New Zealand: The Women's Christian Temperance Union 1885–1895. In Bunkle, P., & Hughes, B. (Eds.), *Women in New Zealand Society.* Sydney: George Allen & Unwin.

———. (1988). *Second Opinion: The Politics of Women's Health in New Zealand.* Auckland: Oxford University Press.

Cameron, J. (1990). *Why Have Children? A New Zealand Case Study.* Christchurch: University of Canterbury Press.

Clay, M. M., & Robinson, V.M.J. (1978). *Children of Parents Who Separate.* Wellington: NZCER.

Department of Education. (1976). *Education and the Equality of the Sexes.* Wellington: Department of Education.

Fletcher, G.J.O. (1978). Division of labor in the New Zealand nuclear family. *New Zealand Psychologist, 7*: 33–40.

Gray, A. (1988). *Teen Angels: Being a New Zealand Teenager.* Wellington: Allen & Unwin/Port Nicholson Press.

Horsfield, A. (1988). *Women in the Economy.* Wellington: Ministry of Women's Affairs.

——— & Evans, M. (1988). *Maori Women in the Economy.* Wellington: Ministry of Women's Affairs.

Koopman-Boyden, Peggy G. (1986). *The Retirement of Older People.* Christchurch: University of Canterbury Sociology Department.

———. (1987). The elderly and the family. *Proceedings of the SSRFC Symposium on New Zealand Families in the Eighties and Nineties.* Christchurch: University of Canterbury Press.

Meade, A. (1988). *Education to Be More: Report of the Early Child Care and Education Group.* Wellington: Government Printer.

——— & Staden, F. (1985). Once upon a time, amongst blocks and car cases . . . *NZCER Set*, No. 2, Item 5.

O'Neill, A.-M. (1990). Gender and education: Structural inequality for women. In Codd, J., Harker, R., & Nash, R. (Eds.), *Political Issues in New Zealand Education,* 2d ed. Palmerston North: Dunmore Press.

Phillips, J. (1987). *A Man's Country? The Image of the Pakeha Male—A History.* Auckland: Penguin.

Podmore, V. N., & Bird, L. (1990). *Parenting and Children's Development in New Zealand.* NZARE State of the Art Monograph, No. 3. Palmerston North: New Zealand Association for Research in Education.

Ritchie, J., & Ritchie, J. (1970). *Child Rearing Patterns in New Zealand.* Wellington: A. H. & A. W. Reed.

———— (1978). *Growing Up in New Zealand.* Sydney: George Allen & Unwin.

Sears, R. R., Maccoby, E. E., & Levin, H. (1957). *Patterns of Child Rearing.* Evanston, IL: Harper & Row.

Smith, A. B. (1985). Teacher modeling and sex-typed play preferences. *New Zealand Journal of Educational Studies, 20*: 39–47.

————. (1988). *Understanding Children's Development,* 2d ed., rev. Sydney: Allen & Unwin/Port Nicholson Press.

Thomson, D. (1991). *Selfish Generations? The Ageing of New Zealand's Welfare State.* Wellington: Bridge Williams Books.

17

Nigeria

Wilhelmina Kalu and
Ogbu U. Kalu

INTRODUCTION

Nigeria is the largest country in West Africa, both in landmass and population. A recent census gives the figure of 89 million people grouped into 250 ethnic relations and with about eighty languages. Geographically, it occupies zones from the littorals of the Sahel through the Plateau of Jos, the semisavanna of the Middle Belt, the deciduous forests of the southwest, to the mangrove forest of the Atlantic Ocean seaboard.

Beyond the wide ecological zone and rich cultural mosaic are shared cultural forms. Indeed, most of the languages fall within the Kwa and Benue-Congo families, and recent scholarship has further narrowed the differences. The large ethnic and cultural affinity of the country with its neighbors (e.g., the Yoruba in Benin and Togo republics, the Shuwa Arabs in the Chad/Borno area, and the Fulani connection with the Fulfulde of Senegal) has ensured that Nigerians are found in most West African countries as traders, artisans, and so on.

OVERVIEW

Discussions of gender roles within such a wide scope must therefore be general; they must also be conscious of changes in time perspective. Nigeria has experienced enormous and rapid changes since its creation in 1914. The shift from traditional to modern socioeconomic and political conditions has affected the perception and status of women in the communities.

Furthermore, gender roles in the traditional setting were controlled by the worldview of the people. This carries two implications: first, the traditional worldview is resilient and is still very much in the present. Western values have not triumphed, nor have emergent values predominated. At each point, three value systems could be perceived. Thus, the issue of gender roles entails the competition of perceptions of women as well as the efforts of women to readjust. Second, one could distill a common denominator or shared aspects of the worldviews among Nigerian peoples. Details may differ while the basic structure is the same. Indeed, all Africans share a basic structure of worldview, which underlies the value system and gender roles (Mbiti, 1969). Further, the onslaught of world religions—Islam and Christianity—has complicated gender-role ideology.

A worldview describes how people perceive and explain the way things are in their environment. Their culture and norms are derived from this and serve as modes of surviving in a particular environment, physical and psychological. From the worldview, people could predict and control space-time events. Culture illuminates and perpetuates differences in sexual status. In this context, the role of culture in defining sexuality is of great importance.

Time and space are the controlling indexes for understanding this worldview. The perception of time among Nigerian peoples is cyclical as life moves from birth through death to a rebirth/reincarnation. This cyclical conception of time is borrowed from the agricultural cycle and the cosmic world. It relates to the myth of eternal return and is typical of subsistence agricultural communities. The celebration of rites of passage indicates clearly the layers of meaning put on each stage of human development. Time itself is not measured as *Kronos*, abstract time units, but as events, *Kairos*.

The conception of space is three-dimensional—the sky; the earth, intricately woven with water; and the spirit world. Each of the three dimensions operates as a viable reality, connected, but not in a hierarchical manner. Although the Supreme Being lives in the sky and major divinities such as lightning, thunder, sun, and moon are near him, there is nothing to suggest that ancestors who live in the Ancestral World are inferior. The spirit world is a mirror of the human world; therefore slaves were buried alive with their masters so as to continue serving them in the spirit world.

The human world itself is an alive universe that man shares with a host of jostling human spirits; guardian spirits of various professions such as hunting, fishing, farming, and so on; animal spirits; evil spirits; and the Earth Deity. Related in a filial manner to the Earth Deity are water deities, who enjoy a kingdom in the water. Human existence is precarious in the effort to tap the resources of good spirits to ward off the machinations of evil spirits. Sociopolitical and economic aspects of life are thus predominated by a highly spiritualized and religious worldview. The basic character of power and power allocation in the society is theocratic and so is the core theory of obligation (Kalu, 1978).

Sex is a biological condition, but gender is a cultural construct. It relates to various ideas, values, and beliefs about men and women expressed through ideology. Though coherent, an ideology may contain conflicting elements. This is most true among Nigerian peoples (Onunwa, 1989). The worldview betrays the fact that the female gender looms large in imagination. For instance, among the Igbo of southeastern Nigeria, a taxonomy study shows that Igbo deities are arranged spatially in four levels. Male deities predominate in the first and fourth levels while females dominate in the second and third levels as follows:

1. Sky—Male
2. Earth—Female
3. Water—Female
4. Ancestral—Male

The deities in the sky, such as lightning, thunder, and sun, who serve as agents of the Supreme Being, are male while the earth and water are under the purview of the Earth Goddess and Queen of the Coast. Female ancestral rituals exist, but most rituals are male, as if the females lose their identity. Indeed, Nigerian communities treat a very old woman as a man (O. U. Kalu, 1989). Key areas, such as land, river, hills, forests, caves, are controlled by female deities. They are also connected with agriculture, fertility, morality, mores, beauty, blessings.

But a certain ambiguity existed: in spite of the importance of the female gender, the African world remains patriarchal. The priests of key female goddesses are male. To take another example from Igboland: an important river goddess such as Idemili in northwest Igboland has a male priest as well as a male consort to whom she pays obeisance (Amadiume, 1987). For the most part women serve as votaries who sweep shrines or as wives of deities. A few exceptions exist.

A number of reasons could be adduced for the marginalization of women at the religious level: (1) myths and proverbs that purveyed negative gender ideology and are inculcated from an early age; (2) dual membership of the female in the family, so that she was marginalized in her marital home; (3) polygyny; (4) power constituting the core in religious practices and used to legitimize the power bases of the society, in terms of hierarchy of political groups, social relationships, control of order, economic sustenance, and protection of the well-being of individuals and lineages. Men tend to dominate the key power nodes. The pattern of distribution and access to scarce resources essential for production, therefore, operated against the womenfolk, unlike the Yoruba myth of origin, which bears many similarities but in which the protagonists are male.

Yam, for instance, is regarded as the king of agricultural products in Nigeria. The yam harvest heralds a new year. The god of yam is accorded primacy all over southern and central Nigeria. Therefore, yam cultivation is a male occupation. Women could cultivate cocoyam, cassava, vegetables, and cereals (in the north). Yam cultivation fetches more money—and is a sign of wealth—than cocoyam or cereal cultivation. Males dominate in the cultivation of cash crops and artisan crafts such as blacksmithing that enable capital accumulation. The marginalization of women at the economic level is assured. In some areas, however, women develop capital-yielding occupations such as weaving, pottery, and salt making. Markets and petty trades in foodstuff remain under female control. These activities give the woman a measure of economic independence. A Nigerian woman could take chieftaincy titles in name only either through her own capital accumulation or through her husband or children, who may wish to honor her by paying for such titles. But females do not inherit land even in matrilineal communities. A woman's male children in such cases inherit the land.

At the social level, sex differentiation is enshrined by emphasis on deference to males. At the family level, the habitat structure in which the man's hut stood apart from his wives, as well as the reverent manner of referring to the head of the family, indicates the general pattern. For instance, a woman cannot call her husband by his name; the most common address would be ''Our Father'' or even ''Master.''

Two aspects moderated the level of female subservience. First, age is important. The society is organized through an age-grade system, consisting of people within three-year age bands and given a name. Within an age-grade, females and males share a joking relationship that relaxes the deference norms (Sudarkasa, 1981). After performing certain age-old roles, a female enjoys some of the exclusively male rights. She can even upbraid a male of any age in public without shocking the community. Second, married women play a role in their patrilineages as daughters (Okonjo, 1976; Allen, 1976; Mba, 1982). They serve as a police force against the wives married into their patrilineages and as ritual specialists dealing with confessions of infidelity or adultery by wives and cleansing the patrilineage of pollutions and abominations. They could, in a group, ''sit on a man'' whose sexual rascality soiled the name of the patrilineage and may prevent the man from sending away his wife. Moreover, a barren, middle-aged woman can ''marry'' a girl to bear children for her and then pay for all the required obligations of a husband whose role she enacts.

COMPARISONS BETWEEN MEN'S AND WOMEN'S GENDER ROLES DURING THE LIFE CYCLE

Infancy and Early Childhood

The worldview described above carries immense implications that determine attitudes toward male and female socialization and gender roles. A new baby's head should touch the ground/soil of its progenitors in which the umbilical cord is ritually buried. This is a form of dedication to the Earth Goddess. The baby's first cry heralds that an ancestor (male or female) has reincarnated. The concept of reincarnation looms large in gender ideology. Thus, being born in the village of one's parents enables the ancestors from either lineage to ''honor'' the family. The eastern Igbo and other groups in Nigeria have a schematized naming pattern—the first son is named after the paternal grandfather while the first daughter is named after the paternal grandmother. In other groups the name is a statement of the father's relationship to his gods or his expectations of life.

Birth rites initiate sex-role orientation at an early age. The child is expected to model after the reincarnated ancestor represented by the godfather or godmother. People point to gestures, character traits, looks, and other signs to confirm that the child really is a reincarnation of a loved one. Thus, a middle-aged man may call a baby "uncle" because he perceives the baby as a reincarnated uncle. From birth, rites of passage are designed to celebrate and initiate the child into the family and community. Customs dictate sex and role differentiations. Male babies are supposed to be more active and to start crawling much earlier and to cry more than female babies. This attribute has been tested cross-culturally and is disputed in Africa (Durojaiye, 1976).

Experience has taught that females (daughters) generally look after their fathers better in old age than males (sons). Yet there is a higher preference for male babies because of the maintenance of family name. "May My Name Never Be Lost" becomes a matter of identity and a guiding principle in the lives of individuals, communities, and the race. A study of the names given to children betrays the desire that one's homestead may always be warmed by people bearing the name of the ancestors. In matrilineal communities the woman (mother) needs male sons to inherit the land and titles due her (Aidoo, 1981). In Nigeria, it is interesting to note that both boys and girls are found to prefer more sons (Abiri, 1981).

A similar struggle goes on to retain the hearth of one's mother. The first female child is pampered as the one who will retain the hearth. Two reasons make the battle crucial. First, a covered calabash is kept near the hearth, containing ash from the hearth. This serves as a shrine for enforcing sexual probity. The site of the shrine must be retained for continuity with one's roots. Second, pots are placed around the hearth; each pot represents a woman in the matrilineage. It is a form of genealogical chart that must not be lost.

Child rearing is the primary concern of the woman and her mother. By puberty, sex typing with tasks, boundaries of behavior, and sex-role preferences emerge. The image of females as a nurturing agent becomes gradually entrenched (Kalu, 1992a). Among Nigerian peoples, there is manifestly little difference in child rearing of male and female babies except that the beautification of girls begins early. The ears of girls are perforated for earrings quite early. The perforation is preserved with black thread as a substitute for an earring. From about two years of age, mothers spend time decorating the child's body with female adornment such as a single line of colorful beads, red ocher, and white calcium powder. Until recently, toys were not part of indigenous culture. European influence led the Ibibio of southeastern Nigeria to produce male and female wooden dolls. The Ibibio are very artistic wood-carvers. These colorfully painted dolls, by a process of cultural diffusion, became prevalent throughout southern Nigeria.

A more typical effort to preoccupy a child is to gather a mound of sand near the child. It cushions a fall, the child may even eat some, and the child may make images on the remainder. As the mothers may start farming again after weaning the baby, supervision falls either to girls who are undergoing puberty rites before marriage or to older siblings of either sex and in any age of childhood (Kalu, 1987).

School Years

By the period of school age, clearer socialization differences and sex-role preferences emerge in male and female children. Colonialism brought schools and created a culture that combined traditional and Western education. Suspicion of missionary intentions and disruptive counterculture led parents to send girls and "disposable" (those considered lazy or too weak to farm) male children to schools. Thus, early educational facilities had more female patronage. English Victorian mores of courtesy and propriety determined a curriculum that focused on home economics, hygiene, and home management rather than academics. However, it did not take long before various communities realized the uses of Western education and turned it into a matter for male domination. The pattern of how they regarded Western education varies markedly. Islam forced colonial policy toward protection from Western education. By the late 1960s there was an awareness of lower female enrollment in all levels of education, especially the tertiary (W. J. Kalu, 1989a). In 1950 there were 36 boys' secondary schools and 3 girls' secondary schools. In 1958, 64.5 percent of primary school enrollment consisted of males, and 34.5 percent females (Nduka, 1964). The figure is higher in Yorubaland and much less in northern Nigeria.

The common and official age of entry into primary school is 6 or 7 years. The age range for school entry is, however, wide—between 5 and 13 years. This is partly because many children are sent to school when the money is available. Some children may attend grade one or two and then have to wait for a number of years before they can continue (Kalu, 1992a). By the 1970s, girls' education enrollment figures were comparable to those of the boys in the primary and secondary schools levels. In 1981, female enrollment was 50 percent in primary schools, 42 percent in secondary, and 14 percent in technical or trade schools (Federal Ministry of Education [FME], 1985).

About 76 percent of primary school children and 71 percent of secondary scholars come from polygamous homes (Durojaiye, 1972). There are many siblings to be considered for formal education. It is, therefore, likely that early primary education may have to be funded by the mother or a relative. The mean number of siblings is 5.6 for primary school children and 7.1 for secondary school children (Durojaiye, 1972).

Sibling relationships are highly focused on the mother as a point of reference because of polygyny. Children from one mother relate to each other with a stronger bond of affection than they do with their half-siblings. In the struggle for limited economic opportunity and education within such settings, sibling rivalry among children of the same mother is reduced but is allowed to operate or even escalate among children of the same father but different mothers in childhood and through adulthood. Children of the same mother are encouraged to present a united front.

Girls are encouraged to be mothers to the brothers, and boys, to be fathers to the sisters. This often persists into adulthood. Great responsibility is placed on the first son and first girl in taking care of younger siblings right from early school years. To help educate the younger ones, many first sons and daughters disrupt their own education early so they can work. Both male and female children help their mother to improve the economic resources of the family by assisting in trading of goods or street hawking. However, more female children are involved than male children (Obikeze, 1984).

About 75 percent of Nigerian children grow up in rural areas. A typical male child tramps into the bush on the outskirts of the village to check his animal and bird traps early in the morning or carry home a keg of palm wine from his father's palm grove before rushing to school. Schools are often located at an extreme end of a village or some distance from it in 67 percent of the cases (Durojaiye, 1972; Kalu, 1992b). Until the mid-1950s, most females did not aim higher than teacher training college or secondary grammar school education (W. J. Kalu, 1989a; Guglier & Flanagan, 1978). Subject preferences for females therefore continued to be related to homemaking and teaching until the 1970s. By the 1980s Obanya (1981) found similar ratings in subject preferences among boys and girls. English language has a high rating, and vernacular has a low rating over a three-year study. But by third year more girls in secondary schools give a lower ranking to mathematics and physics than boys, and more boys give a lower ranking to French and geography than girls.

In early mission schools, boys and girls sat separately while other missions built special domestic centers for girls. But until the 1970s most secondary schools in Nigeria were either for boys or for girls. Mixed education was an uncommon feature reserved for tertiary educational institutions. Missionary practice therefore reinforced the indigenous socialization process that separated boys from girls in sex-role learning.

Young Adulthood

A key index of peer socialization trend is the role of secret societies in the male child's life after the age of six. There is a variety of masquerade and secret society traditions in Nigeria. Each masquerade tradition has gradations, and male children are initiated into the early grades during school age. These societies serve as models of adult society. The boys emulate adult life, and, significantly, the father becomes less of an authority figure in the boy's life. The authority of the leaders of the secret societies substitutes for the authority of the father, though this is not a break in the ties with the parents. Membership separates boys from girls.

Sex-role typing ensures that girls are trained to play domestic roles: they engage in vegetable gardening near the homestead, cooking, child rearing, body beautification, and certain artisan skills such as weaving. Girls model their mothers and stay in female peer groups. Lower education expectations and achievements breed unequal socioeconomic status for males and females in a rapidly changing society. This produces both earlier marriage as well as the problem of teenage pregnancy. Those who enter early marriages tend to move into agricultural production and marketing and hence, the trading sector. This leads to a large number of female traders in West Africa (Oppong, 1983).

The biggest fear of a mother in traditional society, however, is premarital pregnancy of a daughter. Traditional religious values impose a dread of this situation. Crude herbal abortion practices exist but no ethics of confidentiality. It was said in one village that if a girl got pregnant, a palm tree on the bank of a stream dedicated to women would ripen. Observers would make inquiries as to where the new baby was to be born. At night, young boys and girls, in groups, would carry garbage and sing obscene, satirical songs, to the accompaniment of staccato rhythm, to the pregnant girl's homestead and dump the garbage on them. This Dance of Shame is a social stigma. Yet, when the child is born, ululation rents the air. The same people who danced in scorn celebrate the child. There is no concept of the bastard as there is always a known father. The male's family hastily pays a visit with gifts to claim the child, or else the girl's father names the child. Children are desired as much as arrows in a family's quiver. Abortion is frowned upon as an offense against the Earth Deity.

This danger of premarital pregnancy emphasizes the need for disciplined upbringing of teenage families. Sex-role standards are enforced as solution. These include, first, sending the young girl after first menstruation to be prepared for marriage. Second, when people have left for the farms, such girls stay in groups to baby-sit, do house chores, and play. They tend to sleep together in the house of a respected old woman. An indiscreet young male going near would look like a skunk prowling around the chicken coop. Third, courtship is managed through intermediaries, message bearers, and family representatives. Marriages are arranged and regarded as family, rather than private, affairs. The emphasis in marital ethos is female subservience. Childbearing preoccupies females. Early marriages mean that females spend their entire fertile years in childbearing and nurturing children (Oppong, 1983; Kalu, 1987).

The trend in Nigeria today is the rapid growth in the number of educated females. Nationalists heralded the trend in various ways: (1) literacy campaigns focused attention on females; (2) universal primary education (free tuition) removed the hurdle posed by fathers who were unwilling to spend money on female education; (3) the control on exorbitant bride prices ''liberated'' females because exorbitant bride prices paid by the young adult turned the woman into a purchased chattel who must obey the master's voice. Further changes in the political economy accentuated the process of liberation, for instance, the United Nations Woman's Decade. In addition, during the post–civil war period, the intense struggle to recover or rehabilitate themselves bred independence in women. Education was seen as a bulwark. With increased educational expectation and quest for jobs in the modern sector, marriage patterns changed. The individual's choice became more prominent (W. J. Kalu, 1989a). Between 1981 and 1989, 20 percent of Nigerian University enrollment was female; females accounted for about 36 percent of education students, 20 percent of students in the physical sciences, 23 percent in medicine, and 6 percent in engineering.

Young males dropping out of schools in the 1990s are reversing the old trend. Males currently dogmatically pursue opportunities in the business world that do not require much academic training. The great urge is to build financial emporia, following what many illiterate adults have done.

In summary, masculinity dominates the gender ideology in the period, from birth to marriage. The socialization processes nurture this, as in the pattern of sharing work—in the house, farm, and market—as well as the types of sports and relaxation. Wrestling, secret society outings, masquerade and dances, and hunting all reinforce male orientation. Females suffer more restrictions in outings, more subdued play and opportunities to participate in dancing.

Adulthood

Attention has focused on the changing trends in gender ideology and thus raised the question whether adulthood affects perception of gender. The bulk of literature on this matter indicates that the level of stress and strain in gender roles has increased tremendously in the modern adult world. First, the International Labor Organization (ILO, 1984) reports that 78.7 percent of the agricultural labor force in Africa are women and that women constitute 6.1 percent of the industrial labor force as well as 15.2 percent of the public service labor force. Another report (Roodkowsky, 1983) shows that in West Africa, 80 percent of the labor force in trading, including wholesale and retail, are female. In Nigeria, the growth of the number of females in top administrative positions is on the rapid rise. At Lagos State University, for instance, the vice-chancellor, registrar, and bursar (the topmost principal officers) are all women. The increase in education, new career opportunities, and dual-career family structure have taken enormous tolls on traditional family structures and may result in emancipated ideas on sex, obligations, sharing of authority, family planning, child-rearing practices, and possibly a new attitude to divorce (Kalu, 1987). Experimentation in cohabitation has emerged, though frowned upon by the older generation.

It has been noted that considerable numbers of mothers seek a well-rounded development of their daughters' intellect, talent, and energies, beyond the narrow confines of child upbringing and homemaking (Pepitone-Rockwell, 1980; W. J. Kalu, 1989a). Nigerian society, like most African societies, is facing the stark reality that woman's place is no longer confined to the home. Resentment, opposition, and raging controversy have ensued in sections of the society. But among Nigeria's three dominant ethnic groups, the northern Hausa/Fulani have been most resistant to the changes in the female roles, though they accept higher educational opportunities for females. The Igbo have been very open to female education but attempt to break the rate of change with tradition and customs. In

1958 there were 6,620 primary schools in eastern Nigeria, with 787,777 males and 433,494 females enrolled, compared with 2,204 primary schools in the north, with 17,745 males and 58,255 females enrolled (Nduka, 1964). Fafunwa (1974) reports similar findings in the late 1960s. Cultural norms bind the society; indeed, the village so dominates the attitudes of people that even those located in the most sophisticated environment cling to traditional customs and go home to the village regularly for important functions. One can conclude that the Hausa, Fulani, and Igbo are never fully urbanized. The Yoruba have been most open to change and more urbanized. Urbanity carries a different worldview and ethos.

Eleanor Fapohunda (1983) draws a similar conclusion from a different approach. She statistically analyzes urban women's labor force participation in Zaria (north), Ibadan (west), and Onitsha (east) and concludes:

1. In Zaria women's labor force participation rate declines from 8.9 percent for women in the 15–19 age group, reaches a minimum of 3.9 percent for those in the 35–44 age category, and gradually rises to a maximum value of 11.3 percent in the 65–74 age group.
2. In Ibadan, the participation rate rises to 71.6 percent for the age category 25–34, peaks at 74.7 percent in the 35–44 age group, and declines to 70 percent after 65 years of age.
3. In Onitsha, the curve starts at 21.2 percent for ages 20–24, rises to 25.7 percent for those in the 55–64 age category, and falls below 20 percent after 74 years of age. At issue is the fact that traditional social values determine male willingness to permit the women to work outside the home. Fapohunda argues that a higher rate of monogamy among the Onitsha-Igbo partially explains the lower rate compared with Ibadan. The surviving force of traditionalism is the core issue.

In Nigeria, there are little conceptualization and vociferous advocacy of feminism. The popular Better Life for Rural Women Program in Nigeria is not a feminist program in reality. The impact of modernity is subtly corroding the fabric of the family. But beyond customs, social institutions such as the age-grade and the extended family exert enormous restraining influence on the avant-garde woman. She is thus faced with multiple sources of strain—stress generated by her job, the demands of running a home and coping as a mother and wife, and the demands of the extended family and village community (W. J. Kalu, 1989b). Living in so many worlds at the same time is more taxing than is the case for a woman in the Western world.

A clear index of the psychological stress on adult gender roles is the changing pattern of divorce. In traditional society, the divorce rate was low, but separation was a most casual affair. The patriarchal authority pattern ensured that the man easily sent a disobedient wife back to her parents. The term *disobedient* is loaded. It could mean that the woman is obstinate and disrespectful, talks back to her husband, does not feed the husband or accede to his desires, and so on. When the woman is packed home, mediations by relevant family heads settle matters after a few market days, to cool the male tempers (Surdarkasa, 1981). Sometimes the brothers of the women may forcefully rescue their sister from a husband who batters. The husband visits the in-law to ascertain that his runaway wife is there. At a later date, mediation ensues.

Curiously, sexual infidelity does not automatically lead to divorce because it is perceived as a religious offense against the Earth Goddess. Ritual cleansing and propriations follow. However, a rampant recurrence incurs divorce, and allegations of witchcraft and sorcery and poisoning produce instant divorce because life is at stake. In this case, the woman takes custody of the young children as the matrilineage is expected to assist in their succor. The children, however, belong to the man, and he may take custody at any time. Young adults stay with their fathers. When divorce occurs, the bride price is returned to the man. The financial burden persuades the woman's family to discourage their sister from doing anything that would incur divorce.

Dual careers in recent times, Western values in love and marriage engendered by movies, and availability of modern legal facilities (which encourage civil court marriages) have combined to remove the dread and social stigma from divorce. Although the negative stigma is usually on the divorced woman, some churches are nowadays accepting divorced females into the ministry.

Another factor that has affected the divorce rate is the size of family and family planning. A woman with a large number of children is unlikely to have the option of divorce. A proverb says that a hen with chicks does not run fast. Till recently, poor education on family planning and the predominance of male-centered contraceptives stunted family planning programs, especially as the men resisted. But birth control devices have changed to include some that are female-centered. Recent findings indicate that women who work in the modern urban market economy, those in higher status occupations, those working outside the home, and nonfamily employees tended to have lower fertility than the national average. These kinds of jobs give women greater occupational rewards and are likely to cause conflict between maternal and occupational role activities and responsibilities. This combination of factors is seen as pushing women to control their fertility (Oppong, 1989). Males are slow in active participation in modern family planning options (PPFN, 1990).

Political scientists have developed the concept of "two polities" to understand the life pattern of the Nigerian. One polity is the traditional, while the other is the Westernized. Three value systems emerge: traditional, modern, and emergent values that combine both but are neither. Much of the confusion in discussing gender roles arises from unclarified operative value systems. Many Nigerians seek to bestride the polities and operate with emergent values rooted in neither of the polities. This becomes clear as individuals begin to acquire traditional titles both ascribed and achieved. Originally chieftaincy titles constituted a form of reward or social control model designed to support acceptable norms and values by rewarding those who have upheld them. Such titles or rewards made the recipients advisers to the political leadership. It presumed moral probity and possession of certain charisma or gift/talent. Males or females could be so rewarded as the praise name indicated the credentials of the recipient. However, most of the titles referred to male-oriented qualities—strength, military prowess, successful yam cultivation or hunting, eloquence in speech, wisdom in judgment, scion or royal family, and such. Often, membership in a dominant secret society would be a prerequisite for accession to certain titles. In state-organized political structures, such titles are graded. For instance, among the Onitsha of northwest Igboland, the hierarchy is thus:

1. Obi, the Ruler
2. Onowu, the Prime Minister
3. Ajie, Scribe (Secretary)
4. Owelle, Principal Adviser

Before reaching this rung of palace advisers, one would have performed *ozo* title rituals and *Ogbuefi* title rituals. Gender differences rear their heads: when a man takes the lower chieftaincy titles, his wife is accorded the female equivalents of the titles. But when he accedes to the advisory title roles, the wife does not receive any. For instance, if a man became ennobled, the wife becomes a Lady of the Manor, but if the man went to the House of Lords, the wife does not follow. A separation of roles occurs. In Nigerian communities, a woman joins her husband to perform title rituals but does not go further. A woman may accede to other titles by her own wealth or through the children. Status differential is a core aspect of social organization. Such titled women are accorded respect both in the general society as well as in the Council of Women. Even though such women would not sit with men to adjudicate cases and govern, their advice, proffered informally, carries weight because of the moral prerequisite.

In contemporary society, this moral prerequisite has eroded because of emergent values. Individuals could cheat, defraud their employers, and embezzle public funds from the modernized polity and virtually buy chieftaincy titles from the traditional polity. It looks as if the robber who arrives safely with the loot is heralded with the big drum into the palace. He must be a strong man, protected by his ancestors in his daring escapade and venture in the white man's world.

Old Age

After the top layers among the age cohorts have died, the next two age cohorts perform a retirement ritual that literally means "dropping the machete" (a farming and hunting instrument). This is done by both males and females. Such people do not farm as vigorously as usual and do not perform any public tasks such as guarding the village, working on the roads, roofing the schoolhouse, and such. This retirement ritual is performed every seven years.

Thus, there are really two retirements—one from employment in the modern sector and the other from the traditional sector. They may not necessarily coincide. Quite often, people who retire from the lower cadres of employment in the modern sector cut down on their financial burdens by retiring to their villages. The advantages are no house rent, availability of agricultural land for support, the cushion effect of extended family, and the opportunity of playing/leadership role in village politics and in the village church.

Care for senior citizens is not institutionalized, so much depends on the savings of the retiree. For the most part, people have not learned to save. Low wages and high cost of living, combined with the large family sizes, do not provide opportunities to save. In the early 1960s government policy, through the National Provident Fund (NPF), endeavored to force a savings culture. Children are considered the best savings. If the children succeed in life, they will look after the parents accordingly. The quality of care showered on one's parents is an index of one's well-being. Care for widowed and aged parents is an enshrined norm. This may explain why official policy does not usually go beyond pension scheme problems to provide for the aged. First sons and all daughters have a priority to take in and look after aged and ailing parents regardless of their family size. (For the Yoruba tribe widow in Nigeria, the death of her husband does not end the marriage, unless she wishes it. Otherwise the marital rights go to the husband's junior brother or to the son by another wife [Okafor, 1991].)

Beyond their political roles, the aged become moral watchdogs as far as their senses of sight, smell, and mobility allow. Since they do not farm, they observe the younger ones. The old women's homesteads become the rendezvous of young girls. Grandchildren visit and live with grandparents regularly.

In traditional religious worship, people pray that they may die in the soil of their birth, where their umbilical cords were buried. Thus, after the age of 70, depending on the state of health, a retired person prefers to go back to the village and await the journey into the ancestral lands. One obvious risk is the lack of organized health care delivery for the aged. Generally, the life expectancy is higher for females. More females are expected to be widowed (W. J. Kalu, 1989b). In many cultures, women who are first daughters are buried, at death, in their maternal compounds instead of their husband's compounds. The concept of reincarnation explains this, but it causes much stress.

SUMMARY AND CONCLUSIONS

Nigeria is a big country with about 250 ethnic groups—"tribes and tongues," as the colonial officials say. Vast cultural differences vitiate in-depth study of gender roles. This chapter has therefore combined ethnographical data and socio-psychological analyses. Effort has been made to compare the data from various ethnic groups. Obviously, the larger ethnic groups have received more attention.

It has been argued that gender ideology among Nigerian peoples is embedded in the worldview. But, worldview is not static, as changes in the contemporary period have modified perceptions and created emergent values that are neither traditional nor Western. Thus, the modern Nigerian lives in three value systems at once. But a certain stubborn conservatism ensures that the village mentality persists. Sex-role differentiation is strongest in early life and weakens in old age.

Gender ideology is fraught with ambiguities. The female gender looms larger in imagination and is accorded honor and major roles; the pantheon of gods attests to this. Yet women's roles in the house, marketplace, and public square are marginalized. Cases of dual sex roles exist in the political and social arena, but the deference system and the pattern of economic and religious power ensure male domination.

Socialization, as well as restrictive and reward models of social control, reinforces male domination. Paradoxically, Christianity and education, as external change agents, explain much of the liberation of women as Islam explains the *purdah* and marginalization. The contemporary trend is a rise in female enrollment in all levels of educational institutions, even in the Islamic enclaves. The struggle for political power creates new ethos. The growth of female presence in tertiary educational institutions is most astonishing. So also is the ironic decline of male enrollment in secondary schools. Certain professions are still male-dominated, such as engineering, finance, and banking, but others, such as legal and medical professions, are opening up to women. Still, data show that female presence at the executive level is still low.

In the 1930s European observers were still shocked by the impact of the Aba Women's Riot, which engulfed most of southeastern Nigeria. Given the notion of a docile female population, the force of the revolt was inexplicable. Conventional wisdom rested on a certain division of gender roles that left the women contented in their own female world, different from the male world. Thus, the lack of vociferous feminism does not mean that women in Nigeria are not assertive. The direction matters. A certain ambiguity in gender ideology suffuses the whole system beyond the bounds of the psychologist's data, which, at any rate, cannot be applied beyond a certain time frame.

REFERENCES

Abiri, J. O. (1981). Nigeria adolescent pupils' aspirations about the size of their own families. *Ilorin Journal of Education, 1*: 33–44.

Aidoo, A. A. (1981). Asante Queen mothers in government and politics in the nineteenth century. In Stead, Filomina Chioma (Ed.), *The Black Woman Cross-Culturally: An Overview* (pp. 65–78). Cambridge, MA: Schenkman.

Allen, J.V.C. (1976). Ideology, stratification and the invisibility of women. In Hafkin, N. J., & Bay, E. G. (Eds.), *Women in Africa: Studies in Social and Economic Change*. Stanford, CA: Stanford University Press.

Amadiume, I. (1987). *Male Daughters, Female Husbands: Gender and Sex in an African Society*. London: Zed Books.

Durojaiye, M.O.A. (1972). *Psychological Guidance of the School Child*. Lagos: Evans Brothers.

———. (1976). *A New Introduction to Educational Psychology*. Lagos: Evans Brothers.

Fafunwa, A. B. (1974). *History of Education in Nigeria*. London: George Allen & Unwin.

Fapohunda, E. (1983). Female and Male work profits. In Oppong, C. (Ed.), *Female and Male in West Africa* (pp. 32–53). London: George Allen & Unwin.

Federal Ministry of Education (FME). (1985). *Statistics of Education in Nigeria 1980–1984*. Lagos.

Guglier, J., & Flanagan, William G. (1978). *Urbanization and Social Change in West Africa*. Cambridge: Cambridge University Press.

ILO. (1984). *Yearbook of Labor Statistics*. Geneva: ILO.

Kalu, O. U. (1978). Precarious vision: The African's perception of his world. In Kalu, O. U. (Ed.), *Readings in African Humanities: African Cultural Development*. Enugu: Fourth Dimension.

———. (1989). Gods of our fathers: A taxonomy of Igbo deities. Workshop on Igbo Worldview. Institute of African Studies, University of Nigeria, Nsukka.

Kalu, W. J. (1987). Childbearing experiences of contemporary Nigerian working mothers. *Women Studies International Forum, 10* (2): 141–56.

———. (1989a). Motherhood role strains in married female undergraduate students. *Counselling and Development, 14*: 106–13.

———. (1989b). Widowhood and its process in contemporary African society: A psychosocial study. *Counselling Psychology Quarterly, 2*, (2): 143–52.

———. (1992a). Motherhood concept among Igbo women. *Proceedings of Conference on Igbo Women*. Owerri: Institute of African Studies, University of Nigeria, Nsukka.

———. (1992b). Child psychology in Nigeria. In Gielen, Uwe P., Adler, Leonore Loeb, & Milgram, Noach (Eds.), *Psychology in International Perspective*. Amsterdam: Swets and Zeitinger.

Mba, N. E. (1982). *Nigerian Women Mobilized: Women's Political Activities in Southern Nigeria, 1900–1965*. Berkeley: Institute of International Studies.

Mbiti, J. S. (1969). *African Religion and Philosophy*. London: Heinemann.

Nduka, O. (1964). *Western Education and the Nigerian Cultural Background*. Ibadan: University Press.

Obanya, Pai. (1981). A longitudinal study of school subject preferences of a group of Nigerian adolescents. *Illorin Journal of Education, 1* (1): 111–15.

Obikeze. (1984). Agricultural child labor in Nigeria: A case study of Anambra state. In Ebiogbo, Peter O., et al. (Eds.), *Child Labor in Africa Proceedings of the First International Workshop on Child Abuse in Africa*. UNICEF, Enugu: Chuka.

Okafor, N.A.O. (1991). Some traditional aspects of Nigerian women. In L. L. Adler (Ed.), *Women in cross-cultural perspective*. New York: Praeger Publ. Chapter 10.

Okonjo, K. (1976). The dual sex political system in operation. In Hafkin, N. J., & Bay, E. G. (Eds.), *Women in Africa*. Stanford, CA: Stanford University Press.

Onunwa, R. U. (1989). Femininity in Igbo cosmology: Paradoxes and ambiguities. Workshop on Igbo Worldview, Institute of African Studies, University of Nigeria, Nsukka.

Oppong, C. (1983). *Female and Male in West Africa*. London: George Allen & Unwin.

———. (1989). Women's roles and general issues in family planning in Africa in development. In *Family Planning Policies and Program in Africa*. Legon: Regional Institute for Population Studies, University of Ghana.

Pepitone-Rockwell, F. (Ed.). (1980). *Dual Career Couples*. Berkeley, CA: Sage.

Planned Parenthood Federation of Nigeria (PPFN). 1990. Lagos.

Roodkowsky, M. L. (1983). *Women in Agriculture*. Rome: FAO.

Sudarkasa, Niara. (1981). Female employment and family organization in West Africa. In Stead, Filmonia Choma (Ed.), *The Black Woman Cross-Culturally: An Overview* (pp. 49–64). Cambridge, MA: Schenkman.

18

Peru

Maria M. Ragúz and Juana R. Pinzás

INTRODUCTION

Peru is characterized by diversity in its climate, geography, ethnology, and cultures. Due to uneven regional development, more than half the 22 million population lives on the coast, which covers only one-tenth of the territory. A third of the population crowds Lima, the capital city, where government, economy, educational opportunities, and other services are centralized. The majority of Peruvians live in small cities, towns, or communities along the coast, in the Andean highlands, and in the Amazon jungle.

Economic heterogeneity is evident when comparing development in rural highlands with that of modern urban areas. In 1989, an estimated 70 percent of the population lived below the poverty line, making Peru one of the poorest South American countries. In October 1990, the estimated annual inflation rate was 12.74 percent. Since then official inflation has lowered to a monthly average of 4 percent, following drastic economic measures with the strongest impact on the poorest sectors.

Since 1950 rural migration has been taking place, especially from the central highlands toward cities like Lima. In the last three years, many families migrated, escaping terrorist and antiterrorist forces in the Andes. This meant unplanned urban growth and the development of large shantytowns surrounding the cities.

Acculturation and syncretism exhibited by the population can be traced back to the Spanish conquest of the Inca Empire and centuries of native indoctrination by Catholic missionaries. In the last decades, however, migration and the growing influence of mass media have led to new processes of acculturation and syncretism. In response to current living conditions—extreme poverty, terrorism, and violence—Peruvian cultural patterns are changing. This change can also be observed in the realm of traditional sex-typing patterns and gender roles.

Middle-class urban women are now working outside the home, not for self-fulfillment but to contribute to the family's income. Governmental policies offer few social support mechanisms (i.e., day-care centers, part-time jobs) to urban working women. Social support is found in older children, extended family networks, and, if affordable, live-in housemaids.

The economic crisis has been especially hard on the poorest women. With aid from nongovernmental agencies, urban marginal women are developing strategies not only to help families survive but to make their communities more organized and productive and to achieve better health conditions. These women are massively participating in demonstrations, presenting their communities' pleas to legal and political authorities. Strategies such as communal child-care centers, communal meals (an estimated 3,500 in Lima only), more than 8,500 Comités del Vaso de Leche ("Glass of Milk" committees), and thousands of Mothers' Clubs have also become an arena for change in women's way of life, beliefs, and values, affecting their self-esteem, self-concept, and traditional gender stereotypes and roles.

Marginal rural people, including women, have also been fighting terrorism with whatever means they can, until the government agreed to give them arms and military training. They have been participating in large communal defense and development activities (Blondet, 1991; Tamayo & García Rios, 1990) but terrorism has now targeted marginal urban women's organizations. Urban women have started to react massively in defiance, which in some cases has led to their assassination. Despite the threat they continue to be active participants.

The effect of the crisis thus involves changes in women's self-concept and self-esteem. Many women are becoming more economically productive within and outside the family unit (e.g., heading the family, earning more than the partner). More than work experience itself, what seems a critical variable for changes in self-esteem and self-concept is educational level, and education correlates positively with socioeconomic status (SES).

Change, nevertheless, has not yet reached the main issue in women's social and personal identity: maternity and maternal behavior and traits. These remain central in their identity definition and as criteria for femininity and womanhood (Ragúz, 1990, 1991a, 1991b). Studies on identity change in working women yield mixed results (Barnechea, 1985, 1988; Goméz & Gutiérrez, 1987; Guzmán & Portocarrero, 1985; Lora & Anderson, 1985; Mateos, 1991; Ragúz, 1989, 1991b; Stahr & Vega, 1987; Ureña & De Vivanco, 1981). In the case of urban marginal women, gender conflict seems embedded in an ethnic and SES conflict.

The complexity of Peruvian reality implies that it is not possible to generalize about the Peruvian man or woman, since there is no homogeneous model, no shared, single set of values and norms. Middle- and high-SES groups, for example, tend to exhibit a strong Western influence that involves some aspects of gender roles. Thus, one needs to establish some distinctions among different cultures coexisting within the country, especially within Lima.

OVERVIEW

Though Peruvian multidimensionality makes generalizations difficult, some broad tendencies may be traced. Gender roles are nested in a clearly sex-stratified society. Patriarchalism is deeply rooted in Peruvian history since pre-Inca cultures, especially during the Inca Empire. Sociologists believe when the Spaniards conquered Peru, Western culture brought along machismo (Sara-Lafosse, 1979). Though more prevalent in the northern coast—where the Spaniards had a strong influence—it has made its way to the highlands and jungle. Machismo and women's lower SES are considered to be determinants of the high rate of unwanted adolescent pregnancy, which makes Peru a priority for educational and health intervention programs (Ferrando, Sing & Wulf, 1989).

In urban settings, women have clearly become second-class citizens. Inequalities characterize urban social structures, gender being a status indicator. Inequalities are evident in education, employment, and salaries, deepening in the poorest sectors. National surveys, for example, show that while in 1985–1986 only an estimated 16 percent of Peruvians were considered illiterate, 74 percent of them were females. Women double, even triple, males in urban and rural illiteracy (Pinzás, in preparation). Inequalities may underlie a series of legal and tacit obligations and rights, such as a woman's needing her husband's authorization to work or males' control of their partner's sex life and contraceptive practices.

The critical situation of the Andean agrarian economy has led to change in the productive value of motherhood. Before, as many hands as possible were needed to cultivate the land. Now, with no means to feed her children, rural peasant women may want to limit fertility in the family, only she lacks knowledge of contraception means or has no access to them.

High fertility rates currently characterize the less educated and poorest women. Education seems closely linked to feminine self-perception, to traditional sexual attitudes, and to contraceptive behavior. Coinciding with the distribution of educational levels throughout the country, while in the jungle the fertility rate in 1990 was 7.5 and in the highlands 7.2, in the coast it was 3.6, and in Lima, 2.5.

Assuming that the maternal role is natural and unquestionable, women have faced discrimination (including self-discrimination) in economic and political realms. Women, especially rural migrants, have become involved in informal commerce and poorly paid services, earning less than males for equal jobs. A group among them has developed entrepreneurial interests and initiatives and is becoming considerably skilled in buying and selling national or imported goods.

Patriarchalism is evident in males' socially accepted violence against women. The father, brother, and, later, the partner exert violence over women as a means of socialization and control. In the highlands and in the jungle, for instance, a woman may not be expected to defend herself from a man's aggression. Some contend this can be interpreted as social power but not necessarily machismo, given traditional Andean role complementarity, where not being equal does not mean unequal value and where women have other social channels to exert power and influence.

In the Andean view, the world may be seen as divided on the basis of masculine and feminine principles, which complement each other but also compete. Though patriarchal and matriarchal principles rule descendance and inheritance, patriarchalism is usually dominant. Vertical kinship systems are important for males, and horizontal systems are important for females. Additional examples can be found in religion, housing arrangements, marriage, and perception of nature. Residence patterns tend to be on the male's side and may also be neolocal, but rarely are they neolocal on the female's side. Marriage is seen as a promise that undergoes a series of testing stages, through which the boy chooses the girl. He tries to win her agreement to being ritually kidnapped and later searches for their families' approval. Reciprocity, however, is considered by some authors to be at the base of Andean culture since Inca times, with a system of compulsory cooperation among family members, families, neighbors, and communities (*ayllus*). This is why Andean ideology may be found to be patriarchal but not *machista*, with different gender roles but equal value.

Sex typing occurs not only with regard to persons and roles but also in relationship to nature. Rain is considered female; drought, male. Upper sides and lower sides are ascribed gender, as are natural phenomena and the seasons. In the Quechua language, sex is a status indicator; different terms are used when the speaker is male or female. For Andean women, status derives from their role as wife, mother, sister; there is no strong feeling of common gender identity with other women. Marriage highlights gender differences more than any other social activity; in kindred relations, sex typing is less rigid than in marriage relations.

Jungle women's feminine roles also focus on home, children, and community, but since these women work collectively, this allows for the development of a strong gender identity. Due to harsher survival conditions, within-gender cooperation is essential. Male power is expressed in control of religious rituals and political communal entities. Jungle women, however, may have status higher or equal to males as long as trading is not replaced by cash currency, which implies males' traveling to the markets and handling home economics. Nowadays, male dominance—especially political dominance—in the rural Amazon is decaying due to interchange with other ethnic groups and due to migrations.

Migrants to the cities rapidly acculturate to a macho culture. The traditional Andean community support system breaks. Nonresponsible sex and parenthood, one-parent families, and unwanted adolescent pregnancies are considerably frequent. Women migrants are attributed a "nonproductive" reproductive role, losing their power mechanisms and being economically and emotionally subordinate to the male. They try to find a male partner who complements them as it used to be, only to realize that he will abuse and abandon them when they become a burden due to pregnancies that once constituted their value.

Traditionalism can also be found in the most educated and socioeconomically privileged groups (Ragúz, 1981, 1983, 1991b; Williams & Best, 1982). Research findings, however, trace only part of the Peruvian gender roles' reality. In countries as heterogeneous as Peru, cross-cultural studies based on small student samples can be misleading. A trend toward panculturalism in sex typing exists (Ragúz, 1991b) but is to be generalized only to populations with similar degrees of education.

Since the 1970s a trend from patriarchalism and traditionalism toward egalitarianism and liberalism may be observed. More urban women report joint family decisions and husbands' eventual collaboration with some traditionally feminine chores. Society as a whole, however, could still be considered as putting political, economic, and religious power, almost exclusively, in males' hands.

COMPARISONS BETWEEN MEN'S AND WOMEN'S GENDER ROLES DURING THE LIFE CYCLE

In Peru, life cycles with stages of specific responsibilities may be found in coastal populations of Westernized culture. In contrast, in the highlands and jungle, for example, despite rites of passage, it is usual to find children assuming important adult responsibilities and roles regarding younger siblings, land, or cattle. This means that at one stage, characteristics of other stages overlap or prevail.

Research results with a Lima coastal sample of educated late adolescents showed a link between each life stage and the stereotypes of masculinity and femininity. Social masculinity—for example, aggression, dominance, leadership—was expected in young boys; femininity—sensitivity, tenderness, warmth—was expected in young girls. Internal masculinity—assertiveness, independence, self-confidence, self-esteem—was not ascribed to young boys and girls. While young girls were not expected to differ from little girls in this respect, young boys were ascribed more internal masculinity than little boys (Ragúz, 1991b). Adulthood seemed the turning point for social and internal masculinity. Femininity was mostly attributed to females, but when reaching adulthood, women were also attributed masculine traits and behaviors. Nevertheless, men were attributed significantly more masculinity. Lesser masculinity was expected in older persons, but only old females were believed to be feminine.

Infancy and Early Childhood

More than a bias regarding the newborn's sex preference, in Peru this preference may relate to the fact that gender roles are associated with different social functions. For instance, in Puno highlands a newborn girl means happiness to the family. Andean division of labor by gender is also illustrated by a Puno tradition: if the newborn is a boy, the mother buries her afterbirth with small tools; if it is a girl, with miniature cooking utensils. Infants may not be assigned a place in the Andean community until baptized so it is likely that no gender differences in socialization may be appreciated until then. Male and female babies are tightly wrapped with similar clothing.

When walking is mastered, the parents determine a date for the first haircut. This important ceremony marks a gender differentiation and probably a transition from a natural state to a civilized state.

The change in dress code may occur before, after, or simultaneous to the haircut ceremony. While beginning to learn to walk, the child used a skirt (*wara*); from now on, he or she will wear masculine or feminine clothing. For rural children, sex typing probably occurs more on the basis of rituals, daily occupations, and chores than in terms of games and toys.

Toward the end of this life period, Andean children are expected to help with family chores. At play, with their peers, they reproduce adult chores and sex typing. It is said they learn that mother corn tends the crops, and father mountain is both father and mother of plants and animals; that stars are females that seduce young boys; and that the sun is the jealous protector of his sister, the moon.

In urban settings, newborn girls and boys will also have different meaning for the parents, but here female may mean less. While girls are seen as social support systems, endowed with nurturant qualities, boys are seen as economic support systems, ensuring the continuity of the family name in a patrilinear system. Thus, baby boys may be preferred over baby girls, especially so when reproduction is no longer of survival value.

Following tradition, middle- and high-SES families express initial differential attitudes toward girl and boy newborns through, for example, baby's clothing and room decoration. Pink is used for girls, and light blue for boys. Toys' sex typing is not marked in infancy, but it becomes highly emphasized in the preschool years, coinciding with the acquisition of "gender identity" and, later, "sexual identity" (Ragúz, 1991a). Action toys (cars, airplanes, boats), building, and war-related toys are for boys; baby dolls, dolls, houseware, and baby-care and beauty-related toys are for girls. Some toys may be more neutral: tricycles, roller skates, bikes, and educational, computer, and electronic games.

In these groups, panculturalism shows in gender stereotypes and differential socialization. Boys are rewarded for being active, aggressive, and outgoing. Girls are rewarded for being tender, sweet, and docile. Boys are expected to be adventurous, risk taking, independent, and more physically active. Girls are expected to be vulnerable so they are allowed to express publicly feelings of love, fear, and pain. In older boys, social contact may be more rigidly regulated, and kissing or touching is accepted only in heterosexual relations or within family ties.

Though lacking toys or having to create their own, working-class urban children are very well aware of sex typing in toys, games, and behaviors. Mass media modeling (e.g., advertising) and observational and vicarious learning may supplement what direct experience does not provide.

School Years

The large majority of Peruvian elementary students attend public schools (91 percent of the school system), which, with very few exceptions, are coeducational. Middle- and high-SES parents send their children to private schools, also mostly coeducational. The most traditional Peruvians prefer schools for girls only or for boys only. These preferences may be based on the belief that boys and girls have different educational and sociopersonal needs, on a desire to restrict and control frequency and intensity of interaction among them, which is considered risky, and on an assumed need to provide their children with a network of social relations for the future (Pinzás, in preparation).

In working-class families adult behavior is expected and enforced for the majority of youngsters and even for many children. By age seven, or earlier, children are usually expected to take care of infants and younger siblings. They are left alone in charge of them at home, while parents go out to work. With her mother or sisters, the Andean little girl works on home chores, tends the cattle, works the land. With his father and brothers, the little boy also works the land and travels to sell goods. Hence, schooling may become a second priority.

In Andean populations traditional sex typing includes dress codes. It can mean long braids and several colorful skirts for women and *ponchoes* or *ojotas* (sandals) for men, of no cross-sex use.

In the jungle, women's dyeing of long hair and the way each gender decorates face and body with vegetable dyes are also invested with meaning. As in the Andes, once established, dress codes do not change with age: the same pattern is used by girls and by adult and old women or by boys and by adult and old men.

In urban shantytowns differential socialization may be based on the belief in natural gender differences. Socialization, however, responds to family needs more than to individual or gender needs (Schade & Rojas, 1989). Many children, both boys and girls, work as street vendors, car washers, watchmen, or beggars. Thus, the street itself becomes a socialization agent. Peers and older children on the street supplement parental role models (Franco, 1989).

Urban middle- and high-SES children evidence the same pattern of acquisition of gender-role stereotypes as has been found in 23 other countries. The same holds for a university sample in Lima (Best, 1980–1981). Girls showed intermediate sex typing while boys were highly sex-typed.

For many parents in these SES groups the street is male territory. Girls may not go out alone, but in small groups, for specific errands, or accompanied by a maid(s) and only to close surroundings. Football games, skateboarding, surfing, and biking allow the boys to spend free time in sports with male peers, away from home. Girls practice sports at school, in clubs, or in parks. Boys are expected to use coarse and tough language, though not at home; this is much less usual among girls.

Gender-role identity in low-SES urban adolescents in Lima shows they follow traditional models without exploration or questioning—"closed" gender-role identity (Maurial, 1991). Formal schooling contributes to sex typing through textbooks' sexist content (Mansilla, 1983; Mercado, 1985).

Peruvian urban and rural adolescents evidence traditional sexual attitudes (Ferrando, Sing & Wulf, 1989; Loli, 1986). A study of a national sample of adult educators showed traditional gender-role stereotyping. Men were attributed "brains," realism, pragmatism; women were attributed "heart," sensitivity, imagination, and intuition. Men were described as active, street-oriented, vicious, and aggressive, and women, as passive, submissive, peaceful, home-oriented, and more faithful (Bendezú et al., in preparation).

Makeup, earrings, and jewelry still characterize middle- and high-SES girls, as do skirts and long hair, consistent with the sex-object role. A certain cross-gender dressing style (jeans, T-shirts, sneakers) in youngsters may give the impression of a tendency toward more androgynous models. However, in dating, choosing a sexual partner, proposing, and asking for a "love proof," boys generally take the initiative. Also, more male than female youngsters work, and the former receive higher weekly allowances from their parents.

In the urban cultures, changes in clothing codes, especially, use of makeup, may be interpreted as rites of passage to adolescence and young adulthood, in the same way as parties for the fifteen-year-old girls are a "presentation to society." Boys have no equivalent ceremony, except in the small Jewish community. In boys, socially sanctioned behavior is tolerated or accepted earlier: fighting, drinking, smoking, or sexually experimenting.

Young Adulthood

In the Andean cultures the couple, not the individual, may be seen as the major force in economic, social, and ritual life. Marriage, for example, involves a series of testing stages. First, youngsters search and experiment heterosexually at parties. Children who had freely grown up together in mixed-sex groups now become involved in a series of games; joking and courtship behaviors appear. Youngsters dress seductively, trying publicly to impress girls with their abilities. Young women may use colorful laces on their clothing and flowers on their hats; young men use Creole clothing: white sneakers, a kerchief around the neck, or sunglasses. In more traditional groups, young men use laces and buttons over their knitted hats (*chullos*). Girls giggle and whisper secretly to girlfriends, faking indifference in front of boys. These, in turn, start behaving more on their own, walking alone, and playing an Andean flute (*quena*). The boy playfully throws small pebbles at the girl he likes. If her reaction is shame and running away, he says nice words; she responds in front of her friends with faked insults. During feast times, same-gender groups playfully fight each other, even with songs and verses. Boys try to steal girls' clothing accessories. Later, girls claim their property, and after a heated discussion, a couple may be formed. They hide in the countryside or meet in secrecy, with furtive expressions of intimate feelings.

The *rimanakuy* stage follows, brought about by the young woman's pregnancy. Parents may express sadness, worry, and even dislike toward the boy and his family. Formal visits allow reaching an agreement. The young woman goes to live with the man's family, sometimes after a ceremonial kidnapping. A series of ritualized behaviors—crying, faking opposition—may be exhibited by the parents and in-laws, probably to test the couple's strength.

A *servinakuy*, or trial marriage, follows, in which the male tries to prove he is mature and deserves the goods both families may have arranged to give the couple. Parents may show coldness and resentment toward their son, while parents-in-law show hostility for his stealing their daughter. The young woman tries to prove her "feminine" abilities as housekeeper to the mother-in-law and endures her rejection as well as her own pregnancy.

The couple is driven to count on each other more than on the parents. After the baby's weaning, the couple is considered individually "fully achieved." Only then does the community start treating them as adults, proven able as a couple, and at this point they receive their dowries.

This same Andean cultural pattern was found by Harman (1990) in rural Piura (northern coast). Some variations are noted, however, in relation to machismo. The ritual known as *amujerarse* (term coined for "taking a woman") is con- sidered to illustrate gender inequalities and men's power. Falling in love and seduction among rural Piura youngsters resemble Andean patterns more than urban coastal patterns. Instead of the boy and girl's walking hand in hand, it is the same-gender group who teases the other gender group, tainting seduction with intimacy and privacy with the help of their friends. Here, too, courtship occurs after harvesting, when boys have some money. With the girl's consent, the boy kidnaps her from her house, but they stay at a godfather, friend, or other relative's house. The girl's family is to look for her; if they do find the couple, they have the right to hit the boy, because of public ridicule. If the girl is found alone, doubts arise about her prudery and virtue. If the boy is found alone, it is taken as a lack of respect for the family. The couple seeks pardon from the girl's family and makes the necessary arrangements. If everything is accepted, they move to the boy's house. As in the Andes, these unions prevail upon formal civil or religious marriages.

Important differences with regard to the Andes can be appreciated. Here it is not socially approved for the girl to become pregnant. Once the union is for- malized, the families do not feel responsible for their problems or needs. The girl submits now to the boy's authority and also to his mother's and family's authority.

Adulthood

In the Andean culture full adulthood is reached after the *servinakuy*, and the community helps build the couple's house in a ritual and religious ceremony. Shortly after, most couples officially marry. It is a developmental stage where the person is expected to achieve wealth and prestige, following a socialization process of poverty, dependence, and domestication. If the adult fails to meet these expectations, he or she is considered sinful or lazy.

In the urban culture, middle- and high-SES, educated late adolescents (pre-university students) ascribe to adults—especially male adults—high social and internal masculinity; only female adults are attributed high femininity (Ragúz, 1991b). Various psychological, anthropological, and sociological studies attest to traditionalism in urban Lima middle-class adult women, whose identity focuses on the maternal/housewife role, although many of them significantly contribute to family income. A traditional male ideal seems to prevail in all SES groups. Jones (1983) confirmed that dependency behavior and attitudes exist even in professional women. Traditional sex typing prevails even in Peruvian mental health professionals (Ramos, 1987). A gender bias in the professional distribution was noted by Baruch (1989): education, obstetrics, and nursing were female-saturated; medicine, engineering, and business administration were male-saturated. In Baruch's study, women from traditionally "feminine" professions had higher self-perceived femininity than women from "masculine" professions. "Feminine"-profession women's self-perception in the family and in the working context was significantly less masculine-typed than that of "masculine"-profession women. Single professional women—either from "feminine" or "masculine" professions—were more androgynous than the married ones.

Peruvian divorce rates may be considered relatively low. As Peru is a Catholic country, divorce is not favored in urban sectors. In rural sectors, couples tend to stay together due to functional reasons, but the few that separate or divorce may not be socially or religiously sanctioned, as happens in urban settings. The pattern is even more flexible in the rural jungle, but the tendency still favors stable family units.

Old Age

About 6 percent of Peruvians are sixty years old or more. Although not yet systematically studied, marked cross-cultural differences within the country can be expected regarding perception of gender roles among elderly people.

In the rural Andean culture old age may be related to poverty. As sons and daughters marry, the couple starts losing properties but tries to keep a part of them to ensure some power. The younger or unmarried offspring will stay with them and, upon their death, inherit their part. Old people may be expected to be relatively poor. Ortiz (1989) notes these stereotypes are bound to change due to migration patterns and to the fact that rural communities in the Andes are no longer isolated from market economies.

In the Ragúz (1991b) study with preuniversity students, old people were considered highly non-sex-typed (neutral). Female elders, however, were perceived as highly feminine. Both male and female elders were believed to be less masculine (in their internal and social masculinity) than adults and even children and less internally masculine than youngsters.

Comparing perception and attitudes toward old age in middle/high- and low-SES Lima university students and persons older than 60 years, Romero (1989) found no gender, age, or SES differences. But younger persons evidenced a more negative attitude toward old persons.

One may hypothesize that in urban middle- and high-SES groups, what is important, more than age itself, is the way in which retirement is handled. Sex-typed persons, especially men with a masculine gender-role orientation (self-perception), may find it more difficult to accept retirement and find a meaningful source of self-esteem than non-sex-typed persons. Due to differential gender-role socialization, retired men may tend to perceive they are losing their productive role, a main source of status and self-esteem. Many "feminine" old women may not find their self-concept and self-esteem menaced since they continue to display their maternal and nurturant role, supervising or helping with domestic chores or with raising of infant and young grandchildren or even caring for their old partner. Non-sex-typed old people are theoretically expected to have better personality resources to cope with and adapt to situations and crises, as may be implied in retirement or getting older.

Social Security systems in Peru do not cover the minimal economic needs of retired persons. There are living arrangements run by religious and private institutions, varying in cost and quality. It is common for urban families to have old parents living at home, especially when they are widowers. Daughters are expected to assume the care and nurturing of sick and/or old parents, and sons are expected to provide financially for them, if the need arises. Often, only those with no relatives live alone. The most affluent sectors can pay a live-in nurse or maid who takes care of the old person. The less affluent will take care of the elderly themselves. In shantytowns, old people keep on working, but in less demanding jobs (e.g., as street vendors) in the neighborhood, or help with domestic chores and child care.

SUMMARY AND CONCLUSIONS

The aim of this chapter has been to present gender roles in Peru in a framework of diversity of cultures, multiple crisis, and change. In Peru's highest SES levels, sex typing tends to follow what are (or used to be) the traditional Western patterns, due to Peruvians' Westernized education, their access to various mass media, their traveling and becoming acquainted with foreign values and beliefs. The vast majority in Peru, though, are urban and rural people living in extreme poverty and showing different patterns.

Peasants in the Andes adhere to their ancient worldview and their traditional way of life, resulting in a syncretism between patriarchal Catholic and Andean values and beliefs. Large numbers of Andean families have been migrating to the cities, especially to Lima. Their culture clash resulted in new processes of acculturation to several coastal values and beliefs, including machismo.

In the city of Lima, especially in the very large urban slums, poverty and violence characterize life, especially women's lives. The country's severe crisis, however, has significantly led Peruvian women to organize communal strategies for survival that have become an arena for changes in gender relations and in gender-role identity. Women have also developed commerce skills and work in "informal markets" or as street vendors.

Middle-SES urban women have had to start working outside the home, leaving their traditional maternal and housewife roles. This middle-SES group can be characterized as a Creole mixture of cultures, a combination of Western traditional attitudes and values and indigenous values and beliefs from its ancestors. It has been found to be more traditional in its sexual attitudes, gender roles, and sex typing (but not necessarily sexual behavior) than the higher-SES groups.

One cannot easily compare traditionalism between urban and rural low-SES groups, since these latter groups differ considerably from each other. In addition to this, rural groups have rigid sex typing but on different grounds, untainted or less tainted by machismo. In general terms it may be hypothesized that machismo cuts across SES; the upper class may be more liberal in a Western sense, with the middle class being more similar to the Western traditional culture. The urban working class may be characterized by a synthesis of patriarchal and *machista* ideologies.

Little can be said of native Amazon rural groups—a relatively small part of the Peruvian population—except that their within-gender solidarity explains women's higher status and stronger gender identity. Change in these groups due to market economy and to exchange with urban groups has usually led to a worsening of the status of women.

Peru's dynamic psychosocial processes and economic situation may be leading to more compatible and fair gender roles. If there were a large improvement in educational opportunities for all, it could combine with women's current changes to provide them with access to opportunities, to ways of developing further their organization for survival, and to higher living conditions. All of these may allow for experiencing clarification of values and a rise in self-consciousness.

REFERENCES

Barnechea, C. (1985). Organizándose para cambiar la vida. In Lora, C., & Anderson, J. (Eds.), *Mujer: Víctima de opresión, portadora de liberación*. Lima: Instituto Bartolomé de las Casas.

────. (1988). *Autoestima y experiencia de organización en un grupo de mujeres de pueblos ióvenes*. Bachelor diss., Pontificia Universidad Católica del Perú, Lima: P.U.C.

Baruch, M. (1989). *Orientación de rol sexual en mujeres que trabajan en profesiones sexualmente tipificadas*. Bachelor diss., Pontificia Universidad Católica del Perú, Lima: P.U.C.

Bendezú, A., Ragúz, M., Fernández, M., Dughi, P., Londoña, C., & Abad, E. (in preparation). *Capacitación en sexualidad y planificación familiar para profesores de escuelas nocturnas 1990–92*. Lima: Pathfinder Fund.

Best, B. (1980–1981). An overview of findings from children's studies of sex-trait stereotypes in 23 countries. Paper presented at the Fifth International Association for Cross-Cultural Psychology (IACCP) Meeting, India, 28 December–1 January.

Blondet, C. (1991). *Las mujeres y el poder. Una historia de Villa El Salvador*. Lima: IEP.

Bourque, S., & Warren, K. (1981). *Women in the Andes: Patriarchy and Social Change in Two Andean Towns*. Ann Arbor: University of Michigan.

Ferrando, D., Sing, S., & Wulf, D. (1989). *Adolescentes de hoy, padres del mañana: Perú*. New York: Alan Guttmacher Institute.

Franco, R. (1989). Redes de soporte social de niños trabajadores en Lima Metropolitana. *Revista de Psicología de la P.U.C., 7* (1): 79–92.

Gómez, B., & Gutiérrez, C. (1987). *Actitudes frente a pautas de crianza diferencial de los hijos en mujeres pertenecientes a comedores populares en El Agustino*. Lima: AMIDEP.

Guzmán, V., & Portocarrero, P. (1985). *Dos veces mujer*. Lima: Mosca Azul.

Harman, L. (1990). "Ya se ha mujerao." *Anthropologica, 8* (8): 309–18.

Jones, C. (1983). *La dependencia de la mujer y su relación con el trabajo*. Ph.D. diss., Pontificia Universidad Católica del Perú.

Loli, A. (1986). *La sexualidad en la adolescencia: Un estudio peruano*. Lima: SMMISA.

Lora, C., & Anderson, J. (1985). *Mujer: Víctima de opresión, portadora de liberación*. Lima: Instituto Bartolomé de las Casas.

Mannarelli, M. E. (1988). *Algunas reflexiones a propósito de la investigación sobre mujeres y género en el Perú*. Lima: FOMCIENCIAS.

Mansilla, M. E. (1983). Aprendiendo a ser mujer. Estereotipos sexuales en textos escolares. *Debate, 9*: 65–89.

Mateos, Z. (1991). Mi mamá trabaja. Encuesta: Imagen de la limeña. *Debate, 12* (64): 28–30.

Maurial, X. (1991). Las posiciones de identidad del yo en un grupo de adolescentes tardíos de sector popular. Bachelor thesis, Pontificia Universidad Católica del Perú.

Mercado, H. (1985). La familia y el niño. Paper presented at AMIDEP Second National Meeting on Population, Tarma, Peru.

Ortiz, A. (1989). La comunidad, el parentesco y los patrones de crianza andinos. *Anthropologica, 7* (7): 135–70.

Pinzás, Juana R. (in preparation). *Necesidades educativas: La situación de la mujer*. Lima: Pontificia Universidad Católica del Perú.

Ragúz, M. (1981). Actitudes hacia la mujer en estudiantes de post-grado de diversa procedencia étnica y social. License case study, Pontificia Universidad Católica del Perú.

————. (1983). Estereotipos de rol sexual y diferencias sexuales: Realidad y distorsión. *Revista de Psicología, P.U.C.*, *1* (1): 27–37.

————. (1989). Maternidad/maternalidad y trabajo: Efectos del rol dual sobre los hijos y la pareja. *Revista de Psicología, P.U.C.*, *7* (1): 3–21.

————. (1990). Maternidad/maternalidad y trabajo: Efectos del rol dual sobre las madres que trabajan. *Revista de Psicologia, P.U.C.*, *8* (2): 181–201.

————. (1991a, 2 October). Existe el eterno femenino? Paper presented at the Diploma of Studies on Gender Conference, Lima: Pontificia Universidad Católica del Perú.

————. (1991b). Masculinity and femininity: An empirical definition. Ph.D. diss,. Catholic University of Nijmegen, The Netherlands.

Ramos, M. C. (1987). Estereotipos de rol sexual y estándar de salud mental en un grupo de psicoterapeutas y estudiantes universitarios. Bachelor diss., Pontificia Universidad Católica del Perú.

Romero, R. (1989). Percepción y actitud hacia la ancianidad de acuerdo a la edad, sexo y nivel socioeconómico. Bachelor diss., Pontificia Universidad Católica del Perú.

Sara-Lafosse V. (1979). *La familia, la mujer y la socialización de los hijos en contextos sociales diferentes*. Lima: P.U.C.

Schade, B., & Rojas, C. (1989). Niños en extrema pobreza . . . Socialización deficitaria? *Revista de Psicología, P.U.C.*, *7* (2): 139–50.

Singh, S., & Wulf, D. (1990). *Adolescentes hoy, padres del mañana: Un perfil de las Américas*. New York: Alan Guttmacher Institute.

Stahr, M., & Vega, M. (1987). *Efectos de la socialización en la estructura psíquica de las mujeres de sectores populares*. Lima: AMIDEP.

Tamayo, G., & García Rios, J. M. (1990). *Mujer y varón. Vida cotidiana, violencia y justicia*. Lima: Raíces y Alas.

Ureña, C., & De Vivanco, P. (1981). La condicion de la mujer campesina en su familia y comunidad: Huancavelica. Unpublished paper, Lima.

Williams, J., & Best, B. (1982). *Measuring Sex Stereotypes: Cross-Cultural Research and Methodology*. Beverly Hills, CA: Sage.

19

The Philippines

Patricia B. Licuanan

INTRODUCTION

The Philippines is a cluster of 7,100 islands situated in Southeast Asia. The archipelago is bounded by the South China Sea in the west, the Pacific Ocean in the east, Sulu and Celebes Seas in the south, and the Bashi Channel in the north. It has a total land area of 300,780 square kilometers (116,131 square miles) and has the longest discontinuous coastline in the world.

The Philippine population is characterized by a high birthrate and a gradually decreasing mortality rate. Latest data from the national census of 1990 estimate the total number of Filipinos as 60,685,000, with practically equal numbers of males and females. Although the Philippines is predominantly rural, approximately 37.23 percent of the population live in urban areas. This may be attributed to migration from rural areas to urban centers in search of better employment opportunities. Metropolitan Manila is the premier city and has a population of over 8 million. The Philippines has a relatively young population, with 42 percent of the population below 15 years of age.

There are more than 87 languages and dialects spoken in the country. Several religions are practiced with Roman Catholicism (85 percent) predominating. Muslims comprise 4 percent and Protestants 3 percent of the population. Aside from these there are local Christian sects, Buddhists, and indigenous religions.

The Philippines has had a long colonial history under Spain, the United States, and Japan. In its more recent history as an independent country, the Philippines functioned under a U.S.-style constitution and government structure. It went through 20 years of dictatorial rule; but since February 1986, after a popular revolt, it has been a newly restored democracy.

OVERVIEW

Most Filipinos consider the status of Filipino women and men a nonissue. Observing the highly visible women in Philippine society, including a woman president, women in Congress, in the Supreme Court, and in the Cabinet as well as in business and the private sector, most Filipino men (and women) sincerely believe that Filipino women enjoy equal status to men.

Indeed, there are many genuinely positive aspects of the situation of women in the Philippines. There is formal acceptance of the equality of women in basic laws and conventions. The 1987 Philippine Constitution contains an explicit gender equality provision, which affirms that "The State recognizes the role of women in nation building, and shall ensure the fundamental equality before the law of women and men" (Article II, Sec. 14). This is further supported by more specific laws such as the Labor Code, the New Family Code, and the Women in Development and Nation-Building Act. The Philippines is signatory to international conventions and agreements such as the United Nations (UN) Convention on the Elimination of All Forms of Discrimination Against Women (CEDAW) and the Nairobi Forward-Looking Strategies for the Advancement of Women. It has a national government machinery for women, the National Commission on the Role of Filipino Women, and numerous active and committed women nongovernmental organizations (NGOs). In 1989 the Philippine Development Plan for Women was launched as a companion plan to the Medium-Term Philippine Development Plan.

In general, the educational status of women and men is equal, patterns of decision making in the family are egalitarian, and the more blatant forms of discrimination against women that may exist in some countries and cultures are totally absent. However, despite the obvious positive aspects of the situation of women in the Philippines, many problems do in fact exist, as de jure equality does not always flow easily into de facto equality.

COMPARISONS BETWEEN MEN'S AND WOMEN'S GENDER ROLES DURING THE LIFE CYCLE

Infancy and Early Childhood

Philippine society is characterized by a strong positive attitude toward children. The birth of a child is always a joyful event, as most Filipino couples consider children as gifts from God and an intrinsic part of marriage. The typical Filipino family has five children. However, an increasing number of parents desire fewer children.

Filipino parents do not have clear preferences about the gender of their offspring. What is clear is that they want a good balance of male and female children. While male children are valued because they serve to perpetuate the family name, female children are desired because they are more helpful at home and because daughters will care for their parents in their old age. Among low-income families children of both sexes are considered assets as soon as they begin to walk and perform chores, and as they grow older, they become increasingly useful as helpers in income-generating activities.

At a very early age, children are taught the valued traits of obedience and respect for parents and elders. Family solidarity is emphasized, along with the need to place family goals over individual goals. Children of both sexes are trained to be diligent and responsible. While both sexes are taught ideal traits and behaviors and are discouraged from engaging in undesirable activities, sons are excused more readily for their failures. Daughters, on the other hand, are expected to be "good" and to conform more closely to the ideal. They are expected as well to be more pious and closer to God.

For the Filipino child, socialization into sex-appropriate roles begins early. In general, a preschool child can already distinguish male from female and choose sex-appropriate toys, games, and activities. Favorite toys across ages are dolls and stuffed animals for girls and balls and combat toys for boys. Girls, 3–6 years of age, enjoy playing house while boys of the same age enjoy gunfights. Gender stereotyping with regard to toys and games is more obvious among urban middle-class children, who have greater exposure to Western media and whose parents have the means to buy Western-type toys. Low-income and rural children do more improvising and play more gender-neutral games, such as playing in the sand and catching insects.

School Years

In general, the division of labor at home is determined by age and sex considerations. Boys, 3–10 years old, are assigned to clean the yard and fetch firewood and water. On the other hand, the girls take care of setting and clearing the dining table, washing dishes, changing bedding, and, eventually, cooking. Either one may be asked to run errands, watch and play with younger siblings, and care for houseplants.

When they reach adolescence, girls assume greater responsibility for marketing, in addition to cooking. The care of younger children is increasingly thrust upon them. This stage marks the start of more pronounced delineation of gender roles in the household. Girls are expected to stay at home and sharpen their housekeeping skills. Boys begin to work outside the home, usually with their father, in activities such as farming and fishing.

The sexual division of labor, however, does not appear to be rigid. In some cases the main consideration in determining who performs a chore seems to be the availability of the person rather than gender.

In a country where the literacy rate is quite high (93 percent) there is no significant difference in the overall literacy rate between the male and female population. Neither is there a difference in school participation rate, with equal numbers of males and females enrolled at the elementary, secondary, and tertiary levels.

There is, however, a definite pattern of gender tracking in colleges and universities, with women dominating certain courses such as food and nutrition, accounting, nursing, and teacher education. Men dominate in courses such as law, architecture, engineering, and foreign service. However, females are increasingly enrolling in traditionally "male" courses.

In the formal educational system there is the subtle presence of sex-role stereotyping in textbooks used by schoolchildren. A content analysis of elementary textbooks reveals more interesting and varied activities for men and more limited activities for women. Women are given a social role and definition by virtue of relationship with men (i.e., usually introduced as a wife, daughter, or sister). Males have more varied descriptions and more outstanding characteristics, and male characters are highlighted in illustrations, with females generally in the background.

Young Adulthood

As children, girls and boys interact freely with each other at home and in school, with no norms governing their interaction beyond the general norms of proper behavior—respect for elders, consideration for one another (i.e., no quarreling), and safety. As they reach adolescence and young adulthood, when they begin to get interested in the opposite sex or actually start searching for a prospective spouse, more specific norms begin to apply.

The norms governing young adults in the areas of male-female relationships are influenced by such factors as social class, urban-rural background, and gender. While men and women are allowed to mix freely, social roles of both sexes involve important elements of restraint, both in behavior and in language. Modesty is the rule among young women, and conscientiousness is the rule among young men. In dating and in courtship, the woman is expected to play a more passive role, always careful about her reputation. Men, on the other hand, are supposed to be more aggressive and initiate developments in the relationship. At the same time they have the obligation to act responsibly and not take advantage of women, at least not "nice" women.

In more traditional settings, particularly in rural areas, dating is a group activity where a young man and woman go out together in the company of other couples or a group of friends not necessarily paired. Solo dating occurs in more urbanized (and Westernized) groups. Dating patterns among young adults in the city are much more liberal than those of their rural counterparts or of their parents a generation ago.

The place, kind of activity, and dating style are dictated by such factors as financial capability, education, and hobbies or interests. Favored dating places are movie houses, parties, parks, restaurants, and discos, in that order. In most instances, the man shoulders the expenses, but some independent-minded women prefer to pay half or a portion of the bill.

Greater tolerance in the matter of premarital sex has been noted among Filipino men than among women. In the same vein, virginity is more highly valued in females than in males.

A comparison of male and female labor force participation rates shows that while about 87 percent of males are economically active, only slightly more than half of the entire female population aged 15 and above are in the labor force. While females make up half of the household population and possess equal education, males nevertheless outnumber females in the national employment scene. Factors affecting women's access to employment opportunities are many:

1. There is a traditional cultural distinction between men's work and women's work. What is considered women's work reflects the connection with home activities (sewing, cooking), and women are less readily considered for jobs that do not fall into this stereotype.
2. Women's work is viewed as auxiliary in character. Women are tapped by industrial firms only when the seasonal demand is high.
3. Women's work is viewed as marginal and dispensable. Women join the labor force only to augment income during times of difficulty. Otherwise they withdraw into the household, their traditional place.
4. Traditional attitudes that women should not work, should get married, have children, and stay at home and that women should give way to men in getting jobs still hold sway.
5. Women are further handicapped by their relative immobility. They are reluctant to accept work far from home since they have to be physically available to their children. Furthermore, if the husband's job entails a change in location, the woman usually moves with him.
6. Protective legislation for women and higher incidental costs in employing them because of provision for maternity leaves influence employers to favor male applicants.

Despite these obstacles, women who manage to find employment have to face further problems, such as unequal pay for equal work. Women also tend to hold lower positions in the employment ladder. In administrative, executive, and managerial positions there is one female for every four males. Women are promoted much more slowly than men and have less access to training. Because of the lower positions of women and their lack of higher-level skills, the introduction of new technology such as mechanization generally results in the displacement of female labor. More women are laid off or terminated. Studies show that while most terminations in cases involving male workers are motivated by unacceptable actions on the part of the males, for example, violation of rules and unsatisfactory performance, separation cases affecting females are due to economic reasons such as severe financial difficulties, partial shutdown, and retrenchment.

Gender stereotypes continue to plague women workers. In rice agriculture women prepare the seedbeds, transplant, weed, apply fertilizer and insecticide, water, harvest, thresh, winnow, transport, dry, mill, and market, and yet the man is recognized as the farmer because his hands are behind the plow. Thus it is the men who are trained for new farm technology and who have access to credit.

Adulthood

The average age at marriage of females is 23.8 years while that for males is 26.3 years. A ritual usually associated with Filipino marriages is the traditional custom called *pamanhikan*, which literally means "going up" (to the home of the prospective bride). The future groom, accompanied by his parents or a family elder, formally presents his marriage proposal to his fiancée's parents and seeks their blessing and approval. In most instances, the ritual is a mere formality, as prior consent would already have been obtained by the couple informally. During the *pamanhikan* wedding plans are discussed and finalized, as well as the couple's intended living arrangements after the wedding, when they settle down as man and wife. The cultural significance of the *pamanhikan* lies in its embodiment of revered Filipino values such as respect for parents, submission to parental authority, and reverence for the sanctity of marriage.

Traditionally, the future groom shoulders the cost of all the wedding expenses. Modern-day weddings, however, have become increasingly influenced by more practical considerations. Sometimes, both sets of parents share in the wedding expenses. A more recent trend is for young couples who are both professionals and financially independent to make all the arrangements and, from their pooled savings, shoulder all the wedding expenses.

In the traditional Filipino marriage, the wife is expected to care for her husband, the home, and the children. Perceptions of an ideal woman invariably describe her as a wife and mother, with few exceptions related to nondomestic areas. Perceptions of husbands, on the other hand, include areas of family, occupation, and community activities.

Men spend most of their day in income-earning activities as well as in leisure and community involvements. Women spend the greater portion of the day in home management. When a man says of his wife or, for that matter, when a woman says of herself that she does not work, she just stays home, they are saying that cooking, laundering, cleaning, tending the backyard garden, tending the animals, sewing, and caring for the children do not count as work. Women who do work outside the home are responsible for home chores as well and carry a double burden. It is estimated that husbands work only two-thirds as much as their working wives.

Since the husband is not expected to do household work after work, this allows him more time for relaxation, drinking, and socialization with friends outside the home. Socializing while his wife works may be rationalized as fulfilling the husband's responsibility to establish and maintain proper links with the community for the good of his family.

The Filipino family has been described as egalitarian with respect to decision making, with both husband and wife playing important roles in family decisions. Each spouse, however, has a particular area of influence where her or his view predominates. The wife is accepted as the major decision maker in matters related to household management, including family budget, and in most aspects of child care and training. Husbands, on the other hand, exert greater influence in matters of livelihood or occupation and the discipline of older sons. Major areas where joint decision making is the pattern are financial matters, family residence, family leisure, children's education, and family planning.

Much is made of the fact that Filipino wives hold the purse strings in the family. But when a family's income cannot even meet the basic necessities, her role as financial manager is less a source of status than it is an added burden. While the man's duty is to be the breadwinner of the family, the woman's duty is to stretch family resources to make ends meet.

In Filipino marriages there exists a double standard of morality that governs the behavior of husbands and wives. It is generally accepted both by women and men that women should be devoted and faithful to their husbands. The expectations for husbands are considerably less strict, and thus, should a husband stray, this is tolerated because it is believed that men are morally weaker than women.

The media are one of the main instruments of informal education on the roles of men and women in society. In print and broadcast media, particularly in advertisements, soap operas, and sitcoms, women are generally portrayed in stereotyped and unflattering ways—typically as housewives or domestics, as sex objects, or as nice, wholesome creatures whose main goal in life is to attract and keep a man. The "macho man" and the "long-suffering wife" are common cultural stereotypes reinforced by movies and television drama.

Census statistics assure us that marriage in the Philippines is highly stable, with 9 out of 10 marriages still intact. An examination of the provisions of the Philippine Civil Code provides strong support for the value Philippine society has attached to a monogamous and permanent marriage. Although debate on the matter is revived regularly, absolute divorce continues to be prohibited in the Philippines. What is allowed is legal separation or relative divorce, for which a petition may be filed on account of any of the following grounds: sexual infidelity or perversion; an attempt against the life of the petitioner by the spouse; repeated physical violence or grossly abusive conduct directed against the petitioner, a common child, or a child of the petitioner; physical violence or moral pressure to compel the petitioner to change religious or political affiliation; an attempt of the respondent to corrupt or induce the petitioner, a common child, or a child of the petitioner, to engage in prostitution, or connivance in such corruption or inducement; drug addiction or habitual alcoholism of the respondent; formal judgment sentencing the respondent to imprisonment of more than six years, even if pardoned; lesbianism or homosexuality of the respondent; abandonment of petitioner by the spouse without justifiable cause for more than one year.

In case the petition for legal separation is granted, the couple's children who are over seven years of age are given the right to choose the parent who would exercise parental authority over them, unless the parent so chosen is declared unfit. Children under seven years of age automatically remain with the mother, unless there are compelling reasons for other arrangements. In general, custody of the children is awarded to the innocent spouse. A legal separation does not allow the spouses to remarry. Despite the absence of divorce, spouses do separate, whether formally through the mechanism of legal separation or informally by simply living separately, sometimes with new partners. Those who are economically better off may go through foreign divorce and remarriage. Separations and "new arrangements," while becoming more common and more accepted, are still a source of discomfort to the persons and families involved.

Old Age

There are more elderly females than males in the Philippines, confirming the well-documented pattern of a longer life span for women compared with men. There are also more elderly females who never married.

The elderly in the Philippines enjoy a high status in society and in the household. They are viewed to possess such qualities as wisdom and knowledge. Hence, they are held in high esteem and usually take active roles in making decisions, giving advice, and raising the grandchildren.

The family continues to play a central role in the retirement years of its members. Most elderly prefer to live with their children or their relatives. Proportionately more males than females live with their spouses and other family members. On the other hand, proportionately more females than males stay with other family members besides their spouse. This reflects the fact that women have a longer life expectancy than men. When a woman outlives her husband, she is expected to live with other family members. Residential homes for the aged in the Philippines are few and have limited functions. They are not permanent residential or nursing care homes but are rehabilitative in nature. The residents are often transients, needing assistance in regaining self-sufficiency. Thereafter, they are sent back to families who are willing to accept them.

Filipino elderly generally perceive themselves to be in good health. They become less optimistic, however, as they grow older. More males than females report good health in old age. This might appear surprising in light of the fact that women outlive men by an average of 4.8 years, indicating better health and greater resistance against death-causing diseases. Self-assessments that reflect a contrary picture seem to be part of the macho culture, where males are regarded as the more dominant sex and necessarily, stronger, hardier and less-complaining. Their positive self-reports allow them to cling to this masculine self-image for a longer period of time.

Generally, both male and female elderly living in urban areas feel healthier than their rural counterparts. For the urban male elderly, however, this appears to be true only until around 65 years, when they reach retirement age. At this point, there is a drastic decline in the number of urban elderly males reporting good health. This is perhaps related to greater displacement experienced by them as they search for new roles. This does not seem to be the case in the rural areas, where the elderly undergo a smoother shift, with fewer changes in household and community roles.

Nearly two-thirds of all elderly are economically self-reliant while two out of five count on money provided by their children. Nearly half of all elderly females rely on their children's support. Whether a true gender differential exists or just a greater tendency among females to admit that their children give them money is still uncertain.

Among those economically active, differential patterns of participation are evident. The rate for males are almost twice that of females, reflecting a possibly greater tendency for females to favor home responsibilities over productive employment. Three out of every five males aged 65 and above are economically active, compared with only one out of every five females. Furthermore, a greater desire to continue working has been observed among the male elderly than among the female. Dependency is almost certain for both males and females at age 75 and above.

Social activities of the elderly include community activities, socializing with friends, and caring for other family members. Among the most common recreational activities of retired and employed elderly are watching television and movies and listening to the radio. Rural grandparents enjoy telling stories to the young, their stories often containing moral lessons. Elderly females most often stay at home and preoccupy themselves with raising their grandchildren.

SUMMARY AND CONCLUSIONS

Any discussion of gender roles is inevitably a combination of description and prescription. A description of gender roles in the Philippines presents not merely what is but also, implicitly and even explicitly, what should be. The prescriptive dimension of gender roles, however, is expressed in two voices. One voice is that of tradition, crying for the preservation of cultural values and practices and warning against the dangers of tampering with the foundations of some of our sacred cultural institutions such as marriage and family. From this perspective, gender roles are a part of our culture and should be respected as such.

The second voice in the discussion advocates change, pointing directly or indirectly, moderately or militantly, to what is undesirable in the present state of gender roles. From this perspective, much harm may be perpetuated in the name of culture and tradition.

From this review of gender roles in the Philippines, it is obvious that while respect for tradition is important, change is necessary. Filipino women and men have to find the combination that is right for them as equals and as partners in the development of the Philippines.

REFERENCES

Bautista, Cynthia B. (1977). Women in marriage. In Bulatao, Rodolfo A. (Ed.), *Stereotype, Status, and Satisfactions: The Filipina Among Filipinos*. Quezon City: Social Research Laboratory, University of the Philippines.

Bulatao, Rodolfo A. (Ed.). (1977). *Stereotype, Status, and Satisfactions: The Filipina Among Filipinos*. Quezon City: Social Research Laboratory, University of the Philippines.

Castillo, Gelia T. (1981). The Filipino woman: Wife, mother, worker and citizen. Occasional Paper No. 3. NFE/WID Exchange-Asia. University of the Philippines, Los Baños.

Contado, Mina E. (1981). Power dynamics of rural families: The case of a Samar Barrio. *Philippine Sociological Review*, 29 (1–4):73–85.

Cortes, Irene R. (1982). Discrimination against women and employment policies. *NCRFW Research Monograph*, No. 1. Manila: National Commission on the Role of Filipino Women.

David, Rina, & Azarcon-de la Cruz, Pennie. (1985). *Toward Our Own Image: An Alternative Philippine Report on Women and Media*. Quezon City: Philippine Women's Research Collective.

Decaesstecker, Sister Donald. (1978). *Impoverished Urban Filipino Families*. Manila: University of Santo Tomas Press.

Domingo, Lita J., & Zosa-Feranil, Imelda. (1987). *The Filipino Elderly: A Review of Literature and Existing Data*. Demographic Research and Development Foundation.

———. (1990). *Socio-Economic Consequences of the Aging Population: Insights from the Philippine Experience*. Demographic Research and Development Foundation.

Esquillo-Martinez, Natividad. (1976). Conjugal interaction and fertility behavior among Filipino urban working class. M.A. thesis, Department of Sociology and Anthropology, Ateneo de Manila University.

Eviota, Elizabeth U. (1978). Sex as a differentiating variable in work and power relations. *Philippine Sociological Review* 26 (3–4): 151–58.

———. (1982). Time use and the sex division of labor. *Philippine Journal of Industrial Relations*, 4(1–2): 116–33.

Gonzales, Anna Miren, & Hollnsteiner, Mary R. (1976). *Filipino Women as Partners of Men in Progress and Development*. Quezon City: Institute of Philippine Culture, Ateneo de Manila University.

Herrin, Alejandro N. (1981). Economic activities of married women in the Philippines: Conceptual and measurement issues. Paper presented to the PSSC-U.P. Law Center Seminar-Workshop on Development Planning and the Roles of Women. Asian Institute of Tourism, Quezon City.

Illo, Jeanne Frances I. (1977). *Involvement by Choice: The Role of Women in Development*. Quezon City: Social Survey Research Unit, Institute of Philippine Culture, Ateneo de Manila University.

———. (1988). Putting gender up front: Data, issues, and prospects. In Illo, Jeanne

Frances I. (Ed.), *Gender Issues in Rural Development: A Workshop Report* (pp. 9–20). Quezon City: Institute of Philippine Culture, Ateneo de Manila University.

————, & Pineda-Ofreneo, Rosalinda. (1989, 6–10 August). Producers, traders, workers: Philippine women in agriculture. Paper prepared for the FAO/TDRI Regional Workshop on Planning and Implementation Aspects of Programs and Projects Assisting Women Farmers in ASEAN Countries, Chomtien, Thailand.

Ira, Luningning. (1990). *Guidebook to the Filipino Wedding*. Manila: Vera-Reyes.

Jurado, Gonzalo, Alonzo, R., Canlas, D., Ferrer, R., Tidalgo, R., Armas, A., & Castro, J. (1981). The Manila informal sector: In transition? In Sutheraman, S. V. (Ed.), *The Urban Informal Sector in Developing Countries: Employment, Poverty and Environment* (pp. 151–67). Geneva: International Labor Organization.

Licuanan, Patricia B. (1986). *Some Are More Unequal Than Others*. Quezon City: Ateneo de Manila University.

————. (1991). A situation analysis of women in the Philippines. In Illo, Frances I. (Ed.), *Gender Analysis and Planning: The 1990 IPC-CIDA Workshops* (pp. 15–28). Quezon City: Institute of Philippine Culture, Ateneo de Manila University.

————, & Gonzales, Anna Miren. (1976). Filipino women in development. Typescript.

Miralao, Virginia A. (1980). Time use as a measure of women's role in development. Paper presented at the Second National Statistical Convention, Manila.

Philippines (Republic) National Census and Statistics Office (NCSO). (1982). *Vital Statistics Report*. Manila: NCSO.

Philippines (Republic) National Statistics Office (NSO) (1986). *Integrated Survey of Households, Fourth Quarter 1986*. Manila: NSO.

————. (1991a). *Philippine Statistical Yearbook*. Manila: NSO.

————. (1991b). *Singulate Mean Age at Marriage 1948–1990*. Manila: NSO.

Porio, Emma, Lynch, Frank & Hollnsteiner, Mary. (1975). *The Filipino Family, Community and Nation: The Same Yesterday, Today and Tomorrow?* Quezon City: Institute of Philippine Culture, Ateneo de Manila University.

Ramirez, Mina. (1984). *Understanding Philippine Social Relations Through the Filipino Family: A Phenomenological Approach*. Manila: Asian Social Institute Communication Center.

Sempio-Diy, Alicia V. (1989). Major changes introduced by the new family code. Typescript.

Sevilla, Judy Carol C. (1982). *Research on the Filipino Family: Review and Prospects*. Pasig, Metro Manila: Development Academy of the Philippines.

Sycip, Lynne Marie. (1982). Working mothers: Their problems and coping strategies, an exploratory study. *Social Science Information*, *10*(2):1–8.

Torres, Amaryllis Tiglao (Ed.). (1989). *The Filipino Women in Focus: A Book of Readings*. Bangkok: UNESCO.

20

Poland

Halina Grzymala-Moszczynska

INTRODUCTION

More than 1,000 years ago, the Polish state came into being in the area bordered by the Carpathian and Sudeten mountains in the south, the Baltic Sea in the north, the Oder River in the west, and the Bug River in the east, as a result of the unification of related West Slav tribes. A decisive part was played in this process by the Polanie (Polanes) tribe. The Polish state was brought into the sphere of influence of the Mediterranean culture prevailing in Western Europe through a baptism in 966 into the Christian faith of the first historical ruler, Mieszko I. Today Poland is situated between 49 degrees and 54.5 degrees latitude north and 14.07 degrees and 24.08 degrees longitude east. At present Poland occupies 120.733 square miles, which is 2.7 percent of the area of Europe. The population consists of about 38 million people. Women represent 51.3 percent, and men 48.7 percent, of the population. Women are in the majority in the age groups over 45 years; however, this is reversed in the younger age groups, where there are more men, which means that in many regions of the country, particularly in rural areas, men have no chances to find prospective wives. This, then, is one of the main reasons for men to emigrate from rural to urban districts and change from being farmers to city dwellers.

Different periods of the country's history had special importance in shaping contemporary national culture and character. An important period in Polish history for forming social consciousness dates back to 1772. In that year Poland lost its independence and became divided among three countries: Russia, Prussia, and Austria. Partition of Poland produced a chain reaction of dramatic attempts by Polish citizens to regain their country's independence by means of military uprisings against the ruling powers. Nearly all the men of the Polish nobility became—in one way or another—involved in military fights. This struggle caused the death of many of them, as well as the confiscation of their property, long sentences of imprisonment, and, in the part of Poland ruled by Russia, exile to Siberia.

These developments brought about the establishment of the importance in social life of the family and the special role of women within the family. The family became the real and only fortress for preserving the national identity, the culture, and the Polish traditions. At the same time the family was the only institution left that was not infiltrated by an alien political establishment. As a matter of fact, many families of the Polish nobility never allowed any member of the mandatory political authorities to enter their homes.

In a short time the women became the only group that, after the death or the long years of imprisonment of their husbands, was able to carry on the responsibilities connected with the running of their estates and that could make the decisions concerning the future of their children. It was not uncommon for women to resume underground activities against the invaders. All these situations resulted in increasing the prestige of women and creating high standards and expectations with regard to their competence. On the other hand, women became more and more conscious of their responsibilities toward society. They secretly helped to preserve the national consciousness and identity by teaching farmers' children Polish history, including patriotic pieces of Polish literature. They built up their own authority among farmers by means of providing them with medical help in cases of emergency. The situation continued during the Second World War. Women became nearly equally involved in both military battles and conspiracies against the Nazis.

One could have expected that with the high prestige and positions that women held within their families and some small groups, they would in difficult times also be able to secure high positions in professional and political life. However, this did not turn out to be the case.

After 1945 women were free to pursue their political activities, yet they were accepted only in a very limited scope in the state's power structure. The situation stemmed from the fact that the typical Polish family was a patriarchy that had its foundation in a strong agricultural tradition. The head of family was the father, who represented power and constraints. He provided the members of his family with protection against outside dangers. He always represented the family outside the home. The high prestige of women was limited to the family as well as to informal social circles; this, however, did not extend beyond the family circle.

Additional support for the traditional stereotypical divisions between male and female roles during the life span was provided by the Roman Catholic Church, which was a strictly patriarchal institution.

Because farmer families, as a group, comprised the majority of all Polish families, the pattern of the patriarchal family was obviously dominant. Also, within workers' families there existed very strong separation between man's and woman's domains. Male activities belonged to the sphere outside the home, while females' prerogative was concern for the household. Relatively, the intelligentsia families made the strongest efforts for emancipation and attempts to preserve equality, but these families represented only 6 percent of the Polish population.

Therefore the prevailing tradition was deeply rooted in the majority of Polish families. This meant that the dominance of women was in the domain of the internal affairs of the family and household duties, while the role of men as head of family was as representative to the rest of the world. Only during the last two generations was there a change in the social context, since the patriarchal tradition was no longer dominant to the same degree.

The state's policy with respect to the context of the relevant female role also changed throughout the period after World War II (Sokolowska, 1976). Between 1947 and 1954 the dominant trend was directed toward the extremely high professional involvement by women. Women were very much encouraged to enter all professions, even those that were traditionally considered to be male domains (e.g., truck drivers, bricklayers, tractor drivers, metallurgists). A great deal of effort was given to building nurseries and kindergartens. Between 1955 and 1957 the main emphasis was placed on the role women were assigned within the family. Their professional role was diminished. Maternity benefits became somewhat higher, in order to motivate women to stay at home and to take care of their children until they were able to enter kindergarten or school. Since 1958 attempts were made to build a policy that would balance both professional and family involvement by women. Professional activities of women became a matter of necessity, because of the financial situation of many families. To enable women to take care of their children and to earn an additional income, programs of cottage work for women were widely introduced.

In the beginning of the 1980s new regulations were issued. Women were allowed to stay at home until their children would be admitted to kindergarten. For three months after the birth of a child, women were allowed to stay at home with full pay; after that period until the child was four years old, women could stay home on unpaid maternal leave, with fully guaranteed return to her earlier job. However, after two years the existing regulations did not operate anymore. Because of a reduction of jobs, women were afraid to lose their previous employment while they were on maternity leave. Increasingly, the more difficult financial situations experienced by many families prompted women not to take advantage of the maternity benefits. From 1988 on, increasingly fewer women stayed at home after childbirth for more than 3 months.

COMPARISONS BETWEEN MEN'S AND WOMEN'S GENDER ROLES DURING THE LIFE CYCLE

Infancy and Early Childhood

Certain expectations as to the gender of a child are built during pregnancy. The child's sex is inferred from the level of activity of a fetus (the more active fetus must be a boy) and from the looks of the mother. If the mother's face changes and becomes swollen, or if she looks drawn, it "clearly" points to the fact that her baby will be a girl. Popular reasoning stresses the fact that a baby girl takes away all beauty from her mother. On the other hand, if a woman looks unchanged, "without any doubts" she is carrying a boy. Sometimes expectations as to the gender of the fetus are built on the basis of biological rhythms. If the fetus keeps quiet during the day and becomes active during the night, which may reflect the mother's rhythm, the fetus is expected to be a girl.

After birth it is anticipated that an infant boy is more difficult. More often there is crying at night, as well as more frequent suffering from colic and bellyaches. Some expectations continue into later periods in a boy's life. It is anticipated that they are slower in toilet training than girls and somewhat retarded in their speech.

Real sex-role typing begins at birth. Distinctions are made in clothing, toys, and even colors. Colors are especially important during the festive baptism ceremonies, which are performed in church. As the children grow older, pressures for sex-stereotyped roles escalate. Boys are encouraged to be active, brave, and resistant to pain. Behaviors like crying for help and tears are punished by peers and by parents. The usual way of punishing small boys is to tell them that they behave like a woman or like a crybaby. Girls are considered fragile and are taught to be polite, quiet, and helpful to others. If they display some physical, aggressive behavior toward people or objects, they are rebuked, such as, "You behave like a bully."

Concerning preferences for a child's gender, there is a clear pattern. The first child should be a boy in order to inherit and carry on the family name, but the second should be a girl. Parents expect and reinforce children to get involved in gender-appropriate behavior. Boys are expected to help their fathers and to be interested in technical matters and mechanical activities (such as working with the father on maintaining the family car or repairing electrical appliances for the home). Girls are brought up to help their mothers take care of their younger siblings and to help with household chores.

Even though sex-stereotypical practices in child rearing are observed, parents claim—almost unanimously—that they treat their sons and daughters absolutely in the same way, probably because they feel that they share their love and punishments equally and in a just way among all their children. But parents remain largely ignorant of the fact that they have different rules and expectations for their daughters than for their sons. A very interesting pattern occurs during the first period in children's lives; boys, as well as girls, are cared for by women; they have contact with their mother, the nurse, the schoolteacher, and a female pediatrician. Increasing numbers of children are deprived of contact with their male role models. Also, fathers are less accessible because they are working more and often put in extra hours, leaving very little time to spend at home. In many families the father is totally absent because of the parents' divorce. As a side effect of such a situation, one could point to the fact that boys are left to their own devices, where the pattern of the male role is concerned. They might often adopt a movie hero (frequently a violent one) as the only readily available pattern of a "real man." Psychological investigations show that the search for the father figure becomes one of the strongest motivations for boys and young men to affiliate with Poland's new religious groups.

School Years

Compulsory education starts in Poland at the age of six years and lasts until the child has completed the eighth grade (until she or he is 15 years old).

All primary schools are coeducational. While public schools are free of charge, private schools, which opened only about two years ago, are expensive. There is no difference in attendance between boys' and girls in private or public schools. Very clear differences between boys' and girls' educational careers start at the level of the secondary schools. First of all, boys are more often placed in schools that offer a complete professional education and provide those skills that allow them to start employment immediately after finishing school. Girls, on the other hand, are more often placed in secondary schools that do not offer any definite educational goals, just a liberal arts orientation. Such a decision is backed by a point of view that could be summarized as follows: "Girls do not need any special education since they will get married and their husband will provide for them and their children." Another fact is that boys in general—compared with girls—more often have clear interests and educational preferences. There are some interesting differences in the reasons girls and boys consult school psychologists. A typical reason for boys' seeing a psychologist at the end of the primary school years is difficulties in learning or some forms of misbehavior, while a typical reason for girls is to get some suggestions with regard to the direction of their future education. Girls' interests seem to be less clear and definite. Many secondary schools of a general type, or high schools (lyceum), have parallel classes with specialized programs (such as languages, mathematics, chemistry, physics, biology). A general practice is that girls are placed in linguistic or biologically oriented programs, while boys are steered into programs concentrating on mathematics, chemistry, or physics.

At present it looks slightly different in the rural areas. Secondary education for girls plays a role as part of the dowry. Especially in families where the oldest son eventually takes over a farm, the sisters are allowed to learn a profession in a vocational school (to become dressmakers, hairdressers, and so on). In case of the death or illness of the mother, the daughter takes over, almost automatically, her duties and burdens and thereby loses immediately all chances for the continuation of her education beyond the compulsory minimum (Tryfan, 1987).

A university education is not equally available to both sexes. Again there are marked differences between the number of prospective students in rural and urban areas. In rural areas three times as many young men as young women continue their studies. In the cities more young women than young men choose higher education. During the academic year 1989–1990 a total of 194,000 women and 184,000 men began their academic careers at the university. However, only 23,000 women and 25,000 men completed their M.A. thesis (the formal requirement for completion of the academic education) (*Rocznik Statystyczny*, 1991). Women, more often than the men, leave their educational careers, because of their marriage and the birth of their child. The only situation when a young woman could continue her studies in spite of the birth of her child would be when her parents would be willing to take care of the child; in this case she would be free to resume her academic studies.

Unfavorable situations for women to complete their academic education are apparent in all types of educational institutions (*Rocznik Statystyczny*, 1991). Yet it is possible to specify typical male and female study orientations. Women are in the majority in the universities, the pedagogical colleges, and the medical academies. Men, on the other hand, primarily select the polytechnic institutes and the agricultural academies.

Young Adulthood

Adolescent boys enjoy greater freedom in social life than adolescent girls. Parents accept readily their rich social life, coming home late at night, dating girls, spending holidays without any immediate parental control. However, it is different for girls, who are raised more strictly, mostly because of a fear of abuse and pregnancy. Because of the stricter upbringing of girls, they more often pursue their education in the city, especially when their families are living there. Only if there is no alternative for a girl's chosen field of education is she permitted to move to another city, where she stays in a students' hostel or rents a furnished room.

After completing their education, there is no such thing as equal opportunities for professional careers for men and women. Employers prefer men as prospective employees since women are perceived as being less involved with their professional work and having a high rate of absenteeism because of their home duties and caring for their children.

Adulthood

The average age for marriage in Poland is 22 years. In cities it is 24 years, and in the rural areas it is 20 years. In very few cases is the choice of a future spouse left mainly to the involved individuals. Mostly in rural areas, parents might intervene in their children's choices because of financial reasons, for instance, if the prospective spouse is too poor or does not have any property, cattle, or dowry. Generally it is considered a rise in social status for a young woman when she marries a foreigner and emigrates with him to a Western country. For a farmer's daughter it is considered a social step up when she marries a man from the city and then moves with him to the city (Wawrzyniak,

1980). Very few young urban couples start their new life in their own apartment or their own house. The majority of newlyweds share an apartment with the parents or rent a room elsewhere. Statistically 25 percent of couples live with parents for the rest of the parents' lives (GUS, 1985). In the rural districts, young couples live with their parents until they build their own house. Difficulties due to the housing situation are considered one of the chief reasons for getting a divorce.

In the majority of families there is a pretty clear division between male and female duties within households. Typically, men are responsible for the financial support of their families, while women are in charge of running the households. This is so even in situations when women have jobs outside their homes. While a woman works full-time outside her home, it does not diminish her duties in her household. Very few couples share duties, but sharing household responsibilities has become more popular in the cities than in the villages.

As far as typical employment for women is concerned, women work mainly in educational institutions, in health care centers, in banks and insurance companies, and in stores. Despite the fact that women constitute a majority of the work force in these settings, they nearly never occupy managerial positions. Typically, male workplaces include heavy industries, building and construction work, forestry, administration, and transportation.

There are a growing number of women—in comparison to men—who have lost their jobs within the last two years (*Rocznik Statystyczny*, 1991). Working at a job leaves very little time and energy for hobbies and different kinds of relaxation. Therefore the most typical pastime—for men and women alike—is a passive way to relax, such as watching television. Many women feel sorry for wasting their time watching television, and therefore they combine television viewing with knitting. Participation in sports represents only a small portion of time spent by the adult population. Very few people go regularly swimming, jogging, or skiing. Little interest in physical fitness, combined with a low intake of vitamins and a high protein diet, in addition to a high level of stress, results in a steadily increasing rate of different cardiovascular diseases, including fatal infarcts (*Rocznik Demograficzny*, 1989).

Very little free time remains after a baby is born. The care of the baby is entirely a woman's responsibility. There exists a high rate of mortality among children. For 1,000 newly born infants, 16 die before the end of their first year of life. The most frequent cause of death is prenatal diseases or conditions and different kinds of developmental handicaps.

The typical farm family has three children. Thirteen percent of these rural families have more than four children. In the city the typical family has only one child, and only 4 percent have more than four children (*Rocznik Demograficzny*, 1989). Nearly every third marriage is contracted because of an existing pregnancy. Situations such as these provide indirect information about the consequential aspects of Polish religiosity. Ninety-eight percent of the Polish population declare their religious affiliation with the Roman Catholic Church. At the same time the teachings of the Church concerning sexual behavior ("no sex outside marriage") seem to be not widely followed. Pregnancy outside wedlock is considered more repugnant in urban than in rural settings. In many cases farmers consider pregnancy as a natural consequence of dating and as a sui generis proof of a woman's fertility. It is interesting to note that in the case of infertility, women are far more stigmatized than men. Women try to find out reasons for their own infertility; however, men, as a rule, plainly refuse any medical intervention with their problem. Contraceptive devices are little known and are rather rarely used by the population. They are almost never used before marriage or before the birth of the first child. This leads to the not uncommon pregnancies of 15- and 16-year-old girls. The results of an opinion poll reveals (Demoskop, 1992) that 45 percent of the adult population never used any contraceptive devices and that 3.8 percent of the women use intravaginal chemical contraceptives and 3.9 percent use pills. In rural areas 70 percent of the women never use any kind of contraceptives. Nearly the same number do not use contraceptives because they do not know anything about these methods and because they respect the Church's prohibitions (each group constitutes nearly 20 percent of the population). However, 66 percent of the population do not accept the Church's point of view concerning the prohibition of the use of all contraceptive means. Only 6 percent hold the opinion that all kinds of contraceptives should be totally abolished in Poland.

In general the source of information about contraceptives are peer groups and television programs. The topic, however, remains taboo at home and in schools. Teachers generally declare that they feel unprepared for discussing the topic with their students. There are also no books available for introducing sexual education. Parents represent only a limited source of education with respect to sexual behavior. They feel embarrassed to talk about these issues with their children and expect the schools to be the legitimate source for such information for the children.

Another problem is the high rate of divorce. The most frequent reasons for divorce are alcoholism of one spouse and infidelity. Unsatisfactory housing conditions hold the third highest rank.

Every fifth marriage ends in divorce, but divorced people do not necessarily live a solitary existence. A high percentage of men and women remarry within a short time. Very strong barriers against divorce are part of the doctrine of the Roman Catholic Church. Once a church wedding is contracted, there is practically no chance for invalidation of the marriage, that is, for the Church to approve divorce. Divorced people remain stigmatized to the end of their lives. They are not only unable to have another church wedding but excluded from taking Holy Communion, and they are not allowed to be godparents or have priests officiate at their burial. Even their children might be subjected to negative remarks by the priest who gives religious instruction in school. Social stigmatization of once married and later divorced people represents a real problem in the villages. Life in the cities becomes more anonymous, and very few people could trace the marital records of their neighbors. In case of a divorce, 95 percent of the children remain with the mother. However, the father is obliged to pay alimony. In fact, alimonies constitute very small amounts of money for the mother and child or children because of the high inflation rate in Poland. The prescribed sum of money loses a lot of its value after just one year because of the economy.

Old Age

The social image of an old person varies in the city and the village. In rural areas it is more negative. Old people are perceived as less worthwhile because they are not able to carry on with their duties on the farm. In the city the social image of an old person greatly depends on her or his personal characteristics. The elderly are perceived in a more personal way (Susulowska, 1989). The period of life identified as retirement from the job represents very different patterns for men and for women. From the very beginning, women's plans concerning old age concentrate on chances to offer their help to their children and the family. Men's plans are more selfish and concentrate around personal fulfillment (pursuing different hobbies such as fishing, reading, or gardening). A really busy period of satisfactory and rewarding retirement is far more often reached by women than by men. After retirement women get less stressed. They do not have to try to balance both family and job activities. They have more relaxed and tolerant attitudes toward people. As a result they have good inter-actions, as well as the role of confidant for grandchildren. At this time grand-mothers often create better relationships with their grandchildren than they did years before with their own children.

On the other hand, men feel lessened tolerance toward surroundings by men, which stems in part from their own perception of having a lower social status because of the loss of high status and the importance ascribed to their professional role. Women are also willing to accept certain concessions by the family in order to provide better care for the retired mother; men, to the contrary, feel ashamed or hurt when some duties are taken away from them. This involves some deeply rooted guilt feelings because they concentrated all their life around their jobs and related activities, and after retirement they feel that they are not really entitled to take advantage of the family's care. These perceptions might explain why women live longer and why their evaluation of the retirement years is higher than that of men. On the average women have a life expectancy of 76 years, and men have 67 years (*Rocznik Demograficzny*, 1989). Immediately after their retirement women assume the duty of baby-sitter for their grandchildren. In many families the grandmother is willing to help take care of the grandchildren. This is the only option that makes it possible for the wife to continue her work after childbirth. Not only is hiring a baby-sitter very expensive, but in many cases she turns out to be not particularly reliable. Taking over the role of looking after the quality of life and the well-being of the entire family, women could remain in a role of authority. Their competence in household duties and the care of the grandchildren is highly regarded. Men, after losing employment, feel very quickly that their knowledge is obsolete, and thereby they lose their self-respect for the rest of their life. This situation certainly results in a relatively lowered self-image for a man compared with that of a woman. Life for many men after leaving employment is often very empty. They try to keep busy with different chores and hobbies such as repairing the car, gardening, or taking care of the pets, but in the majority of cases they suffer from having too much time on their hands. This might explain why there is a particularly high mortality rate among coal miners and metallurgists during their first year of retirement. Their high occupational prestige and competence are unavoidably lost. Life for them is empty.

Because 90 percent of retired people have their own pensions, they are most often independent of their children in financial terms. In fact, 25 percent give financial help to their own children. To give financial help remains a male domain, while household help continues to be a female domain (GUS, 1985). In general, the cultural pattern for both the rural and the urban environments requires children to take care of their elderly parents. In some cases children are not able to fulfill this obligation. In such a situation the elderly person could apply for a paid nurse from the Polish Red Cross. Nurses come for a few hours a day and basically look after all the needs of the elderly person, such as shopping, cooking, and cleaning the home. According to the current regulations every elderly person who is 75 and lives alone can get this kind of help free of charge or for only minimal payment. Sixty-three percent of the population of elderly citizens who are 75 years and over need regular visits to outpatient clinics and hospitals, but only 10 percent require permanent help in all their everyday activities (Pedich, et al., 1979).

In some cases of very poor health and the lack of any possibilities to get adequate care, old people have to settle in old people's homes, senior citizens' residences, or nursing homes. Around 10,000 elderly persons who are above 65 years live in these residences. It is, however, considered the worst option for the last years of life, mainly because of the bad living conditions. Rooms are shared with many individuals, and real privacy is missing. In addition, rather poor care is delivered, and everyday life is boring. Many conflicts between roommates arise because people who have to live together in one room come from very different backgrounds. People from the city generally consider roommates from the farm of lower social status and less culture (Susulowska, 1989).

The most typical leisure activities for pensioners are listening to the radio, watching television, reading books, household activities, visits with friends and relatives, reading newspapers, and taking walks. A difference in leisure activities for women and men is seen in their hobbies. Women do not have hobbies as such. Their lives are full and busy. By devoting time to hobby activities, men try to find a balance in their somewhat disrupted life-styles (Susulowska, 1989). Generally a stronger social involvement by women can be observed by comparing percentages of male (23 percent) and female (77 percent) participants in universities' continuing education programs (a kind of open university for elderly citizens within the organizational scheme of academic institutions). For a general comparison between the life-styles of men and women, it is possible to state that men prize most highly the self-fulfillment connected with economic success and assurance against becoming helpless and decrepit. Women value most their emotional fulfillment, freedom of choice between their family and their occupational roles, a good marriage, and the successful upbringing of their children (Sawicka, 1975).

SUMMARY AND CONCLUSIONS

Economic and political changes that have taken place in Poland during last few years have a very strong influence on the content of gender roles. First of all, men are confronted with the necessity of taking jobs that were previously considered typical female occupations, such as store personnel, caregivers for the children, and caretakers of the home, so that the women can still keep their job when the men become unemployed. Second, men face relatively strong pressure from women to treat them as partners in different kinds of enterprises. A female boss is no longer an unthinkable or unbelievable phenomenon. There is also growing feministic consciousness among women. Six female organizations in Poland are fighting against political and professional inequalities for women. As a catalyst they have acted on the antiabortion law that was discussed in the Polish Parliament in 1991. Another very hot issue is dating, since women are determined to keep their freedom in their own hands.

REFERENCES

Demoskop (Institute for Public Opinion Research). (1992). Co wiemy o antykoncepcji (What do we know about contraceptives?). *Gazeta Wyborcza* 18–19 stycznia.

GUS (General Statistic Bureau). (1985). *Sytuacja bytowa ludzi star w Polsce* (Life situation of old people in Poland). Seria, Materialy statystyczne.

Kozinska, D. (1986). Problemy mieszkaniowe (Housing problems). In *Encyklopedia Seniora*. Warsaw: Wiedza Powszechna.

Pedich, A., et al. (1979). *Pielegniarstwo geriatryczne* (Geriatric Nursing). Warsaw: State Medical Publisher.

Rocznik Demograficzny (Demographic Yearbook). (1989). Warsaw: General Statistic Bureau.

Rocznik Statystyczny (Statistical Yearbook). (1991). Warsaw: General Statistic Bureau.

Sawicka, H. (1975). Psychologiczne aspekty bilansu zyciowego ludzi starych (Psychological aspects of the life-styles of elderly). *Zeszyty Naukowe UJ. Prace Psych.Ped.* (Scientific issues of the Jagiellonian University), *23*.

Sokolowska, M. (1976). Obraz kobiety w swiadomosci wspolczesnego spoleczenstwa (Image of women in the contemporary society). In *Podsumowanie dorobku nauki polskiej w zakresie studiow nad problemami kobiet, rodziny i macierzynstwa* (Output of the Polish research on problems of women, family and maternity). Warsaw: Polish Academy of Sciences.

Susulowska, M. (1989). *Psychologia starzenia sie i starosci* (Psychology of getting old and old age). Warsaw: State Scientific Publisher.

Tryfan, B. (1987). *Kwestia Kobieca na wsi* (Feminine question in the countryside). Warsaw: State Scientific Publisher.

Wawrzyniak, B. (1980). *Kobieta wiejska* (Countryside woman). Warsaw: LSW (Peasants Cooperative Publishing House).

21

Portugal

Maria das Mercês Cabrita de Mendonça Covas

INTRODUCTION

Continental Portugal[1] is situated on the western side of the Iberian Peninsula. To the west and south it is bordered by the Atlantic Ocean, and to the north and east it is bordered by its only neighbor, Spain. This territory, with its capital in Lisbon, is divided into eighteen districts, has a population of approximately 10 million inhabitants, occupies 88,944 square kilometers (34,341.3 square miles), and has an average population density of 110.1 inhabitants per square kilometer (285.2 inhabitants per square mile). Oporto, Braga, Coimbra, Setubal, and Faro are its principal cities and, like Lisbon, are located in coastal districts (which are the most highly industrialized areas). The northern and central regions of the country are mountainous, and their population is scattered throughout the region on *minifundia* (small plots of land). Farming is done by the family in the traditional manner. The south, particularly the Alentejo, is a region of plains. Here, where *latifundia* (large plots of land) predominate, the population is concentrated in the few cities and many villages throughout the region. As in the north, traditional agricultural processes prevail. The extreme south, the Algarve, has characteristics that are relatively different. The region is less flat than the Alentejo, and it is characterized by a disperse population and by the predominance of small- and medium-sized properties in which modern agricultural techniques are practiced; this region has also developed the tourism sector.

The population of Continental Portugal is distributed rather heterogeneously, concentrated strongly along the coast (Lisbon, Oporto, Braga, Aveiro, and Setubal), where the largest number of industries has been built. This regional demographic imbalance has become progressively severe in the last decades, such that district population densities range from 17.0 inhabitants per square kilometer (44 inhabitants per square mile) in Beja to 771.4 inhabitants per square kilometer (1,997.9 inhabitants per square mile) in Lisbon. The interior districts have not become industrialized but have instead maintained traditional patterns of agriculture. These factors, among others, have contributed to the mass exodus from rural areas of working-age residents and the progressive aging of the rural resident populations.

In the 1960s and early 1970s, when Europe was in a stage of industrial expansion, Portugal did not industrialize, turning instead to its then-colonies (Angola, Guinea-Bissau, and Mozambique) that between 1961 and 1974 were fighting for their independence until the last days of the totalitarian regime, which ended as a result of the revolutionary movement, 25 April 1974. During this fifteen-year period, the country "developed" unharmoniously: first, Portugal opened its doors to emigration; second, large numbers of people moved from the interior regions to coastal areas. Throughout the 1960s the average number of emigrants reached its highest level in the history of the country, 68,000 residents per year, of whom 41.6 percent were female. By 1975, this number had fallen to 50,000. Between 1976 and 1980 the average volume of emigrants fell to 18,000 and continued to fall during the five-year period of 1981–1985, during which time fewer than 10,000 emigrants per year for both sexes left the country. Presently these numbers continue to fall.

The Portuguese population decreased by 2.5 percent between 1960 and 1970, which represents a net loss of 220,000 individuals. During the 1960s only five districts in Continental Portugal showed a population increase: Braga, Aveiro, Lisbon, Oporto, and Setubal. The growth of the Braga district was due, above all, to its high birthrate, whereas the other districts' increase in population was due to internal migrations. During the 1970s and until 1987, these districts evidenced an opposite trend. The population of the country's interior regions (Beja, Castelo Branco, Guarda, Portalegre, and Vila Real) increased as national citizens returned from the former Portuguese colonies (Instituto Nacional de Estatística [INE], Employment Survey, 1989). Between 1970 and 1981 these districts showed a net population increase of 23.5 percent, and between 1981 and 1985, 3.6 percent. While the former rate represents the influx of *retornados* (Portuguese citizens returning from the former colonies), the latter refers to the lower rate of emigration and the return of emigrants from Western Europe.

Even so, the natural growth rate has strongly decreased—from 13.3 percent in 1960 to 2.4 percent in 1988—while the rate of effective growth slipped from 0.4 percent in 1987 to 0.3 percent in 1989. The decrease in the natural growth rate is one of the most significant demographic changes registered in the last three decades. As of the mid-1980s, Portugal is no longer one of Europe's highest natural growth-rate countries; rather, it has come to approximate the most highly developed countries in this demographic indicator.

The birthrate also decreased, principally in the 1980s. The gross birthrate decreased from 24 percent in 1960 to 11.2 percent by 1990. The decrease in the gross birthrate seems to be associated with significant changes in the behavior and the fertility calendar of the Portuguese woman. From the beginning of the 1980s there has been a greater concentration in the number of first- and second-order births, which by 1989 was equivalent to 81.7 percent of the total number of births, while those of the third order (and greater) represented 18.3 percent. The global fecundity rate, which was 85.9 percent in 1960, decreased to 45.7 percent by 1989. This decrease in the intensity of fecundity was reflected strongly in the average number of children per woman. This average halved from three children per woman in 1960 to 1.5 by 1989.

The number of births registered to married women decreased significantly, with the highest values continuing in the northern districts (especially in Braga). On the other hand, the number of births registered to unmarried women increased in general, while maintaining its historical trend of the highest values being in the south.

In relation to the number of weddings, two opposing trends have been seen in the last thirty years. Between 1970 and 1974, there was a slight and continual increase in the number of weddings. In 1975 (one year after the revolution) the highest number of weddings ever was recorded, and this level remained fairly constant until 1977. Between 1977 and 1985 there was a decrease, while beginning in 1986 the number of weddings varied very little, showing a slight increase until 1990. The passing of the Divorce Law of 1975 (for Catholic marriages; for non-Catholic marriages there was already a law in effect) meant that between 1975 and 1977 weddings were concretized between couples who previously were impeded from marrying due to the former law's prohibiting divorce; thus, situations were formalized that previously did not legally exist. After this period, the global volume of weddings reassumed its normal rhythm, showing small annual variations.

Portugal is traditionally Catholic. Still, one of the most significant sociological characteristics regarding weddings is the increase in the number of non-Catholic weddings, principally in the southern districts (especially Setubal and Faro), where its value passes 50 percent. In the northern districts, the majority of weddings are Catholic.

The number of divorces has increased. The gross divorce rate rose from 0.06 percent in 1970 to 0.88 percent by 1989 and then fell slightly to 0.80 in 1990. The districts of Lisbon, Oporto, and Faro registered the highest gross divorce rates, between 1.6 percent and 1.1 percent.

The mortality and morbidity rates were significant in the 1980s. The gross mortality rate decreased from 10.6 percent in 1960 to 9.3 percent by 1989 and then increased to 11 percent in 1990. The most important change was in the significant reduction of the percentage of deaths in the age groups of under 1 year and 1–4 years and, simultaneously, a greater concentration in the number of deaths of those aged fifty and over. The deaths of those in the over-50 age groups represented 65.4 percent of the total number of deaths in 1960 and 87.6 percent in 1985. The infant mortality rate decreased from 56.9 percent in 1970 to 10 percent by 1990.

Beginning in April 1974, Portugal began to have a democratic regime with a system of semi-presidential government.[2] Portugal made commitments to international organizations of which it was a member to develop specific programs regarding equality between the sexes. Among these programs are Strategies for the Progress of Women by the Year 2000, a United Nations program; and Equal Opportunities for Women, initiated by the European Economic Community (EEC), 1986–1990. In addition, Portugal ratified an agreement in 1980 regarding the elimination of all forms of discrimination against women.

In 1986 Portugal joined the EEC, opening new horizons and new challenges to Portuguese citizens. In economic terms, this has implied a tremendous effort to raise Portugal to the level of the other EEC countries, and EEC aid has been made available to assist Portugal in this endeavor through FEDER,[3] FEOGA,[4] and FSE[5] programs. These programs will aid in developing the country in general and, more specifically, the regions that are the most depressed economically due to a lack of compensatory economic activities for the local populations.

OVERVIEW

In theory, one can say that Portugal has "enlightened" legislation in the area of equality. A few articles of the constitution mention equality: equality is considered in a general sense (Article 13); in the family (Articles 36 and 67); in public office (Article 49); in the workplace (access, employment security, choice of profession or type of work and professional development, Article 59); in education and teaching (Article 74), and so forth. Additional legislation has also been passed in the form of Executive Law 392/79, which prohibits discrimination on the basis of sex, access to employment, professional development, career advancement, and equal pay for equal work.

In spite of this theoretical, judicial "equality," opportunities continue to be unequal. To date there is still no tie between the theoretical (or abstract) woman and actual women. This difficulty results, fundamentally, in the group of stereotypical values and ideas carried by the family, the school, the media, and society in general regarding the roles for women and men in Portuguese society. The sexual division of family roles is still the traditional one, which perpetuates obstacles for women and impedes true equality. Portuguese men and women are still indoctrinated and conditioned by sexist values, inherent in the society they inherited, where political, institutional, economic, and judicial power continues to be almost exclusively in the hands of men.

In Portugal one of the greatest inequalities between men and women lies in access to power. Women's access to power, especially economic power, has only recently come to be debated as one of women's rights.

At both the individual and family levels, economic power is defined by the origin of disposable income and by the ability to decide its allocation. The few studies that exist that examine intrafamily divisions of economic power, along with our own empirical observation of reality, suggest that the situation is somewhat heterogeneous. This varies principally as a function of the sphere of economic activities to which women have access. The woman's discretionary income, then, is relative to the position she occupies in the workplace, her socioprofessional category, her age, and her geographical location (urban/rural). Younger families tend to be more egalitarian in the division of economic power, but women of the highest social strata are economically more independent. In families that own small farms the division of economic power is very traditional. To women falls the responsibility of handling those activities that provide the smallest amount of income and will not require her leaving the farm (selling animals, eggs, fruits, and vegetables). The men, on the other hand, are responsible for the more profitable activities (selling cattle, real estate, and agricultural tools and machinery), although they may consult with their wife before completing these transactions.

Due to the emigration of Portuguese males during the 1960s and 1970s, rural women assumed the management of the family farms; this constituted, apparently, a factor in promoting women's access to economic power. There are still no qualitative studies examining how women have adapted to the new situations and the relative impact regarding the management of family resources and the family agricultural enterprise.

In the entrepreneurial domain, there are few cases of women organizing firms, and when they do, they are generally oriented to the continuance of domestic activities (restaurants, hotels, clothing stores, handicrafts, and other personal services). In agricultural and commercial activities, however, there have been a few women who have demonstrated a great deal of entrepreneurial initiative.

Regarding the management of large enterprises, be they public or private, the presence of women is nearly nonexistent. Economic power is still in the hands of those who manage great amounts of money (the wealthy are generally powerful because of their wealth). There exists less discrimination in the division of the wealth than in its management. Many women who have property and capital do not manage them directly, generally transferring that responsibility to the man of the family (husband, son, brother, or other family member).

Women's penetration into the affairs of the local community has been very slow. In this case, this is not due only to weak participation by women in the economic, political, and party power bases but also to the fact that it is through these areas that one has access to city management. Presently no woman heads a political party represented in the National Assembly, although there are some women (in variable percentages) in the National Secretariats or committees of those parties. In the local elections of 1989, 300 men and 5 women were elected to the 305 mayorships. In other cities, women preside due to the substitution of the elected official.

In the area of class organization, where one distinguishes syndical associations and company organizations (of entrepreneurs or economic activities), the presence of women is incomparably less prevalent than that of men. Further, even in instances where women hold directorships, their presence in the public meetings of the partnerships of these organizations is rare. Their speakers are men, who generally preside at the conference tables and fraternize at dinners and other such occasions.

The percentages of women members who act as directors of the labor union affiliates of the two central labor unions are 17 percent in the CGTP-IN (General Confederation of Portuguese Workers-Intersyndical) and 24 percent in the UGT (General Union of Workers). The percentages of women in relation to the total labor union membership are 30 percent in the CGTP-IN and 46 percent in the UGT.

In government-owned institutions, women are equally underrepresented. This fact is due, in part, to the reduced number of women involved in party politics and government. The current constitutional government has 61 offices, of which 4 are occupied by women.

During the 1991 elections for the National Parliament, nineteen women were elected in a total of 230 parliamentarians. A woman was elected vice president of this body. In the government Cabinet, there are still no women. In the June 1989 elections for the European Parliament, three of the twenty-four parliamentarians were women. Two were integrated into the Women's Rights Commission. Women have been almost totally absent in the areas of judicial and magisterial power. Only recently has the first woman judge been appointed, and there is only one woman in the Constitutional Tribunal, the highest court for constitutional questions.

In 1990 the level of schooling of the Portuguese population of those aged 15 and older presented some differences according to sex, as presented in Table 21.1. The percentage of people (both men and women) who have completed college, or even high school, remains very small.

In the work area the differences between men and women are significant, as evidenced by the Employment Survey conducted by the National Statistics Institute (INE, 1989). In the last quarter of 1990, the percentage of women employed was 42.6 percent versus 57.7 percent of men (INE, Employment Survey, 1989), and women represented 43.2 percent of the work force. Unemployment, however, affects women principally: for the same period, 67.3 percent of the unemployed were women. The rate of unemployment for women was 8.1 percent, while for men it was 3.2 percent. Of the total unemployed women, 38.8 percent were below the age of 25. Table 21.2 shows the distribution of female workers in the various employment sectors.

Women represent 23.0 percent of the self-employed who have employees working for them and 48.0 percent of the self-employed who have no employees working for them. They represent 41.9 percent of the workers who work for others and 53.3 percent of family workers receiving no remuneration. These unremunerated family workers represented 6.2 percent of the total number of workers and are concentrated in the areas of agriculture, commerce, restaurants, and hotels.

Working women who have completed secondary education or higher accounted

Table 21.1
Education Level of Portuguese Men and Women Aged 15 and Older in 1990

Highest School Level Attained	Men	Women	Total
Illiterate	8.7	17.0	13.1
Literate (but no formal education)	0.7	0.8	0.8
Obligatory Education (through 9th grade)	79.3	71.0	74.9
High School	6.7	5.9	6.3
Junior College (3-year program)	0.9	2.7	1.8
College (5-year program)	3.5	2.4	2.9
Other	0.2	0.2	0.2
Total	100.0	100.0	100.0

Source: INE, Education Statistics (1990), Lisbon.

for 14.8 percent of the total in 1989, while illiterate women continued to work fundamentally in agriculture and domestic service. Regarding the type of work contract women are given, 80.6 percent of those working for others had a permanent contract or a contract of "indeterminate length," while 19.4 percent were working under a short-term contract. For male workers these figures were 84.4 percent and 15.6 percent, respectively. In 1989 the average monthly salary received by women was 76.7 percent of that received by men generally, except in the area of public administration, agriculture, and domestic services, when these were carried out outside the sphere of the companies, in which cases the compensation is equal (INE, Employment Survey, 1989).

COMPARISONS BETWEEN MEN'S AND WOMEN'S GENDER ROLES DURING THE LIFE CYCLE

Infancy and Early Childhood

In Portugal there are few, if any, scientific studies regarding the preference of parents toward having sons or daughters, but a preference exists. The most evident cases arise in farming or entrepreneurial families, whose management generally passes from father to son. Normally these families have a greater

Table 21.2
Women as Percentage of All Workers Within Employment Sectors

Employment Sector	1988/89	1990
Agriculture	52.4	53.6
Textile Industry	66.4	67.6
Health Services	70.4	69.9
Other Services (including Domestic Services)	55.4	58.0
Scientific and "Liberal Professionals"	54.5	54.2
Directorships and Higher Administrative Positions	16.8	20.5
Administrative Personnel	50.0	52.9
Commercial Personnel	43.0	43.9
Education	77.1	75.8
Pre-Primary	N/A	98.6
Elementary School (Grades 1 through 4)	N/A	92.2
Basic Preparatory School (Grades 5 and 6)	N/A	68.2
High School (Grades 7 through 12)	N/A	62.7
Colleges and Universities	N/A	33.7

Source: INE, Employment Survey (1988, 1989, 1990), Lisbon.

number of children, and at least one male child to whom to pass such responsibilities.

Large families, even ones that are principally nuclear families, are no longer the ones most valued socially. Large families are found most frequently in the wealthiest and in the poorest families, although the origin of these motives is different. Middle-class nuclear families are small (with one or two children), constituting the most common pattern for the Portuguese nuclear family in today's society.

Prior to the 1970s, families with two sons or two daughters often opted to have a third child in an effort to have children of both sexes. This may well have been one of the ways in which couples could satisfy, simultaneously, social expectations and their own expectations regarding children. These expectations may be related to the near future (the management of family resources) and/or to the security of the parents in their old age. Today this situation is less frequent.

Having two children, preferably a boy and a girl, continues to be the ideal for the majority of couples, but there is a tendency toward having a single child. Portuguese society is becoming more democratic and pluralistic in its values. The expectations of parents in relation to their children, as well as social expectations in relation to couples, have evolved qualitatively. Empirical observation of current reality, aligned with the decrease in the birthrate during the last decades, suggests that Portuguese parents tend to value the child, independent of its sex, although its sex continues to affect its socialization.

In families where the husband and wife work outside the home, the children are cared for by public or private institutions (nursery schools, day-care centers, preschools) of varying quality or by nannies or family members.

Especially in institutions outside the home, pre–school-age children, of both sexes openly play together, sharing their toys and games. However, in the family environment, the codes and sex roles become more evident. One of the most common examples is the reaction of families to unisex clothing. Despite being accepted by many parents, the majority buy, intentionally, other types of clothing, jewelry, hair ornaments, and toys that they consider more appropriate for the sex of their child.

During early childhood the sexual distinction begins to manifest itself, principally through the initiative of parents and/or family members by introducing clothing differences and colors and by orienting the preferences of children toward specific toys that they (the adults) feel are appropriate for the sex of the child. Girls continue to be given toys that teach them to be docile, pretty, and loving, while boys are given toys that give them the idea of strength, power, and competitiveness. No one would dare buy dolls, dresses, ovens, kitchen implements and dishes, or a makeup kit for a boy or dress a boy in pink. Boys are given pistols, rifles, toy soldiers, war tanks, car tracks, airplanes, and the like; they are dressed in strong colors. In addition, the power of the media and publicity directed to children, often sexist, reinforces their choices and contributes to an accentuation of these role differences based on sex. Still, there exists an enormous variety of toys, educational games, and instruments that parents, principally those of the middle class, buy either for a boy or for a girl. This attitude, in part consumerist but also educative, varies according to the economic and educational level of the families, which give to their children a socialization model consistent with their financial and intellectual capacities.

School Years

The school phase is extremely important for the young of both sexes, since it is decisive for the children's success or failure during future stages of life. Their life experience assumes various forms and results, intimately related to the level of life and well-being of their families, namely, the educational level, profession, and income of the parents.

Some differences are noted in school-age children with respect to daily chores at home. It is much more frequently the daughters who help the mothers than the sons, just as their fathers before them rarely helped their mothers. These domestic chores include ironing, making the beds, hand-washing clothing or dishes, vacuuming the floor, straightening up one's bedroom and/or the house, dusting, and making meals. However, the assignment of these duties differs according to the social strata of the family, the age of the child, whether the child is a student, and the amount of time the child spends at home.

The large majority of Portuguese families value schooling and education as the best way to grow personally and advance both professionally and socially; they believe in transmitting these values to their children.

In Portugal schooling is mandatory and free through the ninth grade, which, under normal circumstances, is when the child is 14 or 15 years old. Following this are the secondary schools and institutions of higher education, both optional. There has been a significant rise in the number of students of both sexes registered in schools, particularly beginning in the 1980s.

In order to enter an institution of higher education (the university), one must satisfactorily complete secondary-level education (twelfth grade). One's opportunity to attend and register for classes is restricted, however, by the government-determined "numerus clausus." Each year the number of students who are qualified to enter is greater than the number of places; as a result, there is a waiting list; some students must wait for one or two years or, alternatively, choose a course of study that is not their first choice.

In 1988–1989, nearly 52 percent of the students registered in secondary school were females. However, the distribution among subject areas was vastly different between males and females, as shown in Table 21.3. Table 21.3 also shows the percentage of total graduates in each program who are women.

The drop-out rate attains particularly high levels during the years of mandatory schooling, mainly in families with limited economic resources, whose parents are often illiterate. For these families education is still viewed as an obstacle, limiting the amount of help the family can obtain; the boys are expected to find paid work, while the girls are expected to do domestic chores and take care of the younger children. Families with the greatest economic difficulties demonstrate the greatest segregation of masculine and feminine roles, and they exert great pressure on their children to follow the same pattern. These factors, among others, result in their disinterest in schooling and their decision to abandon it without completing the minimum level required either to function professionally

Table 21.3
Rates of Feminine Enrollment and Completion of Higher Education (Percentage of Females in Relation to Total Number of Students) in 1988–1989

	Enrollment	Completion
Languages and Literatures	74.5	79.8
Religion and Theology	23.8	20.8
Educational Sciences / Teacher Education	75.2	80.5
Fine Arts and Applied Arts	56.1	56.9
Architecture and Urban Planning	36.5	40.5
Law	53.6	53.5
Social and Behavioral Sciences	56.8	57.3
Business Education and Management	51.8	60.0
Journalism and Social Information	58.6	20.3
Natural Sciences	62.2	65.7
Mathematics and Computer Science	54.2	69.6
Industrial Engineering	54.7	30.0
Engineering Sciences	24.4	23.2
Medicine, Health Sciences, Hygiene	64.4	61.5
Nutrition	89.8	58.8
Agriculture, Forestry, and Fishery Science	45.3	41.3
Other	43.2	35.5
Total	62.7	54.4

Source: INE, Education Statistics (1989), Lisbon.

or to continue with the studies. Dropping out aggravates their state of poverty, inherited from previous generations and proven to be evermore difficult to escape.

For the young who continue in school and complete the various levels of education, their behavior, opportunities, and horizons are very different. Between siblings, schoolmates, and/or friends, of the same sex or not, a certain competition is generated in terms of their school grades. The students hope to obtain from this effort greater approval and admiration by their family members, schoolmates, friends, and/or teachers. Frequently, young boys and girls make friends with those they feel share equally their interests and abilities, principally those of the same sex. As time progresses and they advance in school, the competition increases and at times even compromises some friendships. From this results the creation of new groups of equals in which the first priority is given to interests or common objectives, already oriented toward their future professional life.

Young Adulthood

No qualitative studies exist in Portugal regarding socialization practices and dating for men and women. This is due partially to the great diversity of possible situations. Empirical observation indicates rural/urban variation and even within each group, the opportunities are not identical throughout the country. In addition, other conditioning factors exist, such as the group of friends to which one belongs, the economic situation in which one finds oneself, the social class from which one comes and wishes to maintain or change, one's educational level, the social milieu in which one moves, the degree to which one practices a religion, one's current status as a student or employee, the degree to which one is integrated into society, whether one maintains a low profile, the degree of independence or dependence that one maintains in relation to one's parents or other family members, and so forth.

Freedom of choice, the types of opportunities in socialization practices and of encounters and social mobility tend to increase with urbanization; it is difficult to establish rules regarding the forms of their occurrence. On the other hand, urban centers, accentuating individualism, contribute to the increase of socialization opportunities for both sexes, permitting more easily one's chance to achieve personal realization, whether at the level of basic necessities or cultural necessities, aesthetics, and self-actualization. Many necessities that are considered "superior" are only rarely acquired through family or school socialization; rather, they are acquired through intensive contact with elites or with the mass media.

In rural areas, traditionally conservative, within social strata and classes very well defined, these situations are somewhat rare and easily sanctioned because the degree of integration is much greater and social control is strong. In these environments women and men have fewer opportunities and freedom of choice; they are not anonymous; there are relatively strict expectations regarding behavior based on one's sex; these rigid expectations govern conduct and impose some limits to self-actualization. Women and men are strongly conditioned by the group to which they belong. Individualist tendencies and the necessity of isolation, when manifest, are neither well understood nor well tolerated, even less so if women demonstrate these tendencies.

In rural areas dating was most frequently done between members of the same social sphere, which made social mobility difficult and perpetuated a static society. Presently, the situation seems to be changing—if only a little—as the young, whether through their studies or work, have greater geographical mobility. This factor brings them in contact with people from other localities, in some cases to marry and start a family.

In areas that are more urbanized, dating is normally between men and women who know each other by frequenting the same leisure spots, by being school or work colleagues, or by having been introduced by a friend or family member. In this way, they seek to deepen their friendship and to establish a closer and more stable relationship, if both desire it. The man takes the initiative to set up the first date. The most common meeting places are cafés, restaurants, nightclubs, movie theaters, parties, theaters, gardens, and the like. If later they decide not to develop the relationship further, both are free to choose other companions. Presently, in the most populous-urban areas the reputation of the woman is not compromised, as in the past, by her having several boyfriends or by having lost her virginity.

In rural areas, while there have been changes, dating still implies that both members of the couple are serious and intend to marry. If marriage does not occur, the woman's reputation will suffer if she does not marry either the first or second fiancé. In the more traditional areas where the woman is not economically independent, she may be accused of being a "lightskirt" and "condemned to definitive celibacy," even if she is a virgin. Still, these cases are becoming rarer.

Regarding career opportunities, there are significant differences in opportunities for women and men in practically all professional categories. Still, this situation is particularly evident for the highly demanding professions (e.g., diplomats, magistrates, university professors, and scientific and technological investigators). The professional demands of these careers are difficult to reconcile with the heavy demands placed on women, especially if they intend to marry and have children. Women have some opportunities for access to, and progression in, a career, but they are fully aware of the innumerable conditions that society imposes on them.

Adulthood

Romantic love and the building of a family in marriage have been, for the majority of Portuguese, two of the objectives to be attained in adult life. In spite of this, significant geographic differences were found in the intensity of nuptiality throughout the 1960s and 1970s. This percentage was lower for men in the southern districts (e.g., 80 percent in Beja) and for women in the northern districts (e.g., 80 percent in Viana do Castelo and 85 percent in Braga). These values compare with the Continental Portuguese averages of 92 percent for men and 87 percent for women. Between 1970 and 1981 there were fewer differences between districts, and there was, simultaneously, an overall increase in nuptiality. The average throughout Continental Portugal for men rose to 94 percent, and for women, to 92 percent, which represents a significant increase in the case of women. At the moment, the data from the last General Census of the Portuguese

Population (1991) have not been published, which prevents the calculation of the most recent indicators and the opportunity to make comparisons. Still, some alterations are predicted in the rates of nuptiality, definitive celibacy, the average age at marriage, and the appearance of new types of families.

The average age at marriage has varied somewhat during the last thirty years, showing a tendency for both sexes to marry at a younger age. For women the marrying age has gone from 24.8 years in 1960 to 22.7 years by 1984. For men, during those same years, the marrying age has gone from 26.9 years to 25.2 years, respectively.[6]

During the 1980s there was a significant increase throughout Continental Portugal in the number of unmarried couples living together and in the number of births conceived outside marriage. In the southern districts of Faro, Setubal, Lisbon, Évora, and Beja these tendencies are even more pronounced. While these common-law marriages are still criticized, they are becoming more tolerated socially. Recently there have been important changes in the area of family law; some types of discrimination have been eliminated regarding the couple as well as children born from these unions, who prior to 1975 were considered illegitimate.

The reasons couples live together without marrying today are different from the reasons of those who did so prior to 1970. Frequently, in poor families, especially in rural areas of the southern districts, the affianced male would run off with his intended, simulating a kidnapping (yet sometimes with the consent of the parents), in order to avoid the expenses of the wedding. The expenses were justified socially only if the woman was still a virgin or was considered one. Primarily economic reasons, therefore, led to the formation of these common-law marriages, which were as stable and lasting as those consecrated by legal marriage. Further, the sexual division of family roles did not depart from traditional patterns.

Presently, common-law marriages occur for other motives and are generally not due to economic factors. While there has been no national study regarding these marriages, it seems that younger couples are more egalitarian in the decision-making process, in the division of roles, and in family responsibilities.

A national study was completed in 1988 by the Direcção Geral da Família (Portuguese Governmental Office of Family Relations) regarding 532 Portuguese families. This study analyzed upper, upper-middle, middle, lower-middle, and lower class families comprising a father, mother, and children aged 15 and younger. This study, which was based on interviews with the mother, revealed that family responsibilities are being shared by both parents (contrary to previous patterns) and that both are responsible for deciding the number of children they will have, ensuring that the children obtain a good education, helping them with their homework, becoming involved in school issues, and punishing them. Mothers are demanding more and more that fathers help them, although the physical caring for the children is still being done by the mothers. The mothers take the children to the doctor or stay at home when the children are sick.

This same study shows that the division of domestic duties is far from being equal. Men's participation tends to be what can be done outside the home, such as shopping (71 percent) or other duties related to the cleaning or maintenance of the house, vehicles, garden, or backyard (44 percent). In the home they help to polish shoes (67 percent), to prepare food (50 percent), and to make the bed (38 percent). Washing clothes, ironing, sweeping the floor, and washing dishes are duties that continue to be done principally by the females of the household (mothers and daughters). In 27 percent of the 532 families studied, the husband does not participate in any domestic duties.

This study also reveals that women dedicate more hours daily to supporting the family than men do, while they spend only a few minutes more per day on their personal appearance or in sleeping. On the other hand, men spend more time traveling and watching television. During the week women dedicate more time than men to religious activities (although the difference is only minutes), while men spend more hours than women in social and sports activities.

The management of the family income, the decision regarding large purchases, and the organization of vacation and holiday periods are generally shared by the couple. Administrative questions are handled mostly by men, while the percentage of couples who handle them jointly is between 23 percent and 33 percent, depending on the social class.

The majority of women interviewed who work outside the home say they feel guilty for not being able to spend more time with their children and at home. They agree with the idea of reducing the number of hours of work, working part-time, altering the number of days of work per week, or working flextime. Of those interviewed, 36 percent believe that in the ideal family the woman has a less "absorbing" profession than the man, 31 percent consider that in the ideal family the professions are equally absorbing, and 28 percent consider that in the ideal family the woman does not work outside the home. The majority of lower-status working women reveal that they neither feel professionally satisfied nor adequately compensated (socially, personally, or by the family) by exercising their profession; thus, given the little they earn, they would prefer to work at home. Women of greater status reveal opposing opinions.

The divorce rate has increased in Portugal, and divorce is instigated most often by the woman. If children are involved, the woman is granted custody of them, unless she is considered by a court to be in a state of dementia or total incapacity (physical or otherwise) to do it. By judicial decision the father becomes authorized to visit the children and is obliged to provide a monetary contribution, in accordance with his economic possibilities, for the child's sustenance and education. The financial help generates some postdivorce problems, principally if the ex-wife is unemployed or if her income is irregular, temporary, or insufficient, as relatively frequently the man will shirk his financial obligation, being regular neither in the amount nor the date of the payment. Among the divorced and widowed, the men most often seek a new marriage.

Old Age

In Portugal the majority of the elderly population have low status due, principally, to their low educational level. In 1987, in the total population of those aged 60 or more, 41.1 percent were illiterate. For each 100 illiterate people aged 60 and more, 67.7 percent are women. This age group, relative to the other levels of education, has extremely limited development of, and participation in, professional life, sharing of the salary pool, presence in civic and political affairs. Through this profile of the aged Portuguese population, one can perceive the innumerable factors that negatively conditioned their lives and, further, their old age. Among these factors, the most fundamental is that these people have lived nearly all of their life during the totalitarian and unenlightened regimes of Salazar and Marcelo Caetano, which lasted nearly 50 years and ended 25 April 1974. The knowledge and life experience of the elderly accumulated throughout the years were supremely devalued. The democratic regime became consolidated, new values arose, and new ideologies and new technologies were developed, resulting in a cultural chasm between the generations, serving to aggravate further the marginalization of the elderly and their feelings of uselessness. As a result, many of the elderly live in tremendous social isolation.

In Portuguese society the aging process assumes different degrees of severity according to one's sex, social class, milieu (urban/rural), and the experiences one has gained through employment. These factors affect the attitudes and behavior of each individual in relation to the different stages of life, principally in the aging process. The situation is especially grave when the person is both elderly and poor. Women and men of the least favored classes fear aging and, at the same time, are confronted by it more quickly, being victims of the social attitude of the social milieu where they live. These individuals are the first to express that they are feeling old and to exhibit a weakening in their self-esteem as well as exterior signs of precocious aging. In the economic classes that are more favored, the attitude toward aging is more positive. Aging is viewed more naturally and with greater optimism, and exterior signs of aging tend to appear later.

Presently, women over the age of 65 form the group that lives under the worst economic conditions. A large percentage of these women are widows (their life span is longer) or unmarried, given that there were fewer married women in this age group. In 1988, according to data from the National Statistics Institute's Employment Survey, second trimester (INE), the percentage of working women over the age of 65 was 7.4 percent; thus, only a small percentage of the women of this age group will be eligible for a pension for having worked.[7] The percentage of working women in this age group has historically been very low; in 1978 the percentage of these women who worked (then aged 55–65 years old) was 5.9 percent, and in 1960 (then aged 35–44 years old) it was 13.7 percent (INE, Employment Survey, 1989).

To alleviate to some degree the incidence of poverty of the elderly, a special social pension was instituted in 1974; this was designed to reach a larger percentage of the population than was covered under the standard provisions of the Social Security Services. This pension began to be paid to individuals of both sexes who never contributed to Social Security and reached, in this case, a great number of women who, never having worked before, would never have the right to receive a retirement check. Still, despite the annual increases, the amounts are insufficient to cover the fundamental necessities and the increase in the cost of living. In this way, the elderly remain in a situation of financial semi-dependence in relation to family members (sons/daughters) or to the Social Security Services.

The aged population presently enjoys judicial protection in the fundamental rights (housing, health, transportation, and so on) and some social benefits. Still, poor dissemination of information, a high rate of illiteracy among this age group, and poor mobility impede the aged from taking better advantage of the benefits they are eligible to receive. The very poor frequently go to the Regional Offices of the Social Security Service asking for help for the payment of health expenses (principally the chronically ill), rent, and necessary repairs, as well as debts for food or other items.

Chronic illnesses are present in 20 percent of the elderly, which results in enormous health expenditures. Morbidity surveys reveal that the principal illnesses of the elderly are hypertension, problems of the respiratory tract, bronchitis, and rheumatism. Bronchitis is found more in males, due probably to the type of work they engage in, working outside during the cold of winter and the heat of the summer. Women, on the other hand, are attacked most often by rheumatism, no doubt a reflection of their household duties (washing clothing in outside tanks and using cold water year-round). Among the principal causes of death are cerebral-vascular diseases, severe heart attacks or myocardia, arteriosclerosis, and malignant tumors.

The number of suicides of those over 65 is significant, with the highest number in the district of Beja, where in 1985 there were 30 cases, 27 in 1986, 32 in 1987, and 16 in 1988. Of these, for the same district and the same years, 23, 22, 26, and 10 suicides, respectively, were committed by men (INE, Health Statistics). We hypothesize that the greater percentage of suicides committed by men is due to the fact that widowers feels greater loneliness than widows and are unaccustomed to taking care of their basic needs. Once their spouse has died, men who have no one else to take care of them may give up on life. Further, in traditional communities one did not remarry after the death of one's spouse. One was expected to "respect the memory" of the spouse. This philosophy is changing.

Physical dependence raises great problems for the elderly when the person lives alone and does not have family or lives far from them. Friends and neighbors assume an important role as effective support or as help in case of an emergency, but not in carrying out routine tasks. When confronted with this situation, the elderly have few options. These days, the elderly prefer not to live with their children (if they have children); rather, they prefer to live near them so that the children can dispense some help and attention without the parents' needing to go to a retirement home. However, when the elderly are physically dependent on others, the help the children can give may not be sufficient due to their work schedule. In addition, there are not enough effective in-home services to give support to the elderly. Thus, the only solution for many is to enter a retirement home. This signifies the loss of liberty and privacy. The retirement home is seen by the elderly as a dumping ground for the elderly and the place where they will die.

As the elderly have a lot of time during their retirement, they are able to occupy themselves in diverse activities, generally related to the activities they practiced in the past, although adapted to their current physical condition. Leisure activities are conditioned by low income, a lack of health, or transportation problems. Elderly men frequently occupy their free time with others in cafés, in a tavern, in the garden, or in another central place (such as the local plaza) where they live. Elderly women leave the home to go shopping or to attend religious ceremonies. At home they occupy their time in domestic tasks, knitting, or crocheting. In addition, men and women occupy themselves by watching television or reading (those who know how to read) and doing routine tasks, generally sedentary. In some communities there are volunteer associations that have activities for the elderly, appropriate to their capacities, necessities and style of life, thus facilitating their social integration.

SUMMARY AND CONCLUSIONS

The focus of this chapter examined some of the aspects that have most influenced the formation of gender roles in Portuguese society and the way they condition the different phases of life for individuals. Until the revolutionary movement of 25 April 1974, sex roles and the socialization processes within the family were greatly segregated at school, at work, and in society in general, following traditional patterns.

With the transition toward the democratic regime, freedom was reinstated to the Portuguese, resulting in an acceleration of all the processes of change. Freedom and equal rights became inalienable, opening new perspectives of life for men and women. The forms of socialization have evolved in a direction favorable to the equality of rights, while the coexistence of the values of previous generations (more conservative) does not always permit as rapid a change as might be desired.

The women of today, principally the young women, seek a different life from that sought by their mothers and grandmothers, for whom marriage and child raising were the only alternatives. Currently, Portuguese women are more alert, they have more opportunities from which to choose, they have become more calculating, they know better what they want, they make decisions about their personal life, they formulate life objectives, they seek economic independence and self-actualization and professional advancement. Marriage and child raising continue to be important, but they are not the highest priorities. Women have become less submissive, they have greater self-esteem, they have become more demanding of themselves and others in family relationships, in work relationships, and in society in general. They have become conscious of their rights and the inequalities of which, historically, they have been victims. They are looking for ways to remove the obstacles that limit their self-actualization, their freedom of living, their choosing, and their going further in their ambitions. Men, in their turn, have come to understand the legitimacy of these rights, and, while they still offer some resistance, they are slowly adopting new models of behavior in the family and/or outside it, participating together with women in the construction of a fairer society for both sexes. One senses an ever-growing change in social attitudes; still, despite everything, there continues to be discrimination, namely, in the opportunities for work and a career, which will disappear only slowly. For this reason, Portuguese women will have to have a great strength of will to work arduously, as only by attaining a high level of competence will they manage to penetrate areas traditionally dominated by men. Legally the opportunities exist, but for women, as opposed to men, these options demand sacrifices. Some cultural obstacles (stereotypical ideas and other cultural and social inequalities) still exist, principally in rural areas and in the least favored classes, which impede women from having greater success in all of society's domains.

NOTES

1. *Continental Portugal* is the term used to describe the portion of Portugal that is part of the European continent. The term thus excludes the archipelagos of Madeira and the Azores, as well as the island of Macau.

2. While there is a president, the major power of the country is vested in the prime minister and the Parliament.

3. FEDER (Fundo Europeu para o Desenvolvimento Regional) is the European Fund for Regional Development.

4. FEOGA (Fundo Europeu de Orientação e Garantia Agrícola) is the European Fund of Orientation and Agricultural Guarantee.

5. FSE (Fundo Social Europeu) is the European Social Fund.

6. One can hypothesize that the 1991 census results will show a turnaround in these figures due to better employment opportunities for women and the difficulty for new couples to find housing.

7. Anecdotal evidence suggests that these women work in order to become eligible for a pension.

REFERENCES

Covas, Maria das Mercês C. M. (1989a). Contributos para a análise da produção familiar de bens e serviços em função do tempo [Contributions for the analysis of goods and services in the function of the time]. In *Comunicações do seminário tempo para o trabalho tempo para a família* [Papers of the seminar time for the work time of the family] (pp. 157–72). Lisbon: Direcção Geral da Família, Ministério do Emprego e da Segurança Social.

———. (1989b). Evolução de algumas situações familiares em Portugal: Sua relação com o desempenho do papel económico e do papel doméstico da família [Evolution of some family situations in Portugal: Its relation with the performance of the economic and the housekeeper roles]. *Economia e Sociologia, 47*: 99–132.

———. (1991, April 10–12). Evolução de algumas características demográficas da família em Portugal Continental nas décadas de 70 e 80: Abordagem distrital [Evolution of some demographic characteristics of the family in continental Portugal in the seventies and eighties: Districtal approach]. Paper presented in the conference entitled Famílias e Contextos Sociais: Os Espaços e os Tempos da Diversidade, [Families and social contexts: The spaces and the time of the diversity], sponsored by the Grupo de Estudos sobre a Família, Lisbon.

Direcção Geral da Família (DGF). (1988). *Alguns dados para o estudo da vida quotidiana das famílias portuguesas* [Some data for the study of the Portuguese families' daily life]. Lisbon: Direcção Geral da Família, Ministério do Emprego e da Segurança social.

Instituto Nacional de Estatística (INE). (1960, 1970, 1981). Recenseamento Geral da População. Lisbon.

———. (1985, 1986, 1987, 1988). Estatísticas da Saúde (Health Statistics). Lisbon.

———. (1986, 1987, 1989, 1990). Estatísticas da Educação (Education Statistics). Lisbon.

———. (1988, 1989). Inquérito Permanente ao Emprego (Permanent Employment Survey). Lisbon.

Portugal: A situação das mulheres [Portugal: The situation of women]. (1991). Lisbon: Comissão para a Igualdade e para os Direitos das Mulheres, Presidência de Conselho de Ministros.

Salgueiro, Gabriela. (1989). *As mulheres e o envelhecimento* [The women and the aging], 2d ed. Lisbon: Colecção Informar as Mulheres 8, Comissão da Condição Feminina.

Salgueiro, Teresa Barata. (1987). Actividade e progresso na carreira [Activity and career progress]. *A mulher e o ensino superior, a investigação científica e as novas tecnologias em Portugal* [The woman and the college education: The scientific investigation and the new technologies in Portugal] (pp. 105–16). Lisbon: Cadernos Condição Feminina *21*.

Silva, Manuela. (1987). A mulher e o poder económico [The woman and the economic power]. *Comunicações do seminário "A Mulher e o Poder"* [Papers of the seminar, "the woman and the power"] (pp. 131–39). Lisbon: Cadernos Condição Feminina *20*.

Silva, Maria Regina T. da. (1988). Intervenção da Presidente da Comissão da Condição Feminina [Intervention of the president of the Commission of Female Condition]. *O direito comunitário e a igualdade e a igualdade jurídica entre mulheres e homens* [The European community law and the juridical equality between women and men] (pp. 13–16). Lisbon: Cadernos Condição Feminina *23*.

Sousa, Maria Reynolds de, Canso, Dina, & Castro, Isabel. 1990. *Portugal: Situação das mulheres 1990* [Portugal: The situation of women 1990], 8th ed. Lisbon: Comissão da Condição Feminina.

22

Singapore

Agnes Chang Shook Cheong

INTRODUCTION

Singapore is an island nation and consists of Singapore island and fifty-eight other islets in its territorial waters. It lies between latitudes 1°09'N and 1°29'N and longitudes 103°38'E and 104°06'E, 136.8 kilometers (84.82 miles) north of the equator. Being so close to the equator, it enjoys uniform temperature, high humidity, and abundant rainfall all year. The average daily temperature is 26.7°C (80°F).

It is among one of the smallest nations in the world, with the main island having an area of only 573.9 square kilometers (221.58 square miles). The total land area, including the islets, is 633.0 square kilometers (244.4 square miles) but is changing year by year as a result of successful land reclamation from the sea.

North of Singapore is Peninsular Malaysia, and the two nations are linked by a causeway 1,056 meters (3,484.8 feet) long. Sabah, Sarawak (part of Malaysia), and Brunei flank the eastern side of Singapore, and the southern neighbor is Indonesia. Due to its strategic position in the midst of bigger land masses, Singapore is well protected from rough weather elements such as typhoons. It is also outside the active volcanic zone.

Singapore is a city-nation, and like all land-scarce countries, the land is carefully planned for industrial and urban development. But Singapore is no concrete jungle. As the native people say, "green lungs" are built in all parts of the island, especially in the public housing estates. The Singapore Botanic Gardens is one of the best public gardens in Southeast Asia, especially known for its orchid varieties.

An aerial view of the country shows many areas of tall housing blocks. In a

Table 22.1

Singapore Residents By Ethnic Group, Age Group, and Sex, June 1990

Ethnic Group	Sex	Total	0-9	10-19	20-29	30-39	40-49	50-59	60-69	70 & over
Total	Males	1,360.5	221.9	216.0	258.3	274.7	166.8	108.6	70.0	44.0
	Females	1,329.6	206.1	201.9	252.1	267.2	163.7	108.0	71.8	58.8
Chinese	Males	1,049.9	159.3	169.8	194.9	218.5	137.6	85.5	49.3	35.0
	Females	1,039.5	146.9	158.7	189.6	212.0	134.7	86.6	58.5	52.5
Malay	Males	193.3	42.4	30.6	42.3	35.1	16.1	12.2	10.0	4.6
	Females	187.3	40.2	28.5	41.2	34.2	17.0	13.3	8.8	4.1
Indians	Males	103.2	16.9	13.7	19.1	18.8	11.6	9.5	9.7	3.9
	Females	87.8	15.8	13.0	18.8	18.0	10.2	6.9	3.7	1.4
Others	Males	14.1	3.3	1.8	2.1	2.4	1.7	1.2	1.0	0.6
	Females	15.1	3.2	1.7	2.6	2.9	1.7	1.3	1.0	0.7

Note: Numbers refer to Singapore citizens and permanent residents. Data may not add up due to rounding off.

Source: *Yearbook of Statistics* (Singapore: Department of Statistics, 1991).

land-hungry country, 87 percent of its citizens are living in flats built by the Housing and Development Board. These flats are reasonably priced and mostly owned by the occupants.

The 1990 population census showed that a total of 3,002,800 persons were living in Singapore (Table 22.1). Chinese residents constituted 77.77 percent of the total population, Malays 14.1 percent, Indians 7.1 percent, and others 1.1 percent. There were slightly more males than females, with a sex ratio of 1.023 males per 1,000 females. Young residents below the age of 15 years formed 23.3 percent of the population in 1990 while the proportion of senior citizens aged sixty years and above has touched 9.1 percent. Improved standards of living and health care reduced the infant mortality rate to 6.7 per 1,000 live births in 1990 and raised life expectancy to 74.1 years in 1989.

The racial composition of Singapore is linked to Singapore's immigrant history. At the end of the nineteenth century, Singapore's population was made up largely of migrant workers who were attracted by the commercial opportunities of flourishing Singapore and by the job opportunities in the rubber plantation economy in Peninsula Malaya. Streams of migrants from the south and southern China, India, and nearby Indonesia came to work in Malaya. It was not until the 1930s that Singapore could speak of having a settled population. The majority of the early migrants were able-bodied males, many of whom were single or, if married, had left their families in their own native countries. In 1911, there were 2,453 males to every 1,000 females.

The earliest immigrants were the Indonesians and Malays, who thus contributed substantially to the early growth of population in Singapore. In 1824, the population comprised 60 percent Malays, 31 percent Chinese, and 7 percent Indians. By 1830, the Chinese had outstripped the Malays in numbers and became the largest ethnic component of the population. This demographic pattern has persisted to the present day.

As the three dominant races in Singapore are Chinese, Malays, and Indians, the official languages are Malay, Chinese, Tamil, and English. Malay is the national language while English is the language of the administration. English is the principal medium of instruction, and all children of Singapore residents and permanent residents have to take their mother tongue as a second language. Bilingual education starts at the preschool level.

The general literacy rate of residents has risen from 84 percent in 1980 to a high 90 percent in 1990. The improved literacy is due to the active promotion of continuing educational and training programs for working adults.

Singapore, being a secular country, allows freedom of religious practice. Eighty-six percent of the population aged 10 years and above professed to some religious belief. Buddhists and Taoists form the largest group (58.9 percent). This is not surprising as Chinese is the largest ethnic group. Islam is the religion of 15.4 percent of the population, of whom 85.9 percent of the believers are Malays. Christianity is taken up by 12.6 percent of the residents, and Hinduism has 3.6 percent of the population.

OVERVIEW

In small but modernizing Singapore, which has no natural resources except its male and female citizens, discrimination against either gender is not affordable. In addition, its sex ratio stands at 1:1, and hence manpower and womanpower alike are equally valued by the country in its course of nation building.

Singapore women today enjoy relatively equal social status compared with men. Women have voting rights; they have equal access to primary, secondary, and tertiary education; they hold and trade property; and they enjoy equal pay with men in the public sector.

The non-Muslim women are protected by the Women's Charter, established in 1961, which outlaws polygamous marriages. There is hardly any formal barrier against women's entry into all kinds of occupations (except medicine), but certain forms of unofficial, overt, and covert discrimination against women still persist in the society.

There is a quota system governing the acceptance of females into the Medical Faculty in the National University of Singapore. For every four undergraduates admitted into the Faculty, only one is a female. Despite the public uproar, the university maintains its stand and argues that some women doctors stop practicing after marriage and female doctors employed in the civil service could not be easily assigned duties. Women generally also shy away from occupations that demand shift duties, frequent overseas travel, and client entertaining. Everything being equal, employers prefer to employ a male worker who is not going to ask for maternity leave.

Compared with their single sisters, married women are less likely to be economically active. Marriage is usually the single biggest barrier to an increase in the female labor force participation rate in Singapore, because women today are still expected to cope with the demands of both work and family life simultaneously. Though more and more modern husbands are willing to lend a helping hand in home chores, the burden of home management still falls on women.

Despite the rapid rise of women's status in the working world, she and her children are considered dependents of her husband if he is still alive. This is indicated by the medical schemes for female employees. Unlike their male counterparts, the medical schemes are not extended to the immediate family members of women, except for single mothers.

Another area that leaves Singapore women seething is the slow acceptance of their foreign husbands as permanent residents of Singapore. Compared with the foreign wives of men, foreign husbands of Singapore women find it more difficult to gain naturalization. From the government's point of view, it has to screen its potential immigrants carefully to ensure that no marriage of convenience has taken place. The government has learned much from the patterns of immigration in the developed countries.

National service is compulsory for all Singapore male citizens and permanent citizens at age 18. Irrespective of their ethnic groups, religious beliefs, and educational qualifications, 18-year-olds undergo 2.5 years of national service. Females in the same age group are free to pursue higher education in tertiary institutions or join the work force. Males with health problems still join the national service but are assigned light duties. It is the aim of the government to have a trim, fit, and healthy nation.

Critics have pointed out that women are not well represented in Singapore politics. It had two women members of Parliament after the 1991 election, both from the ruling political party. Though there are many vocal women's groups in Singapore, few of the women are keen to sacrifice their privacy for a place in Parliament. Similarly, the Ministry of Education has bemoaned the fact that a number of capable female teachers have declined the nomination to become heads of departments and principals.

Despite opportunities for advancement, many Asian women are still traditional in their outlook and prefer to keep a low profile.

All in all, there are more equalities then inequalities between the genders. For an Asian country, Singapore women enjoy higher social status and higher occupational status than their counterparts in many other developing countries.

COMPARISONS BETWEEN MEN'S AND WOMEN'S GENDER ROLES DURING THE LIFE CYCLE

Infancy and Early Childhood

The maternal mortality rate in Singapore has a proud record of 0.1 per 1,000 live births and stillbirths for the last three years. The falling fertility rate is of great concern to the government. The mean number of children born to resident, ever-married females dropped from 3.4 in 1980 to 2.4 in 1990. The figures in Table 22.1 show that the number of males born was higher than the number of females for all the major ethnic groups.

It is a common belief that Asian parents, especially Chinese, prefer boys to girls, as boys carry on the family lineage. The lineage system that was typical and unique in its total dominance of agricultural villages in southern and south-eastern China could not be maintained in Singapore (Freedman, 1958). In urbanized Singapore, new forms of clan, dialect, and territorial associations assumed great significance in the social organization of the Chinese community. The traditional ways of life of immigrants from the different ethnic groups have to be modified in response to the social and economic changes in Singapore. As the literacy rate improves among the residents, views toward female children take a favorable turn.

Female infanticide is unheard of in Singapore. Many parents have found that daughters are more caring and are more likely to visit their parents after marriage. The responsibilities of caring for aged and sickly parents are usually shouldered by female kin.

Male and female infants are brought up very much in the same way, except that parents may be stricter toward the boys, who are usually more active and playful. Working mothers have to make alternative arrangements with regard to child care. According to the *Report on National Survey on Working Mothers* (1986), the most common child-care alternative for children under 6 was provided by grandparents (50.8 percent for first child and 44.3 percent for second child). Relatives, foster day care, and servants each accounts for 10 percent to 18 percent of child-care arrangements. Less than 4 percent of children needing an alternative option are put into child-care centers. However, the 1990 statistics suggest that more older women are joining or rejoining the labor force. Thus fewer grand-mothers, aunts, and foster mothers will be available as child-care givers in the next few years. To keep their female workers happy, some large companies and statutory boards provide child-care facilities. In view of the shortage of alternative child-care givers, the government is encouraging interested individuals and agencies to set up private child-care centers.

Though the traditional blue for boys and pink for girls are still being practiced in the purchase of gifts for newborn infants, young children in the hot, humid Singapore weather are more comfortable in cotton T-shirts and shorts. Frilly frocks and long pants are reserved for special festive days. Sex socialization takes forms other than dressing. Ethnic costumes like the *samfoo* and *cheongsam* (Chinese), *sari* and *choli* (Indians), and *baju kurong* and *sarong kebaya* (Malays) can be restrictive for the young children for daily wear. Hence ethnic costumes are usually worn by the older children on special ethnic festivals.

There is still a tendency to buy Barbie dolls and soft toys for little girls and robots and toy cars for little boys. But educational toys like alphabet blocks, play dough, Leggo blocks, and children's books are getting to be popular Christmas and birthday presents for children of both genders. Cartoon characters like He-Man and Ninja turtles are favorites with most boys and even with some girls.

Traditional games like marbles, five-stones, and hopscotch are seldom played by young children these days. Instead, swimming, bicycle or tricycle riding, and kite flying are favored by Singapore children and their parents. As an island, Singapore gives easy access to the sea for the residents; public swimming pools are available all over the island too.

Preschool education begins at 3 years with nursery class, followed by Kindergarten I for the 4-year-olds and Kindergarten II for the 5-year-olds. Low-cost preschool education is provided by the People's Action Party, People's Association, and National Trade Union Congress. Duration of daily lessons is between two and three hours. Kindergartens are also set up by churches and interested individuals. They usually command a higher fee and provide better facilities. There are not enough places in existing kindergartens for all the young children. It is not uncommon to find parents camping outside the kindergartens in order to secure a place for their children. Preschool education is not under the purview of the Ministry of Education. Since 1990, the government has established 1-year preparatory classes for 5-year-olds in specially selected primary schools.

School Years

The nuclear family is now the predominant family type in Singapore. For the younger families, children seldom exceed three in number. In the 1990 census, 48.1 percent of married women had 1 to 2 children, and a further 26.6 percent had 3 to 4 children. This may have something to do with the effective campaigns on family planning in the earlier years. But couples are now encouraged to have more children. Siblings with an elder brother or sister in a school will be given priority for admission over someone without any connection with the school. This is one way of encouraging parents to have more children and to arrest the declining fertility rate.

As the common family size is small, children, especially those from single-child families, have to rely on cousins, neighbors' children, and classmates for companionship. Many schoolchildren confess to loneliness at home after school and over the weekends. This does not mean that they do not have any homework, tuition, or extra classes to keep them busy. Though education is not compulsory in Singapore, all parents realize that education is the best means to social mobility in a meritocratic society. Besides regular lessons, many parents arrange for their offspring to take music, ballet, swimming, art, speech, and computer lessons. This does not apply only to children of professionals and well-paid officers in management positions. It is not uncommon to have children of taxi drivers and clerical officers taking art and music lessons in Singapore.

More enlightened parents train their children to be independent and encourage them to help out with household chores. But for families who can afford foreign maids, parents usually leave the household chores to the maids and arrange for

Table 22.2

Highest Qualification Attained for Males and Females by Age Group, 1980 and 1990 (percentages)

Highest Qualification	25-29 Years		30-39 Years		40-49 Years	
	1980	1990	1980	1990	1980	1990
Males	100.0	100.0	100.0	100.0	100.0	100.0
Below Secondary	69.0	45.4	72.4	51.4	84.0	62.5
Secondary	16.9	32.9	13.6	29.1	7.9	21.7
Upper Secondary	9.2	13.2	8.8	12.1	4.5	9.6
University	4.9	8.5	5.2	7.4	3.6	6.2
Females	100.0	100.0	100.0	100.0	100.0	100.0
Below Secondary	72.3	35.8	80.5	51.7	92.0	72.7
Secondary 2 Upper Secondary	18.0	44.0	12.1	34.6	4.6	19.3
	6.5	12.2	5.1	9.1	2.4	5.6
University	3.2	8.0	2.3	4.6	1.0	2.4

Note: 1990 data are based on 10% sample.
Source: *Yearbook of Statistics* (Singapore: Department of Statistics, 1991).

their children to spend their time on tuition or extra lessons. Doting parents tend to pamper their children and do the household chores themselves if they have no maids.

Primary education is free, and a place is available for every child who wants to attend school. In 1990, among Singapore residents between the age of 6 and 16, 97 percent were students, an increase from 90 percent ten years ago. Primary education for most pupils takes six years, and secondary education takes four years for the better pupils and five years for the weaker students. At the end of secondary schooling, students sit for the Cambridge G.C.E. "O"-level examination. Junior colleges offer two years of post-secondary education and prepare students for the Cambridge G.C.E. "A"-level examination. There are two universities, three polytechnics, and the National Institute of Education (formerly known as the Institute of Education) providing tertiary education in Singapore.

There is a marked increase in the proportion of students pursuing higher education after secondary school. The proportion of students in upper secondary and polytechnic schools and universities increased from 7 percent in 1980 to 13 percent in 1990.

In 1990 almost as many females as males aged twenty-five to twenty-nine years had upper secondary or university qualifications (Table 22.2). Older males were better qualified than females, and the disparity widened with increasing age. Females have made rapid advancement in educational advancement over the last ten years. The number of younger female graduates rose from 3 percent in 1980 to 8 percent in 1990 while that of male graduates of the same age group increased from 5 percent to 9 percent.

Table 22.3
Percentage of Females in Selected Undergraduate Courses, 1970–1971, 1980–1981, and 1988–1989

Courses	70-71	80-81	88-89
Arts & Soc. Studies	58.2	67.2	75.1
Business Admin.	22.5	44.3	66.1
Science	39.3	55.0	56.8
Law	34.4	53.2	46.9
Medicine	26.8	38.4	32.7
Engineering	2.5	9.9	14.6
TOTAL	33.2	45.5	52.3

Sources: Annual Reports of the National University of Singapore.

Evidence shows more boys are channeled into the lower streams after the streaming exercise at Primary 3. As girls mature faster than boys, early streaming may place boys at a disadvantage. However, selection into the Gifted Program at Primary 3 also sees more boys than girls, in the ratio of 2:1, being successful. In terms of preuniversity education, while more girls are admitted, a larger percentage are enrolled in the 3-year preuniversity centers than in the 2-year junior colleges. As the preuniversity centers stress arts and commerce rather than science, a larger proportion of girls take arts and commerce. Although sex-stereotyping in choice of secondary school subjects is fairly universal, it is less evident in a highly technological society like Singapore, except for obvious subjects like technical studies and home economics. Both parents and children alike foresee a bright future in a career related to science and technology.

Though there has been an increase in university enrollment of females, their choice of courses reflects their bias toward arts and business administration and avoidance of engineering. Surprisingly, more than half of the science under-graduates were females in the 1988–1989 Annual Report of the National University of Singapore (Table 22.3). Education is a caring profession and attracts more females to it, given the societal stereotyping of females as being more caring (Table 22.4). The progressive feminization of the teaching profession is causing some concern to the authorities. Boys, especially those in the secondary schools, need male teachers to be their models, but not many are forthcoming.

Table 22.4
Percentage of Female Enrollments in Tertiary Institutions, 1965, 1970, 1980–1981, and 1988

Institutions	1965	1970	1980/81	1988
University University of Singapore Nanyang University National Univ. of S'pore Nanyang Technological Institute	29.1 26.7	32.3 39.7	43.9	49.2 39.8
Polytechnic (Singapore Polytechnic + Ngee Ann Polytechnic)	9.9	8.1	22.5	30.7
Teachers' Training College Institute of Education College of Physical Education	58.0	69.5	84.9	82.3 58.7
TOTAL	36.0	30.7	37.6	39.0

Source: *Yearbook of Statistics* (Singapore: Department of Statistics, 1965, 1970, 1980–81, Ministry of Labor).

Even in the College of Physical Education, there were more female than male trainees enrolled from 1985 to 1988. Since 1989, the number of males has outstripped the number of females (Table 22.5). Polytechnics, which stress engineering courses, have a lower enrollment of females. The new polytechnic offers courses on designing and business, which attract a large number of female students.

Young Adulthood

Asian parents are generally more protective toward their daughters and take greater interest in the company they keep. Parents are more likely to allow their sons to go out with their friends at a younger age and later into the night. It is not unusual for parents to impose curfew hours on their daughters' outings, and staying out later is rarely granted. This may seem strange to non-Singaporeans as Singapore projects an image of modernity and sophistication and its residents are fed a diet of current Western literature. However, the Asian cultural roots sink deep and are reflected in child-rearing practices.

Most government primary and secondary schools and all junior colleges are coeducational, and hence socialization between young boys and girls takes place at a young age. However, their interest in each other may not be romantic for a long time until they are in their adolescence. Girls in general mature socially

Table 22.5
Enrollment in Institutions of Higher Learning, 1987–1990

Year	National University of Singapore		Nanyang Technological Institute		Singapore Polytechnic	
	Males	Females	Males	Females	Males	Females
1987	7,737	7,229	2,454	1,486	10,529	3,224
1988	8,254	7,946	2,650	1,751	10,479	3,553
1989	8,315	8,311	3,357	2,125	10,676	4,059
1990	8,696	8,646	4,265	2,700	10,864	4,583

Year	Ngee Ann Polytechnic		Temasek Polytechnic		Institute of Education		College of Physical Education	
	Males	Females	Males	Females	Males	Females	Males	Females
1987	6,821	4,037	–	–	218	1,121	53	67
1988	7,066	4,213	–	1	172	802	43	61
1989	7,667	4,704	–	–	296	1,117	69	60
1990	8,180	5,111	185	551	347	1,284	85	65

Source: Ministry of Education.

and emotionally a few years ahead of boys and hence are ready for dating before the boys. Naturally, older boys are preferred.

Group dating is popular among the younger teenagers age 12 to 16. Fast-food joints and shopping centers are favorite haunts of these young groups of mixed genders (Khor, 1988). Many youngsters work part-time in the fast-food restaurants to earn extra money to finance their outings. Older teens in junior colleges and youths in tertiary institutions or at work are more ready to go on double dates and single dates. Romantic dates are tacitly understood to be an invited outing, and the boys pay the expenses incurred. In recent times, career women are quite ready to share the expenditure. Though it no longer raises eyebrows when a woman shows explicit interest in a man and dates him, most women still prefer to be wooed. Singapore men are flattered when they get unsolicited female attention but prefer to be the hunter.

Among the different ethnic groups, some conservative Indian parents who still practice the caste system and are concerned about the perpetuation of their religions have reservations about their children's socializing with young people of other religions and castes. Chinese parents who are more flexible about religions do not object too much to their children's socializing with people of different religious beliefs. Most Malays are Muslims and would like little change in this pattern.

Singapore is not a welfare state, but there is work available for all who are willing to work. Domestic help comes from neighboring countries, and the construction industry is supported solidly by workers from the same source countries. Of the total population age 15 years and above in 1990, 65 percent were economically active. The remaining 35 percent of economically inactive persons were mainly students, homemakers, retirees, and other aged persons. Over the last ten years, the labor force has expanded by an average rate of 3.1 percent.

The overall increase in labor force participation is due to more females' entering the labor market. The female participation rate improved from 44 percent in 1980 to 50 percent in 1990. In contrast, there was a decline in the male participation rate from 82 percent in 1980 to 79 percent in 1990. The male participation rate showed a decline in almost all age groups, the largest being for the youngest and oldest age groups. This is quite understandable, as the younger men were at school and the elderly persons had retired and left the labor market.

There were substantial increases for the prime working age groups for females, reflecting the stronger career orientation among women and abundant job opportunities. The progress made by women in academic pursuits enabled them to have greater access to a variety of jobs formerly denied to them. As a matter of fact, the level of education of female workers has tended to be generally higher than that of their male counterparts (Table 22.6).

In 1988 it was found that the participation rate for married females peaked at 20–29 years and fell between 30 and 39 years. This was because some married

Table 22.6
Distribution of Employed Males and Females by Education Attainment,
1980 and 1988

Sex / Year	Never attended school	No qualification	Primary/ Post Primary	Secondary	Post Sec/ Tertiary
1980					
Male	10.0	15.7	36.3	25.1	9.0/3.5
Female	13.9	10.3	27.2	36.0	10.1/2.5
1988					
Male	5.9	13.9	33.3	27.6	13.4/5.9
Female	9.0	9.9	25.0	37.4	13.9/4.8

Source: Report of Labor Force Survey of Singapore (Singapore: Ministry of Labor, 1988).

women preferred to leave the labor force in order to start and raise their families. As their children grew older, some rejoined the work force. For the older age group of 40–49 years, married females were less likely to leave, as their families were older and their family life was more stabilized. There were significant increases in single female participation in all prime working age groups.

There was a gradual upgrading of the occupational structure of the work force, with a higher proportion in the more highly skilled jobs. In 1990, professional and technical workers constituted 16 percent of the work force, compared with 12 percent in 1980. Administrative and managerial officers also increased from 6 percent to 8 percent. Clerical, sales, production, and other lower-skilled jobs still accounted for 76 percent of the work force.

The proportion of female professional workers has shown significant increase in the last decade, edging out their male counterparts in the race (Table 22.7). The increase from 12 percent in 1980 to 16 percent in 1990 reflected higher educational achievement among women. Male workers appeared to show a slower rate of improvement (12 percent to 15 percent). There was a shift away from blue-collar jobs. Administrative and managerial positions were still dominated by males (11.0 percent versus 3.9 percent) while females were the pillars in clerical, sales, and service positions (38.5 percent versus 18.9 percent).

Males find clerical work boring and unchallenging. Nursing is another occupation that is stereotyped as being feminine, and few parents would encourage their sons to go into nursing. Despite great effort and much publicity on the part of the Ministry of Education to attract males into the teaching profession, the increase in the number of male teachers in recent years is negligible. All trainee teachers in Singapore are given a generous scholarship during their training, but the incentive does not lure the restless males. On the other hand, airlines are

Table 22.7
Occupational Distribution of Males and Females, 1980 and 1990

Occupation	Number ('000)				Percent			
	Males		Females		Males		Females	
	1980	1990	1980	1990	1980	1990	1980	1990
Total	704.6	912.2	368.7	573.6	100.0	100.0	100.0	100.0
Professional & Technical	81.4	139.5	44.0	94.4	11.5	15.3	11.9	16.4
Administrative & Managerial	60.3	100.0	7.1	22.3	8.6	11.0	1.9	3.9
Clerical, Sales & Services	158.3	172.3	146.5	220.7	22.5	18.9	39.8	38.5
Production & Others	404.6	500.3	171.0	236.3	57.4	54.8	46.4	41.2

Note: 1990 data are based on 10% sample.
Source: Department of Statistics.

Table 22.8
Marital Distribution, 1980 and 1990 (percentages)

Marital Status	Total		Chinese		Malays		Indians		Others	
	1980	1990	1980	1990	1980	1990	1980	1990	1980	1990
Total	100.0	100.0	100.0	100.0	100.0	100.0	100.0	100.0	100.0	100.0
Single	48.0	41.2	47.7	41.8	50.5	39.5	46.1	37.8	43.8	37.5
Married	46.0	52.0	46.0	51.5	44.4	54.1	49.2	54.8	48.6	54.6
Widowed	5.2	5.6	5.5	5.6	4.0	4.9	3.9	6.0	5.4	5.7
Divorced	0.8	1.2	0.8	1.1	1.5	0.8	1.1	1.4	2.2	2.2

Source: Department of Statistics.

less likely to employ a female commercial pilot. Occupations involving high risks (e.g., criminal investigation, Central Narcotic Affairs) are usually held by males too. Discrimination may occur in certain areas of work, but the psychological and biological makeup of the genders is a principal contributing factor.

Adulthood

Among Singapore residents aged 15 years and above, the proportion that was married increased from 46 percent in 1980 to 52 percent in 1990 while there was a decline in the proportion of singles from 48 percent to 41 percent (Table 22.8).

One of the observable changes in the age pattern of marriage in Singapore after the Second World War was the postponement of marriage. This is reflected

Table 22.9
Proportion Single, 1980 and 1990

Age Group	Males		Females	
	1980	1990	1980	1990
20 - 24	92.1	94.3	73.7	78.8
25 - 29	54.8	63.7	33.6	38.6
30 - 34	21.4	33.0	16.6	20.4
35 - 39	10.6	17.1	8.5	14.4
40 - 44	8.1	10.1	5.8	11.2

Source: Department of Statistics.

in the rising proportion of singles among both males and females in the younger age groups (Table 22.9). In 1980, the median marriage age for grooms was 27.8, and for brides 24.6. There was a steady rise through the decade. By 1990, the median marriage age for grooms was 29.6, and for brides 26.4.

In recent years, the government has been very concerned with the trend of male graduates' marrying down and the increasing number of female graduates' staying single. A 1990 survey found that one out of every four female graduates remained single. To ameliorate the situation, the government made worldwide news in establishing an official matchmaking bureau known as the Social Development Unit (SDU). This unit is entrusted with the task of creating opportunities for single graduates to meet and socialize. Besides the usual teas, lunches, dinners, and dances, subsidized overseas trips and educational courses are also organized to attract participants. There has been moderate success in this official social engineering attempt. More male graduates are now found to look for their life partners among female graduates instead of "A"-level and "O"-level holders. Single female graduates are also encouraged to look for their soul mates among nongraduates. This would, indeed, increase their opportunities and choices.

On the whole, love marriages are the norm in modern Singapore, especially among the Chinese, European races, and Eurasians. Arranged marriages are still quite common among Indians, even for girls who are holders of master's and doctoral degrees.

Registration of marriage is compulsory in Singapore. Marriages other than Muslim marriages are registered under the Women's Charter, 1961. Notices of such marriages have to be lodged with the Registrar of Marriages, irrespective of the venue of solemnization. Under the Women's Charter, de facto marriages

Table 22.10
Ever-Married Females by Number of Children Born 1980 and 1990 (percentages)

Number of children born	Total		Chinese		Malays		Indians		Others	
	1980	1990	1980	1990	1980	1990	1980	1990	1980	1990
Total	100.0	100.0	100.0	100.0	100.0	100.0	100.0	100.0	100.0	100.0
0	8.5	10.5	8.2	10.5	9.9	9.4	9.2	11.6	12.5	16.4
1 - 2	36.2	43.3	36.4	43.9	34.1	38.9	36.1	42.7	45.5	48.1
3 - 4	27.5	27.8	28.7	27.8	21.3	27.7	26.8	28.7	26.2	26.6
5 & Over	27.7	18.4	26.7	17.8	34.7	24.0	27.9	17.0	15.8	8.9
Mean Number	3.4	2.9	3.4	2.9	3.9	3.4	3.4	2.8	2.8	2.4

Note: 1990 data are based on 10% sample.
Source: Department of Statistics.

are not recognized, and palimony does not exist in the Singapore legal system. Registration of Muslim marriages in Singapore became compulsory from 1 July 1909, when the Mohammadan Marriage Ordinance, 1908, was enacted. Religious rites in marriages are common among Christians, Muslims, Hindus, and Buddhists. Hence church weddings for Christians and temple weddings for Hindus and Buddhists are frequent occurrences over the weekends.

As more women delay their marriage to establish their career, their child-bearing years are also reduced. Hence the family size is becoming smaller. The average number of children born to ever-married females has dropped from 3.4 in 1980 to 2.9 in 1990. The number of childless couples increased from 9 percent in 1980 to 11 percent in 1990 (Table 22.10). More older females had no children after marriage. Some childless couples have gone overseas to China, Taiwan, Malaysia, Indonesia, and India to adopt children.

In Singapore, many educated couples are dual earners. This suggests that both husband and wife are contributing toward the family home and hence should share the household duties. If a maid is engaged to take care of the household chores, both husband and wife need only to clean up the house on the maid's off-days. Eating out in Singapore is relatively inexpensive and convenient. Hence cooking has never posed a problem to young couples without children. For families without domestic help, some enlightened husbands do their fair share of the household chores. But the belief that a man should not be kitchen-bound still persists in some families, and the wife ends up in bringing home the bacon plus bending over the cooking pot. It is little wonder that a number of career wives suffer from burnout due to job-parent conflict (Aryce, 1991). Fathers are increasingly encouraged to enjoy the development of their children by actively participating in their children's upbringing.

As more women become financially independent and the nation becomes more affluent, the divorce rate has also accelerated. In 1983 there were 1,602 divorces, and the number went up to 2,662 in 1990 (Table 22.11). This increase affected

Table 22.11
Divorces of Couples, 1983–1990

Year	Women's Charter	Muslim Law Act
	Total	Total
1983	1,602	711
1984	1,676	637
1985	1,606	738
1986	1,822	786
1987	1,912	796
1988	2,023	893
1989	2,002	907
1990	2,662	972

Source: Department of Statistics.

all ethnic groups. Divorces appeared to peak in the twenty-five to thirty-nine age group for both males and females.

Non-Muslim divorces are governed by the Women's Charter, which is "more favorable to women." Under the Women's Charter, either spouse may petition for divorce on any one of the following grounds: (1) adultery, (2) desertion after three years, (3) cruelty, (4) living separately and apart for seven years, or (5) mental illness with medical treatment for the preceding five continuous years. Muslim divorces are governed by Muslim laws and handled by the Muslim Law Court known as the Shariah Court. Traditionally a Muslim couple could be divorced simply by the husband saying, "Talak" (I divorce you) three times. After the ordinance was implemented in 1958, all divorces must take place at the Shariah Court. Desertion and adultery are most commonly cited as reasons for divorce in Singapore. Most court fights over custody of children are usually settled amicably.

For couples whose elderly parents are staying with them, weekends usually see the brothers and sisters who moved away making home visits to their elderly parents. Together with their parents, they usually go for a nice meal in one of the many restaurants in Singapore. Eating out has become a national hobby. There is little countryside to talk about, but there are many attractive shopping centers. Hence window-shopping is another national passion. Many families drive over the causeway to Malaysia for the weekend.

Places of interest like the Science Center, Zoological Garden, Bird Park, Chinese Garden, Japanese Garden, Haw Par Villa, Sentosa, and the Botanic Gardens are very popular with young children and their parents on weekends.

For the sporting types, squash courts, gyms, tennis courts, golf greens, and jogging tracks are available all around the island. Sea sports like waterskiing, yachting, windsurfing, and sailing are becoming popular with the yuppies. Nightclubs, pubs, and *karaoke* lounges are favorites with the night birds. Traveling overseas for holidays is now affordable to a large proportion of the residents. For the low-income wage earners, Association of Southeast Asian Nations (ASEAN) countries are within their budget. Places like California, London, Paris, and Sydney are the playground of the sophisticates.

Old Age

The retirement age from public service is 60 years while from most statutory boards (including tertiary institutions) it ranges from 55 years to 60 years. The private sector takes the cue from the government, and most firms retire their employees at 55 or 60 years. As the life expectancy of Singapore residents rises (71.9 for males and 76.5 for females), the government appeals to the private firms that have set their retirement age at 55 to raise this to 60 years. As an incentive, the government lowered the Central Provident Fund, the employers' contribution for employees over 55 years old, to encourage employment of retirees. The 1990 statistics show that for the last ten years, 30 percent to 40 percent of males above the age of 60 were still gainfully employed. The employment figure for females registered less than 10 percent for the same age group. Older women generally prefer to stay home to look after their grandchildren.

In a Confucian society like Singapore, where filial piety is strongly valued and exhorted, parents are revered, and occasional incidents of parent abuse are given much publicity in the media. The erring children are treated with great disdain by the neighbors and public at large. The government encourages children to stay with their parents so that the elderly will benefit from the love and care of their loved ones. While money may not be a great problem in affluent Singapore, senior citizens on their own may feel very lonely. A recent survey carried out on the 1985–1988 population reveals that there are more suicides in the 65 + age group than in the 10–64 age group. In most cases, loneliness and ill health are cited as the major causes. Among the Chinese, females are more likely to take their lives compared with males. For the Indians, the picture is reversed while the difference between the genders was insignificant. As an incentive, the government encourages young families and their parents to apply for public housing flats in the same block. This serves the dual purpose of having able-bodied children to look after old parents, who, in turn, can take care of the young grandchildren while their parents are at work.

With a graying population, social services are offered by both government agencies and voluntary groups:

1. The Befriender Service is a good-neighbor program, made up of kind befrienders who advise and assist lonely citizens and act as contacts in terms of crises. This service

is organized by the Ministry of Community Development and the Senior Citizens' Club of the People's Association.

2. Counseling and advice services are provided by six agencies to help senior citizens settle their personal and family problems and disputes.

3. Senior citizens' health care centers set up by the government polyclinics provide domiciliary services to frail senior citizens at central locations. They also offer basic nursing and simple physiotherapy for senior citizens who need follow-up rehabilitative care after discharge from hospitals. For senior citizens sixty-five years and above, the polyclinics charge half-price for consultations and medicine.

4. Social day centers and senior citizens' clubs cater to the social activities of senior citizens while their family members are at work. Hence the elderly can participate in games, hobbies, keep-fit exercises, and educational courses at nominal fees.

5. Many community centers and voluntary organizations provide nutritious meals free or at nominal cost from once a month to three times a week. Some centers even deliver meals to homebound senior citizens.

6. Health screening is offered to senior citizens by the government and private agencies. It includes physical examination, weight and height measurement, blood pressure and blood glucose checks, eye and dental checks.

7. Residential care is available for those of physical or mental infirmity who cannot be taken care of by family members. The Ministry of Community Development has set up three welfare homes under the provisions of the Destitute Persons Act. There are also nongovernment homes run by voluntary organizations. Homes for the aged, run on a commercial basis, are also available.

8. Respite service providing nursing and personal care is available to senior citizens who are convalescing or are unable to maintain themselves temporarily in their own home. It gives a break to family members who have to care for the senior citizen.

9. Senior citizens over 60 years are offered discounts in transport (bus and mass rapid transit), continuing education, sports, recreational activities, and places of interest.

A very active volunteer organization known as the Singapore Action Group of Elders (SAGE) has done much to better the quality of life of senior citizens. Besides organizing the usual social and recreational activities for senior citizens, it has launched a massive project to build the SAGE Elders' Village. On completion, the village will be able to offer 50 rooms for temporary stay to senior citizens. The village hopes to provide a library, conference and exhibition facilities, employment services, and day-care center for senior citizens.

As with all old people around the world and especially for a humid country like Singapore, rheumatism and arthritis are common health complaints of the elderly. For females, problems of menopause are not uncommon, but the Well Women Clinic gives medical advice to those who avail themselves of its services. However, many Asian women choose to suffer in silence as they still consider menopause a private matter that should not be publicized and will go away after some time.

In recent years, deaths from heart attacks and cancer top the chart on causes of death in Singapore (Table 22.12). Cancer is the top killer for men, followed closely by ischemic and heart diseases. Women tend to fall victim to ischemic

Table 22.12
Major Causes of Death, 1989

Cause of Death	Rate per 100,000 population		
	Men	Women	Total
Total	581	464	524
Ischemic & other heart disease	140	107	124
Cancer	144	99	122
Cerebrovascular disease	52	63	58
Pneumonia	40	45	42
Injuries	53	24	39

Source: Ministry of Health.

Table 22.13
Deaths from Cancers That Are Amenable to Early Detection and Treatment Among Women, 1985–1988

Year	Breast Cancer	Cervical Cancer
1985	157	67
1986	158	92
1987	178	77
1988	170	97

Source: Ministry of Health.

and heart disease more frequently than cancer. Cardiovascular disease is also a high risk for women, more so than for men. Probably men are involved in work that is more accident-prone, and hence, deaths from injuries for males are more than double those for females. As society becomes more affluent and life more hectic, people also consume more animal fat in their diet. Fat-rich and meat-rich diets are linked to heart problems, some types of cancer, and cerebrovascular illnesses. There is evidence that there is an increase in Singapore women's suffering from breast and cervical cancer (Table 22.13). High blood pressure and diabetes are also on the increase among women.

SUMMARY AND CONCLUSIONS

Singapore is at the crossroads where modernization juxtaposes tradition. With its strategic position in Southeast Asia and its predominantly Asian population, Singapore residents need to preserve their cultural heritage and Oriental values. For progress and advancement, a tiny nation like Singapore has to go along with the tide and acquire knowledge of Western technology to ensure foreign investments, full employment, and economic stability. With manpower and womanpower as its only resource and a sex ratio of approximately 1:1, Singapore cannot afford to practice sex discrimination. Hence educational and occupational opportunities are based largely on merit. Female residents have improved their lot through better access to education and, in turn, to jobs with greater responsibilities and higher salaries.

However, covert discrimination may still work against females because of their biological function as mothers and also the traditional expectation of a woman to be a homemaker and caregiver. As many as 72.3 percent of married women stop working, citing child care, marriage, and household reasons for their decision to leave the work force (*Report on National Survey on Working Mothers*, 1986:1). Again, more working mothers suffer from burnout as a result of job-parent conflict (Aryce, 1991). Singapore is making rapid industrial progress and is facing labor shortage. At this moment it is relying on foreign workers to fill the vacancies. But Singapore should look to its own population to fill up the labor shortage. In order for a woman to fulfill her maternal responsibilities and to maximize her intellectual potential, both her family and her employer will have to lend a helping hand.

In more developed countries, the government and employers have recognized the need to change the corporate culture and have begun to bring changes in work design that accommodate the family demands of their employees. Schemes like flexible work schedules, parental leave, job sharing, and part-time work are introduced to attract capable females back into the work force. In recent years, to encourage female employees in the public sector in Singapore to stay in service and to have more children, part-time work has been offered as one of the many incentives to mothers with children below six years old. Attractive tax rebate is also enjoyed by working mothers with two or three children. Another right move is to allow mothers to take unpaid leave up to four years to attend to their young families. However, only women whose families do not need a second paycheck can afford to avail themselves of this scheme.

Young mothers are most appreciative of the sick–child leave scheme. This scheme enables working mothers in Singapore to claim 5 days of leave per child up to the third child. All these schemes indicate that the problems faced by mothers are gaining recognition and attention. However, the fact that all the schemes are directed at women, represents an undisguised belief that child care is primarily a woman's concern. What about the father? Some employers have responded to the call by the government to provide child-care centers as part of their welfare scheme. But many more, affordable child-care centers are needed to provide enough places to meet the demands of working mothers.

Women in Singapore can and should stand shoulder to shoulder with their male counterparts in the economic development of their nation. They have come a long way since the time when they came to Singapore as brides of immigrants or as maids. Equality in access to education has opened the door to a bright future of economic independence, social mobility, and competitive status in work.

There are right moves on the part of the government to boost further the economic power of females. It is now up to the women to set their priorities. The policymakers are mostly men, who believe that, given the necessary conditions to assuage the occasional hiccups present in the homes, women should have no problems in adroitly juggling their multiple roles as employee, wife, and mother.

Compared with many women in other Asian countries, Singapore females are considered very fortunate. They are treated with respect and can retain their femininity while holding high-status positions. They do not have to take to the street and picket government buildings in order to have their voices heard. Female residents are confident that tomorrow will be even better for them than today.

REFERENCES

Aryce, S. (1991, 28 September). Burnout in dual-earner couples. Paper presented at the forum "Work and Family: The Challenges Ahead."

Census of Population 1990: Advance Data Release. (1991). Singapore: Department of Statistics.

Chang, C. T. (1979). Nuptiality patterns among women of childbearing age. In Kuo, E.C.V., & Wong, A. K. (Eds.), *The Contemporary Family in Singapore* (pp. 117–41). Singapore: Singapore University Press.

Chang S. C., A. (1991). Women and health issues in Singapore. Paper presented at the Forty-ninth Annual Convention of the International Council of Psychologists, San Francisco.

Dead men shed no tears. *The Straits Times*, 10 November 1991, Life Section, p. 2.

Freedman, M. (1958). *Lineage Organization in Southeastern China.* London: Athlone Press.

Gopinathan, S. (1991). Higher education in Singapore: A study of policy, development, financing and governance, 1960–1990. Draft paper prepared for World Bank, National Institute of Education, Nanyang Technological University, Singapore.

Khor, S.Y.P. (1988). Boy-girl relationships and the Singapore adolescent: Some insights. Unpublished paper, Institute of Education, Singapore.

Kuo, E.C.Y. & Wong, A. K. (1979). Some observations on the study of family change in Singapore. In Kuo, E.C.Y., & Wong, A. K. (Eds.), *The Contemporary Family in Singapore* (pp. 3–16). Singapore: Singapore University Press.

Report on National Survey on Working Mothers. (1986). Singapore: Research Sections, Ministry of Community Development.

Saw, S. H., & Wong, A. K. (1981). *Youths in Singapore: Sexuality, Courtship and Family Values*. Singapore: Singapore University Press.

Sim, W. K. (1991). Education for equality in a changing society. *Singapore Journal of Education, 11* (2): 12–20.

Singapore 1991. (1991). Singapore: Publicity and Promotions Division, Ministry of Information and the Arts.

Singapore Council of Women's Organization. (1991, 28 September). Integration of work and family responsibilities—Redesigning work; redefining corporate concerns. Paper presented for the forum "Work and Family: The Challenges Ahead."

Tai, C. L. (1979). Divorce in Singapore. In Kuo, E.C.Y., & A. K. Wong, (Eds.), *The Contemporary Family in Singapore* (pp. 142–67). Singapore: Singapore University Press.

Wong, A. K. (1979). Women's status and changing family values. In Kuo, E.C.Y., & Wong, A. K. (Eds.), *The Contemporary Family in Singapore* (pp. 40–61). Singapore: Singapore University Press.

Yearbook of Statistics: Singapore 1990. (1991). Singapore: Department of Statistics.

23

South Africa, Republic of

Dap A. Louw and Anet E. Louw

INTRODUCTION

South Africa forms the southernmost part of the African continent. It borders several countries: Namibia, Botswana, Zimbabwe, Mozambique, and Swaziland. Completely enclosed by South African territory is Lesotho, a totally independent kingdom. Within the borders of South Africa one also finds the so-called independent Republics of Transkei, Bophuthatswana, Ciskei, and Venda. As these "independent republics" are the result of the apartheid policy, they are not recognized by any other country in the world.

South Africa is surrounded on three sides by ocean: the South Atlantic and southern Indian Oceans.

On the whole, South Africa has a healthy climate that favors outdoor living in all seasons. It has an average annual precipitation of 502 millimeters as against a world mean of 857 millimeters. The total surface area is 1,127,200 square kilometers (347,860 square miles).

Concerning the peoples of South Africa, the Bushmen (San) were there first. There is evidence to suggest that they entered Southern Africa about 1,500 years ago. Next to arrive were the Hottentots (Khoi), who were followed by the Negroid peoples. The Westernization of South Africa, however, dates from the first Dutch settlement at the Cape of Good Hope in 1652.

The total population of South Africa is nearly 40 million: about 1 million Asians, about 30 million Blacks, about 3 million so-called Coloreds, and about 5 million Whites.

OVERVIEW

There are mainly four reasons writing a chapter like this is not easy.

First, as a result of the apartheid system laws kept apart the different racial groups until about two years ago. Although most of these laws have been removed and apartheid will hopefully be destroyed by the time this book is published, the aftereffects remain, and the different racial groups still tend to be concentrated in specific areas and neighborhoods. The overall result is the tragedy that the different racial groups do not know much about each other. It is therefore a formidable task for a person from one race to write about other South Africans.

Second, not all the different groups in South Africa have written literature on their history, culture, and customs. This is especially true for the black groups. The result is that, for example, the development and delicate shades of meaning are not known or accessible to outsiders. Only in this century did some publications on this topic start to make their appearance—and they were mostly written by Whites.

Third, the black people of South Africa are in different stages of Westernization, and the white population is in separate stages of Africanization. The result is that it is very difficult, if not impossible, to describe a "typical" South African at this time. This is aggravated by the fact that, next to the different races mentioned, there are numerous ethnic groups, each with its own specific culture and resulting customs. For example, among black South Africans one of the ethnic groups is the Sotho, which again is divided in the North and South Sotho. Just like among white South Africans one finds, for example, Afrikaners, English-speaking South Africans, Portuguese, Greeks, and Jews from Europe.

Fourth, Ramphele and Boonzaier (1988) rightly state:

The issue of gender does not constitute an obvious element in the political discourse in South Africa. It is commonly felt that race relations form the core of the political debate and that concern about gender relationships is either irrelevant or overshadowed by the more pressing problems associated with relationships between different races, ethnic groups, cultures, tribes and so on. The issue of gender has been, and continues to be, a neglected topic. (P. 153)

Against the abovementioned background and because most black South Africans still have traditional roots, the present authors decided to use gender roles in the traditional black cultures as a starting point and basis, after which attention is paid to the white culture. More specifically, the traditional black cultures and the white culture should be regarded as the two extremes with many (mostly black) people lying on varying points on this continuum. It should be underlined, however, that the focus is mainly on information thought by the authors to be unique and/or interesting.

COMPARISONS BETWEEN MEN'S AND WOMEN'S GENDER ROLES DURING THE LIFE CYCLE

Infancy and Early Childhood

Although Van der Vliet (1974) implies that before the age of six years, few differences are evident in the early existence of boys and girls in the traditional black nations, some other authors indicate interesting variations in gender roles.

According to Mönnig (1967), among Pedi children a natural division occurs between the sexes. This difference is notable by the differences in clothing. Young boys usually wear loincloths, and their hair is usually shorn close to their heads. Young girls, on the other hand, wear a short string apron (*lebole*) in front around the loins and a triangular skin apron (*nthepana*) to cover the buttocks. Their hair is fashioned in a characteristic manner (*leetse*) in long, separate strings treated with fat and graphite. From an early age boys are expected to tend to the family's livestock. They start off by looking after the calves that remain in the kraals, but soon they join the other boys in herding the sheep and the goats and eventually the cattle. The young boy's education is left largely in the hands of his peers. The activities of his group are mostly controlled by the group of boys just older than he is. Similarly, Pedi girls have to start domestic duties early in life. These activities (grinding corn, fetching water and wood) are also performed communally, and older girls also control the activities of the younger group. The process of acculturation takes place through these activities: the boys acquire the essential knowledge of pastoralism, and the girls of agriculture. In this way they are introduced into crafts of their gender.

Although Zulu children of both sexes are also expected to do chores from an early age, Krige (1950) points out that traditionally Zulu children spend a lot of time playing games. Binns (1974:170) also comments on the "merry laughter and happy spirit of camaraderie" as they fulfill their duties. As in Western cultures, the boys engage in rougher games while the girls tend to indulge in the more feminine or housekeeping games. On the other hand, many play groups include children of both sexes, and they tend to share the same games and pastimes.

In the white culture the sex of a child still remains an important issue, although this seems to be more important in the lower socioeconomic classes, probably because of the (especially Afrikaner) viewpoint that the oldest son not only is the main heir but also is expected to take over the father's important role if he is no longer there. Among the lower socioeconomic classes there is even a belief among some that the sex of the child is an indication of the virility of the father: if the baby is a boy, the father's virility is no longer in question.

The sex of a child has a direct influence on the behavior of the parents, as they not only treat boys and girls differently but also manipulate the environment of the sexes in different ways. For instance, in South Africa pink is regarded as the appropriate color for a girl, with the result that not only is a baby girl usually dressed in pink clothes but her room has, for example, pink curtains and pink baby blankets. Blue is regarded as "the color for a boy."

As children grow older, their sex determines many other ways in which they will be treated. Baby girls are seen as more fragile and as belonging to the "weaker sex." They are also expected to be more ladylike. Boys are seen as tougher, and their behavior is reinforced for behaving in such a way. Phrases like "Boys don't cry" and "Don't be a sissy" illustrate that parents, especially fathers, tend to reinforce this macho role.

The toys given to the children also reinforce the different sex roles. Parents, for example, buy dolls and housekeeping toys for their daughters and cars and military toys for their sons. (During the twenty-year war South Africa was fighting in Namibia ''to protect the borders,'' most white South African boys had some military toy or another with which they fought their own war against black ''terrorists.'')

Just as in the United States of America and Europe, the South African mass media, especially television and books, reinforce sex roles. Most television programs are dominated by men who play the more important and stronger part, with women in the ''typical'' roles of mother or housewife or at least in a subordinate role. The same applies to children's books, where the boy is usually portrayed as the stronger sex, who is likely to rescue himself and the girl from some danger. The girl is usually portrayed (also in the illustrations) as the more passive and feminine one.

School Years

During the prepuberty years the child in the traditional black culture learns most of the social behavior that will be required of him or her as an adult (Van der Vliet, 1974). Boys engage in behavior very similar to that of same-age children of Western cultures. They fight for leadership and try to make an impression on girls, but they also acquire knowledge of the veld and its wildlife. As they grow older, their responsibilities increase. Games played during this stage are ideally suited to fit them for their future careers: these games not only train them to be courageous but also develop them to such a degree of physical fitness that, by the time full manhood is reached, they are able to stand up to amazing feats of hardship and endurance without complaint (Binns, 1974).

According to Van der Vliet (1974), the life of girls in the traditional black cultures does not change much in the years prior to puberty. Unlike a boy, a girl, for the most part, remains tied up with domestic duties. At first her main duty is nursemaid to her younger brothers and sisters, but gradually she learns all the other skills required to run her own home. Initially, her contributions are small. She is taught those techniques that match her strength—bringing small bundles of kindling, fetching small calabashes of water. Skills like grinding corn or maize, smearing walls and floors, and making fires are acquired gradually over this period. The girl is usually able to run a household long before puberty.

The onset of puberty is probably the most dramatic event in the developmental life cycle of the traditional black child. It is usually marked by a period of intensive ritualization aimed at integrating the child formally into the adult world (Van der Vliet, 1974).

Among many traditional tribes the boy's first nocturnal emission signals physical maturity (Binns, 1974; Krige, 1950; Van der Vliet, 1974). The Zulu mark the event with an extensive ritual, the *thomba*, in which the boy is given strengthening medicine and secluded in a hut and must observe food taboos and contact with women. A certain amount of instruction concerning sexual behavior is given, but in general the isolation period is uneventful. Seclusion is terminated after a ritual sacrifice of a beast or goat has been made to the ancestors. After feasting, singing, and dancing by the whole community, the boy is taken down to the river by his comrades where he is washed and given a new name by which he will be known for the rest of his life by people of his own age or younger. (Older people will still call him by his boyhood name, but should the younger ones not recognize his new status by using his new name, it would be considered abusive.) Hereafter the seclusion hut is freshly smeared, the boy receives new clothes, and, amid much singing, dancing, and beer drinking, he is reincorporated into the society as a mature man and may start courting girls.

Among the Lobedu and Tsonga the event is marked simply by treating the boy with medicine to strengthen and protect him. The Venda boy's puberty ceremony, *vhutumba vhutuka*, on the other hand, differs from others in that, on experiencing his first emission, a boy must wait until a number of boys reach the same stage before the rite takes place (Van der Vliet, 1974). The ritual also includes several days of physical hardening like immersion in icy river water. Boys are taught tribal etiquette and customs and also given sexual instruction. This rite is regarded as the first stage on their "journey to manhood," and they may indulge in "playful familiarities with girls" (Stayt, 1931). Among the Pedi, there is no social recognition of puberty for the boy. This is indicative of the Pedi conception of the importance of the procreative ability of women, while the fertility of men is accepted as a biological fact (Mönnig, 1967).

Puberty rites for girls are rites of passage underlining an important change of life. Although puberty ceremonies usually occur at the time of first menstruation, this is not invariably so. The Mpondo ceremony, *manthombisa*, for instance, must be held sometime between a girl's first menstruation and marriage. The Venda rite, *vhusha*, may be postponed until two or three girls have begun to menstruate, and they then go through the ceremony together (Van der Vliet, 1974).

For most tribes like the Pedi, Lobedu, the northern Tsonga clans, Zulu, and Cape Nguni, the puberty rites basically follow the same pattern (Van der Vliet, 1974), although the Pedi practice a simplified form with minimal community involvement. The Pedi ceremonies are regarded as a family affair in which the changing status of the girl is recognized, but she is not yet initiated into tribal status (Mönnig, 1967).

In some tribes (e.g., Pedi and Zulu) the girl reports the event of her first menstruation to her mother, while in some other tribes it is reported to the mother via an intermediary or indirectly by the girl's crying or running away and hiding (Binns, 1974; Mönnig, 1967; Van der Vliet, 1974). The initiation rite for most tribes includes a period of seclusion for the duration of the first menstrual period. During this period she must not be seen by the community, especially by men, although she spends her evenings singing, dancing, and feasting with fellow initiates. During the seclusion she may also be subjected to certain hardships. Among the Tsonga and Lobedu she is forced to sit in icy river water for long periods, and she may be beaten or forced to eat porridge without relishes (Lobedu) or scratched, pinched, and teased (Tsonga). Zulu and Bhaca girls are treated more leniently but must observe a taboo on sour milk. This is lifted at the end of the seclusion period when a goat is killed. Pedi girls are ritually bathed in the river before sunrise. Since menstruation is considered to be impure, she is taught to eat and drink from separate utensils during this period, lest she should contaminate others. Pedi, Lobedu, and Tsonga girls are given sex instruction during seclusion, including warnings on how to behave during the menstrual period. She is specifically warned not to have any relations with men during this period.

The end of the seclusion period is signified by a feast and beer drinking. The girl's emergence from childhood is recognized by a symbolic act—she is given new clothes (Pedi) or the clothes normally worn by married women (Zulu and, formerly, Bhaca), her head is shorn (Lobedu and Zulu), or something associated with the seclusion period is destroyed; for example, the grass floor of the seclusion hut is burned (Bhaca) or the grass ropes (skirt) worn by the girl during this period are burned (Zulu) (Binns, 1974; Van der Vliet, 1974).

White children in South Africa experience their middle childhood and adolescent years in very much the same way as their European and especially their American counterparts. Their first encounter with the ''real world'' is when they enter school. (Due to the apartheid system schooling is compulsory for Whites but not for Blacks.) At school gender differences are apparent in many ways. As the wearing of school uniforms is compulsory in South Africa, the difference between the sexes is more conspicuous than, for example, among American children: the girls look very neat and ladylike in their school dresses, while the boys wear shirts and trousers, which also give them a neat but not always ''with it'' appearance. The latter is emphasized by the fact that schoolboys in South Africa are not allowed to wear long hair.

In the classroom there is a difference in the attitude of the teachers toward the sexes. The girls are treated more ''softly'' than the boys, and even their punishment differs; for example, it is not uncommon for a boy to be caned for a (more serious) offense, while this type of punishment for girls is not permissible.

On the sports field gender differences are also apparent. Except for sports like gymnastics and tennis, which are equally popular among boys and girls, boys have ''their'' sports, like rugby, soccer, and cricket, while girls compete with each other in sports like netball. To illustrate: the authors' son, while in seventh grade in the United States of America during his parents' sabbatical, was chosen for the first soccer team of his school. Although he was very proud of that, he was also shocked that girls were also included in the team. He actually requested that this should never be revealed to his friends in South Africa, regardless of the fact that the star of their team was a girl!

Double standards regarding sexual expectations for the sexes, described in most international textbooks, also prevail in South Africa. The adolescent boy is regarded as the "hunter" and the girl as the "innocent victim," whose main task is to protect her virginity. The result is that girls who are promiscuous have bad reputations, while promiscuous boys are often regarded as sexual heroes by their peer group. These double standards are kept intact by the mass media as well as the parents, who reinforce the social expectation that women should be less interested than men in sexual activity.

One of the few research projects on gender roles in South Africa (Le Roux, 1989) tried to determine the view of 550 adolescent Afrikaner girls in eleventh grade on gender roles (Afrikaners are generally regarded as more conservative in most life spheres than white, English-speaking South Africans). Her main findings were:

- The attitudes of the girls toward sex roles are in the process of changing, more specifically, becoming more acceptable concerning the absence of differentiation of gender roles. This is especially true for career differentiation.
- There is a statistically significant correlation between the attitudes of the girls and the attitudes of their parents. In other words, the more traditional the parents are concerning sex roles, the more conservative the girls are, and vice versa. This clearly shows the already mentioned influence of parents on sex roles.
- The girls view the attitudes of their teachers toward sex roles as more conservative than their own. Le Roux comes to the conclusion that Afrikaans schools do not keep pace with the changes in the South African society regarding sex roles.
- Girls in girls' schools are less traditional toward gender roles than girls in coeducational schools.
- Daughters of full-time professional mothers are less traditional.
- Girls from a higher socioeconomic status are less traditional.

Le Roux strongly recommends that provision should be made in the training syllabi of teachers to accommodate sex-role socialization and that such programs presently used in countries like the United States of America and Great Britain be implemented in South African schools.

Young Adulthood

The most dramatic rite of passage for traditional Blacks occurs during the initiation schools, where the initiates undergo a collective status change surrounded by elaborate ceremonies (Van der Vliet, 1974). Like all transitional ceremonies the initiation ceremony is characterized by preparation and separation rites, followed by a period of seclusion and, finally, incorporation rites. The initiation is a sacred institution. The initiation of boys is taboo to all women and uninitiated children, and the initiation of girls is taboo to all men. Generally women know very little about male initiation, and men know little about female initiation, as everyone is extremely reticent in speaking about it (Mönnig, 1967). Van der Vliet (1974) reports that although the initiation rituals are considered of major importance in the life cycle of the individual, it is difficult to determine the significance of the institution for any particular group. Many ethnographers indicate that the initiation confers adulthood or manhood on the initiate without defining whether this means sexual, jural, social, religious, political, or economic adulthood or a combination of these statuses. Mönnig (1967), on the other hand, states that, for the Pedi at least, initiation is one of the cornerstones of the whole social and political organization. As an institution it is a means of investing the initiate with the status of citizenship of the community and participation in the social, political, and jural activities of the tribe, according to the sex of the initiate. Regarding the political and jural organization of the community, women are always under the guardianship of men, and the politicojural functions are performed by men, although the prinicipal wife of the chief has a position of importance in the political organization.

According to Van der Vliet (1974), the boy's initiation follows, in broad outline, a similar pattern in all tribes. In preparation for the opening of initiation school, boys often spend time together: the Lobedu boys spend a fortnight out in the veld, learning songs; the South Sotho boys meet daily, going out with the cattle and returning at night, collecting firewood, making ropes for the lodge, and learning a number of secret songs, while Pedi boys must spend this preparatory period working for the chief. In preparation for the school the fathers of the Cape Nguni initiates kill a goat, while among the Xhosa and Mfenga the boy is given meat from the right foreleg. This practice is said to prevent the boy from going mad or dying during the initiation.

The separation stage is characterized by a physical separation of the boys from the rest of the community. Usually a lodge is built in a secluded place, some distance from the village. A symbolic act usually precedes the separation of the initiate from his former state; for example, some tribes shave the boy's head, while others hold a ritual killing and a feast. A custom commonly associated with male initiation is circumcision. This operation finally separates the boy from his childhood. Often, specific reference is made to this fact; for instance, after the cut, the boy is told to say, "I am a man." Other tribes (e.g., South Sotho) are more understanding, and cries are drowned by the loud singing of onlookers.

After circumcision, the wound is usually treated by medicines varying from healing leaves to antibiotic cream, brandy, and paraffin in recent years. The initiates are then taken to the lodge of seclusion, where they spend between two to three months secluded from normal community life, although the degree of isolation varies among the tribes. Besides this physical separation their special state is further emphasized by numerous taboos and observances: in various tribes the initiates' bodies are painted white; often a special language or special words for everyday objects and actions are used, and contact with women is forbidden or discouraged.

A feature characteristic of all initiation schools is the subjection of the initiates to a number of hardships and ordeals. Beatings, unsavory food, little drinking water, uncomfortable sleeping conditions, and bathing in icy rivers (traditionally the schools are held in winter) are some of the ordeals most commonly encountered. Sometimes this severe treatment can even lead to the death of an initiate. His death, however, is not publicly mourned, which suggests the boy they had known was "dead" anyway and the "man" had not been born yet.

Another important feature of the initiation schools is the formal teaching given by the tribesmen during the seclusion period. The content of the material, however, varies among the tribes: some boys receive sex instruction, while others learn secret formulas and songs that are used as passwords in establishing the individual's identity as an initiated tribesman when traveling among strangers. The Sotho groups favor teachings of a nationalistic content: tribal loyalty and values and the rights and obligations of citizenship are stressed. Important pastimes are hunting and dancing, of which the latter is often quite spectacular.

The termination of the period of seclusion is marked by rites releasing the boy from his marginal status. The boys bathe ritually to wash off the white clay, after which they are smeared with red ocher (except the Lobedu). Their heads are again shaved (South Sotho, Lobedu, Venda, Tsonga, and Pedi), and they are given new clothes (Pedi, Tswana, Tsonga, Bomvana, Thembu, Mpondomise, Mfengu, and Xhosa). A final symbol of termination of their boyhood is the burning of the seclusion hut and its contents. The retreating boys are forbidden to look back as their past is burned behind them.

The initiates are now ready to be incorporated into the community. They are generally received with feasting and celebration. In many cases, though, the boys do not return to their homesteads immediately. Bomvana boys have to spend three or four days in the kraal of the "father" of the school; Pedi youths spend ten days in the royal kraal, where they are reminded of their new duties and responsibilities; Venda boys must spend six days working for the chief before they return home.

Although the boy is now reincorporated into the community and his new status is recognized, he is not necessarily regarded as being completely adult in all spheres of life. He must undergo another session in order to attain the full status of manhood. The outstanding difference in the conception of the roles of men and women appears with this last session for boys. Girls do not undergo this final process of initiation. During the last session the boys are incorporated into the society of men. Here they attain full politicojural status and a strong bond of solidarity, and mutual cooperation is created, which is often a lifelong commitment (Mönnig, 1967).

This last session usually occurs a year or two after the first session. Generally it is a repetition of the previous rites but is not as formal or as harsh. The lodge is usually much closer to the village, and the boys are allowed much more freedom and also have a greater variety of food. During the school the initiates again receive formal instruction and sing and repeat formulas. With the Tswana this is usually accompanied by many painful forms of discipline (Schapera,

1940). For the Tswana the school is terminated when the boys have successfully performed a task as a regiment (unit), after which they are regarded as men and are free to marry. The Pedi perform a ceremony in which a pole, topped by a woven grass bird, representing the regiment, is planted by the boys near the tribal fire in the chief's gathering place. This signifies the formal incorporation of the members of the regiment. After the announcement, "On this day you are men," their new status is officially recognized (Mönnig, 1967). This, on the other hand, does not necessarily mean that the young man has reached full adulthood—this is attained only upon marriage.

Among many of the tribes (the Lobedu, Venda, Pedi, South Sotho, and Tswana) the scope and size of the girl's initiation school resemble those of the boys' circumcision lodges (Van der Vliet, 1974). In some tribes the schools are closely linked with the school held for boys of the same age. For example, the Tswana initiate a girls' regiment shortly after the boys' regiment is formed. They also share the same name; the Lobedu girls' initiation (*byali*) takes place at the same time and in conjunction with the boys' *buchvera*; the Pedi girls' *byale* starts at the close of the boys' *bogwera* and also brings a new women's regiment into being, while the Venda's *domba* is a combined school for boys and girls.

The schools vary in their duration and could last anything from one month (Tswana and Pedi) to one (Lobedu) or two years (Venda). Special areas are assigned for the seclusion huts. Preparatory rites are usually performed in many of the tribes: their girls' hair is shaved, they receive special clothing, their bodies are smeared with red ocher, and they are treated with protective medicines.

A rite similar to the circumcision of the boys is performed. South Sotho girls may undergo some physical operation where the hymen is broken; the Lobedu girl is given a tiny cut above the clitoris. Tswana and Pedi girls do not undergo a specific operation but have rites imitating circumcision: the girl lies under a blanket, and a knife is pressed between her legs; although she is not actually injured, she does cry out in fright, and to enhance further the realistic nature of circumcision, the women who perform the "operation" emerge with their hands covered with red plant juices to simulate blood (Mönnig, 1967). This rite finally separates the girls from their previous status.

During the period of seclusion girl initiates must, like the boys, observe certain taboos and are subjected to certain hardships and ordeals, but these are less severe than those imposed upon male initiates. Singing and dancing are important in girls' initiation schools. During this period they receive formal instruction on the work and duties of women—domestic, agricultural, and marital, especially their relationship with men. They are told to respect all men and are also instructed in sexual matters. In some instances girls have to assist one another to elongate, through continued stretching, the labia minora, which is said to ensure greater sexual gratification for men (Mönnig, 1967). They are also taught special songs and formulas.

Toward the conclusion of the period of seclusion the girls bathe ritually, they are formed into a regiment, their hair is shaved, and they receive new clothes.

Their physical maturity is generally acknowledged, and they are regarded as being fully initiated into the tribe. They are now entitled to marry.

Among the white population of South Africa one of the prominent gender differences of young adulthood centers around career choice. In the past a man's choice of a career was regarded as more important than a woman's since it determined both his and his family's status (Thom, 1991). A woman's career was seen as something to do before she married. Over the last decade or two, however, important changes in career possibilities for women in South Africa have been taking place as a result of changes like the woman's status in the husband-wife relationship, changes in the family and in society, greater financial needs, and more support systems for the working woman. Nowadays more young girls in South Africa are undergoing tertiary training and becoming career women before marriage and are thus marrying later. More women are also returning to the working world after the birth of their children than in the past.

More young female adults are now entering occupations that were previously reserved for men, for example, engineering. Women, however, are still a minority in many occupations like medicine, law, and engineering.

The choice of a career in South Africa is thus still influenced by the traditional gender roles. According to research by Gerdes (see Thom, 1991) it appeared that the career choice for males was predominantly in favor of professions needing skilled labor (e.g., carpenters, electricians, mechanics, and engineers), while the career choice of females was predominantly in favor of the service professions (e.g., teaching, nursing, and social work). An interesting finding of the Human Sciences Research Council in Pretoria was that the reason females do not often choose certain professional and technical occupations is not because they lack the necessary skills and abilities but rather because they are not socialized enough to see that such occupations are open to them (see Thom, 1991).

Although career choice differences between the sexes are diminishing in South Africa, a man's role is still very much seen as primarily that of breadwinner, and a woman's role is seen as a partner and mother. Her pursuance of a career is thus perceived as of secondary importance. Discrimination based on gender is also the order of the day. For example, although much more than 50 percent of all teachers in South Africa are female, less than 10 percent of all school principals are female. Women are also underrepresented at South African universities (CSD Bulletin, 1992). Male academics constitute 71 percent of the national academic population. At the universities of the North, Natal, Orange Free State, Potchefstroom, Rhodes, and Stellenbosch, between 77 percent and 81 percent of the academic staff are male. At Medunsa, Vista, and Unisa between 41 percent and 39 percent of the academics are women. Women seem to be concentrated at the lower levels of university hierarchies. In other words, they are underrepresented not only in absolute terms but also in terms of occupying the well-paid and prestigious positions in university structures. The University of the North has a single woman professor, and the highly regarded Rhodes University has not one!

Women constitute 61 percent of all junior lecturers in the country, 44 percent of lecturers, 22 percent of senior lecturers, 17 percent of associate professors, and 5 percent of professors.

UDASA, the mouthpiece of the Union of Democratic Staff Associations, cites several reasons for this:

- Women entered the academic world later—during the 1960s—than men. State regulations also curbed the employment of women at some universities.

- Overt discrimination against women continues in the form of differential conditions of service for men and married women. Married women, for instance, are denied a housing subsidy and have unequal access to pension funds.

- The presence or absence of university child-care facilities has a strong impact on a woman's ability to progress in her academic career and to manage a family at the same time. Maternity leave was not available in most universities until the 1980s.

- Many women bear greater loads of teaching and administration and therefore have less time for research and to study for higher degrees, which are widely seen as important bases for promotion.

- The importance of a department's culture—the way different people are treated and the expectations that exist below the surface—is often overlooked in understanding power relations among academics. Many women are of the opinion that there is a "male culture" in their departments.

- Some women do not actively seek promotion, because they are already financially secure.

Adulthood

Initiation for traditional black South Africans can be viewed as instrumental in the defining of roles, statuses, and social relationships. Despite these important functions, initiation does not confer instant adulthood in all social roles—it mostly is regarded as a necessary step to later acceptance into complete adult status. Marriage and parenthood in many cases confer final adult status (Van der Vliet, 1974).

Marriage among the Zulus, for instance, can be regarded as a rite of passage for the couple concerned, as both are transferred from the status of the unmarried to that of the married. For the girl this is a double transition. She has to loosen herself from her own group and be incorporated into the group of her husband. During this transition certain rites are imposed: separation rites (e.g., the wearing of a veil); seclusion rites (she is secluded for the greater part of the marriage ceremonies, and her behavior is generally quiet and restrained); and finally a series of aggregation rites by means of which she is incorporated into her husband's group. The Pedi regard the marriage ceremonies as stages in a legal act, not as religious rites. Marriage is not considered the shedding of former status and acquiring a completely new one, and therefore no rite of preparation, purification, or seclusion is imposed (Mönnig, 1967). Marriage, however, does confer an advanced status on the couple in terms of an increase in the powers, obligations, and duties already conferred on them. Attaining guardianship over the bride (who was acquired by the communal property of the group) entitles the groom to powers over the properties of the group. This gives him full legal status within the group. The groom thus attains full adulthood. The bride's status changes from mature girl to tribal initiate to woman. She, however, attains full adulthood only with the birth of her first child, when, with the legal powers she attains as a mother over her child, she acquires a certain standing within the group and also becomes entitled to partake of the possessions of the group (Mönnig, 1967).

Generally marriage is not an individual affair but a group concern where a relationship between two groups of relatives is legalized (Krige, 1950; Mönnig, 1967). This legal act involves the transfer of certain marriage goods from the relatives of the groom to the relatives of the bride. In return for this presentation the bride is publicly transferred by her relatives to the place of her in-laws. The contraction of marriage has broad similarities in most of the black societies and is based on three basic marriage rules. First, a woman may have only one spouse while a man may have more than one wife if he so wishes. Second, a woman should join her husband after marriage, either at his own homestead or at that of his father's or brothers'. Third, marriage is brought about by the transfer of bridewealth from the agnatic group of the groom to that of the bride. These three rules have important implications: that polygamy is allowed, that patrivirilocal residence is ensured, and that certain vital rights over a woman are transferred from her father or guardian as representative of her family, to her husband and his family (Preston-Whyte, 1974). This transfer has important implications since it decides the filiation of children and influences the interpersonal relationships between husband and wife, between the spouses and their respective affines, and between the affinal groups linked by marriage.

Traditionally relationships between parents-in-law and children-in-law are quite formal. The relationship between the father-in-law and his daughter-in-law, for example, is characterized by bashfulness, respect, and a revered psychological distance on the part of the daughter-in-law (Finlayson, 1978). She is expected to respect her new home by refraining from addressing her father-in-law directly (only by means of a mediator) and by avoiding the use of words containing sounds related phonetically or morphonetically to his name (Department of Linguistics, 1983). This results in using substitute words, which are transmitted from generation to generation of women. This not "only saves the new bride the trouble of inventing a whole new vocabulary all by herself, but also ensures the maintenance of status and dependency relationships between men and women across generations" (Louw-Potgieter, 1991: 331). The relationship between father-in-law and son-in-law is generally more congenial.

The traditional maternal attitudes of love and tenderness are greatly absent in the mother-in-law's relationship with her daughter-in-law (Reader, 1966). This relationship is often characterized by a certain critical sternness and even hostility.

This is mostly due to the young wife's need to prove to the mother-in-law that she is prepared to work and cooperate with her new descent group. The adjustment could be quite trying for the young wife, for not only does she have to contend with an often unreasonable and demanding mother-in-law, but also her husband has to side with his mother as long as he lives in the parental kraal. Certain speech avoidances are also evident—mother-in-law and daughter-in-law address each other not by their names, but in kinship terms. In time, however, the relationship seems to relax, and the husband's mother assumes the role of mother to his wife (Jackson, 1976; Reader, 1966).

Reader (1966) reports that among the Makhanya tribe no trace of mother-in-law/son-in-law avoidances could be found and that in fact the wife's mother shares the same close relationship her husband bears with his son-in-law. Jackson (1976) and Raum (1973), on the other hand, report a formal relationship between mother-in-law and son-in-law, characterized by a number of avoidances such as no direct communication and using kinship terms rather than their names.

A woman is subjected to the authority of her husband; she has to respect and obey him. The relationship relaxes in time and becomes more spontaneous (Jackson, 1976). The transfer of the wife to her husband and his agnatic group implies that he has certain rights over her. These rights include rights as a wife and as a mother (Preston-Whyte, 1974). Rights as a wife include rights of sexual access and rights of labor, both domestic and in the fields. Rights as a mother imply that the husband and his lineage acquire legal control over all children born to a woman unless the marriage is dissolved, in which case the bridewealth is returned. The transfer of the childbearing capacities of the woman to her husband is so complete that whoever fathers her children, her husband is regarded as their father (an impotent man may, for example, ask one of his kinsmen to father his children) (Preston-Whyte, 1974).

In a polygamous family the grading of wives is of great importance. Senior wives wield authority over junior wives, while children's rights and social position are influenced by the status of their mother as cowife. Therefore a man's status is determined not only by the place of his father in the descent group but also, if his father is a polygamist, by the status of his mother within the compound family (Preston-Whyte, 1974).

The main role of a husband toward his wife implies the duties of guardianship, provision, support, procreation, and kindness, while the wife's main role toward her husband implies cooperation, housekeeping and cultivation, nursing, hospitality, and consultation (Reader, 1966).

The role of the father toward his children is provider. Traditionally his relationship toward his children is strict authoritarian who expects complete obedience (Jackson, 1976). Generally he plays an unimportant role in their upbringing (Reader, 1966). The mother's role toward her children is nurturer and educator (in conjunction with the grandmother). Generally her relationship with her children is characterized by warmth, intimacy, and spontaneity (Jackson, 1976).

Adulthood in the white population in South Africa also centers around the work role and the family role. The white family is monogamous and is structurally a nuclear family. According to Gerdes et al. (1988), three types of family systems occur: the traditional system, in which the husband is the only breadwinner and the undisputed head of the family; the companionate system, in which the husband is the main breadwinner and the head of the family but the wife is consulted more often and there is greater cooperation between marriage partners, as when the wife supports her husband in a subordinate but complementary role; and the egalitarian system, in which the husband and wife each has a career, in which authority is shared on the basis of equality, and in which there is a more equitable sharing of roles regarding domestic and parenting functions.

A South African study, however, indicates that inequalities of role division with regard to parenthood exist (Gerdes & Van Ede, 1991). From a comparison of the perceptions of role division by men and women, it appeared that women performed approximately twice as many tasks as men in the rearing of children from birth to age 12. The greatest difference occurred in the physical care of children, and the smallest difference occurred in discipline and control. It was obvious that men's perceptions of the extent of their contribution to the fulfillment of parental tasks differed from those of women: men felt they did more than what the women believed they did. Another finding was that similar differences applied whether the woman was a full-time housewife or employed.

An aspect of South African life where gender seems to play an important role is the custody of children in divorce cases. Regardless of the fact that international data show that a father could be an equally good parent for young children, Hahlo (1985:391), a well-known South African jurist, notes that "as a rule the custody of young . . . children is given to the mother." The reason for this could be found in a statement by a South African judge: "There is no one who quite takes the place of the child's mother. There is no person whose presence and . . . affection can give a child the sense of security and comfort that a child desires from his own mother" (Cumes & Lambiase, 1987:123). At present, however, South African courts seem slowly to be moving away from this viewpoint and rather give custody to the best parent, regardless of sex.

Old Age

While marriage and parenthood confer full adult status on the individual, in many tribes full political, jural, and religious status is attained only after middle age (Van der Vliet, 1974). Krige and Krige (1943:123) describe this as follows:

The bride is of small consequence even in her own home; for long she serves an apprenticeship under the control of her mother-in-law, who also takes her child out of her hands and bathes and feeds it. Only as an old woman does she reach the peak of her life. With a man the position is no different. After the initiation he has a kind of legal status. After marriage he advances a further stage, but in his marital relations and as a father he is a child dependent upon advice from his elders. In public activities, such as the courts, he sits and listens, but the old men may entrust a case to him and his age-mates to teach them a sense of responsibility.

Traditionally among the black peoples of South Africa, advancing age brings increased power and authority to both men and women. Aging brings the prospect of new roles that generally suit the individual's capacities. For the man, advancing age means obtaining respect. Young people generally accept his judgments, experience, and authority. For the woman, middle age marks a period of increased influence in both domestic and community affairs (Van der Vliet, 1974).

Brindley (1985, 1986a,b) examined the role of old women in traditional Zulu culture. Old age in Zulu culture seems to be primarily linked with physiological change, like the attainment of menopause (the absence of menstrual periods is seen to confer purity upon the woman). Old age is secondarily associated with the acquisition of new roles (parent-in-law and grandparent) and accumulated knowledge and experience. For a woman, the positions of mother-in-law and paternal grandmother, in particular, enable her to wield considerable power and influence. The Zulu grandmother plays an indispensable and stabilizing role in the families of her sons and daughters. Because of her kinship position, knowledge, age, and ceremonial purity, she is involved in the major stages of procreation, in every aspect of the development of the young, and her influence continues undiminished during adolescence. She is, for instance, intimately involved in ceremonies demarcating adolescents' puberty, coming of age, and preparation for marriage.

Due to acculturation, however, the position of elderly people within the society is changing rapidly. Aging in any society constitutes the easing into new roles in each successive phase of life. Generally, the main problem in modern society is thought to be the role loss associated with retirement from the mainstream of adult life. Moller (1990:4) states the following: "Although retirement may be a typically modern problem, traditional societies moving into the urban-industrial world are not spared the modern dilemmas of growing old. Traditional society will have to decide whether to discard or reshape existing aging patterns in the process of becoming modern." According to Moller, such decisions can be painful, but one solution to the problem could be "educare" programs, which aim to restore the dignity of the traditional senior female role by infusing it with a new meaning for urban-industrial society. This means that grandmothers are trained as child minders to meet the requirements of the modern, Western educational system in meeting the four basic needs of children: health and hygiene, physical development, social-emotional security, and mental and moral development. Theoretically, therefore, senior black women could be assisted to regain the respect that was their due in traditional society. Other communities have started reading and storytelling programs at their local libraries in an effort to demonstrate new roles for the elderly in their townships, since many older adults feel that their traditional role in the black culture has been eroded (Hildebrandt, 1991).

Whereas the aging of the black population in South Africa follows the Third World pattern (5 percent of black South Africans are expected to be in the 60 + cohorts by the year 2020) (Moller, 1990), the aging of the white population follows that of the Western world (the growth rate for people older than 65 is higher than the growth rate for the population as a whole). Whereas traditional Zulu society defines old age in terms of roles or physiological changes, traditional Xhosa society determines age in adult males in terms of initiation associations, resulting in three adult male categories: young men, junior men, and senior or old men. Adult females are organized primarily according to the length of their married status and the number of children born in wedlock. This results in four adult female age categories: young women, junior women, women in the middle, and senior or old women (Van Eeden, 1991). Among Western societies chronological age is generally regarded as an indication of old age. The United Nations and the World Health Organization both define the elderly as people older than 65. The South African Elderly Persons Act of 1967 states that women of 60 and older and men of 65 and older are elderly (Raubenheimer, 1991).

Throughout the human life span the mortality rate for males is higher. For example, although at present 105 white boys are born for every 100 white girls in South Africa, above age 65 there are only 71 males for every 100 white females (Republic of South Africa, 1988). The same trend is found in other population groups. The possibility of an elderly man's remarrying is also greater than the possibility of an elderly woman's remarrying.

Few comparative studies on sex-role identity in adulthood and old age have been done. What information there is, however, indicates that a change does not occur in certain aspects of masculinity and femininity. Neugarten and Gutman (1958) found in their comprehensive study of middle age that women become more accepting of their aggressive and egocentric tendencies, whereas men become more accepting of their protective and affiliative tendencies. These changes become conspicuous during the empty nest stage, and they increase particularly during the man's retirement stage (Sinnott, 1977). These findings could be applicable to South Africans as well. Due to a mainly patriarchal society, where the male is seen as the head of the household and the major breadwinner and the female is nurturer and housekeeper, the role of the male changes drastically after retirement, while the female role continues. Raubenheimer (1991) reports, however, that happy marriages that have withstood the test of time often achieve a partnership style in which the traditional sex roles are less important.

Activities for the aged are usually group-related, and both men and women take part. Activities include handiwork, exercising, fund-raising, and excursions. The elderly of all population groups may belong to various clubs like seniors' clubs, luncheon clubs, and church clubs. A study conducted by Moller and Nkosi (1992) found that black seniors in particular benefit from excursions organized by luncheon clubs. Considering that black township dwellers reported depressed well-being in response to quality of life studies conducted during the past decade, these excursions provide men and women with a special event to which to look forward. These outings are learning experiences that contribute to individual growth, improved self-esteem and self-confidence, and a generally enhanced sense of well-being.

SUMMARY AND CONCLUSIONS

The introduction of Western culture has influenced traditional culture to a large extent, with the result that black children currently grow up in a distinctly different cultural milieu and are trained toward distinctly different adult roles. This changing milieu already affects the preschool child. Traditionally girls and boys learned their respective roles by imitating and observing their parents in the house or in the fields. Currently, with both parents often working away from home, boys and girls are cared for by grandparents or other caregivers. The appearances and behavior of the children, especially those in the city areas, are also changing. Both boys and girls tend to dress like their white counterparts while their toys are also Western or modifications thereof.

The onset of school age brings a dramatic change between the old and the new in both the method and content of training. (Although schooling is not compulsory for Blacks in South Africa, many black parents do recognize its importance and send their children to school.) Boys, for instance, enter school at an age when they normally would have started tending to cattle. Initiation school has to be postponed or held at a time that would not interfere with their schooling. In other cases initiation schools are discouraged by either missionary or government action or by the attitude of the tribesmen themselves. For instance, being a schoolboy or working in town may be regarded as a confirmation of adulthood by many tribes (Schapera, 1940; Hammond-Tooke, 1962). Entering the work force also means that a young man may become independent at an earlier age than during more traditional times.

Schooling also means that a girl is withdrawn from her traditional role as caregiver for the younger brothers and sisters and that of help to the mother. Entering the work force after schooling could mean a further disengagement from her traditional role. The traditional moral values usually transmitted by their mothers and grandmothers have greatly disappeared, while school and church have failed to provide the children with adequate cultural mores. The result is an alarmingly high incidence of teenage pregnancies and illegitimacy. Traditionally sexual instruction was given during the initiation schools. Intercrural intercourse was allowed, and couples were careful to stick to the rules so that no defloration took place. Girls were generally inspected by the older women of the tribe, and should defloration be discovered, ridicule, isolation, and fines could be the result.

Urbanization and Westernization have also influenced economic life. In tribal society the family was the unit of production and consumption and was largely self-contained. Most of the roles were age- and gender-specific. Modernization has brought about a less formal division of labor within the family and has made its members less dependent upon each other (Dubb, 1974).

Westernization has not only changed the economic role of the family but also contributed toward the loosening of kinship relationships and the decline of the patrilineally extended household. These factors have important consequences for family life. Parents have to accept educational, economical, and emotional responsibilities and functions that were once performed by a group of kin. New patterns of behavior between parents and children evolved to meet the new demands. These include close cooperation between husband and wife and consultation about money matters and children's upbringing. Although this may seem the ideal situation, which could benefit not only modern family life but also the aspirations of professional and middle-class women, such a break from traditional values is not accepted by all men. Frequently families are under strain because of the unresolved conflict between the husband's partriarchal conduct and his wife's role as wage earner, manager of the household budget, and educator of the children. Men, including educated men, seem to resist the emancipation of women that modern conditions promote (Dubb, 1974).

The disappearance of apartheid, where the whites with their Western culture had a powerful impact on the traditional cultures, means that black leaders from a more traditional background will lead the country. Whether this will have a diminishing effect on the Westernization process and a resulting strengthening of traditional customs remains a question to be answered.

REFERENCES

Binns, C. T. (1974). *The Warrior People. Zulu Origins, Customs and Witchcraft.* Cape Town: Howard Timmins.

Brindley, M. (1985). Old women in Zulu culture: The old woman and childbirth. *South African Journal of Ethnology, 8*: 98–108.

———. (1986a). The role of old women in Zulu culture: Old women and child-nurture. *South African Journal of Ethnology, 9*: 26–31.

———. (1986b). The role of old women in Zulu culture: The old woman and adolescence. *South African Journal of Ethnology, 9*: 120–28.

CSD Bulletin. (1992, May). *University Discrimination Entrenched*, p. 3.

Cumes, J. W., & Lambiase, E.A.A. (1987). Legal and psychological criteria for the determination of custody in South Africa: A review. *South African Journal of Psychology, 17*: 119–26.

Department of Linguistics, Unisa. (1983). *Guide 2 for LNG100-5.* Pretoria: Unisa.

Dubb, A. A. (1974). The impact of the city. In Hammond-Tooke, W. D. (Ed.), *The Bantu-Speaking Peoples of South Africa* (pp. 441–68). London: Routledge & Kegan Paul.

Finlayson, R. (1978). A preliminary survey of hlonipha among the Xhosa. *Taalfasette, 24*: 17–21.

Gerdes, L. C., Moore, C., Ochse, R., & Van Ede, D. (1988). *The Developing Adult*, 2d ed. Pretoria: Butterworths.

Gerdes, L. C., & Van Ede, D. M. (1991). Adulthood. In Louw, D. A. (Ed.), *Human Development*. Pretoria: HAUM.

Hahlo, H. R. (1985). *The S.A. Law of Husband and Wife*. Cape Town: Juta.

Hammond-Tooke, W. D. (1962). *Bhaca Society: A People of the Traskeian Uplands, South Africa*. Cape Town: Oxford University Press.

Hildebrandt, E. (1991). Duduza self-help project. *Thambodala*, 2 (2): 7.

Jackson, A. O. (1976). 'n Ondersoek na die ontwikkelingsprosesse en -probleme by die Xolo van Suid-Natal. Ph.D. diss., Rand Afrikaans University, Johannesburg.

Krige, E. J. (1950). *The Social System of the Zulus*. Pietermaritzburg: Shuter & Shooter.

———, & Krige, J. D. (1943). *The Realm of a Rain Queen*. London: International African Institute.

Le Roux, T. (1989). Geslagsrolsosialisering en adolessente dogters se siening van geslagsrolle. Ph.D. diss., Rand Afrikaans University, Johannesburg.

Louw-Potgieter, J. (1991). Language and identity. In Foster, D., & Louw-Potgieter, J. (Eds.), *Social Psychology in South Africa* (pp. 317–44). Johannesburg: Lexicon.

Moller, V. (1990). A role for black seniors in educare: A community assessment. *Cooperative research program on aging*. Pretoria: HSRC.

Moller, V., & Nkosi, L. (1992). The benefit of excursions for seniors: A consumer survey. *Thambodala*, 3 (1):4.

Mönnig, H. O. (1967). *The Pedi*. Pretoria: Van Schaik.

Neugarten, B. L., & Gutman, D. L. (1958). Age-sex roles in middle age: A thematic apperception study. *Psychological Monographs*, 72.

Preston-Whyte, E. (1974). Kinship and marriage. In Hammond-Tooke, W. D. (Ed.), *The Bantu-Speaking Peoples of South Africa* (pp. 177–203). London: Routledge & Kegan Paul.

Ramphele, M., & Boonzaier, E. (1988). The position of African women: Race and gender in South Africa. In Boonzaier, E., & Sharp, J. (Eds.), *South African Keywords. The Uses and Abuses of Political Concepts* (pp. 153–66). Cape Town: David Philip.

Raubenheimer, J. R. (1991). Late adulthood. In Louw, D. A. (Ed)., *Human Development*. Pretoria: HAUM.

Raum, O. F. (1973). *The Social Functions of Avoidances and Taboos Among the Zulu: Monographien zur Völlerkunde*. Berlin: Walter de Gruyter.

Reader, D. H. (1966). *Zulu Tribe in Transition*. Manchester: Manchester University Press.

Republic of South Africa. (1988). *Demographic Trends in South Africa*. Cape Town: Government Printer.

Schapera, I. (1940). *Married Life in an African Tribe*. London: Faber & Faber.

Sinnott, J. D. (1977). Sex-role inconsistency, biology, and successful aging. *Gerontology*, 17: 459–64.

Stayt, H. A. (1931). *The Bavenda*. London: Oxford University Press.

Thom, D. P. (1991). Adolescence. In Louw, D. A. (Ed.), *Human Development*. Pretoria: HAUM.

Van der Vliet, V. (1974). Growing up in traditional society. In Hammond-Tooke, W.

D. (Ed.), *The Bantu-Speaking Peoples of Southern Africa* (pp. 211–34). London: Routledge & Kegan Paul.

Van Eeden, J. A. (1991). Aging and seniority in a rural Xhosa community. *Thambodala*, 2 (2): 8.

24

The Soviet Union and Post-Soviet Era

Harold Takooshian,
Anie Sanentz Kalayjian, and
Edward Melkonian

INTRODUCTION

On 25 December 1991, the Union of Soviet Socialist Republics (USSR) suddenly and officially ceased to exist. During its 74 years, this nation grew into the world's largest, occupying one-sixth of the planet's entire land surface. Its population of 291 million was the third largest on earth. It grew from an underdeveloped nation in 1917 into a world leader, uniting 15 diverse republics under one banner—Russia, Armenia, Azerbaijan, Byelorussia, Estonia, Georgia, Kazakhstan, Kirghizia, Latvia, Lithuania, Moldavia, Tajikstan, Turkmenestan, Ukraine, Uzbekistan. Russia was by far the largest of the republics, containing 72 percent of the union's territory and 52 percent of its population. Since 1991, these fifteen republics have become fully independent—with even more fractionation likely in the coming decade, as at least some of the former USSR's 50 ''autonomous regions'' and ethnic enclaves similarly press for sovereignty from their republics. This would make the former USSR a region of fragmentation at precisely the time when nearby Western Europe is rapidly coalescing.

What were gender roles for men and women in the closing years of the Soviet era? Equally important, what is the likely future of post-Soviet gender roles now that this communist nation has so irrevocably dissolved? For lack of a better term, this chapter uses the term *post-Soviet* to describe this region of 15 republics that are now independent but that share a common Soviet heritage of up to 74 years.

OVERVIEW

Few nations so early and fully recognized the legal equality of women and men as did the USSR in 1917. Still, the picture here is mixed. Despite de jure egalitarianism, Soviet-era men and women experienced de facto inequality in many ways. From the outset, it is useful to note here four general points about gender roles in the Soviet and post-Soviet era.

First, the 15 republics are remarkably varied in culture, including gender roles. Contrast the six Muslim republics in the east (collectively known as Turkestan), now swinging toward religious fundamentalism, the two southern Caucasus republics of Armenia and Georgia with a Christian heritage going back 1,500 years, the three radical Baltic republics to the north (Estonia, Latvia, Lithuania), and the westward-looking Slavic republics (Russia, Byelorussia, Moldavia, Ukraine). To discuss Soviet gender roles is to recognize the wide variations within this diverse region.

Second, there is a huge gap between the official and unofficial status of Soviet women and men. Judging by official sources, the USSR is a paradise for those who value equality for women and men. Yet the schism between theory and practice existing in most nations is uniquely wide in the Soviet Union. In the official picture, Article 35 of the All-Union Soviet constitution (adopted in 1977) guarantees:

Women and men have equal rights in the U.S.S.R. Realization of these rights is insured by affording women equal access with men to education and professional training, equal opportunities in employment, wages and promotion, in social, political, and cultural activities, and by special labor and health protection measures for women; by providing conditions enabling mothers to work; by legal protection, material, and moral support for mothers and children, including paid leaves and other benefits for expectant mothers and mothers, and gradual reduction of working time for mothers with infants, toddlers, and preschool children. (In Zhernova, 1991: 69–70)

Compared with women in other nations, Soviet women reportedly have unusually long life expectancy (75 years); high participation in the labor force (71 percent of adult women) with 51 percent of all Soviet workers being women; low fertility (2.4 births); remarkably high adult literacy (98 percent); exactly 1:1 ratio of women-to-men enrolled in higher education. Yet on an unofficial level, post-Soviet authorities today recognize their multiple shortfalls; compared with men, women are underpaid, and segregated at school and work and shoulder a "double burden" of household duties (Clayton & Millar, 1991). From 1917 to 1991, Soviet communism was an unusually radical system suddenly imposed upon an unusually conservative culture—a clash of stateways and folkways never quite resolved in the nation's 74-year history. In the case of gender roles, there always was "status ambiguity" (Takooshian & Kalayjian, 1991), in which women and men were seen simultaneously as equal yet unequal. Though there is little social science writing on Soviet men, there is a rich (albeit scattered) literature on Soviet women, which is cumulated in the references below.

Third, the feminist movement has had long but tenuous roots in Russia. In the 1890s, under the czar, early feminists pushed unsuccessfully for greater gender equality in Russia. The 1905 revolution galvanized reformers, including feminists, who hosted the first major political meeting of women in Russian history—in St. Petersburg on 10 April 1905. Such efforts for women's suffrage were crushed in 1908. Meanwhile, V. I. Lenin's wife, Nadezhda Krupskaya, was a feminist revolutionary who had penned *The Woman Worker* in 1900 and rallied for gender equality as an integral part of Bolshevism. Indeed, communist legislation immediately after the 1917 revolution made the total equality of women and men official state policy. A new wave of feminist reform kindled, beginning in the 1960s, to try to put this policy more into practice. In 1979 feminists began publishing a women's journal, *Samizdat*, but Soviet authorities quickly crushed feminists' demands by exiling or imprisoning four women founders of *Samizdat*. Even into the 1980s the two major women's groups, Women and Russia and Club Maria, have had limited impact (Ruthchild, 1983). So the Soviet push for gender equality has had a long yet checkered history (Adler, 1991).

Fourth, the USSR is the nation with the greatest "surplus" of women over men, with a sex ratio of 111:100 (McFarlan, 1992: 196). This compares with a global ratio of near equality, 99 women per 100 men. This means the Soviet population of 291 million has 15 million "redundant women," a term used by Soviet sociologists. The imbalance is even greater than 111:100 in Russia than in the large Muslim republics, with women outnumbering men up to 6:1 within some specific Russian areas. This is due to the many wars in the past 200 years that have decimated the Russian male population. To the extent that even a small surplus of marriage-age women over men is a potent yet subtle contributor to sexism (Guttentag & Secord, 1983), this pushes Russian and Soviet society in the direction of gender inequality in a nation officially dedicated to the equality of women and men.

COMPARISONS BETWEEN MEN'S AND WOMEN'S GENDER ROLES DURING THE LIFE CYCLE

Infancy and Early Childhood

From its start in 1917, Soviet Russia was "the first republic in the world to recognize motherhood as a social, and not a private family responsibility" (Holland, 1985: 145). Historically, most Russian babies were delivered by *babki* (folk healers), with only 5 percent of women attended by trained medical personnel. But Soviet authorities quickly established an extensive system of specialized maternity clinics that, by 1925, had cut nearly in half the rate of infant mortality of 1914. Today, nearly 100 percent of urban and 90 percent of rural births occur in these maternity clinics, some 80 percent of which are units within larger polyclinics. The mother and infant normally leave the clinic within seven days of delivery and return monthly the first year for follow-up attention. Like all health care, this maternity care is entirely free of charge—from prenatal (pregnancy tests, health education, counseling) and delivery to postnatal follow-up. Since 1990, hospitals are openly offering their patients the option of paying for above-average attention, a practice formerly done only in secret.

In the six Muslim republics there is at least some tradition of preference for male offspring, in line with Islam. Males are somewhat preferred in Georgia and Armenia, too, to maintain the family name. Gender preference is less common in Russia and the western republics. In observant Soviet Jewish families there is no clear preference since the son says the mourning prayers for his dead parents (Izraeli & Safir, 1993), while the mother transmits the religion in traditional Judaism. For the preschool years, a survey on "the perfect child" by the USSR Institute for Sociological Research asked preschool teachers to describe the best and the worst child in their experience; some 59 percent of the "best" children were girls, and only 13 percent of the "worst" children were girls (Solodnikov, 1989).

Right from birth, it is common to distinguish children by gender with the traditional colors of light blue for boys and pink for girls. "Even the casual observer in the Soviet Union cannot fail to notice the abundance of feminine frills and bows with which girls of the youngest ages are adorned; surely this would serve to inform children of both sexes that such attention to one's appearance is an exclusively female concern" (Holland, 1985:62). Toys, too, are different—for boys, the more technical toys such as building sets, sports, electrical and mechanical items; for girls, kitchen, sewing, dolls, and domestic activities.

In theory, Marxism-Leninism is egalitarian, aiming for the full realization of each individual's potential, apart from all stereotypes of gender or nationality (Raiklin & McCormick, 1988). In practice, this approach has changed over the decades, with shifts in Soviet pedagogy. For example, two Soviet pedagogists advise:

Girls are more emotional and subjective than boys. They are more sensitive, taking praise and censure to heart. They are less brave than boys (hence raise their hands less often in class, for fear of giving the wrong answer).... They are better than boys at understanding simple and commonplace ideas, but worse regarding more specialized concepts. ... Girls are neater, more accurate, conscientious, industrious, and responsible.... Girls tend towards arts subjects such as history and literature, especially poetry, and dislike physics, biology, and math; while boys are more interested in handcrafts and sport. (Holland, 1985: 66–67)

Such views in turn shape child-rearing practices (Aidarova, 1983; Azarov, 1983; Valsiner, 1988). Soviet pedagogy not only recognizes these tendencies as "natural" (i.e., inborn) but sees the aim of the school and family to recognize and reinforce them in socially productive ways. Expert advice on child rearing is offered to the "sensible family," such as:

The attitude towards the boy is stricter, demands on his physical strength and bravery are decisively higher, and defeats and failures are criticized more sharply. . . . The boy's bed is harder, the mother's caresses are more restrained, the look of the father is more stern and punishment stricter. . . . Even from the first class it is important to demand of boys that they defend girls, giving up their places to them, letting them go first, not allowing them to do heavy physical work. (Holland, 1985: 68–69)

Key Soviet scientists like Igor Kon see such differences as naturally extending into adulthood: "Men of all ages are more assertive and persistent than women, and more emotionally stable; women's greater fragility makes them more prone to neurosis, and results in a greater need for a stable environment and human contact" (Holland, 1985:61).

Such gender stereotypes are not inherently anti-Marxist if we consider that Karl Marx, in dialogue with his own daughter, reportedly answered her that he valued "strength in a man and weakness in a woman," that the natural tendency of woman is to be supportive of man while man is to be protective of woman—surely a sexist conservatism by Western standards, yet a conservatism that permeated the Soviet era.

School Years

There are 83 million children in the USSR, some one-third of the population. The government considers itself responsible for children's health and welfare. Besides care to newborns and their families, the state provides free services for preschoolers—including hobbies, entertainment, athletics, nutrition. The *USSR Yearbook* (Hippocrene Books, 1990: 9) noted:

Among the recreation facilities for children . . . there are Young Pioneer clubs, young technicians' centers, amusement railway and ship lines, not to mention numerous parks, libraries and sport centers. Over a million schoolchildren also attend specialized music, art and ballet schools. During summer and winter holidays schoolchildren attend over 60,000 camps. The biggest health resort is the Artek Young Pioneer camp in the Crimea, on the Black Sea coast.

Foreign youth exchanges and tours are also offered through the Sputnik Youth Travel Agency, formed in 1958. As of its thirtieth anniversary in 1988, this agency had sent overseas 330,000 students to socialist nations, 96,000 to capitalist nations, and 17,600 to developing nations.

At the same time, government recognizes shortfalls in its care of youngsters. In June 1989 the Congress of People's Deputies heard stark statistics: annually 700,000 children lose one or both parents; 900,000 are detained for delinquency or vagrancy; 6,000 die of cancer, and tuberculosis is rising in northern republics; 1,299 were murdered (in 1987), and 2,194 committed suicide. Infant mortality and juvenile delinquency rates are higher than in most other nations, and they are increasing. A Lenin Soviet Children's Fund, which operated from 1924 to

1938, was restored in 1987 to supplement government efforts with private phi-
lanthropy by groups of workers and others. The fund has since provided all sorts
of services to youngsters—health, education, and social welfare.

Probably because of the abuse of children common in the pre-Soviet Russian
Empire, Soviet policy toward children is protective. Both boys and girls are to
be nurtured, not overworked, carefully shaped by the state into socially responsible adults. Similarly, families are expected not to make excessive demands on
children, as in doing more than their share of home cleaning and preparations.
School tasks are expected to be the focus of the child's responsibility.

Universal secondary education through grade 11 is required of all Soviet boys
and girls. Upon completion, students are eligible to take competitive exams to
enter college or professional schools (which require 4–6 years to complete) and
beyond that, graduate school. There is no discrimination against females in
admissions. In fact, women are sometimes more represented than men—58
percent of students in secondary schools, 55 percent in colleges, 33 percent in
graduate schools. Such "data on education show absolute equality between men
and women, but at the university level departments tend to be divided into
masculine and feminine subjects" (Fabris, 1977). Men are drawn to scientific
and managerial fields—engineering, math, law, politics—while women are
drawn to service and artistic school subjects—teaching, medicine, psychology,
linguistics, music, art.

Young Adulthood

Dating practices vary widely by region. In the more traditional republics
(Georgia, Armenia) as well as in Muslim Turkestan, adolescent dating is not
widely accepted, even in cities. Teenagers date little, often with chaperones,
sometimes furtively. Though arranged marriages are uncommon today, parents
retain a clear voice in dating as well as marriage—so, too, in rural areas throughout the Soviet Union. In contrast, teen dating is the norm in urban culture in
the western republics, including the Baltics. In Moscow and St. Petersburg, it
is typical for boys and girls over 13 to be dating and sexually active. This is
reflected in the sharp drop in age of marriage, as well as the rates of teen
pregnancy, illegitimacy, and abortion. Those in the conservative republics regard
Russian teens as too liberal, if not promiscuous.

In 1920 the USSR became the first nation formally to legalize abortion on
request. After 1936 and the temporary illegalization of abortion during the Stalin
years, abortion was reliberalized in 1955, so it is now available on request in
state clinics through the first trimester. With hardly 15 percent of Soviet women
having access to any form of contraception, abortion has become a crude means
of birth control. The average Russian woman has 6–8 abortions in her lifetime,
and the number often goes as high as 25 for some. Women are limited to one
abortion every six months. In the late 1980s in the USSR, there were an estimated
2.1 abortions for every live birth (compared with 0.4 in the U.S.A.), a far higher

abortion rate than in any other nation. A state-performed abortion takes eight minutes and costs only 5 rubles (U.S. $7), compared with an average $213 in the U.S.A.

Illegitimacy, too, is a burgeoning problem, hand in hand with teenage pregnancy. Some 10 percent of all live births are out of wedlock. In 1989, feminist Tatyana Mamonova noted, "Pervasive fatherlessness, or *bezottsovschchina*—a term which arose out of the tragedies of World War II—is making a comeback" (Zelkowitz, 1989: 2). She estimates that only one-third of pregnancies are conceived in wedlock. "Men do not take responsibility for pregnancy despite the rise of premarital sex, so 27 percent of pregnancies are aborted, and 14 percent lead to births by unwed mothers" (Mamonova in Zelkowitz, 1989: 1).

Adulthood

Weddings also vary by republic. There are 2.7 million marriages annually in the USSR. All marriages must be registered with the state and require a one-month waiting period after filing. Minimum age is 18 in all but two of the republics (Ukraine and Uzbekistan), where it is 17. Over 80 percent of women and 70 percent of men are married by age 25, a lower percentage married in Russia than in the Caucasus or Muslim republics. Similarly, even while divorce rates escalate, a 1990 survey found 82 percent of Soviets feel married life is preferable. Young couples starting a family face the obstacles of money and housing, so it is typical to rely on one's parents for assistance during the start-up. About half of all newly married couples must live with their parents upon marriage, forcing two or more families where one once lived. Government helps at least somewhat, offering newlyweds interest-free loans of up to 1,500 rubles to form a new household and cash bonuses for each child the family has after marriage.

The Soviet-era state was extremely pronatalist in its policies, doing whatever was possible to increase marriage and childbearing to replenish its tens of millions lost in war, famine, and genocide in this century. The fertility rate in the USSR overall is 19.6 per 1,000 population. Still, the fertility rate is declining in Russia, while rising in the six Muslim republics. In 1990, one Western traveler described it thus: "When I visited Moscow and Leningrad, I noted that in these cities most couples have no more than one or two children, whereas many Central Asian women have five, six, seven or more" (Halsell, 1990: 32). Meanwhile, the smallest families are in the western republics—the Baltics, Russia, Byelorussia, Ukraine—largely due to financial hardships and the fears of family instability and divorce. Children are provided free breakfast and lunch at school, a bounty to their parents, and other supportive amenities by the state.

There is no legislation regulating equality within the home, and, indeed, men shoulder less of this burden—cooking, cleaning, laundry, child rearing, waiting on lines, shopping—particularly considering the scarcity of modern appliances in this onerous work. The average time per week devoted to household duties by men (12 hours) is less than half that of women (twenty-eight hours) (Mamonova, 1984b). One Russian feminist opines, "Men feel no sense of duty to help out with the shopping, standing in lines, preparing meals from scratch, and taking care of children" (Mamonova in Zelkowitz, 1989: 1). This is even more so in the sprawling Soviet countryside, where "surveys of rural attitudes make it clear that women . . . are increasingly unwilling to tolerate husbands' lack of consideration, rudeness, heavy drinking and indifference toward the care of their children. . . . Women are resentful at what they clearly see as parasitic behavior by many men" (Holland, 1985: 196).

A recent survey asked schoolchildren, "Who supervises your study and public activity?" Some 23 percent identified their father, and 64 percent their mother. How much time do women spend on household duties? Some 14 percent of women report 1–2 hours, 32 percent 2–3 hours, and 54 percent 3 or more hours daily. This might explain why Soviet women surpass men in education but lag in later on-the-job skills, since they have less time than men to devote to their work life.

A few sociological surveys confirm this gender imbalance of household duties. A 1975 survey of 1,000 Moscow families found working women's husbands shared no responsibility for housework, and they lacked even simple appliances to do this work (Iankova, 1975). Similarly, a 1983 survey of 500 urban families in Muslim Kazakhstan found that 63 percent of males endorsed an egalitarian attitude towards sharing household duties, yet, in their behavior, only 30 percent mended clothing, 34 percent cooked, 35 percent laundered, 48 percent washed dishes, 58 percent cleaned house (Junusbajev, 1985). In an econometric analysis over time, "time-budget data show that between the 1920s and the 1960s there was no change in the extent to which males share in the housework" (Sacks, 1977: 48).

The Soviet constitution of 1977 guarantees equal treatment for women and men, in work as well as school. This includes access to jobs, promotion, and salary. Though women are more educated than men, accounting for 60 percent of workers with specialized higher education, women occupy only 6 percent of all executive positions. Women dominate certain fields, particularly low-paying service industry jobs—95 percent of secretaries, 94 percent of cashiers, 83 percent of retailers, 82 percent in public health and social welfare, 75 percent of teachers, 74 percent of social workers. Even in medicine, for instance, women are large in number but subordinate in status—comprising 99 percent of nurses, 90 percent of primary physicians, 50 percent of managers, 40 percent of specialists, 20 percent of professors, and 10 percent of members of the Academy of Medicine. From necessity, many also work in physically demanding labor, such as railroad maintenance, construction, road building. A 1991 survey of 417 Soviet women found them dissatisfied for earning far less than their male counterparts in the same jobs and resenting the "double burden" of doing housework as well as their salaried job (Clayton & Millar, 1991).

How about recreation? Almost all of a family's time is spent to "make ends meet.'' Neither husband nor wife has much leisure time after a five-day work-week, family chores, and hours of waiting on long lines for even the most basic foods and supplies. In fact, in major cities clever pedestrians often dart into nascent lines even before knowing what they are queued for, aware that it is later much easier to exit a line if they do not need the product than to enter the line for a product they badly need. Despite limited leisure, government offers subsidized recreation for adults as well as youngsters—cinemas, clubhouses, athletic facilities, and heavy subsidies for arts and culture. Domestic travel is inexpensive and common, with over 195 million citizens (over half the population) vacationing each year to resorts, festivals, or other activities. Foreign travel is unusual, since the ruble exchange rate is so prohibitive, and (until 1988) visas were hard to obtain. Cafés are popular.

Sperling (1990) notes that domestic violence is a barometer of male oppression of women; she finds not only that ''in the USSR, crimes against women, such as domestic violence and rape, are widespread'' (p. 16) but also that the legal system often winks at this problem—indicating an excessive tolerance of such oppression. Indeed, such domestic violence seems a leading cause of the escalating divorce rate in Soviet cities (Holland, 1985: 132), particularly in Russia. Fully 60 percent of all murders and 50 percent of serious physical injuries are committed within families at home. Officially, rape is punishable by 3 to 7 years' imprisonment, sexual harassment by up to 3 years' prison. Yet in reality, only some 2 percent of rapes are ever reported (Mamonova, 1984a), due to embarrassment and lack of confidence in the legal system, and this reporting approaches zero percent in the Muslim regions.

Freedom to divorce was granted by decree in 1917. In cases of uncontested divorce with no minor children, divorce can be granted without the need of courts, simply with a 50-ruble fee and at least a three-month waiting period. The court must approve any divorce that is contested or that involves minors. Some 15 percent of divorce suits end in a successful reconciliation before the court hearing. Soviet courts try to prevent divorce and require a three-month waiting period for the couple to reconsider their plans. Of those who divorce, some 50 percent of men remarry within 10 years, compared with only 25 percent of women who remarry.

In 1990, 1 million Soviet families divorced, affecting some 775,000 children (Hippocrene Books, 1990). The Soviet divorce rate increased dramatically over the past 40 years—from 3.4 per 100 marriages in 1950, to 10.7 in 1960, to 28 in 1970, to over 40 in 1990. This makes it number two in the world, behind the United States of America. On the average divorce occurs only 3 years after marriage in the USSR, indicating Soviet families' great instability.

Divorce rates vary greatly by republic. In one example, a Moscow-based yearbook speaks admiringly of the ''family cult in Armenia,'' that ''Armenia is like an island of tranquility amidst a stormy sea of divorces,'' with a divorce rate 72 percent below the Union's average (Novosti Press Agency, 1987: 79).

Divorce is highest in the liberal northwest republics, lowest in the conservative Caucasus and Turkestan.

Reasons for divorce also vary by republic. In Russia, alcohol abuse is the key factor. The husband's alcohol abuse is the prime reason cited by 47 percent of Russian women and is a subsidiary reason in many of the other half (intertwined with husbands' physical and verbal abuse and malingering). Meanwhile, Russian husbands' two key reasons for filing for divorce are wives' incompatibility and marital infidelity. Adultery is given as the reason in Estonia twice as often as in Georgia. In-law friction is a widespread reason in Armenia, Georgia, Uzbekistan—a rare reason in the Baltics. A spouse's reluctance to have children rarely leads to family breakup in Estonia yet is the most cited reason in Georgia. Overall, some 60–70 percent of all divorce suits are filed at the wife's initiative. The ex-wife normally takes custody in divorces involving youngsters.

Russia's pronatalist policy is troubled by abortion and divorce, since these depress fertility. ''In an effort to stem the rising divorce rates a number of analysts have proposed that the waiting period prior to marriage be lengthened, that marriage counseling be introduced on a wide scale, that sex education be included in secondary school programs'' (Lapidus, 1978: 300–301). Meanwhile, through the 1980s there has been an increase in couples living together without marriage, particularly in Russia and the Baltics, though guesstimates on this trend are unavailable. Another possible, though rarely discussed practice is ''fictional divorces,'' in which a married couple may feign official divorce in hopes of qualifying for two separate apartments, which they can use for increased space if successful.

How do Soviets regard the ideal of equality between the sexes? In the west, Soviet society has the twofold image of being more egalitarian on paper yet more sexist in practice. To test this notion of ''status ambiguity,'' the authors conducted two studies of adult gender attitudes in the USSR during 1987–1990— a questionnaire survey of women and a more in-depth interview study of men.

Some 115 women in Yerevan, the capital city of Armenia, completed an Armenian version of the Feminism Survey (Beere, 1990), which had previously been used in the United States of America and other nations (Takooshian & Stuart, 1983). On its 24-point scale, Armenian women proved far less egalitarian (mean = 8.3) than American women (mean = 13.8, p < .0001), particularly in acceptance of household and child-rearing duties. As in the United States of America, the younger and more educated women of Armenia were more egalitarian (Takooshian, 1991).

One of the present authors, Anie Sanentz Kalayjian, interviewed 35 men in Armenia, ages 30 to 60. The interview began with an open-ended question: ''Tell me about your perception of the male-female relationship here.'' This was followed by more specific questions: ''Who is responsible for housework?'', ''Who takes care of the children?'' ''If your child gets sick, what procedure do you follow?'', ''If you have an unexpected meeting after work, what do you do?''

In response to the first open-ended question, 97 percent of males agreed that they shared freedom and equality with their female counterparts. They substantiated this by emphasizing how their wives were educated and employed: "My wife is a doctor; she works as I do" or "My wife is an engineer; she has been working longer than I have." The majority (97 percent) expressed having "no problem" with their wives' education or career. However, in responding to the more specific questions, an overwhelming majority (91 percent) stated that housework was a woman's responsibility, with the remaining 9 percent stating that sharing might be a good idea. Child care was universally viewed as a woman's responsibility (100 percent). Men perceived their role as being provider—paying the bills, buying theater tickets, and so on. When asked what would happen should their children get sick, 91 percent agreed their wives would be the ones to attend to the children's needs—taking a day off, rearranging schedules, and so on. Women were perceived as better qualified for child care; after all, they were the ones "bearing them," or this was "God's will." The purpose of the final question ("If you have an unexpected meeting after work, what do you do?") was to gain an understanding of spouses' communication patterns. A majority (86 percent) felt that they were under no obligation to "report" back to their wives; they believed that it would be "cowardly" to have to discuss their schedule with their wives. The remaining 14 percent stated that they would call their wives only after they had made their decision to attend the meeting, simply to "inform" them. At the conclusion of the interview, the author asked if the interviewees had anything to add. An overwhelming majority (91 percent) reasserted their belief in the total equality of women and men; they then proceeded to qualify their statement by saying that this would be the case so long as women knew "their place."

Old Age

Soviet life expectancy is 65 years for men and 75 years for women. In traditional European and Asian culture, the grandparents occupy a position of respect. This has changed in Russia in particular. One analyst writes of the "vanishing *babushka*" (grandmother)—that prototypical elderly, stout Russian woman who seems everywhere in Russian cities and countrysides. Due to economic difficulties, Russian women over age 55 find their pensions inadequate and increasingly must sacrifice self-reliance to appeal to their families for aid (Sternheimer, 1985). This *stariki v dome* ("old people in the home") is a dilemma in millions of Soviet households; on one hand, this may be a source of family solidarity, in which elders help greatly to tend youngsters while receiving much needed room and board; on the other hand, they may add friction and burden in an already struggling household.

Retirement is a problem for women and men alike. Official retirement age is 60 for men, 55 for women, and 50 for women with 5 or more children. Government recognizes that its pensions are inadequate, forcing the elderly to rely on their families for support, live in crowded and substandard retirement homes, or eke out an independent existence in their twilight years. The future of the Soviet elderly seems one of increased doubling up and deprivation in the twilight years.

SUMMARY AND CONCLUSIONS

What does the post-Soviet era portend about the future of gender roles in these republics? A few trends seem clear. First, as the likely absence of mass war and famine allow the sex ratio to normalize in the next two generations, we can expect a trend toward more egalitarian gender roles (Guttentag & Secord, 1983).

Second, there will likely be greater tension, as Kremlin suzerainty subsides, unleashing both radical and conservative forces. On the radical side, feminists like the exiled Tatyana Mamonova will use their new freedoms to press for stronger Russian bonds with world feminism and mobilize into professional and activist associations. Meanwhile, the conservative forces of the countryside will be unleashed as well, where "the rural traditions of higher birth rates, more authoritarian families, greater religious emphasis, male scorn for women . . . and lack of institutional supports for child care and housework [will] help perpetuate sex stratification" (Shoemaker, 1983: 35), as the central government loses its grip. Indeed, Mamonova warns that "rising ethnic tensions are giving strength to patriarchal religions, which historically have forced women into subordinate roles. A similar phenomenon is occurring in Poland, where the Catholic Church is using its influence with Solidarity to curtail the availability of contraceptives and abortion" (1989: 2). The ultimate outcome of this clash of Scylla and Charybdis is less predictable. Perhaps post-Soviet women and men will be more equal than ever. Alternately, post-Soviet women will opt to end their double burden of work-plus-home duties by forsaking their claims of equality outside the home.

Third, there will inevitably be a greater spread among the 15 republics as they proceed unhampered in remarkably different directions, unbridled by any centripetal pressure.

REFERENCES

Adler, L. L. (Ed.). (1991). *Women in Cross-Cultural Perspective*. New York: Praeger.

Aidarova, L. (1983). *Child Development and Education*. Moscow: Progress.

Arndt, R. (1990). Muslims in the U.S.S.R. *Aramco World, 41* (1): 2–3.

Azarov, Y. (1983). *A Book About Bringing up Children*. Moscow: Progress.

Beere, C. A. (1990). *Gender Roles: A Handbook of Tests and Measures*. New York: Greenwood.

Clayton, E., & Millar, J. R. (1991). Education, job experience and the gap between male and female wages in the Soviet Union. *Comparative Economic Studies, 33*: 5–22.

Fabris, M. (1977). The woman in the USSR: Contradictions and problems. *Rivista di Sociologia, 1:* 233–63.

Gregory, P. R., & Collier, I. L. (1988). Unemployment in the Soviet Union: Evidence from the Soviet interview project. *American Economic Review, 78:* 613–32.

Guttentag, M., & Secord, P. (1983). *Too Many Women?* Beverly Hills, CA: Sage.

Halsell, G. (1990). A visit to Baku. *Aramco World, 41* (1): 30–33.

Hippocrene Books. (1990). *USSR Yearbook '90.* Moscow: Author.

Holland, B. (Ed.). (1985). *Soviet Sisterhood.* Bloomington: Indiana University Press.

Iankova, Z. A. (1975). The development of women in Soviet society. *Sotsiologicheskie Issledovaniya, 2:* 42–51.

Izraeli, D. N., & Safir, M. P. (1993). Israel. In Adler, L. L. (Ed.), *International Handbook on Gender Roles.* Westport, CT: Greenwood Press.

Junusbajev, M. D. (1985). Household division in the Kazakh family. *Sotsiologicheskie Issledovaniya, 12:* 106–9.

Lapidus, G. W. (1978). *Women in Soviet Society: Equality, Development, and Social Change.* Berkeley: University of California Press.

McFarlan, D. (1992). *Guiness Book of World Records.* New York: Bantam.

Mamonova, T. (1984a). The USSR: It's time we began with ourselves. In Morgan, Robin (Ed.), *Sisterhood Is Global: The International Women's Movement Anthology* (pp. 683–89). New York: Anchor.

————. (Ed.). (1984b). *Women and Russia.* Boston: Beacon.

Moses, J. C. (1986). The Soviet Union in the women's decade, 1975–1985. In Iglitzin, L. B., & Ross, R. (Eds.), *Women in the World 1975–1985* (pp. 385–413). Santa Barbara, CA: ABC-Clio.

Novosti Press Agency. (1987). *Yearbook USSR '87.* Moscow: Author.

Raiklin, E., & McCormick, K. (1988). Soviet men on the road to utopia: A moral-psychological sketch. *International Journal of Social Economics, 15:* 3–62.

Ruthchild, R. (1983). Sisterhood and socialism: The Soviet feminist movement. *Frontiers, 7:* 4–12.

Sacks, M. P. (1977). Sexual equality and Soviet women. *Society, 14:* 48–51.

Shoemaker, S. (1983). The status of women in the rural USSR. *Population Research and Policy Review, 2:* 35–51.

Solodnikov, V. V. (1989). The perfect child: Views of teachers. *Sotsiologicheskie Issledovaniya, 16:* 87–90.

Sperling, V. (1990). Rape and domestic violence in the USSR. *Response to the Victimization of Women and Children, 13:* 16–22.

Sternheimer, S. (1985). The vanishing babushka: A roleless role for older Soviet women? *Current Perspectives of Aging in the Life Cycle, 1:* 315–33.

Swirski, B., & Safir, M. P. (1991). *Calling the Equality Bluff: Women in Israel.* New York: Macmillan.

Takooshian, H. (1991). Soviet women. In Adler, L. L. (Ed.), *Women in Cross-Cultural Perspective* (pp. 78–88). New York: Praeger.

Takooshian, H., & Kalayjian, A. S. (1991, April). Not knowing her place: The ambiguous status of soviet womanhood. Presentation to the Symposium on Cultural Studies of the Soviet Union, Columbia University, New York City.

Takooshian, H., & Stuart, C. R. (1983). Ethnicity and feminism among American women: Opposing social trends? *International Journal of Group Tensions, 13:* 100–105.

Valsiner, J. (1988). *Developmental Psychology in the Soviet Union*. Bloomington: Indiana University Press.

Vianello, M., & Siemienska, R. (1990). *Gender Inequality: A Comparative Study of Discrimination and Participation*. Newbury Park, CA: Sage.

Zelkowitz, J. (1989). Feminism and Soviet society. *Harriman Institute Newsletter, 3*(3): 1.

Zhernova, L. (1991). Women in the USSR. In Adler, L. L. (Ed.), *Women in Cross-Cultural Perspective* (pp. 68–77). New York: Praeger.

25

Sri Lanka

*Suneetha S. de Silva,
Deborah A. Stiles, and
Judith L. Gibbons*

INTRODUCTION

Lotus ponds surround dagabas built in honor of the Buddha. Sacred Bo trees rustle with families of langur monkeys feeding and grooming. Nearby civil war rages. Two groups of people, descendants of one subcontinent, engage in battle. Dead and dying soldiers lie beside effigies built to pay homage to a philosophy that calls for peace and love. This could be a scene from any time in the history of this beautiful yet turbulent country of Sri Lanka. For almost 15 centuries its two major ethnic groups have been in conflict, and intentions have not changed. Still each group fights to assert its identity in terms of culture, language, religion, and control of the land.

Then, as now, men went to battle while women played the subordinate role of wife and mother. Yet history is etched with the occasional Sinhala queen or ruling woman who led her armies to the north. Today the young Tamil woman chooses to join a militant group, perhaps because she lacks a dowry to marry (Hodgin, 1990). She sacrifices the roles of wife and mother to go to battle for a cause in which she believes.

Sri Lanka, the pearl of the Indian Ocean, lies just south of the subcontinent of India and 60 degrees to the north of the equator. This location makes the climate tropical and the land lush in beauty. Its rain forests teem with exotic flora, beautiful mountains where gemstones are found in abundance, and serene white beaches. Tea, spices, coconut, and rubber are but a few of its natural products.

To understand a culture as complex as that of the inhabitants of Sri Lanka, one has to include its ethnic origins, varied history, geography status, multiple religions, caste system, and continuously changing social structure. The major ethnic groups are the Sinhalese, the Tamils, the Muslims, and the Burghers.

Stone Age dwellers lived in Sri Lanka before its recorded history of five centuries B.C. The first Sinhalese people were descendants of Indo-Aryan origin. An important recording of this is the *Mahavamsa* (1912), which is a chronicle of ancient Ceylon. The story recorded is of an Indian prince who succumbs to the charms of a Veddha princess. This was the beginning of the Sinhalese or lion-blooded race. The Sinhalese now comprise about 70 percent of the population. They are predominantly Buddhist and speak Sinhalese. Twenty percent of the population are of Indian origin; they speak Tamil and are mainly Hindus. According to the *Mahavamsa*, the first group from India arrived around the third century B.C. They are called Ceylon Tamils and form about 13 percent of the total population. Arab traders in spice came in search of wealth and stayed. Descendants of these traders constitute about 7 percent of the population and are known as Muslims. They speak Tamil and Malay.

Christianity was introduced to this island in 1505 with the arrival of the Portuguese. They were succeeded by the Dutch in 1658. Descendants of these colonies are the Burghers, who are predominantly Christian and are set apart in appearance and cultural habits from the rest of the country; they comprise less than 1 percent. The English occupied the country in 1796. They brought over Indian laborers to work in the tea plantations. These newcomers are known as Indian Tamils and form 6 percent of the total population (Keuneman, 1984).

This migration pattern accounts for the many different ethnic groups in Sri Lanka, who have different customs, religions, and languages. However, the majority of the Sri Lankan people today speak some English as well as their ethnic languages.

The caste system was handed down from India, along with art and architecture. When the kings governed and exercised absolute rule, the caste system determined the occupations of the people. There were as many castes as there were chores (i.e., farmer, jeweler, drummer). Today there are still about twenty castes, even though foreign occupations have erased many traditions (Farmer, 1983). Castes play a major role in determining marriages and people's status at rituals.

Two generations ago Sri Lankans were born, lived, and died in the same town or village. After independence in 1948 and then during the next 20 years there were glimpses of freedom and a promise of a peaceful life. But in the last two decades the country has been in social upheaval.

Modern Sri Lanka has seen drastic political, economic, and social changes (Committee for Rational Development, 1984; Hodgin, 1990; Rupensinghe, 1988; Thambia, 1990). A loss of faith in religious philosophies has accompanied an increase in senseless violence. According to newspaper reports, the younger generation have killed innocent people in their efforts to gain power, and the government has retaliated. The social structure was completely changed when the lower and middle classes obtained work in the Middle East and returned as the new rich.

Electricity has made its way into the deepest villages, changing lamplit evenings that tended to segregate men, women, and children, into evenings when families watched late night television shows. The presence of television introduced a global view, drastically changing the quiet, sedate life-style in rural areas.

The family structure has destabilized as mothers who once stayed home now go to work and leave children to be brought up by relatives, servants, or older siblings. "The increase of women in the workplace has not been welcomed and . . . there is a lurking fear that employment may threaten the stability of family life" (Jayaweera, 1979:167).

Many of the recent political and economic changes in Sri Lanka have been reported in the news media; however, there is a paucity of information about contemporary gender roles in Sri Lanka in the social science literature. The first author of this chapter, Suneetha de Silva, is a native of Sri Lanka, an educator, and is knowledgeable about the development of gender roles in Sri Lanka. In order to get a picture of the most recent changes in gender roles as well as a broader perspective, twenty-four cultural informants were consulted. These persons included Buddhists, Hindus, Muslims, and Christians and represented a variety of geographical areas and socioeconomic groups. Both men and women, as well as different age groups, were included. Twenty Sri Lankans answered a detailed questionnaire about contemporary gender roles; four were interviewed in depth. Because the Sinhalese comprise 70 percent of the population, much of the information we present on gender roles concerns their customs. Important variations in beliefs and behavior for the Tamils, Muslims, and Burghers are included throughout the chapter.

OVERVIEW

During infancy boys and girls are dressed and treated alike. Gender differentiation occurs increasingly during childhood as boys and girls engage in different activities in the family and at school. During puberty, girls symbolically prepare for their lesser role in society as they participate in a celebration known as "stepping into the house." During adulthood "the social climate is still influenced by traditional myths and prejudices that present women in an inferior and subservient role . . . [and] behavioral norms that require women to be docile, 'innocent' and protected" (Jayaweera, 1979:167)

Men have superior status and dominate at home and at work. Many Sri Lankans believe that men have been reincarnated as males because of the more righteous lives they led in their previous lifetimes. Men are given many privileges, including being fed better food at meals and always being served first. Eye contact between men and women is avoided; females are taught that they will suffer embarrassment if they make eye contact with men. Men have more employment opportunities and receive higher compensation.

Currently the most dramatic changes in gender roles can be seen in the lives of women. In some instances the silent, smiling Sri Lankan woman is being replaced by a young woman in search of an identity. Young women have protested the traditional judgments of elders and moved away from home to live in cities or foreign countries. A few women have left the traditional roles of wife and mother to emerge "in leadership roles and make significant contributions to national life" (Jayaweera, 1979: 165). Sri Lanka was the first country to elect a woman prime minister. Today some of the most emancipated women have joined the militant Tigers, a women's rights organization, and march together in battle for the LTTE (Liberation Tigers of Tamil Elam) (Hodgin, 1990).

COMPARISONS BETWEEN MEN'S AND WOMEN'S GENDER ROLES DURING THE LIFE CYCLE

Infancy and Early Childhood

"Children are a valuable investment. It is they who take care of us when we are sick. It is they who continue our traditions of our culture and they will not discard us when we are old" (Rajagopalan, 1989, personal communication).

During pregnancy a woman is treated with much care, fed the best foods, given oil massages, and given special herbs to drink for the good of the child. This is the one time that she will be given more food and better treatment than her husband. However, the announcement of pregnancy is kept within the immediate family to ensure protection against the "evil eye" or "evil word." In Sri Lanka there is a superstition that giving compliments to babies causes them harm.

In the old patriarchal tradition, Sinhalese, Tamils, and Muslims preferred to have sons, to continue the family name, to bring in wealth in the form of a dowry, and to maintain land and money within the family. According to recent questionnaire responses, sons and daughters are now equally preferred. A teacher from the southern province explained: "Preference for boys was very strong 30–40 years ago. With time and more job opportunities these ideas have become obsolete."

When a child is born, his or her mother's first milk is placed in a spoon, then it is rubbed with gold and is given as the baby's first meal. Both boys and girls receive this milk, which is called *Ran-kiri* and brings them good fortune. Also at birth a horoscope is cast and is used to find a suitable name for the child. The same horoscope guides males throughout their lives, but females receive a new horoscope at menarche.

Love is lavished on infants. Boys and girls are rocked to sleep, and lullabies are sung to them. In poorer families the primary caretakers are mothers or are siblings if the mothers are at work. In middle-class families, servant girls are employed to help with child care. Upper-class families have Ammas, who are older women who give full-time care to children. During early childhood independence is not encouraged in either boys or girls unless the children are from low-income families. Physical needs such as getting dressed or being fed or bathed are attended to by mothers or female servants.

Girls and boys are treated alike at infancy. In the past, both boy and girl babies wore smocked dresses. Now they wear Western-style sweat suits or whatever else might be in fashion. Infants and toddlers seldom have their hair cut because superstition states that a haircut during the first stages of speech will make a baby stutter.

Boys and girls are often seen wearing jewelry: a bracelet of black and white beads to ward off the evil eye and evil mouth. A necklace with a gold sovereign with five gold weapons, called a *panchayudha*, is also worn for protection.

Reincarnation is an important religious belief with relevance for understanding child development in Sri Lanka. About age three, children may begin remembering their previous lives, which may include existence as the opposite gender (Cook, Pasricha, Samararatne, Maung, & Stevenson, 1983).

Evenings are a close time for families. Beginning in early childhood, evenings are spent listening to stories told by parents and other relatives. The Jataka stories are about the Buddha's previous lives, and each of these stories has a moral and is told and retold to children many times in their lives. The stories are about being good, respectful, and kind. Following these virtues is rewarding to people in their reincarnation (Fenton, Hein, Reynolds, Miller & Nielson, 1983; Wickramasinghe, 1956). Children who don't listen or follow the rules are not physically punished, but they are told that they are bad. The stories communicate expectations for moral behavior, and in some instances, they indirectly describe gender roles. The Buddha always appears as a good male personage; sometimes the other males in the stories represent powerful evil or good forces. In general, the female characters have milder and more peripheral roles; female heroines are mentioned as goddesses or temptresses.

Young children's toys are determined by both gender and where they live. Boys growing up in urban areas play with cars and imported toys. Boys in rural areas play with sand, rocks, seashells, and coconut shells. Girls living in urban areas play with dolls and pots and pans. Rural girls play with sand, coconut shells, and available pots and pans. Girls and boys are not segregated at early ages, so friendships are formed as they play together, and this socializing between genders usually occurs only during early childhood. In years past when mothers stayed at home, children stayed with them. Now, preschools are fashionable in urban areas and have been established through necessity in the rural areas by Buddhist temples (Prosser, 1986).

School Years

Gender differentiation occurs increasingly during this stage as boys and girls engage in different activities in the family and at school. Although at this age children enter the world to go to school, in most ways they remain sheltered from the outside, and thus family life is extremely important. Boys and girls don't travel to town or the marketplace without being chaperoned by parents or servants. Thus, children learn their gender roles mostly within the family, by observing their parents and their siblings.

For example, during holidays, children observe their parents' roles in the celebration and help out. Two Buddhist holidays with gender-differentiated customs are the Sinhalese New Year and Wesak. During the New Year, which takes place in April, the women of the family play the major role in the preparations. For several weeks they cook sweetmeats, just before New Year's Day they whitewash their houses, and finally, at an auspicious time, they boil milk until it overflows; this is believed to bring prosperity in the coming year. While the boys light firecrackers, the girls stay indoors with the women who are cooking festive meals. They serve and entertain the many guests who visit.

Wesak, which takes place during the full moon in the month of May, is a holiday in which fathers play a dominant role. During Wesak fathers help children make and decorate *kudu*. As with other family events, fathers and the other males in the house are more involved than mothers with the physical and light-hearted activities. According to our consultants and researchers who have studied play among Sri Lankan children, it is the man's role to do the most enjoyable activities with the children (Prosser, 1986).

Although age may be the most important factor in interaction with siblings and cousins, gender has an effect. Siblings support and respect each other, and older siblings are looked up to and obeyed by younger ones. Even a child who is one month younger than his cousin will respect and listen to the slightly older cousin. Older children give orders to younger children, but boys are treated more leniently and expected to do less.

Girls are expected to do more housework than boys, who spend their free time playing with friends. The Sinhalese, Tamil, and Muslim respondents to our questionnaires all agreed that there are different requirements for boys and girls in terms of household chores. A Sinhalese woman explained that boys "watch TV [television] and make excuses to work" while girls do sweeping and wash clothes. A Tamil woman stated that boys do "practically nil" and girls "help in the household chores." A Muslim woman explained that "girls usually help mother in household chores; boys help in outdoor work."

Play and sports also tend to follow gender-role stereotypes. While fathers and sons engage in outside activities, mothers and daughters are busy with inside activities such as sewing dolls' clothes and play-cooking. Cricket, rugby, football, and volleyball are boys' games, occasionally tried out by females, while netball, hopscotch, and "changing posts" are saved for girls. Girls play with dolls, tea sets, pots and pans, and play with other girls. Boys ride bicycles, climb trees, and play with other boys.

Most schools are sex-segregated and have a dress code. In contrast to early childhood, boys and girls at this age dress differently. Girls wear white uniforms and a tie that represents their school. Boys wear blue shorts and a white shirt. Teachers tend to encourage boys to work with tools and learn mathematics. Girls seem to prefer home science, music, and languages. According to our consultants, girls are often the more serious students, whereas "boys don't give a hoot." Girls are described as neater and more obedient. They are taught to speak softly and sit with their feet together. "Boys choose a more outgoing sort of behavior and do their studies in a playful manner which is a combination of studies and games."

At adolescence, there is increasing gender differentiation with regard to ceremonies surrounding puberty and continued gender segregation in education, with most boys and girls attending separate schools.

In Sri Lanka the physical changes associated with puberty are acknowledged in a special way for girls. Menarche is referred to as "stepping into the house," which may symbolize the entry into adult women's roles. Buddhist girls at menarche undergo a special ceremony to mark their entry to womanhood. At the first menstruation, the girl has to stay in seclusion, with only older women to tend to her needs, and horoscopes are consulted as to the best time for her presentation. In the meantime, jewelry is purchased, new clothes are bought, and all the relatives from far and near gather in the house of the girl's family. All the women relatives, young and old, spend time with the young woman reminiscing, gossiping, and teasing the young girl about being a woman now. At an auspicious time, days or weeks later, she is cleansed in oils and boiled herbs, bathed, and taken indoors. Dressed in fine jewels, she is greeted as a woman.

Buddhist, Christian, and Hindu boys pass through puberty without ceremony. Muslim boys go through a period of isolation, and after a ceremony of circumcision, feasting, and celebration, they enter manhood. Gradually they earn access to the adult world.

Social life for Sri Lankan adolescents is differentiated according to gender. "Difficult" adolescents, that is, those who are disobedient or talk back to adults, are usually sent to live with relatives until astrological times are better. Boys are sent away so that they do not mix with delinquent boys. Some difficult girls are sent away whereas others might be kept within the house, helping with housework.

Most girls are chaperoned to school or extracurricular activities, and elders are treated with much respect. Socializing between sexes is very limited. Young boys group together and try out driving cars or smoking cigarettes. Parties and dating are rare, yet family gatherings might enable young people to meet, mingle, and socialize. Relationships between cousins are common. If a serious relationship is noticed, separation follows unless they are of marriageable age. Eloping was common years ago. If pregnancy occurs, it is considered a shame shared by the family. Thus the baby might be given up for adoption to someone outside or within the family. At no time is the teenager asked for an opinion, nor is she given sympathy. Alone in a world of angry adults, she faces shame, guilt, and sadness.

Education is highly valued in Sri Lanka. Among its close neighbors, Sri Lanka has the highest literacy rate (85 percent in 1980) and was the first to achieve universal primary education (Robinson, 1989). Despite the high literacy rate there is a gender difference in the ability to read and write (91 percent of men and 81 percent of women). Although attendance at primary and secondary schools is evenly distributed according to gender, at the university level only 38 percent of students are females (McCurdy, 1986).

For secondary schooling, girls and boys may be sent to boardingschools to receive a better education than what is available in the rural areas. At ninth grade parents advise students in choosing between science (biology, math, chemistry, and physics) or arts (art, history, geography, and languages). Occupational choice follows from the school subjects chosen. The most desirable occupations are doctor, lawyer, engineer, or teacher. Girls idealize doctors and teachers because they help other people (de Silva, Stiles & Gibbons, in press). Some young men may choose to be a Buddhist priest, since higher educational opportunities are available to them.

Very recently education has been often interrupted because of political strife. Girls and boys may attend tutorials rather than sex-segregated schools. This allows mingling of the sexes and the formation of friendships between boys and girls.

After school, baby-sitting or working at jobs is not usual as most after-school hours are also spent in some type of learning program. Boys from "business owner" families are trained in the trade while continuing school. Most girls are taught to play the piano and go for classes in spoken English or dancing.

Education plays so much importance that junior and high school years are spent trying to obtain four passes in the advanced-level certificate of education, which determines adolescents' future (Jayaweera, 1979). According to the education system, at eighteen, young people sit for the general certificate of education, advanced level. This is a deciding point. Those few who succeed in gaining entrance to university with acceptable grades go on to further their education. The others never go to university. Instead they have to make other choices: a career or marriage for women, a technical school or trade for men.

Most respondents to the questionnaire replied that there were equal opportunities for boys and girls to attend higher educational institutions. However, some disagreed, saying that "boys are given all the opportunities . . . girls are often discouraged [from] higher education." As pointed out above, a smaller percentage of young women than of men actually attends university.

There was some disagreement among our consultants as to whether males and females differ in their preferences for academic disciplines. For example, one of two Islamic respondents from Galle had the opinion that "preferences for academic disciplines depend on individual capabilities and not on sex" whereas the other stated: "Males prefer to be doctors, lawyers, females, teachers." For whatever reason, women are underrepresented among university students in engineering and architecture (McCurdy, 1986).

Late adolescence is a time when most young people are either in the university or working. For those who enter college this might be the first encounter with a large group of mixed sexes without supervision. Though most young men and women stay home with their parents while going to university or while working, living in dormitories is a great stride that some young men and women take toward independence.

Young Adulthood

The dramatic social changes in Sri Lanka can be seen most clearly in the changes in values, habits, and mores in the lives of young adults. In the past, higher education was available to the English-speaking elite. Beginning in 1959 the university education entrance examinations were offered in the indigenous languages; this opened up educational opportunities (Jayaweera, 1979). Now, with a stronger ethnic consciousness, a new generation of college-educated youth exert their authority. The intense ethnic and religious conflicts have mobilized young people into a political force (Thambia, 1990). The traditional social organization according to caste, creed, social background, and gender has eroded and no longer determines employment and social life of young adults.

One notable change has been the migration to take advantage of job opportunities in the Middle East and Europe. Economically disadvantaged Sri Lankans take jobs in foreign countries as maids, bellhops, drivers, and cooks, returning to Sri Lanka relatively affluent.

Career opportunities for men and women within Sri Lanka have also changed over the years. Earlier, work was a man's place, and the home was for the woman. Today, more work opportunities are opening up for women. Since career choices follow from fields of study at the university or trade school, there is often gender differentiation. According to one of our respondents, young women often choose teaching, nursing, and civil service. Men more often choose engineering, medicine, law, and business management. Another Sri Lankan noted that "boys set their hearts on top-level jobs, and girls settle for more secondary type of jobs."

The data on women's employment in Sri Lanka coincide with these comments. In office work, a male might be a young executive, but a woman would not unless the business was family-owned. Only 7 percent of administrative positions in Sri Lanka are held by women (United Nations, 1991). Girls with less education might choose to be typists or shop girls. But even the clerical positions are more often held by men (65 percent). Most businesses and shops are owned by families, and the men of these families run the business. Since shop owners are wealthy, their wives and daughters stay at home and enjoy leisurely lives (Perera, 1991, personal communication). On the other hand, men and women appear equally likely to be agricultural workers. For example, almost all tea pluckers in Sri Lanka are women. Seager and Olson (1986) have described the job of tea picker as a "job ghetto" for women because it carries low pay, low status, and little security.

Family ties remain strong during young adulthood, with parents exerting powerful influences on the lives of young adults. Although most unmarried young adults continue to live with their parents, a very recent trend is "clubbing," young adults of the same sex getting apartments together.

Dating (men and women going out alone together) may be strictly prohibited or allowed only for men. A respondent said, "Men would be allowed to date anyone they like but if a female does, society would say that her morality is low."

Because parents influence decisions about the social lives of young adults, they may feel stress if parents disapprove of a relationship. Parental criticism and unrealistically high expectations, especially for the oldest child, can also lead to poor self-esteem.

As virginity is very important, women are constantly chaperoned, whereas men have more freedom to explore. However, there are various ways for eligible men and women to become acquainted. Being a bridesmaid to an older sister, relative, or friend at this time is a way of being presented to the clan as an eligible young woman. The Burghers arrange mingling between the sexes by encouraging young men to visit the homes of eligible girls. Other communities arrange marriages through newspaper advertisements:

- Jaffna Vellala tamil, Roman Catholic couple seek for tall, fair 29-year-old son a pretty girl with good dowry.
- Well-connected Kandyan Govi Buddhist parents seek educated partner for daughter, 23 years, fair, 5'4", teacher, Kethu 7th house.
- A Buddhist Govi family seek for daughter, 22, fair, tall, English-educated, attractive. Dowry over 1 million rupees including cash and home in Colombo.
- Ceylonese family with U.S. citizenship, so doctor, 30, seeking Tamil girl, educated, fair complexioned, and slim. Request horoscope and full details.

The Sunday paper, about thirty pages in all, usually has at least three pages of advertisements under brides and bridegrooms. The ads specify religion, caste, ethnic origin, physical characteristics, dowry, and occasionally disposition or personality traits. A physical characteristic desirable for women, but not for men, is to be light-skinned. For a man, the older members of his family make the choice of his bride, with female members having more influence; for a woman, older male members have more influence in the final decision. The young man and young woman concerned see very little of each other. Visiting rights and privileges occur only after a formal agreement (Perera, 1991, personal communication).

Marriage agreements are reached by families after extensive comparing of horoscopes, agreement on the dowry, and a visit to the bride's home by the bridegroom and a few selected relatives. Most decisions are made only after a glimpse of one's future partner and the influence of the elders. After a formal engagement, which takes place after confirmation of dowry, the young couple are able to get to know each other.

In Sri Lanka there are more than 20 castes, and traditionally marriages occurred within a caste. Marriage out of caste was frowned upon and could have meant expulsion from the family. Today, young men and women have more opportunities to meet and fall in love. According to several Sri Lankan informants, in spite of parental disapproval, young people of today sometimes go ahead and get married.

Adulthood

Monogamy is the law in Sri Lanka, although Muslims follow their own laws, which permit men to have more than one wife. Sinhalese and Tamil men and women are expected to stay loyal in monogamous relationships. Rural women in Sri Lanka used to practice polyandry (Jayawardana, 1986). Today, this is rare since marriages are expected to be registered.

Child marriages do not affect the women of Sri Lanka (Jayawardana, 1986). The average age of marriage for women is 24.4, and for men 27.9 (United Nations, 1991).

A dowry is an essential part of a marriage. The late age of marriage may reflect the postponement of marriage and childbearing in order to collect a dowry for oneself. Lack of dowry may be a reason for women to join the LTTE rebels or to take a job in a foreign country.

Sri Lankan marriages are religious and social affairs that take planning. The wedding arrangements, including the cost, decorations, and clothing, will be a topic at tea parties, birthday parties, and Galle Face Green (a beach resort) conversations. Marriage ceremonies vary according to religious tradition. Christian weddings take place in church. Brides dress in white and wear veils. Afterward, guests go to a ballroom of a hotel, where bands play music and some people dance. Until a few years ago, young girls were not allowed to dance, though they did anyway when not watched by parents. Food is served on trays. Family and friends meet and have fun. Hindu brides wear red, blue, or gold but never white, which is a color for funerals. Ceremonies are held under a "roofed" area and are conducted by a religious official. The ceremony is identical to that conducted by Hindus in India and other parts of the world. Muslims all over follow the same ceremony. The weddings are elaborate and take place at night. Muslim brides traditionally wear a red sari. Women celebrate in the women's quarters, and men celebrate along with other men, except for the bridegroom and his family and young boys, who join the bride and the other women. Buddhist weddings occur on auspicious days, according to horoscopes. The bridegroom's family may be expected to bring the cake and the bouquet for the bride and maids and pay for half the expenses to the reception. The bride's family gives a dowry, the reception, and gifts to all the members of the groom's family.

The wedding ceremony is very formal. The Porura, surrounded by lighted coconut oil lamps and tender coconut blossoms, is made ready. The bride, wearing white, and the groom, wearing a suit, stand on rice, money, and grains. After much chanting the marriage is confirmed by the tying of the two little fingers with a gold thread.

Marriage brings with it different expectations for men and women. Virginity is expected of a woman. It is not uncommon in the villages for a new bride to be returned if her virginity is questionable. In addition, the woman is made to feel that she is leaving her family and joining her husband's family.

In the past many young married couples went to live in the husband's home. A young wife was expected to wait hand and foot on her mother-in-law. The mother-in-law's role was to pressure the young wife to have children and to present the family with a son and heir.

In the past the men went to work; the women stayed at home. Men made all of the financial decisions, and women were given an allowance. The men had a free life-style; they enjoyed the company of other males and some females (who were well aware of the marital status of the man but needed the extra income). The women stayed at home and, with the help of mostly women servants, cooked, cleaned, took care of and disciplined the children. The men who came home in the evening were served with tea. After tea they would sit and either read the papers or listen to the tales their wives related. The children played and studied and around 8:00 P.M. the family ate together. Always, the father was served first; if food was scarce, the mother did without.

In a family that had servants, the male servants drove the car, polished the floor, cut wood, tended the garden, and served the evening dinner. The female servants cooked, cleaned, and did child care. As children the girl servants, boy servants, and children of the house played together. This changed with adulthood. Adult male servants slept in the garage. The female servants did not mix with them but served them with respect. They made the men their meals and washed their plates.

Today more young couples are living alone. With the tendency for both men and women to work, men sometimes change their ways and help their wives. According to responses on the questionnaires, some responsibilities in the home are now shared. Yet most men prefer to watch television and relax while wives tend to household duties. There are fewer female servants than in the past because many servants have left Sri Lanka for the Middle East. Many women have two jobs; they leave for work just like men, and they return to housework, cooking, and taking care of the children. Society has by and large a narrow concept of women's role in economic life and is apt to view women as "secondary earners" (Jayaweera, 1979: 167).

For relaxation people like to go to the beach. For years the tradition has been to spend Sunday afternoon at Galle Face Green. Traditionally, women dressed in finery and sat in their cars. Fathers and children went for a walk or flew kites. In their leisure time women attend cooking classes, play the piano, and learn etiquette and entertainment. The women stay with other women and go to the matinee or tea at other homes. Some women swim and play tennis. Men spend their free time with other men. Men's hobbies include swimming, tennis, squash, and sailing.

This is a patriarchal society. One respondent explained, "The husband takes pride in having a child and calling them his children, but the wife brings up the children and sees to their needs." Women have learned to gain power by using feminine charms. "Gahanu Mayang Hata-Hathara" is a Sri Lankan saying that a woman is born with 64 charms (or guiles). Women have to learn to live with a lot of blame. If a family is not doing well, it might be blamed on the horoscope of the woman or a daughter of the house. If a husband prospers, it is the fortunate horoscope of the wife. If a husband dies, be it accidental or a shooting, again it is because the wife's horoscope brought misfortune.

Alcoholism is sometimes a problem in Sri Lanka, more common among men than among women (Samarasinghe, 1989; Samarasinghe, Dissanayake & Wijesinghe, 1987). A highly potent drink called *arrack* is available. Physical violence against wives is related to alcohol consumption and the expectation that women's place in society is to obey. To avoid shame and discomfort for her children, a woman may put up with much suffering. There are no battered women's shelters in Sri Lanka (Seager & Olson, 1986).

Divorce is not common in Sri Lanka. The annual average divorce rate is less than 0.25 percent (Seager & Olson, 1986). According to our consultants, divorce is regarded as a shame, and a woman's returning home to live with her parents might not be desired. Mothers are awarded custody of their children.

Old Age

Respect for the elderly has always been strong in Asian cultures. In an age-graded society the older you get, the more love and respect you receive. There was strong agreement among the respondents to our questionnaire that "during old age men and women are respected for their knowledge and loved greatly." Failing to love and respect the elderly is considered morally wrong. In a famous ancient poem that is learned by all Sinhalese-speaking children, evil is personified by a daughter-in-law who refuses to give rice to her old and starving mother-in-law.

When one elderly partner dies, the other usually goes to live with a favorite child or the oldest son. All ethnic groups follow a similar pattern. Grandparents help their children look after the grandchildren. The closeness between grandparents and the younger generation has kept a beautiful heritage cohesive and continuous. Unrecorded family history, folk stories, and traditions are handed down. Some Sri Lankans regret the introduction of television because precious moments of intergenerational communication are now replaced by television viewing. Homes for the aged are rare but do exist for those few who do not have family to care for them.

Old age is a restful period. As no work is expected of them, the elderly spend their last years in leisure reminiscing about the good old days. However, there are differences according to where they live and their gender.

In villages, older men sleep in separate quarters on a wooden bed in the veranda of the house. Clad in sarongs, they are often seen gathered together reminiscing about old times. Considered storehouses of family and traditional history, they are often consulted on such matters. Older men in towns usually wear trousers when they are going out; they get together in clubs, play bridge or cards, and again talk of how good things were in the past. Evenings are spent telling stories to the children of the house. Cigar smoking and betel chewing are common among the older men.

On the other hand, both rural and urban older women move in to live with their favorite child or with relatives and play a more useful role than older men. In some instances, they take on the supervision of house and servants and take care of the needs of the children of the house.

The older women are a storehouse of family recipes, cook or give instructions on cooking, and tell stories of how they lived during olden times, clothes they wore, cruises they went on or even simple stories about what they learned in a small village school.

Both sexes are treated equally by the younger generation, but among the elderly, males are given food first. Women do not eat or drink till the older men are taken care of.

The elderly spend a lot of time meditating or in religious activities. Men and women spend more time in the church, temple, or *kovil*. Muslims continue to worship separately. Among the Buddhists, time is spent in meditation and listening to Bana (the words of the Buddha) and Pirith (prayers chanted by Buddhist priests). By this time socializing between men and women is not frowned upon. Even in the temples, men and women meditate and recite prayers together. However, the men lead and play a dominant role in the temple, and the priest addresses and looks primarily at them rather than the women.

The belief in reincarnation keeps the older generation busy collecting merits to help in another life. A Buddhist and Hindu belief is that one is reborn according to merit. The better you are—kind, wise, helpful, good to the poor—the better chance of being born a man. Otherwise, one might be reborn as a woman or even as a lower form of life.

Death is not looked on as a parting. Hindus and Buddhists cremate the dead. Funeral rites are the same for men and women. Most Buddhists cremate the dead, and the surviving relatives offer alms to priests. The alms give merits to the deceased and help him or her to have a better new life. In the past men had burial plots separate from those of women. Now with the scarcity of land, this practice does not seem to be an issue.

SUMMARY AND CONCLUSIONS

The majority of men and women live their lives in a stage of foreclosure, never questioning the decisions made for them concerning education, careers, or marriage. They keep tradition alive, educating their sons and daughters with behaviors, actions, and reactions that they learned from their mothers and fathers.

The predominant beliefs about gender roles are that a man's role in society is higher than a woman's. A man is reincarnated as a male because of a more virtuous life he led previously. It is believed that the man deserves to be served by his mother, his wife, and his daughters yet he should sacrifice his own happiness for the protection and care of the women in his family. The woman's role is to serve, obey the command of elders, and treat males with respect.

Changes in gender-role behaviors can be seen as women are becoming more authoritative and making strides into what was once a man's domain. Many women now work outside the home. A few women have become political leaders and militant fighters and in doing so have followed in the tradition of the women leaders in ancient Sri Lankan history.

These social changes are occurring during a time of political turmoil. The future for those once peaceful and gentle islanders who kept their doors open to welcome anyone looks bleak. There is an old saying that a crow cawing is a forewarning of visiting relatives who arrive laden with gifts. Today that caw might be interpreted as a calling card from either of the fighting parties, who come empty-handed, but take away the male family members, never to return.

Astrologers have been unable to predict the future of this ancient society that is now rapidly changing. In the past Sri Lanka was a completely segregated society; as modern Sri Lanka surges toward the twenty-first century, the disparity between gender roles seems to be narrowing. Today we see some instances of men and women cooking, taking care of children, driving cars, building bridges, and marching to war side by side.

NOTE

The authors would like to thank Sheila Perera, Rosemund Setukavalar, Nelun Perera, Vijaya Rajagopalan, Saku Suntha, Courtney Beers, Varsha de Silva, Cele Cummiskey, Roy Tamashiro, and Dan Sebben for their assistance in the preparation of this chapter.

REFERENCES

Committee for Rational Development. (1984). *Sri Lanka: The Ethnic Conflict*. New Delhi: Navrang.

Cook, E. W., Pasricha, Samararatne, Maung, & Stevenson. (1983). A review and analysis of ''unsolved'' cases of the reincarnation type: I. Introduction and illustrative case reports. *Journal of the American Society for Physical Research*, 77: 45–62.

de Silva, S., Stiles, D. A., & Gibbons, J. L. (in press). Girls' identity formation in the changing social structure of Sri Lanka. *Journal of Genetic Psychology*.

Farmer, B. H. (1983). *An Introduction to South Asia*. London: Methuen.

Fenton, J. Y., Hein, N., Reynolds, F. E., Miller, A. L., & Nielson, N. C. (1983). *Religions of Asia*. New York: St. Martin's Press.

Hodgin, D. (1990). An ethnic inferno in island paradise. *Insight, 6*: 8–18.

Jayawardana, K. (1986). *Feminism and Nationalism in the Third World*. London: Zed Books.

Jayaweera, S. (1979). Education. Aspects of the role and position of women. In Fernando, T., & Kearney, R. N. (Eds.), *Modern Sri Lanka: A Society in Transition* (pp. 131–54, 165–80). Syracuse, NY: Syracuse University Press.

Keuneman, H. (1984). *Sri Lanka*. Singapore: Tien Mah Litho Printing.

McCurdy, J. (1986). Women in Sri Lanka. In Wilgosh, L. (Ed.), Counselling women: Information from diverse ethnic cultures. *Eleventh International Round Table for the Advancement of Counseling*. Also in *International Journal for the Advancement of Counselling, 9:* 35–46.

Mahavamsa or the Great Chronicle of Ceylon, trans. W. Geiger. (1912). London: Oxford University Press.

Prosser, G. V. (1986). Children's play in Sri Lanka: A cross-cultural study. *British Journal of Developmental Psychology, 4:* 170–85.

Robinson, F. (Ed.). (1989). *Cambridge Encyclopedia of India, Pakistan, Bangladesh, Sri Lanka, Nepal, Bhutan, and the Maldives*. Cambridge: Cambridge University Press.

Rupensinghe, K. (1988). Ethnic conflicts in South Asia: The case of Sri Lanka and the Indian peace-keeping force (IPKF). *Journal of Peace Research, 25:* 337–50.

Samarasingha, D. (1989). Treating alcohol problems in Sri Lanka. *British Journal of Addiction, 84:* 865–67.

Samarasingha, D., Dissanayake, S. A., & Wijesinghe, C. P. (1987). Alcoholism in Sri Lanka. *British Journal of Addiction, 82:* 1149–53.

Seager, J., & Olson, A. (1986). *Women in the World: An International Atlas*. New York: Simon & Schuster.

Thambia, S. J. (1990). Sri Lanka: Introduction. In Peebles, P., Colonization of ethnic conflict in the dry zone of Sri Lanka. *Journal of Asian Studies, 49:* 30–53.

United Nations. (1991). *The World's Women: Trends and Statistics 1970–1990*. New York.

Wickramasinghe, M. (1956). *The Buddhist Jataka Stories and the Russian Novel*. Colombo: Lake House.

26

Taiwan

Wen-Ying Lin and Hsiao-Chin Hsieh

INTRODUCTION

Taiwan, the Republic of China (ROC), is located approximately 100 miles off the southeastern coast of the Chinese mainland in the western Pacific Ocean. The whole area includes Taiwan Island and several small archipelagoes, approximately 36,000 square kilometers (13,900 square miles) in size. Taipei, located in the northern portion of the island, is the capital city and the economic, political, and cultural center of the ROC.

The people of Taiwan are composed of a number of different ethnic groups. The Han race is predominant. Approximately 300,000 residents are aborigines who live primarily on reservations on the east coast of Taiwan. Those who came to Taiwan after 1949 are commonly referred to as "mainlanders," whereas those who are descendants of immigrants who came from the coastal provinces of mainland China over the last three centuries are referred to as "Taiwanese." Approximately 85 percent of the population are "Taiwanese," 13.5 percent are "mainlanders," and 1.5 percent are aborigines. As Taiwan is a stronghold of traditional Chinese culture, Buddhism and Taoism are predominant, although Christianity and Islam are also represented.

The population of Taiwan was 20 million as of the end of July 1989, with a density of 558.5 persons per square kilometer—among the highest in the world—and a sex ratio of 107.1 males per 100 females. The country's crude birthrate was as high as 49.9 per 1,000 in 1951, but had fallen to 16 per 1,000 by 1989, a trend that should continue. The population growth rate decreased from 3.7 percent in 1951 to 1.1 percent in 1989, projecting zero population growth by the year 2030. Due to the improvement in public health, medical facilities, and standard of living, life expectancy has increased from 61.8 in 1960 to 71.0 in 1990 for men and from 67.1 to 76.1 in the same time period for women.

In the last thirty years, Taiwan has experienced rapid economic growth. Its economic structure has been transformed from a predominantly agricultural to an industrial[1] basis. The per capita income of Taiwan has increased from U.S. $186 in 1952 to U.S. $7,332 in 1990, the average annual increases being 6.4 percent. From 1953 to 1989, the proportion of the population employed in agriculture decreased from 56 to 13 percent, while that in industry changed from 17 to 42 percent and that in tertiary activities increased from 27 to 45 percent. The labor participation rates of men and women were 83 percent and 33 percent, respectively, in 1965. By 1989, the labor force in the ROC numbered 8.3 million, with a participation rate of 75 percent for men and 45 percent for women. The unemployment rate was lower than 1 percent for the year.

OVERVIEW

Under the processes of modernization and industrialization, various gaps between men and women in Taiwan have narrowed since the beginning of the postwar era. Equal rights for men and women are incorporated in the centra's Constitution. Article 7 of the 1947 Constitution states: ''All citizens of the Republic of China, irrespective of sex, religion, race, class or party affiliation, shall be equal before the law.'' A nine-year compulsory education ensures equal educational opportunities for boys and girls between the ages of six and fifteen. The Labor Standards Law, passed in 1984, forbids discrimination against any worker on the basis of sex. Special protection for women's political rights, motherhood, and family is further specified in the Constitution.

Equality de jure, however, is not quite the same as equality de facto. To date, men in Taiwan still enjoy significant social, educational, economical, and political advantages over women. Son preference remains popular in Taiwanese society. While boys and girls have equal access to schooling at the compulsory level, discrepancies between the sexes are still found at postcompulsory levels and widen as the years of schooling increase. In higher education, sex segregation is evident in fields of study, which is discussed later.

Sex segregation is also prevalent in the workplace. Women are concentrated in traditional female jobs, with restricted choices and much less stable labor force participation than men have. Women employees suffer disadvantages in the areas of promotion, salary, and fringe benefits when compared with men. Moreover, married female wage earners are doubly burdened as household work is still considered to be the wife's duty.

The patriarchal characteristics of the Taiwanese society are explicitly reflected in the legal status of men and women in the family. The Family Law grants the man the headship of the conjugal family by preserving his authority over the management of family property, place of residence, and the child's surname.

Politics in Taiwan, as in many other societies, is almost exclusively a male domain. The political participation of women has increased in the past four decades, but they are still significantly underrepresented across all levels of public offices, especially in high-ranking government positions.[2] Recently, local women's organizations and associations for various purposes have emerged, indicating a rapid rise in women's social participation. However, these groups primarily consist of well-educated women with white-collar jobs and/or middle-class housewives.

COMPARISONS BETWEEN MEN'S AND WOMEN'S GENDER ROLES DURING THE LIFE CYCLE

Infancy and Early Childhood

Son preference was strong in traditional Chinese society due to the agricultural mode of production, which demanded intensive manual labor, and the mandate of the family system that the son carry on the family line as well as support the family and his parents in old age. This legacy continues in contemporary Taiwan. A 1988 statistic shows that, even among women themselves, the average ideal number and sex of children are 1.50 boys and 1.19 girls. Nevertheless, as a consequence of economic growth, women's increasing participation in extra-domestic life, and their closer ties with their natal families, there is a gradual lessening of the attitude of "emphasizing the man, de-emphasizing the woman" (Hu, 1985; Chiang, 1989). In studying working women in urban Taiwan, Tsui (1987) reported a decreasing preference for sons among the highly educated, white-collar working women. Their husbands, however, still showed a strong son preference.

Son preference is also shown in contraceptive practices. In their study, Chiang, Shyu, and Wu (1985) found that, of the 1,420 tubal ligation cases, 21 percent acceptors had boy(s) only, and 5 percent had girl(s) only. This implies that Taiwanese women are less likely to accept tubal ligation if there is no male heir in the family.

In the Chinese naming system, one's surname is adopted from the father's family, and the first name can be the combination of any one or two Chinese characters. A survey (Liao, 1991) examining the naming of children between 1950 and 1987 reveals that the grandfathers are more often requested to choose the names for their grandsons than for their granddaughters, whereas mothers are chosen as name givers for girls more often than for boys. It is also found that the meanings of boys' names are mostly related to qualities suggestive of high ambition and to refined characteristics such as auspicious prospects, great achievement, erudition, and moral rectitude. By contrast, names given to girls are usually either without any special significance or are related to attractive appearance, polite manners, virtues, jewelry, and flowers. Differential values and expectations are thus revealed in the naming of boys and girls.

In child rearing, most mothers denied that their ways of taking care of their infants vary according to the sex of babies (Su & Jong, 1985). Wang and Lu (1985) also found no significant effect of parental gender-role rearing on preschoolers' preference for gender-specific toys and work. However, Lee's (1983) study reveals that five-year-old boys and girls have developed clearer concepts of stereotypical male roles than of female roles. While boys hold preference for stereotypical male roles, girls tended to prefer androgynous gender roles. Recent findings (Lin, 1989) indicate that when parents do not observe traditional parental division of household tasks, the less traditional are their children's sex-role attitudes. Thus, a further challenge for research lies in interventions that foster sex typing in childhood through the parents' child-rearing philosophies and practices.

School Years

Education is emphasized greatly in Chinese culture. As a consequence of the global educational expansion, the educational level of Taiwan's population has escalated considerably since the early 1950s. By 1980, the literacy rate had increased from 74 percent in 1961 to 93 percent. The number of university students per 1,000 persons increased from 2.5 to 8.6 in the same period of time.

However, women were grossly deprived of educational opportunities until the turn of the century. The gap in educational attainment between the sexes has narrowed over the past forty years. By 1980, the proportion of female students at the compulsory level reached 48 percent and higher. At the postcompulsory levels, senior high schools observed rapid growth from 28 percent up to 47 percent in female student population during the years from 1950 to 1989. The proportion of female students in junior college and above also rose from 11 percent in 1950 to 45 percent in 1989.

Significant sex inequalities in educational opportunities nevertheless remain. As shown in Table 26.1, the higher the level of schooling, the lower are women's participation rates. More specifically, while public schools are more prestigious than private ones, girls are offered smaller admission quotas in public senior high schools than are boys (Hsieh, 1991). From college and beyond, men are concentrated in the sciences and technology, while women are in the humanities and social sciences. Since the recent expansion in higher education centers of departments in sciences and technology, primarily out of the concern for economic growth, men, not women, benefit more from such increasing opportunities for higher learning.

Sex segregation by fields of study does not exist by chance. Rather, it has been maintained and reinforced by the interaction of the educational system and social values. First of all, in 1947, a high school organization regulation stated that "students should be divided into different schools by sex." The article was revised in 1970 to read, "Students should be divided into different classes by sex." The policy was in effect until 1981 for senior high schools and until 1983 for junior high schools. Although the influence of single-sex education on students' sex-role development waits to be verified (Tsou, 1989), the awareness of its restriction on the interactions between boys and girls has brought forth a new

Table 26.1
Percentage of Women at Different Educational Levels

	TOTAL		IN PUBLIC SCHOOL
	1950	1989	
Kindergarten	43.52	47.79	48.89
Primary Ed.	38.99	48.47	48.52
Junior High	28.66	48.78	49.24
Senior High	27.09	46.71	45.85
Vocational High	15.51	53.72	47.87
5-year College		43.61	36.81
3-year College	10.89	51.20	36.32
2-year College		52.46	36.32
4-year Col. & Univ.		45.64	41.94
Master	---	24.79	22.00
Doctor	---	15.77	14.77

Sources: Adopted from *Educational Indicators of the R.O.C.* (Taipei: Ministry of Education, 1991), 32, and calculated from *Educational Statistics of Republic of China* (Taipei: Ministry of Education, 1991), 61.

trend toward coeducation. Second, teachers who serve as role models are segregated in their fields of teaching by sex (Hsieh, 1989). In addition, teachers and characters represented in the mass media usually manifest interests and skills adapted to stereotypical sex roles.

Third, primary and secondary school textbooks constantly portray stereotypical gender roles and convey male-centered messages (*A Handbook*, 1988; Ou, 1988). For instance, 98 percent of the characters presented in the twelve volumes of elementary school social studies textbooks are males who play a wide variety of roles. The 2 percent female characters include three fictional figures, one empress portrayed negatively, and one heroine (*A Handbook*, 1988: 12). Another analysis of elementary school Chinese readers documents the same sex discriminatory treatment. Some possible consequences are indicated by empirical research: primary school boys significantly more frequently identify themselves with same-sex roles than do girls (Lu, 1989); boys also give higher appraisal to male characters in storybooks than to female ones (Sheu, 1987).

Finally, social values still support traditional gender roles. A recent survey reveals differential educational expectations for males and females in Taiwanese

Table 26.2
Labor Participation Rate in Taiwan (percentages)

YEAR	MALE	FEMALE
1965	82.62	33.11
1968	80.23	34.36
1970	78.87	35.45
1973	77.13	41.53
1975	77.61	38.56
1978	77.96	39.16
1980	77.11	39.25
1983	76.36	42.12
1985	75.47	43.46
1988	74.83	45.56

Sources: *Council for Economic Planning and Development* (1984); *An Analysis of the Utilization of Female Labor Force in Taiwan* (Labor Committee, Executive Yuan, 1990); *Male and Female Labor Statistics, Taiwan Area* (R.O.C., 1990).

society. For example, teacher education and home economics are considered most suitable for women, while technology, engineering, and medical science are for men. Furthermore, people expect that girls should receive at least a junior college education and that men should at least finish university studies. As a result, even among students of National Taiwan University, the most prestigious university in Taiwan, the average level of aspirations for graduate studies is significantly lower for females than for males. Although both men and women aspire to professional jobs, men are more inclined to be employers themselves, whereas women are more apt to be employees (Tsai & Chiu, 1988).

Young Adulthood

Both the increasing level of educational attainment and the industrialization of Taiwan's economy contribute to rapid growth of female participation in the labor market. Table 26.2 shows that the labor force participation rate for females between the ages of fifteen and sixty-five increased from 33 percent in 1965 to 46 percent in 1988, whereas that for males decreased from 83 percent to 75 percent for the same time period. In their review of the status of women in Taiwan, Chiang and Ku (1985) noted that women enter the labor force earlier and spend longer periods of time looking for jobs than men. This may be due to women's relatively shorter period of education as well as to the greater number of jobs in technical fields than in humanities and greater chances for men to be employed, especially when there is competition for a job between the sexes (Chiang & Ku: 10). Empirical studies also suggest that a higher level of education is required for women than for men for jobs of the same level (Tsai, 1987).

Conditions of employment are different for men and women. For instance, men tend to create their own job opportunities and become self-employed, whereas women tend to secure jobs through friends and job interviews. Upon job selection, occupational interest is the major concern of men, while the compatibility of job and family demands is the chief concern of women (Kao, 1985). The female employment rate marks an M shape: highest in the 20–24 age group, then declining and rising again between the ages of 35 and 44. Along with the growth of female labor force participation, the slope of the M shape diminishes slowly over time (Chang, 1978).

Although jobs traditionally held by men are increasingly performed by women due to the latter's increasing education, statistics for 1989 show that women continue to concentrate in sales, service, commerce, and manufacturing; they constitute 48, 47, 44, and 42 percent of the labor force, respectively. Except for manufacturing, none of these sectors is regulated by the Labor Standards Law. Even within the same industry, men are likely to concentrate in the core administrative and research levels, with women mostly in the less productive and low-skilled sectors (Yeh, 1990).

Numerous studies have documented wage differentials between men and women in Taiwan. In 1989, the average salary for women of senior high school education was 66 percent of that for men of the same educational level. At the junior college level and beyond, the average salary for women was 69 percent of that for men. Liao and Cheng (1985) found that discrepancies in pay between the sexes is larger in private industries than in government employment. Lin's (1988) study further indicated that unequal pay for equal work directly contributed to the wage differential by sex. The discriminatory treatment against women in promotion, salary increase, and in-service training is significantly more frequently and seriously perceived by women than by men (Yu, 1991).

Marriage is no longer arranged by parents in modern Taiwan. As a consequence what a man looks for in a marriage partner is quite different from that in traditional society. In old days, the so-called feminine characteristics were what counted in a woman's marital values. By contrast, a recent study on a sample of 875 young adults in Taipei suggested that, when selecting a spouse, men now put a premium on women's willingness or motivation to work with them for family goals. On the other hand, a woman continues to emphasize the mannishness and the sense of responsibility in a man. Research also reveals that, compared with their male counterparts, females are more conservative in their attitudes toward sexuality and sexual behavior but are more liberal in their attitudes toward female independence in family and marital relationships (Li, 1981). Although overt sexuality remains a taboo among Taiwanese, single motherhood is gradually gaining social acceptance.

Due to the prolongation of schooling and changes in socio-economic structure, late marriage is now a characteristic feature of contemporary Taiwanese society. The unmarried rate of women between 20 and 24 rose from 59 percent to 77 percent between 1978 and 1990, and from 17 percent to 32 percent for women between 25 and 29. At the same period of time, the average marriage age extended from 21.1 to 21.9. Despite the facts that divorce is increasingly common[3] and that many couples delay childbearing, marriage and parenthood are still the central life involvements for the majority of adult men and women in Taiwan. The patterns of marriage and parenthood, however, seem to vary for people of different educational levels. The higher-educated females are inclined to marry late and have fewer children. The average marriage age of female university graduates is 26, and the average number of children is 1.7, far fewer than the number for all married women, which stands at 3.2.

Adulthood

The Family Law, revised in 1985, endorses the joint ownership of property for husband and wife; however, only the husband is granted the right to manage and use the union property. The child is allowed to bear the mother's surname only if she has no brother and the father gives his consent. Divorce by mutual consent is effected by requiring at least two witnesses' signatures and registration at a district office. One party may apply to the court for a divorce if proof is provided the other party has committed an offense specified in the civil code.

However, in a divorce either by consent or by court judgment, the custody of the child goes to the husband unless otherwise agreed upon. No visiting rights are ensured for the mother, nor are there provisions of alimony in a divorce by consent. Consequently, many divorced women encounter social discrimination and financial difficulties through losing their status of being married and are deprived of their maternal identity as well. Before the law, women are put at a great disadvantage when they enter into a marriage contract.

Taiwan's traditional culture designates housekeeping and child rearing as women's primary responsibilities, which should be carried out voluntarily. When there is conflict between career and motherhood, women are inclined to give up their career in order to fulfill their maternal role (Lu, 1981). Married women who have small children and who wish to continue working are more likely to choose informal, rather than formal, employment because of the compatibility of the former with their familial roles (Lu, 1991).

As shown in Table 26.2, the formal employment rates for females fluctuate, indicating the marginality of the female labor force. Their participation in the labor market is largely affected by factors such as marriage, childbearing and child rearing, and age.[4] In 1990, 30 percent of married women left their jobs due to marriage, and about 80 percent of them never returned to the job market because of the decidedly limited job opportunities (Executive Yuan, 1991).

Among married women, however, especially the highly educated, a declining trend of taking care of children personally is observed. The overall percentage of married women nurturing children themselves is 75 percent, while only 28 percent of college-educated women do so. When mothers work outside the home, grandparents, relatives, and baby-sitters become the main caretakers of children. Since more than 60 percent of families in all economic classes in urban areas are nuclear families, public nurseries remain an urgent need for working women in Taiwan.[5]

Compared with research on women's changing social status, research on men's attitudes toward gender roles is quite primitive and few. One such interesting research is the work of Hsu (1991), who reported that in current advertisements in the mass media, males are no longer portrayed as authoritative husbands explaining to their ignorant and incompetent wives how the products work. More and more men are characterized as being caring and considerate, doing the shopping, washing the dishes, and operating electric home appliances. In many urban Taiwanese families married couples are now sharing in decision making regarding domestic affairs; the wife, in fact, preserves power in appropriating family income and in child rearing (Yi & Tsai, 1988; Lu, 1991).

The 1989 ICP (Integrated Consumer Profile) indicated that women between age 15 and 29 were the main consumers and patrons of literary and artistic activities. By far, more women than men are found eagerly participating in a variety of intellectual activities such as speeches, language or skill learning, career planning, and education tours to enhance personal growth (Hsu, 1991). Chen's (1985) study found that married working women in Taipei are more interested in restful than children-related activities, and yet, in practice, they attend children-related activities more than others. Based upon a field study of three newly founded women's groups,[6] Lu (1991) concluded that the maternal role is a major motivation for women's self-growth. Thus, women's maternal identities function as catalysts in their search for social resources and intellectual pursuits. On the other hand, Taiwanese men are found to be more interested in sports activities for their own pleasure.

Old Age

The proportion of the civilian population aged 65 and over was 5.9 percent in 1990 and is estimated to reach 8.4 percent in the year 2000. Public Social Security for the elderly is not yet available in Taiwan. According to a survey administered in 1989 by the Executive Yuan, while 73 percent of the old-age population believed living with their children (permanently or in turn with several children) to be the ideal living arrangement, only 66 percent actually do so. Although there is a trend toward the nuclear family, the tradition that places the responsibility of caring for aged parents on adult children still prevails. Sixty percent of elderly males and 72 percent of females live with children. The sex differences may be largely due to the fact that aged females are economically less advantaged: 73 percent of females, as opposed to 46 percent of males, depend upon children economically.

For elderly people, adapting themselves from being a source of aid for others to being a needy recipient of their support seems to be crucial; this is true for both sexes. Although male-female role reversal in late life has been suggested in Lin's (1989) study (i.e., aged males manifest female attributes, with aged females showing male personalities), more empirical studies are needed to support this claim in Taiwan and elsewhere.

As for stimulating activities of the aged, 88 percent of them seldom go out for any kind of leisure activity, only 3 percent participate in intellectual sessions, and 4 percent take part in voluntary work. Except for religious activities, which are participated in by both sexes across all ages, statistics on the elderly indicated that, in general, the younger, the more educated, and the males engage in all kinds of activities more than the older, the less educated, and the females.[7]

SUMMARY AND CONCLUSIONS

In the Tang Dynasty, a famous Chinese poet, Pai Chu-i, wrote: "Never be a female, because centuries of joy and sorrow are under the control of others."[8] Just a few decades ago in Taiwan, women who worked outside the home were viewed as divorced, widowed, or having a husband who could not adequately provide for the family, and so they were socially looked down upon or pitied. One could hardly imagine any possibilities outside the strict stereotyped roles.

Nowadays, the lengthening of schooling and the broadening of areas of study have exposed both men and women to a wide variety of perspectives, values, and standards of behavior. The rapidly changing social situation has facilitated a wide-ranging critique of discriminatory treatment of women in Taiwan. The end result has been a higher percentage of women attaining postmarriage working careers and participating in social activities. Despite many women having to fulfill dual roles as a wage earner and homemaker in order to achieve social recognition, their presence and performance in the public sphere have contributed to bringing into focus the theme of equality between men and women.

As Taiwan moves from an industrial- to an information-based society, automation and intellect-intensive types of industry increasingly blur the sex division of labor. This allows further participation of women in economic activities, which, in turn, helps to enhance their status in the family as well as in society. Together with women's awareness of the importance of education and independence and with active participation in a variety of professional fields, one can reasonably expect an increasing prominence of females in all walks of life.

However, as previously indicated, the structural discrimination of women's social and legal status still exists. Also, biases against women built upon traditional value systems still prevail in one's attitude toward gender roles at work and in family life. It is evident that the quality of male and female relationships depend greatly on the social context of the various stages and factors influencing an individual's life cycle. It is hoped that this presentation has provided a context for further discussion and that constraints and barriers will be removed as Taiwan progresses to a more egalitarian society.

NOTES

1. The major industries are electronics, petroleum, textiles, and construction.

2. According to the statistics published by the Ministry of Personnel, Examination Yuan, in 1983, women comprised 23 percent of all government employees. Among the women, 0.4 percent were of high rank, 8.4 percent of middle rank, and 91 percent of low rank, while 3.7 percent of men were of high rank, 24 percent of middle rank, and 72 percent of low rank. The proportion of women being elected to the General Assembly, the Legislative Yuan, and the Control Yuan in 1986 was 19 percent, 10 percent, and 14 percent, respectively.

3. The divorce rate was .38 percent in 1965 and increased to 1.2 percent by 1989.

4. For example, married women's employment rate of 42 percent is much lower than the 57 percent rate among unmarried women. A recent survey found that 7.6 percent of the employers interviewed reported forced resignation of women upon marriage or childbirth in their firms, despite maternity protection regulated in the Labor Standards Law (Yu, 1991).

5. For example, only 23 percent of the applying families fulfilled their wishes to use public nurseries in the Taipei area in 1991.

6. The New Environmental Homemakers' Association founded in 1987, the Taipei Women's Development Center in 1984, and the Warm Life Association in 1984.

7. This can be shown by the composition of the participants of the Silver Threaded Noble, a program organized by the Bureau of Social Affairs of Taipei in 1991 for the elderly: 65 percent are of college and above education, 37 percent are female, and only 28 percent are above seventy years old.

8. The line is drawn from the poem "Tai Hang Lu" by Pai Chu-i.

REFERENCES

An Analysis of the Utilization of Female Labor Force in Taiwan. (1984). Taipei: Council for Economic Planning and Development.

Chang, C. H. (1978). A review of female labor force participation. *Economic Essays,* 8: 275–84.

Chen, C. I. (1985). Leisure interests, leisure participation and life-styles of married working women in Taipei. *Journal of Education & Psychology, 9:* 191–209.

Chen, L. C. (1983). The study of the college graduates' identity status development. *Bulletin of Educational Psychology, 16:* 89–98.

Chiang, C. D., Shyu, C. E., & Wu, P. H. (1985, March). Follow-up survey on the tubal litigation acceptors in Taipei City. Paper presented at the Conference on the Role of Women in the National Development Process in Taiwan, Taipei.

Chiang, L. H. (1989). The new social and economic roles of Chinese women in Taiwan

and their implication for policy and development. *Journal of Developing Societies*,
5: 96–106.

Chiang, L. H. & Ku, Y. (1985). *Past and Current Status of Women in Taiwan*. Taipei:
National Taiwan University, Center for Population Studies—Women's Research
Program.

Educational Indicators of the R.O.C. (1991). Taipei: Ministry of Education.

Educational Statistics of the R.O.C. (1991). Taipei: Ministry of Education.

A Handbook for Equal Education for the Two Sexes. (1988). Taipei: Awakening Foundation.

Hsieh, H. C. (1989). Gender ideology in the school system. *Humanistic Education*, 7:
30–35.

Hsieh, H. C. (1991, June). Sex differences in educational opportunities: The case of two
Taipei junior high schools. Paper presented in Conference on Gender and Society,
National Tsing-Hua University, Taipei.

Hsu, H. L. (1991). Portraits and values as reflected in the late 1980s women's magazine
advertisements. Master's thesis, Fu Jen Catholic University, Taipei.

Hu, T. L. (1985). The influence of industrialization of Taiwan rural area on the status
of women. In Chiang, N. (Ed.), *The Role of Women in the National Development
Process in Taiwan* (pp. 339–55). Taipei: National Taiwan University, Center for
Population Studies—Women's Research Program.

Kao, S. K. (1985). A comparison between men and women in Taiwan on the selection
of occupations. In Chiang, N. (Ed.), *The Role of Women in the National Development Process in Taiwan*. Taipei: National Taiwan University, Center for Population Studies—Women's Research Program.

Lee, J. Y. (1983). A study on gender role development of Chinese children. Master's
thesis, National Taiwan Normal University, Taipei.

Li, M. C. (1981). The construction of sex trait inventory and the comparisons of four
sex trait categories on achievement motive and attitudes toward marriage, career
and sex. *Acta Psychologica Taiwanica*, *23*(1): 23–37.

Liao, K. F. (1991). A survey of child naming and value change in Taiwan. Master's
thesis, Fu Jen Catholic University, Taipei.

Liao, L. L., & Cheng, W. Y. (1985, March). The contributions of female labor force
to economic growth in Taiwan. Keynote speech delivered at the Conference on
the Role of Women in the National Development Process in Taiwan, Center for
Population Studies, National Taiwan University, Taipei.

Lin, C. C. (1988). Sex differences in wage among the first-job holders. *Economic Essays*,
16(3).

Lin, M. C. (1989). A study on gender role and personality of the middle-aged and the
elderly. In *Proceedings of the Conference on Gender Role and Social Development*. Taipei: National Taiwan University, Center for Population Studies.

Lin, T. M. (1989). The influence of parental gender role attitudes on those of their
children's—An analysis of patterns of parental division of household tasks and
its effect on children's household task assignment. Master's thesis, National Taiwan Normal University, Taipei.

Lu, C. C. (1989). A study of children's identification objects in Taiwan. Master's thesis,
National Taiwan Normal University, Taipei.

Lu, H. S. (1991, June). Women's self-growth groups and empowerment of the ''uterine family'' in Taiwan. Paper presented at the Conference on Gender and Society, National Tsing-Hua University, Taiwan.

Lu, Y. H. (1981). Career attitudes of women in a changing society. *Bulletin of the Institute of Ethnology. Academia Sinica, 50*: 25–66.

———. (1991, June). Women's informal employment in Taiwan. Paper presented at the conference on Gender and Society, National Tsing-Hua University, Taiwan.

Male and Female Labor Statistics in Taiwan Area. (1990). Taipei: Labor Committee.

Ou, Y. S. (1988). Gender ideology in elementary school textbooks. In Chen, B. C. (Ed.), *Ideology and Education* (pp. 255–72). Taipei: Hsu-Ta.

Report on Fertility and Employment of Married Women in Taiwan Area. (1988, 1991). Taipei: Directorate-General of Budget, Accounting and Statistics.

Sheu, M. H. (1987). A study of how children appraise males and females in children's storybooks. *Bulletin of Counseling, 10*: 341–55.

Social Indicators in Taiwan Area of the ROC. (1990). Taipei: Directorate-General of Budget, Accounting and Statistics.

Su, C. W., & Jong, J. T. (1985). A study about how mothers take care of their infants. *Bulletin of Educational Psychology, 18*: 117–48.

Tsai, S. L. (1987). Occupational segregation and differential educational achievement: A comparison between men and women. *Chinese Journal of Sociology, 11* (Spring): 61–91.

Tsai, S. L., & Chiu, H. Y. (1988). Gender and achievement aspirations: The case of Tai-Ta students. *Chinese Journal of Sociology, 12*: 125–68.

Tsou, H. Y. (1989). The relationship between gender segregation, school formation and high school students' sex role development and achievement motivation. Master's thesis, National Kao-hsiung Normal College, Taiwan.

Tsui, Y. L. (1987). *Are Married Daughters Spilled Water?—A Study of Working Women in Urban Taiwan.* Monograph 4. Taipei: National Taiwan University, Center for Population Studies—Women's Research Program.

Wang, H. C., & Lu, T. M. (1985). The influence of parental gender role attitude and distribution on preschoolers' gender role. *Home Economics Education, 9*(6): 76–88.

Yearbook of Manpower Statistics in Taiwan Area. (1990). Taipei: Directorate-General of Budget, Accounting and Statistics.

Yeh, C. H. (1990). *A Study on Labor Policies Protecting Female Workers—Empirical Analysis of Labor Standards Law of R.O.C.* Taipei: Graduate Institute of Public Policy, National Chung-Hsing University.

Yi, C. C., & Tsai, L. Y. (1988, August). An exploratory analysis of marital power in Taipei area: The case of family decision making. Paper presented at Conference on Taiwan Social Phenomena, Institute of Sun Yet-Sen, Academia Sinica, Nankang, Taiwan.

Yu, H. Y. (1991, September). Sex discrimination in labor market in Taiwan area. Paper presented at the Conference on Sex Equality in the Workplace, Center for Population Studies—Labor Committee and Women's Research, National Taiwan University, Taiwan.

27

Tanzania

Issa M. Omari

INTRODUCTION

Any attempt at a thorough and adequate analysis of the concept of gender roles in African cultures is bound to be surrounded by both theoretical and methodological limitations. At one level, it is reasonable to contend that there are as many cultures in Africa as there are tribes, and there are 120 tribes in Tanzania alone, which is one medium-size country out of about 50 countries in Africa. Besides these spatial differences, there are situational, temporal, and cross-generational differences (Doob, 1967). In Africa extreme forms of poverty, illiteracy, and underdevelopment coexist with modernity, literacy, and very rich modes of existence. In this context, it is more than pretentious to assume the responsibility for a critical analysis and presentation of a coherent view about generalizable gender roles in Africa—or Tanzania, for that matter (Omari, 1982). Gender roles differ with levels of education, family occupations, anthropological traits (matrilineal, matrilocal, patrilineal, patrilocal), or a combination of these. On a methodological plane, attempts to use any survey methods to delineate differences in social arrangements across countries, ethnic groups, and age levels present logistical problems that cannot be overestimated. Thus the present attempts are based on an examination of existing literature, which is, by and large, based on experiences of the authors rather than on concrete studies, coupled with the author's observations and experientially acquired insights. This might lead to the development of a mere caricature but should be an acceptable risk for an exercise of this nature. The chapter concentrates on gender roles in Tanzania, where the author hails from and about which the author thus has better insights into gender dynamics.

Tanzania as a nation-state has a very short history. After about three centuries of Arab slave trade and commercial plunder of a fragmented society by external forces (A.D. 1500–1850), the country was formally acquired by the Germans as a colony at the Berlin Conference of 1885. After the First World War, in 1918, the country changed hands and became a British protectorate territory, and after the Second World War in 1945 it became a United Nations trusteeship under British administration. In 1961, after long and protracted negotiations, it became an independent country known as Tanganyika, which united with Zanzibar in 1964 to become Tanzania. The present family system and social structures are, by and large, a product of both these historical circumstances, spanning over three centuries of Arabic, German, and British influences, and the current political, social, and economic policies and activities that circumscribe individual actions.

Tanzania is a relatively large country that lies on the East African coast of the Indian Ocean. The long coastline of about 6,000 miles between Kenya and Mozambique opened up lines of cultural contacts among Arabs, Africans, and Indians. The Arabs from Oman and the Gulf states brought with them Islamic influence and Koranic education system along the coast and on the routes into the interior that were used for trade in slaves and ivory tusks. The Arabs came with Islamic cultures, which encouraged large families and allowed marriage of four wives by one man. The Asians from the Indian subcontinent introduced other versions of Islamic and Hindu cultures. They established closed societies in the main cities of Tanzania, with their own educational, cultural, business, and social systems, quite different and separate from those of the African cultures.

On the other hand, the Africans, mostly of Bantu origin, with their own traditional educational system and dialects, could not resist the cultural and economic penetration from organized external forces; hence the Kiswahili language emerged, which is an adaptation of Bantu language structures to Arabic, Indian, and Portuguese lexicons, and vice versa. It is now the only common language that is intelligible to all tribes and peoples of Tanzania and is spoken in the neighboring countries as well. The complexities of this background make Tanzania a quite heterogeneous society with respect to family traditions, social organization, and anthropological practices.

Tanzania has an area of 945,000 square miles of landmass and 60,000 square miles of inland waters, consisting of the African Great Lakes (Lakes Victoria, Tanganyika, and Nyasa) and an assortment of long and large rivers, such as the Great Ruaha, Rufiji, Ruvu, and Pangani, and small lakes, such as Natron, Eyasi, and Jipe. There are some man-made lakes, too, such as Nyumba ya Mungu and Mtera dams, used for both irrigation and hydroelectric power. The landscape of Tanzania is characterized by high mountain peaks, such as Meru and the famous Kilimanjaro, which is 20,000 feet high and the only permanently snowcapped peak in Africa. There are mountain ranges of about 8,000–10,000 feet high in the northeast and southwest. The Great East African Rift Valley, which stems from the Middle East, forms deep inland troughs and hills that create different farming cultures and family life patterns.

Besides irregular volcanic eruptions on top of Kilimanjaro and regular river floods, Tanzania is a relatively stable landmass. The process of desertification in central Tanzania that has been taking place in the last 50 years is being arrested by a government afforestation campaign, but spells of drought and long dry seasons make continued and productive farming activities impossible. The geographical features determine rain distribution patterns and hence agricultural activities. Thus, while the whole country experiences hot, wet summers and cool, dry winters, the mountainous areas have cold, dry winters, and coastal areas have mildly cool, dry winters. The early missionaries who introduced Christianity and modern Western education preferred the cool highlands while the Arabs preferred the hot coastal areas. Thus, educational and cultural developments followed these early settlement patterns and thus led to great inequalities in the distribution of educational opportunities, economic and cultural advancements, and environmental management practices.

Thus most of the coastal areas practice Islamic cultures that allow marriage of four wives while the Christian inland areas acquired a Western concept of family life, capitalizing on one man, one wife, and the gender roles thus differed dramatically between the two civilizations and marriage systems.

OVERVIEW

Tanzania conducts periodic national population censuses. The 1967 census indicated a population of 12,313,469 people, and by the 1978 census, the population was 17,527,564 people, giving a rate of annual increase of 3.3 percent and a population density of 19.8. Currently the population is estimated at 25 million people, with women forming about 52 percent of the total population. The age distribution is greatly skewed in favor of those below 15 years of age, characteristic of developing countries' demographic features. The current growth rate per annum is about 2.8 percent.

The 1978 census gave the proportion of households in urban area as 20 percent and an urban male-female ratio of 9:6. However, the Tanzania population is predominantly rural as it is estimated that about 87 percent of the people live in rural areas. The main cities are the regional headquarters, but most of them are medium-size cities of populations between 50,000 and 160,000 people only. The capital city of Dar-es-Salaam approaches 1 million people. As a general policy, the government attempts to distribute development projects evenly throughout the country, and great efforts are being made to develop the rural areas so as to curb urban migrations. However, the urban population growth rate of 9.34 is relatively higher than anticipated (Government of Tanzania, 1969) and poses a threat to smooth resource allocation and tranquil urban family and social lives.

Ethnically Tanzania is a very homogeneous country, as most of the population is African (95.6 percent), with small Indian, Arab, and European minority groups engaged in either business or plantation farming. However, linguistically Tanzania is a very heterogeneous country, as there are about 120 tribes speaking different languages all over the country, although Kiswahili is intelligible to all of these groups and is used both as a national language and as a medium of instruction in primary schools and in lower-level training institutions. Among 120 tribes, however, a few tribes are particularly large: the Wasukuma of Mwanza, the Wachaga of Kilimanjaro, the Wahaya of Kagera (West Lake), and the Wanyakyusa of Mbeya. Besides their great economic and educational advancements, these tribes enjoy relatively advantaged social positions. On the other hand, family life and hence gender roles and child-rearing styles differ widely from the famous nomadic Masai of northern Tanzania, the cave people (Hadza) of central Tanzania, the modern life-styles of these large tribes mentioned above, and the urban elite, which despite the economic constraints, has adapted very well to current international standards of social life and nutritional habits.

The employment and class structure in Tanzania can be meaningfully analyzed only in the context of its national ideology. Over the years since independence in 1961, Tanzania has evolved a coherent socialist ideology that emphasizes collective ownership of the major means of production and living together in communal villages. The type of socialism advocated in Tanzania is clearly articulated in the official policy document called *The Arusha Declaration* (1967), in which the major means of production were declared nationalized. These included land, buildings, industries, and financial institutions such as banks and insurance companies. Furthermore, communal villages or collectives were established as the basic units of production in the rural areas. The policy pronounced the intention to fight all forms of exploitation of one person or group by another and declared that Tanzania society will be composed exclusively of workers and farmers. The declaration abolished the system whereby one received more than one salary and civil servants were not allowed to own private property such as houses for rent, shops, and farms. Tanzania is currently engaged in struggles to make all these intentions a reality but has faced very serious reversals, especially after the collapse of the Eastern socialist structures. The collectivization of peasants into communal villages was ideally not only socialist in intent but also a practical strategy to facilitate effective provision of water, electricity, transport, health, and educational services to the greatest number of families. However, the resultant economic dislocations and the world economic crisis of the 1970s and 1980s mitigated against these efforts. The Tanzania government had deliberately followed a strict income control policy through control of ownership of major means of production, progressive taxation system, price controls, and pay raise freeze for high-income groups, but all these efforts are currently crumbling.

The per capita income of the Tanzanian population was about $650 by 1990. Incomes do not vary very much due to all these controls, although gender-related variations in appointment and promotion to key positions are quite apparent. In Tanzania, therefore, only the bureaucratic and business classes seem to feature strongly, as there are no large upper classes based on ownership of the means of production. The private sector was greatly diminished by the socialist policies of nationalization of the means of production. Officially, the policies do not have apparent gender-based discriminative orientations, as anyone can now acquire land for productive purposes or own some property, but at family and informal levels, females have been facing more negative responses than men in their quest for property ownership, and thus there have been claims of gender biases inherent in the Tanzania culture and government practices.

Tanzania pursues a planned approach to the development and management of the economy. The overall emphasis of the planning exercises has been first to change from a colonial economy which was truncated in favor of the export sector at the expense of within-country interlinkages that would have created an internally coherent economy. Second, the planning thrusts encouraged participation of all the peoples in the country in the development process irrespective of gender, class, ethnicity, or religion. Therefore, theoretically, in all planning exercises, the strategy has been to plan from below rather than from above, although in practice this has been difficult, given the entrenched government and party bureaucracies at the top. Third, planning has emphasized balanced and harmonious development, both in space (geographical regions) and in the types of projects. Likewise, there has been a shift from overreliance on a few agricultural crops for export (sisal, coffee, and cotton) to a more diversified economy that includes processed industrial products, mining, and an assortment of other crops such as tea, tobacco, cloves, cashew nuts, and pyrethrum. Finally, planning has emphasized attainment of high-level manpower self-sufficiency, and this has been vigorously pursued irrespective of gender so that currently there are a few female full ministers and permanent secretaries in the government, although the situation is still greatly skewed in favor of the male folk.

The question of the changing family in the African context needs to be examined in the context of rural poverty and limited resources for governments to create child-supporting structures, such as day-care centers and kindergartens. Tanzania had 2,752 day-care centers in June 1983, catering to 184,694 children. However, compared with the population of children of that age, this enrollment is very small and typically urban. In addition, the quality of preschool education and facilities in general leaves a lot to be desired. In urban areas where young families have working mothers and fathers, children are left to the vagaries of street life or, if lucky, in the care of uneducated grandmothers or untrained *ayahs* (nannies) and day-care center attendants, who are predominantly female, as child rearing and day-care roles are characteristically assigned the females.

In Tanzania, there have been legal provisions regulating marriages that have a bearing on family life and the welfare of children. Formally, three types of laws exist. First, there is the traditional law, by which a man can marry as many wives as he wishes, irrespective of whether he can support them or not. Theoretically, marrying another wife required the approval of the first wife, but in practice this is not so, given traditional, asymmetric gender power relations. While economic constraints curtail the continuation of this practice, in some rural areas it is quite prevalent, with one helpless father having 10 children from three to five wives. Second, there are the Islamic laws, by which a man can marry as many as four wives. Some Islamic families also insist that children attend exclusive Koranic schools, which tend to retard their social and intellectual development of the mainstream in national culture and education. Third, there are modern national laws as passed by Parliament, by which one man is allowed to marry only one wife in court but can marry a second wife with the consent of the first wife. This has tended to militate against marriage of many wives, although determined men have resorted to customary laws, which are not as stringent as modern laws. Half of the Tanzanian population, however, practice Western Christianity, which prohibits formal marriage of two wives, a prohibition resisted by men of traditional belief systems. There are no studies comparing family life-styles in these different settings and the enforcement of the legal requirements therein, but it seems that social problems of large families, multiple wives, and discrimination in gender-based succession and inheritance practices exist.

One final legal provision with a bearing on family life is maternity leave. All mothers, married or not, are entitled to 84 days of maternity leave within three-year cycles. They receive pay and other privileges, such as promotion and salary increments. This gives them an opportunity to take care of the young baby. However, there are no provisions for paternity leave; therefore discrimination in childbearing and child-rearing practices and formal welfare provisions exist in the workplace.

COMPARISONS BETWEEN MEN'S AND WOMEN'S GENDER ROLES DURING THE LIFE CYCLE

In the current psychological taxonomies of human developmental processes, the human being is conceived as moving through stages: conception, infancy, childhood, and adulthood. Psychologists are interested in the behaviors that distinguish one period or stage of development from another. It is quite obvious now that the stage model theories provide an attractive and theoretically valid way for analyzing human developmental processes. Yet most observations suggest that developmental stages greatly overlap. Thus, rigid differential expectations of stage and age-related behaviors and gender roles may not be fully warranted. The task of this chapter is to delineate characteristic role expectations, role prescriptions and performance, and behaviors, including inhibitions, as circumscribed by gender specifications from childhood to adulthood in an African context.

Ideally, gender roles and preferences start with differential gender expectations right from birth, including inheritance patterns and social development of the family. In principle, in patrilineal societies boys are preferred to girls while in matrilineal settings girls are most valued and gender roles relating to child rearing gravitate along the female lines, especially through the aunt, as opposed to the uncle in patrilineal setups. However, there are many variations to these practices, depending on social status of the families involved. In general, mothers and grandmothers seem to prefer girls while fathers, especially in warrior traditions, prefer boys. Boys are socially expected to concentrate their energies on masculine activities such as hunting, identifying and fighting imaginary and real enemies, playing with appropriate toys, for example, bows and arrows, and building minihouses. They are naturally expected to keep out of the house and completely out of the kitchen and spend most of their time looking after cattle, while girls are expected to stay in and around the house to get more exposure to kitchen chores such as cooking, fetching firewood and water, and hair plaiting.

In the African cultures within Tanzania (it is best to use the word *cultures* since there is no one single African culture here) conceptions and expectations of childhood vary from one group to another, depending on the ethnicity and its level of modernization and development and whether the group is patrilineal or matrilineal. However, one element that seems to be common is the gradations and steps that the child has to pass through to become an adult. Thus adulthood is not by automatic accession; this status is bestowed through a variety of actions, steps, and rituals after careful formal and informal observations of the growing child. In each step or event toward adulthood, the child is expected to become more confident, and adults give more freedom for role differentiation and performance. Table 27.1 compares the modern and traditional conceptions of the transitions from infancy to childhood and adulthood.

The child in the African family occupies a special position, and thus its development becomes a matter of utmost mutual concern of both parents and the grandparents. As Raum (1940:70) observed, in the traditional cultures: "The child creates the family. Sexual attraction between man and woman leads to intercourse but it is the desire for offspring which insists on a social character for the prolongation of the relationship." Thus, when the child is born through the legitimate union of the parents, it becomes their particular joint concern and responsibility to bring up the new individual strictly within the socially accepted role differentiations.

Infancy and Early Childhood

Lijembe (1967), recounting his picture of the traditional African culture, had this to say about childbirth and familyhood among the Baluya of Kenya:

It is at birth, as the account of my advent into the family and tribe has made clear, that Baluya children are socially accepted and accorded a place in the community. Indeed childbirth is a highly welcome event in our society, where only through parenthood can men and women achieve honored status. Not even the introduction of European schools has done much as yet to detract from this ideal. (P. 23)

However, the status of the child and the mother depends on the legitimacy of marriage and procreation. Illegitimate children and their mothers carry a lower,

Table 27.1
Some Taxonomies of Developmental Stages of the Child

| Age Levels | Piagetian | Categorization Tradition | | |
		General Psychology	School Educators	African Cultures
0-2 yrs	Sensor Motor Period	Infancy Period	Toddler House	Teething Period
2-5	Preconceptual Period	Early Childhood Period	Nursery School	Weaning Period
5-7	Intuitive Period	Middle Childhood Period	Kinder- garten School	Milk teeth- cutting period
7-12	Concrete Operations Period	Late Child- hood period	Primary School	Circumcision Period
12-18	Formal Operations Stage	Adolescence Period	Secondary School	Initiation Ceremonies Period
18-30	Early Adulthood	Young Adulthood	University Education	Marriage Period
30+	Adulthood	Adulthood	Adulthood Continuing Education	Adulthood

generally negative status in most African cultures. In fact, in some tribes, girls who gave birth to "illegitimate" children were ostracized by being separated from their families to live in isolation; often such children were killed, but there were no efforts to hunt for male culprits in these events, and thus the taboos and practices relating to legitimacy of children were inherently biased against women.

It is important to note, however, that childhood in African cultures operates in a myriad of familial relations, including parents, grandparents, ancestors, cousins, and the community at large. Thus child rearing in terms of administration of discipline and moral sanctions is the concern not just of the immediate parents but of the clan; and gender roles are similarly determined in that wider context, with females specializing in handling girls (and boys under the age of 7), and men concentrating on boys (over the age of 7).

School Years

From birth, one observes a series of natural and social events meant to signify that childhood is waning and adulthood is ensuing. The first event is the growth of the milk (frontal) teeth. This normally signifies that the child is growing up and that the mother may, at any time now, become pregnant again. Therefore, training for independence begins immediately, and children are entrusted with some duties in the family. As Vankerviser (1969:71) observed in Sukumaland, Tanzania, "When the child has reached the age of three, the mother sees to it that he is gradually entrusted with some light tasks." In fact, mastery of complex tasks and performance of gender-related roles are a signal to the adult community that the child deserves to be promoted to higher status and finally to adulthood. Thus, childhood wanes as mastery of ascribed roles improves. The girls follow their older sisters when they go to collect water or firewood. They start washing dishes and help prepare the food. In the Wapare culture in the Kilimanjaro area of northern Tanzania, for example, the father gets a thrill when the daughter prepares a good quality and adequate maize meal called *ugali* or *sima* and covertly and sometimes overtly says, "Yes, now I have a grown-up daughter who is ready to be engaged to be married." The daughter, in turn, takes pride in her mastery of these roles, not as an end in itself but because she is about to be promoted from childhood to senior positions or roles and thus become accepted among adult women.

Normally a young girl of 10 years of age is expected to be able to make a fire by herself, boil porridge for the family, and possibly cook sweet potatoes and vegetables. The duties become heavier as the girl grows older and demonstrates mastery of these adult duties. Boys herd the cows and water the calves, while girls start milling flour and make the fire for men to sit around during the evenings during the cold seasons. Gradually, the girls take over all the responsibility for looking after themselves and, to an increasing extent, assist their mothers in taking care of younger brothers and sisters. In the Sukuma and Wapare cultures, education for girls is considered complete when she is about twelve years old, though the skills in performing her roles may need improvement. For a boy, this state is considered reached when he has built his own hut at the age of about sixteen, can take care of the cattle, and shows signs that he can establish and maintain his own homestead. In some tribes, in effect, boys and girls cease to live in the main house. They get their own gender-specific quarters so that they may be able to entertain their age-mates. Among the Maasai of Tanzania, boys have to prove their manhood by killing a lion or leopard, although there are no similar expectations for the girls.

Young Adulthood

Childhood ends at adolescence after mastery of adult roles. However, physiological changes also played a role in cuing the adult community to the effect that it was high time something was done to have the individuals change roles. In the Kwapim tribe of Ghana, for instance, the onset of puberty in girls is recognized as the sign of approaching womanhood, and the occasion of a girl's first menstruation is marked by a special feast, followed by an elaborate pubertal rite involving seclusion and wifery instruction, ritual purifications, and keeping an elaborate program of taboos and sex-role training, and overt differential expectations are expressed by the adult community.

In fact, Van Gennep's (1960) concept of rites of passage characterizes the waning of childhood in African culture very well. In this tradition as elaborated by Van Gennep, the life of an individual in any society is seen as a series of passages from one age to another and from one occupation or role to another. He observes a pattern of ceremonial events in many cultures that accompany a passage from one age group to another. Three types of rites of passage appear quite self-evident in the Tanzania cultures. There are rites of separation or what are sometimes called preliminal rites. Then there are rites of transition or liminal rites, and there are rites of incorporation or postliminal rites. Typically, the rites of separation consist of symbolic behaviors signifying the detachment of the individual or group from an earlier fixed point in the social structure, from a set of cultural conditions, or from both. Thus, in the traditional African cultures, rituals characterize these rites, marking the transition from childhood to adulthood, and gender-role differentiation and prescriptions are inherently circumscribed in these rites.

In the Nyakyusa society of southern Tanzania, for example, Wilson (1963) observed that boys remain and work in their parents' house until age ten or eleven. After that they stop herding their father's cows. Their younger brothers take over this duty while they themselves start their own farms and raise their own cattle. They also now join an age village of boys away from their parents' villages. Within the villages, the senior boys of sixteen and eighteen refuse to let the younger ones join their cottages since, as Wilson reports, "they are children" (p. 21). Thus, even within the boys' village there are strata. The boys remain in their villages until the age of twenty, when they are officially integrated into the adult community. As Wilson observed, "The process of becoming an adult in the Nyakyusa society is consummated in the coming out ceremony in which young and old people together recognize that the boys have acquired a new social status as *men*" (p. 21).

This new status as men enables them to gain political powers. They can become leaders like village headmen, and economically, socially, and politically these young men are now expected to play roles consonant with adult responsibility, cultivating their fields and establishing and supporting their own families. Failure to be independent economically and to behave like a grown-up would be like abdicating an adult status lately conferred upon them. All young men work hard to retain the adult status and enhance their social responsibilities among the much older colleagues who accept them in their group. But this acceptance is gender-specific such that girls play with young women and boys with older men until marriage, when young men can participate in ceremonies including both married men and women.

In the Wapare tribe of northern Tanzania, in their traditional cultures, childhood does not end until boys have attended an elaborate initiation ceremony called *Mshitu*. This is an institution for males only. Boys at the age of about 15 years are taken to a sacred forest that no women or children below 15 years are allowed to visit. The boys remain there for about three weeks, learning adult masculine roles such as good citizenship in the tribe, qualities of a good husband, tolerance, and courage in terrifying situations such as when faced by dangerous animals like lions and when passing through dangerous gorges and underground caves. On some occasions, they get military training too. One does not become a *man* and does not become accepted in the community of *men* before one has successfully undergone this ritual process of role learning and performance. After this event, the young men are allowed to drink with adults, marry, smoke, and build their own houses, and they become overtly more respected, especially by women and children. A man is accorded the highest respect and becomes almost immortal or infallible after this ritual process. He is expected to be independent, self-respecting, hardworking, and courageous and should court more ladies as a sign that he is ready for marriage. In fact, after this ritual process, a father would not be surprised but, in effect, would be delighted to see a son courting and outshining others in role performance, especially in dancing during ceremonies and demonstrating bravery during dangerous periods, for example, attacks by enemies.

Likewise for the women, in the Pare culture, there is a ritual of separation and incorporation. The onset of puberty signifies that the girl should go through a ritual called *Kuekwa*, in which girls of the same age or similar pubertal characteristics are secluded from their homes, especially from children and men. They are confined to one house of a respected old woman in that culture within that village. For one or two weeks the girls undergo strenuous training in the roles of womanhood, including sex play, tendering to husband and children, respect for in-laws, and childbirth rituals. After this ritual process, the girls come out of seclusion in a colorful ceremony. This practice is widespread in East Africa. As Kaye (1962) pointed out, chastity is observed for girls who conceive before their pubertal rites. However, postpubertal but premarital chastity is not strictly observed in many African cultures provided that the girl can produce the responsible man, who is naturally expected to marry her.

Naturally boys are supposed to make approaches to girls with respect to sex and marriage, and not vice versa. Marriages are arranged by the family after mutual acceptance of each other by the boy and the girl. Uncles and aunts play key roles in setting up situations for boys and girls to meet and befriend each other. Wedding arrangements depend on whether the family is in a matrilineal-matrilocal, or patrilineal-patrilocal society. In a matrilineal society, the girl's family is quite active in the arrangements for marriage while in a patrilineal setup it is the reverse. In fact, in matrilineal-matrilocal settings, the man gets married and moves into the woman's place. Dowry, however, is always expected of the boy's family. In some tribes the dowry varies with the beauty of the girl, her level of education, and how rich the suitor is, although this practice of paying dowry is slowly losing appeal.

In a traditional setting, parents prefer that boys go to school as far as possible while girls are expected to stop going to school when they reach marriageable age. This is reflected in the differential encouragement and distribution of family resources, which are skewed in favor of boys. At home, girls are expected to concentrate on kitchen chores while boys are expected to review their schoolwork and help in protecting family property. While the situation has changed dramatically in the last decade or so, this differential treatment of children by gender accounts for the differential performance rates in higher education, with girls faring quite poorly. Girls were traditionally expected to follow feminine careers such as nursing, cookery, needlework, teaching, and secretarial jobs while boys were expected to choose masculine schooling paths such as engineering, medicine, accounting, and computers. While this is changing, one can see pockets of resistance and girls experiencing fear of success, as one might not easily get married if she belongs to a masculine profession such as mechanical and civil engineering.

Adulthood and Old Age

At adulthood and old age, the roles are quite differentiated and stabilized so that the man is expected to be the breadwinner and custodian of family discipline, property, and moral values. In a traditional setting, a wife is a sex object and an object of labor, occupying a central role in house chores and the feeding of the family while the man undertakes more laborious, masculine tasks outside the house and in the community. Divorce is quite rare and never sanctioned by local cultures, but when it happens, children remain in the custody of the father in a patrilineal setup while the reverse is true in a matrilineal culture. Men are expected to relax and play masculine sports outside the house, including hunting, felling trees, and drinking beers, but formal dancing is done jointly with women in a quite colorful way. Hobbies and sporting activities are quite limited, but often work and play are quite integrated in the cultural activities. As families grow old, dependency shifts from the wife being dependent on the husband and to parents being dependent on the children. Thus boys are expected to take care of their parents as they grow old. Since daughters are expected to be married and the dowry has been paid, they are naturally not expected to take care of their parents, due to both physical separation and role definition, unless the sons cannot adequately take care of the aging parents. Old age can thus be miserable when the family has no educated and able male children. There are no homes for the aged and urbanization tends to pull children to urban areas, leaving the aged alone and lonely in the rural areas. Dependency on sons is total but there is great respect and reverence for the aged people, who are seen as the source of wisdom and life itself as they have the power of cursing their offspring. Therefore, under normal circumstances children repatriate financial and food resources to the rural folks. Health facilities are poor but the tropical weather is not as hostile to old age as cold winter weather is. Their hobbies consist of visiting friends and taking care of grannies and looking after calves and guarding crops against wild animals.

SUMMARY AND CONCLUSIONS

This presentation of the concept of gender roles in African cultures has to be understood within the context of a changing people and changing cultures. The institutions of schooling and religiosity have eroded much of what traditionally regulated the age- and gender-related activities and the relationships between people of different sexes. Some of the oppressive traditions are being discarded. Some conceptions are now viewed as pernicious, especially the insistence on compliance with traditions, fear of ancestors, spirits, taboos, excessive respect for elders and men, and rigid observation of ascribed gender-specific social norms and forms of behavior. In this respect, Castle (1966) observed: "In the authoritarian Baganda home obedience is the highest virtue and rebellion the greatest sin. Submission and pliability are the characteristics most praised in Baganda children" (p. 66). Some of these orientations are still pervasive and transpire in family and classroom authority relationships between teachers and pupils, boys and girls, men and women. Some of them, indeed, hinder the process of active participation of the total population in the process of liberation and development of families and countries. Yet some are worthy of reexamination since they played regulatory and educative roles. For instance, the initiation ceremonies were greatly used for regulating the development of sex-related roles and behaviors. Thus, aggressive behaviors in the family were discouraged. In addition, there were sex education, family planning, and marital life education during the initiation ceremonies. Adolescence was carefully regulated, and the transition was gradually directed toward productive adult sex roles. Adolescent pregnancy was frowned at and was a rare misfortune in a family. Thus these traditional practices and belief systems might have mitigated against the development of deviant behaviors during adolescence. It is not self-evident that missionaries and schooling have adequately replaced the role of traditional cultural practices and events that regulated development of positive gender roles. Of course, some of the discriminatory practices are and should be in the process of being slowly eliminated. Yet some of the productive and educational processes might be inadvertently eliminated too. Educators concerned about cultural changes in African societies should be challenged to develop more productive and constructive adaptations of the traditional conceptions of gender-related roles and behavior prescriptions so as to retain some of the useful devices of the cultures and progressively drop the negative aspects of the practices.

REFERENCES

Castle, E. B. (1966). *Growing Up in East Africa.* Nairobi: Oxford University Press.

Doob, L. W. (1967). Psychology. In Lystad, A. (Ed.), *The African World: A Survey of Social Research* (pp. 373–415). London: Pall Mall Press.

Government of Tanzania. (1961, 1964, 1969). *The First, Second, and Third Development Plans* (1961–64; 1964/69; 69/74), Dar-es-Salaam: Government Printer, 1961, 1964, 1969.

Government of Tanzania. (1981). *National Census 1978.* Dar-es-Salaam: Government Printer.

Kaye, B. (1962). *Bringing Up Children in Ghana.* London: George Allen & Unwin.

Lijembe, J. A. (1967). The valley between: A Muluya's story. In Fox, E. (Ed.), *East African Childhood* (pp. 1–41). Nairobi: Oxford University Press.

Omari, I. M. (1982). *Psychology and Education in Changing Societies.* Dar-es-Salaam: University of Dar-es-Salaam Press.

Raum, O. F. (1940). *Chaga Childhood.* London: Oxford University Press.

Van Gennep, A. (1960). *The Rites de Passage.* Chicago: University of Chicago Press.

Vankerviser, C. M. (1969). Growing up in Sukumaland. In CESO (Ed.), *Primary Education in Sukumaland Tanzania* (pp. 42–82). Groningen: Wolters Noordhoff.

Wilson, M. (1963). *Good Company: A Study of Nyakyusa Age Villages.* London: Oxford University Press.

28

Thailand

Aree Petchpud

INTRODUCTION

Thailand is a newly industrialized country in Southeast Asia that maintained its independence throughout the colonial period, though King Rama V ceded some parts of his territory, in the east to France and in the south to Britain, so that Thailand could maintain independence of the remainder. In fact, this policy was successful at a time when most of the countries in this region had been colonized.

Bangkok celebrated its bicentennial in 1982, as the Chakri Dynasty started ruling Thailand in 1782 by absolute monarchy. For a long time, since the reign of King Rama IV (King Mongkut), Thailand had started to modernize the country. He openly accepted many Western influences and ideas (Office of the Prime Minister, 1979). When he died in 1898, King Chulalongkorn, his son, succeeded him and continued the policy of Westernization. During his reign, he sent young students, including his own sons, to study in European countries; when they came back, they started modernizing the country by building up infrastructures, schools, and hospitals.

In 1932 a group of civil and military officers who had studied in Europe and had embraced democratic ideals made a bloodless coup and changed the absolute monarchy into a constitutional monarchy, which it still is today. The monarchy influenced Thai people's ways of life. There is no caste system in Thailand, but there are classes, rich and poor, royalty and commoners, farmers and officers. Under the law, everybody has equal rights, but in practice it is not the same between males and females or between high class and low class.

The population of Thailand, reported by the National Statistics Bureau (1986) as 53.5 million, became 60 million in 1992; males and females are equal in number but fewer females than males are in the labor force. However, after

1986 the number of females in the labor force increased steadily in industrial and commercial jobs but decreased in agricultural jobs.

Since 1932 Thailand has changed by coup d'état many times, and constitutional laws were canceled and rewritten again and again. Three violent changes occurred because the people and students campaigned for democracy and wanted to throw out the dictators. The first violent change occurred in 1973, the second in 1976, and the last in May 1992. Those events showed instability in the Thai political and socioeconomic situation. Thailand started to restore the political and economic situation again by holding a democratic election to form a democratic government. However, the king of Thailand played the most important role in solving conflicts among the confrontation groups and creating compromises either in politics or in the economy.

The groups that campaigned for social justice and democracy were composed of people from almost every occupation, men and women, boys and girls; that event showed no difference between males and females in their social justice and their democratic way of life.

OVERVIEW

Thai society is growing very rapidly, and social change in Thailand has had a great impact on the quality of life of Thai children.

In the past, family life in urban and rural areas was not different. Typical Thai families were extended families: parents and offspring, including grand-parents and other relatives. All members were living together in the same house or compound. The family represented security and stability in an uncertain world. Grandparents actively helped to raise their grandchildren and great-grandchildren until they grew up into adulthood. Nowadays industries promoted in the cities cause the migration of young people or young couples from rural areas to the cities. Besides working in factories, they work as construction workers so the family structure in the cities changed from extended families to nuclear families, especially neolocal families, that migrated from rural to urban areas and work in construction sites.

Males and females are born equal, but when they grow up, physiological structure shows differences; females are weaker than males because they have a less muscled and smaller body so females take lighter work, such as household jobs, taking care of youngsters, and also serving the men. Because women are weaker than men, the community assumes their roles and jobs to be appropriate to their physical capacity (Praperudee, Pimisuthi & Srihong, 1977).

Besides the limitation of physiological factors, the long history of customs and culture also influences gender roles. Thai history shows the power of men in protecting the country, either ruling or fighting enemies. Men are also dominant in religious roles and practices. Women cannot become monks in Buddhism and also cannot be religious leaders in the Islamic religion or other religions. Female roles are limited by cultural and religious principles. Thai women accept their roles and status; that is, they are under the power of men (Kanasutra, Kampoo & Kamolnavin, 1979).

Thailand is a Buddhist society; about 95 percent of Thai people are Buddhists, and 5 percent are other religions, such as Muslim, Christian, Catholic, Hindu, and so on. However, in religious practices Thai women can become nuns and practice Buddhist principles. Some Thai nuns tried to help the poor people in rural areas by promoting projects in handicrafts, sewing, and weaving and joined the division of women career development. There are about 20,000 nuns in Thailand. Besides those jobs, nun volunteers work as baby-sitters, teach in poor areas, and lead meditation for people who want to meditate (Committee of Long-Run Development of Women, 1981).

In some *wats* (temples) in rural Thailand senior monks set up orphanages for children from poor families. Nuns are teachers, caretakers, and advisers, especially for girls.

COMPARISONS BETWEEN MEN'S AND WOMEN'S GENDER ROLES DURING THE LIFE CYCLE

Infancy and Early Childhood

When a couple get married, especially in the provinces, they carry a traditional way of life. They hope the first baby will be a boy rather than a girl. They believe that boys carry the family names for life while girls change after they marry and become a member of another family. Parents pay less attention to girls and give better care to boys (Siam Rath, 1992).

Child care is primarily the responsibility of mothers. Fathers play a very small role in this, especially in rural areas. In urban areas mothers have to work outside the home and leave their children to the care of others. Thai middle-class families usually hire live-in maids to help them take care of their children and home chores. Now young people prefer working in factories to becoming maids, so day-care centers become popular places to take the children.

Poor families that cannot afford to pay for servants let their oldest female child take care of the younger ones. Traditionally, Thai mothers breast-fed their children, but now they have to go out to work so babies are fed sweet condensed milk, which is cheap but has very little nutritional value.

Santaputra (1988) reported that about 10,000 children in urban areas such as Bangkok under age fourteen were left to fend for themselves when they were very young, but children in rural areas, though the families were very poor, still had somebody to look after them at home.

Traditionally, Thai children have been trained in obedience, respect for authority, nonaggression, gratitude, and kindness (Suvannathat, Kamnuanmasok & Bhunapirom, 1971; Suvannathat, 1979). They were trained to practice a seniority system; they call older persons such as older brothers or sisters *phii* and younger persons *nhong*, though they may not be related to them. They were also taught to control their tempers and not to show aggression and hostility to others, especially senior persons; that is why Thai children are polite and docile.

Almost all Thai children in rural areas are raised naturally with little specific training or supervision. When they are babies, mothers breast-feed them whenever they cry and carry them to work. They are weaned when mothers become pregnant; they are bottle-fed sweet condensed milk at about 1 1/2–2 years and then start eating adult food with their families. Children have to help themselves when they are very young; they are trained to be independent and to stand on their own feet (Suntaputra, 1988).

When children in urban, low-income families are about three–four years old, they have been trained to do the same household jobs as five- to six-year-old children in rural families with similar income. Girls are trained to cook, sew, take care of younger brothers and sisters, and take care of the house, including feeding the fowl. Boys are trained to help their fathers, working in the field, feeding cattles, collecting wood, plowing, and doing other jobs (Jongwatana & Manaspaiboon, 1986).

In early childhood, Thai children in the villages lack everything. They never have toys or dolls to play with; when they are about 2–3 years old, they can go out to play in open places with anything they collect from around their homes and gardens, such as banana trees, coconut leaves, clay, gravel, and sticks. In the cities, children from the middle class or upper class play with dolls, toys, or teddy bears as in Western countries, but poor children, especially from construction-worker families, always play in construction sites, jump rope, or play football, like children in slum areas (Santaputra, 1988). Poor children have less opportunity to play because they have to work to help the family. However, when they are free, they like to play at least with rubber bands or pebbles or anything they can find.

Boys like to play rough games such as football, boxing, and wrestling while girls like to play with dolls, small cooking utensils, and small baskets. Modern technology games are played only in rich families. Play activities and play objects are inadequate in rural, slum, and disadvantaged areas. Children in these areas are more delayed in mental development than children in adequate surroundings in the cities (Chugcharoen, 1988).

School Years

Boys and girls have an equal right to go to school. By law, parents have to send their children to primary school at 7–8 years old. If any parents don't follow the law, they are punished by imprisonment, but in remote areas, not every parent knows the law, so some children miss the chance to go to school and are illiterate.

In the cities, children are sent to school at a very young age; some families send their sons or daughters to nursery schools or kindergarten when they are only 2 1/2–3 years old because both parents work and would otherwise have to leave the children with servants inexperienced in child care. Children are in nursery schools and kindergarten about 2–3 years and then move to primary school.

In the past, schools began in the temples (wats); the monks became teachers and taught Buddhist principles and some academic subjects such as mathematics, the Thai language, reading, and writing. Only boys had opportunities to study because they could stay with monks and work to serve the senior monks. Girls were forbidden to touch the monks or stay close to them. The oldest and most famous schools were founded in the compounds of temples.

Modern education began in King Rama V's reign. More boys' schools were founded, and the first girls' school that was founded was supported by her Majesty the Queen. The first courses related to handicrafts, cooking, and Thai classical dancing. In 1920 King Rama VI announced compulsory education laws for all children who were eight years old. These children had to go to primary school and study for four years. In 1970 compulsory education was raised to 7 years, and at present it requires 6 years of schooling.

Secondary schools, separate for boys and girls, were also founded in King Rama V's reign. In 1943, a coeducational school was founded, a two-year preuniversity school; now almost all secondary schools are coed. Opportunities to attend secondary school, especially in the provinces, are very small compared with opportunities in the cities because country children come from poor families. If parents have to choose between boys and girls to send to secondary school, they prefer to choose boys, while the girls have to stay home and work to earn money for their brothers' education.

Only in families with no financial problems can boys and girls have similar opportunities for education. When the first university was founded about 70 years ago, boys and girls had an equal chance to go to university for every faculty besides engineering and forestry. Nowadays there is no gender discrimination in education, and larger numbers of girls are going to university than in the past, especially in the past two decades.

Though boys and girls have equal chances, there are more boys in engineering, veterinary science, and forestry, while girls are more numerous in arts and social sciences. There are military colleges and police colleges for boys only, while nursing colleges are for girls. In vocational schools, more boys enrolled for mechanics, electronic engineering, and courses with high-risk practice while more girls enrolled in cooking, food processing, designing, sewing, and so on. Parents also influence their children's education. Almost all parents prefer their daughters to study for a low-risk occupation, and some parents prefer their daughters to work for the government or in offices rather than in outdoor jobs or jobs with high risk. In conclusion, parents prefer their children to study for their future occupations (Jongwatana & Manaspaiboon, 1986).

Young Adulthood

Setho, Pirokes, Petcharat, and Jamikorn (1978) studied 521 students' attitudes toward dating at Kasetsart University and found that boys started going out on dates earlier than girls. They began dating at age fifteen while girls started at seventeen, but the average age was eighteen. Sometimes students, especially girls, asked for permission from their parents before going out on dates.

The beginning of dating occurred at home when both boys and girls, after they knew each other, went out to movies or went shopping. Almost all subjects said that they preferred dating in the daytime to nighttime and just liked to talk to each other, have fun, or enjoy walking side by side around town. Very few couples had sexual relations before getting married.

Since most dating couples expect to get married or become a permanent couple, they do not start dating when they are young. Real dating always happens in colleges or universities or at least in high school or vocational schools. After they finish their education, they look for jobs and get married.

Stien Koset wrote about parental attitudes toward dating and showed that parents of girls look at dating as inappropriate behavior since if girls go out with boys very often, they might be looked down upon by neighbors. Dating also causes them to waste time and money, so it is not appropriate when they still have no jobs. Almost all Thai parents have negative attitudes toward sexual relations before marriage.

On the other hand, modern parents look at dating as a means for young people to adjust their behavior and personality. Boys learn to be polite to girls, to be gentlemen, to take care of young ladies, and to learn social etiquette.

In the past, marriage was arranged by parents, relatives, and matchmakers. They considered a mate's background, including social class, economic status, education, and similar ages. When the families arranged marriages, boys and girls never disagreed with their parents. This mating arrangement is still in practice in the provinces and even in the cities among high-society families. However, nowadays boys and girls have more freedom to choose their mates and prepare their marriages, but they need approval and support from their families (Jongwatana & Manaspaiboon, 1986).

Adulthood

When males and females mature and are ready to get married, both should have permanent jobs, or at least the man should have a job with which he can support the new family. Among the farming families in the provinces young couples about to marry sometimes need support from their parents, through either land or money. They have to work on their parents' land and stay in their parents' house until they can settle into their own home. Before getting married, men have to pay a dowry in gold or money, depending on the woman's parents. Among educated middle-class and upper-class people, the marriage arrangement is made by both sides; it is not fixed who will pay for the wedding ring, the wedding celebration, and the new house. Thai women marry at an average age of 20.2 years (Leoprapai & Sirirasmi, 1988). Sometimes the couple plan and share the cost together, depending on economic status. Frequently, they are supported by their parents, who also prefer their married children to stay close to them (Jongwatana & Manaspaiboon, 1986).

In the past, when a young couple started their new home, men went out to work, and women stayed home and took care of the house, but now both husband and wife go out to work. The house was looked after by servants. If a couple did not have either a servant or relatives to do the household duties, they shared with each other, the wife doing the cooking, the husband cleaning the house and doing the laundry. In the Thai traditional way of life, taking care of the baby was the woman's job because men went to work on the farm, in the government, or in other occupations, but now, since the wife also goes out to work, household jobs and caring for the children are chores shared by both husband and wife.

If husband and wife have problems and conflicts, they always consult their parents or senior relatives and follow their suggestions. Very few couples go to court for divorce. One cause of divorce is polygamy, which often causes conflict with the wife. Divorce is difficult, and Thai culture has tried hard to prevent it. After divorce, almost all children stay with their mothers rather than their fathers because people believe that mothers are closer to their sons and daughters than are fathers. Men will find another wife quickly, while women are concerned about their children's security and therefore may not marry again.

Another situation, homosexuality, is more popular among males than females. Thai society accepts this situation, so there are a gay society, gay clubs, gay bars, and gay shows in tourist areas such as Pattaya and Chiengmai. In the past two decades, gays were not accepted and were forced to conceal their sexuality, but now they are able to live their lives openly. There are no occupational restrictions against homosexual persons either in government jobs or in private jobs, but most homosexuals are employed as dress designers, hair designers, entertainers, and cooks.

Boys and girls play similar games and sports when they are still young, but adults seldom play sports or games because they do not have much time. Only people in high society always have leisure or spare time; they usually belong to some kind of sports club for which they pay a high membership fee, sometimes joining the club because of its socioeconomic status.

If they want to learn to play a game and they are healthy, males have more chances than females for sports and games. For some sports they have to pay membership fees, such as golf, tennis, sailing yachting, where numbers are limited. However, with Thailand's big gap between the poor and the rich, games and sports are for city people, not for the rural residents, and for the individuals with higher income, not lower income. Yet, in the city, there are not enough public sports arenas or stadiums.

Industry Magazine reported in 1990 that half of the national population are females and that they are very important to the labor force. In 1983, about 67.5

percent of women worked in textile factories, canning factories, and work related to skilled labor, such as gem cutting, dressmaking, shoe cutting, and food processing. However, there are many obstacles for working women: they receive lower wages than men and they seldom achieve high status, since men still hold higher positions as leaders in industry.

Nowadays, more women come into the business world; some run their own business or share with others so they can get to the top or to a higher position in their business. Of the women who hold higher positions, almost all of them have a higher education.

Another factor that supports women is their parents' occupation. When the parents run their own business, the children have more opportunity to train and take over this business after they have gained more experience and their parents become older.

In the past, Thai people believed that the highest security in life could be earned by working with the government because after retirement, they could get a pension. Nowadays, the values of working have changed. People who run their own business, even though they have to take higher risks, earn more money and can use their money for their own security.

Prapreudee, Pimisuthi & Srihong (1977) wrote that by law, in the past, women were inferior to men and men could have more than one wife at the same time. The wife had to take care of the husband, the house, all the possessions in the house, and also the animals and trees. Women became the men's belongings. The marriage laws were passed in 1936; men and women had to register at the local office after they married. At present, by law men have only one wife, and women can choose to use either their own maiden name or their husband's name. Husbands and wives have equal rights to the belongings they acquire after getting married. If women are not satisfied with married life—for example, if they are abused or battered—they can go to court and ask for a divorce. This actually happens with middle- or high-class people rather than lower-class people. In general, men and women have equal chances in education, business, politics, and administration.

In the past, Thai society did not offer women status mobility; women could not move from lower class to middle class or upper class because society expected women to play their part in the family rather than outside the home. In 1990, the Committee of Economic and Social Development investigated women's attitudes toward society and found that Thai women tend to prefer freedom and believe that good individuals make a good society and that women should devote themselves to working for society.

Nowadays Thai women form Thai Women's Societies and groups of housewives, such as army housewives, navy housewives, air force housewives, police housewives, ministry housewives, so that they can develop the communities and help society. They also support their husbands. Women also play important roles in protecting the environment (Siam Rath, 1992).

Praperudee, Pimisuthi & Srihong (1977) wrote that politics was related to social organization. Men dominate Thai politics and administration. The Committee of Economic Development reported that very few women were elected to be representatives in Parliament. Very few women can become judges. Although women can work in government, very few reach the top positions compared with men. They summarized the results of their investigation as follows:

1. Women who completed higher education have more opportunities to become leaders.
2. Women lack self-confidence because very few can reach top positions.
3. Very few women like to hold power and authority so they lack opportunities to become top leaders.
4. Women do not like to commit themselves to their occupations; they like to hold back so they do not attain their leader's positions.
5. Women possess low ambition so they have fewer opportunities to become leaders.
6. Thai society praises men to be leaders more than women.

In 1973 considerable change occurred in women's political roles. It started from university students' activities in their campuses, then extended to factories and the labor force. Women began campaigning for social justice and status, as well as for equal rights in politics, the economy, and administration. In 1974 three women were elected to Parliament, and in 1991, ten women were elected and one was made a minister. Thai women stood up for their rights, which were written into constitutional laws (Siam Rath, 1992).

Women—compared with men—play a more important role in health development, family planning, child care, and community health care. Women take care of children and other members of the family concerning their nutrition, physical health, mental health, and social health. Mothers influence their children's development more than fathers, so women are the most important people in family health development. In family planning programs, Thai women (90 percent) accept birth control more than men, especially in rural areas; very few Thai men have vasectomies.

Jantaravitoon (1979) reported that because of economic problems, women have to work outside the home. At first, women, especially in the provinces, with low education and lack of industrial skills, worked on the farm; when they shifted to industrial factories, they received lower wages than men. According to Jantaravitoon, the problems of women in industry are:

1. They receive lower wages than male workers.
2. They are forced to retire earlier than men.
3. Small industries prefer to hire women, but they are provided with fewer facilities and less welfare and so are more tense and highly stressed and have poor health.
4. Fewer women join the labor union so they have less power to negotiate when they have problems at work. They are always exploited by employers.

Manaspaiboon, Dilokvithayaratana, Manaspaiboon, and Uthaiori (1984) investigated human rights in four industrial factories and twelve other organizations, such as hospitals, hotels, and transportation throughout the country. The findings showed the following:

1. Employers prefer to hire male workers to female workers in every type of industry except textile factories. Women are treated worse than men.
2. Men tend to receive higher wages than women in similar jobs, except in textiles, though by law men and women have equal rights to receive the same salary for the same job.
3. Women have fewer opportunities for advancement, though they start at the same level and in similar jobs, because men have stronger physical attributes and can work physically harder.

Liewrungreang, the Head of the Government Correction Home, said in an interview to *Siam Rath Daily Magazine* that boys commit crimes because they are stronger and are not tied to the families and to Thai custom. Thai girls, in contrast, are taught to obey authorities and to follow Thai custom and discipline.

Old Age

Old people hold high status in the community because in Thai culture, children and younger people are trained to respect authority (Suvannathat, Kamnuanmasok & Bhunapirom, 1971; Boesch, 1977). After their retirement, old people become consultants or advisers to their juniors. Thai families are extended families; old parents always stay with their children to help take care of the younger generation. No generation gap occurs among Thai families; in families with grandparents staying with them, the children are more secure and happier than in families without grandparents. People who retire from their full-time jobs in business, government, and industry, become farmers, gardeners, flower growers, and do other kinds of jobs and spend their retirement happily.

People over 60 years old are provided social welfare support for health care. If they have worked with the government over 25 years, they receive a pension and other facility supports from the government until the last day of their lives.

Some senior people who retire from the government shift to the private sector as consultants or senior managers. If they retire from government universities, they apply to work with private universities until 65–70 years old. They can also stop full-time work and live on a pension.

SUMMARY AND CONCLUSIONS

Gender roles have changed from traditional to modern times. Thai women in traditional roles had to stay home, take care of children, and do housework as housewives and housekeepers. They had to serve their husbands and all members of their families. Nowadays women go out to work so men have to change their role to share household chores and take care of children. Life becomes more cooperative, neither husband nor wife dominates, all generations share the responsibilities, and old persons help to take care of grandsons and granddaughters. Thai families are close and warm; there is no formal discrimination between men and women in education, occupation, and social activities in modern life in Thailand.

REFERENCES

Boesch, E. (1977). Authority and work attitude of Thais. In Wenk, K., Rosenberg, K. (Eds.), *Thai in German Eyes* (pp. 176–231). Bangkok: Kled Thai with cooperation of Erdmann Verlag.

Chugcharoen, C. (1988). A case study of the woman workers' education through home-based instruction program at Din Daeng [slum] community. In Ekberg, K., & Mgaavatn, Per Egil (Eds.), *Growing into a Modern World* (pp. 498–508).

Committee of Long-Run Development of Women. (1981). *The Long-Run Women's Development Planning*. Bangkok: Kurusapa.

The democratic protecting group. (1992). *New Way, 6* (3): 26–30.

Jantaravitoon, N. (1979). *Thai Labor Force*. Bangkok: Karaweg Press.

———. (1989). Women's role and industrial development. *Industrial Magazine, 2*: 101–5.

Jongwatana, N., & Manaspaiboon, J. (1986). *The Survey of the Cost of Children in Rural-Urban Northeastern Thailand*. Bangkok: Population Study Institute, Chulalongorn University.

Kannasutra, K., Kampoo, T., & Kamolnavin, S. (1979). *Thai Women's Image Reflection*. Bangkok: Thaikaset Press.

Leoprapai, B., & Sirirasmi, B. (1988). *Health Status and Public Health Usage of Rural People*. Bangkok: Mahidol University Press.

Manaspaiboon, S. (1984). *Human Rights and Employees in Thailand*. Bangkok: Thamasart University Press.

Manaspaiboon, S., Dilokvithayaratana, L., Manaspaiboon, J., & Uthaiori, R. (1984). *Human Rights and Employees in Thailand*. Bangkok: Thamasart University Press.

National Statistics Bureau. (1986). *Annual Report on the Labor Force*. Bangkok.

Office of the Committee of Economic and Social Development. (1990). *Present Status of Thai Women*. Bangkok: Anongsilpakarnpim.

Office of the Prime Minister. (1979). *Thailand into the Eighties*. Bangkok: Thai Watana Panich.

Praperudee, B., Pimisuthi, T., & Srihong, Ch. (1977). *Thai Women: Role as Administrative Leaders*. Bangkok: Faculty of Political Sciences, Ramkamhang University.

Santaputra, S. (1988). Growing up in Thai society. In Ekberg, K., & Mgaavatn, Per Egil (Eds.), *Growing into a Modern World* (pp. 897–907).

Satienkosate. (1976). *Thai Cultures and Tradition*. Bangkok: Klangvithaya.

Setho, R., Pirokes, S., Petcharat, K., & Jamikorn, S. (1978). *Behavior and Attitudes of Kasetsart University Students Toward Dating and Mating*. Bangkok: Faculty of Social Sciences, Kasetsart University.

Siam, Rath. (1992). Political role of Thai women. *Siam Rath Weekly Magazine, 45*.

Suvannathat, C. (1979). The inculcation of values in Thai children. *International Social Sciences Journal, 31*: 477–85.

Suvannathat, C., Kamnuanmasok, N., & Bhunapirom, L. (1971). Summaries of studies of social influences on the development of Thai children in village of Ban-Pran-meun and U-meng. In *Research Bulletin*. Bangkok: Bangkok Institute for Child Study.

Tongurai, P. (Ed.). (1991). *Siam Rath Weekly Magazine, 38* (21): 3.

29

Traditional Tibetan Societies

Uwe P. Gielen

The father is the family's head, the mother is the base.
—Tibetan Proverb

INTRODUCTION

The road from Srinagar, capital of the Indian state of Jammu and Kashmir, to Leh, capital of the district of Ladakh within Kashmir, is one of the world's great mountain roads. Starting in the lush valley of Kashmir, the 434-kilometer (269 mile) road snakes across 4,000-meter-high passes till it reaches the stark mountain desert of Ladakh, the "Land of the Moon." The traveler starts in the subcontinent of India but ends up, geographically and culturally, in Central Asia. The road traverses two radically different cultural zones. While the valley of Kashmir and the surrounding mountain ranges are centers of conservative Islam, Ladakh forms one of the last bastions of Western Tibetan Buddhism. Here, in their villages alongside the upper Indus valley under the immense dark blue dome of the Tibetan sky and surrounded by the soaring peaks of the Karakorum and the Himalayas, lives a hardy race of peasants, nomads, traders, monks, astrologers, and "oracles," together with their sheep, goats, yaks, dzo (a cross between a yak and a cow), donkeys, and invisible armies of ever-present demons and spirits.

Due to military considerations all of Ladakh remained off-limits to foreigners until 1974, and thus much of its unique culture has survived intact to this day. Ladakh provides ideal opportunities for the study of traditional Tibetan culture with its unique religious belief systems and social customs. To the student of gender roles it is a fascinating place. Ladakh and other Western Tibetan societies form the largest remaining cultural zone in which fraternal polyandry (a wife is married to several brothers) is practiced to this day. Tibetan women have traditionally occupied a relatively high position in society, especially when compared with their lower and more restricted positions in the neighboring Muslim and Hindu societies. On the walls of every Ladakhi monastery one finds mystic representations of the Tibetan cosmos: religious liberation is symbolized by the sexual union of male and female deities, symbolically representing the unity of "male" compassion with "female" wisdom. The union of male and female principles represents the very archetype that to the Tibetan embodies the ultimate goal of human striving.

The trip from Srinagar to Leh introduces the traveler to two divergent conceptions of how males and females should relate to each other. In the streets of Srinagar, the women are hidden beneath the *chador*, a black, tentlike contraption designed to protect women and their sexual purity against temptations and the greedy stares of assertive, impulsive, "uncontrollable" men. As the traveler leaves the city and makes his way along the winding mountain road, Muslim peasant women without their *chador* step away from the road and turn their backs toward him. It quickly becomes apparent that sharp dividing lines are expected to separate women from men, non-Muslims from Muslims, and strangers from in-group members.

As the road descends into Ladakh's Buddhist villages, the traveler may encounter gangs of obviously poor road workers. Smiling easily, they readily share their meager fare with the visitor. But the real surprise to the visitor may be this: a good many members of these little troops of Ladakhi road workers are women—a situation simply unthinkable in the Muslim areas of Kashmir. No Muslim father would ever permit his daughter to work in a road gang, and it is most unlikely that his daughter would ever wish to do so. The dividing lines between men and women and between strangers and in-group members are drawn much more softly in Buddhist Ladakh than in Islamic Kashmir. Relationships between Ladakh's men and women are more relaxed, cheerful, open, and egalitarian than corresponding relationships in Kashmir.

This chapter discusses traditional Ladakhi and Tibetan conceptions of gender roles, their place in the structure of Tibetan societies, and Tibetan conceptions of the life cycle. The Tibetan journey through life combines pragmatic, cheerful adaptation to the harshness of the land with spiritual depth and beauty and a keen awareness that the present journey is only one in a long chain of reincarnations. While women and men pursue somewhat different journeys, it should be pointed out that traditional Tibetans tend to be more interested in human commonalities than in gender differences. They tend to experience gender roles as belonging to an unchanging natural social order.

Ladakh is located in the northwestern area of India and forms a part of the state of Jammu and Kashmir. About half as large as England, it has approximately 130,000 inhabitants. More than 99 percent of the land is a high-altitude mountain desert, but barley, buckwheat, potatoes, turnips, and walnut and apricot trees are planted in the valleys. Ladakh borders on Pakistan and on Tibet, the latter now forming part of China. There is one town, Leh, which has about 9,500 inhabitants. The other Ladakhis live in villages, but some nomadic pastoralists roam the more remote, high areas. Most Ladakhis are farmers, craftsmen, small-business men, government officials, or members of the Buddhist clergy. They speak Ladakhi, a Tibetan language. Hindi, Urdu, "high Tibetan," and English are spoken by some Ladakhis in business or government transactions or by the Buddhist clergy. Literacy levels vary greatly by region, social class, gender, and age. The author estimates that perhaps 35–45 percent of all adults in the central Leh region are literate to varying degrees. More women than men are illiterates. The majority of children in Leh and surrounding villages are now attending primary school. About 60 percent of Ladakh's population profess the Buddhist faith while most other inhabitants of Ladakh belong to the Sunni and Shiite traditions of Islam. The present chapter confines itself to the Buddhist population.

The upper Indus valley forms the cultural center of Buddhist Ladakh. Here are located many of the monasteries that traditionally have dominated the spiritual life of Buddhist Ladakh. The monasteries belong to a variety of Tibetan lineages, such as the Gelugpa ("Yellow Hat"), the Kargyupa (including Digunkpa and Dukpa), the Nyingmapa, and the Sakyapa.

Almost as large as Western Europe in area, Tibet (*Bod* in Tibetan) has since 1965 been known as the Tibetan Autonomous Region of the People's Republic of China. The "Roof of the World" forms the largest and highest plateau on earth, with an average elevation of 4,600 meters (15,000 feet). Ringed by many of the world's highest mountains, Tibet borders in the south on Pakistan, India, Nepal, Bhutan, and Burma. Through its valleys flow some of the largest rivers of Asia, such as the Yarlung Zangpo River (Brahmaputra) and the Senge Khabab (Indus River). While the great northern high plateau, the Chang Thang, is only very thinly populated, the mountains in the southern and southeastern regions are cut into ridges and fertile, more densely populated valleys. Here lie the major cities of Tibet, including its capital, Lhasa, and many important monasteries.

At present, the estimated population of the Tibetan Autonomous Region includes close to 2 million Tibetans, 150,000 Chinese settlers, and 250,000 Chinese soldiers. The Tibetans are distinguished from the Han Chinese by their language, their religions (Vajrayana or Tibetan Buddhism and the native Bon religion), their customs, and their conscious identity as Tibetans. Only about 35 percent of all Tibetans live in the Autonomous Region of Tibet. More than 2 million additional Tibetans may be found in the Chinese provinces of Qinghai, Sichuan, and Yunnan. Other societies strongly shaped by Tibetan traditions include Buddhist Ladakh, various regions in Nepal, Sikkim (now part of India), Bhutan, and the Lahoul-Spiti region of northwest India. In addition, approximately 100,000 Tibetan refugees live in India under the leadership of the Dalai Lama's government-in-exile.

This chapter focuses on a number of Tibetan societies that have until recently remained isolated for geographic and political reasons. These societies include Buddhist Ladakh, the Nyinba and other Bhotia (Tibetans) in northwest Nepal, nomads from the Kham and Amdo areas in the eastern and northern areas of the Tibetan cultural zone, Tibetan refugees from the D'ingri area of southern central Tibet, and the famous Sherpas from the Mt. Everest region. The concept of "Tibetan society" is used in a cultural and sociological sense regardless of present political boundaries. The concept refers to societies that have been shaped by Tibetan Buddhism, share Tibetan customs, and speak Tibetan dialects and languages. Many members of these societies identify themselves as Tibetans, but others derive their primary identity from the geographic region or nation they belong to. It should be noted that due to considerations of space, the chapter downplays important regional variations in social customs and beliefs.

During the 1950s and 1960s the social structures of traditional Tibet were largely destroyed by the incorporation of Tibet into the People's Republic of China and the ensuing "Great Proletarian Cultural Revolution." The revolution attempted to gut Tibet of its very soul, devastating the country in the process. Large numbers of people were killed, and only 15 of Tibet's 3,500 monasteries were left standing (Lehmann & Ullal, 1983). But outside Tibet, in India, Nepal, and Bhutan, many aspects of traditional Tibetan culture have remained intact to this day.

Although many Tibetans, a few Ladakhis, and numerous outsiders have written extensively about traditional Tibetan society and culture, reliable social scientific information about gender differences and gender-specific development is limited in scope. Above all, there is a dearth of relevant psychological research. Basic statistical data are scarce and often unreliable. The authors of traditional Tibetan writing are usually monks who prefer to write about religious and historical matters. Though feminine principles, including frank sexual yet sublimated representations, are much emphasized in the traditional symbolic world (Paul, 1982), women are frequently considered to be temptresses intent on diverting monks from their difficult path toward religious liberation and salvation. In contrast to traditional religious writings, standard ethnographies of Tibetan societies and descriptions by travelers and Christian missionaries often include observations on Tibetan and Ladakhi family life, emphasizing forms of marriage and the relatively high status of women in Tibetan society (Duncan, 1964; Bell, 1928; Prince Peter, 1963; Fuerer-Haimendorf, 1964). In addition, more specialized social scientific studies have been published. They include Hermanns's (1959) detailed analysis of the family system prevailing among the nomads of the Amdo region (located in the northeastern corner of the Tibetan cultural realm), anthropological investigations of life cycle and other rituals (Brauen, 1980), healers and their patients (Kuhn, 1988), worldviews and religious conceptions (Gielen, 1985, 1990; Gielen & Chirico-Rosenberg, 1993), the social structure (Kaplanian, 1981), and social change (Friedl, 1984), all in Ladakh, and analyses of fraternal polyandry in northwest Nepal (Levine, 1988; Schuler, 1983, 1987). Taken together, these and other studies can be used to draw a realistic portrait of family life, gender roles, and gender-specific socialization practices in Ladakh and Tibet.

The worldviews of traditional Tibetans simultaneously reflect pragmatic economic interests, deeply held religious convictions, individualistic forms of self-assertion, and collectivistic orientations toward life in the family and community. There is a great diversity of family systems and forms of marriage, including monogamy, fraternal polyandry, polygamy, common-law marriage, and spinsterhood. Swaggering nomads with laughing eyes, pleasure-loving aristocrats, hardy yet timid peasants, shrewd traders, married and celibate monks, nuns who have illegitimate children and return to the worldly life, ''mad'' saints in remote mountain caves, robbers who give liberally to monasteries, witches, compassionate *bodhissatvas* (saviors) reincarnated as *tulkus* (high-ranking reincarnations), walking corpses, bisexual deities, sky-walking fairies, spirits of the sky, the earth, the rivers, and the house, ogres, goblins, hordes of demons, and countless other invisible beings live side by side, often in symbiosis but sometimes in opposition to each other. The visible social order is gender-specific, while the symbolic Tibetan cosmos is based upon the intertwining of the masculine and feminine principles. Women are freer than in the neighboring societies, but their social and metaphysical status does not equal that of men. Women strive for the highly valued goal of religious salvation but in a less individualistic fashion than the monks.

OVERVIEW

Four major fissures run through the social structures of many Tibetan societies. These include divisions between (1) monks, nuns, and laypersons; (2) agriculturalists and nomads; (3) nobility (*ger pa*), taxpaying peasant-serfs owning considerable tracts of land (*drong pa*), small householders owning little or no land (*d'u ch'ung*), merchants, and craftsmen; and (4) women and men.

Traditional Tibet (prior to the 1950s) has sometimes been described as the world's most ''priest-ridden'' society, ruled by a theocracy with the Dalai Lama at its head. Approximately 25–30 percent of its adult males are monks. While some of the monks are married (if they follow Nyingmapa or Bon traditions), monks following the predominant Gelugpa or state church tradition are not allowed to marry, thus creating a surplus of marriage-age women. This is one important reason (polyandry is another) why there are many spinsters in Tibet, a situation quite unusual in preindustrial societies. Nuns usually play a subordinate role in institutionalized religion, constituting perhaps 5–10 percent of all religious specialists. Their status is both low and ambiguous (Reis, 1983). Only rarely do they receive sufficient religious instruction to strive effectively for the ultimate goal in traditional Tibetan culture, religious salvation and liberation. Indeed, a good many Tibetans believe that ''woman ranks very low in the scale of birth, she must be reborn as a man before she can get started upon the road to Nirvana'' (Duncan, 1964).

The division between nomadic pastoralists and peasants runs deep throughout Tibetan history, though many Tibetan families succeed in combining agricultural pursuits with animal husbandry. Perhaps 30 percent of the Tibetan population consists of nomadic pastoralists who live mostly on the bleak northern high plateau, the Chang Thang, and the northeastern areas of Amdo. There they herd *nor* (including *yak*, *bod*, and *dri*), sheep, goats, and horses. Nomads are often economically better off than most villagers, whose economic and legal status frequently approaches that of serfs. Many villagers are attracted to the nomadic life-style, which combines (relative) economic prosperity with a significant amount of freedom, although the nomadic pastoralists, too, owe taxes and allegiance to their worldly or ecclesiastical overlords. The nomads, in turn, believe that they are the true Tibetans. Some of the nomad tribes, such as the Golok, are quite warlike and frequently attack caravans.

The psychology of the nomad differs from that of the peasant. Nomads are the rulers of space, whose mobile life-style demands alertness, independent, quick decision making, risk taking, courage, farsightedness, physical and mental strength, hardiness against brutal weather conditions, self-confidence, and self-control. Impatient of restraint, Tibetan nomads are often fierce, stubborn, yet generous and hospitable individualists, who like to assert their will in competitive games (Ekvall, 1968; Hermanns, 1959). While these psychological characteristics are especially demanded of men in their fierce struggles against nature and sometimes each other, nomad women tend to possess similar, if more muted, personality characteristics. The self-assured "mistress of the tent" knows that without her there is no family life or survival. On the whole, Tibetan women have a higher status among the nomadic pastoralists than among the peasants.

In contrast to nomads, peasants are tied to their land and often subject to tight control by their masters: the government, the local monastery, or the local lord. Peasants—and especially so in Ladakh—tend to be less assertive, aggressive, willful, and individualistic than the nomads. Instead, they value peace, serenity, discretion, humility, and obedience in their children. Ladakh is, indeed, one of the most peaceful societies on earth (Gielen & Chirico-Rosenberg, 1993). The ideal Ladakhi is hardworking, cooperative, and mild-mannered. Above all, women are expected to live up to those ideals, and most do.

Traditional Tibetan societies are stratified societies whose members are highly aware of status and economic differences. Aziz's (1978) investigation of the social structure prevailing in the D'ingri area of southern central Tibet may serve as an illustration. She distinguishes among six socioeconomic layers:

1. Elite:
   ngap pa = religious leadership (religious "aristocracy")
   ger pa = "worldly" aristocracy
2. Subjects (*mi ser*):
   dr'ong pa = property-holding, taxpaying peasant-serfs
   tsong pa = independent traders (small–medium scale)
   d'u ch'ung = "small smoke": artisans, landless workers, families subleasing land
   from *dr'ong pa*, nontaxpayers
3. Outcastes:

(*ya wa*): fishermen, smiths, butchers, tanners, persons responsible for dismemberment of corpses

Tibet's aristocracy consists of about 200 families who control landed estates and participate in the government of Tibet. Among the *mi ser* (subjects), a crucial distinction must be drawn between the taxpaying *dr'ong pa* (who hold inalienable rights to property leased from the government, monasteries, or the *ger pa*) and the landless *d'u ch'ung*, a mobile group of laborers and craftsmen. In Ladakh, however, most peasants own their land and often are surprisingly well off.

This discussion of gender roles and gender differences emphasizes the conditions prevailing among the *dr'ong pa* of Tibet and the landowning peasants of Ladakh, since they play a central role in the social structure of Ladakhi and Tibetan villages. Fraternal polyandry, for instance, is especially prevalent among the *dr'ong pa* since it is the purpose of polyandry to hold together family property.

Table 29.1 outlines the sexual division of labor in Ladakh and Tibet. The table is, in part, based upon a similar scheme depicted by Levine (1988: 208). In addition, the table integrates information from studies conducted in Ladakh (Brauen, 1980; Friedl, 1984; Kuhn, 1988; Ribbach, 1940), among Tibetan nomads (Goldstein & Beall, 1990; Hermanns, 1959), and among villagers in various Tibetan societies (Aziz, 1978; Chorlton, 1982; Dargyay, 1982; Schuler, 1983), as well as Gielen's (1985, 1990) observations on Ladakh. When one surveys the table, the fluid character of Tibetan society should be kept in mind. While many tasks are said to have a masculine or feminine character, that does not mean that they are invariably performed by men only or by women only. For instance, men are often away on long-distance trading expeditions. During that time, their wives frequently perform various "masculine" tasks, especially when no other men are available.

The sexual division of labor is experienced by both men and women as being part of the natural order of things. Men who perform women's tasks (cooking, housekeeping, and so on) may be ridiculed by their peers and lose status in the eyes of women. It is believed that due to their greater physical and mental strength, men are naturally suited to physically strenuous and dangerous tasks. It is generally understood that the women work harder than the men and that the hard work of wives contributes in a decisive way to the economic situation of the family. Men, in turn, must "go out into the world," where they may be required to undertake dangerous and physically demanding journeys across steep mountain passes and barren highlands for weeks and months at a time. When Goldstein and Beall (1990: 95) "asked the nomad women whether they sometimes resented the men's lack of help in the milking cycle, many could hardly understand our question, so alien was it to their view of a 'natural' division of labor. Nyima, who has seven children and a large herd to care for, one day responded to our suggestion of inequality and oppression with an air of incredulity." Similarly, Ladakhis do not discuss gender roles and gender differences in terms of abstract notions of equality, although in the sexual sphere they

Table 29.1
Sexual Division of Labor in Tibetan Societies

Tasks	Mostly/Only Men	Both	Mostly/Only Women
Child Rearing			
(esp. infants, small children)			+
Taking care			
of young siblings		(sometimes boys)	girls
House/Tent Keeping			+
Control of household			
money, storage			+
Food & drink preparation			+
Fetching water			women & children
Cleaning			+
Collecting dung/			
thistles/firewood			+
Making Things			
Spinning wool, knitting		+	
Weaving, sowing		(local variations)	
Preparing leather			
materials	+		
Making handicrafts		+	
Construction	+	(some types)	
Masonry, carpentry,			
heavy labor	+		
Erecting tents			
Guidance, heavy labor	+		
Helping, less heavy labor		+	
Felling trees (also for			
firewood)	+		
Constructing terrace walls	+		
Road repair		+	
Agriculture		+	
Sowing	+		
Plowing	+		(taboo for women)
Watering, threshing,			
chafing, bagging grain,			
harvesting, gathering hay		(more women)	
Weeding, spreading manure			
kitchen gardening, clearing			
fields of stones, brush,			
watering fields			+
Digging new channels	+		
Repairing channels		(more women)	
Herding and Dairy Farming			
Yak, horses, lassoing	+		
Sheep, goat, cattle		(adults and children)	
Sheep shearing	+		
Milking			+
Castrating, slaughtering	+ (polluting)		(taboo for women)
Selling of animals	+		
Trading and Moving			
Local trading, peddling,			
shopkeeping		+	
Long-distance trading,			
guidance of caravans	+		
Porters		+	
Mountain guides (Sherpa)	+		
Running local inns/tents		+	
Saddling horses	+	(sometimes)	
Loading yaks and horses	+		
Truck driving	+		

Table 29.1 (continued)

Tasks	Mostly/Only Men	Both	Mostly/Only Women
Politics			
State leadership	+		(occasionally women)
Tribal councils	+		(sometimes widows)
Village councils	+		(sometimes widows)
Giving public speeches (wedding, etc.)	+		
Occupational Specialists	+		
Doctor-pharmacists (amchi)	+		
Blacksmiths	+ (low caste)		
Gold/silversmiths, metal workers	+		
Musicians		+ (often low status)	
Actors (theater & opera)		+	
Bards, minstrels	+		
Beggars		+ (low status)	
Prostitutes			+
Jeep drivers, tourist guides	+		
Traditional teachers	monks, elderly men		
Modern teachers		+	
Assertive/Aggressive Action	+		
Gambling	+		
Wrestling, horse racing, polo, archery contests	+		
Hunting	+		
Law enforcement	+		
Production & handling of weapons	+		(often taboo for women)
Defense, raiding, war, soldiers	+		
"Sky burial" (dismemberment of corpses)	+ (low caste)		
Religion			
Reincarnations	+		
Leadership in monastic institutions	+		
Ordained monks/nuns	+		(ordained nuns rare)
Hermits, meditators	+		(a few women)
Itinerant religious specialists		(more men)	
Mediums (village oracles)		(more men)	
Astrologers, diviners (laymen and monks)	+		
Religious artisans (scroll painters, stone carvers, religious poets)	+		
Constructing prayer walls	+		
Pilgrimages; circumambulation of sacred places and buildings; spectators and participants in religious festivals; beneficiaries of religious rituals; prayers		+	
Sacrifices to house god		variable	
Witches			+

sometimes hold intuitive notions about "the battle of the sexes." At harvest festivals groups of young men and women taunt each other, singing ironic songs about faithless lovers, stuck-up maidens, and bumbling suitors whose sexual prowess leaves something to be desired (Bell, 1928).

The Ladakhis occasionally explain the sexual division of labor in terms of "natural" personality differences between men and women. Women are thought to have "small hearts" (poor self-control, emotionality, high levels of anxiety, shyness) when compared with men, making them less able to perform leadership tasks. It is said that women are by nature suited to, and interested in, children and child rearing. Almost all women want children, and those who do not or cannot have any are pitied by the other women (Kuhn, 1988). In the words of a Tibetan proverb, a woman without children is frequently ill.

The gender-typed social order outlined in Table 29.1 reflects tendencies fairly similar to those found in other peasant and nomad societies. Women are responsible for the raising of infants and young children. They are the mistresses of the tent and the house; there they rule the kitchen and the cash box. Their tasks tend to keep them close to home, with some exceptions to be discussed later. Agricultural tasks and tasks related to dairy farming and herding are divided between the sexes in such a way that men tend to perform those tasks requiring the most physical strength. Since long absences from home would be incompatible with the feminine task of child rearing, women often supervise local, small-scale trade, inns, and drinking places while men are more likely to engage in large-scale, long-distance trading enterprises. Unmarried and poor women, of whom there are quite a few in Tibetan society, are nevertheless hired for road repair work and as porters for caravans. It should be added that long-distance trading engages both laymen and monks from wealthy monasteries.

Women's tasks are more repetitive in nature and less varied in character than the more specialized tasks of men. The work of men is seen as more skillful, and on the whole it is valued more highly than women's drudgery. Men represent their household in the outer world, although widows sometimes take the place of their deceased husbands in political assemblies and as heads of merchant enterprises. Men control the political, symbolic, and religious spheres of life, the means to religious salvation, and the more prestigious social positions. They are far more likely than the women to engage in risky, assertive, and aggressive behaviors. Men drink, gamble, and fight much more often than women, and unlike women they engage in competitive sports such as wrestling, horse races, and archery competitions. Taboos forbid women to hunt, slaughter animals, handle weapons, or engage in the raiding of caravans. It should be added that these activities are regarded as sinful by everybody.

The social order reflects a more or less universal division of labor, but superimposed upon this division are the typical characteristics of most Tibetan societies: fluidity of social relationships, openness of social and sexual relationships between men and women, flexibility in task assignment and marriage arrangements, and opportunities for headstrong men and women to bend the social norms to their advantage or liking. Tibetan societies provide considerable opportunities for determined men or women to find their own special social and religious niches and to "follow their own drummer." Such choices, however, may not be easy to make. The individual may have to trade in economic security and comfort for romantic attachments, inner freedom, and spiritual development (Aziz, 1978).

COMPARISONS BETWEEN MEN'S AND WOMEN'S GENDER ROLES DURING THE LIFE CYCLE

People everywhere distinguish between different stages in the life cycle. The nomads of Amdo, for instance, have separate categories for little babies regardless of sex (*zha zhe*), early childhood boys (*zhe lu*) and girls (*zhe mo*), older boys/sons (*bu*) and girls/daughters (*bo mo*) during the late childhood and unmarried teenage years, youth (*ho sar*), teenage girls or young women (*bu nyid*), and so on (Hermanns, 1959). Mature adults, whether related or not, are often addressed with kinship terms that express respect, familiarity, and personal warmth. Terms such as elder brother, auntie, or grandpa simultaneously reflect Tibetan conceptions of the life cycle, of kinship, and of the gender-typed social order.

Ladakh's sociocultural order recognizes birth, marriage, and death through rites of passage that mark entrance into this life, the establishment of a new family, and one's transition through death and the intermediate *bardo* state into a future form of reincarnation. The religiously oriented rites de passage are shaped according to heavenly archetypes. The rituals protect society and the individual from the terrors of chaos and uncertainty, helping to reestablish new balances among the changing individual, society, and the cosmos. The life cycle is embedded in a field of visible societal and invisible religious/magical/cosmic forces that can be predicted through divination and astrology and guided or diverted through defensive religious rituals.

A person's present life cycle is considered merely one among many. Past and future are linked through the iron chain of reincarnation that has been forged by the inevitable effects of karma. The Tibetan asks, Is it not superior wisdom to know that all life must end in death, that our self is merely an illusion, that all created forms are like a mirage, like bubbles in the water, like images in a dream? One can read in a fairy tale: "Behind the lamp was the Buddha, the giant statue that had calmly watched the lives of people drift by, a continual circle of birth, old age and death, to start once again, birth, old age and death never ceasing, forever turning the wheel of life that balances the good and the bad, the happiness with the suffering, the years of plenty with the years of want. Only the people could dictate their futures by the way they lived each day" (Thurlow, 1975: 81). The Buddha's benign detachment represents a powerful cultural ideal, especially for the elderly and the religiously inclined, although most men and women readily acknowledge that they cannot live up to it.

Tibetans sometimes compare the life cycle with the changing of the seasons. After the icy sleep of winter, springtime awakens the seeds of life. Just as the plowman helps to open and fertilize mother earth, so the husband "plows" the fertile field of his wife. Summer brings bright sunshine and fullness of life, helping to prepare mellow autumn when some of the fruits of karma ripen, and the person reaps what he or she has sowed. When the fierce blizzards of winter race over the frozen land, life goes temporarily underground. The person must be prepared to die and be reborn into a new womb. Buddhist conceptions of karma and reincarnation reflect agricultural conceptions of the cycle of life and death, in which men and women play their appointed but different roles, jointly creating and protecting life. The web of "karmic interconnectedness" reflects the web of agricultural life.

The nomad, pilgrim, and caravanner encounter the infinite in the vast silences and immense spaces of the land. Traveling on foot for months across the boundless grassy oceans and stony mountain deserts of the Chang Thang or trying desperately to live through a Himalayan snowstorm, the Tibetan experiences this as ultimate truth: all is vanity, and beneath the ever-changing, magiclike world of forms there exists only *tongpanyi*, that is, Emptiness or the Void. *Tongpanyi* represents the timeless principle underlying all reality, a principle that is reflected by the stainless mirror of one's own True Mind. A full realization of this truth constitutes the ultimate goal of the human journey through life, a realization that the Buddhist calls nirvana. While ignorant human beings can grasp this ultimate truth only with great difficulty, they must attempt to do so. Otherwise, their journey through life has been in vain and must be repeated many times over at the lower levels of existence.

The Tibetan vision of ultimate reality is expressed in symbolic representations of invisible, cosmic forces that provide a sacred background to the mundane events of daily life. All life is suffering, all life is ephemeral, and people's very selves are no more solid than the ever-shifting clouds that sail silently across the endless sky. These are the truisms of Tibetan Buddhism, yet the Tibetan perception of the vanity of all things often goes hand in hand with gutsy involvement in daily events, keen appreciation of economic opportunities, talkative gaiety, a ready sense of philosophical humor, and a cheerful acceptance of life's hardships. The paradoxical integration of the sacred and the profane, of philosophical detachment with cheerful involvement in the mundane world, of inner serenity in the face of the terrors of impermanence, of abstract metaphysical speculation and naive belief in the mythopoeic imaginations of legend, magic, and dreams gives the Tibetan worldview a quality found perhaps nowhere else on earth. Keeping this worldview in mind is especially crucial for an understanding of the monks, nuns, and many elderly who pursue the quest for deliverance.

Infancy and Early Childhood

Much has to happen before a Ladakhi arrives in this uncertain world. Prior to the advent of modern medicine, mortality rates for infants and young children in Ladakh and other Tibetan societies were extremely high, reaching perhaps 40–80 percent (Duncan, 1964; Levine, 1988). While poor hygiene and the short-comings of traditional medicine must be held responsible for this desperate state of affairs, it is clear to the traditional Ladakhi family that only the relentless attacks of the ''100,000 child-demons'' can explain this misery. Monks thus have to be called into the pregnant mother's home to exorcise the powerful demons with their beady eyes and cannibalistic desires, by chanting sacred texts and hurling ever more powerful spells against them (Ribbach, 1940).

Birth takes place in the home, although not in the kitchen, where the hearth goddess has taken up her residence. The mother-in-law and some women from neighboring houses assist in the birth, although modern women sometimes give birth in Leh's hospital. The newborn child is washed and may be rubbed down with butter or oil. Most parents appear to prefer boys over girls, although this preference is not as pronounced as in Hindu India, Muslim Pakistan, or Confucian China. The preference for boys is, in part, based on the expectation that the oldest son will take over the family property and ensure the economic well-being of the aged parents.

Since birth and death bring ritual pollution to the parents, they may not go out into the fields for at least a week since this would evoke the ire of the earth and water spirits. The mother may not touch cooking utensils. These taboos appear to be adaptive in nature since they protect the weakened mother from excessive demands, leaving her with the time to establish a close bond to the newborn. A few days after birth, the newborn receives a black stripe on the forehead, which will protect the little one against the envy and evil eye of the neighbors and perhaps against some of the more benighted demons. The midwife must also be careful, since malicious spirits have been known to turn a boy into a girl! Soon thereafter, the parents visit the local astrologer and soothsayer to ask for the child's ever-so-important horoscope. Relatives and visitors arrive to congratulate the family, bringing with them butter-porridge to celebrate the arrival of the child.

A few weeks after the child's birth, the father visits the nearby monastery, asking the abbot for his blessing, a printed prayer for the protection of his child, and a name. The abbot often chooses pious names, such as Dolkar (White Goddess or Savioress), Padma (Lotus Flower), Lhamo (Protector Goddess of Tibet), Geldan (Full of Virtue), or Sherab (Wisdom). Other names reflect more concrete hopes, such as Tsetsen (Safe Life) or Tsewang (Vital Life Power). These names reflect the parents' fervent desire that their child may live long and prosper—something not to be taken for granted in this world of suffering. Many popular names such as Tsering (Long Life) are given to both girls and boys, indicating that sexual differentiation is not an overpowering concern in Ladakh. There are no family names; rather, a person is recognized by his or her ''house-name.'' This custom reflects the deep bonds that connect the peasant to his land, which he almost never sells.

Infants and young children are warmly welcomed into their family and treated with great affection and patience. Grandparents and their grandchildren tend to be especially close to each other. There is much hugging, and children are breast-fed for two to four years. Toilet training is lenient, and many a toddler may be seen with a vertical cut in the back of his or her trousers to facilitate defecation. Abandonment of (usually illegitimate) babies is probably very rare, always hushed up, and regarded as a very great sin. Little children are present at many social gatherings, running here and there among the laughing, drinking, and dancing guests. Merry and mischievous, they play with their homemade toys and marbles, throw snowballs and stones, build snowmen, and enjoy games such as Wolf and Sheep or Tiger Play, Sheep Play. The girls also play at keeping house.

From early on, the boys and even more so the girls, carry infants on their backs and take care of younger siblings. Differences between boys and girls are not much emphasized at such a young age, but the games of the boys are a bit wilder and louder than the more quiet games of the girls. The girls are asked to take on responsibility quite early, to show modesty, to stay closer to home than the boys, and perhaps to carry water. Except for some children of very poor families and a few adopted children, much human sunshine reaches Ladakh's young children (Norberg-Hodge, 1991).

School Years

Life in traditional Tibetan societies has an almost medieval quality quite different from the quality of life in other twentieth-century societies. This has influenced conceptions of the life cycle that do not focus on distinctions between preschool and school-age children since very few of the girls and only some of the boys went to (an informal kind of) school in the old days. Instead, children around the ages 6–10 were expected to become responsible herders of animals, to help out in the kitchen, and so on. Modern conceptions of the life cycle stress schooling and a long period of adolescence while traditional Tibetan conceptions emphasize the smooth integration of the child-adolescent into the economic order of things.

Around five to six years of age, children are gradually drawn into the production process. Girls from early on may be asked to clean kitchen utensils, do the laundry, fetch water, collect dried dung and firewood, help with the cooking, help out with some of the lighter agricultural tasks, and look after some of the animals. Boys may be given more time to play, but they, too, are drawn into the world of work at an early age (Ludwar, 1975). Children as young as six or seven may be asked to look after herds of goats, sheep, dzo, and yaks in the mountains and the grassy fields of the Chang Thang. This is a major responsibility since much of the wealth of nomadic families is invested in these animals. It can also be a very scary and lonely activity since wolves, snow leopards, and eagles regularly attack the sheep and goats. Using a slingshot to control the animals, boys at seven or eight years of age are considered to be effective herders (Goldstein & Beall, 1990). In traditional Tibet, one became an adult taxpayer at the age of thirteen. Similarly, children at a surprisingly early age may be asked to make major life decisions, such as whether to join a monastery. Gender roles are thus learned early, and they are learned primarily on the basis of concrete task assignment. Whiting and Edwards (1988) have pointed out the importance of task assignment for the learning of gender roles in other traditional societies as well.

In old Ladakh there were no public schools, yet a surprisingly high percentage of the men—perhaps 20–25 percent—could read and write more or less effectively. Boys were sent to a local "schoolmaster," often a monk or elderly gentleman. Very few girls received such an education. In recent decades the government has established a network of schools throughout Ladakh. More and more parents send their children to public school, yet some parents do so only reluctantly or not at all, since they want their children to work in the fields or the mountain pastures. More girls than boys are kept from going to school, a situation common in many other developing societies.

Traditional conceptions of gender roles are also nourished by hearing traditional stories, fairy tales, proverbs, miraculous stories of saints and old Tibetan or Ladakhi kings, the epos of the culture hero Gesar, the compassionate *jataka* stories of the former lives of the Buddha, poetry, and song. During long winter evenings around the family hearth, Grandma or Grandpa will entertain everybody by telling wonderful tales about clever foxes, evil stepmothers, poor folk who miraculously find pots of gold at the end of a rainbow, evil giants who are vanquished by courageous young men, poor but gentle-hearted and pretty maidens who are discovered by a prince and live happily ever after, unhappy young lovers who are kept apart through the machinations of their greedy elders, and merciful *bodhissatvas* who descend from heavenly heights to help suffering humanity. These stories are shaped by universal archetypes and reflect the hopes, desires, ideals, fears, worldviews, and wisdom of the common people. Ribald stories are by no means missing in this collection, and everybody breaks out into broad smiles when sex-starved uncles and not-so-chaste monks set out on their deliciously funny misadventures with the other sex. Although sexual discretion is highly valued in Ladakh, an earthy peasant humor insists that sex represents a natural appetite that must be satisfied.

Young Adulthood

Proverbs and traditional stories tell us much about popular conceptions of ideal men and women: ideal young men are tall, courageous but with a sense of compassion, resourceful but aware of traditional pieties. Clever rogues may be surreptitiously admired when they get the better of the greedy rich, but they themselves will surely remain stuck in the mire of desire and delusion. Desirable young maidens are cheerful, pious, hardworking, compassionate, gentle-hearted, and, of course, beautiful.

Tibetan boys and girls grow up together and know each other from early on.

There are no adolescent initiation ceremonies or men's clubs. Boys and girls often stay overnight in huts on pasturelands on the mountainside, far from adult supervision. There is much drinking and singing, and casual sexual contacts are by no means rare. Although Ladakh tends to be a more conservative and restrained society than most of the other Tibetan societies, premarital and extramarital affairs, if discretely handled, tend to evoke only muted criticism or no criticism at all. Boys and girls also meet each other at festivals such as the popular *cham* dances, which all large monasteries celebrate once a year. The *cham* dances take place in the monastery courtyard where monks don rich costumes and masks to personify the invisible but ever-present world of gods, spirits, and demons. The dances celebrate the victory of good over evil, of Buddhism over the old, native Bon religion with its animal sacrifices, secret magic and adoration of ghouls, ghosts, spirits, and demons. A lively festival atmosphere surrounds the dances, a wonderful opportunity for giggling girls to look over the boys, flaunt their rich jewelry, gossip, buy antiques from Tibetan traders, or haggle over cheap plastic shoes with a Kashmiri merchant (Gielen, 1990). The boys try to snatch a ribbon or ring from some not-so-unwilling girl, who must redeem the ribbon at a later tryst under the cover of darkness.

Adulthood

While boys and girls meet at festivals, parties, or in the daily rounds of their existence, they may not necessarily be allowed to marry their sweethearts. The family has much to say about choosing a marriage partner. As in many other traditional societies, marriage represents not merely the union of two individuals in love but the establishment of concrete obligations and bonds between two kinship groups. In Tibetan societies, the house and the land associated with it represent the basic unit of production, which must be sustained over time. The oldest son inherits all of the land (primogeniture), younger siblings coming under his authority after the father's retirement. Should there be no son, either the oldest daughter inherits the land or a young boy will be adopted into the family to become the father's successor.

Tibetan societies know a great diversity of marriage systems, which vary according to region, social class, family composition, and individual choice. Monogamy is most common, prevailing in the eastern regions of the Tibetan cultural zone, among nomads, the landless, the poor, and Tibetans exposed to modern influences. Fraternal polyandry is most commonly practiced in western Tibetan societies such as the Nyinba of northwest Nepal and Ladakh. Although on the decline during recent years and actually outlawed since 1942 by Kashmir's Muslim-oriented state laws, polyandry continues to be practiced in the more remote regions of Ladakh. In these regions, an estimated 25–60 percent of all marriages were based upon polyandry during the late 1970s. Prior to the 1950s, polyandry was the morally preferred and statistically predominant form of marriage in Ladakh (Prince Peter, 1963), as it remains to this day among the Nyinba of Nepal (Levine, 1988).

In Tibet, polygamous marriages were sometimes contracted among the noble and well-to-do families. Other forms of marriage, such as more or less formally established ''group marriages'' or a father's sharing a wife with his son (the son's stepmother) existed but were practiced only in exceptional circumstances.

Arranged marriages and traditional weddings continue to play a major role in present-day Ladakh. The family chooses a bride or bridegroom based mostly upon practical considerations. The prestige and amount of property that a family owns constitute important criteria for the choice. The bride-to-be should be known as a hardworking, competent, and pious person. Sweetness of character and beauty are added but not necessarily decisive criteria in this context. The bride is typically between 12 and 24 years of age and often is from a neighboring village. After the family council has agreed on its choice, the son (or sons) have to give their agreement, which is only rarely withheld.

An astrologer is asked to compare the horoscopes of the young people, which must match reasonably well for the family to proceed further. Provided the stars and elements do not send any serious warning signals, a family delegation or go-between is sent to the family of the bride-to-be. Much beer flows during the negotiations, eloquent speeches are given, and good-natured but quite real haggling about the ''Price for the Mothermilk'' begins. This price is given to the young girl's parents to compensate them for all the trouble they took in bringing her up.

Weddings organized by well-to-do families can be grand affairs. Taking place during the winters when there is more time for celebration, they may involve several hundred guests. The guests drink beer and salted butter tea, give speeches, gossip, recite poetry, ask age-old riddles, dance, and sing the ancient, poetic folk songs till late into the night.

On the evening of the wedding day, a group of young men appears at the doorstep of her family's house, shouting for the bride to appear. After much begging and ''threatening,'' she appears in tears on the doorstep—tears that are ritual in nature yet often also quite real. Since most marriages are virilocal (the bride moves into her husband's home, which tends to be in another village), she must now leave the warm nest of her family to prove herself in her new home under the critical eyes of her mother-in-law. For the first time in her life, she is wearing her *perak* on her head, a broad leather band covered with numerous turquoises and silver or gold boxes containing sacred mantras for protection. Her mother has just handed the family heirloom over to her. Soon a wedding procession will bring the bride to her new home.

Meanwhile monks pray in the bridegroom's house for the welfare of the family ''and all sentient beings,'' performing religious rituals to chase out ghosts and demons that may have been lurking around or brought in by the wedding procession! Since every house is protected by house and hearth gods, the bride must formally take leave from the deities of her former home and make obeisance to the deities of her new home. These will, from now on, watch and guard her, provided she performs her sacrifices and avoids polluting actions and events.

Traditional Ladakh recognizes two major forms of marriage, the virilocal form (the wife moves into her husband's house) and the uxorilocal form (the husband moves into his wife's home). The virilocal form occurs most frequently and is called *bag ma* by the Ladakhis. The uxorilocal form occurs in 10–15 percent of all marriages and is called *mag pa*. *Bag ma* marriages may be based upon monogamy or polyandry while *mag pa* marriages are usually monogamous. *Mag pa* marriages are contracted when there is no son in the house and the daughter inherits the property. In such cases the wife has much power, especially during the early stages of the marriage when she may divorce her husband without much ado.

The most common form of polyandry involves a *bag ma* marriage between two or three brothers and one wife. The wife is formally married to the oldest brother, who alone can divorce her. The second brother may spend a good deal of time away on trading expeditions, in the army, and so on. Alternatively, he may at a later time move out of the household and become a *mag pa* in his new wife's household. The youngest brother may prefer or be asked to join a monastery where he can look after the spiritual welfare of the family.

The emotional and sexual aspects of polyandry have frequently evoked the curiosity of outsiders. The wife needs to exercise a great deal of discretion and has to avoid favoritism or even the appearance of favoritism with respect to her husbands. Public opinion tends to hold her, rather than her husbands, responsible for the marriage's success or failure. The husbands, in turn, typically claim that no jealousy exists among them. Polyandry demands from them that they subdue egoistic forms of self-assertion and give priority instead to the greater good of the family. Elderly Ladakhis sometimes state that they cannot afford the "luxury" of individualistic self-assertion and choice. They feel that to enter into a polyandrous marriage reflects a moral and altruistic choice (Prince Peter, 1963). While polyandry demands emotional sacrifices, it is nevertheless based upon the search for the good life: by not dividing up the land, families assure themselves and succeeding generations of a reasonable living standard and economic security (Goldstein, 1987). The search for the good life appears to have been successful since Ladakh knows much less grinding poverty than the adjacent, non-Buddhist areas of India and Pakistan.

Children in the family address both the elder and the younger brother(s) as "father," often calling the younger brother *aba chung* or "little father." Assignment of paternity appears to vary from family to family. While all of the children are frequently considered to be the children of the "elder father" (older brother), there exists in some families a more or less tacit understanding that the younger brother(s) are the "real" fathers of some of the children. Ladakhis tend to treat these issues with admirable tactfulness, making a great effort to protect family harmony.

The wife's treatment of her husbands may subtly shift over time. During the early years of her marriage, her relationship to the oldest husband tends to be of crucial importance. At this time the younger husband may still be a child or young teenager, and she may treat him almost as a kind of stepson rather than as her husband. As he comes of age, she initiates him into the sexual life, possibly preferring him over his older brother. He, in turn, may feel that his wife is growing old, that the time has arrived to leave the household and to find a new wife. Younger brothers may also get involved in extramarital affairs, which public opinion tolerates as long as they are not flaunted.

The stability of Tibetan family arrangements varies by region, social class, and type of family structure, but on the whole it is not very great. While family structures tend to endure in conservative Ladakh and Zanskar, they are more unstable among the Nyinba of Nepal (Levine, 1988) and the inhabitants of the D'ingri area of southern-central Tibet (Aziz, 1978). Polyandrous marriages devolve so frequently in the course of time that the departure of younger husbands is not even recognized by formal divorce. But regardless of the form of marriage, a wife's position is strengthened substantially by the arrival of children. She has become the center of family life. The husband develops closer bonds with his wife, participates in the children's upbringing, and is less likely to spend time with drinking companions and girlfriends.

In the case of divorce, arrangements for child custody depend on personal arrangements, economic considerations, the age of the child involved, and local custom. Frequently, infants and very young children remain with their mothers, as do many of the older girls. In contrast, older boys may be asked or elect to join their fathers. In some cases, custody of a child changes over time. Illegitimate children are reasonably well accepted in most Tibetan societies. One crucial question is whether illegitimate boys are entitled to inherit family property. Although villagers may claim that "boys born out of wedlock forfeit their rights to inherit any family property . . . this sanction is rarely, if ever, invoked" (Chorlton, 1982: 84). Tibetan social relationships and family arrangements tend to have a very fluid character, responding as they do to economic pressures, personal preference, age-related personality changes, spiritual interests, and the considerable power of public opinion. Frequently, informal arrangements take precedence over stipulations laid down in formal law.

Old Age

Prior to World War II, many Ladakhi parents retired during middle age. On the day of the usually polyandrous wedding of their sons, the parents would move from the family's main house into a small side building, yielding the headship of the family to the oldest son. The parents kept a few pieces of land, on which they would plant vegetables and barley. The new wife became the mistress of the kitchen, traditionally the center of the family's activities. The parents began their gradual withdrawal from this world of illusion to prepare themselves for a life of prayer and reduced worldly authority. The focus of their lives gradually shifted toward a concern for a favorable future reincarnation.

New laws, which became effective in 1942, have gradually undermined the old system, although it survives to varying degrees in the more remote areas of Ladakh and Zanskar. Younger sons may now ask for a partitioning of family property while many parents retire later than they used to in the old days. But the religious goals inherent in the traditional way of life remain convincing to many of Ladakh's elderly. The many aged who spin their prayers wheels, murmur mantras (sacred invocations of deities), and send sweet-smelling juniper smoke to the numina in the sky are much admired by society. Some embark on pilgrimages to holy places in order to acquire religious merit and improve their chances for a favorable reincarnation. In Tibet itself elderly pilgrims wander across the endless open spaces, perhaps to visit the city of Lhasa or sacred Mt. Kailash in West Tibet, a stunning mountain that symbolizes the center of the Buddhist and Hindu cosmos. Some especially pious pilgrims prostrate themselves during their entire circumambulation of the sacred mountain. Others die during their pilgrimage, secure in the knowledge that the purity of their endeavor has helped them to ensure a favorable future existence—maybe even admission to the Western Paradise of the Lord Buddha, Amithaba.

For most elderly Ladakhi the gradual disengagement from their daily round of existence is only very partial. Many elderly become loving and much-beloved grandparents whose wisdom, good humor, patience, forbearance, storytelling talents, and baby-sitting skills provide warm support and guidance for the growing generation. In recent years the position of many grandparents in the web of family life has strengthened since an increasing number of fathers accept full-time or part-time jobs outside their homes and their communities. In addition the number of children has increased due to the spreading influence of modern medicine.

For traditional Ladakhis, death is merely a point of departure that separates one life cycle from the next. Upon physical death the *nam shes* (consciousness or "spirit") leaves the body to enter the phantasmagoric state of *bardo*, which traditionally is said to last forty-nine days. It is the all-important task of the monks to guide the *nam shes* through the transitory *bardo* state so that it may not be swept down into a subhuman existence.

Upon the death of a person, his or her *pha spun* (a kind of mutual aid group) sends for a monk and an astrologer. While the astrologer works out the death horoscope, the monk attempts to direct the free-floating *nam shes* back into the body of the deceased. Should he succeed in this, he then redirects the *nam shes* through the fontanel on top of the head, thereby helping the *nam shes* along its way to the limitless light of the Western Paradise of Amithaba (Brauen, 1980).

Subsequently the members of the *pha spun* wrap the deceased in an embryonic position. For several days, the monks read the *Bardo Thodol* (The Tibetan Book of the Dead) to the *nam shes*, which is believed to hover in the vicinity of the corpse. Driven by the winds of karma—the aftereffects of the dead person's actions—the *nam shes* swirls through a confusing labyrinth of self-created visions, at first benign and later on terrifying in nature. These mockeries of karma ultimately push and pull the *nam shes* into a womb, leading to the rebirth of the person (Fremantle & Trungpa, 1975). By reading the *Bardo Thodol* to the *nam shes*, the monks help the *nam shes* to recognize the subjective nature of its own confusing visions, thereby guiding it on its way to liberation from the bondage of past existences.

After the reading of the *Bardo Thodol*, a procession of monks accompanies the body of the deceased on its last journey to the cremation oven. During deadly epidemics a corpse may also be given a water burial during which it is thrown into a fast-flowing river.

In contrast to Ladakhi customs, Tibetans follow the custom of "sky burial." The cadaver is placed on a remote hill and hacked into pieces, which are then fed to vultures and wild dogs. The custom reflects the Buddhist belief that even in his death a person should be of benefit to other sentient beings. A more pragmatic interpretation suggests that sky burials are adaptive in a land with few trees, many rocks, and long periods during winter when the ground remains frozen.

Most monks and laypersons in Ladakh and Tibet do not believe that after their deaths they will reach ultimate liberation—the timeless bliss of nirvana—or the culturally valued goal of becoming a *bodhissatva*, a savior who out of compassion for all suffering beings refuses to enter nirvana. The road to liberation is indeed steep, and only a few *rinpoches* (high-ranking reincarnations) and lifelong hermit-meditators are thought to reach liberation "in one lifetime."

Women are especially disadvantaged in their search for liberation. With one exception, all *rinpoches* are men while the number of theologically trained female hermits remains minuscule. Many nuns receive very little religious education and remain subservient to the monks, while other nuns sustain a marginal existence at home or become mendicant singers of Buddhist prayers. Traditional Tibetan society exhibits a curious ambivalence toward the religious strivings of women while greatly admiring similar strivings in men.

Pious women are valued by society, but the same society fails to support women on their path toward ultimate liberation. Because society must reproduce itself, women must have children, yet this necessity "postpones" women's disciplined search for liberation to some future round of the wheel of life. Many Tibetans perceive that women remain chained to their daily rounds of existence yet these perceptions encourage the very attachments that Tibetans find so regrettable from a religious point of view. It is clear that these cultural contradictions hide a clash in which the concrete necessities of society remain victorious over the professed goals of Buddhism. All the same, elderly women form one of the most religious groups in Tibetan society.

SUMMARY AND CONCLUSIONS

During the last two decades social and cultural changes have come to the Himalayas with lightning speed. The change agents include new employment opportunities in the state administration or the army, radio stations, modern schools, the introduction of new agricultural methods, the building of roads and airports, and the pervasive effects of tourism. In 1977 there existed just a few small guesthouses and one hotel in Leh, but by 1981 tourists could choose among some 60 guesthouses and hotels, including a modern hotel of the Oberoi chain. Ladakhis now watch sentimental Hindu movies in the Leh cinema while others buy videos representing a mentality in complete opposition to the tenets embodied in Ladakh's traditional culture. Old customs disappear or weaken, and the traditional mythopoeic-magical worldview is confronted with modern, scientifically oriented worldviews that are taught in the schools. The clash between the different value systems leads to alienation among some of the young, and it increases differences in worldview between the generations. Younger Ladakhis reject some of the beliefs and customs of the older generation, claiming that these represent superstition and outdated tradition. Political tensions between Muslim traders and Buddhist Ladakhis have recently flared up, and it is clear that the former equilibrium among nature, society, religion, and the strivings of the individual has been irrevocably upset. Ladakh has become more prosperous, but the people's desires may have increased more rapidly than their living standards.

The effects of these changes on gender roles and conceptions of the family are manifold. They include the following:

1. *Decrease in the practice of polyandry.* Because new employment opportunities have opened up, younger brothers have become less willing to settle for a subordinate position in their families, joining instead the army or seeking jobs as taxi drivers, tourist guides, or civil servants in the "big city," Leh. The influx of Hindu, Muslim, and Western cultural influences is sweeping away the cultural support for polyandry. Modern ideologies emphasize the priority of private desires over the interests of the family, thus undermining the collectivistic basis of polyandry.
2. *Rapid population increases.* As polyandry is abandoned and modern preventive medicine reduces infant and child mortality, the population increases rapidly. Since the land cannot support the rising population, more and more young men enter specialized careers or migrate to the big cities of India. On the whole these events lead to more pronounced gender differences, despite the "liberating" effects of modern education, which would appear to counteract pressures toward more differentiated gender roles.
3. *Fewer but better-educated monks.* While in former times younger sons were often sent to the local monastery at an early age, modernistic ideologies taught in schools and elsewhere tend to make traditional religious choices less attractive and convincing. The monasteries are forced to "compete" with divergent worldviews and career options, a process that in recent years has led to improvements in the quality of Buddhist education.
4. *Increase in individualism, male violence, and gender differences.* Traditional Ladakhis are "embedded" in collectivistic social structures and worldviews that ask the individual to give priority to family and village interests and to cooperate in collective activities. Modernization inevitably disrupts this "embedding" process, thereby both liberating and alienating the individual from networks of social constraint and support. Young men, especially, grow to be more assertive, self-oriented, and impulsive. Given

the right circumstances, they may even get involved in physically aggressive actions. In Ladakh at least, modernization appears to lead to the emergence of greater gender differences since traditional society restrained male tendencies toward self-assertion to an amazing degree (Gielen & Chirico-Rosenberg, 1993; Norberg-Hodge, 1991). In Ladakh, the effects of modernization on gender-role differentiation and equality between men and women appear to be opposite to those reported for other Third World countries. While industrialization and modernization lead in most countries to greater equality between the sexes and in extreme cases even to ideals of androgyny, the recent changes in Ladakh appear to undermine the traditionally rather egalitarian relationships between men and women.

It is unclear to what extent the reported changes in Ladakh mirror transformations in other Tibetan societies. Changes in Tibetan societies outside China may have followed patterns fairly similar to those reported for Ladakh, especially if these societies were exposed to comparable outside influences.

Life in the Sherpa villages of the Mt. Everest region has already undergone profound changes, and prosperous Sherpa traders may now be found in Kathmandu, Bangkok, and Hong Kong. In contrast, life in the Tibetan villages of northwest Nepal has retained a much more traditional character. In Tibet itself changes have followed a unique pattern. During the 1960s and 1970s the Han Chinese–led government eliminated almost all monasteries and nunneries, dispossessed the aristocracy, and ''liberated'' the serfs but forced everybody to work for state communes (Lehmann & Ullal, 1983). Communism endorsed an ideology of equality between men and women, both of whom had now to work exclusively for the government. In spite of many killings the population increased because infant and child mortality rates were substantially reduced.

During the 1980s, however, the government acknowledged that many ''mistakes'' had been made during the Cultural Revolution. Reports indicate that there is a gradual drifting back to more traditional ways of living. Goldstein and Beall (1990) describe this process of drifting back among a group of nomadic pastoralists from western Tibet. Their description of the division of labor among men and women and of gender roles and gender-specific socialization practices is largely compatible with earlier reports of life among Tibetan nomads (Ekvall, 1968; Hermanns, 1959).

Tibet has changed greatly since the Chinese takeover during the 1950s. Roads now connect the major cities, sterile-looking modern buildings stand next to older buildings built in the beautiful, traditional Tibetan style, and more Han than Tibetans live in the holy city of Lhasa. The quiet atmosphere of Drepung, Tibet's largest monastery, is disturbed by shots ringing out from a nearby army shooting range. The Chinese have strategically placed it there to remind the monks who has become the master of Tibet. Chinese soldiers may be seen everywhere in and around Lhasa, while above Tibet's major roads the ruins of once-thriving monasteries and forts stare sadly into the sky.

Yet everywhere traditional Tibetan life tries to reassert itself. Small groups of monks have been allowed to return to their monasteries, and with the help of volunteers and state support, they have rebuilt some buildings in some of the monasteries. High above Lhasa on the roof of the Potala, a group of women construction workers chant the traditional work songs while in the Jokhang— the "cathedral" of Lhasa—pilgrims circumambulate the statute of *Jowo-Rin-poche*, "the gem of majesty." Foreign travelers are incessantly asked to hand out pictures of the Dalai Lama, suggesting that in the eyes of many Tibetans the Chinese-led government still lacks legitimacy.

Throughout history Tibetan men and women have responded to the harsh demands of high-altitude living with vigorous economic activities, a unique family system, and profound metaphysical conceptions of human nature, the cosmos, and the infinite. As in other traditional societies, the burdens of life have fallen more heavily on the shoulders of women than of men. Tibetan society also exhibited a troublesome ambivalence toward women's religious quest for liberation. At the same time, relationships between Tibetan women and men have always been more egalitarian, open, and cheerful than corresponding relationships in all neighboring, traditional societies.

In Tibet itself the traditional way of life was brutally interrupted, and an imported, materialist rival vision of history and the meaning of life was imposed upon the people. In Ladakh and other Himalayan regions the enticements of modern life have begun to act as corrosive, if seductive, forces that slowly but steadily undermine traditional customs and belief systems. Soon, many Tibetan traditions will have receded into the mists of history. This must be judged a great cultural and spiritual loss for all humanity.

REFERENCES

Aziz, B. (1978). *Tibetan Frontier Families: Reflections on Three generations from D'ing-ri*. New Delhi: Vikas.

Bell, C. (1928). *The People of Tibet*. Oxford: Clarendon Press.

Brauen, M. (1980). *Feste in Ladakh*. Graz, Austria: Akademische Druck u. Verlagsanstalt.

Chorlton, W. (1982). *Cloud-Dwellers of the Himalayas. The Bhotia*. Amsterdam: Time-Life Books.

Dargyay, E. (1982). *Tibetan Village Communities—Structure and Change*. Warminster: Aris & Phillips.

Dolkar, T. (1971). *Girl from Tibet*. Chicago: Loyola University Press.

Duncan, M. H. (1964). *Customs and Superstitions of the Tibetans*. London: Mitre Press.

Ekvall, R. B. (1968). *Fields on the Hoof: Nexus of Tibetan Nomadic Pastoralism*. New York: Holt, Rinehart, & Winston.

Epstein, I. (1983). *Tibet Transformed*. Beijing: New World Press.

Fremantle, F., & Trungpa, C. (1975). *The Tibetan Book of the Dead. The Great Liberation Through Hearing in Bardo*. Boulder, CO: Shambhala.

Friedl, W. (1984). Die Kultur Ladakhs erstellt anhand der Berichte and Publikationen der Herrnhuter Missionare aus der Zeit von 1853–1924. Ph.D. diss., Universitaet Wien.

Fuerer-Haimendorf, C. von (1964). *The Sherpas of Nepal*. Berkeley: University of California Press.

Gielen, U. P. (1985). Some themes in the ethos of traditional Ladakh. In Dendaletche, C. (Ed.), *Ladakh, Himalaya Occidental. Ethnologie, écologie. Recent research no. 2* (pp. 235–46). Pau, France: Université de Pau.

———. (1990). Ladakh—die letzte Bastion des westtibetischen Buddhismus. *Kleine Beitraege aus dem staatlichen Museum fuer Voelkerkunde Dresden*, 11: 25–31.

Gielen, U.P., & Chirico-Rosenberg, D. (1993). Traditional Buddhist Ladakh and the ethos of peace. *International Journal of Group Tensions*, 23 (1): 5–23.

Goldstein, M. C. (1987). When brothers share a wife. *Natural History*, 96: 38–49.

Goldstein, M. C., & Beall, C. M. (1990). *Nomads of Western Tibet. The Survival of a Way of Life*. Berkeley: University of California Press.

Hermanns, M. (1959). *Die Familie der Amdo-Tibeter*. Freiburg: Vlg. K. Alber.

Kantowsky, D., & Sander, R. (Eds.). (1983). *Recent research on Ladakh: History, Culture, Sociology, Ecology*. Muenchen: Weltforum Vlg.

Kaplanian, P. (1981). *Les Ladakhi du Cachémire*. Paris: Hachette.

Kuhn, A. S. (1988). *Heiler und ihre Patienten auf dem Dach der Welt*. Frankfurt a.M., Germany: Verlag Peter Lang.

Lehmann, P. H. & Ullal, J. (1983). *Tibet. Das stille Drama auf dem Dach der Welt*, 2d ed. Hamburg: Geo/Gruner & Jahr AG.

Levine, N. E. (1988). *The Dynamics of Polyandry. Kinship, Domesticity, and Population on the Tibetan Border*. Chicago: University of Chicago Press.

Lha-mo, R. (1926). *We Tibetans*. London: Seeley Service.

Ludwar, G. (1975). *Die Sozialisation Tibetischer Kinder im soziokulturellen Wandel*. Wiesbaden: Steiner Verlag.

Norberg-Hodge, H. (1991). *Ancient Futures. Learning from Ladakh*. San Francisco: Sierra Club Books.

Norbu, T. J., & Turnbull, C. M. (1972). *Tibet*. New York: Simon & Schuster.

Paul, R. A. (1982). *The Tibetan Symbolic World*. Chicago: University of Chicago Press.

Peter, Prince of Greece and Denmark. (1963). *A Study of Polyandry*. The Hague: Mouton.

Reis, R. (1983). Reproduction or retreat: The position of Buddhist women in Ladakh. In Kantowsky, D. & Sander, R. (Eds.), *Recent Research on Ladakh: History, Culture, Sociology, Ecology* (pp. 217–29). Muenchen: Weltforum Vlg.

Ribbach, S. H. (1940). *Drogpa Namgyal. Ein Tibeterleben*. Muenchen: Barth-Verlag. (Trans. J. Bray (1986) as: *Culture and Society in Ladakh*. New Delhi: Ess Ess.)

Rizvi, J. (1983 [1989]). *Ladakh: Crossroads of High Asia*. New Delhi: Oxford University Press.

Schuler, S. R. (1983). Fraternal polyandry and single women: A study of marriage, social stratification and property in Chumik, a Tibetan society of the Nepalese. Ph.D. diss., Harvard University.

———. (1987). *The Other Side of Polyandry*. Boulder, CO: Westview Press.

Taring, R. D. (1970). *Daughter of Tibet*. London: Camelot Press.

Thurlow, C. (1975). *Stories from Beyond the Clouds. An Anthology of Tibetan Folktales*. Dharamsala, India: Library of Tibetan Works and Archives.

Whiting, B. B., & Edwards, C. P. (1988). *Children of Different Worlds*. Cambridge, MA: Harvard University Press.

30

Turkey

Güler Okman Fifek

INTRODUCTION

Turkey is a relatively unique country in many respects. Geographically, it spans two continents (Europe and Asia), and its ecology is very varied for its size (about 800,000 square kilometers or 308,880 square miles). Historically it has been host to a multitude of cultures (Hittite, Greek, Roman, Byzantine, Seljuk, Ottoman, to cite a few), which have blended to produce today's sociocultural mix. It is the only predominantly Islamic country with secular law, it is a democracy with a long history of imperial absolute rule, and it is a Third World country by some standards and a relatively developed country by others. Finally it is a relatively traditional culture undergoing extremely rapid sociocultural, economic, and political change. Timeless tradition coexists with dynamic change.

Making generalizations about such a culture is a difficult enterprise, and this chapter is written with that awareness. Further, the fact that some essential topics regarding gender roles have not yet been researched in the Turkish context adds a further limitation. Thus this chapter presents the available literature on gender and the life cycle, followed by a conclusion statement about the current situation and directions of change.

OVERVIEW

Turkish society is undergoing a transformation from a traditional, rural, agricultural, patriarchal society to an increasingly modern, urban, industrial, egalitarian one. As of 1985, 51.10 percent of a population of close to 60 million was urban, as compared with 18.67 percent in 1950. The constitution upholds secular, egalitarian democracy. Women have had the right to vote in national elections since 1934. Universal elementary education is a legal requirement, and higher levels are encouraged by the state.

However, not all areas of social functioning have changed equally rapidly; cultural values, norms, and attitudes lag behind economics and even actual practices. This is nowhere as evident as in the case of interpersonal relations in general and gender politics in particular. In that context the culture can still be described as somewhat traditional, authoritarian, and patriarchal.

First, as to the quality of social relationships in general, familial and relational values are predominant in Turkey (Ergüder, Kalaycìo°lu & Esmer, 1992), as befitting its being classed as a "culture of relatedness" (Ka°ìtçìbafì, 1986). Most social relationships are structured on the basis of expectations of reciprocal support and loyalty among kinship groups, especially in the countryside (Fifek, 1982). While the majority of households are nuclear in structure (67 percent in 1988), the functionally extended family is a very viable form of social interaction and support (Kandiyoti, 1974; Ka°ìtçìbafì, 1982; Timur, 1972). The individual tends to be embedded in a network of hierarchically ordered relationships, in which the welfare of the group often takes precedence over that of the individual (Fifek, 1982; Ka°ìtçìbafì, 1989).

Gender relations revolve around one basic concept, male supremacy, the belief that women are lower in value, prestige, and power than men (Fifek, 1982; Ka°ìtçìbafì, 1982; Kiray, 1976; Sunar, in press). It is a fair statement to say that patriarchy or gender hierarchy is a basic structural feature of this society, along with generational hierarchy (Fifek, 1990; Fifek & Wood, 1991).

The basic nature of this issue can be seen in a perusal of the law regarding male-female relationships. The family is legally considered the foundation of the society and is under the protection of the law. The man is considered the head of the household and is responsible for being the provider. He also has certain rights over his wife and children, including, until recently, the right to decide whether his wife can work. Thus gender inequality is structured into the law along with statements regarding equal rights for all citizens.

This, in short, is the arena in which the relations between the sexes are played out in Turkey. However, the matter appears much more complex and varied when one takes a closer look at different corners of the arena and at different cross-sections of the life cycles. Variations are mostly associated with rural-urban differences and social class indexes such as educational level, level of professionalism of occupations, and the like, and they will be pointed out as appropriate.

COMPARISONS BETWEEN MEN'S AND WOMEN'S GENDER ROLES DURING THE LIFE CYCLE

Infancy and Early Childhood

Turkish culture is pronatalist, so children occupy a large part in the societal consciousness (Çanakçi, 1992). However, as in all patriarchal societies, sons are preferred over daughters (Ka°ìtçìbaƒì, 1982; Kiray, 1976; Yörüko°lu, 1978), more so in rural than urban areas (Duben, 1982). This attitude is based mostly on the fact that children are desired for their economic value, as insurance against old age, and as carriers of the family name. In all these cases, sons have an advantage over daughters (Ka°ìtçìbaƒì, 1982; Sunar, in press).

While the value attributed to children is changing toward an emotional fulfillment dimension in more modern sectors (Ka°ìtçìbaƒì, 1982; Ka°ìtçìbaƒì & Sunar, in press), the preference for boys continues. The reason for this will become more clear when intrafamily dynamics and changes in the woman's status in the family and society are discussed.

Children are reared in an atmosphere of love and control, where control does not have the connotation of lack of love, as might be the case in Western cultures (Ka°ìtçìbaƒì, 1972). "Emotional attachment and loyalty" are key words (Sunar, in press). Both genders are brought up with an emphasis on obedience, dependency, conformity, and quietness, with autonomy, initiative, activity, and curiosity being discouraged (Ka°ìtçìbaƒì & Sunar, in press; Öztürk, 1969). While indulgence prevails over discipline for infants and very young children, the general attitude is protectiveness and restriction of autonomous activity (Fiƒek, 1982).

Discipline can be inconsistent (Helling, 1966). Common methods are forms of power assertion such as threats of bodily harm, beating, scaring with supernatural agencies, and shaming, with reasoning seldom being used (Ka°ìtçìbaƒì, Sunar & Bekman, 1988; Öztürk, 1969; Yörüko°lu, 1978). These attitudes are giving way to more egalitarian approaches, with reports of increased autonomy, avoidance of corporal punishment, and more democratic expectations among urban middle and upper classes (LeCompte, Özer & Özer, 1978; Fiƒek, 1982; Sunar, in press).

The above statements apply to both sexes; however, there are differences in expectations of boys and girls, especially in terms of preparing them for adult roles. Thus boys are allowed more freedom of movement, are expected to be more rambunctious and aggressive, while girls are expected to be less assertive and more subservient, especially in rural areas (Yörüko°lu, 1978). These expectations start early (Ka°ìtçìbaƒì & Sunar, in press), and empirical findings are consistent with these expectations as early as the preschool years (Kozcu, 1987).

From early ages on, girls are encouraged to engage in activities and games that can lay the groundwork for their eventual domestic roles, and boys are encouraged to practice male skills (Öztürk, 1969). For girls, restriction of their freedom of movement increases with age (Baƒaran, 1974), with inevitable negative impact. For example, in a study of urban, lower middle-class, adolescent girls, the subjects indicated a high degree of affiliative concern but did not display a similar degree of initiative and instead focused on external blocks to their needs (Tunalì, 1983). Similarly, female adolescents have been found to score lower on ego strength, to be more anxious and pessimistic, more helpless and nervous (Fiƒek, 1982; Yanbastì, 1990).

While socialization differences influence boys' and girls' behavior and perceptions, socioeconomic status (SES) seems to be an important mediator of final
outcomes. For example, Sìlay (1987) explored urban children's pictorial depic-
tions of interaction in same-sex and mixed-sex dyads. Boys tended to depict
more aggression, skill orientation, and competition, indicating a power and
dominance emphasis, than girls, who were more interpersonally oriented. However, high SES children of both sexes were more interpersonally oriented while
lower SES children were more skill-oriented. Gender and SES interacted in many
areas, indicating that the higher the social class, the less rigid the sex-role
stereotypes of children of both sexes.

School Years

Elementary education, which is five years, is compulsory in Turkey. While
this rule is adhered to in urban sectors, it has to be followed up in the countryside,
where girls are concerned, especially in the least developed east and southeast
regions. This is not surprising since education does not have much of an impact
on the life or labor force participation of rural women (Özbay, 1982). Since they
are expected to marry out, there is no benefit to the family in educating them
(Gök, 1990).

About half of elementary school graduates of both sexes do not go on to middle
school; of those who do, only 35 percent are females. The figures for high school
are 57 percent boys and 43 percent girls. Only a small proportion of high school
graduates are able to attend university; of those only 32 percent are women (Gök,
1990). These figures indicate that education beyond elementary school is not a
given for the majority, male or female but even less so for girls (Özbay, 1982).

A large number of girls in the more traditional sectors of society are either
kept home or oriented toward technical and occupational training, in such sex-
typed occupations as dressmaking, nursing, teaching, and secretarial work, which
are labor-intensive and do not pay well (Gök, 1990). Boys who do not go on
in school are encouraged to find apprenticeships in some trade so that they will
be able to provide for their families later on. In effect, the majority of the youth
are directed toward activities that will provide the basis of their adult roles, in
a sex-stereotyped fashion.

Such strong emphasis on preparing for adult life in concrete ways to the
detriment of education would seem to reflect the economic priorities of the
populace as well as the government. In fact, a nationwide survey of priorities
in spending indicated that housing and other needs involving economic maintenance far outstripped education for all social strata (Esmer, Fiʃek & Kalay-
cìoʻlu, 1987).

While education may lose out to overall economic survival, it is nevertheless
important, especially to the urban elite. Interestingly, though, gender is not an
issue vis-à-vis education for this sector. Daughters and sons of the elite are
strongly and similarly encouraged to pursue professional educations, even in

traditionally so-called male-dominated areas such as engineering (Acar, 1989; Erkut, 1982). When one looks at the educational attainment of those who continue in regular academic training, women tend to be more persistent and successful than their male peers (Erkut, 1982).

The educational encouragement of elite women has been explained by referring to the notions that their success does not represent as much of a threat to the power of elite men as the success of lower-class males would be (Erkut, 1982; Öncü, 1981) and that elite women benefit from the supportive domestic services of lower-class uneducated women, which obviates the necessity of sharing the domestic load with their spouses, thereby reducing potential conflict (Ka°ìtçìbafì, 1986). Finally, perhaps because female professionalism is a relatively recent phenomenon that coincided with other democratic reforms, the professions were opened up to women before they could be sex-typed (Öncü, 1981). Be that as it may, there is no overall translation into increased status for women with education (Gök, 1990).

Young Adulthood

Consistent with the enforcement of early sex segregation, there is a clear preference for same-sex friendships. While this tends to be true of adolescents in most cultures, Turkish youth seem to be closer to their same-sex friends than, for example, are American youth (Bekata, 1980). Next to their friends, the young tend to prefer their mothers over their fathers for intimacy (Hortaçsu, 1989). Friendship elicits expectations of loyalty, investment of time, and sharing of decision processes (Gökçe, 1976; Hortaçsu, 1989).

Given the strong normative support of same-sex socialization, opposite-sex socialization is remarked upon. For example, opposite-sex dyads are considered to be necessarily romantically involved rather than just being friends (Helling, 1966; Hortaçsu, Düzen, Arat, Atahan, & Uzer, 1990).

The emphasis on sex segregation is based on the concept of honor (*namus*) prevalent in most parts of the Middle East and the Mediterranean. A man's honor and social prestige are intimately linked to the sexual chastity of his female relatives; therefore, in order to preserve his place in the community of men, he has to impose strict controls over the conduct of his women (Ka°ìtçìbafì & Sunar, in press; Kandiyoti, 1987). This, in turn, is tied to the Muslim view of women as highly sexual creatures who would lead men astray if they were not kept separate (Kandiyoti, 1987). These two constructs together combine to keep the two genders in separate worlds.

Urban youth, under the influence of coeducation and Western media, have increasingly sought mixed-sex socialization, but opportunities are limited outside school (Ka°ìtçìbafì & Sunar, in press). However, there is increasing debate about the need for more permissiveness, and all sectors are speaking out. For example, a public statement in 1990 by an ultraconservative member of a previous government that flirting is synonymous with prostitution led to an enormous uproar among the young and old alike, especially among women.

Women comprise 30.6 percent of the active labor force as of 1989. While this is not a high percentage, it is large enough to indicate that gainful female employment is here to stay. However, a recent nationwide survey revealed some ambivalence on this topic (Ergüder, Kalaycìo°lu & Esmer, 1991). A large majority saw the woman's primary responsibilities as her home and children. Yet both women and men endorsed the claim that the road to emancipation for a woman is through employment and that a working mother can be as nurturing as a nonworking mother. Further, the idea that women should contribute to the family income was also endorsed.

Overall, women are represented in the lower ranks in all types of work (Kabasakal, 1991). The percentage of women decreases as one moves up the managerial ranks, and this fact is consistent with attitudes (Smith, 1990). The sectors that employ more women and more women managers tend to be lower-paying sectors such as textiles (Kabasakal, 1991). Further, these women have little impact in their workplace. Women have to rely more on their own personal qualifications than other sources of power available to men (Kabasakal, 1991).

However, the situation is somewhat different for professional women. Women are highly involved in high-prestige professions such as medicine and law (Öncü, 1981). Estimates in 1970 of the percentage of women in medicine and law in Turkey were 14 percent and 19 percent, respectively, while the United States of America estimates were 10 percent and 5 percent, respectively (Erkut, 1982).

The divergence between the overall low status of women with regard to employment and the situation in the most modernized sectors parallels the educational divergence mentioned before and is reflected in values, too. For example, the work-related values of a sample of university students indicate that females are more androgynous than males, are willing to work in male-dominated jobs, and do not fear success. Further, they tend to score higher than males in achievement motivation and work ethic, while there are no sex differences in financial aspirations and competitiveness (Balkìr, 1990).

Contrast this with public sector employees, who say they work mainly because of economic need and show a preference for a domestic role (Özbay, 1989; Özkalp, 1989), and the divergence becomes clear. The roots of this divergence have to be sought, at least in part, in the fact that there is almost no institutional or normative support for the working woman. Since employment is associated with low status outside the elite realm, most women prefer their family roles (Özbay, 1989).

A study of female participation in academic careers demonstrates some of the dilemmas of the professional group (Acar, 1989). Female faculty members comprised 32.2 percent of the total in 1989, with no exclusive concentration in so-called female fields and no complaints of formal discrimination. However, this state of affairs does not translate into power in any wider sense (Acar, 1989). First, academic science has weak links to societal power; where the links exist, as in schools of political science, women are underrepresented. Second, these women tend to occupy the lower ranks of professorship and they still give evidence of informal discrimination in terms of access to networks of power.

Last, one of the biggest drawbacks seems to be in the area of role conflict. There is no decrease in the traditional domestic expectations of women because of employment, regardless of the status of the job (Erkut, 1982; Özkalp, 1989). Consequently, these women feel pressure to reduce standards of professional performance and otherwise balance home and workplace responsibilities (Acar, 1989). The fact that fully 48.9 percent of academic women and 29.8 percent of women in high-level academic administrative posts are single, compared with 38.15 percent and 3 percent, respectively, for men, is an index of the situation.

Another area where women are underrepresented is politics; Turkey has had, and continues to have, female ministers, but the percentage of women in Parliament today is close to zero. Thus women have only a "symbolic" presence in political life (Tekeli, 1981). They do not show much interest in politics and vote under the influence of their families. This is understandable, since in the division of labor between men and women, politics falls squarely within the male sphere (Tekeli, 1981). Those women who are politically active complain about male dominance and control (Arat, 1985; Ayata, 1989).

Adulthood

In the traditional sectors marriage is still a social and economic transaction between two families more than an individual decision by two autonomous individuals, leading to a preference for arranged marriages and marriages among relatives (Fifek, 1982; Ka°itçìbafì, 1982). However, there is increasing emphasis on choosing one's partner oneself (Imamo°lu, 1991).

The nuclear family is structured hierarchically in terms of generation and gender, with the latter being primary (Fifek, 1982, 1990). This hierarchy is mainly reflected in role differentiation and separation of spheres of activity of the spouses (Kìray, 1976; Olson, 1982). In fact the two factors of the woman's low status and clear separation of spheres of activity have implications for all areas of family life.

To begin with, the woman's low status prevails regardless of differences in urban/rural residence, educational status, or employment status, the only exception being highly educated, professional, urban women (Çanakçì, 1992; Kandiyoti, 1974; Ka°itçìbafì, 1986; Kuyaf, 1982).

In traditional areas, a woman gains status through giving birth to a son, thereby ensuring the continuation of the family name and future economic security for the parents, and through aging, which brings domestic high status vis-à-vis her daughters-in-law (Kìray, 1976). Clearly, these are powerful reasons for preferring sons.

The extreme segregation involved in the historic practice of seclusion of women is scarcely an issue today. However, residual attitudes and ongoing division of labor along gender lines seem to have resulted in a family structure that has been described as being duofocal, with husband and wife living in somewhat different worlds (Olson, 1982).

In traditional sectors spousal relationships tend to revolve around economic maintenance and child rearing, rather than emotional companionship (Olson, 1982). Traditional sex-role expectations pervade decision-making functions. The husband is responsible for major decisions involving the household (Timur, 1972), whether rural or urban (Gökçe, 1976).

Communication between spouses is not a high priority in the more traditional families, so that even topics such as family planning do not get discussed (Kandiyoti, 1977; Ka°ìtçìbafì, 1982; Olson, 1982). Emotional expression and self-disclosure between spouses may even be frowned upon in traditional, rural areas (Kandiyoti, 1977). In fact, spousal emotional intimacy in the Western European sense may be said to be irrelevant in this kind of marital partnership (Fifek, 1992). This idea is borne out by the finding that there are no sex differences in the amount of self-disclosure engaged in; however, self-disclosure tends to be a within-sex phenomenon (Kìzìltepe, 1982).

The marital relationship is one area in which increased education and urban residence are leading to changes. Highly educated, high SES, urban couples show more egalitarian attitudes and intimacy expectations regarding spousal relationships and intrafamily status (Bahar, 1982; Ka°ìtçìbafì, 1986; Kuyaf, 1982). Their participation in, and satisfaction with, family decision-making processes also increase (Imamo°lu, 1991; Yalçìnkaya, 1990).

The more egalitarian marriages of well-educated, urban, dual-career couples also show a trend toward a more egalitarian division of labor. However, this trend still moves more slowly for men, in that while women more readily take on male roles, the reverse is not true for men (Imamo°lu, 1991).

Overall there is a tendency for women to admit to more psychological problems than men, especially if they are married (Imamo°lu, 1991). For example, women score higher than men in neuroticism and conformity. Married women who express depressive feelings tend to attribute their problems to spousal and other familial causes (Savafìr, 1990). While these results are consistent with Western findings, it is not clear how similar the dynamics are. It should also be noted that the studies were done mostly with urban samples, whose stresses and expectations are different from those of their rural counterparts.

The hierarchic structure of the family has an effect on the interpersonal relationships in the family, as follows. Since the father is distanced from the domestic sphere due to his sex-role mandate, his relationships with the children and his wife are somewhat limited and hierarchic (Fifek, 1982; Hortaçsu, Düzen, Arat, Atahan, & Uzer, 1990). While the father-daughter relationship may be characterized by some degree of affection (Kandiyoti, 1977), the father-son relationship tends to be more formal and authoritarian (Kìray, 1976).

The mother and daughter are close and share much time together, but the especially important relationship is that between mother and son. Obviously, the fact that a son confers status upon his mother is one reason for this closeness (Kìray, 1976). Further, in terms of hierarchy, the highly valued son is close enough to his low-worth mother in power and status that boundaries between the two are especially prone to be blurred (Fifek, 1982; Fifek & Wood, 1991). When one considers the distance of the woman from her husband and her relative isolation in the domestic arena, it is natural to expect the woman to turn to her children, especially her valued son (Fifek, 1982).

Isolation in the domestic sphere seems to have its advantages in that women can attain a certain amount of autonomy in the absence of immediate male control (Ka°ìtçìbafì, 1986; Kìray, 1976). The closeness with the children, especially the son, can also lead to a fairly central role for the mother in the domestic sphere, where she can be a buffer in father-child conflicts as well as forming coalitions against the father (Kìray, 1976). While this kind of experience leads to a certain strengthening of the female character and a fairly strong female subculture, it is not clear how and if this strength gets manifested in community life (Kìray, 1976).

As would be expected of the separation of activities, leisure time is also spent separately in traditional families. Housewives get together with relatives and other neighboring women, both informally, in doing household tasks together, and formally on "visiting days" (Kìray, 1976). Men tend to spend their leisure time outside the home, in the neighborhood coffeehouse. More modern sectors are showing a strong trend toward more joint activities, however (Kìray, 1976).

While increasing in numbers, divorce is still a somewhat rare occurrence in Turkey despite the fact that the laws are quite permissive (Levine, 1982). The divorce rate has never risen above 1 percent (Özbay, 1989). It appears that increases in the divorce rate are linked with periods of expansion of the economy, increased availability of housing, and decreases in the inflation rate (Levine, 1982). Thus the prevalence of divorce says more about the possibilities of economic independence, especially for women, than it does about intrafamilial unhappiness.

When one looks at the sectors with the highest rate of divorce, the just literate, semiskilled, urban poor seem to be most affected (Levine, 1982). This, of course, is the group that is most likely to experience the crunch of increased aspirations without opportunities. Thus it seems that while this group suffers the most from the uneven progress of social change, it also is the group most willing to challenge traditional norms, especially regarding female submission.

However, women and men do not suffer the same fate once they are divorced. Remarriage is not viewed in the same light for men and women. While a divorced woman is stigmatized, this is not the case for men; remarriage is an accepted and common practice for divorced men (Özbay, 1989).

A number of studies exploring sex-role expectations and stereotypes among urban, middle-class respondents offer consistent results (Gürbüz, 1985; Kandi-yoti, 1978; Sunar, 1982). Overall, there is agreement among males and females that male and female roles are quite distinct in the expected direction. However,

Turkish respondents seem to differ from their American counterparts on some points. Thus, the female role elicits more disagreement among Turkish men and women, with men seeing women in a more extremely sex-typed fashion, such as being very dependent, childish, and ignorant (Sunar, 1982).

There is more agreement on the masculine role, which is different from American masculinity. A strict instrumental-expressive dichotomy does not hold for Turkish sex-role stereotypes; expressive characteristics such as good communication are positively evaluated, while independence and individuality are negatively evaluated for both sexes (Gürbüz, 1986; Sunar, 1982). Fewer characteristics related to achievement, competence, and instrumentality are attributed to Turkish males than to American males (Gürbüz, 1985; Kandiyoti, 1978). In terms of androgyny, the masculine component has a closer association with self-esteem than the feminine component (Gürbüz, 1985). Thus the cultural definition of femininity cannot be said to be conducive to self-esteem.

Intergenerational studies indicate that the older generation tends to be more stereotypical in their expectations than the younger (Kandiyoti, 1978; Sever, 1985; Sunar, in press). A comparison of husbands' and wives' perceptions of marital roles indicated that men were more satisfied with the division of labor and spousal relationships than women, while women complained about lack of communication and support (Imamo°lu, 1991).

Old Age

As in most traditional cultures, traditional Turkish culture demands a reverence of the elderly. In the most patriarchal sectors, the oldest male is still the head of the household, and the oldest woman is the head of the domestic sphere with all the attendant privileges. However, their centrality is diminishing with increasing economic independence of the younger generation (Kìray, 1976).

When the culturally ascribed status of the elderly diminishes, their welfare and life satisfaction become issues of psychological importance. Studies of retirees indicate that female retirees find ways of making their lives meaningful and useful more easily, thus experiencing less anxiety and more life satisfaction (Sa°lam, 1986; U°ursal, 1981). Women can offer child care and other domestic services to the younger generation; in fact, such services are indispensable in many families where the mother works. The meaning of work for men and women plays a role here, with men giving it a more central role in their self-definition than women. Thus men who can maintain their male identity through reemployment suffer fewer ill effects (Sa°lam, 1986).

The traditional familistic values are evident in the fact that elderly parents tend to live with their offspring in larger numbers than would be true in the West (Ka°itçibaƒì & Sunar, in press). This is probably also related to the fact that services such as retirement homes are basically negligible and do not provide the elderly with a meaningful option (Imamo°lu & Imamo°lu, in press). In some cases the adult generation, among women at least, seem to prefer to live alone, at least to have that option. If they have to live with an adult child, the majority seem to prefer their son, in the traditional manner (Özbay, 1989).

SUMMARY AND CONCLUSIONS

The implications of the above survey of the literature on gender roles in Turkey can be stated very shortly. Patriarchy or gender hierarchy continues to be one of the most basic structural features of the society. Given this fact, there is also a great deal of movement in many aspects of social life, not all of which has been researched, let alone understood. It would appear that gender relations in Turkey will be subject to increasing change, with its unavoidable concomitants of uncertainty and conflict.

This survey also indicates that not all aspects of gender roles have been equally thoroughly researched from a psychological perspective. The most comprehensively studied areas tend to be in other fields of the social sciences, such as politics, education, and especially sociology. The fact that psychology is a relatively recent field in Turkey is one reason for this.

Further and much more importantly, most of the studies fit broadly into the field of women's studies, excluding the study of men. While this was certainly needed to correct the errors of gender bias in earlier studies, it has also led to some limitations in the studies of gender roles and relations.

It would appear that the time is now ripe to begin focusing on a more comprehensive analysis and understanding of gender relations in contemporary Turkish society. This is especially important when one considers that fully half the population of Turkey is under the age of 25. Given such a young population, one has to ask how gender relations are different for this generation, and if they are not different, why not. At that point we can begin to understand some of the socioeconomic, social-structural, and psychological variables contributing to the perpetuation and change of gender relations in Turkey.

REFERENCES

Acar, F. (1989). Women's participation in academic science careers: Turkey in 1989. Paper presented at the meeting of the UNESCO-Vienna Center joint project "Women's Participation in Positions of Responsibility in Careers of Science and Technology," Lisbon.

Arat, Y. (1985). Obstacles to political careers: Perceptions of Turkish women. *International Political Science Review*, 6 (3): 355–66.

Ayata, A. G. (1989). Women's participation in politics in Turkey. In Tekeli, P. (Ed.), *Women in the Turkey of the 1980s from Women's Perspective* (pp. 269–87). Istanbul: Iletifim.

Bahar, M. (1982). Marital communication and its relationship to marital satisfaction. Master's thesis, Bo°aziçi University, Istanbul.

Balkìr, B. (1990). Gender differences in work values of middle- and upper-class freshman college students in Turkey. Master's thesis, Bo°aziçi University, Istanbul.

Baᶠaran, F. (1974). *Psychosocial Development: A Study on 7–11 Year-Old Children.* Ankara: Ankara University Press.

Bekata, F. (1980). The natural history of friendship: A cross-cultural study. Ph.D. diss., St. Louis University.

Çanakçì, Ö. (1992). The psychological well-being and marital satisfaction of involuntarily childless women in Turkey. Master's thesis, Bo°aziçi University, Istanbul.

Duben, A. (1982). The significance of family and kinship in urban Turkey. In Ka°ìtçìbaᶠì, Ç. (Ed.), *Sex Roles, Family and Community in Turkey.* Bloomington: Indiana University Press.

Ergüder, Ü., Kalaycìo°lu, E., & Esmer, Y. (1992). *The Values of Turkish Society.* Istanbul: TUSIAD.

Erkut, S. (1982). Dualism in values toward education of Turkish women. In Ka°ìtçìbaᶠì, Ç. (Ed.), *Sex Roles, Family and Community in Turkey. Bloomington: Indiana University Press.*

Esmer, Y., Fiᶠek, H., & Kalaycìo°lu, E. (1987). The Socioeconomic Situation and Outlook of the Turkish Household. Istanbul: TUSIAD, Report no. T/87.12.107.

Fiᶠek, G. O. (1982). Psychopathology and the Turkish family: A family systems theory analysis. In Ka°ìtçìbaᶠì, Ç. (Ed.), *Sex Roles, Family and Community in Turkey.* Bloomington: Indiana University Press.

———. (1990). A cross-cultural examination of proximity and hierarchy as dimensions of family structure. *Family Process, 30*: 121–33.

———. (1992, May). The feminization and romanticization of intimacy: A Western cultural phenomenon. A.F.T.A. [American Family Therapy Association] *Newsletter.*

Fiᶠek, G. O., & Wood, B. (1991). Gender: An essential factor in the organization of proximity and hierarchy in families. Paper presented at the Colloquium on Current Topics in International Psychology, Washington, DC.

Gök, F. (1990). Education and women in Turkey. In Tekeli, P. (Ed.), *Women in the Turkey of the 1980s from Women's Perspective.* Istanbul: Iletiᶠim.

Gökçe, B. (1976). *Shantytown Youth.* Ankara: Hacettepe University Press.

Gürbüz, E. (1985). A measurement of sex-trait stereotypes. Master's thesis, Bo°aziçi University, Istanbul.

Helling, G. A. (1966). The Turkish village as a social system. Unpublished monograph, Occidental College, Los Angeles.

Hortaçsu, N. (1989). Targets of communication during adolescence. *Journal of Adolescence, 12*: 253–63.

Hortaçsu, N., Düzen, E., Arat, S., Atahan, D., & Uzer, B. (1990). Intrusions upon same-sex or different-sex dyads in a Turkish university dining hall. *International Journal of Psychology, 25*: 33–37.

Imamo°lu, O. (1991). Changing intra-family roles in a changing world. Paper presented at the seminar, "The Individual, the Family and the Society in a Changing World," Istanbul, Turkey.

Imamo°lu, O. & Imamo°lu, V. (in press). Life situations and attitudes of the Turkish elderly toward institutional living within a cross-cultural perspective. *Journal of Gerontology Psychological Sciences.*

Kabasakal, H. (1991). Women, organizations and power allocation. *Toplum ve Bilim (Society and Science), 53*: 55–63.

Ka°ìtçìbafì, Ç. (1972). *The Psychological Dimensions of Social Change*. Ankara: Turkish Social Science Association.

———. (1982). *Value of Children in Turkey*. East-West Center, Honolulu, Hawaii: Current Studies on the Value of Children.

———. (1986). Status of women in Turkey: Cross-cultural perspectives. *International Journal of Middle East Studies, 18:* 485–99.

———. (1990). Family and socialization in cross-cultural perspective: A model of change. In Berman, F. (Ed.), *Nebraska Symposium on Motivation,* No. 37. Lincoln: Nebraska University Press.

Ka°ìtçìbafì, Ç., & Sunar, D. (in press). Family and socialization in Turkey. In Roopnarine, J. P., & Carter, D. B. (Eds.), *Parent-Child Relations in Diverse Cultural Settings: Socialization for Instrumental Competency.* Ablex.

Ka°ìtçìbafì, Ç., Sunar, D., & Bekman, S. (1988). Early enrichment project. IDRC manuscript report, Ottawa.

Kandiyoti, D. (1974). Some social psychological dimensions of social change in a Turkish village. *British Journal of Sociology, 15,* (1): 47–62.

———. (1977). Sex roles and social change: A comparative appraisal of Turkey's women. *Signs: Journal of Women in Culture and Society, 3:* 57–73.

———. (1978). Intergenerational change among Turkish women. Paper presented at the Ninth World Congress of Sociology, Uppsala, Sweden.

———. (1987). Emancipated but unliberated? Reflections on the Turkish case. *Feminist Studies, 43* (2): 317–39.

———. (1988). Bargaining with patriarchy. *Gender and Society 2* (3): 274–90.

Kìray, M. (1976). Changing roles of mothers: Changing intra-family relations in a Turkish town. In Peristiany, J. G. (Ed.), *Mediterranean Family Structures.* London: Cambridge University Press.

Kìzìltepe, Z. F. (1982). Self-disclosure. Master's thesis, Bo°aziçi University, Istanbul.

Kozcu, Pt. (1987). An investigation of aggressive behaviors in preschool children and their mothers' reactions. *Psikoloji Dergisi (Journal of Psychology), 6* (21): 19–22.

Kuyaf, N. (1982). Female labor and power relations in the urban Turkish family. In Ka°ìtçìbafì, Ç. (Ed.), *Sex Roles, Family and Community in Turkey.* Bloomington: Indiana University Press.

LeCompte, G., Özer, A., & Özer, S. (1978). Child-rearing attitudes of mothers from three socioeconomic levels in Ankara: Adaptation of an instrument. *Psikoloji Dergisi (Journal of Psychology), 1:* 5–8.

Levine, N. (1982). Social change and family crisis—The nature of Turkish divorce. In Ka°ìtçìbafì, Ç. (Ed.), *Sex Roles, Family and Community in Turkey.* Bloomington: Indiana University Press.

Olson, E. A. (1982). Duofocal family structure and an alternative model of husband-wife relationship. In Ka°ìtçìbafì, Ç. (Ed.), *Sex Roles, Family and Community in Turkey.* Bloomington: Indiana University Press.

Öncü, A. (1981). Turkish women in the professions: Why so many? In Abadan-Unat, N. (Ed.), *Women in Turkish Society.* Leiden: E. J. Brill.

Özbay, F. (1982). Women's education in rural Turkey. In Ka°ìtçìbafì, Ç. (Ed.), *Sex Roles, Family and Community in Turkey.* Bloomington: Indiana University Press.

———. (1989). Family and household structure in Turkey: Past, present, and future.

Paper presented at the conference on "The Changing Family in the Middle East," Amman, Jordan.

Özkalp, E. (1989). Employment reasons and problems of female public sector employees. Paper presented at the Second National Congress of the Social Sciences, Ankara, Turkey.

Öztürk, M. O. (1969). Inhibition of autonomy and initiative in the Anatolian personality. Paper presented at the Fifth National Congress of Neuropsychiatry.

Sa°lam, N. (1986). Anxiety and depression in middle-aged Turkish retirees. Master's thesis, Bop°aziçi University, Istanbul.

Savafìr, B. (1990). Content analysis of women's letters written to a television program. Master's thesis, Bo°aziçi University, Istanbul.

Sever, L. (1985). Change in women's perceptions of parental child-rearing practices, attitudes and beliefs in the context of social change in Turkey: A three-generation comparison. Master's thesis, Bo°aziçi University, Istanbul.

Sìlay, P,. (1987). Nature of boys' and girls' perceptions of interactions in same-, opposite- and mixed-sex dyads. Master's thesis, Bo°aziçi University, Istanbul.

Smith, P,. T. (1990). Obstacles for women on the way to management: A study of business students' images of the ideal manager. *Journal of Contemporary Management*, *3*: 77–88.

Sunar, D. (1982). Female sterrotypes in the United States and Turkey: An application of functional theory to perceptions in power relations. *Journal of Cross-Cultural Psychology*, *13* (4): 445–60.

———. (in press). Turkish child-rearing practices in three generations.

Tekeli, P,. (1981). The woman's place in Turkish political life. In Abadan-Unat, N. (Ed.), *Women in Turkish Society*. Leiden: E. J. Brill.

Timur, S. (1972). *Family Structure in Turkey*. Ankara: Hacettepe University Press.

Tunalì, B. (1983). An investigation on need affiliation and its relation to family cohesion in Turkish adolescents. Master's thesis, Bo°aziçi University, Istanbul.

U°ursal, B. (1981). Retirement and life satisfaction. Master's thesis, Bo°aziçi University, Istanbul.

Yalçìnkaya, A. (1990). Decision making in the Turkish family. Master's thesis, Bo°aziçi University, Istanbul.

Yanbastì, G. (1990). Self-evaluation of mental health by male and female students: A comparison. *Psikoloji Dergisi* (*Journal of Psychology*), *8*: 57–63.

Yörüko°lu, A. (1978). *Child Mental Health*. Ankara: Türkiye I*f* Bankasì Press.

31

United States of America

Florence L. Denmark,
Karen A. Nielson, and
Kristin Scholl

INTRODUCTION

The United States of America is an industrialized nation located on the continent of North America. It is bordered by Canada to the north and by Mexico to the south. It lies between two oceans, the Atlantic Ocean on the east, and the Pacific Ocean on the west. Forty-eight of the fifty states that comprise this country lie within its mainland and are contiguous. The state of Alaska lies to the northwest of the mainland, bordering Canada, and the fiftieth state of Hawaii, which is surrounded by the Pacific Ocean, lies southwest of California. Altogether, the United States contains nearly 3,618,770 square miles.

The population of the United States of America is approximately 260 million. Its population distribution is 75 percent urban and 25 percent rural. This country has been called a melting pot, for most of its population consists of immigrants from virtually every country in the world. Its earliest settlers up until 1840 were predominantly from England and Scotland. Settlers from other European nations, such as Ireland, Germany, and Scandinavia, were the next to arrive. A new wave of immigrants from Italy and the Slavic countries began to make the U.S.A. their home beginning in the 1860s. Through slavery, a forced immigration of Blacks from Africa began in the early 1600s and continued until the beginning of the nineteenth century. Although displaced by European settlers, the Native American people of the U.S.A. are found in all 50 states but have higher population concentrations in the Great Plains and the West. The newest inhabitants of this country include Spanish Americans, primarily from Puerto Rico, Mexico, and Central America, as well as Asian settlers from China, Japan, Korea, and Vietnam. As in the past, the most recent wave of newcomers to settle in the United States of America did so to escape overpopulation, famine, war, economic hardship, and religious persecution in their countries of origin (Kellogg, 1990).

Another characteristic of the United States of America that has had a great impact on its citizens and immigrants is its prosperous climate. It is one of the world's leading productive powers, and its economy is primarily free enterprise. It is a nation rich in natural resources, with farms, fisheries, mines, and industry.

The intermingling or cultural blending that has occurred in the United States of America, as well as its evolving economic character and opportunities, has contributed greatly to the acquisition and maintenance of specific and unique gender roles.

OVERVIEW

In such a nation, which is rich both in its economy and in its cultural diversity, the concept of gender roles and exploring how they have evolved and currently manifest themselves are interesting. Historically, distinct gender roles in this country have been clearly established, although recently there has been a change toward a greater appreciation for the work performed by women and more participation in housework and child care by men.

However, throughout the history of the U.S.A., women have been faced with balancing their productive and reproductive work (Anderson, 1988). Regardless of their contributions, either professionally or domestically, the social position of women has essentially remained the same, with little change in power or status. A man's sphere and role consist of more visible and material pursuits. His elevated status in the world and position as head of the household have almost always been a dynamic of the couple, the family, and society itself.

For a greater understanding of how gender roles have come to be defined in the United States of America today, it is important to appreciate the evolution of these roles from the earliest beginnings of the nation to the present day. In colonial times, due to the abundance of land, women had some independence and were able to own property. Frontier conditions required that all members of the community, male and female, work together. Women's work was consequently both socially apparent and essential. There were more men than women, thus women were in greater demand, which in turn offered them wider choices in husband selection. They were also allowed opportunities for paid work. Wives and husbands worked together in productive activities and shared in child rearing. Nevertheless, the social status of women was seen as a reflection of their spouses' positions. Should a wife receive wages, her salary contributed to that of the household (Anderson, 1988).

The early nineteenth century brought with it many changes: westward expansion, the commercialization of agriculture, and the beginning of the era of industrialization. These changes made women less visible as they remained working within the household, while men were free to engage in work outside the home. Women's roles began to be redefined as more interpersonal, while the work of men came to be seen as more physically demanding and productive (Cott, 1977).

While the church and community had played a role during colonial times, by supporting families emotionally and by acting as mediator in domestic disputes, women in the nineteenth century were given the responsibility of socializing their children, as well as providing emotional support for their husbands. These responsibilities, coupled with the many daily domestic chores faced by women, were stressful, time-consuming, and exhausting, yet women were expected to fulfill their roles with patience and self-denial (Anderson, 1988). Work outside the home, which was predominantly performed by men, increasingly began to be seen as more important and more physically and emotionally demanding than domestic work. Thus, work performed by women was devalued. Home for the man represented a haven from the workplace, where he could find rest and relaxation.

Women who worked outside the home during this time period were largely employed as domestic servants. Some women needed to help support their families while remaining at home. They did this by taking in others' laundry and sewing, running a boardinghouse, or creating products at home on a piecework basis (Anderson, 1988).

The industrialization of the 1820s and 1830s offered the opportunity for factory work for both men and women. However, women's status and pay were lower than those of the male factory workers. Women usually performed low-skill jobs, with little opportunity for skill development and advancement. Accelerated urbanization, advances in transportation and communication, and the development of large corporations of the late nineteenth century offered alternative employment opportunities. Most importantly, traditionally assigned gender roles began to change. Women began to shift from domestic service to clerical and sales positions. This change became evident as the percentage of women who were employed as clerical or sales workers increased to 29 percent in 1940, up from 8 percent in 1900 (Anderson, 1988). During this same time, men who had previously filled positions now assumed by women were being upgraded to managers, engineers, technicians, and administrators. The "feminization" of these lower clerical positions, as well as the lower factory positions filled by women, served to characterize all female employment as being of lower pay and lower mobility and requiring lesser skills than when those positions were filled by men.

The formation of labor unions in the 1920s helped to improve working conditions for women, but by and large, they remained unable to obtain recognition. Other female-dominated professions began to emerge in nursing, teaching, and social work. Not surprisingly, even these professional vocations were deemed consistent with a "woman's role"—and required qualities such as nurturance, empathy, and motherliness. The Great Depression further served to demonstrate a clearly defined division of labor by gender, for unemployed men seldom displaced women in female-dominated jobs.

Women began to enter the labor force in greater numbers during World War II to replace the male workers who were enlisted for the war. The men went off to war and followed their prescribed masculine role as protector and aggressor. Women were needed and trained for positions in defense plants. Even older and married women sought out such employment. Once the war ended, however, it was expected that these women would resume their domestic roles, thus allowing men to return to their jobs. As a result, a postwar baby boom came about in the 1950s.

The 1960s contributed to a shift in the concept of gender roles to an even greater extent. The times were turbulent, with the controversial Vietnam War, the explosion of the civil rights movement, the sexual revolution, and campus unrest all occurring at the same time. Values that had once been accepted were now being seriously questioned. The advent of birth control at this time allowed couples to forestall having families, as well as limiting family size.

These things, together with a recent economic recession, have contributed to today's decline in birthrates and a growing number of women currently entering the labor force (Denmark, Schwartz & Smith, 1991). The employment opportunities for women today are slowly expanding to areas that were formerly both dominated by men and outside traditional female-dominated spheres.

The status of men and women in the U.S.A. is most like that of Canadian men and women. One reason for this may be that industrialization in both nations changed the economies from a household to a market system. This in effect reduced the importance of the domestic role (Denmark, Schwartz & Smith, 1991). In fact, there is a rise in the number of men entering previously female-dominated professions, such as nursing and teaching, while at the same time, women are entering male-dominated professions in increasing numbers.

Yet despite these changes, the U.S.A. basically follows a traditional and conservative trend. The Equal Rights Amendment to the Constitution was not adopted, although a vast majority of women currently work outside the home and many support households single-handedly. While there has been a reduction of strict gender-role adherence, traditional gender roles continue to predominate in the United States of America today.

COMPARISONS BETWEEN MEN'S AND WOMEN'S GENDER ROLES DURING THE LIFE CYCLE

Infancy and Early Childhood

Gender-role expectations and assignments are set forth at birth, sometimes even prenatally, for many American couples elect to find out the sex of their child during the mother's pregnancy. Early preparations can then be made, such as the selection of nursery room color and decor and the purchase of gender-appropriate toys and clothing. Traditionally, the predominant color for newborn boys' clothing, bedding, and/or room has been, and continues to be, blue.

Similarly, the traditional color representing girls is pink. While children of both genders may initially receive soft, cuddly toys to play with, it is considered most unusual for the growing female child to be given male toys, such as footballs and trucks. Often couples in the U.S.A. hope that the firstborn children will be male, based on the assumption that if a female child is born afterward, she will have an older brother to look out for her (Jaccoma & Denmark, 1974).

At birth, there are some behavioral differences by gender, but they are few. Males appear to have an advantage in grip strength and are able to hold their heads up better than females—but these differences are so small that they are not significant (Jacklin, 1992). Hormonal levels at birth surprisingly do not determine later behavior. For example, children born with high testosterone levels do not necessarily engage in rough-and-tumble play later on (Jacklin, 1992).

Early socialization of infants may differ according to the child's, as well as the parent's, gender. Many parent-infant interactions in the United States of America are based upon the nonverbal behaviors of parent gazing and touching, along with infant gazing. Mothers touch their sons more when their sons look at them, whereas mothers react to their daughters' gazes with a visual rather than physical response. Fathers respond to their sons' visual behavior with physical contact (Roggman & Peery, 1989). Gross motor behavior in infant sons is responded to with greater frequency by parents than the same activity in infant daughters (Lewis, 1972; Moss, 1967). Additionally, female infants and toddlers are often treated as if they were more fragile than infant boys (Sidorowicz & Lunney, 1980). Perhaps this is the beginning of differentiation by gender that is socially and culturally determined.

Fathers are often more likely than are mothers to reinforce gender-typical play in their preschool children, especially in sons (Langlois & Downs, 1980). The role of fathers in the early socialization of males appears to be qualitatively different in physical play. Mothers touch more frequently when boys look at them, but fathers touch longer with boys who look less. In the area of discipline, boys are more likely to be physically punished (Maccoby & Jacklin, 1974), while girls are more likely to receive verbal reprimands (Serbin, O'Leary, Kent, & Tonick, 1973). Boys may also be given greater freedom in their physical environments than girls at a much earlier age. That is, they are given more freedom to explore without the accompaniment of a parent or adult (Nerlove, Munroe & Munroe, 1971). Thus, it appears that early parent-child social interactions may contribute to the beginnings of distinct social environments for male and female children. Such findings suggest that parents may have expectations of how boys and girls should be treated differentially, from infancy on.

Actual physical differences between males and females may play a role in attitudes toward the growing child's cognitive development (Anastasi, 1985). Females accelerate developmentally faster than males, even prior to birth. They reach puberty earlier. They are more advanced in height, weight, and skeletal development throughout childhood. The early growth of girls in infancy has been used to account for more rapid acquisition of language, giving females a verbal head start. Females also have an early advantage in manual dexterity and in fine motor control, which may arise from their initial developmental acceleration. Males, however, have greater muscular strength, larger general overall body size, and greater speed and coordination of gross bodily movements. These biologically determined differences may thus also contribute to the acquisition of subsequent skills and interests by gender. Girls' accelerated verbal communication and boys' greater ability to move about and manipulate objects may provide a clue to female-male differences in problem-solving approaches. That is, girls tend to solve problems via social communication, whereas boys tend to solve problems via spatial exploration and independent action. Gender-role stereotypes as culturally transmitted may perpetuate these early physical differences.

Early awareness of these differences is supported by cognitive developmental theory (Bem, 1981). This gender schema theory postulates that children are able to divide their world into male and female by the age of three years. Regardless of parental views on gender, children process information from other sources as well, such as the media, peers, and other adults. However, the gender expectations of parents have been shown to be the largest predictor, followed by teacher expectations, of how children perceive they should behave as girls and as boys.

In terms of later achievement and self-confidence, these early patterns and differences may lead both girls and boys to strive for success in tasks that they perceive as appropriate to their gender roles. Anastasi (1985) speaks not of fear of success by females, but of fear of deviating from gender-role standards and the social consequences connected with such deviations. Any deviation from a gender-role standard for males may have strong social consequences as well. Gender differences in interests thus have relevance to cognitive achievement and in the development of aptitudes. Training and experiential history may play a role in the development of individual and group differences.

A cultural examination of gender differences supports the concept of how society, not just biology, impacts on perceived abilities of males and females. Culture therefore influences social climate and expectations of gender roles.

School Years

Parents in the United States of America further foster gender-role assignments by requesting their children to assist in chores around the home (Etaugh & Liss, 1992). Traditionally girls assist with meal preparation and engage in more household chores than do boys. The latter may be encouraged to engage in more masculine tasks, such as helping their fathers with car or plumbing repairs. Boys' rooms are more often furnished with sports equipment, vehicles, and military toys, while girls' rooms are frequently equipped with dolls, dollhouses, and domestic-type toys.

On gift-giving occasions such as birthdays, Christmas, and Chanukah, children most often want, ask for, get, and enjoy gender-typical toys. They are not as likely to receive gender-atypical toys, even if they ask for them. Not surprisingly, children's preferred activities and job aspirations follow gender-typical paths. Interestingly, as children become older, both girls and boys tend to prefer male friends and masculine toys. However, there do not seem to be any gender differences in favorite or least preferred school subjects (Etaugh & Liss, 1992).

This gender differentiation continues in various other ways in school. Classrooms for preschool boys and preschool girls are equipped with different types of play materials (Rheingold & Cook, 1975). Teacher responses vary as well (Etaugh & Harlow, 1975). Boys are given more praise and work-related contacts yet also receive more negative sanctions. Girls are responded to less frequently. Later on, school subjects may be perceived as being either more feminine or more masculine, with reading and art being more socially feminine and appropriate for girls to enjoy and math being more socially masculine and challenging for boys (Stein & Smithells, 1969). This early interest in particular school topics may serve as a basis for the choice of later occupational goals (Hilton & Berglund, 1973). As children progress throughout their education, the increased impersonal environment of middle and junior high schools may be better suited to the learning styles of boys rather than girls. Females are seen as more concerned with their relationships with others, while males are encouraged to assert their independence (Huston & Alvarez, 1990).

Expectations of how children will perform differentially in school abound in the United States of America. Girls are believed to be better in reading, boys in mathematics. Yet these are cultural expectations, not actual ability differences. Studies in England and Germany do not reveal the gender differences in reading performance that were found among schoolchildren in the United States of America (Nash, 1979).

As a result of perceived differences in mathematics and reading, the Standardized Achievement Tests were changed to correct for this seeming disparity. Verbal subtests were modified because of perceived male verbal inferiority, without similar changes made in mathematical areas, the realm of perceived female inferiority (Jacklin, 1992).

During the school years, various activities that children participate in further solidify gender-role behaviors. Extracurricular school activities appear to play a critical role in the transmission of gender-role assignments. Eder and Parker (1987) found this to be so when performing a study at a midwestern middle school, where they investigated the communication of gender differences among students. Because many aspects of schooling reflect the values and beliefs of society, school serves as a vehicle in which such gender differences are learned and encouraged.

While athletics has been a featured activity of secondary school for males in this country, female participation in athletic activities has not typically been promoted. Male athletes attain higher status among their peers than do male nonparticipants, whereas females tend to achieve higher status as cheerleaders than as athletes themselves. The values and attributes assigned to these two roles further serve to differentiate boys from girls (Eder & Parker, 1987). Male athletes are encouraged to be achievement-oriented, competitive, and aggressive. Female cheerleaders, on the other hand, are encouraged to be poised and cheerful. Personality and attractive appearance are seen as essential characteristics for girls. These attributes carry through to other spheres as well, particularly in the selection of an occupation. Traditional male occupational roles emphasize competitiveness and achievement-related skills (Kohn, 1969). There is less emphasis on competition for females, who often prepare for careers as assistants or helpers. Females have traditionally been encouraged to be part of a labor force that not only is secondary but has little mobility (Felmlee, 1982). It is not difficult to see how boys in the United States of America are easily socialized to become future breadwinners for their families, while feminine socialization involves preparation for domestic roles as wife and mother.

Young Adulthood

Some researchers suggest that there is heightened pressure to conform to traditional male and female roles in adolescence as differences between males and females, both biologically and psychologically, become more pronounced with the onset of puberty (Galambos, Almeida & Petersen, in press; Hill & Lynch, 1983). This gender intensification hypothesis implies that others, such as parents, teachers, and peers, encourage teens to adhere to prescribed gender-role assignments. Bancroft (1990) posits that the introduction of sexuality at this stage further influences gender behavior. The middle and late childhood preference for same-sex friends (Maccoby, 1990) begins to include a desire to form relationships with those of the other sex.

The action and example set by parents also have an impact on gender development. Mothers in the U.S.A. traditionally tended not to be employed outside the home. Today, however, more and more women are entering the work force on either a full- or part-time basis. This trend has been found to influence adolescents' understanding of adult roles (Huston & Alvarez, 1990). As a result, young peoples' perceptions of male and female roles are becoming less stereotypic. Hoffman (1989) found that daughters of employed mothers tended to have higher educational and occupational aspirations than daughters whose mothers were not employed outside the home. The mass media also influence adolescent gender development (Huston & Alvarez, 1990). Teens often identify with idealized television characters and advertisement models from whom they receive strong messages of appropriate gender behavior. Unfortunately, television often portrays women as sexual objects, while men are shown as being more dominant, aggressive, competent, and autonomous (Williams et al., 1986).

As children mature and become young adults, their concerns about future plans, family planning, and occupational issues become more pressing. In examining gender differences in identity development, by looking at American adolescent identity concerns, we see that males and females view the identity process in much the same way (Archer, 1989). One may believe that females are more concerned with interpersonal relationships and caring and that males are more concerned with ideologies, individuation, and occupations. However, occupational choice, religious beliefs, and gender-role orientations are equal in importance to all adolescents (Archer, 1989). Yet, males do not consider a conflict between family and work to be their concern, nor do they anticipate such a conflict. Females, on the other hand, identify this conflict and do believe it to be their problem. Female adolescents in the United States of America exhibit substantial anticipated role conflict and more role articulation concerning future family plans (Kramer & Melchior, 1990). A study by Kramer and Melchior investigating these attitudes found that not one male assumed responsibility for child care (1990). Males appear blind to the complexity of a family-work problem and thus are unable to see the importance of a resolution or compromise.

Males and females also approach political ideology differently, with females showing more apathy or minimal interest. Additionally, adolescent females in the U.S.A., compared with their male counterparts, experience identity awareness sooner and are further apt to achieve more earlier in school (Archer, 1989). Females also use highly developed decision-making skills in the areas of sexuality and family roles (Archer, 1989). This may be due to the fact that women are predominantly responsible for child rearing, despite their increasing employment outside the home. Females also continue to have the primary responsibility for contraception (Archer, 1989).

Today growing numbers of women in the U.S.A. plan to combine work and family and search for relationships where role sharing is possible. Many men and women consider life to include time with children, mates, and occupations. Yet a discrepancy between the genders exists. In general, women continue to show more planning and concern for anticipated role conflict, whereas men do not appear to acknowledge, anticipate, or experience any conflict, assuming for the most part that wives will abandon their careers in favor of their husbands' (Gilbert, Dancer, Rossman, & Thorn, 1991). Not surprisingly, young adults in the U.S.A. maintain the widespread belief that a man's career is of greater importance than a woman's. American high school students' attitudes concerning the experience of dual-career couples show that a vast majority of students believe that a female should withdraw from her career to take care of children as a solution to a relationship with career conflicts. Any other solutions, such as the male's helping with child care or helping to find an alternate caregiver for the child, are almost nonexistent (Janman, 1989). The appearance of attitudes and beliefs that support a traditional male role as breadwinner and female role as mother provides evidence of how deeply entrenched gender-role assignment becomes by young adulthood in the United States of America.

Adulthood

These adolescent beliefs and gender assignments carry on into adulthood. There have been two worlds in the United States of American—a female world containing a love and duty ethic and a male outside-the-home, monetary-valuing world. However, women, to a greater and greater extent, are achieving in the world of work. Although women are still paid less than men, 72 cents for every dollar a man earns, they have progressed from the 60 cents on a dollar of 12 years ago (Aburdene & Naisbitt, 1992). Women have entered, in greater numbers, male-dominated fields, including politics, the sciences, the professions, and business, as well as blue-collar occupations, including construction and road maintenance. Conversely, more men than ever before are entering female-dominated fields and are becoming, for example, nurses and flight attendants. There are more women-owned businesses than ever before. However, women continue to face barriers in reaching the higher levels of their chosen careers.

Women face a dilemma. While they acknowledge and value caring and nurturing pursuits, they do not want to be at a disadvantage in a man's world (Voydanoff, 1988). The female love and duty ethic appears to be disappearing in the United States today without a comparable replacement. Women are sharing the provider role significantly more than men are sharing family work. Unfortunately, a redistribution of responsibilities in the home does not seem to be taking place. Although some men are increasing their participation in household work, employers are slow to accept responsibility for assisting in the coordination of work and family roles. Unless employers design policies and programs to be used by men as well as women, women will continue to be at a disadvantage in the workplace.

Stress is often the outcome for women struggling to meet the demands of both family and employment. For dual-income couples with at least one child under the age of 12, women seem to experience more stress than men. This stress, predominantly experienced by employed women, is due to "role overload" and role strain (Anderson & Leslie, 1991).

Interestingly, when women combine work and homemaking, role conflict is not always the outcome. Researchers Kibria, Barnett, Baruch, Marshall, & Pleck (1990) examined women's employment/homemaking roles in relation to their experience of distress and psychological well-being. If women have a good homemaking role experience, they are more likely to experience psychological well-being and lower psychological distress. This association is even higher when a woman is paid fairly for her work. Thus, psychological well-being for many women depends upon the quality of their homemaking and paid work roles (Kibria et al., 1990). Additionally, women in more feminine occupations have an easier time combining work and family. This is most likely due to more opportunities for part-time work in predominantly feminine fields (Olson, Frieze & Detlefsen, 1990).

The division of household labor in the United States of America and its relationship to gender-role orientation are predictable in working couples. Women, on the whole, assume more responsibility for household labor than for financial tasks. This suggests that as women's occupational roles increase, their domestic chores do not decrease. Hearteningly, a greater number of domestic tasks are fulfilled by both feminine and androgynous-oriented males compared with masculine-oriented males. Androgynous men also experienced the least amount of role conflict regarding domestic tasks (Denmark, Shaw & Ciali, 1985).

While still unequal in carrying out household chores, men and women of the United States of America seem to be changing some of their attitudes and behavior regarding the division of labor issue. Married women in the U.S.A. spend increasing amounts of time with their children and decreasing amounts of time preparing meals. Men have increased the amount of time spent in both child care and meal preparation. However, much of the increased meal preparation time for men occurs on weekends. While fathers are becoming more sensitive to the fact that there are children needing attention in the home, they still do not appear to be as sensitive to their wives' occupational status (Douthitt, 1989). However, these trends indicate that over a ten-year period, both parents are spending more time with their children, thus breaking from a well-established pattern of traditional gender roles.

Job performance and selection are another area where gender-role adherence is found. American male wage earners are more likely to place priority on extrinsic rewards for job performance and selection. Women, in particular, married women workers, who have traditionally been secondary-income workers, are more interested in the intrinsic rewards of an occupation (Martin & Shehan, 1989). Different wage-earning responsibilities for women and men, due to their prescribed roles, help to explain these differences. Secondary wage-earning women, who have traditionally been involved in homemaking, may opt for jobs that are convenient and enable them to carry out their responsibilities at home. Because the primary support of the family, in the past, did not rest on their shoulders, women were able to concentrate on occupations providing intrinsic value to them. However, since the 1970s, women's need to earn a decent wage has greatly increased due to the rise of divorce, female-headed families, and inflation. Currently, economic responsibility, rather than gender, determines whether an individual chooses an occupation for intrinsic or extrinsic rewards (Martin & Shehan, 1989).

Those who earn more appear to have less responsibility for domestic chores. Steil and Weltman found "spouses who earned more viewed their careers as more important and had more say at home than spouses who earned less . . . men, overall had more say in financial matters, less responsibility for the children and the household, and saw their own careers as more important than their wives' careers" (1991: 161). Women, hesitant to assert the importance of their careers and invested in maintaining the husband as head of the household/breadwinner, did not try to attain or sustain an equitable allocation of domestic tasks.

This may be a phenomenon of first marriages in those who remarry. Men and women in the U.S.A. who remarry do not differ in their expectations of a balanced relationship, but men and women come to these expectations from a different self-other orientation in their first marriages (Smith, Goslen, Byrd, & Reece, 1991). Often, both males and females in a first marriage hold traditional sex-role expectations. Men in first marriages were found to exclude others (most often their wives) in terms of emotional outreach. This perspective is in keeping with how men are socialized—which includes an emphasis on individual rights versus caring for others. This corresponds to female socialization in the U.S.A., which stresses a caring for others first and an exclude-the-self perspective. In considering a second marriage, both men and women frequently reevaluate themselves in terms of a care perspective. Some men and women appear to have learned from experience that traditional gender-role orientations are not productive and that it is important for them to change this culturally prescribed behavior and move toward a more equitable stance in order for future relationships to be successful (Smith et al., 1991).

Old Age

Gender roles are not set in stone throughout the life span. Men and women often incorporate aspects of gender-opposite traits due to changing life events, such as the death of a spouse. Older men in the United States of America often experience various psychosocial crises. Many older men have great difficulties adapting to events such as widowerhood, retirement, dependency, and changes in health. While various researchers claim that older males become more feminized as time goes on, Solomon (1984) concludes that "gender role behavior does not change throughout life unless there is a conscious effort made to do so. . . . Some of their outward behaviors may change, but for reasons other than a change in gender roles." Solomon believes role constancy throughout life serves to "maintain the older person's status within his immediate community and family, and to protect against rolelessness, anomie, alienation, boredom, and psychopathology" (p. 125).

Retirement often contributes to psychological difficulties, particularly for the man whose identity is wrapped up in his work role. In the United States of America, men often experience themselves and their status as an extension of their occupational success (Solomon, 1984). A man's work role is closely tied to his job as the family provider. Once this is gone, a man sometimes experiences a loss in status and a loss of relationships and contact with former friends and associates. He must often develop a new identity, with new relationships, particularly with his wife and family, which may require him to be more intimate and vulnerable. Leisure time is yet another new experience that is often quite difficult to adjust to, particularly for the man whose life was his work.

Widowerhood is another life event that drastically affects some older men, not only emotionally but in the sense that they have to take over a new feminine role. Practically and psychologically, men may not be prepared to cook, shop, grieve, express their feelings, or deal with newfound attention from other women. Dependency needs are no longer being met, which may lead to feelings of helplessness and depression.

Older people face deteriorating strength and health. Men, more than women, are often threatened by physical concerns due to their sense of invulnerability. Illness of any sort, particularly of a chronic nature for the older man, may contribute to a man's refusal to accept medications or treatment, outbursts of anger, feelings of frustration, or depression. Overall, older men face the issue of rolelessness unless they find meaningful new roles. Loss of self-esteem, helplessness, and depression may occur if a man or woman accepts society's stereotypes that an older person is useless and is a noncontributing member of the community. Finally, the man or woman who is most androgynous or least tied to a specific gender role appears to be best suited to adapt to changes in the life span.

Women face similar problems in old age. Yet much of the research literature does not address these concerns. Retirement, for example, is an issue that many women have to face, yet because many women have derived satisfaction and social status from their husband's occupations, retirement and its effects on women are often minimized. Women of the United States of America often retire much earlier than their male counterparts. This early retirement is due to close adherence to a woman's gender role. Society itself pressures women to retire and perhaps take care of an ailing or retired husband (Matlin, 1993). However, women may have more problems with retirement than men, and it often takes them longer to adjust (Szinovacz, 1983).

Many women (and men), however, look forward to retirement; it is frequently not the traumatic experience that many have believed it to be. Additionally, women often experience widowhood as a mixed phenomenon rather than as a completely traumatic event. Despite the emotional loss, widowhood is often also experienced as a time for growth and self-exploration. These findings point to the idea that men and women do change later in life and that they in fact often become more alike, even exchanging personality traits as they get older. As men and women age, they appear to become or feel more at liberty to express feminine and masculine parts of themselves. This may be due to the fact that environmental and life pressures are no longer as strong in later years (Wainrib, 1992).

SUMMARY AND CONCLUSIONS

Gender roles in the United States of America have undergone metamorphoses in much the same way that the nation itself has grown. They have followed the economic, social, and political trends of the country's history. While aspects of male and female roles have changed, many traditional attitudes concerning gender codes of conduct remain.

Women in the country's work force are making progress toward advancing to higher positions held by men, although the glass ceiling remains an obstacle. On the other hand, men's adherence to traditional male-dominated professions is changing with the increase of men entering typically female professions such as nursing, teaching, and social work.

Women continue to contribute more to domestic tasks and child care, whether or not they work outside the home. However, couples in the U.S.A. today are more willing to share in both child care and household responsibilities.

What we may want to strive for is a sharing of masculine and feminine roles, experiences, and expectations. In the United States of America we are moving toward a society, albeit slowly, in which activities are not rigidly designated as appropriate only for men or for women. Hopefully, both women and men will be free to express themselves as individuals without adherence to fixed gender roles.

REFERENCES

Aburdene, P., & Naisbitt, J. (1992). *Megatrends for Women*. New York: Villard Books.

Anastasi, A. (1985). Reciprocal relations between cognitive and affective development with implications for sex differences. In Sonderegger, T. B. (Ed.), *Psychology and Gender* (pp. 1–36). Lincoln: University of Nebraska Press.

Anderson, E., & Leslie, L. A. (1991). Coping with employment and family stress. *Sex Roles, 24*: 233–37.

Anderson, K. (1988). A history of women's work in the United States. In Stromberg, A. H., & Harkees, S. (Eds.), *Women Working: Theories and Facts in Perspective*, 2d ed. (pp. 25–41). Mountain View, CA: Mayfield.

Archer, S. L. (1989). Gender differences in identity development: Issues of process, domain and timing. *Journal of Adolescence, 12*: 117–38.

Bancroft, J. (1990). The impact of sociocultural influences on adolescent sexual development: Further considerations. In Bancroft, J., & Reinisch, J. M. (Eds.), *Adolescence and Puberty*. New York: Oxford University Press.

Bem, S. L. (1981). Gender schema today: A cognitive approach of sex-typing. *Psychological Review, 88*: 354–64.

Cott, N. (1977). *The Bonds of Womanhood: ''Woman's Sphere'' in New England, 1780–1835*. New Haven, CT: Yale University Press.

Denmark, F. L., Schwartz, L., & Smith, K. M. (1991). Women in the United States of America and Canada. In Adler, L. L. (Ed.), *Women in Cross-Cultural Perspective* (pp. 1–19). New York: Praeger.

Denmark, F. L., Shaw, J. S., & Ciali, S. D. (1985). The relationship among sex roles, living arrangements, and the division of household responsibilities. *Sex Roles, 12*: 617–625.

Douthitt, R. A. (1989). The division of labor within the home: Have gender roles changed? *Sex Roles, 20*: 693–704.

Eder, D., & Parker, S. (1987). The cultural production and reproduction of gender: The effect of extracurricular activities on peer-group culture. *Sociology of Education, 60*: 200–213.

Etaugh, C., & Harlow, H. (1975). Behaviors of male and female teachers as related to behaviors and attitudes of elementary school children. *Journal of Genetic Psychology, 127*: 163–70.

Etaugh, C., & Liss, M. B. (1992). Home, school, and playroom: Training grounds for adult gender roles. *Sex Roles, 26*: 129–47.

Felmlee, D. H. (1982). Women's job mobility processes within and between employers. *American Sociological Review, 47*: 142–51.

Galambos, N. L., Almeida, D. M., & Petersen, A. C. (in press). Masculinity, femininity, and sex role attitudes in early adolescence: Exploring gender intensification. *Child Development*.

Gilbert, L. A., Dancer, L. S., Rossman, K. M., & Thorn, B. L. (1991). Assessing perceptions of occupational-family integration. *Sex Roles, 24*: 107–19.

Hill, J. P., & Lynch, M. E. (1983). The intensification of gender-related role expectations during early adolescence. In Brooks-Gunn, J., & Petersen, A. C. (Eds.), *Girls at Puberty: Biological and Psychosocial Perspectives*. New York: Plenum.

Hilton, T. L., & Berglund, G. (1973). Sex differences in mathematics achievement—A longitudinal study. *Journal of Educational Research, 67*: 231–327.

Hoffman, L. W. (1989). Effects of maternal employment in the two-parent family. *American Psychologist, 44*: 283–92.

Huston, A. C., & Alvarez, M. (1990). The socialization context of gender-role development in early adolescence. In Montemayor, R., Adams, G. R., & Gulotta, T. P. (Eds.), *From Childhood to Adolescence: A Transitional Period?* Newbury Park, CA: Sage.

Jaccoma, G., & Denmark, F. L. (1974). Boys or girls: The hows and whys. Master's thesis, Hunter College.

Jacklin, C. N. (1992, February). Gender and developmental psychology. Paper presented at the meeting of the Council of Graduate Departments of Psychology, Tampa, FL.

Janman, K. (1989). One step behind: Current stereotypes of women, achievement and work. *Psychology of Women Quarterly, 3*: 209–30.

Kellogg, J. B. (1990). Forces of change. In Schultz, F. (Ed.), *Education 90/91* (pp. 144–49). Guilford, CT: Dushkin.

Kibria, N., Barnett, R. C., Baruch, G. K., Marshall, N. L., & Pleck, J. H. (1990). Homemaking-role quality and the psychological well-being and distress of employed women. *Sex Roles, 22*: 327–45.

Kohn, M. (1969). *Class and Conformity: A Study in Values*. Homewood, IL: Dorsey Press.

Kramer, D. A., & Melchior, J. (1990). Gender, role conflict and the development of relativistic and dialectical thinking. *Sex Roles, 23*: 553–74.

Langlois, J. H., & Downs, A. C. (1980). Mothers, fathers, and peers as socialization agents of sex-typed play behaviors in young children. *Child Development, 51*: 1217–47.

Lewis, M. (1972). State as an infant-environmental interaction: An analysis of mother-infant behavior as a function of sex. *Merrill-Palmer Quarterly, 18*: 95–211.

Maccoby, E. E. (1990, June). Gender and relationships: A developmental account. Paper presented at the meeting of the American Psychological Society, Dallas, TX.

Maccoby, E. E., & Jacklin, C. N. (1974). *The Psychology of Sex Differences*. Stanford, CA: Stanford University Press.

Martin, J. K., & Shehan, C. L. (1989). Education and job satisfaction: The influence of gender, wage-earning status, and job values. *Work & Occupation, 16*: 184–99.

Matlin, N. W. (1993). *The Psychology of Women*, 2d edition. Fort Worth, TX: Harcourt Brace Jovanovich.

Moss, H. A. (1967). Sex, age and state as determinants of mother-infant interaction. *Merrill-Palmer Quarterly, 13*: 19–36.

Nash, L. C. (1979). Sex role as a mediator of intellectual functioning. In Wittig, M.A.

& Petersen, A.C. (Eds.), *Sex-Related Differences in Cognitive Functioning: Developmental Issues* (pp. 263–302). New York: Academic Press.

Nash, L. C. & Parker, S. (1987). The cultural production and reproduction of gender: The effect of extracurricular activities on peer-group culture. *Sociology of Education, 60*: 200–213.

Nerlove, S., Munroe, R., & Munroe, R. (1971). Effect of environmental experience on spatial ability: A replication. *Journal of Social Psychology, 84*: 3–10.

Olson, J. E., Frieze, I. H., & Detlefsen, E. G. (1990). Having it all? Combining work and family in a male and a female profession. *Sex Roles, 23*: 515–33.

Reisman, J. M. (1988). An indirect measure of the value of friendship for aging men. *Journal of Gerontology, 43*: 109–10.

Rheingold, H. L., & Cook, K. V. (1975). The contents of boys' and girls' rooms as an index of parents' behavior. *Child Development, 46*: 459–63.

Roggman, L. A., & Peery, J. C. (1989). Parent-infant social play in brief encounters: Early gender differences. *Child Study Journal, 19*: 65–79.

Serbin, L., O'Leary, K., Kent, R., & Tonick, I. (1973). A comparison of teacher response to the preacademic and problem behavior of boys and girls. *Child Development, 44*: 796–804.

Sidorowicz, L. S., & Lunney, G. S. (1980). Baby X revisited. *Sex Roles 6*: 67–73.

Smith, R. M., Goslen, M. A., Byrd, A. J., & Reece, L. (1991). Self-other orientation and sex-role orientation of men and women who remarry. *Journal of Divorce and Remarriage, 14*: 3–32.

Solomon, K. S. (1984). Psychosocial crises of older men. *Hillside Journal of Clinical Psychiatry, 2*: 123–34.

Steil, J. M. & Weltman, K. (1991). Marital inequality: The importance of resources, personal attributes, and social norms on career valuing and allocation of domestic responsibilities. *Sex Roles, 24*: 161–79.

Stein, A. H., & Smithells, J. (1969). Age and sex differences in children's sex-role standards about achievement. *Developmental Psychology, 1*: 252–59.

Szinovacz, M. E. (1983). Beyond the hearth: Older women and retirement. In Markson, E. W. (Ed.), *Older Women: Issues and Prospects* (pp. 93–120). Lexington, MA: Lexington Books.

Voydanoff, P. (1988). Women, work, and family: Bernard's perspective on the past, present, and future. *Psychology of Women Quarterly, 12*: 269–80.

Wainrib, B. R. (1992). *Gender Issues Across the Life Cycle*. New York: Springer.

Williams, T. M., Baron, D., Phillips, S., David, L., & Jackson, D. (1986, August). The portrayal of sex roles on Canadian and U.S. television. Paper presented at the conference of the International Association for Mass Media Research, New Delhi, India.

Select Bibliography

Abiri, J. O. (1981). Nigeria adolescent pupils' aspirations about the size of their own families. *Ilorin Journal of Education*, *1*: 33–44.

Adler, L. L. (Ed.). (1977). *Issues in Cross-Cultural Research*. New York: The New York Academy of Sciences Annals, Vol. 285.

———. (1982). *Cross-Cultural Research at Issue*. New York: Academic Press.

———. (1989). *Cross-Cultural Research in Human Development: Life-Span Perspectives*. New York: Praeger.

———. (1991). *Women in Cross-Cultural Perspective*. New York: Praeger.

———, & Gielen, U. P. (Eds.) (1994). *Cross-Cultural Topics in Psychology*. Westport, CT: Praeger.

Afigbo, A. E. (1966). Revolution and reaction in Southeastern Nigeria, 1900–1929. *Journal of the Historical Society of Nigeria*, *3* (3): 539–57.

Ahmed, L. (1982). Western ethnocentrism and perceptions of the harem. *Feminist Studies*.

Ahmed, R. A. (1989). The development of number, space, quantity, and reasoning concepts in Sudanese schoolchildren. In Adler, L. L. (Ed.), *Cross-Cultural Research in Human Development: Life-Span Perspectives* (chapter 2). New York: Praeger.

———. (1991). Women in Egypt and the Sudan. In Adler, L. L. (Ed.), *Women in Cross-Cultural Perspective* (chapter 9). New York: Praeger.

Aidarova, L. (1983). *Child Development and Education*. Moscow: Progress.

Aidoo, A. A. (1981). Asante Queen mothers in government and politics in the nineteenth century. In Chiomastead, Filomina (Ed.), *The Black Woman Cross-Culturally: An Overview* (pp. 65–78). Cambridge, MA: Schenkman.

Alexander, N. (Ed.). (1936). *We Soviet Women*. New York: E. P. Dutton.

Allen, J.V.C. (1976). Ideology, stratification and the invisibility of women. In Hafkin, N. J., & Bay, E. G. (Eds.), *Women in Africa: Studies in Social and Economic Change*. Stanford, CA: Stanford University Press.

Almeida, E., Ramirez, J., Limon, A., De la Fuente, E., & Sanchez de Almeida, M. E.

(1987). Aplicacion de la prueba de premisas socioculturales en tres medios escolares culturalmente diferenciados. *Revista de Psicologia Social y Personalidad*, *3* (1): 35–49.

Almeida, E., Rodriguez, G., Mercado, D., Rivero, M., & Sanchez de Almeida, M. E. (1983). Psychological characteristics of male and female students and the status of women in Mexico. *International Journal of Psychology*, *18* (1–2): 67–81.

Almeida, E., & Sanchez de Almeida, M. E. (1983). Psychological factors affecting change in women's roles and status: A cross-cultural study. *International Journal of Psychology*, *18* (1–2): 3–35.

Amadiume, I. (1987). *Male Daughters, Female Husbands: Gender and Sex in an African Society*. London: Zed Books.

Amato, Paul. (1987). *Children in Australian Families: The Growth of Competence*. New York: Prentice-Hall.

An Analysis of the Utilization of Female Labor Force in Taiwan. (1984). Taipei: Council for Economic Planning and Development.

Anastasi, A. (1985). Reciprocal relations between cognitive and affective development with implications for sex differences. In Sonderegger, T. B. (Ed.), *Psychology and Gender. Nebraska Symposium on Motivation*. Lincoln, NE: University of Nebraska Press.

Anderson, K. (1988). A history of women's work in the United States. In Stromberg, A. H., & Harkees, S. (Eds.), *Women Working: Theories and Facts in Perspective*, 2d ed. (pp. 25–41). Mountain View, CA: Mayfield.

Andreas, C. (1971). *Sex and Caste in America*. Englewood, NJ: Prentice-Hall.

Apo, Satu. (1989). Suullinen runous - vuosisatainen traditio. In Nevala, Maria Liisa (Ed.), *Sain roolin johon en mahdu*. Keuruu: Otava.

Arat, Y. (1985). Obstacles to political careers: Perceptions of Turkish women. *International Political Science Review*, *6* (3): 355–66.

Archer, S. L. (1989). Gender differences in identity development: Issues of process, domain and timing. *Journal of Adolescence*, *12*: 117–38.

Arndt, R. (1990). Muslims in the U.S.S.R. *Aramco World*, *41* (1): 2–3.

Assaad, M. (1980). Female circumcision in Egypt: Social implications, current research, and prospects for change. *Studies in Family Planning*.

Atkinson, D., Dallin, A., & Lapidus, G. W. (Eds.). (1977). *Women in Russia*. Stanford, CA: Stanford University Press.

Ayandele, E. A. (1973). The collapse of Pagandom in Igboland. *Journal of the Historical Society of Nigeria*, *7* (1): 125–40.

Ayata, A. G. (1989). Women's participation in politics in Turkey. In Tekeli, P. (Ed.), *Women in the Turkey of the 1980's from Women's Perspective* (pp. 269–87). Istanbul: Iletifim.

Azarov, Y. (1983). *A Book About Bringing Up Children*. Moscow: Progress.

Aziz, B. (1978). *Tibetan Frontier Families: Reflections on Three Generations from D'Ingri*. New Delhi: Vikas.

Azuma, H. (1984). Secondary control as a heterogeneous category. *American Psychologist*, *39*: 970–71.

———. (1986). Why study child development in Japan? In Stevenson, H. Azuma, H., & Hakuta, K. (Eds.), *Child Development and Education in Japan* (pp. 3–12). New York: W. H. Freeman.

Bancroft, J. (1990). The impact of sociocultural influences on adolescent sexual development: Further considerations. In Bancroft, J., & Reinisch, J. M. (Eds.), *Adolescence and Puberty*. New York: Oxford University Press.

Barakat, H. (1985). The Arab family and the challenge of social transformation. In Fernea, E. (Ed.), *Women and the Family in the Middle East*. Austin: University of Texas Press.

Barnechea, C. (1985). Organizándose para cambiar la vida. In Lora, C., & Anderson, J. (Eds.), *Mujer: Víctima de opresión, portadora de liberación*. Lima: Instituto Bartolomé de las Casas.

Barroso, C. (1975a). Participação da mulher no desenvolvimento científico brasileiro (Women's participation in Brazilian scientific development). *Ciência e Cultura*, *27* (6): 613–20.

———. (1975b). Porque são tão poucas as mulheres que exercem actividades científicas? (Why do so few women engage in scientific activities?). *Ciência e Cultura*, *27* (7): 703–10.

Barroso, C., & Mello, G. (1975). O acesso da mulher ao ensino superior brasileiro (Women's access to higher education in Brazil). *Cadernos de Pesquisa*, *15*: 47–76.

Barry, K. (1979). *Female Sexual Slavery*. Englewood Cliffs, NJ: Prentice-Hall.

BaSaran, F. (1974). *Psychosocial Development: A Study on 7–11-Year-Old Children*. Ankara: Ankara University Press.

Bassi, Tina Lagostena. (1991). *L'avvocato delle donne, Dodici storie di ordinaria violenza* (The women's lawyer, twelve stories of ordinary violence). Milan: Arnoldo Mondadori.

Batcher, E. (1987). Building the barriers: Adolescent girls delimit the future. In Nemiroff, G. H. (Ed.), *Women and men: Interdisciplinary readings on gender* (pp. 150–165). Canada: Fitzhenry & Whiteside.

Bautista, Cynthia B. (1977). Women in marriage. In Bulatao, R. A. (Ed.), *Stereotype, Status, and Satisfactions: The Filipina Among Filipinos*. Quezon City: Social Research Laboratory, University of the Philippines.

Beasley, W. G. (1990). *The Rise of Modern Japan*. New York: St. Martin's Press.

Beere, C. A. (1990). *Gender Roles: A Handbook of Tests and Measures*. New York: Greenwood.

Befu, H. (1986). The social and cultural background of child development in Japan and the United States. In Stevenson, H., Azuma, H., & Hakuta, K. (Eds.), *Child Development and Education in Japan* (pp. 13–27). New York: W. H. Freeman.

Bell, C. (1928). *The people of Tibet*. Oxford: Clarendon Press.

Bellocchio, Lella Ravasi. (1987). *Di madre in figlia* (From mother to daughter). Milan: Raffaello Cortina.

Belotti, Elena Gianini. (1973). *Little Girls*. Milan: Giangiacomo Feltrinelli. (English translation published in 1975, London: Writers & Readers Publishing Cooperative.)

Bem, S. (1974). The management of psychological androgyny. *Journal of Consulting and Clinical Psychology*, *42*: 155–62.

———. (1981). Gender schema today: A cognitive approach of sex-typing. *Psychological Review*, *88*: 354–64.

BenTsvi-Mayer, Shoshana, Herz-Lazerovitz, Rachel, & Safir, Marilyn P. (1989). Teacher's selections of boys or girls as prominent pupils. *Sex Roles*, *21*: 231–47.

Bernstein, Deborah. (1983). Economic growth and female labor: The case of Israel. *Sociological Review, 31*: 263–92.

Bijoux, Legrand. (1982). Contrôle de la chance dans le milieu Haitien. *Traditions et Innovations Cours International d'Été: La femme Haitienne en milieu rural.* Collection CHISS, 175–82.

Binns, C. T. (1974). *The Warrior People. Zulu Origins, Customs and Witchcraft.* Cape Town: Howard Timmins.

Black, N. (1988). The Canadian women's movement: The second wave. In Burt, S., Code, L., & Dorney, L. (Eds.), *Changing Patterns: Women in Canada* (pp. 80–102). Toronto: McClelland & Stewart.

Blekher, F. (1979). *The Soviet Woman in the Family and in Society: A Sociological Study.* New York: Wiley.

Bloom, Anne R., & Bar-Yosef, Rivka (1985). Israeli women and military experience: A socialization experience. In Safir, Marilyn, Mednick, Martha T., Izraeli, Dafna, & Bernard, Jessie (Eds.), *Women's Worlds: From the New Scholarship.* New York: Praeger.

Boesch, E. (1977). Authority and work attitude of Thais. In Wenk, K., & Rosenberg, K. (Eds.), *Thai in German Eyes* (pp. 176–231). Bangkok: Kled Thai.

Bonamigo, E., & Rasche, V. (1980). O processo de socializaçao da criança em familias de classe popular (The socialization process in children of low-income families). *Psicologia: Teoria e pesquisa, 4* (3): 295–315.

Bottomley, Gill, & De Lepervanche, Marie. (Eds.). (1984). *Ethnicity, Class and Gender in Australia.* Sydney: George Allen & Unwin.

Bourque, S., & Warren, K. (1981). *Women in the Andes: Patriarchy and Social Change in Two Andean Towns.* Ann Arbor: University of Michigan Press.

Brauen, M. (1980). *Feste in Ladakh.* Graz, Austria: Akademische Druck u. Verlagsanstalt.

Bridger, S. (1987). *Women in the Soviet Countryside: Women's Role in Rural Development in the Soviet Union.* New York: Cambridge University Press.

Briggs, Freda, & Potter, Gillian. (1990). *Teaching Children in the First Three Years of School.* Melbourne: Longman Cheshire.

Brindley, M. (1985). Old women in Zulu culture: The old woman and childbirth. *South African Journal of Ethnology, 8*: 98–108.

———. (1986a). The role of old women in Zulu culture: Old women and child-nurture. *South African Journal of Ethnology, 9*: 26–31.

———. (1986b). The role of old women in Zulu culture: The old woman and adolescence. *South African Journal of Ethnology, 9*: 120–28.

Brown, D. R. (Ed.). (1968). *The Role and Status of Women in the Soviet Union.* New York: Teachers College Press.

Bryson, L. (1985). Gender divisions and power relationships in the Australian family. In Close, P., & Collins, R. (Eds.), *Family and Economy in Modern Society* (pp. 83–100). Houndmills, Hampshire: Macmillan Press.

Buckley, M. (1989). *Women and Ideology in the Soviet Union.* Ann Arbor: University of Michigan Press.

Bulatao, Rodolfo A. (Ed.). (1977). *Stereotype, Status, and Satisfactions: The Filipina Among Filipinos.* Quezon City: Social Research Laboratory, University of the Philippines.

Bunkle, P. (1980). The origins of the women's movement in New Zealand: The Women's

Christian Temperance Union 1885–1895. In Bunkle, P., & Hughes, B. (Eds.), *Women in New Zealand Society.* Sydney: George Allen & Unwin.

———. (1988). *Second Opinion: The Politics of Women's Health in New Zealand.* Auckland: Oxford University Press.

Burton, Clare. (1987). Merit and gender: Organizations and the "mobilization of masculine bias." *Australian Journal of Social Issues* (22).

Callan, Victor. (1986). *Australian Minority Groups.* Sydney: Harcourt Brace Jovanovich.

Cameron, J. (1990). *Why Have Children? A New Zealand Case Study.* Christchurch: University of Canterbury Press.

Campbell, J., & Sherrard, P. (1968). *Modern Greece.* London: Ernest Bern.

Campbell, R., & Brody, E. M. (1985). Women's changing roles and help to the elderly: Attitudes of women in the United States and Japan. *Gerontologist, 25*: 584–92.

Campos, M., & Esposito, Y. (1975). Relação entre o sexo da criança e aspirações educacionais da mãe (The relationship between child's sex and mother's educational aspirations). *Cadernos de Pesquisa, 15*: 37–46.

Cardella, Lara. (1989). *Volevo i pantaloni* (I wanted trousers). Milan: Arnoldo Mondadori.

Cassirer, S. (1975). *Teaching About Women in the Foreign Languages: French, Spanish, German, Russian.* Old Westbury, NY: Feminist Press.

Castle, E. B. (1966). *Growing Up in East Africa.* Nairobi: Oxford University Press.

Caudill, W. (1973). Tiny dramas: Vocal communication between mother and infant in Japanese and American families. In Lebra, W. P. (Ed.), *Mental Health Research in Asia and the Pacific*, vol. 2 (pp. 25–48). Honolulu: East-West Center.

Celmina, H. (1985). *Women in Soviet Prisons.* New York: Paragon House.

Chang, C. H. (1978). A review of female labor force participation. *Economic Essays, 8*: 275–84.

Chang, C. T. (1979). Nuptiality patterns among women of childbearing age. In Kuo, E.C.V., & Wong, A. K. (Eds.), *The Contemporary Family in Singapore* (pp. 117–41). Singapore: Singapore University Press.

Chen, C. I. (1985). Leisure interests, leisure participation and life-styles of married working women in Taipei. *Journal of Education & Psychology, 9*: 191–209.

Chen, L. C. (1983). The study of the college graduates' identity status development. *Bulletin of Educational Psychology, 16*: 89–98.

Cheung, F. M., Lam, M. C., & Chau, B.T.W. (1990). Caregivers' techniques and preschool children's behavior in Hong Kong. In Chan, B.P.K., & Smilansky, M. (Eds.), *Early Childhood in the 21st Century: A Worldwide Perspective* (pp. 403–12). Hong Kong: Yew Chung Education.

Cheung, T. S., & Tam, S. Y. (1984). *An Analysis of the Self-Esteem of Adolescents in Hong Kong.* Hong Kong: Center for Hong Kong Studies.

Chiang, L. H. (1989). The new social and economic roles of Chinese women in Taiwan and their implications for policy and development. *Journal of Developing Societies, 5*: 96–106.

Cho, B. E. (1990). Intergenerational family solidarity and life satisfaction among Korean aged parents. *Journal of Korea Gerontological Society, 10*: 105–24.

Chorlton, W. (1982). *Cloud-Dwellers of the Himalayas. The Bhotia.* Amsterdam: Time-Life Books.

Clay, M. M., & Robinson, V.M.J. (1978). *Children of Parents Who Separate.* Wellington: NZCER.

Clayton, E., & Millar, J. R. (1991). Education, job experience and the gap between male and female wages in the Soviet Union. *Comparative Economic Studies*, *33*: 5–22.

Collman, J. (1979). Women, children and the significance of the domestic group to urban aborigines in Central Australia. *Ethnology*, *18*(4): 379–97.

Connidis, I. (1989). The subjective experience of aging: Correlates of divergent views. *Canadian Journal on Aging*, *8*(1): 7–18.

Contado, Mina E. (1981). Power dynamics of rural families: The case of a Samar barrio. *Philippine Sociological Review*, *29* (1–4): 73–85.

Cook, E. W. (1983). A review and analysis of "unsolved" cases of the reincarnation type: I. Introduction and illustrative case reports. *Journal of the American Society for Physical Research*, *77*: 45–62.

Cormack, M. (1961). *The Hindu Woman*. Bombay: Asia Publishing House.

Cortes, Irene R. (1982). Discrimination against women and employment policies. *NCRFW Research Monograph*, No. 1. Manila: National Commission on the Role of Filipino Women.

Cott, N. (1977). *The Bonds of Womanhood: "Woman's Sphere" in New England, 1780–1835*. New Haven, CT: Yale University Press.

Covas, Maria das Mercês C. M. (1989a). Contributos para a análise da produção familiar de bens e serviços em função do tempo. In *Comunicações do seminário tempo para o trabalho tempo para a família*. (pp. 157–72). Lisbon: Direcção Geral da Família, Ministério do Emprego e Segurança Social.

———. (1989b). Evolução de algumas situações familiares em Portugal: Sua relação com o desempenho do papel económico e do papel doméstico da família. *Economia e Sociologia*, *47*: 99–132.

Crean, S. (1988). *In the Name of the Fathers: The Story Behind Child Custody*. Toronto: Amanita Enterprises.

Cumes, J. W., & Lambiase, E.A.A. (1987). Legal and psychological criteria for the determination of custody in South Africa: A review. *South African Journal of Psychology*, *17*: 119–26.

D'Amorim, M. A. (1987). Valores e atitudes em relação ao futuro em universitários brasileiros (Values and attitudes toward the future in Brazilian undergraduates). *Arquivos Brasileiros de Psicologia*, *39* (4): 21–38.

———. (1988). Estereótipos de gênero em universitários (Gender stereotypes in Brazilian undergraduates). *Psicologia: Reflexão e Crítica*, *3* (1–2): 3–11.

Danilova, Y. Z. (Ed.). (1975). *Soviet Women: Some Aspects of the Status of Women in the USSR*. Moscow: Progress.

Dargyay, E. (1982). *Tibetan Village Communities—Structure and Change*. Warminster: Aris & Phillips.

Das, V. (1976). Indian women. Work, power and status. In Nanda, B. R. (Ed.), *Indian Women: From Purdah to Modernity*. New Delhi: Vikas Publishing House.

———. (1979). Reflections on social constructions of adulthood. In Kakar, S. (Ed.), *Identity and Adulthood*. Delhi: Oxford University Press.

Davies, B. (1989). *Frogs and Snails and Feminist Tails: Preschool Children and Gender*. Sydney: Allen & Unwin.

de Silva, S., Stiles, D. A., & Gibbons, J. L. (In press). Girls' identity formation in the changing social structure of Sri Lanka. *Journal of Genetic Psychology*.

De Vos, G. A. (1985). Dimensions of the self in Japanese culture. In Marsella, A., De Vos, G. A., & Hsu, F. (Eds.), *Culture and Self*. London: Tavistock.

Deaux, K., & Lewis, L. (1984). Structure of gender stereotypes: Interrelationships among the components of gender label. *Journal of Personality and Social Psychology, 36* (9): 927–40.

Decaesstecker, Sister Donald. (1978). *Impoverished Urban Filipino Families*. Manila: University of Santo Tomas Press.

Dempsey, K. (1989). Gender exploitation and the domestic division of labor among the elderly: An Australian case study. *Australian Journal on Ageing, 8* (3).

Denmark, F. L., Schwartz, L., & Smith, K. M. (1991). Women in the United States of America and Canada. In Adler, L. L. (Ed.), *Women in Cross-Cultural Perspective* (pp. 1–19). New York: Praeger.

Denmark, F. L., Shaw, J. S., & Ciali, S. D. (1985). The relationship among sex roles, living arrangements, and the division of household responsibilities. *Sex Roles, 12*: 617–25.

Department of Education. (1976). *Education and the Equality of the Sexes*. Wellington: Department of Education.

Diaz-Guerrero, R. (1972a). Occupational values of Mexican schoolchildren. *Totus Homo, 4* (1): 18–26.

———. (1972b). Una escala factorial de premisas historico-socio-culturales de la familia mexicana. *Revista Interamericana de Psicologia, 6* (3–4): 235–44.

———. (1973). Interpreting coping styles across nations from sex and social class differences. *International Journal of Psychology, 8* (3): 193–203.

———. (1974). La mujer y las premisas historico-socioculturales de la familia mexicana. *Revista Latinoamericana de Psicologia, 6* (1): 7–16.

———. (1975). *Psychology of the Mexican: Culture and Personality*. Austin: University of Texas Press.

———. (1982). El Yo del Mexicano y la piramide. In Diaz-Guerrero, R., *Psicologia del Mexicano* (chapter 12). Mexico, D.F.: Trillas.

———. (1986). Historio-sociocultura y personalidad: Definicion y caracteristicas de los factores de la familia mexicana. *Revista de Psicologia Social y Personalidad, 2* (1): 15–42.

Diaz-Guerrero, R., & Iscoe, I. (1984). El impacto de la cultura iberoamericana tradicional y del estres economico sobre la salud mental y fisica: Instrumentacion y potencial para la investigacion transcultural, I. *Revista Latinoamericana de Psicologia, 16* (12): 167–211.

Diaz-Guerrero, R., & Lara Tapia, L. (1972). Diferencias sexuales en el desarrollo de la personalidad del escolar mexicano. *Revista Latinoamericana de Psicologia, 4* (3): 345–51.

Diaz-Guerrero, R., & Salas, M. (1975). *El Diferencial Semantico del Idioma Español*. Mexico City: Trillas.

Dikaiou, M. (1989). Peer interaction in migrant children. Observational data and parents' evaluations. *International Migration, 27*: 49–67.

Dikaiou, M., Sakka, D., & Haritos-Fatouros, M. (1987). Maternal attitudes of Greek migrant women. *International Migration, 25* (1): 73–86.

Dolkar, T. (1971). *Girl from Tibet*. Chicago: Loyola University Press.

Doob, L. W. (1967). Psychology. In Lystad, A. (Ed.), *The African World: A Survey of Social Research* (pp. 373–415). London: Pall Mall Press.

Doumanis, M. (1983). Mothering in Greece: From collectivism to individualism. In *Behavioral Development: A Series of Monographs*. New York: Academic Press.

Douthitt, R. A. (1989). The division of labor within the home: Have gender roles changed? *Sex Roles*, *20*: 693–704.

Douyon, Chavannes. (1982). Image de soi de la femme Haitienne en milieu rural. *Traditions et Innovations Cours International d'Été: La femme rurale en Haiti et dans les Caribes*, 183–204.

Dragona, Th. (1987). *Birth*. (In Greek.). Athens: Dodoni.

du Boulay, J. (1974). *Portrait of a Greek Mountain Village*. Oxford: Clarendon Press.

Dubb, A. A. (1974). The impact of the city. In Hammond-Tooke, W. D. (Ed.), *The Bantu-Speaking Peoples of South Africa* (pp. 441–68). London: Routledge & Kegan Paul.

Duben, A. (1982). The significance of family and kinship in urban Turkey. In Kaºitçìbafì, Ç. (Ed.), *Sex Roles, Family and Community in Turkey*. Bloomington: Indiana University Press.

Dulude, L. (1988). Getting old: Men in couples and women alone. In McLaren, A. T. (Ed.). *Gender and Society: Creating a Canadian Women's Sociology* (pp. 205–20). Toronto: Copp Clark Pittman.

Durojaiye, M.O.A. (1972). *Psychological Guidance of the Schoolchild*. Lagos: Evans Brothers.

———. (1976). *A New Introduction to Educational Psychology*. Lagos: Evans Brothers.

Dwyer, D., & Bruce, J. (1988). *A Home Divided: Women and Income in the Third World*. Stanford, CA: Stanford University Press.

Eder, D., & Parker, S. (1987). The cultural production and reproduction of gender: The effect of extracurricular activities on peer-group culture. *Sociology of Education*, *60*: 200–213.

Edgar, Patricia, & ors. (1974). *Under Five in Australia*. Melbourne: Heinemann.

Ehrlich, M., & Vinsonneau, G. (1988). Representations differentielles des sexes: Attributions et prises de roles dans les equipes de travail. *Bulletin de Psychologie*, *41*: 785–801.

Eisenstein, Hester. (1991). *Gender Shock*. Sydney: Allen & Unwin.

Ekvall, R. B. (1968). *Fields on the Hoof: Nexus of Tibetan Nomadic Pastoralism*. New York: Holt, Rinehart, & Winston.

El Guindi, F. (1983). *Veiled Activism*. Egyptian Women in the Contemporary Islamic Movement. *Femmes de la Mediterranee*.

El Saadawy, N. (1980). *The Hidden Face of Eve: Women in the Arab World*. London: Zed Books.

Elu de Leñero, M. C. (1969). *Hacia donde va la mujer mexicana?* Mexico City: Instituto Mexicano de Estudios Sociales, A.C.

Ergüder, Ü., Kalaycioºlu, E., & Esmer, Y. (1991). *The Values of Turkish Society*. Istanbul: TUSIAD.

Erkut, S. (1982). Dualism in values toward education of Turkish women. In Kaºitçìbafì, Ç. (Ed.), *Sex Roles, Family and Community in Turkey*. Bloomington: Indiana University Press.

Etaugh, C., & Harlow, H. (1975). Behaviors of male and female teachers as related to behaviors and attitudes of elementary school children. *Journal of Genetic Psychology*, *127*: 163–70.

Etaugh, C., & Liss, M. B. (1992). Home, school, and playroom: Training grounds for adult gender roles. *Sex Roles, 26*: 129–47.

Etzion, Dalia. (1988). Experience of burnout and work and non-work success in male and female engineers: A matched pairs comparison. *Human Resource Management, 27*: 163–79.

Eviota, Elizabeth U. (1978). Sex as a differentiating variable in work and power relations. *Philippine Sociological Review, 26*(3–4): 151–58.

————. (1982). Time use and the sex division of labor. *Philippine Journal of Industrial Relations, 4*(1–2): 116–33.

Fabian, Sue, & Loh, Morag. (1980). *Children in Australia*. London: Oxford University Press.

Fabris, M. (1977). The woman in the USSR: Contradictions and problems. *Rivista di Sociologia, 1*: 233–63.

Fafunwa, A. B. (1974). *History of Education in Nigeria*. London: George Allen & Unwin.

Fapohunda, E. (1983). Female and male work profits. In Oppong, C. (Ed.), *Female and male in West Africa* (pp. 32–53). London: George Allen & Unwin.

Farmer, B. H. (1983). *An Introduction to South Asia*. London: Methuen.

Felmlee, D. H. (1982). Women's job mobility processes within and between employers. *American Sociological Review, 47*: 142–51.

Fenton, J. Y., Hein, N., Reynolds, F. E., Miller, A. L., & Nielson, N. C. (1983). *Religions of Asia*. New York: St. Martin's Press.

Ferro Bucher, Júlia. (1991). Recasamento e recomposição familiar: questões metodológicas, de linguagem e das teorias (Remarriage and family recomposition: Methodological, language and theoretical questions. *Psicologia: Teoria e pesquisa, 6* (2): 155–69.

Ferro Bucher, J., & Vale, J. A. (1987). O acidente, o acidentado e o contexto sócio-familiar. *Arquivos Brasileiros de Psicologia, 39* (1): 95–108.

Findlay, Bruce, & Lawrence, Jeannette, A. (1991). Who does what? Gender-related distribution of household tasks for couples, their families of origin and their ideals. *Australian Journal of Marriage & Family, 12* (1): 3–7.

Fifek, G. O. (1982). Psychopathology and the Turkish family: A family systems theory analysis. In Ka°itçibafî, Ç. (Ed.), *Sex Roles, Family and Community in Turkey*. Bloomington: Indiana University Press.

————. (1990). A cross-cultural examination of proximity and hierarchy as dimensions of family structure. *Family Process, 30*: 121–33.

————. (1992, May). The feminization and romanticization of intimacy: A Western cultural phenomenon. *AFTA* [American Family Therapy Association] *Newsletter*.

Fletcher, G.J.O. (1978). Division of labor in the New Zealand nuclear family. *New Zealand Psychologist, 7*: 33–40.

Franco, R. (1989). Redes de soporte social de niños trabajadores en Lima Metropolitana. *Revista de Psicología de la P.U.C., 7* (1): 79–92.

Fremantle, F., & Trungpa, C. (1975). *The Tibetan Book of the Dead. The Great Liberation Through Hearing in Bardo*. Boulder, CO: Shambhala.

Freyre, Gilberto. (1964). *Casa grande e senzala* (The masters and the slaves). Porto Alegre: Globo.

Friedman, Ariella. (1987). Getting powerful with age: Changes in women over the life cycle. *Israel Social Science Research: A Multidisciplinary Journal* (special issue on Women in Israel, Dafna N. Izraeli guest editor), *5*: 76–86.

Galel el-Din, M. E. (1984). The discrimination between masculines and feminines and its reflections on woman's positions and her role in the society. (In Arabic.) *Journal of the Social Sciences (Kuwait)*, *12* (3): 7–35.

Gaskell, J. (1988). The reproduction of family life: Perspectives of male and female adolescents. In McLaren, A. T. (Ed.), *Gender and Society: Creating a Canadian Women's Sociology* (pp.146–68). Toronto: Copp Clark Pittman.

———, & McLaren, A. (1987). Introduction. In Gaskell, J., & McLaren, A. (Eds.), *Women and Education: A Canadian Perspective* (pp. 5–20). Calgary: Detselig Enterprises.

Gee, E. (1988). The life course of Canadian women: An historical and demographic analysis. In McLaren, A. T. (Ed.), *Gender and Society: Creating a Canadian Women's Sociology* (pp. 187–204). Toronto: Copp Clark Pittman.

Georgas, J. (1985a). Cooperative, competitive and individual problem solving in sixth-grade children. *European Journal of Social Psychology*, *15*: 67–77.

———. (1985b). Group interactions and problem solving under cooperative, competitive and individual conditions. *General Psychology Monographs*, *3*: 349–61.

———. (1986). Cooperative, competitive and individualistic goal structures with seventh-grade Greek children: Problem-solving effectiveness and group interactions. *Journal of Social Psychology*, *126*: 227–36.

———. (1987). Effect of intelligence on group interactions and problem solving: Cooperative, competitive and individual goal structures with Greek children. *International Journal of Small Group Research*, *3*: 16–37.

Gerdes, L. C., Moore, C., Ochse, R., & Van Ede, D. (1988). *The Developing Adult*, 2d ed. Pretoria: Butterworths.

Gerdes, L. C., & Van Ede, D. M. (1991). Adulthood. In Louw, D. A. (Ed.), *Human Development*. Pretoria: HAUM.

Gielen, U. P. (1985). Some themes in the ethos of traditional Ladakh. In Dendaletche, C. (Ed.), *Ladakh, Himalaya Occidental. Éthnologie, Écologie. Recent research no. 2* (pp. 235–46). Pau, France: Université de Pau.

Gielen, U. P., Adler, L. L., & Milgram, N. (Eds.). (1992). *Psychology in International Perspective*. Lisse, The Netherlands: Swets & Zeitlinger.

Gielen, U. P., & Chirico-Rosenberg, D. (1993). Traditional Buddhist Ladakh and the ethos of peace. *International Journal of Group Tensions*, *23* (1): 5–23.

Gilbert, L. A., Dancer, L. S., Rossman, K. M., & Thorn, B. L. (1991). Assessing perceptions of occupational-family integration. *Sex Roles*, *24*: 107–19.

Glezer, Helen. (1990). Fathers are parents too. *Family Matters* (27).

Gök, F. (1990). Education and women in Turkey. In Tekeli, P$_t$ (Ed.), *Women in the Turkey of the 1980's from Women's Perspective*. Istanbul: Iletifim.

Goldberg, M. A., Baptista, M. T., Arruda, N.C., Barreto, E. S., & Menezes, S. M. (1975). Concepções sobre o papel da mulher no trabalho, na política e na família (Views about woman's role at work, in politics and in the family). *Cadernos de Pesquisa*, *15*: 86–123.

Goldstein, M. C. (1987). When brothers share a wife. *Natural History*, *96*: 38–49.

Goldstein, M. C., & Beall, C. M. (1990). *Nomads of Western Tibet. The Survival of a Way of Life*. Berkeley: University of California Press.

Gonzales, Anna Miren, & Hollnsteiner, Mary R. (1976). *Filipino Women as Partners of Men in Progress and Development*. Quezon City: Institute of Philippine Culture, Ateneo de Manila University.

Gray, A. (1988). *Teen Angels: Being a New Zealand Teenager.* Wellington: Allen & Unwin/Port Nicholson Press.

Gray, F. du P. (1990). *Soviet Women: Walking the Tightrope.* New York: Doubleday.

Green, M. G. (1964). *Igbo Village Affairs,* 2d ed. London: Frank Cass.

Greenglass, E. (1987). A social-psychological view of marriage for women. In Nemiroll, G. H. (Ed.), *Women and Men: Interdisciplinary Readings on Gender* (pp.290–302). Canada: Fitzhenry & Whiteside.

Gregory, P. R., & Collier, I. L. (1988). Unemployment in the Soviet Union: Evidence from the Soviet interview project. *American Economic Review, 78*: 613–32.

Guglier, J., & Flanagan, William G. (1978). *Urbanization and Social Change in West Africa.* Cambridge: Cambridge University Press.

Guichard, J. (1988). The French school system and sexual differentiation of social roles. *International Journal for the Advancement of Counselling, 11* (4): 323–32.

Guttentag, M., & Secord, P. (1983). *Too Many Women?* Beverly Hills, CA: Sage.

Guzmán, V., & Portocarrero, P. (1985). *Dos veces mujer.* Lima: Mosca Azul.

Hahlo, H. R. (1985). *The S.A. Law of Husband and Wife.* Cape Town: Juta.

Hall, Trish, & ors. (1990). Women and work: Challenges for the 1990s—A panel. In *National Women's Conference 1990 Proceedings.* Queanbeyan: Write People.

Halle, F. W. (1938). *Women in the Soviet East.* New York: E. P. Dutton.

Halsell, G. (1990). A visit to Baku. *Aramco World, 41* (1): 30–33.

Hammond-Tooke, W. D. (1962). *Bhaca Society: A People of the Traskeian Uplands, South Africa.* Cape Town: Oxford University Press.

A Handbook for Equal Education for the Two Sexes. (1988). Taipei, Taiwan: Awakening Foundation.

Hannson, C., & Lidén, K. (1983). *Moscow Women.* New York: Pantheon.

Haritos-Fatouros, M., Sakka, D., & Dikaiou, M. (1988). A study of migrant mothers: Return home and role change. *International Journal for the Advancement of Counselling, 11*: 167–81.

Harman, L. (1990). ''Ya se ha mujerao.'' *Anthropologica, 8* (8): 309–18.

Hassan, Manar. (1991). Growing up female and Palestinian in Israel. In Swirsky, Barbara, & Safir, Marilyn P. (Eds.), *Calling the Equality Bluff: Women in Israel.* New York: Teacher's College Press.

Hatem, M. (1986a). The enduring alliance of nationalism and patriarchy in Muslim personal status laws: The case of modern Egypt. *Feminist Issue.*

———. (1986b). Underdevelopment, mothering and gender within the Egyptian family. *Arab Studies Quarterly.*

Heaven, Patrick, & Callan, Victor. (1990). *Adolescence: An Australian Perspective.* Sydney: Harcourt Brace Jovanovich.

Heitlinger, A. (1979). *Women and State Socialism: Sex Inequality in the Soviet Union and Czechoslovakia.* London: Macmillan.

Hess, R., Holloway, S., NcDevitt, Azuma, H., Kashiwagi, K., Nagano, S., Miyake, K., Dickson, W. P., Price, G., & Hatano, G. (1986). Family influences on school readiness and achievement in Japan and the United States: An overview of a longitudinal study. In Stevenson, H., Azuma, H., & Hakuta, K. (Eds.), *Child Development and Education in Japan* (pp. 147–66). New York: W. H. Freeman.

Hijab, N. (1988). *Woman Power: The Arab Debate on Women at Work.* Cambridge: Cambridge University Press.

Hildebrandt, E. (1991). Duduza self-help project. *Thambodala, 2* (2): 7.

Hill, J. P., & Lynch, M. E. (1983). The intensification of gender-related role expectations during early adolescence. In Brooks-Gunn, J., & Petersen, A. C. (Eds.), *Girls at Puberty: Biological and Psychosocial Perspectives*. New York: Plenum.

Hilton, T. L., & Berglund, G. (1973). Sex differences in mathematics achievement—A longitudinal study. *Journal of Educational Research, 67*: 231–327.

Hirayama, M., Ando, M., Takano, Y., Takamura, K., Nomura, T., Fukaya, M., Moriue, S., & Yunoki, F. (Eds.). (1988). *Encyclopedia of Modern Children*. (In Japanese.) Tokyo: Chuohoki.

Hirschon, R. (1989). *Heirs of the Greek Catastrophe. The Social Life of Asia Minor Refugees in Piraeus*. Oxford: Clarendon Press.

Ho, D.Y.F. (1976–77). Traditional patterns of socialization in China. *Psyche* 7:39.

———. (1986). Chinese patterns of socialization: A critical review. In Bond, M. H. (Ed.), *The Psychology of Chinese People* (pp. 1–37). Hong Kong: Oxford University Press.

Hoffman, L. W. (1989). Effects of maternal employment in the two-parent family. *American Psychologist, 44*: 283–92.

Hoffman-Ladd, V. (1987). Polemics on the modesty and segregation of women in contemporary Egypt. *International Journal of Middle Eastern Studies*.

Holland, B. (Ed.). (1985). *Soviet Sisterhood*. Bloomington: Indiana University Press.

Holtzman, W. H., Diaz-Guerrero, R., & Swartz, J. D. (1975). *Personality Development in Two Cultures*. Austin: University of Texas Press.

Horsfield, A. (1988). *Women in the Economy*. Wellington: Ministry of Women's Affairs.

Horsfield, A., & Evans, M. (1988). *Maori Women in the Economy*. Wellington: Ministry of Women's Affairs.

Hortaçsu, N. (1989). Targets of communication during adolescence. *Journal of Adolescence, 12*: 253–63.

Hortaçsu, N., Düzen E., Arat, S., Atahan, D., & Uzer, B. (1990). Intrusions upon same-sex or different-sex dyads in a Turkish university dining hall. *International Journal of Psychology, 25*: 33–37.

Hsieh, H. C. (1989). Gender ideology in the school system. *Humanistic Education, 7*: 30–35.

Hu, T. L. (1985). The influence of industrialization in Taiwan's rural area on the status of women. In Chiang, N. (Ed.), *The Role of Women in the National Development Process in Taiwan* (pp. 339–55). Taipei: National Taiwan University, Center for Population Studies—Women's Research Program.

Huston, A. C., & Alvarez, M. (1990). The socialization context of gender-role development in early adolescence. In Montemayor, R., Adams, G. R., & Gulotta, T. P. (Eds.), *From childhood to adolescence: A Transitional Period?* Newbury Park, CA: Sage.

Iankova, Z. A. (1975). The development of women in Soviet society. *Sotsiologicheskie Issledovaniya, 2*: 42–51.

Iglitzin, L. B., & Ross, R. (Eds.). (1976). *Women in the World: A Comparative Study*. Santa Barbara, CA: Clio Books.

———. (1986). *Women in the World, 1975–1985: The Women's Decade*, 2d ed., rev. Santa Barbara, CA: Clio Books.

Imamo°lu, O., & Imamo°lu, V. (in press). Life situations and attitudes of the Turkish elderly toward institutional living within a cross-cultural perspective. *Journal of Gerontology and Psychological Sciences*.

Ikels, C. (1983). *Aging and Adaptation: Chinese in Hong Kong and the United States.* Hamden, CT: Archon Books.

Illo, Jeanne Frances I. (1977). *Involvement by Choice: The Role of Women in Development.* Quezon City: Social Survey Research Unit, Institute of Philippine Culture, Ateneo de Manila University.

Inagaki, T. (1986). School education: Its history and contemporary status. In Stevenson, H., Azuma, H., & Hakuta, K. (Eds.), *Child Development and Education in Japan* (pp. 75–92). New York: W. H. Freeman.

Ira, Luningning. (1990). *Guidebook to the Filipino Wedding.* Manila: Vera-Reyes.

Jacobs, J. B. (1975). Continuity and change in the contemporary Chinese family. *Asian Survey, 15* (8): 882–91.

Jancar, Barbara W. (1978). *Women Under Communism.* Baltimore: Johns Hopkins University Press.

Janman, K. (1989). One step behind: Current stereotypes of women, achievement and work. *Psychology of Women Quarterly, 3*: 209–30.

Jantaravitoon, N. (1979). *Thai Labor Force.* Bangkok: Karaweg Press.

———. (1989). Women's role and industrial development. *Industrial Magazine, 2*: 101–5.

Jayawardena, K. (1986). *Feminism and Nationalism in the Third World.* London: Zed Books.

Jayaweera, S. (1979). Education. Aspects of the role and position of women. In Fernando, T., & Kearney, R. N. (Eds.), *Modern Sri Lanka: A Society in Transition* (pp. 131–54, 165–80). Syracuse, NY: Syracuse University Press.

Johnson, F. A. (In press). *Dependency, Interdependency and Amae: Psychoanalytic and Anthropological Observations.* New York: New York University Press.

Jones, F. L. (1983). Sources of gender inequality in income: What the Australian census says. *Social Forces, 62*: 134–52.

Junusbajev, M. D. (1985). Household division in the Kazakh family. *Sotsiologicheskie Issledovaniya, 12*: 106–9.

Kabasakal, H. (1991). Women, organizations and power allocation. *Toplum ve Bilim (Society and Science), 53*: 55–63.

Ka°itçìbafì, Ç (1986). Status of women in Turkey: Cross-cultural perspectives. *International Journal of Middle East Studies, 18*: 485–99.

———. (1990). Family and socialization in cross-cultural perspective: A model of change. In Berman, F. (Ed.), *Nebraska Symposium on Motivation.* Lincoln: Nebraska University Press.

Ka°itçìbafì, Ç, & Sunar, D. (In press). Family and socialization in Turkey. In Roopnarine, J. P., & Carter, D. B. (Eds.), *Parent-Child Relations in Diverse Cultural Settings: Socialization for Instrumental Competency.* Norwood, NJ: Ablex.

Kakar, S. (Ed.). (1979). *Identity and Adulthood.* Delhi: Oxford University Press.

Kalu, O. U. (1978). Precarious Vision: The African's perception of his world. In Kalu, O. U. (Ed.), *Readings in African Humanities: African Cultural Development* (chapter 3). Enugu: Fourth Dimension.

Kalu, W. J. (1979). Functions of nursery school education in Nigeria. *Nigerian Journal of Psychology, 2 & 3*: 73–97.

———. (1981). The social environment. In Ohuche, R. O., & Otaala, B. (Eds.), *The African Child in His Environment* (pp. 14–21). London: Pergamon.

———. (1982). Development of a concept for childhood survival in modern Nigeria. *School Psychology International*, *3*: 161–68.

———. (1989a). Motherhood role strains in married female undergraduate students. *Counselling and Development*, *14*: 106–13.

———. (1989b). Widowhood and its process in contemporary African society: A psychosocial study. *Counselling Psychology Quarterly*, 2 (2): 143–52.

———. (1992). Child psychology in Nigeria. In Gielen, Uwe P., Adler, Leonore Loeb, & Milgram, Noach (Eds.), *Psychology in International Perspective*. Amsterdam: Swets & Zeitinger.

Kandiyoti, D. (1974). Some social psychological dimensions of social change in a Turkish village. *British Journal of Sociology*, *15* (1): 47–62.

———. (1977). Sex roles and social change: A comparative appraisal of Turkey's women. *Signs: Journal of Women in Culture and Society*, *3*: 57–73.

———. (1987). Emancipated but unliberated? Reflections on the Turkish case. *Feminist Studies*, *43* (2): 317–39.

———. (1988). Bargaining with patriarchy. *Gender and Society*, 2 (3): 274–90.

Kannasutr K., Kampoo, T., & Kamolnavin, S. (1979). *Thai Women Image Reflection*. Bangkok: Thaikaset Press.

Kantowsky, D., & Sander, R. (Eds.). (1983). *Recent Research on Ladakh: History, Culture, Sociology, Ecology*. Muenchen: Weltforum Vlg.

Kao, S. K. (1985). A comparison between men and women in Taiwan on the selection of occupations. In Chiang, N. (Ed.), *The Role of Women in the National Development Process in Taiwan*. Taipei: National Taiwan University, Center for Population Studies—Women's Research Program.

Kaplanian, P. (1981). *Les Ladakhi du Cachémire*. Paris: Hachette.

Kapur, P. (1973). *Love, Marriage and Sex*. Delhi: Vikas Publishing House.

Kashiwagi, K. (1986). Personality development of adolescents. In Stevens, H., Azuma, H., & Hakuta, K. (Eds.), *Child Development and Education in Japan* (pp. 167–85). New York: W. H. Freeman.

Katakis, Ch. (1984). *The Three Identities of the Greek Family*. (In Greek.) Athens: Kedros.

Kaye, B. (1962). *Bringing Up Children in Ghana*. London: George Allen & Unwin.

Kellogg, J. B. (1990). Forces of change. In Schultz, F. (Ed.), *Education 90/91* (pp. 144–49). Guilford, CT: Dushkin.

Keuneman, H. (1984). *Sri Lanka*. Singapore: Tien Mah Litho Printing.

Kharchey, A. G. (1964). *Communism and the Family: Women and Family Life in the Soviet Union*. New York: Crosscurrents.

Kibria, N., Barnett, R. C., Baruch, G. K., Marshall, N. L., & Pleck, J. H. (1990). Homemaking-role quality and the psychological well-being and distress of employed women. *Sex Roles*, *22*: 327–45.

Kim, J. U. (1972). Parent-child relationship in the Korean family. *Non Chong (Journal of the Korean Cultural Research Institute)*.

Kiray, M. (1976). Changing roles of mothers: Changing intra-family relations in a Turkish town. In Peristiany, J. G. (Ed.), *Mediterranean family structures*. London: Cambridge University Press.

Koopman-Boyden, Peggy G. (1986). *The Retirement of Older People*. Christchurch: University of Canterbury, Sociology Department.

———. (1987). The elderly and the family. *Proceedings of the SSRFC Symposium on*

New Zealand Families in the Eighties and Nineties. Christchurch: Canterbury University.

Kramer, D. A., & Melchior, J. (1990). Gender, role conflict and the development of relativistic and dialectical thinking. *Sex Roles, 23*: 553–74.

Krige, E. J. (1950). *The Social System of the Zulus.* Pietermaritzburg: Shuter & Shooter.

Krishnan, V. (1987). Preference for sex of children: A multivariate analysis. *Journal of Biosocial Science, 19*(3): 367–76.

Kuhn, A. S. (1988). *Heiler und ihre Patienten auf dem Dach der Welt.* Frankfurt a.M., Germany: Verlag Peter Lang.

Kuo, E.C.Y., & Wong, A. K. (1979). Some observations on the study of family change in Singapore. In Kuo, E.C.Y., & Wong, A. K. (Eds.), *The Contemporary Family in Singapore* (pp. 3–16). Singapore: Singapore University Press.

Kuyas, N. (1982). Female labor and power relations in the urban Turkish family. In Ka°ìtçìbafì, Ç. (Ed.), *Sex Roles, Family and Community in Turkey.* Bloomington: Indiana University Press.

La Rosa, J., & Diaz-Loving, R. (1991). Evaluacion del autoconcepto: Una escala multidimensional. *Revista Latinoamericana de Psicologia, 23* (1): 15–33.

Lage, E. (1991). Boys, girls, and microcomputing. *European Journal of Psychology of Education, 6* (1): 29–44.

Langlois, J. H., & Downs, A. C. (1980). Mothers, fathers, and peers as socialization agents of sex-typed play behaviors in young children. *Child Development, 51*: 1217–47.

Lapidus, G. W. (1978). *Women in Soviet Society: Equality, Development, and Social Change.* Berkeley: University of California Press.

———. (Ed.). (1982). *Women, Work, and Family in the Soviet Union.* Armonk, NY: M. E. Sharpe.

Lau, S. K., & Kuan, H. C. (1988). *The Ethos of the Hong Kong Chinese.* Hong Kong: Chinese University Press.

le Camus, J. (1987). Les pratiques de nursing chez les parents d'enfants de creche, *Enfance, 40* (3): 245–61.

LeCompte, G., Özer, A., & Özer, S. (1978). Child-rearing attitudes of mothers from three socioeconomic levels in Ankara: Adaptation of an instrument. *Psikoloji Dergisi (Journal of Psychology), 1*: 5–8.

Le Vine, R. A. (1970). Sex roles and economic change in Africa. In Middleton, J. (Ed.)., *Black Africa.* London.

Lebra, T. S. (1984). *Japanese Women: Constraint and Fulfillment.* Honolulu: University of Hawaii Press.

Leclerq, J., & Rault, C. (1989). Les systèmes éducatifs en Europe. *Éditions la Documentation Francaise, 6.*

Lehmann, P. H., & Ullal, J. (1983). *Tibet. Das stille Drama auf dem Dach der Welt,* 2d ed. Hamburg: Geo/Gruner & Jahr AG.

Leñero-Otero, L. (1968). *Investigacion de la familia en Mexico.* Mexico City: Instituto Mexicano de Estudios Sociales, A.C.

Leoprapai, B., & Sirirasmi, B. (1988). *Health Status and Public Health Usage of Rural People.* Bangkok: Mahidol University.

Levine, N. (1982). Social change and family crisis—The nature of Turkish divorce. In Ka°ìtçìbafì, Ç. (Ed.), *Sex Roles, Family and Community in Turkey.* Bloomington: Indiana University Press.

————. (1988). *The Dynamics of Polyandry. Kinship, Domesticity, and Population on the Tibetan Border*. Chicago: University of Chicago Press.

Lewis, M. (1972). State as an infant-environmental interaction: An analysis of mother-infant behavior as a function of sex. *Merrill-Palmer Quarterly*, *18*: 95–211.

Li, M. C. (1981). The construction of sex trait inventory and the comparisons of four sex trait categories on achievement motive and attitudes toward marriage, career and sex. *Acta Psychologica Taiwanica*, *23*(1): 23–37.

Liburn, James. (1982). Las castas y las classe. *Pueblo Haitiano*, 243.

Licuanan, Patricia B. (1986). *Some Are More Unequal Than Others*. Quezon City: Ateneo de Manila University.

————. (1991). A situation analysis of women in the Philippines. In Illo, Jeanne Frances I. (Ed.), *Gender Analysis and Planning: The 1990 IPC-CIDA Workshops* (pp. 15–28). Quezon City: Institute of Philippine Culture, Ateneo de Manila University.

Lieblich, Amia. (1991). A comparison of successful Israeli and American career women at mid-life. In Swirsky, Barbara, & Safir, Marilyn P. (Eds.), *Calling the Equality Bluff: Women in Israel*. New York: Teacher's College Press.

Lijembe, J. A. (1967). The valley between: A Muluya's story. In Fox, E. (Ed.), *East African Childhood* (pp. 1–41). Nairobi: Oxford University Press.

Lin, C. C. (1988). Sex differences in wage among the first-job holders. *Economic Essays*, *16*(3).

Lin, M. C. (1989). A study on gender role and personality of the middle- and the old-aged. In *Proceedings of the Conference on Gender Role and Social Development*. Taipei: National Taiwan University, Center for Population Studies.

Louw-Potgieter, J. (1991). Language and identity. In Foster, D., & Louw-Potgieter, J. (Eds.), *Social Psychology in South Africa* (pp. 317–44). Johannesburg: Lexicon.

Lu, Y. H. (1981). Career attitudes of women in a changing society. *Academia Sinica*, *50*: 25–66.

Ludwar, G. (1975). *Die Sozialisation Tibetischer Kinder im soziokulturellen Wandel*. Wiesbaden: Steiner Verlag.

Luling, Virginia. (1982). *Aborigines*. London: MacDonald.

Luxton, M. (1987). Two hands for the clock: Changing patterns in the gendered division of labor in the home. In Salamon, E. D., & Robinson, B. W. (Eds.). *Gender Roles: Doing What Comes Naturally* (pp. 213–26). Toronto: Methuen.

Maccoby, E. E., & Jacklin, C. N. (1974). *The Psychology of Sex Differences*. Stanford, CA: Stanford University Press.

Mc Curdy, J. (1986). Women in Sri Lanka. In L. Wilgosh (Ed.), Counselling women: Information from diverse ethnic cultures. *International Journal for the Advancement of Counselling*, *9*:35–46.

McDaniel, S. (1988). The changing Canadian family: Women's roles and the impact of feminism. In Burt, S., Code, L., & Darney, L. (Eds.), *Changing Patterns: Women in Canada* (pp. 103–28). Toronto: McClelland & Stewart.

McDonald, Peter. (1991). Migrant family structure. In Funder, Kathleen (Ed.), *Images of Australian Families*. Melbourne: Longman Cheshire.

Mackie, M. (1987). *Constructing Women and Men: Gender Socialization*. Toronto: Holt. Rinehart & Winston.

Mackinnon, Alison. (1986). *The New Women*. Netley: Wakefield Press.

Mamonova, T. (Ed.). (1984). *Women and Russia*. Boston: Beacon.

Manaspaiboon, S. (1984). *Human Rights and Employees in Thailand*. Bangkok: Thamasart University Press.

Mandel, W. M. (1975). *Soviet Women*. Garden City, NY: Anchor.

Manninen, Merja, & Setälä, Päivi. (1990). *Lady with a Bow. The Story of Finnish Women*. Helsinki: Otava.

Mansilla, M. E. (1983). Aprendiendo a ser mujer. Estereotipos sexuales en textos escolares. *Debate*, *9*: 65–89.

Marjoribanks, K. (1987). Gender/social class, family environments and adolescents' aspirations. *Australian Journal of Education*, *31* (1): 43–54.

Markus, H. R., & Kitayama, S. (1991). Culture and the self: Implications for cognition, emotion, and motivation. *Psychological Review*, *98*: 224–55.

Martin, Jeanne. (1984). *Non English-speaking women: Production and social reproduction*. In Bottomley, G., & De Lepervanche, M. *Ethnicity, Class and Gender in Australia*. Sydney: George Allen & Unwin.

Massel, G. J. (1974). *The Surrogate Proletariat: Moslem Women and Revolutionary Strategies in Soviet Central Asia, 1919–1929*. Princeton, NJ: Princeton University Press.

Mateos, Z. (1991). Mi mamá trabaja. Encuesta: Imagen de la limeña. *Debate*, *12* (*64*): 28–30.

Mattioni, Marina. (1990). *Dossier Donne '90* (Special report on women in the '90s). Milan: Edimoda.

Mello, G. (1975). Estereótipos sexuais na escola (Gender stereotypes at school). *Cadernos de Pesquisa*, *15*: 141–44.

Mernissi, F. (1985). *Beyond the Veil: Male-Female Dynamics in Muslim Society*. London: El Saqui.

Mies, M. (1980). *Indian Women and Patriarchy*. New Delhi: Concept.

Minas, N. (1981). *Women in Islam: Tradition and Transition in the Middle East*. London: John Murray.

Mitchell, R. E. (1972). Husband-wife relations and family-planning practices in urban Hong Kong. *Journal of Marriage and the Family*, *34*: 134–46.

Mohsen, S. (1974). The Egyptian woman: Between modernity and tradition. In Matthiasson, C. (Ed.), *Many Sisters: Women in Cross-cultural Perspective*. London: Free Press.

———. (1985). *New Images, Old Reflections: Working Middle Class Women in Egypt*. Austin: University of Texas Press.

Momsen, J. H. (1991). *Women and Development in the Third World*. London: Routledge.

Mönnig, H. O. (1967). *The Pedi*. Pretoria: Van Schaik.

Moore, S. M., & Rosenthal, D. A. (1980). Sex-roles: Gender, generation, and self-esteem. *Australian Psychologist*, *15*: 467–77.

Morgan, R. (Ed.). (1984). *Sisterhood Is Global*. Garden City, NY: Anchor Press/Doubleday.

Morgan, S. P., & Hirosima, K. (1983). The persistence of extended family residence in Japan. *American Sociological Review*, *48*: 269–81.

Mori, S. (1992). *Education Based on Philosophy of Play*. Nagoya: Reimei.

Morrill, W. T. (1965). Immigrants and associations: The Ibo in 20th-century Calabar. *Comparative Studies in Social History*, 4.

Moussourou, L. (1985). *Family and Child in Athens*. (In Greek.) Athens: Hestia.

Muñoz-Izquierdo, C. (1987). Actitudes ante el trabajo. In Medina, A. H., & Rodriguez,

L. N. (Eds.), *Como Somos los Mexicanos*. Mexico City: Centro de Estudios Educativos, A.C.

Mura, R., Kimball, M., & Cloutier, R. (1987). Girls and science programs: Two steps forward, one step back. In Gaskell, J., & McLaren, A. (Eds.), *Women and Education: A Canadian Perspective* (pp. 133–49). Calgary: Detselig Enterprises.

Muraro, Luisa. (1991). *L'ordine simbolico della madre* (The symbolic order of the mother). Rome: Riuniti.

Naffine, Ngaire. (1990). *Law and the Sexes: Exploration in Feminine Jurisprudence*. Sydney: Allen & Unwin.

Nagaraja, K., (1991 May 25–June 7). The missing women. Frontline. *National Press*, Madras.

Nakamura, T. (1986, December). Boys' and girls' participation in extra-curricular activities in elementary school. *Child Psychology*, 76–85.

Nakane, C. (1970). *Japanese Society*. Berkeley: University of California Press.

Nascimento, M. C. (1988). Nível de categorização de estereótipos sexuais (Level of characterization of sexual stereotypes). *Psicologia: teoria e pesquisa, 4* (2): 137–48.

Nash, L. C., & Parker, S. (1987). The cultural production and reproduction of gender: The effect of extracurricular activities on peer-group culture. *Sociology of Education, 60*: 200–213.

National Agenda for Women Implementation Report. (1991). Canberra: Office of the Status of Women.

National Policy on Women's Health: A Framework for Change. (1988). Canberra: Australian Government Publishing Service.

Nduka, O. (1964). *Western Education and the Nigerian Cultural Background*. Ibadan: University Press.

Neil, C. C., & Snizek, W. E. (1987). Work value, job characteristics, and gender. *Sociological Perspectives, 30*: 245–65.

Nelson, C. (1984). Islamic tradition and women's education in Egypt. In Acker, S., et al. (Eds.), *The World Yearbook of Education*. London: Nichols.

Nerlove, S., Munroe, R., & Munroe, R. (1971). Effect of environmental experience of spatial ability: A replication. *Journal of Social Psychology, 84*: 3–10, 109–10.

Neugarten, B. L., & Gutman, D. L. (1958). Age-sex roles in middle age: A thematic apperception study. *Psychological Monographs*, 72.

Ng, P.P.T. (1981). Social factors contributing to fertility decline. In, King, A.Y.C., & Lee, R.P.L. (Eds.), *Social Life and Development in Hong Kong*. Hong Kong: Chinese University Press.

Niemi, Päivi. (1988). *Adolescents and the Family. Images and Experiences of Family Life in Finland*. Annales Universitatis Turkuensis, Series B, 181. Turku: University of Turku.

Nittetsu Human Development. (1988). *Nippon: The Land and Its People*. Tokyo: Gakuseisha.

Noller, Patricia, & Gallan, Victor J. (1991). Images of the typical Australian family. In Funder, Kathleen (Ed.), *Images of Australian Families*. Melbourne: Longman Cheshire.

Nolte, J. (1987). Sexuality, fertility and choice: On becoming a woman in the eighties. In Nemiroff, G. H. (Ed.), *Women and Men: Interdisciplinary Readings on Gender* (pp. 202–23). Canada: Fitzhenry & Whiteside.

Norberg-Hodge, H. (1991). *Ancient Futures. Learning from Ladakh*. San Francisco: Sierra Club Books.

Norbu, T. J., & Turnbull, C. M. (1972). *Tibet*. New York: Simon & Schuster.

Novak, M. (1985). *Successful Aging: The Myths, Realities and Future of Aging in Canada*. Markham, Ontario: Penguin Books.

Obanya, Pai. (1981). A longitudinal study of school subject preferences of a group of Nigerian adolescents. *Illorin Journal of Education*, 111–15.

O'Connell, A. N., & Russo, N. F. (Eds.). (1991). *Women's Heritage in Psychology: Origins, Development, and Future Directions*. New York: Cambridge University Press. Special Centennial issue, *Psychology of Women Quarterly*, Whole No. 4.

Office of the Committee of Economic and Social Development. (1990). *Present Status of Thai Women*. Bangkok: Anongsilpakarnpim.

Okafor, N.A.O. (1991). Some traditional aspects of Nigerian women. In Adler, L. L. (Ed.), *Women in Cross-Cultural Perspective* (chapter 10). New York: Praeger.

Okonjo, K. (1976). The dual sex political system in operation. In Hafkin, N. J., & Bay, E. G. (Eds.), *Women in Africa*. Stanford CA: Stanford University Press.

Olson, E. A. (1982). Duofocal family structure and an alternative model of husband-wife relationship. In Ka°ıtçıbafı, Ç. (Ed.), *Sex Roles, Family and Community in Turkey*. Bloomington: Indiana University Press.

Olson, J. E., Frieze, I. H., & Detlefsen, E. G. (1990). Having it all? Combining work and family in a male and a female profession. *Sex Roles*, *23*: 515–33.

Omari, I. M. (1982). *Psychology and Education in Changing Societies*. Dar-es-Salaam: University of Dar-es-Salaam Press.

Öncü, A. (1981). Turkish women in the professions: Why so many? In Abadan-Unat, N. (Ed.), *Women in Turkish Society*. Leiden: E. J. Brill.

O'Neill, A.-M. (1990). Gender and education: Structural inequality for women. In Codd, J., Harker, R., & Nash, R. (Eds.), *Political Issues in New Zealand Education*, 2d ed. Palmerston North: Dunmore Press.

Oppong, C. (1983). *Female and Male in West Africa*. London: George Allen & Unwin.

———. (1989). Women's roles and general issues in family planning in Africa. In *Development in Family Planning Policies and Program in Africa*. Legon: Regional Institute for Population Studies, University of Ghana.

Orasanu, J., Slater, M., & Adler, L. L. (Eds.). (1979). *Language, Sex, and Gender: Does "la différence" make a Difference?* New York: The New York Academy of Sciences Annals, Vol. 327.

Ortiz, A. (1989). La comunidad, el parentesco y los patrones de crianza andinos. *Anthropologica*, *7* (7): 135–70.

Osgood, C. E., May, W. H., & Miron, M. S. (1975). *Cross-Cultural Universals of Affective Meaning*. Urbana: University of Illinois Press.

Ottenberg, S. (1989). *Boyhood Rituals in an African Society*. Seattle: University of Washington Press.

Ou, Y. S. (1988). Gender ideology in elementary school textbooks. In Chen, B. C. (Ed.), *Ideology and Education* (pp. 255–72). Taipei, Taiwan: Hsu-Ta.

Özbay, F. (1982). Women's education in rural Turkey. In Ka°ıtçıbafı, Ç. (Ed.), *Sex Roles, Family and Community in Turkey*. Bloomington: Indiana University Press.

Paul, R. A. (1982). *The Tibetan Symbolic World*. Chicago: University of Chicago Press.

Peck, R. F., & Diaz-Guerrero, R. (1967). Respeto y posicion social en dos culturas.

Proceedings of the 7th Interamerican Congress of Psychology (pp. 79–88). Mexico City: Sociedad Mexicana de Psicologia, A.C.

Pedersen, P. (Ed.). (1985). *Handbook of Cross-Cultural Counseling and Therapy*. Westport, CT: Greenwood Press.

Pedich, A., et al. (1979). *Pielegniarstwo geriatryczne* (Geriatric nursing). Warszawa: State Medical Publisher.

Pepitone-Rockwell, F. (Ed). (1980). *Dual Career Couples*. Beverly Hills, CA: Sage.

Peres, Yohanan, & Katz, Ruth. (1983). Stability and centrality: The nuclear family in modern Israel. *Social Forces*, *59*: 687–704.

Perham, M. (1987). *Native Administration in Nigeria*. London.

Peter, Prince of Greece and Denmark. (1963). *A Study of Polyandry*. The Hague: Mouton.

Phillips, J. (1987). *A Man's Country? The Image of the Pakeha Male—A History*. Auckland: Penguin.

Pitsiou, E. (1986). *Life-Styles of Older Athenians*. Athens: National Center of Social Research.

Podmore, V. N., & Bird, L. (1990). *Parenting and Children's Development in New Zealand*. NZARE State of the Art Monograph, No. 3. Palmerston North: New Zealand Association for Research in Education.

Pöntinen, Seppo. (1990). Koulutuksen kehityslinjoja. In Riihinen, Olavi (Ed.), Suomi 2017. Jyväskylä–Helsinki: Gummerus.

Poole, Millicent. (1983). Influences on job choices of young women and girls—Problems of technological change. *Australian Educational Researcher*, *10* (2): 24–46.

Porio, Emma, Lynch, Frank, & Hollnsteiner, Mary. (1975). *The Filipino Family, Community and Nation: The Same Yesterday, Today and Tomorrow?* Quezon City: Institute of Philippine Culture, Ateneo de Manila University.

Porter, Paige. (1986). *Gender and Education*. Melbourne: Deakin University.

Portugal: A situação das mulheres. (1991). Lisbon: Comissão para a Igualdade e para os Direitos das Mulheres, Presidência de Conselho de Ministros.

Pozas, R., & H. de Pozas, I. (1972). *Los Indios en las Clases Sociales de Mexico*. Mexico City: Siglo XXI Editores.

Prapreudee, B., Pimisuthi, T., & Srihong, Ch. (1977). *Thai Women: Role as Administrative Leaders*. Bangkok: Faculty of Political Sciences, Ramkamhang University.

Preston-Whyte, E. (1974). Kinship and marriage. In Hammond-Tooke, W. D. (Ed.), *The Bantu-Speaking Peoples of South Africa* (pp. 177–203). London: Routledge & Kegan Paul.

Prince, Rod. (1985). *Haiti Family Business*. London: Latin American Bureau.

Prosser, G. V. (1986). Children's play in Sri Lanka: A cross-cultural study. *British Journal of Developmental Psychology*, *4*: 170–85.

Raday, Frances. (1991). The concept of gender equality in a Jewish state. In Swirsky, Barbara, & Safir, Marilyn P. (Eds.), *Calling the Equality Bluff: Women in Israel*. New York: Teacher's College Press.

Radice, J. (1987). Papéis sexuais no nordeste do Brasil: Sua desejabilidade e possíveis consequências para a auto-realização da mulher (Gender roles in Brazil's northeast: Their desirability and possible consequences for women's self-realization). *Revista de Psicologia*, *5* (1): 93–103.

Ragúz, M. (1983). Estereotipos de rol sexual y diferencias sexuales: Realidad y distorsión. *Revista de Psicología, P.U.C.*, *1* (1): 27–37.

————. (1989). Maternidad/maternalidad y trabajo: Efectos del rol dual sobre los hijos y la pareja. *Revista de Psicología P.U.C., 7* (1): 3–21.

————. (1990). Maternidad/maternalidad y trabajo: Efectos del rol dual sobre las madres que trabajan. *Revista de Psicología, P.U.C., 8* (2): 181–201.

Raiklin, E., & McCormick, K. (1988). Soviet men on the road to utopia: A moral-psychological sketch. *International Journal of Social Economics, 15*: 3–62.

Ramphele, M., & Boonzaier, E. (1988). The position of African women: Race and gender in South Africa. In Boonzaier, E., & Sharp, J. (Eds.), *South African Keywords: The Uses and Abuses of Political Concepts* (pp. 153–66). Cape Town: David Philip.

Raubenheimer, J. R. (1991). Late adulthood. In Louw, D. A. (Ed)., *Human Development*. Pretoria: HAUM.

Raum, O. F. (1940). *Chaga Childhood*. London: Oxford University Press.

————. (1973). *The Social Functions of Avoidances and Taboos Among the Zulu: Monographien zur Völlerkunde*. Berlin: Walter de Gruyter.

Rauste-von Wright, Marja-Liisa. (1987). On the life process among Finnish adolescents: Summary report of a longitudinal study. *Commentationes Scientiarum Socialium, 35*.

————. (1989). Body image satisfaction in adolescent girls and boys: A longitudinal study. *Journal of Youth and Adolescence, 18*: 71–83.

Reader, D. H. (1966). *Zulu Tribe in Transition*. Manchester: Manchester University Press.

Reis, R. (1983). Reproduction or retreat: The position of Buddhist women in Ladakh. In Kantowsky, D., & Sander, R. (Eds.), *Recent Research on Ladakh: History, Culture, Sociology, Ecology* (pp. 217–29). Muenchen: Weltforum Verlag.

Reisman, J. M. (1988). An indirect measure of the value of friendship for aging men. *Journal of Gerontology, 43*: 109–10.

Republic of South Africa. (1988). *Demographic Trends in South Africa*. Cape Town: Government Printer.

Rhee, K. O. (1990). The theoretical framework and indicators of social care for the aged. *Journal of Korean Gerontological Society, 10*: 147–62.

Rheingold, H. L., & Cook, K. V. (1975). The contents of boys' and girls' rooms as an index of parents' behavior. *Child Development, 46*: 459–63.

Richard, Abbott M. (1983). *Masculine and Feminine—Sex Roles over the Life Cycle*. Reading, MA: Addison-Wesley.

Ritchie, J., & Ritchie, J. (1970). *Child Rearing Patterns in New Zealand*. Wellington: A. H. & A. W. Reed.

————. (1978). *Growing Up in New Zealand*. Sydney: George Allen & Unwin.

Rizvi, J. (1983 [1989]). *Ladakh: Crossroads of High Asia*. New Delhi: Oxford University Press.

Roadburg, A. (1985). *Aging: Retirement, Leisure and Work in Canada*. Agincourt, ON: Methuen.

Robinson, B. W., & Salamon, E. D. (1987). Gender role socialization: A review of the literature. In Salamon, E. D., & Robinson, B. W. (Eds.), *Gender Roles: Doing What Comes Naturally* (pp. 123–42). Toronto: Methuen.

Robinson, F. (Ed.). (1989). *Cambridge Encyclopedia of India, Pakistan, Bangladesh, Sri Lanka, Nepal, Bhutan, and the Maldives*. Cambridge: Cambridge University Press.

Rocznik Statystyczny (Statistical yearbook). (1991). Warsaw: General Statistics Bureau.

Rocznik Demograficzny (Demographic yearbook). (1989). Warsaw: General Statistics Bureau.

Roggman, L. A., & Peery, J. C. (1989). Parent-infant social play in brief encounters: Early gender differences. *Child Study Journal, 19*: 65–79.

Romer, N. (1981). *The Sex-Role Cycle: Socialization from Infancy to Old Age.* Old Westbury, NY: Feminist Press.

Rosemberg, F. (1975). A escola e as diferenças sexuais (School and gender differences). *Cadernos de Pesquisa, 15*: 78–85.

Rosenthal, Doreen, & Grieve, Norma. (1990). Attitudes to the gender culture: A comparison of Italian-Australian and Anglo-Australian female tertiary students. *Australian Psychologist, 25* (3): 282–92.

Rossiter, C. (1986). Housing tenure and costs of older Australians: Gender issues. *Australian Journal of Ageing, 5* (May): 4–12.

Rubin, V., & Schaeldel, R. (1982). *The Haitian Potential: Research and Resources.* New York: Teacher's College Press, Columbia University.

Rugh, A. (1984). *Family in Contemporary Egypt.* Syracuse, NY: Syracuse University Press.

Ruthchild, R. (1983). Sisterhood and socialism: The Soviet feminist movement. *Frontiers, 7*: 4–12.

Sacks, M. P. (1977). Sexual equality and Soviet women. *Society, 14*: 48–51.

———. (1982). *Work and Equality in Soviet Society.* New York: Praeger.

Safir, Marilyn P. (1983). Sex role education/socialization on the kibbutzim. In Palgi, Michal, Blassi, Joseph, Rosner, Menachem, & Safir, Marilyn P. (Eds.), *Sexual Equality: The Israeli Kibbutz Tests the Theories.* Philadelphia: Norwood Press.

———. (1986). Nature or nurture effects on sex differences in intellectual function. *Sex Roles, 14*: 581–90.

———. (1991). How has the kibbutz experiment failed to create sex equality? In Swirsky, Barbara, & Safir, Marilyn P. (Eds.), *Calling the Equality Bluff: Women in Israel.* New York: Teacher's College Press.

Salaff, J. W. (1981). *Working Daughters of Hong Kong.* Cambridge: Cambridge University Press.

Salem, T. (1981). Mulheres faveladas. Com a venda nos olhos (Shantytown women. With closed eyes). *Perspectivas Antropológicas da Mulher.* Rio de Janeiro: Zahar.

Salgueiro, Gabriela. (1989). *As mulheres e o envelhecimento*, 2d ed. Lisbon: Colecção Informar as Mulheres 8, Comissão da Condição Feminina.

Salgueiro, Teresa Barata. (1987). Actividade e progresso na carreira. In *A mulher e o ensino superior, a investigação científica e as novas tecnologias em Portugal* (pp. 105–16). Lisbon: Cadernos Condição Feminina 21.

Samarasingha, D. (1989). Treating alcohol problems in Sri Lanka. *British Journal of Addiction, 84*: 865–67.

Samarasingha, D., Dissanayake, S. A., & Wijesinghe, C. P. (1987). Alcoholism in Sri Lanka. *British Journal of Addiction, 82*: 1149–53.

Santaputra, S. (1988). Growing up in Thai society. In Ekberg, K., & Mgaavatn, Per Egil (Eds.), *Growing into a Modern World* (pp. 897–907).

Sarti, C. (1989). Reciprocidade e Hierarquia: Relação de gênero na periferia de São Paulo (Reciprocity and hierarchy: Gender relationships on the outskirts of São Paulo). *Cadernos de Pesquisa, 70*: 38–40.

Saw, S. H., & Wong, A. K. (1981). *Youths in Singapore: Sexuality, Courtship and Family Values*. Singapore: Singapore University Press.

Sawicka, H. (1975). Psychologiczne aspekty bilansu zyciowego ludzi starych (Psychological aspects of the life-styles of elderly). *Zeszyty Naukowe UJ.Prace Psych. Ped.*, 23 (*Scientific Issues of the Jagiellonian University*).

Schade, B., & Rojas, C. (1989). Niños en extrema pobreza . . . Socialización deficitaria? *Revista de Psicología, P.U.C.*, 7.

Schuler, S. R. (1987). *The Other Side of Polyandry*. Boulder, Co.: Westview Press.

Scott, S. (1990). O Homem na Matrifocalidade: Gênero, percepção e experiência do domínio doméstico (Men in matrifocality: Gender, perception, and experiences in the domestic domain). *Cadernos de Pesquisa, 73*: 38–47.

Seager, J., & Olson, A. (1986). *Women in the World: An International Atlas*. New York: Simon & Schuster.

Serbin, L., O'Leary, K., Kent, R., & Tonick, I. (1973). A comparison of teacher responses to the preacademic and problem behavior of boys and girls. *Child Development, 44*: 796–804.

Setho, R., Pirokes, S. Petcharat, K., & Jamikorn, S. (1978). *Behavior and Attitudes of Kasetsart University Students Towards Dating and Mating*. Bangkok: Faculty of Social Sciences, Kasetsart University.

Sevilla, Judy Carol C. (1982). *Research on the Filipino Family: Review and Prospects*. Pasig, Metro Manila: Development Academy of the Philippines.

Sharma, U. (1980). *Women, Work & Property in North-West India*. London: Tavistock.

Sheu, M. H. (1987). Children's preferences in rating males and females in storybooks for children. *Bulletin of Counseling, 10*: 341–55.

Shoemaker, S. (1983). The status of women in the rural USSR. *Population Research and Policy Review, 2*: 35–51.

Siam Rath. (1992). Political role of Thai women. *Siam Rath Weekly Magazine, 45*.

Silva, Manuela. (1987). A mulher e o poder económico. In *Comunicações do seminário "A Mulher e o Poder"* (pp. 131–39). Lisbon: Cadernos Condição Feminina 20.

Silva, Maria Regina T. da. (1988). Intervenção da Presidente da Commissão da Condição Feminina. In *O direito comunitário e a igualdade jurídica entre mulheres e homens* (pp. 13–16). Lisbon: Cadernos Condição Feminina 23.

Sim, W. K. (1991). Education for equality in a changing society. *Singapore Journal of Education, 11* (2): 12–20.

Sinkkonen, Sirkka, & Haavio-Mannila, Elina. (1981). The impact of the women's movement and legislative activity of women MPs on social development. In Rendel, Margarita (Ed.), *Women, Power and Political Systems*. London: Groom Hel.

Sinnott, J. D. (1977). Sex-role inconsistency, biology, and successful ageing. *Gerontology, 17*: 459–64.

Smith, A. B. (1985). Teacher modeling and sex-typed play preferences. *New Zealand Journal of Educational Studies, 20*: 39–47.

———. (1988). *Understanding Children's Development*, 2d ed., rev. Sydney: Allen & Unwin/Port Nicholson Press.

Smith, P. T. (1990). Obstacles for women on the way to management: A study of business students' images of the ideal manager. *Journal of Contemporary Management, 3*: 77–88.

Smith, R. M., Goslen, M. A., Byrd, A. J., & Reece, L. (1991). Self-other orientation and sex-role orientation of men and women who remarry. *Journal of Divorce and Remarriage*, *14*: 3–32.

Smock, A., & Youssef, N. (1977). *Egypt: From Seclusion to Limited Participation*. In Giele, J., & Smock, A. (Eds.), *Women: Role and Status in Eight Countries*. New York: Wiley.

Sokolowska, M. (1976). Obraz kobiety w swiadomosci wspolczesnego spoleczenstwa (Image of women in the contemporary society). W: *Podsumowanie dorobku nauki polskiej w zakresie studiow nad problemami kobiet, rodziny i macierzynstwa* (In Output of the Polish research on problems of women, family and maternity). Warsaw: Polish Academy of Sciences.

Solodnikov, V. V. (1989). The perfect child: Views of teachers. *Sotsiologicheskie Issledovaniya*, *16*: 87–90.

Solomon, K. S. (1984). Psychosocial crises of older men. *Hillside Journal of Clinical Psychiatry 2*: 123–34.

Sousa, Maria Reynolds de, et al. (1990). *Portugal: Situação das mulheres 1990*, 8th ed. Lisboa: Comissão da Condição Feminina, *8*.

Spence, J. T., & Helmreich, R. L. (1978). *Masculinity and Femininity*. Austin: University of Texas Press.

Sperling, V. (1990). Rape and domestic violence in the USSR. *Response to the Victimization of Women and Children*, *13*: 16–22.

Spinelli, C., Vassilioiu, V., & Vassilioiu, G. (1970). Milieu development and male and female roles. In Seward, G., & Williamson, R. (Eds.), *Sex Roles in a Changing Society*. New York: Random House.

Stein, A. H., & Smithells, J. (1969). Age and sex differences in children's sex-role standards about achievement. *Developmental Psychology*, *1*: 252–59.

Steinmann, A., & Ramos, E. (1974). Percepções masculino-femininas do papel feminino no Brasil (Male-female perceptions of the feminine role in Brazil). *Arquivos Brasileiros de Psicologia Aplicada*, *26* (4): 85–91.

Sternheimer, S. (1985). The vanishing babushka: A roleless role for older Soviet women? *Current Perspectives of Aging in the Life Cycle*, *1*: 315–33.

Stevenson, H., Lee, S., Stigler, J., Kitamura, S., Kimura, S., & Kato, T. (1986). Achievement in mathematics. In Stevenson, H., Azuma, H., & Hakuta, K. (Eds.), *Child Development and Education in Japan* (pp. 201–16). New York: W. H. Freeman.

Su, C. W., & Jong, J. T. (1985). A study about how mothers take care of their infants. *Bulletin of Educational Psychology*, *18*: 117–48.

Sukemune, S. (1983). Japan, Japanese children and adults, and Japanese psychology today. *International Psychologist*, *24* (2): 16–18.

Sunar, D. (1982). Female stereotypes in the U.S. and Turkey: An application of functional theory to perceptions in power relations. *Journal of Cross-Cultural Psychology*, *13* (4): 445–60.

Susulowska, M. (1989). *Psychologia starzenia sie i starosci* (Psychology of getting old and old age). Warsaw: State Scientific Publisher.

Suvannathat, C. (1979). The inculcation of values in Thai children. *International Social Sciences Journal*, *31*: 477–85.

Swirski, B., & Safir, M. P. (Eds.). (1991). *Calling the Equality Bluff: Women in Israel*. New York: Macmillan.

Sycip, Lynne Marie. (1982). Working mothers: Their problems and coping strategies, an exploratory study. *Social Science Information*, *10*(2):1–8.

Szicom, T. (1988). *Teaching gender? Sex education and sexual stereotypes*. North Sydney: Allen & Unwin.

Tai, C. L. (1979). Divorce in Singapore. In Kuo, E. C. Y., & Wong, A. K. (Eds.), *The Contemporary Family in Singapore* (pp. 142–67). Singapore: Singapore University Press.

Takahashi, K. (1986). Examining the strange-situation procedure with Japanese mothers and 12-month-old infants. *Developmental Psychology*, *22*: 265–70.

Takooshian, H. (1991). Soviet women. In Adler, L. L. (Ed.), *Women in Cross-Cultural Perspective* (pp. 78–88). New York: Praeger.

Takooshian, H., & Stuart, C. R. (1983). Ethnicity and feminism among American women: Opposing social trends? *International Journal of Group Tensions*, *13*: 100–105.

Tamayo, G., & García Rios, J. M. (1990). *Mujer y varón. Vida cotidiana, violencia y justicia*. Lima: Raíces y Alas.

Taring, R. D. (1970). *Daughter of Tibet*. London: Camelot Press.

Tekeli, P. (1981). The woman's place in Turkish political life. In Abadan-Unat, N. (Ed.), *Women in Turkish Society*. Leiden: E. J. Brill.

Thambia, S. J. (1990). Sri Lanka: Introduction. In Peebles, P., Colonization of ethnic conflict in the dry zone of Sri Lanka. *Journal of Asian Studies*, *49*: 30–53.

Thom, D. P. (1991). Adolescence. In Louw, D. A. (Ed.), *Human Development*. Pretoria: HAUM.

Thomson, D. (1991). *Selfish Generations? The Ageing of New Zealand's Welfare State*. Wellington: Bridge Williams Books.

Timur, S. (1972). *Family Structure in Turkey*. Ankara: Hacettepe University Press.

Tinker, I. (Ed.). (1990). *Persistent Inequalities: Women and World Development*. New York: Oxford University Press.

Toda, K., & Katada, Y. (1987). Experimental analysis of the conscious structure of sex-role acceptance in female adolescents: Girl students in their final period of moratorium in Hokkaido. *Japanese Journal of Psychology*, *58*: 309–17.

Torres, Amaryllis Tiglao. (Ed.). (1989). *The Filipino Women in Focus: A Book of Readings*. Bangkok: UNESCO.

Triandis, H., & Vassiliou, V. (1972). A comparative analysis of subjective cultures. In Triandis, H. C. (Ed.), *The Analysis of Subjective Culture*. New York: Wiley.

———. (1987). Frequency of contact and stereotyping. *Journal of Personality and Social Psychology*, *7*: 316–28.

Tryfan, B. (1987). *Kwestia Kobieca na wsi* (Feminine question in the countryside). Warsaw: State Scientific.

Tsai, S. L. (1987). Occupational segregation and differential educational achievement: A comparison between men and women. *Chinese Journal of Sociology*, *11*: 61–91.

Tsai, S. L., & Chiu, H. Y. (1988). Gender and achievement aspirations: The case of Tai-Ta students. *Chinese Journal of Sociology*, *12*: 125–68.

Tzougas, J., & Tziafetas, G. (1989). The impact of international migration on fertility: An econometric population model. *International Migration*, *27* (4): 581–94.

United Nations. (1991). *The World's Women: Trends and Statistics 1970–1990*. New York.

Vaillant, G. C. (1960). *The Aztecs of Mexico*. Baltimore, MD: Penguin Books.

Valkonen, Tapani. (1990). Väestönkehitys. In Riihinen, Olavi (Ed.), *Suomi 2017*. Jyväs-kylä–Helsinki: Gummerus.

Valsiner, J. (1988). *Developmental Psychology in the Soviet Union*. Bloomington: Indiana University Press.

Van der Vliet, V. (1974). Growing up in traditional society. In Hammond-Tooke, W. D. (Ed.), *The Bantu-Speaking Peoples of Southern Africa* (pp. 211–34). London: Routledge & Kegan Paul.

Van Gennep, A. (1960). *The Rites de Passage*. Chicago: University of Chicago Press.

Vankerviser, C. M. (1969). Growing up in Sukumaland. In CESO (Ed.), *Primary Education in Sukumaland Tanzania* (pp. 42–82). Groningen: Wolters Noordhoff.

Vassiliou, G., & Vassiliou, V. (1982). Promoting psychosocial functioning and pre-venting malfunctioning. *Pediatrician*, *11* (1–2): 90–98.

Veras, R. P. (1987). Crescimento da população idosa no Brasil: Transformações e con-sequências na sociedade (Growth of the older population in Brazil: Transformations and consequences for society). *Revista Saúde Pública*, *21*(3): 225–33.

Vianello, M., & Siemienska, R. (1990). *Gender Inequality: A Comparative Study of Discrimination and Participation*. Newbury Park, CA: Sage.

Vogel, Joachim. (1991). *Social Report for the Nordic Countries. Living Conditions and Inequality in the late 1980s*. Copenhagen: Nordisk Statistisk Skriftserie 55.

Voydanoff, P. (1988). Women, work, and family: Bernard's perspective on the past, present, and future. *Psychology of Women Quarterly*, *12*: 269–80.

Wainrib, B. R. (1992). *Gender Issues Across the Life Cycle*. New York: Springer.

Wang, H. C., & Lu, T. M. (1985). The influence of parental gender role attitude and distribution on preschoolers gender role. *Home Economic Education*, *9*(6): 76–88.

Wawrzyniak, B. (1980). *Kobieta wiejska* (Countryside woman). Warsaw: LSW (Peasants Cooperative Publishing House).

Whiting, B. B., & Edwards, C. P. (1988). *Children of Different Worlds*. Cambridge, MA: Harvard University Press.

William, J. (1953). The structure of the Brazilian family. *Social Forces*, *31*: 340–75.

Williams, J., & Best, B. (1982). *Measuring Sex Stereotypes: Cross-Cultural Research and Methodology*. Beverly Hills, CA: Sage.

Wilson, M. (1963). *Good Company: A Study of Nyakyusa Age Villages*. London: Oxford University Press.

Wong, A.K. (1979). Women's status and changing family values. In Kuo, E.C.Y., & Wong, A. K. (Eds.), *The Contemporary Family in Singapore* (pp. 40–61). Sin-gapore: Singapore University Press.

Wong, F. M. (1975). Industrialization and family structures in Hong Kong. *Journal of Marriage and the Family*, *37*: 985–1000.

———. (1981). Effects of the employment of mothers on marital role and power dif-ferentiation in Hong Kong. In King, A.Y.C., & Lee, R.P.L. (Eds.), *Social Life and Development in Hong Kong*. Hong Kong: Chinese University Press.

Working Group on Women in Sport. (1985). *Women, Sport and the Media*. Canberra: Australian Government Publishing Service.

Yamaguchi, M. (1989). Two aspects of Masculinity-Femininity II. *Japanese Journal of Psychology*, *59*: 350–56.

Yamamoto, M., Matsui, Y., & Yamanari, Y. (1982). The structure of perceived aspects of self. *Japanese Journal of Educational Psychology*, *30*: 64–68.

Yanbasti, G. (1990). Self-evaluation of mental health by male and female students: A comparison. *Psikoloji Dergisi (Journal of Psychology)* 8: 57–63.

Yates, Lyn. (1990). *Theory/Practice Dilemmas. Gender, Knowledge and Education.* Geelong: Deaking University.

Yedlin, T. (Ed.). (1980). *Women in Eastern Europe and the Soviet Union.* New York: Praeger.

Yeh, C. H. (1990). *A Study on Labor Policies Protecting Female Workers—Empirical Analysis of Labor Standards Law of R.O.C.* Taipei: Graduate Institute of Public Policy, National Chung-Hsing University.

Yoon, H. Y. (1983). Developmental stages and psychological maladjustment: psychology in late adulthood. *Journal of Korea Gerontological Society, 3:* 5–15.

Yörüko°lu, A. (1978). *Child Mental Health.* Ankara: Türkiye If Bankasì Press.

Yu, A. Y., & Bain, B. C. (1985). *Language, Social Class and Cognitive Style: A Comparative Study of Unilingual and Bilingual Education in Hong Kong and Alberta.* Hong Kong: Hong Kong Teacher's Association.

Zhernova, L. (1991). Women in the USSR. In Adler, L. L. (Ed.), *Women in Cross-Cultural Perspective* (pp. 68–77). New York: Praeger.

Index

About the Editor
and Contributors

LEONORE LOEB ADLER was born in Karlsruhe, Germany; she was educated there and in Lausanne, Switzerland, and came to the United States of America during the Hitler era. She received her Ph.D. in Experimental Social Psychology from Adelphi University. She is the Director of the Institute for Cross-Cultural and Cross-Ethnic Studies and a Professor in the Department of Psychology at Molloy College, Rockville Centre, New York. Dr. Adler is active in many professional organizations and most recently was elected to the American Psychological Association's Committee on International Relations in Psychology. She has received both the Kurt Lewin Award and the Wilhelm Wundt Award from different Divisions of the New York State Psychological Association, the Distinguished Contributions of the Decade Award from the International Organization for the Study of Group Tensions, and the Certificate of Recognition from the International Council of Psychologists. Dr. Adler is involved in several cross-cultural and cross-national research projects. She has published over 70 professional papers and chapters and is the author, editor, or coeditor of 14 books.

LISE BIRD is a Senior Lecturer in Education at Victoria University of Wellington in New Zealand/Aotearoa. Born in the United States, she moved with her family to Australia in her teenage years. She completed a Ph.D. in Psychology in Australia, then settled in New Zealand, where she has lived for the past 14 years. Dr. Bird's research concerns feminist critiques of accounts of girls, schooling, and achievement. She is currently on the National Council of the New Zealand Educational Research Association.

AGNES CHANG SHOOK CHEONG was born and brought up in Singapore. She received her B.Sc., Dip. Ed. (Credit), and M.Ed. (Educational Psychology) from the University of Singapore and her Ph.D. from Macquarie University, Sydney, Australia. She held the position of science teacher with St. Joseph's Institution before she joined the Institute of Education. Dr. Chang was involved in a cross-cultural study on Life Possibilities in Australia and she is currently collaborating with the Hebrew University of Jerusalem on a research study of values. Her research interests include early childhood development, giftedness, bilingualism, metacognition, learning strategies, and motivation. Dr. Chang is a consultant to the International Development Research Center and the Singapore Gifted Education Program (Ministry of Education). She was elected worldwide as Director-at-Large (1989–1992) and Area Chair of the International Council of Psychologists.

NICHOLAS V. CIACCIO is currently Professor of Psychology at the American University in Cairo and Director of the University's Counseling Center. He is also founder and Director of the Child Development Center in Cairo, whose members consult on a wide range of issues affecting the psychosocial well-being of the Egyptian child.

MARIA DAS MERCÊS CABRITA DE MENDONÇA COVAS was born in Faro, Portugal. She completed her undergraduate studies in Sociology. Since 1980 she has been a Lecturer in the Rural Extension Division of the Sociology Department of the University of Évora, teaching Introductory Sociology, Family Resources Management, and Sociology of the Family. In 1981 she received a grant from the U.S. AID (Agency for International Development) program to advance her knowledge of teaching Family Resources Development, which she did at the University of Georgia in the United States of America. She successfully completed an exam that earned the equivalent of a Master's Degree in the Management of Family Resources. Currently she has a grant from the National Institute of Scientific Investigation (INIC: Instituto National de Investigação Cientifica) to complete her doctoral dissertation in the area of Sociology of the Family. Maria Covas has published various articles in the areas of Portuguese families, family roles, and the situation of women in Portugal.

MARIA ALICE D'AMORIM is a Brazilian psychologist and received her Ph.D. in Social Psychology from the Université Catholique de Louvain, Belgium. She held a Faculty position at the Université du Québéc à Trois Rivières, Canada, and the Federal University of Paraiba, Brazil, before she came to the University of Brasília, where she was a Professor of Psychology. Dr. D'Amorim did her postdoctoral work in Community Psychology as Fellow in the Psychiatric Department at the University of North Carolina at Chapel Hill in the U.S.A., at the University of Waterloo, Canada, and at the Université Catholique de Louvain, Belgium. Dr. D'Amorim is currently with the Graduate Program at the Universidade Gama Filho in Rio de Janeiro. Her special interests are the research areas of gender roles and stereotypes, attitudes and values, and expectations.

ROSELINE D. DAVIDO is the author of the CHAD (Childhood Hand Disturbs) drawing technique, a projective test. She is a School Psychologist and has been Associate Professor of Psychology at the University of Paris VII. Currently she teaches psychology at the École des Psychologues Praticiens in Paris, France. Dr. Davido is the author of a novel, *Le Cachalot*, and several books on children's drawings (translated into Japanese and Portuguese). A book on the CHAD is forthcoming.

D. ELAINE DAVIS spent some years with the Counselling Centre at St. John's University in the early 1970s and returned early in 1980 to the Counselling Center at Memorial University, St. John's, Newfoundland. She is involved in a variety of areas, including personal counseling; career counseling; coordinating the Career Planning Centre, including the selection and supervision of student assistants; supervision of practicum students; conducting assertiveness training. Dr. Davis lived and worked in British Columbia in the mid to late 1970s, where she did career planning in an industrial setting and had both counseling and administrative duties at a community college. Her past experience also includes university teaching. She is a past president of the Association of Newfoundland Psychologists and holds a cross-appointment to the Department of Psychology. Her interests include interpersonal communication and the psychology of women, particularly as related to changing sex roles, sexual abuse, and AIDS.

NALINI DEKA received her Ph.D. in Social Psychology from Delhi University in India. She is currently on the Faculty of the Indraprastha College of Delhi University, where she actively took part in committees to improve teaching and administrative standards. Dr. Deka was the recipient of the B. R. Gupta Award and the Most Distinguished Contribution Award. Her special interests include social psychology, social issues, gender roles, development of moral judgment, and religious issues. Her current area of interest and research involves the developmental problems of adolescents in single-parent families.

FLORENCE L. DENMARK received her Ph.D. in Social Psychology from the University of Pennsylvania. She was the president of the American Psychological Association, 1980–1981; the Eastern Psychological Association, 1985–1986; the New York State Psychological Association, 1972–1973; the International Council of Psychologists, 1989–1990; and Psi Chi, the National Honor Society in Psychology, 1978–1980. In addition, she served as vice president for the New York Academy of Sciences and the International Organization for the Study of Group Tensions and is currently a Member of the Advisory Board of the Institute for Cross-Cultural and Cross-Ethnic Studies, Molloy College. Dr. Denmark has been the Thomas Hunter Professor of Psychology at Hunter College of the City University of New York and at present is the Robert Scott Pace Professor of Psychology at Pace University, where she is the Chair of the Department of Psychology. She has authored or edited sixteen books and monographs and has written numerous chapters and articles. She is the recipient of numerous awards, including the American Psychological Association's Distinguished Contributions to Education and Training (1987), APA's Division 35 (Psychology of Women) Carolyn Wood Sherif Award (1991), and the APA's Award for Distinguished Contributions to Psychology in the Public Interest (1992).

SUNEETHA S. DE SILVA was born in Nuwara Eliya Ceylon (now Sri Lanka). She was educated in Sri Lanka, at the Trinity College in England, and at Webster University in St. Louis, U.S.A. She has served as a Director of Montessori Schools in Sri Lanka, England, and the United States of America. She was an Adjunct Instructor at Webster University and is currently the Project Development Specialist with Project Headstart at the Southern Illinois University at Edwardsville. Suneetha de Silva investigates gender roles among adolescents of different nationalities with Drs. Deborah Stiles and Judith Gibbons.

ROGELIO DIAZ-GUERRERO received an M.D. at the National University in Mexico City, Mexico, and then received an M.A. in Psychology and a Ph.D. in Psychology and Neurophysiology from the State University of Iowa (SUI). His residencies in Psychiatry and Neurology were completed at SUI and his Senior Residency in Psychiatry at the University of Miami. Dr. Diaz-Guerrero combined a private practice in neuropsychiatry with teaching psychology, first at Mexico City College and then currently at the National University of Mexico. He initiated research on culture and personality (psychology of the Mexicans), as well as cross-cultural research. Dr. Diaz-Guerrero has made extensive contributions to the areas of culture and personality and cross-cultural psychology, including *Understanding Mexicans and Americans*, which he coauthored with L. B. Szalay in 1991. Presently Dr. Diaz-Guerrero is Research Professor, Faculty of Psychology, National University of Mexico, and is also a Member of the Advisory Board of the Institute for Cross-Cultural and Cross-Ethnic Studies, Molloy College.

MARIA DIKAIOU was born in Arkadia, Greece. After receiving her B.A. with Honors from the University of Thessaloniki, Department of Psychology and Education, she worked as Research Assistant in the same Institute, where she currently holds the position of Assistant Professor. Previously she held positions at the University of Dar-es-Salaam in Tanzania, as well as at the Center for Studies of Education, NUFFIC, The Hague, in the Netherlands, and at the University of British Columbia, Canada. Dr. Dikaiou received her Ph.D. from the Department of Psychology, Stirling University, Scotland. She is a member of several professional organizations, representing her interests in social-psychological problems of minority groups (such as migrants and gypsies) and time perspective. These interests are also reflected in her publications.

CHAVANNES DOUYON was born in Cayes, Haiti, and spent his school years in Haiti. He studied for his License in Psychology at the Université d'État d'Haiti;

he received his Master's Degree in Psychology from Fisk University in Nashville, Tennessee, U.S.A., and his Ph.D. from the Université René Descartes, Sorbonne, Paris, France. His postgraduate studies and specializations were pursued in Manchester, England (Graduate Diploma), the Institut de Psychologie de l'Université de Paris, France (Diplôme de Psychologie Pathologique), and the Universidad Central del Ecuador (Certificate in Exceptional Children). Dr. C. Douyon's research projects and experimentations spread from Paris to Canada, to Massachusetts, Florida, and California, and to Caraibes (University of Montreal). His list of affiliations and employments end with his present position at the Faculty of Ethnology, and as Ministre de l'Éducation National, Jeunesse des Sports. Dr. Douyon is a member of many national and international professional organizations, and he has attended symposia, conferences, and congresses worldwide; he has received many honors, including a *Doctor Honoris Causa* from the Université de l'État d'Haiti.

OMNIA SAYED EL SHAKRY is a graduating senior at the American University in Cairo. She is studying psychology and has conducted past research on crosscultural differences in sex typing and women and eating disorders. She also works as a research assistant for the Child Development Center in Cairo. She plans on continuing her postgraduate studies in the United States in psychology.

JÚLIA FERRO BUCHER was born in Belém, Pará, Brazil. She is Professor at the Institute of Psychology of the University of Brasilia and a Member of the Advisory Board of the Institute for Cross-Cultural and Cross-Ethnic Studies, Molloy College. She studied at the Catholic University of Rio de Janeiro and at the University of Louvain in Belgium, where she completed her doctorate in the area of Family Sciences and Sexology. Dr. Ferro Bucher pursued her postdoctoral studies at the University of Giessen, Germany. She received a Fulbright Fellowship from St. John's University in New York and obtained a grant from the Ford Foundation to do research on motivation for paternity and maternity in Brazil. In addition, Dr. Ferro Bucher has lectured at the Southwest Family Institute in Dallas, Texas, the Mental Research Institute in Palo Alto, California, the University of California at Los Angeles, and other American and Canadian institutions. She has written numerous papers on interpersonal relations and interactions relating to marriage and the family.

GÜLER OKMAN FIƒEK was born in Ankara, Turkey. She completed her secondary education in Turkey and her university and graduate education in the U.S.A., where she received her Ph.D. in Clinical Psychology from the University of Connecticut. She worked in the U.S.A. for some years in a psychiatric hospital for children and a community mental health center. Since 1977 she has been at Boğazici University in Istanbul, Turkey, where she is a member of the Psychology Department. Her areas of interest include individual and family therapy, cross-cultural analysis of family therapy theory, family interaction patterns, gender issues, and psychology of women.

CYNTHIA FRAZIER is a clinical psychologist in private practice in Manhattan and Carmel, New York. She received her doctorate from the New School for Social Sciences in New York City. She holds a B.S. degree from the University of California, Los Angeles, a M.Sc. degree in Educational Psychology from the University of California, Santa Barbara, and a M.Sc. from the New School for Social Research. She completed the psychology *grunnfag* program at the University of Bergen, Norway. In her work, locally and abroad, Dr. Frazier studies the influence of culture upon behavior and the determination of psychopathology. In 1984, she presented a minicourse on behavior therapy in Port-au-Prince, sponsored by the Haitian Association of Mental Health. Later, she and Dr. Chavannes Douyon conducted a cross-cultural study on social support in the elderly, which was published in *Cross-Cultural Research in Human Development: Life-Span Perspectives*, edited by Dr. Leonore Loeb Adler (1989). Dr. Frazier currently teaches at the university level, consults with organizations and hospitals on therapeutic programming and management strategies, and conducts cross-cultural research. She has presented her findings internationally and has published several articles in the areas of aging, Alzheimer's disease, and culture. Presently she is conducting a study on couples therapy in Indonesia.

JUDITH L. GIBBONS received her Ph.D. in Psychology from Carnegie-Mellon University and is currently a Professor of Psychology and Director of Women's Studies at Saint Louis University. For the past six years she has been studying values, gender roles, and views of the future among adolescents of different nationalities. She also does research with Suneetha de Silva and Dr. Deborah Stiles.

UWE P. GIELEN received his Ph.D. in Social Psychology from Harvard University, where he studied with Lawrence Kohlberg. From 1980 to 1990 he served as Chairman of the Psychology Department at St. Francis College where he is Professor of Psychology. He has lived in the Indian subcontinent on five occasions and spent two summers doing fieldwork in Ladakh. Dr. Gielen has been elected by the membership of the International Council of Psychologists to serve as President-Elect (1993–1994) and then as President from 1994–1995. A specialist in cross-cultural psychology, he has published a series of papers concerning moral development in Asian-American, Caribbean, European, and Middle Eastern societies. He is coeditor (with L. L. Adler and N. Milgram) of *Psychology in International Perspective* (1992) and coauthor (with L. Kuhmerker and R. Hayes) of *The Kohlberg Legacy for the Helping Professions* (1991).

HALINA GRZYMALA-MOSZCZYNSKA is Associate Professor of Psychology at the Jagiellonian University in Cracow, Poland, where she carries out her research on the psychology of religion, cross-cultural studies on youth, and analyses of the influence of various religious systems on mental health. She has many publications, including *Structure of the Religious Attitudes of Polish Youth*, *Everyday Life and Religion* and *Psychology of Religion: Selected Problems*. She contributed chapters to several edited books, and she is the author of over 80 scientific papers. She is a Member of many international psychological and sociological associations and organizations, which are furthering the studies of psychology of religion. She is a Member of the Advisory Board of the Institute for Cross-Cultural and Cross-Ethnic Studies, Molloy College. In the summer of 1992 Dr. Grzymala-Moszczynska, together with Dr. Leonore Loeb Adler, was the co-organizer and cochair of a conference on ''Current Topics in International Psychology'' at the Jagiellonian University in Cracow, Poland.

HSIAO-CHIN HSIEH is Associate Professor in the Center for General Education, National Tsing-Hua University in Hsin-chu, Taiwan. She received her M.A. from the Department of Philosophy, Southern Illinois University-Carbondale, and her Ph.D. from the Department of Educational Policy Studies, University of Wisconsin-Madison. Dr. Hsieh's academic interests include the fields of sociology of education, philosophy of education, and women's studies. Her recent research focuses on the differential educational opportunities between males and females in Taiwan.

LIISA HUSU works as a national research coordinator in the Council for Equality Between Men and Women. The Council is a permanent advisory council within the state administration, promoting equality between men and women in Finland. She is the editor of the Finish National Newsletter for Women's Studies and Research on Women (*Naistutkimustiedote*) and coedited (with W. Richter and A. Marks) a European inventory on ongoing research projects on women titled *The Changing Role of Women in Society—A Documentation of Current Research 1984–1987* (1989). She maintains an extensive information service on women's studies for researchers and students. She is also actively involved in international—especially European and Nordic—cooperation in women's studies.

DAFNA N. IZRAELI is an Associate Professor in the Department of Sociology and Anthropology at Bar-Ilan University, Israel. A graduate of McGill University, Hebrew University, and Manchester University, Dr. Izraeli's current research interests include the interface of family and work life; public policy and gender; and organizational politics. She is coeditor (with N. Adler) of *Women in Management Worldwide* (1988) and coeditor (with S. Lewis and H. Hootsmans) of *Dual-Earner Families: International Perspectives* (1992).

OGBU U. KALU is a Professor of Church History in the Department of Religion at the University of Nigeria. He was Dean of Social Sciences and Director of

General Studies at the University for many years. He has written profusely and developed postgraduate programs for African studies, the humanities, traditional religion, and church history. He participated in many international projects on these topics.

WILHELMINA KALU is a Senior Lecturer in Special Education and Educational Psychology, Faculty of Education, University of Nigeria, Nsukka. She has lectured there for the past 16 years and developed programs for undergraduate and postgraduate levels in Special Education and Educational Psychology. She is also involved in research and community advocacy programs with children, women, and families. She has a number of publications in the areas of child psychology, abuse, family violence, challenges in Nigerian special education, and women.

TAE LYON KIM received most of her education in Korea: her B.A. from the Department of Psychology, College of Education, Ewha Woman's University, in Seoul; her M.A. in Psychology from the Graduate School of the same university; and her Ph.D. in Psychology from the Graduate School of the Sung Kyun Kwan University. She participated in a Special Educational Training Program, which was sponsored by a French Government Grant at the University of Paris, France, where she was a Visiting Professor. She was also a Visiting Professor at Cheong Joo University and a Visiting Scholar at the University of California at Los Angeles. Dr. Kim has for many years been very active in many national and international professional organizations. Among these is her Membership on the Advisory Board of the Institute for Cross-Cultural and Cross-Ethnic Studies, Molloy College. She is at present Professor and Chairperson of the Department of Educational Psychology at Ewha Woman's University. She has published many books and articles and presented papers, including at international conventions and meetings.

PATRICIA B. LICUANAN was born in Manila, Philippines. She received her B.A. in English Literature from St. Theresa's College in Manila, her M.A. in Psychology from Cornell University, and her Ph.D. in Social Psychology from The Pennsylvania State University. Dr. Licuanan is currently the Academic Vice President and Professor of Psychology at the Ateneo de Manila University. She has served as President of the Psychological Association of the Philippines and was Chair of the Philippine Social Science Council. Dr. Licuanan is currently the Chair of the National Commission on Women, a government policy body on women's affairs, and is also the Philippine Representative to the United Nations Commission on the Status of Women. Dr. Licuanan's main research areas are national development, social and political psychology, and women.

WEN-YING LIN is an Associate Professor in the Department of Applied Psychology at the Fu Jen Catholic University in Taipei, Taiwan. She received her

M.A. and Ph.D. in Educational Psychology from Keio University in Tokyo, Japan. Professor Lin's current research interests are cross-cultural study in moral development, social justice, and value development. She has published articles on these topics in *Psychologia, Education Today, Taiwan Education, Journal of Japanese Educational Psychology*, and *Journal of Chinese Applied Psychology* and has given numerous presentations to academic audiences.

ANET E. LOUW attended the University of Pretoria in South Africa to complete her B.A., as well as a Teacher's Training Diploma. She received a B.A. (Honors) and a M.A. in Psychology from Potchefstroom University. Ms. Louw was Lecturer in the Department of Psychology at Vista University and is currently Lecturer in the Department of Psychology at the University of the Orange Free State. She specializes in Developmental Psychology and has coauthored a textbook in developmental psychology and a study guide for this textbook, as well as several articles. She is a Member of several professional organizations, among them the International Council of Psychologists and the Psychological Association of South Africa.

DAP. A. LOUW was born and raised in Namibia. He went to the University of Pretoria in South Africa, where he completed his Ph.D. in Criminology. He decided to change careers and completed a Ph.D. in Psychology at Potchefstroom University and then registered as a Clinical Psychologist at the South African Dental and Medical Council. In 1976 he was a Visiting Professor at the University of Idaho, in the U.S.A. From 1970 to 1980 he studied at Rutgers University and Temple University, both in the U.S.A., under the supervision of Drs. Joseph Wolpe and Arnold Lazarus. Upon his return to South Africa, Dr. Louw became Chair of the Department of Psychology and Vice-Dean of the Faculty of Arts at the Vaal Triangle Campus of the Potchefstroom University. At present he is a Professor in the Department of Psychology at the University of the Orange Free State. He is the author of 12 books, which are widely assigned in classes at South African universities. He has visited numerous universities in many countries in South America, North America, Europe, the East, and Australia and presented papers at several international conventions.

DIOMEDES C. MARKOULIS was born in Nicosia on Cyprus. He received a B.A. (Honors) from the University of Thessaloniki in Greece. He studied at the University of Toronto, Canada, in the Department of Psychology and received his Ph.D. from the University of Thessaloniki, where he is an Associate Professor in the Department of Psychology and Education. Dr. Markoulis is a Member of many national and international professional organizations. His fields of interest focus on cognitive and sociocognitive development and sociomoral reasoning processes. He is the coauthor of *Prosocial and Antisocial Dimensions of Behavior* and has published many articles in professional journals.

JUNKO TANAKA MATSUMI is an Associate Professor of Psychology at Hofstra University, Hempstead, New York. She received her Ph.D. in Clinical Psychology from the University of Hawaii and was an East-West Center (Honolulu) degree scholar in Japan. Her current research interests include investigations of social roles and interactive behaviors of depressed people, communication of role behaviors, and cross-cultural research methods to facilitate these investigations. She serves as a consulting editor to the *Journal of Cross-Cultural Psychology* and *Psychological Assessment: A Journal of Consulting and Clinical Psychology*.

MARINA MATTIONI graduated summa cum laude from the University of Milan in 1978 with a degree in Modern History (and a graduate thesis on the Literacy of Italian Social Classes in the Nineteenth Century). She began teaching Italian and history in secondary schools in Milan. At the same time, she worked with feminist-oriented community organizations in lower socioeconomic neighborhoods. In 1980 she left for North and South America, where she successively worked as an archaeological dig assistant in Mexico and as a governess in Ecuador, and in general she traveled extensively throughout the continent. She returned to Italy at the end of 1981 and became a contributing editor at the Milan-based *Donna* magazine, where she is now a full-time journalist and editor.

EDWARD MELKONIAN received his Ph.D. in Cultural Anthropology from the University of Yerevan, Republic of Armenia. He is currently head of social research in the Department of Armenian Diasporan Studies, Academy of Sciences in Yerevan, Armenia.

ROSEMARY MERENDA graduated from Tufts University with a B.A. in Italian Studies, having spent her junior year abroad in Florence, Italy, at Gonzaga University. She moved to Palermo, Sicily, where she worked as research assistant/translator for the Working Group on Psychology under the auspices of the Italian National Research Council, at the University of Palermo. After a year in Milan, she returned to the U.S.A., where she took courses in journalism at the University of Rhode Island and worked as director of the Congress of Ethnic Neighborhoods Organization in Providence. She moved back to Italy and became a translator/journalist with *Donna*, a newly created woman's magazine with an international circulation. Over the years she extended her range of activity, working in the same role as translator/journalist for both fashion establishments and magazines throughout Italy and abroad.

KAREN A. NIELSON is a second-year doctoral candidate at Pace University in New York, where she works as a Graduate Assistant for Dr. Florence L. Denmark. She received her B.A. in Psychology at St. John's University, where she graduated summa cum laude. She has worked with the elderly in a community-based senior citizens' center. Karen Nielson's interests include cross-cultural studies, in particular, Native American studies.

PIRKKO NIEMELÄ is Associate Professor in the Department of Psychology at the University of Turku, Finland. She studied in Turku, Uppsala, Stockholm, and the University of California at Berkeley and Los Angeles. Her earlier research included psychophysiological studies in stress and anticipation; and now, for nearly 20 years, she has concentrated on studies in women's psychological processes and needed support systems in women's lives when milestones are reached, such as motherhood, abortion, divorce, and change from being a home mother to becoming a working mother. Dr. Niemelä is presently studying parents' decision processes. She is particularly interested in ambivalent feelings about motherhood, idealization of motherhood, mothers' support systems, peace research, and enemy stereotypes. Dr. Niemela is Chair of Feminist Psychology of the International Council of Psychologists. She works as family therapist, psychoanalyst, and group therapist, besides her activities in organizing women's studies and research in equality.

MARY ANN O'DONOGHUE completed her undergraduate education at Trinity College, Washington, DC, and earned graduate degrees at Catholic University (M.A. in Religious Education) and at Montclair State College (M.A. in General Psychology). She received her Ph.D. from Hofstra University in both Clinical and School Psychology. She is currently Associate Professor of Psychology at Molloy College, Rockville Centre, New York, and is a licensed psychologist in New York State. She has served on the faculty of Kenyatta University in Kenya and has conducted field research in Japan and in Europe in the area of women's issues. Among Dr. O'Donoghue's research publications and papers are reports on violence in northern Ireland, reviews of the career impact of Peace Corps experiences, and investigations of upward mobility among women in management positions. Prior to her current position, she served as Associate Professor of Psychology at Mercy College, Dobbs Ferry, New York.

ISSA M. OMARI was born in Kilimanjaru, Tanzania. He received his B.A. from the University of East Africa, University College, Dar-es-Salaam in History, Economics, and Education. He received both his M.A. and Ph.D. from Columbia University, New York, U.S.A., in Educational Psychology, Educational Evaluation, and Developmental Education. Dr. Omari's current position is Senior Program Officer and Regional Representative, Fellowships and Awards, Eastern and Southern Africa; he has also acted as Acting Regional Director on many occasions since 1984. Previously he was the Dean Designate, Faculty of Education, Chair of the Department of Education, and Professor of Education and Psychology at the University of Dar-es-Salaam, Tanzania. Dr. Omari spent some time as a Senior Research Fellow at the Center for Studies of Education, NUFFIC, The Hague, the Netherlands, as well as Adjunct Professor at the

University of British Columbia, Canada. His current interests are education at all levels, institutional capacity building, and human resources issues.

MARIE O'NEILL is a fifth-generation Australian who was educated at Sydney University (B.A., T.C., and M.A.) and in Toronto; Canada (Ph.D.). She taught in schools, colleges, and universities in Australia and in Canada. Her present appointment in Adelaide is Principal Clinical Psychologist with the Department for Community Welfare. She is responsible for a statewide clinical service to the public. During 1990 Dr. O'Neill was an Invited Visiting Professor at Memorial University in Newfoundland, Canada, where she had founded a Diagnostic and Remedial Unit in 1972. Dr. O'Neill is a Member of several national and international professional organizations and was nominated for President of the International Council of Psychologists.

AREE PETCHPUD was born in the south of Thailand. She spent two years in Chiengmai under the sponsorship of the Fulbright Foundation for her preuniversity studies. She obtained her B.Ed., M.Ed. (Developmental Psychology), and her M.A. (Community Development) from universities in Thailand and obtained her Ph.D. (Industrial Psychology) from the University of Western Australia in Perth, Australia. Currently she is the Chairperson of the Postgraduate Program in Industrial Psychology and holds a position of Professor of Psychology at the Kasetsart University in Bangkok, Thailand. Dr. Petchpud was elected Director-at-Large (1990–1993) of the International Council of Psychologists; she is a Member of the Australian Psychological Society, the American Psychological Association, and STAR.

JEANNE PHILIPPE was born in Santo Domingo of Haitian parents. She received her M.S. in Anthropology and Sociology and her doctorate in Medicine from the Université d'État d'Haiti. Dr. Philippe also holds a Specialist's Diploma in Child Psychiatry from the Ministry of Foreign Affairs in France and a doctorate in Psychology, with an emphasis on social psychopathology, from the Sorbonne in Paris. Currently Dr. Philippe is a Professor with the Faculty of the Humanities and Social Sciences and a Professor of Library and Documentation of Social Psychopathology with the faculty of Ethnology at the Université d'État d'Haiti. Dr. Philippe is also the Director of the National Television Programs, as well as the Director of the National Radio.

JUANA R. PINZÁS holds a B.A. in Psychology (Catholic University of Peru), M.Sc. in Social Psychology (LSE), M.Sc. in Methodology for Developmental and Social Psychology (University of Strathclyde, Glasgow, Scotland), and is finishing her doctoral dissertation (Catholic University of Nijmegen, Nijmegen, Netherlands). Grants awarded include Ford Foundation, National Council for Science and Technology, Catholic University of Nijmegen, and Fulbright Visiting Scholar. She is Associate Professor of Psychology at Catholic University of Peru, Elementary Counseling Director of the American School in Lima, and consultant for different organizations. Her research concerns improved educational opportunities in Peru, especially for women, emphasizing cognitive and social aspects of learning.

MARIA M. RAGÚZ received her B.A. from the Catholic University of Peru (PUC) and her M.S. from the University of Wisconsin, U.S.A. When she returned to PUC, she became an Associate Professor in the Department of Psychology. After a lengthy study on sex-role orientation, which included several stays in the Netherlands, she received her Doctoral Degree from the Catholic University of Nijmegen, in the Netherlands. She has participated in workshops and meetings in the Netherlands, Canada, Mexico, and Germany.

MARIA LUCY RODRIGUEZ DE DIAZ was born in Lima, Peru, and was raised in La Paz, Bolivia, during her school years. She received her Teacher Certificate from the Normal Catholic School of Cochabamba, Bolivia, and gained her teaching experience in both private and state schools in Bolivia. When she received a scholarship, she stayed for two years of studies and research on personalized education in Spain and Italy. Upon her return to Bolivia, she became the Director of the Pedro Poveda private school in Cochabamba. She completed her professional studies in Psychology at the Universidad Iberoamericana (UI) in Mexico City, where she received the Master's Degree in Psychology and the Ph.D. in Clinical Psychology at UI. Dr. Rodriguez de Diaz worked for the Secretariat of Public Education in Mexico in the Direccion General de Educacion Indigena and developed textbooks and didactic materials in aboriginal languages to be utilized in the different ethnic schools in Mexico. She also held the position of School Psychologist in a private school in Mexico City and at the same time maintained a private practice in which she used test batteries in conducting psychotherapy with children.

NANCY FELIPE RUSSO is Professor of Psychology and Director of Women's Studies at Arizona State University. Before that, she was the first Administrative Officer for Women's Programs of the American Psychological Association (APA). She is a former President of APA's Division of the Psychology of Women and Associate Editor of the *Psychology of Women Quarterly* and currently serves on APA's new Board for the Advancement of Psychology in the Public Interest. She is author of more than 100 publications related to sex roles and the psychology of women. Dr. Russo is the recipient of the Distinguished Leadership Certificate of APA's Committee on Women in Psychology.

MARILYN P. SAFIR is an Associate Professor in the Psychology Department of the University of Haifa, where she founded and directs the Women's Studies Program since its inception following the First Interdisciplinary International Congress on Women: Women's Worlds, which she chaired. She is a Founding Member of the "New" Israeli Feminist Movement. Dr. Safir is coeditor of

Sexual Equality: The Israeli Kibbutz Tests the Theories (1983); *Women's Worlds: From the New Scholarship* (1985); and *Calling the Equality Bluff: Women in Israel* (1991); and is coauthor (with D. N. Izraeli) of a chapter on Israeli women in L. L. Adler (Ed.), *Women in Cross-Cultural Perspective* (1991). Dr. Safir is a licensed Clinical Psychologist and Clinical Supervisor and one of the first behavioral, sex, and feminist psychotherapists in Israel. She served as Chairperson of the National Commission for the Status of Women 1986–1991. She is a Founding Executive Member of the Israeli Women's Network. She was appointed by the President and the Rector of Haifa University to investigate the status of women. Dr. Safir is currently a Member of the Advisory Board of the Institute for Cross-Cultural and Cross-Ethnic Studies, Molloy College.

ANIE SANENTZ KALAYJIAN completed her Master's and Doctoral degrees in Psychiatric Mental Health Nursing at Columbia University and is currently a Visiting Professor at Pace University. Dr. Kalayjian is the cofounder of the Psychiatric Mental Health Outreach Program to Armenia, in the wake of the Soviet-Armenian earthquake of 1988. She collected the interview data for the chapter in this book during her several stays in the Soviet Union.

KRISTIN SCHOLL received a B.A. in American Studies from Colby College. Prior to college, she was an exchange student for a year in France, and she spent much of her junior year in Italy. She traveled extensively throughout Europe, Asia, Africa, parts of South America, and the Caribbean. Kristin Scholl is a Psy.D. candidate at Pace University and works as a Graduate Assistant for Dr. Florence L. Denmark. Her interests include cross-cultural studies and gender and sexual abuse issues.

TOSHIYUKI SHIRAISHI was born in Fukuoka, Japan. He is presently working for his Ph.D. in Psychology of Early Childhood under the sponsorship of Dr. Seisoh Sukemune. His interests include language development, communication in preschool children, and peer relations in schoolchildren. Mr. Shiraishi is a member of several Japanese professional organizations.

YOSHIKO SHIRAKAWA was born in Nagasaki, Japan. She received her B.E. from Nagasaki University and her M.E. from Hiroshima University. She continues her studies in the Psychology of Early Childhood at Hiroshima University under the sponsorship of Dr. Seisoh Sukemune. She holds a membership in several professional Japanese associations. Ms. Shirakawa's interests include social development in children and parent-child relationships in early childhood.

DEBORAH A. STILES received her Ph.D. in Educational Psychology from Boston College and is currently Associate Professor of Education at Webster University. She has taught courses on intercultural communication, education, and women's studies in the United States of America, the Netherlands, and

Iceland. Her research concerns the cross-cultural study of values, gender roles, and views of the future of adolescents. Dr. Stiles has also conducted cross-cultural studies with Suneetha de Silva and Dr. Judith Gibbons.

SEISOH SUKEMUNE was born in Hiroshima, Japan, where he received his B.A. (Psychology), his M.A., and his Ph.D. (Developmental Psychology) from Hiroshima University. He was a Fulbright Graduate Student and did his studies at Ohio State University in the U.S.A. Dr. Sukemune's present position is Professor at Hiroshima University. He is also the Director of the Research Institute of Early Childhood Education, as well as the Graduate School, and Director of the Institute for International Education, all at Hiroshima University. Dr. Sukemune is a member of the Advisory Board of the Institute for Cross-Cultural and Cross-Ethnic Studies, Molloy College. His present interests include children's prosocial (altruistic) behavior, children's concept attainment, modeling (observational) learning, early childhood education and care programs, stress and coping, and cross-cultural studies.

HAROLD TAKOOSHIAN completed his Ph.D. in Social-Personality Psychology at the City University of New York and is currently Associate Professor in the Social Science Division of Fordham University. He served as Visiting Professor of Psychology in Latin America and as an American Fulbright Scholar to the Soviet Union in 1987–1988, teaching and studying in Yerevan, Tbilisi, Moscow, and Leningrad (St. Petersburg). Dr. Takooshian is active in cross-cultural research and has published widely. He is affiliated with numerous professional associations and is prominent in several divisions of the American Psychological Association, the International Council of Psychologists, and the Society for Armenian Studies.

AGNES YINLING YU was born in Hong Kong, where she received a bilingual education, and moved to Canada in 1967. She received her B.A. (Honors) in Psychology from the Universidad de las Americas in Mexico. The focus of her work was in cross-cultural studies. She then returned to Canada. She completed her M.Ed. in Counseling Psychology and her Ph.D. in Cross-Cultural Psychology, both from the University of Alberta, Canada. Since the early 1970s Dr. Yu has researched and worked in various countries: Hong Kong, People's Republic of China, Canada, Mexico, and France. Her research interests are ethnographic studies in cross-cultural settings, immigrant and minority studies, child and family psychology, and psychology of second language acquisition. She currently works as a psychologist for immigrant students in Edmonton Public Schools and has a private practice devoted to counseling immigrant families.